D1239001

Economic complexity: chaos, sunspots, bubbles, and nonlinearity

International Symposia in Economic Theory and Econometrics

Editor
William A. Barnett, *University of Texas at Austin*

Other books in the series
William A. Barnett and Kenneth J. Singleton *New approaches to monetary economics*
William A. Barnett, Ernst R. Berndt, and Halbert White *Dynamic econometric modeling*

Economic complexity: chaos, sunspots, bubbles, and nonlinearity

Proceedings of the Fourth International Symposium in Economic Theory and Econometrics

Edited by

WILLIAM A. BARNETT
University of Texas at Austin

JOHN GEWEKE
Duke University

KARL SHELL
Cornell University

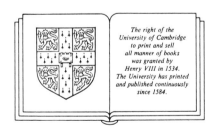

The right of the
University of Cambridge
to print and sell
all manner of books
was granted by
Henry VIII in 1534.
The University has printed
and published continuously
since 1584.

CAMBRIDGE UNIVERSITY PRESS

Cambridge
New York   Port Chester   Melbourne   Sydney

Published by the Press Syndicate of the University of Cambridge
The Pitt Building, Trumpington Street, Cambridge CB2 1RP
32 East 57th Street, New York, NY 10022, USA
10 Stamford Road, Oakleigh, Melbourne 3166, Australia

First published 1989

Printed in the United States of America

Library of Congress Cataloging-in-Publication Data
International Symposium in Economic Theory and Econometrics (4th :
1987 : Austin, Tex.)

Economic complexity : chaos, sunspots, bubbles, and nonlinearity :
proceedings of the Fourth International Symposium in Economic Theory
and Econometrics / edited by William A. Barnett, John Geweke, Karl
Shell.

p. cm. – (International symposia in economic theory and
econometrics)
Includes bibliographies.

ISBN 0-521-35563-X

1. Econometrics – Congresses.   I. Barnett, William A.   II. Geweke,
John.   III. Shell, Karl.   IV. Title.   V. Series.
HB139.I566   1987
330'.028 – dc19   88-29945
                                                                 CIP

British Library Cataloguing in Publication Data
Economic complexity: chaos, sunspots, bubbles, and
nonlinearity: proceedings of the Fourth
International Symposium in Economic Theory and
Econometrics. – (International symposia in
economic theory and econometrics)

1. Econometric models
I. Barnett, William A.   II. Geweke, John
III. Shell, Karl   IV. Series
330'0724

ISBN 0 521 35563 X hard covers

Contents

Editor's introduction

The subject of this volume is economic complexity, which can be taken to be the analysis of complicated outcomes in relatively simple economic models.[1] Examples are stochastic outcomes from nonstochastic economies, as define the concept of sunspot equilibria, and stochastic-appearing outcomes from nonstochastic economies, as can define the concept of deterministic chaos. More conventional examples include nonchaotic nonlinear processes, hyperinflation, and some bubble phenomena.

The contents of this volume comprise the proceedings of a conference held at the IC[2] Institute at the University of Texas at Austin on May 27–29, 1987.[2] The conference, entitled "Economic Complexity: Chaos, Sunspots, Bubbles, and Nonlinearity," was organized to bring together presentations of some of the fundamental new research that has begun to appear in those areas. The organizers of the conference and editors of this proceedings volume are John Geweke, Karl Shell, and I.

The volume is divided into five parts spanning the scope of the conference. Part I is on sunspot equilibria, which is a growing field pioneered by David Cass and Karl Shell. Part II is on bubbles, instability, and hyperinflation. Part III contains contributions to the very recent literature dealing with empirical tests for chaos and strange attractors in time-series data. Part IV is on chaos and informational complexity in economic theory. Part V is on testing for and using nonlinearity in econometrics.

This volume is the fourth in the conference series called *International Symposia in Economic Theory and Econometrics,* which is under my general editorship.[3] Individual volumes in the series generally have coeditors, and the series has a permanent Board of Advisory Editors. The symposia

---

[1] For this definition of economic complexity, see the Cass and Shell chapter in the present volume.

[2] IC[2] stands for Innovation, Creativity, and Capital.

[3] The title of the series recently was changed from "Austin Symposia in Economics," as a result of the increasingly international nature of the symposia in the series.

in the series are sponsored by the IC^2 Institute at the University of Texas at Austin and by the RGK Foundation. The fourth conference was sponsored also by the Department of Economics, Graduate School of Business, Center for Statistical Sciences, and Richard J. Gonzalez Regents Chair at the University of Texas at Austin.

The first conference in the series was organized by Ronald Gallant and me, who also coedited the proceedings volume. That volume has appeared as the volume 30, October/November 1985 edition of the *Journal of Econometrics*. The topic was "New Approaches to Modelling, Specification Selection, and Econometric Inference."

Beginning with the second symposium in the series, the proceedings appear as volumes in this Cambridge University Press monograph series. The organizers of the second symposium and coeditors of its proceedings volume were Kenneth Singleton and I. The topic was "New Approaches to Monetary Economics." The organizers of the third symposium, "Dynamic Econometric Modeling," were Ernst Berndt and I; and the coeditors of that proceedings volume were Ernst Berndt, Halbert White, and I. The organizers of the fourth symposium and coeditors of the current volume on economic complexity were John Geweke, Karl Shell, and I.

The organizers of the fifth symposium, held at Duke University on May 29–30, 1988, and entitled "Nonparametric and Semiparametric Methods in Econometrics and Statistics," were James Powell, George Tauchen, and I, who also are the coeditors of the proceedings volume.[4] The sixth symposium in the series is currently being organized for June 1989 by Claude d'Aspremont, Bernard Cornet, Jean Jaskold Gabszewicz, Andreu Mas-Colell, and me as a joint IC^2 Institute and CORE conference on "Equilibrium Theory and Applications." That conference will be held at CORE in Belgium in honor of Jacques Drèze, and the proceedings volume will be the fifth volume in this monograph series.[5]

The intention of the volumes in the proceedings series is to provide refereed journal–quality collections of research papers of unusual importance in areas of currently highly visible activity within the economics profession. Because of the refereeing requirements associated with the editing of the proceedings, the volumes in the series will not necessarily contain all of the papers presented at the corresponding symposia.

---

[4] The sponsors of that conference included the National Science Foundation, the Institute of Statistics and Decision Sciences at Duke University, and the Conference in Econometrics and Mathematical Economics program of the National Bureau of Economic Research, along with the sponsors of the earlier conferences in the series.

[5] CORE stands for the Center for Operations Research and Econometrics, at the Universite Catholique de Louvain in Louvain-la-Neuve, Belgium.

I am indebted to John Geweke and Karl Shell for the great effort that they have invested as coeditors of this volume and as coorganizers of the conference that produced this volume.

University of Texas at Austin   William A. Barnett

Contributors

William A. Barnett
Department of Economics
University of Texas at Austin

Michele Boldrin
Department of Economics
University of California at Los Angeles

L. Broze
D.U.L.B.E.A.
Université Libre de Bruxelles
Bruxelles, BELGIUM

David Cass
Department of Economics
University of Pennsylvania

Pierre-André Chiappori
Centre d'Etudes Quantitatives
EHESS
Paris, FRANCE

Seungmook S. Choi
University of Nebraska

Richard H. Day
Department of Economics
University of Southern California

Duncan K. Foley
Department of Economics
Barnard College

John Geweke
Department of Economics
Duke University

C. Gourieroux
CEPREMAP
Paris, FRANCE

Jean-Michel Grandmont
CEPREMAP
Paris, FRANCE

Roger Guesnerie
Centre d'Etudes Quantitatives
EHESS
Paris, FRANCE

Melvin J. Hinich
Department of Government
University of Texas at Austin

Blake LeBaron
Department of Economics
University of Wisconsin at Madison

Albert Marcet
Graduate School of Industrial
    Administration
Carnegie Mellon University

Douglas M. Patterson
Department of Finance
Virginia Polytechnic Institute

James Peck
Managerial Economics and Decision
    Sciences
Kellogg Graduate School of Management
Northwestern University

Thomas J. Sargent
Hoover Institution on War, Revolution,
    and Peace
Stanford University

José A. Scheinkman
Department of Economics
University of Chicago

Karl Shell
Department of Economics
Cornell University

Stephen E. Spear
Graduate School of Industrial
    Administration
Carnegie Mellon University

James H. Stock
Kennedy School of Government
Harvard University

A. Szafarz
C.E.M.E.
Université Libre de Bruxelles
Bruxelles, BELGIUM

Jean-Luc Walter
Department of Mathematics
University of Southern California

Michael Woodford
Graduate School of Business
University of Chicago

PART I

Sunspot equilibria

CHAPTER 1

Sunspot equilibrium in an overlapping-generations economy with an idealized contingent-commodities market

David Cass and Karl Shell

Abstract: We analyze a highly idealized infinite-horizon, overlapping-generations economy in which trading in a full spectrum of contingent commodities takes place before the beginning of economic time. We postulate that participation in the market is unrestricted. Hence, individuals are able to insure against all economic risks, even those that are resolved before their birthdates. We construct an example that possesses a sunspot, nonmonetary equilibrium. It Pareto dominates the nonsunspot, nonmonetary equilibrium, but it is Pareto dominated by a nonsunspot, monetary equilibrium.

In earlier work, we have established that restricted market participation is a source of sunspot equilibria. Because market restrictions are assumed away in the present chapter, our example establishes that the "double infinity" of consumers and dated commodities is another, logically separate source of sunspot equilibria.

Our example suggests that the social contrivance of sunspots can be an imperfect substitute for the social contrivance of money in attenuating the effects of oversaving. Our sunspot equilibrium also provides an example of a weakly Pareto-optimal allocation that can be seen to be not fully Pareto optimal from observing the state-contingent allocation for only a finite number of periods.

1   Introduction and summary

a   *Economic complexity*

The subject of this volume is economic complexity, which can be taken to be the analysis of *complicated solutions to relatively simple economic*

Research support from National Science Foundation grants SES-8509957 and SES-8606944 is gratefully acknowledged. The chapter is based on notes dated 10/16/81, which were prepared for a CARESS workshop. We thank Roger Guesnerie for his stimulating discussion in Austin, Texas and Walt Heller, Jim Peck, Steve Spear, and Raghu Sundaram for

3

models. Consider, for example, the chapters devoted to economic dynamics. A focus of these contributions is on the nonstationary paths that arise in economies with stationary environments. We know that business cycles (periodic solutions) and even "chaotic" fluctuations (aperiodic solutions) can occur even though all the economic fundamentals are nonfluctuating (stationary). In some of the other chapters, including ours, the focus is on stochastic outcomes in nonstochastic economic environments. We know that economic outcomes can be random even though all the economic fundamentals (such as preferences, endowments, and technology) are nonrandom. In particular, "sunspots" can affect the allocation of resources even though the economic fundamentals are unaffected by sunspots.

b   *Stochastic outcomes in nonstochastic economies*

The current chapter is on *sunspot equilibrium;* we analyze the stochastic outcomes to a rational-expectations model of a competitive economy in which the fundamentals are nonstochastic. The fact that economies generate uncertainty – as well as transmitting uncertainty arising from outside the economy – should come as no surprise. An economy is a social system in which the individual participants cannot be certain of the behavior of the others. In seeking to optimize his own actions, an economic actor must attempt to predict the moves of all other economic actors. Because he is uncertain about the moves of others, he is also uncertain about economic outcomes (such as prices), even if he is completely certain about the economic fundamentals. Nor should the existence of sunspot equilibria come as a surprise to the economist conversant with game theory. Pure-strategy equilibrium is not the only type of solution to nonstochastic games. Mixed-strategy equilibrium and, more generally, correlated equilibrium are staples of noncooperative game theory. There is no obvious reason that the stochastic equilibria that arise in game-theoretic models of imperfect competition must vanish in the limit as the economy becomes competitive.

Thinking of an economy as a social system composed of strategic decision makers should lead one to accept as natural the idea that the market economy itself creates uncertainty. The reader of business and financial news is well aware of the important role of market uncertainty. Businessmen face uncertainties that are not based on their uncertainty about

Footnote *(cont.)*
their comments. We take this opportunity to record our debt to Paul Samuelson, whose overlapping-generations model serves as a foundation for intelligent macroeconomics and provides two sources of sunspot equilibria.

economic fundamentals; they are, for example, uncertain about the overall level of consumer confidence, the confidence and financial plans of their customers, the production and marketing plans of their rivals, and the tax and regulatory plans of government agencies. For these reasons, we should expect sunspot equilibria to be the rule rather than the exception.

c   *The overlapping-generations model and sunspot equilibrium*

The histories of the OG model and sunspot equilibrium are intertwined.[1] It is our ambition to persuade the reader that, although sunspot equilibrium is an essential aspect in the analysis of overlapping-generations economies, sunspot phenomena are far more general. However, we first return to the original source of sunspots: the overlapping-generations model.

The overlapping-generations model began with Samuelson (1958)[2] who provided an example of perfect-foresight nonmonetary, competitive equilibrium that is not Pareto optimal. For his example, there is also a very simple monetary competitive equilibrium that is Pareto optimal.[3] His example also establishes that the public debt need not be retired in perfect-foresight economies.[4]

What is the source of possible inoptimality in Samuelson's model? The overlapping-generations model differs from the Arrow–Debreu model in two ways:

1   The time horizon is unbounded and the generations overlap. Hence, in the discrete model, there is both a countable infinity of dated commodities and a countable infinity of traders.
2   Trades are restricted by the natural vitality and mortality of the economic actors.

Property 1, the so-called double-infinity property (including the stipulation of the overlapping structure of the generations), is *the* source of the possible failure of Pareto optimality of perfect-foresight (i.e.,

---

[1] A major reason for this is, of course, that the earliest research on sunspot equilibrium was based on either the overlapping-generations model or closely related models. Perhaps another reason has to do with proximity. At the time of our discovery of sunspots, CARESS was a leading center of research on the overlapping-generations model. Even at the time we discovered sunspots, both of us were listing as our prime research interest "overlapping-generations models."

[2] For a detailed and very enthusiastic account of the many virtues of the OG model for macro and monetary analysis, see our propaganda piece, Cass and Shell (1980).

[3] For an up-to-date welfare analysis of the OG model, see Balasko and Shell (1980, sect. 2, 4, and 5).

[4] For an analysis of fiscal policy, equilibrium, and welfare in the perfect-foresight OG model, see Balasko and Shell (1981). For an analysis of debt retirement and equilibrium in the OG model, see Balasko and Shell (1986).

nonsunspot), competitive equilibrium. See Shell (1971) and Cass (1985). Property 2, the restricted-participation property, has been incorrectly cited in the literature as causing the failure of optimality in perfect-foresight, overlapping-generations economies. Shell (1971) establishes that this property is not binding for perfect-foresight (i.e., nonsunspot) equilibria: The set of perfect-foresight equilibria derived on the assumption that traders are constrained by property 2 is identical to the set of perfect-foresight equilibria derived on the assumption that market participation is unrestricted.

Although property 2 plays no role in the analysis of nonsunspot equilibrium, it is important in the analysis of sunspot equilibrium. In Cass and Shell (1983), we showed how such restrictions on market participation are a source of sunspot equilibrium. Here we show how the double infinity (property 1) of the OG model is yet another source of sunspot equilibrium.

The first work on sunspot equilibrium was reported in Shell (1977), which is based on our joint research efforts on the infinite-horizon, overlapping-generations economy. In this unpublished paper, it was assumed that there is no intrinsic uncertainty. The only randomness is in the level of sunspot activity, which has no effect on the economic fundamentals. We showed that there is an equilibrium in which rational individuals believe that the general price level is affected by the level of sunspot activity and that these beliefs are self-justifying. It was assumed that the economy is "shocked" by sunspots in each period. In this first example of sunspot equilibrium, economic fluctuations are generated within the private sector, and the stabilizing (contrasunspot) fiscal policy must be perpetually active. This is contrary to the notion that erratic behavior in rational-expectations economies is solely the fault of the erratic behavior of the government.

In a very nice paper, Azariadis (1981) translated our pure-exchange overlapping-generations model into the simple production-consumption model popular with macroeconomists. Azariadis and Guesnerie (1982, 1986) and Spear (1984) provided sufficient conditions for the existence of *stationary* sunspot equilibria. Peck (1988) showed how nonstationary sunspot equilibria can be constructed for a very wide class of one-good OG models. His method of construction would seem to extend beyond the one-good case. His result suggests that sunspot equilibria are not flukes in the overlapping-generations model.

d   *The sources of sunspot equilibria*

We previously argued (Subsection 1b) that since an economy is a social system in which individuals must attempt to predict the moves of others, it should not be surprising that the economy generates uncertainty. Because extrinsic uncertainty is so likely to affect economic outcomes, it is natural to ask: Which economies, if any, are immunized against the effects of extrinsic uncertainty?

We answer this question in Cass and Shell (1983, sect. VII, pp. 215–18). In an economy with convex preferences and convex technologies, a sunspot-equilibrium allocation is never Pareto optimal. Hence, in a convex environment, if the preconditions of Pareto optimality are met, we know that extrinsic uncertainty cannot matter.

Such is the hold on economists of the basic Arrow–Debreu model that we are frequently asked for "the cause" of or "the reason" for sunspot equilibria. (These questions have the same roots as the idea that failures in Pareto optimality and other nice properties of Arrow–Debreu equilibrium must necessarily be identified with some particular "market failures.") In attempting to respond to these questions, we have pursued the following program: Relax the usual preconditions for Pareto optimality of equilibrium allocations, one at a time, and provide, for each weakening of the assumptions, an example of sunspot equilibrium.[5] In what follows, we list some of these sources of sunspot equilibrium.

(i)   *Restrictions on market participation*
In Cass and Shell (1983), we relaxed the perfect market assumption in a way that is motivated by intertemporal economic theory. All markets are assumed to be open and competitive, but participation in these markets is restricted to economic actors who are alive when the market convenes. In particular, the members of the "young" generation cannot participate in a market for securities based on a state of nature that is revealed before their births. It was shown that sunspot equilibria can be generated in an economy that is Arrow–Debreu except for restrictions on market participation. If there is no intrinsic uncertainty, then the Walrasian equilibria are unaffected by the restrictions on market participation. They are thought of as the nonsunspot equilibria. We showed that there can also be new equilibria, the sunspot equilibria, in which the allocation of resources is affected by extrinsic uncertainty. Balasko, Cass, and Shell (1988) provided some comparative statics for the Cass and Shell (1983) economy. In the effect on the existence of sunspot equilibrium, varying the proportion

---

[5] Our joint program is referred to as the Philadelphia Pholk Theorem by Shell (1987) in his *Palgrave* entry on sunspots. The PPT is the assertion: "In each 'class' of models in which Pareto-optimal allocations are not guaranteed, one can find an example of sunspot equilibrium." The "proof" is based on several examples constructed by us and our co-authors. Of course, time does not stand still. The pholk theorem is now also identified with Ithaca, Geneva, Evanston, New Brunswick, Paris, New York, Pittsburgh, ...

of market-restricted consumers is similar to varying the endowments of the economy.

Natural restrictions on market participation obviously arise in the over-lapping-generations model. Hence, in that model, restricted participation is *a* source of sunspot equilibria. There is one other source of sunspot equilibria in OG models – the double infinity of consumers and dated commodities (along with the structure of generational overlap), which is analyzed in Sections 2 and 3.

(ii)   *Incomplete markets*

Cass (1989) showed that, in an example with securities markets that are not complete, there is a continuum of sunspot competitive equilibria if the endowments are not Pareto optimal (see also Siconolfi, 1987). Cass's securities are purely financial, but subsequent work has indicated that missing markets in general, whether for financial or real commodities, can cause sunspot equilibria to exist.

One is free to interpret an economy with externalities as nothing more than an economy with incomplete markets. Hence, by showing that incomplete markets can be a source of sunspot equilibria, one also establishes that externalities can be sources of sunspot equilibria. Spear (1988) worked out an interesting dynamic model with an externality in the private investment process. He showed that sunspots can affect the equilibrium outcome, and he generated equilibria that seem to be in agreement with some features of actual economic time series.

(iii)   *Imperfect competition*

Peck and Shell (1985) analyzed the role for extrinsic uncertainty in a general-equilibrium model of imperfect competition. The model is like the Arrow–Debreu model except that the price-taking assumption is replaced by the assumption of strategic behavior. For this model, there is a sunspot Nash equilibrium if and only if endowments are not Pareto optimal. Allowing for asymmetric information even further broadens the class of sunspot Nash equilibria. The work of Peck and Shell provided the first formal link between the relatively well-established tradition of extrinsic uncertainty in game theory and the relatively recent tradition of extrinsic uncertainty in formal economic equilibrium models. They showed that, in the market-game environment, every correlated equilibrium is a sunspot equilibrium but that some sunspot equilibria are not correlated equilibria.

(iv)   *Nonconvexities*

Guesnerie and Laffont (1987) provided examples of sunspot equilibria in economies with nonconvex preferences. In contrast, Cass and Polemarchakis (1988) proved that sunspots cannot matter in competitive equilibrium if preferences are strictly convex, even if there are nonconvexities in production.

e   *Sunspot equilibria in the idealized overlapping-generations economy: overview and summary of Sections 2 and 3*

We first found sunspot equilibria during the course of our joint research on Samuelson's model of overlapping generations. Two features distinguish the overlapping-generations model from the standard Walrasian model:

1 Participation in markets in the overlapping-generations economy is naturally restricted by the lifetimes of the individual traders.[6] In the standard Walrasian model, market participation is unrestricted.
2 In the overlapping-generations economy, there is the double infinity of traders and dated commodities[7] along with the overlapping structure of generations.[8] The standard Walrasian model is based on a finite number of commodities and a finite number of consumers.

We know that the first feature, restricted market participation, is a source of sunspot equilibrium.[9] To isolate the sources of sunspot equilibria, we construct in Section 3 a highly idealized overlapping-generations economy in which the first feature, restricted market participation, is assumed away. We postulate in the spirit of Shell (1971) that the market for contingent commodities meets before the beginning of economic time and that each consumer can purchase a full spectrum of contingent claims, even those based on states of nature that were revealed before the consumer's birthdate.

A special case of the model developed in Section 2 is further specified in Section 3. For this example, we find three rational-expectations competitive equilibria:

1 a nonsunspot, nonmonetary competitive equilibrium (which is autarky);
2 a nonsunspot, monetary competitive-equilibrium; and
3 a sunspot, nonmonetary competitive equilibrium.

In our example, the nonsunspot, monetary competitive-equilibrium allocation is Pareto optimal. It also Pareto dominates the sunspot, nonmonetary competitive-equilibrium allocation, which in turn Pareto dominates

---

[6] See Cass and Shell (1983) and Subsection 1d(i).
[7] See Shell (1971).   [8] See Cass (1985).   [9] See Cass and Shell (1983).

the nonsunspot, nonmonetary competitive-equilibrium allocation. The two nonmonetary equilibria are not Pareto optimal, but they are weakly Pareto optimal. Even though the sunspot equilibrium allocation is weakly Pareto optimal, the planner could not convert it to full Pareto optimality without intervening in the first period.

We conclude that *a* source of sunspot equilibria in the overlapping-generations economy is the second distinguishing feature of the model, the double infinity property.

Our example also suggests that sunspots might conceivably be useful as a coordinating device to attenuate a tendency toward oversaving. Lump-sum transfers of outside money to the private sector attenuate any tendency to oversaving and do so costlessly because these transfers do not distort economic decisions. Wagers on sunspots might, under some circumstances, serve to attenuate oversaving, but they are always costly in strictly convex economies because they introduce individual risks into situations in which there is no aggregate risk.

In Samuelsonian prose: The "social contrivance of sunspots" may serve as an imperfect substitute for the "social contrivance of money."

2   An idealized overlapping-generations model with sunspots

In each generation there is only one consumer, labeled by his birthdate $t = 0, 1, \ldots$ and referred to as Mr. t. Mr. 0 is active only during period 1, while Mr. $t > 0$ is alive and active during both periods t and $t+1$. In each period $t = 1, 2, \ldots$ there is only one standard commodity. The economy's level of sunspot activity s is a random variable, realized at the beginning of period 1 and taking on the values α or β. All consumers share the same probability beliefs about the occurrence of sunspots, and these common probabilities $\pi(\alpha)$ and $\pi(\beta)$ satisfy $0 < \pi(\alpha) < 1$ and $\pi(\beta) = 1 - \pi(\alpha)$.

Let $x_t^\tau(s) \in \mathbb{R}_+$ denote consumption by Mr. t in period τ and state s, and

$$x_0 = [x_0^1(\alpha), x_0^1(\beta)] \quad \text{and} \quad x_t = [x_t^t(\alpha), x_t^{t+1}(\alpha), x_t^t(\beta), x_t^{t+1}(\beta)],$$

$$\text{for } t = 1, 2, \ldots.$$

Assume that Mr. 0 has a utility function $v_0 : \mathbb{R}_+^2 \to \mathbb{R}$ with the von Neumann–Morgenstern representation

$$v_0(x_0) = v_0[x_0^1(\alpha), x_0^1(\beta)]$$
$$= \pi(\alpha)\phi[x_0^1(\alpha)] + \pi(\beta)\phi[x_0^1(\beta)],$$

where $\phi : \mathbb{R}_+ \to \mathbb{R}$ is smooth, strictly increasing, and strictly concave. Similarly, assume that Mr. $t > 0$ also has a von Neumann–Morgenstern utility function $v_t : \mathbb{R}_+^4 \to \mathbb{R}$, but with the special form

$$v_t(x_t) = v_t[x_t^t(\alpha), x_t^{t+1}(\alpha), x_t^t(\beta), x_t^{t+1}(\beta)]$$

$$= \pi(\alpha)\psi[ax_t^t(\alpha) + bx_t^{t+1}(\alpha)] + \pi(\beta)\psi[ax_t^t(\beta) + bx_t^{t+1}(\beta)],$$

where $0 < a < b$ and $\psi: \mathbb{R}_+ \to \mathbb{R}$ is smooth, strictly increasing, and strictly concave. So, in particular, Mr. t's certainty utility function ψ exhibits a constant marginal rate of substitution that is less than one,

$$\frac{\partial\psi(ax^1 + bx^2)/\partial x^1}{\partial\psi(ax^1 + bx^2)/\partial x^2} = \frac{a}{b} < 1.$$

Let $\omega_t^\tau(s) \in \mathbb{R}_+$ denote the endowment of Mr. t in period τ and state s, and

$$\omega_0 = [\omega_0^1(\alpha), \omega_0^1(\beta)] \quad \text{and} \quad \omega_t = [\omega_t^t(\alpha), \omega_t^{t+1}(\alpha), \omega_t^t(\beta), \omega_t^{t+1}(\beta)]$$

$$\text{for } t = 1, 2, \dots .$$

Specify that sunspots do not affect endowments and assume that endowments are stationary so that, independent of state and birthdate, Mr. t's endowment is, say, $\omega^1 > 0$ when young and $\omega^2 > 0$ when old. Then we have

$$\omega_0 = (\omega^2, \omega^2) \quad \text{and} \quad \omega_t = (\omega^1, \omega^1, \omega^2, \omega^2) \quad \text{for } t = 1, 2, \dots .$$

Assume for the moment that there is no outside money in the economy, but that there is a complete set of Arrow securities markets or, what amounts to the same thing, a complete set of contingent-claims markets, and that all consumers can participate on all these markets. Let $p^t(s)$ denote the price (before sunspot activity is observed) of a claim for one unit of commodity in period t if state s is realized. Given these contingent-claims prices and the fundamentals (i.e., preferences and endowments) described earlier, we can proceed to characterize consumer behavior.

Mr. 0's optimal consumption bundle x_0 solves the problem:

$$\text{maximize} \quad \pi(\alpha)\phi[x_0^1(\alpha)] + \pi(\beta)\phi[x_0^1(\beta)]$$

$$\text{subject to} \quad p^1(\alpha)x_0^1(\alpha) + p^1(\beta)x_0^1(\beta) \le p^1(\alpha)\omega^2 + p^1(\beta)\omega^2 \quad (1)$$

$$\text{and} \quad x_0 \ge 0,$$

whereas Mr. t's optimal consumption bundle x_t solves the problem:

$$\text{maximize} \quad \pi(\alpha)\psi[ax_t^t(\alpha) + bx_t^{t+1}(\alpha)] + \pi(\beta)\psi[ax_t^t(\beta) + bx_t^{t+1}(\beta)]$$

$$\text{subject to} \quad p^t(\alpha)x_t^t(\alpha) + p^{t+1}(\alpha)x_t^{t+1}(\alpha) + p^t(\beta)x_t^t(\beta) + p^{t+1}(\beta)x_t^{t+1}(\beta)$$

$$\le p^t(\alpha)\omega^1 + p^{t+1}(\alpha)\omega^2 + p^t(\beta)\omega^1 + p^{t+1}(\beta)\omega^2 \quad (2)$$

$$\text{and} \quad x_t \ge 0.$$

Interior solutions to these problems are characterized by the Lagrangean conditions, which, after some simplification, can be written as

$$p^1(\alpha)[x_0^1(\alpha) - \omega^2] + p^1(\beta)[x_0^1(\beta) - \omega^2] = 0 \tag{3}$$

and

$$\frac{\phi'[x_0^1(\alpha)]}{\phi'[x_0^1(\beta)]} = \frac{p^1(\alpha)/\pi(\alpha)}{p^1(\beta)/\pi(\beta)} \tag{4}$$

for equation (1), and

$$p^t(\alpha)[x_t^t(\alpha) - \omega^1] + p^{t+1}(\alpha)[x_t^{t+1}(\alpha) - \omega^2]$$
$$+ p^t(\beta)[x_t^t(\beta) - \omega^1] + p^{t+1}(\beta)[x_t^{t+1}(\beta) - \omega^2] = 0, \tag{5}$$

$$\frac{p^t(\alpha)}{p^{t+1}(\alpha)} = \frac{p^t(\beta)}{p^{t+1}(\beta)} = \frac{a}{b}, \tag{6}$$

and

$$\frac{\psi'[ax_t^t(\alpha) + bx_t^{t+1}(\alpha)]}{\psi'[ax_t^t(\beta) + bx_t^{t+1}(\beta)]} = \frac{p^t(\alpha)/\pi(\alpha)}{p^t(\beta)/\pi(\beta)} \tag{7}$$

for equation (2).

Definition.   *The contingent-claims price sequence*

$$p^1(\alpha), p^1(\beta), p^2(\alpha), p^2(\beta), \dots, p^t(\alpha), p^t(\beta), \dots \tag{8}$$

is said to be a nonmonetary competitive equilibrium *if we have*

$$x_{t-1}^t(s) - \omega^2 = -[x_t^t(s) - \omega^1] \quad \text{for } t = 1, 2, \dots \tag{9}$$

where x_0 is the optimal solution to (1), and x_t is the optimal solution to (2) for $t = 1, 2, \dots$. The sequence of these optimal consumption bundles

$$x_0, x_1, \dots, x_t, \dots$$

is the associated nonmonetary competitive equilibrium allocation.

Equations (9) are the materials balance conditions; and when consumers optimize, they are the (contingent-claims) market-clearing conditions. Next we provide the corresponding nonsunspot and sunspot concepts.

Definition.   *A nonmonetary competitive equilibrium is said to be non-sunspot if, in addition, the associated allocation sequence satisfies*

$$x_0^1(\alpha) = x_0^1(\beta) \quad \text{and} \quad [x_t^t(\alpha), x_t^{t+1}(\alpha)] = [x_t^t(\beta), x_t^{t+1}(\beta)]$$
$$\text{for } t = 1, 2, \dots . \tag{10}$$

Otherwise, it is said to be a sunspot, nonmonetary competitive equilibrium.

We shall also need the concept of a monetary competitive equilibrium. Suppose that the economy is as described previously with the sole exception that the government transfers to Mr. 0, in period 1, one unit of paper money independent of the state of nature. Let $p^m(s)$ be the money price in state s. Then Mr. 0's problem becomes finding the optimal consumption bundle x_0 that solves

$$\text{maximize} \quad \pi(\alpha)\phi[x_0^1(\alpha)] + \pi(\beta)\phi[x_0^1(\beta)]$$

$$\text{subject to} \quad p^1(\alpha)x_0^1(\alpha) + p^1(\beta)x_0^1(\beta)$$

$$\leq p^1(\alpha)\omega^2 + p^1(\beta)\omega^2 + p^m(\alpha) + p^m(\beta) \qquad (1^m)$$

$$\text{and} \quad x_0 \geq 0.$$

Interior solutions to (1^m) are characterized by the simplified Lagrangean conditions

$$p^1(\alpha)[x_0^1(\alpha) - \omega^2] + p^1(\beta)[x_0^1(\beta) - \omega^2] - [p^m(\alpha) + p^m(\beta)] = 0 \qquad (3^m)$$

and (4).

Definition. *A* monetary competitive equilibrium *is a money price vector* $[p^m(\alpha), p^m(\beta)]$ *and a contingent-claims price sequence* (8) *with the property that both the contingent-commodities market-clearing equation* (9) *and the money-market–clearing conditions* $-p^1(s)[x_1^1(s) - \omega_1^1(s)] = p^m(s)$, *for* $s = \alpha, \beta$, *hold when* x_0 *is the optimal solution to* (1^m), *and* x_t *is the optimal solution to* (2) *for* $t = 1, 2, \ldots$. *If, in addition, property* (10) *is satisfied, then we have a* nonsunspot, monetary competitive equilibrium.

In the following section we present three (stationary) competitive equilibria for this example. The nonsunspot nonmonetary and the nonsunspot monetary equilibria are simple and straightforward to display. The sunspot nonmonetary equilibrium, however, requires further specification of the parameters in the example.

3   Three competitive equilibria and their properties

a   *A nonsunspot nonmonetary competitive equilibrium*

Using the simplified Lagrangean conditions (3), (4), (5), and (7), it is easily verified that the autarkic (and thus stationary) allocation described by

$$x_0^1(s) = \omega^2 \quad \text{for} \quad s = \alpha, \beta$$

and $\qquad\qquad\qquad\qquad\qquad\qquad\qquad\qquad\qquad\qquad (11)$

$$[x_t^t(s), x_t^{t+1}(s)] = (\omega^1, \omega^2) \quad \text{for} \quad t = 1, 2, \ldots \text{ and } s = \alpha, \beta$$

is a nonsunspot, nonmonetary competitive equilibrium allocation when supporting prices are defined (up to some normalization) by

$$\frac{p^1(\alpha)}{\pi(\alpha)} = \frac{p^1(\beta)}{\pi(\beta)} > 0$$

and   (12)

$$p^{t+1}(s) = \left(\frac{b}{a}\right) p^t(s) \quad \text{for } t = 1, 2, \dots \text{ and } s = \alpha, \beta.$$

Because, by hypothesis, we have $b/a > 1$, the second condition in (12) implies that "present-value" contingent-claims prices explode, that is,

$$\lim_{t \to \infty} \frac{p^t(s)}{p^1(s)} = \infty \quad \text{for } s = \alpha, \beta.$$ (13)

Now, because it is a competitive equilibrium allocation, we know that the sequence defined by (11) is weakly (or, equivalently, short-run) Pareto optimal. Property (13), however, suggests that this autarkic allocation is not (fully) Pareto optimal. This conjecture is in fact established by the next equilibrium we display.

b   *A nonsunspot monetary competitive equilibrium*

Consider the stationary allocation described by

$$x_0^1(s) = \omega^1 + \omega^2 \quad \text{for } s = \alpha, \beta$$

and   (14)

$$[x_t^t(s), x_t^{t+1}(s)] = (0, \omega^1 + \omega^2) \quad \text{for } t = 1, 2, \dots \text{ and } s = \alpha, \beta.$$

Because, again by hypothesis, we have

$$\left. \frac{\partial \psi(ax^1 + bx^2)/\partial x^1}{\partial \psi(ax^1 + bx^2)/\partial x^2} \right|_{(x^1, x^2) = (0, \omega^1 + \omega^2)} = \frac{a}{b} < 1,$$

it is easily verified [e.g., by attempting to improve on Mr. 0's welfare by perturbing the sequence (14)] that this particular stationary allocation is Pareto optimal. Moreover, because of the strict monotonicity of ϕ and ψ, we have

$$\phi(\omega^1 + \omega^2) > \phi(\omega^2) \quad \text{and} \quad \psi[b(\omega^1 + \omega^2)] > \psi(a\omega^1 + b\omega^2),$$

so that the allocation (14) clearly Pareto dominates the autarkic allocation (11); this demonstrates directly that the autarkic allocation is not Pareto optimal. Finally, the sequence (14) is also a nonsunspot, monetary competitive equilibrium allocation when supporting prices are defined by

$$\frac{p^m(\alpha)}{\pi(\alpha)} = \frac{p^m(\beta)}{\pi(\beta)} > 0 \quad \text{and} \quad p^m(\alpha) + p^m(\beta) = p^1(\alpha)\omega^1 + p^1(\beta)\omega^1 \quad (15)$$

and

$$\frac{p^1(\alpha)}{\pi(\alpha)} = \frac{p^1(\beta)}{\pi(\beta)} > 0$$

and   (16)

$$p^{t+1}(s) = p^t(s) \quad \text{for } t = 1, 2, \dots \text{ and } s = \alpha, \beta.$$

[The last claim is now easily verified by using the simplified Lagrangean conditions (3^m) and (4) together with (5),

$$\frac{p^t(s)}{p^{t+1}(s)} > \frac{a}{b} \quad \text{for } s = \alpha, \beta,$$

and (7), because the latter constitutes the (simplified) Kuhn–Tucker conditions characterizing an optimal solution to (2), for which $x_t^i(s) = 0$ and $x_t^{t+1}(s) > 0$ for $s = \alpha, \beta$.]

c   *A sunspot nonmonetary competitive equilibrium*

The aim in this section is to specify in more detail the parameters of our example in order to construct a sunspot nonmonetary competitive equilibrium. In such an equilibrium, at least one consumer chooses (and thus strictly prefers) an optimal consumption bundle different from his endowment. Hence, this construction guarantees that the associated allocation Pareto dominates the (autarkic) nonsunspot nonmonetary equilibrium allocation (11).

Our strategy is to restrict attention to allocations that are stationary after the level of sunspot activity is revealed. (So, in this sense, all three of our displayed equilibria are "stationary.") Consider an allocation of the form

$$x_0^1(s) = x^{2,s} \quad \text{for } s = \alpha, \beta$$

and   (17)

$$[x_t^i(s), x_t^{t+1}(s)] = (x^{1,s}, x^{2,s}) \quad \text{for } t = 1, 2, \dots \text{ and } s = \alpha, \beta.$$

Choose the parameters in (17) so that Mr. $t > 0$ will be better off in state α than in autarky, but better off in autarky than in state β. In particular, consider $(x^{1,s}, x^{2,s})$ for $s = \alpha, \beta$ that satisfy the following conditions:

$$0 < x^{1,\alpha} < \omega^1 < x^{1,\beta}, \quad 0 < x^{2,\beta} < \omega^2 < x^{2,\alpha};$$

$$x^{i,\alpha} - \omega^i = -(x^{i,\beta} - \omega^i) \quad \text{for } i = 1, 2; \tag{18}$$

$$x^{2,s} - \omega^2 = -(x^{1,s} - \omega^1) \quad \text{for } s = \alpha, \beta.$$

The properties described by (18) are illustrated in Figure 1, together with the relationship between the stationary allocation (17) and (18) and the

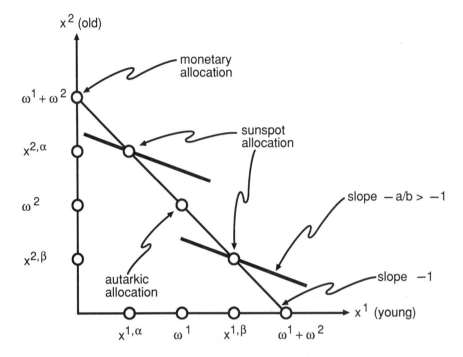

Figure 1

nonsunspot monetary and nonsunspot nonmonetary allocations. Note, especially, that the last equation in (18) implies that the market-clearing conditions (8) are satisfied and [together with the first inequalities in (18)] that we have

$$x^{2,\alpha} - x^{2,\beta} = -(x^{1,\alpha} - x^{1,\beta}) > 0. \tag{19}$$

If an allocation satisfying conditions (17) and (18) is to be supported as a competitive equilibrium allocation, then from Mr. t's first-order condition (6), the real rate of interest after sunspot activity is revealed must equal his constant marginal rate of substitution a/b, so that

$$p^{t+1}(s) = \left(\frac{b}{a}\right)p^t(s) \quad \text{for } t = 1, 2, \dots \text{ and } s = \alpha, \beta. \tag{20}$$

Make the further specification that

$$p^1(\alpha) = p^1(\beta) > 0, \tag{21}$$

which in conjunction with (20) yields

$$p^t(\alpha) = p^t(\beta) > 0 \quad \text{for } t = 1, 2, \dots. \tag{22}$$

At contingent-claims prices satisfying (22), the middle equation in (18) implies that both budget constraints (3) and (5) are satisfied.

Now substitute from (17) and (22) into Mr. t's other first-order condition, (7), which after simplification yields

$$\frac{\psi'(ax^{1,\alpha}+bx^{2,\alpha})}{\psi'(ax^{1,\beta}+bx^{2,\beta})} = \frac{1-\pi(\alpha)}{\pi(\alpha)}. \tag{23}$$

Condition (19), together with the assumption that $0 < a < b$, implies that

$$ax^{1,\alpha}+bx^{2,\alpha} = ax^{1,\beta}+bx^{2,\beta}+(-a+b)(x^{2,\alpha}-x^{2,\beta}) > ax^{1,\beta}+bx^{2,\beta},$$

or that, by strict concavity of ψ, the left-hand side of Eq. (23) must be less than one. So we can solve Eq. (23) for $0 < \pi(\alpha) < 1$, in which case both of Mr. t's first-order conditions (6) and (7), will be satisfied.

Given the foregoing specification of consumption [in (17) and (18)], prices [in (20) and (21)], and probabilities [in (23)], all that remains is to guarantee that Mr. 0's first-order condition (4) is also satisfied. This is accomplished by further restricting ϕ to exhibit the property

$$\frac{\phi'(x^{2,\alpha})}{\phi'(x^{2,\beta})} = \frac{1-\pi(\alpha)}{\pi(\alpha)} < 1,$$

which is possible because ϕ is strictly concave whereas, from the first inequalities in (18), we have $x^{2,\alpha} > x^{2,\beta}$.

We have displayed a sunspot nonmonetary competitive equilibrium.

Remark 1: Constructing this sunspot equilibrium required balancing various considerations (e.g., Mr. t's risk aversion against his relative welfare improvement in state α over state β). This balancing does not seem to be so delicate as to lead us to believe that we are dealing with a razor's edge situation. In particular, the simplifying assumption of linear indifference curves is not essential even for our specific example. From Figure 1, one can see that we basically need only the property that the marginal rate of substitution along some line $x^1+x^2 = k > 0$ be equal and less than unity (for at least two distinct points). Thus, for instance, a more general specification that would justify our specific construction is

$$\psi(x^1, x^2) = f[ax^1+bx^2+cg(x^1+x^2)],$$

where $0 < a < b$, $c > 0$, and both f and g are smooth, strictly increasing, and strictly concave.

Remark 2: As we mentioned at the beginning of this subsection, the sunspot allocation (17) and (18) Pareto dominates the nonsunspot, nonmonetary competitive equilibrium allocation (11). However, although weakly Pareto optimal, it in turn is itself not Pareto optimal; it also is Pareto dominated by the nonsunspot, monetary competitive equilibrium allocation (14). This fact is easily deduced by employing the relationships displayed in Figure 1, together with the strict monotonicity of ϕ and ψ, which yield

$$\phi(\omega^1+\omega^2) > \max_s \phi(x^{2,s}) > \pi(\alpha)\,\phi(x^{2,\alpha}) + \pi(\beta)\,\phi(x^{2,\beta})$$

and

$$\psi[b(\omega^1+\omega^2)] > \max_s \psi(ax^{1,s}+bx^{2,s})$$
$$> \pi(\alpha)\,\psi(ax^{1,\alpha}+bx^{2,\alpha}) + \pi(\beta)\,\psi(ax^{1,\beta}+bx^{2,\beta}).$$

d   *Sunspots, money, and welfare*

We reemphasize the following welfare considerations:

1   The nonsunspot monetary competitive equilibrium allocation (14) is Pareto optimal; it also (strictly) Pareto dominates both the nonsunspot nonmonetary competitive equilibrium allocation (11) and the sunspot nonmonetary competitive equilibrium allocation (17) and (18).

2   Both nonmonetary allocations are weakly Pareto optimal. Although sunspot allocations cannot be Pareto optimal, the sunspot allocation from our example Pareto dominates the nonsunspot, nonmonetary competitive equilibrium allocation from our example. In other words, our example suggests that, in an overlapping-generations setting, sunspots might be employed as a coordinating device to attenuate a tendency toward oversaving; that is, *sunspots can serve as imperfect substitutes for the social contrivance of money.*

The sunspot allocation has another striking welfare property. Even though it is weakly Pareto optimal, a planner seeking to restore Pareto optimality would have to intervene in the first period.[10] This distinguishes this more complicated OG model from the one-good, one-state OG model. In the latter case the planner could wait any finite number of periods before intervening and still convert a weakly Pareto optimal allocation to Pareto optimality.

To paraphrase Samuelson (1967), one might question the importance of distinguishing between weakly Pareto-optimal allocations and fully Pareto-optimal allocations on the grounds that *based solely on a finite*

---

[10] The sunspot allocation is not *observationally Pareto optimal* (see Burke, 1987) because we need only observe a *finite* history to determine that it is not (fully) Pareto optimal. Clearly, in the finite history, the complete contingent allocation (*not* merely the realized allocation) must be observed.

history one cannot observe a difference between weak Pareto optima and full Pareto optima. The importance of Samuelson's point aside, it is accurate for the one-good, one-state model. Samuleson's point is, however, not accurate for one sunspot equilibrium allocation. This weakly Pareto optimal allocation can be detected (or *observed*) to be not Pareto optimal immediately after the first-period contingent allocation has been assigned.[11] Once the allocation has been contaminated by sunspots, it cannot be extended to be Pareto optimal.

Perhaps, in future work, one can move from constructing examples to establishing theorems for economies with many commodities per period, many consumers per generation, more general demographic structure, and naturally restricted market participation. Can the existence of sunspot, nonmonetary competitive equilibria in the general case be related as in our special example to the structure of the set of nonsunspot (monetary and nonmonetary) competitive equilibria? If so, the idea that sunspots may partly fill the same role as money would be strengthened.

REFERENCES

Azariadis, C. (1981), "Self-fulfilling prophecies," *Journal of Economic Theory,* 25(3), 380–96.
Azariadis, C., and Guesnerie, R. (1982), "Prophéties créatice et persistance des théories," *Revue Economique,* 33, 787–806.
(1986), "Sunspots and cycles," *Review of Economic Studies,* 53(5), 725–38.
Balasko, Y., Cass, D., and Shell, K. (1988), "Market participation and sunspot equilibria," CAE Working Paper No. 88-11, March 1988, Cornell University and CARESS Working Paper No. 88-08, March 1988, University of Pennsylvania.
Balasko, Y., and Shell, K. (1980), "The overlapping-generations model, I: The case of pure exchange without money," *Journal of Economic Theory,* 23(3), 281–306.
(1981), "The overlapping-generations model, II: The case of pure exchange with money," *Journal of Economic Theory,* 24(1), 112–42.
(1986), "Lump-sum taxes and transfers: Public debt in the overlapping-generations model," in *Essays in Honor of Kenneth J. Arrow, Volume II: Equilibrium Analysis,* ed. by W. P. Heller, R. M. Starr, and D. A. Starrett, New York: Cambridge University Press, 121–53.
Benveniste, L., and Cass, D. (1984), "Segregated commodity markets and sunspots," CARESS Working Paper No. 84-22, October, University of Pennsylvania.
Burke, J. (1987), "Bounded foresight, efficiency, and the core of overlapping-generations economies," mimeo., November, Texas A&M University.

---

[11] Our example need not necessarily be interpreted as a sunspot equilibrium. It is, of course, also an example of equilibrium for a two-good, one-state OG model. The equilibrium is weakly Pareto optimal; and after the first period allocation is made, it is revealed that the intertemporal allocation could not be fully Pareto optimal. If symmetry-breaking occurs in the first period, it can never be repaired.

20   **David Cass and Karl Shell**

Cass, D. (1985), "Optimality with unbounded numbers of households: I. Overlapping (or overlapping-generations) structure and the first basic theorem of welfare," in *Optimalité et Structures: Mélanges en Hommage à Edouard Rossier,* ed. by G. Ritschard and D. Royer, Paris: Economica, 17–42.

(1986), "Sunspots and incomplete financial markets: The leading example," CARESS Working Paper No. 84-06RR, University of Pennsylvania, March, forthcoming in *Joan Robinson and Modern Economics,* ed. by G. Feiwel.

Cass, D., and Polemarchakis, H. M. (1988), "Convexity and sunspots: A comment," CARESS Working Paper No. 88-06, January, University of Pennsylvania.

Cass, D., and Shell, K. (1980), "In defense of a basic approach," in *Models of Monetary Economies,* ed. by J. Kareken and N. Wallace, Federal Reserve Bank of Minneapolis, 251–60.

(1983), "Do sunspots matter?," *Journal of Political Economy,* 91(2), 193–227.

Guesnerie, R., Laffont, J.-J. (1987), "Tâches solaires en horizon fini," preliminary mimeo., October, EHESS, Paris.

Peck, J. (1988), "On the existence of sunspot equilibria in an overlapping-generations model," *Journal of Economic Theory,* 44(1), 19–42.

Peck, J., and Shell, K. (1985), "Market uncertainty: Sunspot equilibria in imperfectly competitive economies," CARESS Working Paper No. 85-21, University of Pennsylvania, July. Revised version appears as "Market uncertainty: Correlated equilibrium and sunspot equilibrium in imperfectly competitive economies," Center for Analytic Economics Working Paper No. 88-22, May, Cornell University.

Samuelson, P. A. (1958), "An exact consumption-loan model of interest with or without the social contrivance of money," *Journal of Political Economy,* 66(6), 467–82.

(1967), "A turnpike refutation of the golden rule in a welfare-maximizing many-year plan," in *Essays on the Theory of Optimal Economic Growth,* ed. by K. Shell, Cambridge: MIT Press, 269–80.

Shell, K. (1971), "Notes on the economics of infinity," *Journal of Political Economy,* 79(5), 1002–11.

(1977), "Monnaie et allocation intertemporelle," mimeo., November 21, CNRS Séminaire d'econométrie de M. Edmond Malinvaud, Paris. [Title and abstract in French; text in English.]

(1987), "Sunspot equilibrium," in *The New Palgrave: A Dictionary of Economics,* ed. by J. Eatwell, M. Milgate, and P. Newman, New York: The Stockton Press, Vol. 4, 549–51.

Siconolfi, P. (1987), "Sunspot equilibria and incomplete financial markets," CARESS Working Paper No. 87-20, August, University of Pennsylvania.

Spear, S. E. (1984), "Sufficient conditions for the existence of sunspot equilibria," *Journal of Economic Theory,* 34(2), 360–70.

(1988), "Growth, externalities, and sunspots," mimeo., Carnegie-Mellon University.

CHAPTER 2

On stationary sunspot equilibria of order k

Pierre-André Chiappori and Roger Guesnerie

1   Introduction

This chapter is devoted to the study of stationary sunspot equilibria in a one-dimensional, one-step forward-looking dynamical system. Such dynamical systems describe economies, indexed by time, in which the state variable at time t is one-dimensional and the relevant forecasting horizon of the agents is of one period. Although many relevant economic questions with time dimensions cannot be captured within such an elementary structure, a number of simple variants of the popular overlapping-generations model do fit this framework. Other examples of the relevance of the simplified structure under scrutiny, outside of the overlapping-generations class of model, include the model described in Chapter 13 by Woodford (1988).

The attention to one-dimensional, one-step forward-looking systems is justified not only by possible economic relevance but also by simplicity and exemplarity. The study of stationary sunspot equilibria in more complex systems – for example by Guesnerie (1986) or Woodford (1986) – should benefit from progress in the understanding of stationary sunspot equilibria (SSE) in one-dimensional, one-step forward-looking systems.

Our point of view in this chapter has two characteristics that should be emphasized. First, in the line of Guesnerie (1986), we describe the system through an abstract excess-demand function; we formulate axiomatically a certain number of requirements, which are minimal for the theory and which should result, in more specific versions of the model, from the conclusions of consumer or producer theory. This abstract description of the system is justified, in our opinion, by its simplicity and generality. Second, we take a specific line of investigation that differs from other

We are very grateful to two anonymous referees for their patience in deciphering a (somewhat incomplete) previous manuscript and in making sense of its roughest parts. We hope that this version is responsive to their comments. Of course, any remaining errors are ours.

21

approaches in the literature. Such a line, which in its techniques as well as its perspectives can be traced back to the work of Azariadis and Guesnerie (1982, 1986), leads to emphasizing the stochastic properties of the singular, extrinsic (in the sense of Shell, 1977, and Cass and Shell, 1983) sunspot process on which beliefs are based. Other approaches using different techniques lead to existence results of SSE (around the stationary state in Woodford, 1986, or of global nature in Grandmont, 1986a) in which the stochastic properties of the sunspot process are neither directly nor necessarily completely apprehended. Naturally, the various competing perspectives and techniques are complementary rather than opposing. We do think, however, that what could be termed the Azariadis–Guesnerie perspective, which is taken here, is well adapted to a full understanding of some important features of the sunspot phenomenon.

The plan of this chapter is as follows: In Section 2 we describe the model, and in Section 3 we apply the Poincaré–Hopf argument, first introduced by Azariadis and Guesnerie (1982) for the existence of stationary sunspot equilibria, to the abstract system under consideration. Specifically, considering systems with a unique "indeterminate" stationary equilibrium, we extend to sunspots of order k the sufficient conditions previously obtained for sunspots of order 2 in a simple OG framework. In particular, we characterize a broad class of Markov matrices that are associated with sunspots of order k. The set of SSE of order k is considered from a differential viewpoint in Section 4; we show that, in some sense, "many" sunspot equilibria of strict order k do exist "close to" sunspots of order $k-1$. Section 5 introduces a few results on the bifurcations of the system near the stationary state and gives brief indications on the route for obtaining local counterparts of the global results obtained in Section 3.

2   The model

a   *Excess demand under certainty*

The basic model is a very simple variant of Guesnerie (1986). We define an abstract, deterministic, one-dimensional system through a mapping:

$$Z: \mathbb{R}_+ \times \mathbb{R}_+ \to \mathbb{R}.$$

Here, $Z(p_t, p_{t+1})$ can often (but not necessarily) be interpreted as the excess demand for the unique good when present price (in terms of money) is p_t and the (perfectly foreseen) future price is p_{t+1}. Under the (perfect foresight) dynamics described by Z, perfect foresight equilibria are defined by

$\forall t, \ Z(p_t, p_{t+1}) = 0.$

In particular, a stationary equilibrium is a price $\bar{p}$ such that

$Z(\bar{p}, \bar{p}) = 0.$

The equations describing the evolution of the usual overlapping-generation (OG) model with a representative consumer define a one-dimensional, one-step forward-looking system of the kind we are considering. The system may have one or several stationary equilibria (or steady states). Often, as in the next section, we shall assume that it has only one (as is the case for the simple OG model with representative consumer and no government expenditures).

From Z, we can define a vector field ZZ over $\mathbb{R}_+$ by

$$ZZ: (p_1, p_2) \to [Z(p_1, p_2), Z(p_2, p_1)].$$

b   *Uncertainty and sunspots*

Assume now that expectations are stochastic. Tomorrow the price can take any of k different values $p_{t+1}^1, \ldots, p_{t+1}^k$ with respective probabilities $\pi^1, \ldots, \pi^k$. The excess demand of the system can still be defined; but now it is a mapping,

$$\tilde{Z}^k: \mathbb{R}_+^{k+1} \times S^{k-1} \to \mathbb{R},$$

where S^{k-1} is the simplex in $\mathbb{R}^k$. In words, $\tilde{Z}^k$ is a function of present price p_t, future prices $p_{t+1}^1, \ldots, p_{t+1}^k$, and probabilities $\pi^1, \ldots, \pi^k$ (with $\sum_\ell \pi^\ell = 1$). Again, $\tilde{Z}^k$ can easily be derived from consumers' utilities in a usual OG context. In what follows, we shall assume that Z and $\tilde{Z}^k$ are *smooth* (of class C^2) for all $k \in \mathbb{Z}$.

We now come to the definition of a *stationary sunspot equilibrium (SSE)*. The intuition is the following. Consider a random exogenous Markovian phenomenon with k different states; it is described by $k \times k$ Markov matrix M. Let M_ℓ denote the ℓth line of M; that is, $M_\ell = (m_{\ell 1}, \ldots, m_{\ell k})$, where $m_{\ell s}$ is the probability of being tomorrow in state s, given that the present state is ℓ. In particular,

$$\sum_s m_{\ell s} = 1, \quad \text{for each} \ \ell.$$

Associated with M is a price vector $p = (p_1, \ldots, p_k)$ of $\mathbb{R}_+^k$. Suppose that the agents in the economy believe that the price of the unique good in period t will be p_ℓ if and only if the exogenous process is in state ℓ at that date. Under such a "theory," the *present* state of process brings information on the *future* price of the good; namely, if the present state is ℓ, then the probability of the price being p_s tomorrow is exactly $m_{\ell s}$. That is, under this theory, the present excess demand will be $\tilde{Z}^k(p_\ell, p, M_\ell)$. Now we say that the vector p is an SSE associated with the matrix M if this theory is self-fulfilling; that is, if, given the agents' behavior, the price that clears the market when the process is in state ℓ is exactly p_ℓ, as predicted.

This leads to the following formal definition. First, we define the mapping

$$\hat{Z}^k: \mathbb{R}_+^k \times \mathfrak{M}_k \rightarrow \mathbb{R}^k$$

by $\hat{Z}^k(p, M) = [\tilde{Z}^k(p_1, p, M_1), ..., \tilde{Z}^k(p_k, p, M_k)]$, where $\mathfrak{M}_k$ is the set of $(k \times k)$ Markov matrices. In words, the ℓth component of $\hat{Z}^k$ is the excess demand when present price is p_ℓ and the process is in state ℓ. Now we have the following.

Definition 1. *A pair (p, M), for which the components $(p_1, ..., p_k)$ of p are not all identical, define an SSE of cardinal k if $\hat{Z}^k(p, M) = (0, ..., 0)$.*

In the same way, *local* SSE are defined as follows.

Definition 2. *The economy exhibits local SSE (of cardinal k) around the steady state if, for any neighborhood $\mathfrak{N}$ of $(\bar{p}, ..., \bar{p})$, there exists a SSE (p, M) such that $p \in \mathfrak{N}$.*

In words, we speak of local SSE when SSE exists in any, however small, neighborhood of the steady state.

Note that we have defined the *cardinal* of the SSE as the number of components of p. Now, the number of *different* components in p will be called the *order* of the SSE. Note that, from Definition 1, the order of a SSE is at least 2.

c   *Basic axioms*

A number of requirements are in order. First, we need some consistency axioms that describe the relationship between excess demands under certainty and uncertainty. We shall state a few regularity assumptions concerning the "certain" excess demand Z at the stationary state. In what follows, the partial mapping $\hat{Z}^k(\cdot, M)$, for given M, is denoted $\hat{Z}_M^k(\cdot)$.

(i)   *Quantity consistency (A1)*
Assume that $p_{t+1} = (p_{t+1}^1, ..., p_{t+1}^k)$ is such that $p_{t+1}^i = p_{t+1}^j$ (with $i < j$). Define $p_{t+1}' \in \mathbb{R}^{k-1}$ by

$$p'_{t+1} = p_{t+1}^{-j} = (p_{t+1}^1, \ldots, p_{t+1}^i, \ldots, p_{t+1}^{j-1}, p_{t+1}^{j+1}, \ldots, p_{t+1}^k).$$

Then $\tilde{Z}^k$ depends only on the probability distribution of the p_{t+1}; that is, for any p_t and any $\pi \in S^{k-1}$,

$$\tilde{Z}^k(p_t, p_{t+1}, \pi) = \tilde{Z}^{k-1}(p_t, p'_{t+1}, \pi'),$$

with $\pi' \in S^{k-2}$ equal to $(\pi^1, \ldots, \pi^i + \pi^j, \ldots, \pi^{j-1}, \pi^{j+1}, \ldots, \pi^k)$.

In particular, if $p_{t+1}^j = p$ for all j, then whatever π,

$$\tilde{Z}^k(p_t, p_{t+1}, \pi) = Z(p_t, p).$$

(ii)   *Consistency of derivatives (A2)*

$\forall \pi$, $\forall \bar{p}_{t+1} = (\bar{p}, \ldots, \bar{p})$, we have

$$\frac{\partial \tilde{Z}^k}{\partial p_t}(p_t, \bar{p}_{t+1}, \bar{\pi}) = \frac{\partial Z^k}{\partial p_t}(p_t, \bar{p}),$$

and $\forall \ell$, we have

$$\frac{\partial \tilde{Z}^k}{\partial p_{t+1}^\ell}(p_t, \bar{p}_{t+1}, \bar{\pi}) = \bar{\pi}_\ell \cdot \frac{\partial Z}{\partial p_{t+1}}(p_t, \bar{p}).$$

(iii)   *Boundary assumptions (A3)*

(A3a)   Consider the rectangle $R = [b_t, B_t] \times [b_{t+1}, B_{t+1}]$ in $\mathbb{R}_+^2$. For b_t, b_{t+1} small enough and B_t, B_{t+1} large enough, ZZ, considered as a vector field over R^2, points inward.

(A3b)   For any given Markov matrix M, consider the rectangle $\tilde{R} = \prod_{\ell=1}^k [b_{t+1}^\ell, B_{t+1}^\ell]$ in $\mathbb{R}_+^k$. For $b_{t+1}^1, \ldots, b_{t+1}^k$ small enough, and $B_{t+1}^1, \ldots, B_{t+1}^k$ large enough, $\hat{Z}_M^k$, considered as a vector field over $\tilde{R}$, points inward.

These axioms generalize in a straightforward way those in Guesnerie (1986). We see that (A1) essentially says that $\tilde{Z}$ depends only on the probability distribution of future *prices* (and not of the sunspot per se). In particular, whenever the future price is known *with certainty* to be p_{t+1}, then $\tilde{Z}^k$ and Z coincide. Incidentally, an immediate consequence of (A1) is that $\tilde{Z}_M^k[\bar{p}] = 0$, where $\bar{p} = [\bar{p}, \ldots, \bar{p}]$ is a stationary state, for all M. When future price is certain, the derivatives of Z and $\tilde{Z}^k$ with respect to present price p_t must also coincide; this is the meaning of the first relation in (A2), which, incidentally, could simply be deduced from (A1). Also consider, at the margin of this certainty situation, an infinitesimal change dp_{t+1}^ℓ in p_{t+1}^ℓ. Because this introduces only an infinitesimal uncertainty, the change is equivalent to a *sure* change of magnitude $\bar{\pi}^\ell \cdot dp_{t+1}^\ell$ (i.e., the *expected value* of the initial change, hence the second relation in

(A2). Last, (A3a) is a standard boundary assumption, and (A3b) is its unsurprising extension to stochastic forecasts.[1]

It must be stressed that the consistency properties (A1) and (A2) are derived (as the reader can check) from utility maximization, in the context of an usual OG model with representative consumer; no specific assumption is needed upon utilities apart from strong quasiconcavity and sufficient differentiability. However, they hold true in more general frameworks. Note, for instance, that they are preserved by aggregation of individual demands; hence, they do *not* require, in fact, anything like a representative consumer.

We now state a regularity assumption.

(iv)   *Generic regularity of a stationary equilibrium (GR)*
In a stationary equilibrium $\bar{p}$, we have

$$\frac{\partial Z}{\partial p_{t+1}}(\bar{p}, \bar{p}) \neq 0,$$

$$\frac{\partial Z}{\partial p_t}(\bar{p}, \bar{p}) + \frac{\partial Z}{\partial p_{t+1}}(\bar{p}, \bar{p}) \neq 0,$$

$$\frac{\partial Z}{\partial p_t}(\bar{p}, \bar{p}) - \frac{\partial Z}{\partial p_{t+1}}(\bar{p}, \bar{p}) \neq 0.$$

It is clear that if Z is extracted from a "rich" enough set, (GR) is generic (hence, the terminology). A more precise meaning of the genericity assumption can be given in more specific models (e.g., representative consumer and finite number of consumers); this task is left to the reader.

In what follows, we shall note Z_1 (respectively, Z_2) for $(\partial Z/\partial p_t)(\bar{p}, \bar{p})$ [respectively, $(\partial Z/\partial p_{t+1})(\bar{p}, \bar{p})$]. A first remark is that the boundary assumption (A3a), together with uniqueness of stationary equilibrium, determines the sign of $Z_1 + Z_2$.

Result 1.   *Assume* (A3a). *If the stationary equilibrium $\bar{p}$ is unique and regular (in the sense of* GR*), then*

$$Z_1 + Z_2 < 0.$$

Proof: An elementary proof is the following. Consider the mapping

$$z: \mathbb{R}_+ \to \mathbb{R},$$

---

[1] That assumption holds, for example, in the simple OG model without government expenditures. For a more comprehensive discussion of the boundary assumption as well as of the others, the reader can refer to Guesnerie (1986).

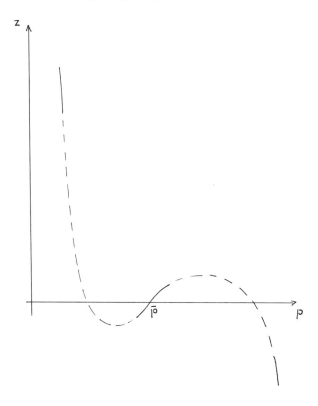

Figure 1

$$p \rightarrow Z(p, p) \stackrel{\text{def}}{=} z(p).$$

Then (A3a) implies $z(p) > 0$ if p is "small enough" and $z(p) < 0$ if p is "large enough." Also,

$$\frac{dz}{dp}(p) = \frac{\partial Z}{\partial p_t}(p, p) + \frac{\partial Z}{\partial p_{t+1}}(p, p).$$

Assume $(dz/dp)(\bar{p}) = Z_1 + Z_2 > 0$. Then the boundary properties imply that the equation $z(p) = 0$ has two solutions in addition to $\bar{p}$ (one smaller than $\bar{p}$ and one greater than $\bar{p}$). So there must exist at least three stationary equilibria, which is a contradiction. ∎

The idea of the proof is summarized by Figure 1.

The conclusion given here is nothing but a particular case of a powerful result in differential topology, the Poincaré–Hopf theorem. Since the general version of the theorem will be used later, it may be useful to give a very simplified presentation of the basic argument. Let S be a manifold with boundaries of $\mathbb{R}^n$, and z a smooth vector field on S with regular, isolated zeros; assume that z points inward at all boundary points of S. If $\bar{p}$ is a zero of z, define the index $i(p)$ of z at $\bar{p}$ by

$$i(p) = +1 \quad \text{if} \quad \Delta_p z(\bar{p}) > 0,$$

$$i(p) = -1 \quad \text{if} \quad \Delta_p z(\bar{p}) < 0,$$

where $\Delta_p z(\bar{p})$ is the Jacobian determinant of z in $\bar{p}$.

The Poincaré–Hopf theorem then implies that the sum of the indices at the zeros of z is a topological invariant of S; in particular, it does not depend on the particular choice of vector field. Moreover, if S is diffeomorphic to a disk of dimension k, then this sum is equal to $(-1)^k$.

How does this result apply here? Take $S = (b, B)$, defined as in (A3a), so that the vector field z points inward at the boundary points. Because $k = 1$, the sum of the indices at the zeros of z must be (-1). But, in this one-dimensional case, the index at p is simply the sign of $(dz/dp)(p)$. If $(\partial z/\partial p)(\bar{p}) > 0$, then the index at $\bar{p}$ is $+1$; so there must be at least two other zeros, with index (-1) [and possibly an equal number of zeros with indices $(+1)$ and (-1)], which is a contradiction.

Of course, this argument can be generalized to any $k \geq 1$. Let $\bar{p}$ be a zero of z, such that the sign of the Jacobian determinant $\Delta_p z(\bar{p})$ is $(-1)^{k+1}$. Then there must be at least two other zeros with index $(-1)^k$. This argument will be used extensively in the next section.

3   Existence of SSE of cardinal k

In this section we state sufficient conditions for a (given) Markov matrix of dimension k to be associated with an SSE. The conditions generalize those obtained by Azariadis and Guesnerie (1982) for matrices of dimension 2 (associated with sunspots of order 2). More precisely, Azariadis and Guesnerie show, in the context of the simple OG model, that if

1   the wage elasticity of savings (under perfect foresight) at the stationary equilibrium ϵ is lower than $-\frac{1}{2}$; and
2   the 2×2 matrix

$$M = \begin{pmatrix} m_{11} & m_{12} \\ m_{21} & m_{22} \end{pmatrix}$$

satisfies $m_{12} + m_{21} > -1/\epsilon$, then there exists an SSE associated with M.

Using the same techniques (which rely basically upon the Poincaré–Hopf theorem), we show that condition 1 and an equivalent version of condition 2 apply to $(k \times k)$ matrices for any $k \geq 2$.

a   Preparation lemmas

The forthcoming results rely upon some technical preliminaries that are gathered here in four lemmas. In what follows, we denote by $\bar{p} = (\bar{p}, \dots, \bar{p})$ the stationary state of the model and by $\Delta \hat{Z}_M^k(p)$ the Jacobian determinant of $\hat{Z}_M^k$ in $p = (p_1, \dots, p_k)$.

Lemma 1. *Assume that there exists a unique stationary equilibrium and that the boundary assumptions* (A3) *are fulfilled. If a Markov matrix M' is such that*

$$(-1)^k \Delta \hat{Z}_{M'}^k(\bar{p}) < 0, \tag{1}$$

then there exists an SSE (p, M') where $p \in \mathbb{R}^k$.

Proof: Lemma 1 says that the index of $\hat{Z}_M^k$ at $\bar{p}$ is $(-1)^{k+1}$. This implies from the Poincaré–Hopf theorem that the equation $\hat{Z}_{M'}^k(p) = 0$ has at least two solutions other than $\bar{p}$; these must be SSE associated with M'. ∎

Thus the existence of SSE can be deduced from the sign of $\Delta \hat{Z}_M^k(\bar{p})$. The next step is to compute this determinant; this task can easily be performed using the consistency axioms (A1) and (A2) and the generic regularity condition (GR).

Lemma 2. *Assume that* (A1), (A2), *and* (GR) *are fulfilled. Then, for any Markovian matrix M,*

$$\Delta \hat{Z}_M^k(\bar{p}) = (Z_2)^k \operatorname{Det}\left(M + \frac{Z_1}{Z_2} I\right), \tag{2}$$

where I is the $(k \times k)$ identity matrix.

Proof: The generic term $\hat{z}_{ij}$ of the Jacobian matrix of $\hat{Z}_M^k$ at $\bar{p}$ is

$$\hat{z}_{ij} = \frac{\partial \tilde{Z}^k}{\partial p_{t+1}^j}(\bar{p}, M_i) + \delta_i^j \frac{\partial \tilde{Z}^k}{\partial p_t}(\bar{p}, M_i),$$

where $\delta_i^j = 1$ if $i = j$, and 0 otherwise.

It follows from (A2) that

$$\Delta \hat{Z}_M^k(\bar{p}) = \begin{vmatrix} Z_1 + m_{11}Z_2 & \cdots & m_{1k}Z_2 \\ \vdots & & \vdots \\ m_{k1}Z_2 & \cdots & Z_1 + m_{kk}Z_2 \end{vmatrix}.$$

Since, from (GR), $Z_2 \neq 0$, this relation can be written as

$$\Delta \hat{Z}_M^k(\bar{p}) = (Z_2)^k \operatorname{Det}\left(M + \frac{Z_1}{Z_2}I\right). \qquad \blacksquare$$

A first consequence is that relation (1) cannot hold unless $|Z_1/Z_2| \leq 1$ [note that (GR) then implies a strict inequality]; also, the set of Markov matrices satisfying (1) for a given value of Z_1/Z_2 can be characterized in the following way:

Lemma 3. *Assume the uniqueness of stationary equilibrium, boundary condition* (A3), *and genericity condition* (GR).

(i) *If* $|Z_1/Z_2| > 1$, *then, for any Markov matrix M,*

$$(-1)^k(Z_2)^k \operatorname{Det}\left(M + \frac{Z_1}{Z_2}I\right) > 0. \tag{3}$$

(ii) *Suppose that* $|Z_1/Z_2| < 1$. *Let M be a Markov matrix; assume that* (Z_1/Z_2) *is not an eigenvalue of M. Then the relation*

$$(-1)^k(Z_2)^k \operatorname{Det}\left(M + \frac{Z_1}{Z_2}I\right) < 0 \tag{4}$$

holds if and only if the number of real eigenvalues of M, inferior to $-Z_1/Z_2$, *is odd.*

Proof: From Result 1 of Section 2, the assumptions imply that $Z_1 + Z_2 < 0$. Now, a first remark is that relation (3) must hold for $M = I$. Otherwise, from Lemma 1, there would exist a SSE associated with I; but, clearly, this would contradict uniqueness of stationary equilibrium. Assume, now, that $|Z_1/Z_2| > 1$. Suppose that there exists a matrix that does not satisfy (3). Then, from the previous remark, the mapping

$$M \to \operatorname{Det}\left(M + \frac{Z_1}{Z_2}I\right)$$

must change its sign over the (connected) set of Markov matrices; hence, there exists a Markov matrix $\bar{M}$ such that $\operatorname{Det}[\bar{M} + (Z_1/Z_2)I] = 0$. This implies that $\bar{M}$ has an eigenvalue equal to (Z_1/Z_2), which is a contradiction because all eigenvalues of a Markov matrix are within the unit circle.

To the contrary, suppose that $|Z_1/Z_2| < 1$. Clearly, $\mathrm{Det}[M + (Z_1/Z_2)I]$ is a polynomial $P(x)$ of degree k in $x = -Z_1/Z_2$; the real roots of this polynomial are nothing but the real eigenvalues of M. Now, the sign of $P(x)$ depends only on the position of x with respect to the real roots of P and, more precisely, on the *parity* of the number of real roots of P below x. In particular, for any given k, the sign of the left-hand side (l.h.s.) of (4) depends only on whether the number of real eigenvalues of M, below $-Z_1/Z_2$, is even or odd.

Last, let us prove that this number must be odd. Indeed, suppose the contrary. Because the only (multiple) eigenvalue of I is 1, this implies that the number of eigenvalues of I below $-Z_1/Z_2$ is zero (i.e., an even number). So (4) holds for I, which is a contradiction to the preceding remarks.

Of course, the fact that the number of eigenvalues below $-Z_1/Z_2$ must be odd can also be checked directly. Assume, first, that k is even. Then $(Z_2)^k$ is positive, so Poincaré–Hopf (PH) applies if $\mathrm{Det}[M + (Z_1/Z_2)I] < 0$. But the characteristic polynomial of M is of even degree, which implies that the number of roots under $-Z_1/Z_2$ must be odd (Figure 2a).

Assume, now, that k is odd. If Z_2 is negative, then also $(Z_2)^k$, and PH again requires $\mathrm{Det}[M + (Z_1/Z_2)I] < 0$. The characteristic polynomial of M is of odd degree. It is negative for "high" values of $-Z_1/Z_2$, specifically for $-Z_1/Z_2 > 1$; but this is excluded by Result 1. So we need the number of eigenvalues of M below $-Z_1/Z_2$ to be odd (Figure 2b). Last, the case with k odd *and* Z_2 positive is ruled out because Result 1 implies $-Z_1/Z_2 > 1$ for that case.   ■

Incidentally, a by-product of this proof is that the PH characterization does not apply unless $Z_2 < 0$; indeed, $Z_2 > 0$ and $Z_1 + Z_2 < 0$ implies that $|Z_1/Z_2| > 1$. In words, excess demand is "backward-bending" at $\bar{p}$ in the sense that an increase in future price decreases today's excess demand.

A last question is whether the set of Markov matrices satisfying (4), when $|Z_1/Z_2| < 1$, is nonempty. The answer is positive.

Lemma 4. *If* $|Z_1/Z_2| < 1$, *then there exist* $(k \times k)$ *Markov matrices* M, *such that* $\Delta \hat{Z}_M(\hat{p}) < 0$.

Proof: From Lemma 3, it is sufficient to show that, given any real number $x(= -Z_1/Z_2)$ in $(-1, 1)$, there exists a Markov matrix M such that the number of eigenvalues of M below x is odd. Now, take any $-1 < \lambda_1 < x$, and any $\lambda_2, \ldots, \lambda_{k-1}$ such that $1 \geq \lambda_i > \mathrm{Max}(x, 0)$, $i = 2, \ldots, k-1$. The Markov matrix

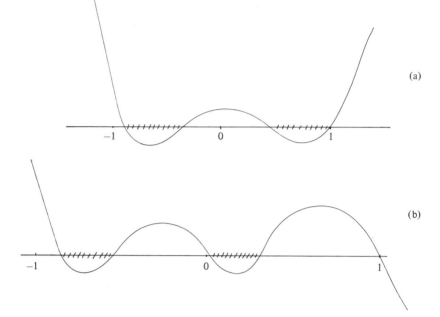

(a)

(b)

Figure 2

$$M = \begin{bmatrix} (\lambda_1+1)/2 & (1-\lambda_1)/2 & 0 & \cdots & 0 \\ (1-\lambda_1)/2 & (1+\lambda_1)/2 & 0 & \cdots & 0 \\ 1-\lambda_2 & 0 & \lambda_2 & \cdots & 0 \\ \vdots & & & & \\ 1-\lambda_{k-1} & 0 & 0 & \cdots & \lambda_{k-1} \end{bmatrix}$$

has exactly one eigenvalue below x (namely, λ_1).   ■

b   *The result*

The economic substance of the preceding results can be summarized as follows:

Proposition 1.   *Assume that there exists a unique stationary equilib-rium, and that conditions* (A1), (A2), (A3) *and* (GR) *are fulfilled. If*

$$\left| \frac{Z_1}{Z_2} \right| < 1, \tag{5}$$

then for any Markov matrix M having an odd number of eigenvalues below $-Z_1/Z_2$, there exists a price vector p such that (p, M) is an SSE. In particular, since the set of such matrices is nonempty, (5) is a sufficient condition for the existence of SSE.

Two remarks may help in understanding this result.

Remark 1: Suppose $k = 2$; then

$$M = \begin{pmatrix} m_{11} & m_{12} \\ m_{21} & m_{22} \end{pmatrix}$$

has two eigenvalues, namely, 1 and $\lambda = m_{11} + m_{22} - 1 = 1 - m_{21} - m_{12}$. Thus an SSE is associated with M if

$$m_{12} + m_{21} > 1 + \frac{Z_1}{Z_2}, \tag{6}$$

that is, loosely speaking, if the process changes its state with a "high enough" probability (a result in the spirit of Azariadis and Guesnerie). In fact, we shall see that in the usual one-dimensional OG model, (6) is identical to the Azariadis–Guesnerie's relation.

Remark 2: It can easily be checked that Proposition 1 applies to matrices of cycles of even order. Indeed, the eigenvalues of a $(\ell \times \ell)$ cycle matrix are the ℓ roots of unity. In particular, if ℓ is even, then the matrix has exactly two real eigenvalues, 1 and -1, so the sufficient conditions of Proposition 1 are fulfilled. Note, however, that the SSE associated with a $(\ell \times \ell)$ cycle matrix is not necessarily a cycle of order ℓ; it may be degenerate, in the sense that the corresponding price vector p has identical components. This aspect will be investigated in Section 4.[2]

c   *Application: the one-dimensional OG model*

Let us apply this result to the usual, one-dimensional OG model. Here "young" people only work (and save their wage through money holdings

---

[2] In fact, in many situations it is necessarily the case that our sufficient conditions signal only *degenerate* cycles because no cycle of order k exists (cf. the general theory of cycles in one-dimensional systems).

with a zero interest rate), and "old" people consume only their wealth. We can assume that the total quantity of money is 1, so total demand at period t is 1 in nominal terms and $1/p_t$ in real terms. Also, under perfect foresight, the young peoples' supply (or savings) is a function s of real wage p_t/p_{t+1} (i.e., the nominal wage today p_t deflated by the price of the consumption goods tomorrow p_{t+1}). So the excess demand under certainty is

$$Z(p_t, p_{t+1}) = \frac{1}{p_t} - s\left(\frac{p_t}{p_{t+1}}\right).$$

The reader can easily check that, under standard assumption on preferences, assumptions (A1)–(A3) are fulfilled. Hence,

$$\frac{\partial Z}{\partial p_t} = -\frac{1}{p_t^2} - \frac{1}{p_{t+1}} s'\left(\frac{p_t}{p_{t+1}}\right),$$

$$\frac{\partial Z}{\partial p_{t+1}} = \frac{p_t}{p_{t+1}^2} s'\left(\frac{p_t}{p_{t+1}}\right).$$

As the stationary equilibrium is characterized by

$$Z(\bar{p}, \bar{p}) = \frac{1}{\bar{p}} - s(1) = 0,$$

then

$$\bar{p} = \frac{1}{s(1)}$$

and

$$Z_1 = -s(1)^2 - s(1)s'(1),$$
$$Z_2 = s'(1)s(1).$$

Thus,

$$-\frac{Z_1}{Z_2} = \frac{s(1)}{s'(1)} + 1 = 1 + \frac{1}{\epsilon(1)},$$

where $\epsilon(1)$ is the wage elasticity of savings (or of labor supply).

The condition $|Z_1/Z_2| < 1$ gives $\epsilon(1) \le -\frac{1}{2}$. This is merely the usual condition of local indeterminacy of the stationary equilibrium. Note that, in particular, $s'(1)$ must be negative: the labor supply curve is backward bending. A consequence is that Z_2 must be negative.

Last, assume $k = 2$ (Azariadis–Guesnerie case). Then condition (6) gives

$$m_{12} + m_{21} > 1 + \frac{Z_1}{Z_2} = -\frac{1}{\epsilon(1)},$$

which (as predicted) is exactly the Azariadis–Guesnerie result.

4 The local structure of the set of SSE: a differential viewpoint

The previous results exhibit sufficient conditions for the existence of SSE of cardinal k. However, nothing has been said so far on the order of those SSE. Clearly, the SSE might be degenerate in the sense that the associated price vector has (at least) two identical components; in this case, its order is less than k.

In this section, we investigate the structure of the set of degenerate SSE. We show that under some regularity assumptions "almost all" SSE are nondegenerate; specifically, the set of SSE of order k is shown to be, locally, an open, dense subset of the set of SSE of cardinal k. In other words, an SSE (p, M) can of course be degenerate, but in that case there exist nondegenerate SSE arbitrarily close to (p, M).

The tools used in this section are borrowed from differential topology. This approach is very natural because an SSE is defined as a zero (with nonidentical components) of the smooth mapping $\hat{Z}^k$. That is, the set of SSE of cardinal k is included in the set

$$E^k = \{(p, M) \in \mathbb{R}_+^k \times \mathfrak{M}_k / \hat{Z}^k(p, M) = 0\};$$

and for any (p, M) in E^k, either (p, M) is an SSE or $p_1 = \cdots = p_k = \bar{p}$ from the assumptions made above.

However, our approach is local rather than global. The reason is that E^k is *not*, in general, a manifold (globally). To see this, suppose that the conditions of Proposition 1 are fulfilled. Then there exists a matrix $\bar{M}$ such that

$$\Delta \hat{Z}_{\bar{M}}^k(\bar{p}) = 0.$$

A direct consequence of consistency axioms (A1) is that, at $\bar{p}$, $\hat{Z}^k$ does *not* depend on M:

$$\forall M, \forall i, \quad \tilde{Z}^k(\bar{p}, M^i) = Z(\bar{p}, \bar{p}) = 0.$$

This implies that $(\bar{p}, \bar{M})$ is a singular point and consequently that 0 is a singular value of $\hat{Z}^k$. In fact, it will be shown in the next section that $(\bar{p}, \bar{M})$ is a *bifurcation* of the system: Local SSE appear in any neighborhood of $(\bar{p}, \bar{M})$. So the structure of E^k, in a neighborhood of $(\bar{p}, \bar{M})$, is not diffeomorphic to $\mathbb{R}^n$ for some n. We shall argue, however, that, generically over the excess demand $\tilde{Z}^k$, the *local* structure of E^k around any (p, M) is that of a smooth manifold, at least if $p_i \neq \bar{p}$ for all i; in particular, the usual tools can be applied locally.

a   *Preparation lemmas*

We first introduce the notion of a *regular* sunspot.

Definition. *A point* (p, M) *in* E^k *is regular if it is a regular point of the mapping* $\hat{Z}^k$.

Here, *regular* is intended in the usual sense: The derivative $D\hat{Z}^k$ at (p, M) must be onto $\mathbb{R}^k$. Technically, (p, M) is regular if one can extract, from the $(k \times k^2)$ matrix $D\hat{Z}^k$, a nonzero determinant of order k.[3]
If $(p, M) \in E^k$ is regular, then the structure of E^k around (p, M) is very simple:

Lemma 5. *Assume* $(p, M) \in E^k$ *is regular and that M is within the interior* $\overset{\circ}{\mathfrak{M}}_k$ *of* $\mathfrak{M}_k$. *For any "small enough" open neighborhood U of* (p, M), $E^k \cap U$ *is a smooth manifold of dimension* $k^2 - k$.

Proof: Since $\hat{Z}^k$ is smooth, for U small enough, any point in U is regular. In particular, 0 is a regular value for the restriction of $\hat{Z}^k$ to U. Then, from the inverse image theorem (see Milnor, 1965), $E^k \cap U$ is a smooth manifold of U. Last, $\hat{Z}^k$ maps $U \subset \mathbb{R}_+^k \times \mathfrak{M}_k$ in $\mathbb{R}^k$, and $\mathfrak{M}_k$ is a manifold (with boundaries) of dimension $k^2 - k$; so the dimension of U is $k + (k^2 - k) - k = k^2 - k$.   ∎

We now consider the case of degenerate SSE. Define

$$E_{ij}^k = \{(p, M) \in E^k \text{ s.t. } p_i = p_j\}.$$

An SSE in E_{ij}^k is degenerate in the sense that the price in state i is the same as in state j. Thus, though there are k possible *states* for the sunspot, there are only (at most) $(k-1)$ possible *prices*. Because excess demand depends only on *prices*, this suggests that an SSE in E_{ij}^k should be "similar" (in a sense to be defined) to some SSE of cardinal $(k-1)$, with well-chosen transition probabilities.
This intuition can be developed in a (slightly) more technical way. To simplify notation, we assume that $i = 1$, $j = k$. Let (p, M) be an SSE in E_{1k}^k. By definition, it satisfies

$$\tilde{Z}^k(p_1; p, M_1) = 0,$$

$$\tilde{Z}^k(p_i; p, M_i) = 0, \quad i = 2, \dots, k-1,$$

$$\tilde{Z}^k(p_k; p, M_k) = \tilde{Z}^k(p_1; p, M_k) = 0.$$

---

[3] As an illustration, consider for any Markov matrix M the point $(\bar{p}, M)$; then $(\bar{p}, M)$ is in E^k, and $D_M \hat{Z}^k(\bar{p}, M) = 0$. This $(\bar{p}, M)$ is regular if and only if $D_p \hat{Z}^k(\bar{p}, M)$ is of full rank; that is, if and only if $\Delta \hat{Z}_M^k(\bar{p}) \neq 0$.

Now, the idea is to construct an SSE of cardinal $(k-1)$ – say (q, N) – by "melting" states 1 and k of the initial SSE (p, M), thus reducing the number of states. Obviously, $q = (p_1, ..., p_{k-1})$. Also, to define the ith row of matrix N, *for* $2 \le i \le k-1$, we proceed as follows:

  i The transition probabilities between i and j $(2 \le j \le k-1)$ are unchanged:

$$n_{ij} = m_{ij}, \quad 2 \le i \le k-1, \ 2 \le j \le k-1.$$

  ii Any transition between state i and either state 1 or state k (in the SSE of cardinal k) is equivalent to a transition between i and 1 (in the SSE of cardinal $k-1$); hence,

$$n_{i1} = m_{i1} + m_{ik}, \quad 2 \le i \le k-1.$$

It can easily be checked that, from the consistency axiom (A1),

$$\tilde{Z}^{k-1}(q^i; q, N_i) = \tilde{Z}^k(p^i; p, M_i) = 0 \quad \text{for } 2 \le i \le k-1.$$

However, there are two possible ways to define the first line of N. Take, for instance,

$$n_{11} = m_{11} + m_{1k} \quad \text{and} \quad n_{1i} = m_{1i}, \quad 2 \le i \le k-1.$$

Then,

$$\tilde{Z}^{k-1}(q_1; q, N_1) = \tilde{Z}^k(p_1; p, M_1) = 0.$$

But, $n'_{11} = m_{k1} + m_{kk}$ and $n'_{1i} = m_{ki}$ $(2 \le i \le k-1)$ also gives

$$\tilde{Z}^{k-1}(q_1; q, N'_1) = \tilde{Z}^k(p_1; p, M_k) = \tilde{Z}^k(p_k; p, M_k) = 0.$$

In summary, from matrix M we can, by adding the kth column to the first, construct exactly k vectors of S^{k-2} – say $N_1, ..., N_k$ – such that $\tilde{Z}^{k-1}(q_i; q, N_i) = 0$ $(2 \le i \le k-1)$ and

$$\tilde{Z}^{k-1}(q_1; q, N_1) = \tilde{Z}^{k-1}(q_1; q, N_k) = 0.$$

In particular, if

$$N = \begin{pmatrix} N_1 \\ N_2 \\ \vdots \\ N_{k-1} \end{pmatrix} \quad \text{and} \quad N' = \begin{pmatrix} N_k \\ N_2 \\ \vdots \\ N_{k-1} \end{pmatrix},$$

both N and N' are $(k-1) \times (k-1)$ Markov matrices, and both (q, N) and (q, N') are SSE of cardinal $(k-1)$.

At this point, it is natural to extend the notion of regularity to degenerate SSE. The argument just developed suggests the following definition.

Definition.   *An SSE (p, M) in $E_{1,k}^k$ is regularly degenerate if the vector $(q, N_1, \ldots, N_k)$ is a regular point of the mapping $\Psi_{1,k}^k$ defined by*

$$\Psi_{1,k}^k : \mathbb{R}_+^{k-1} \times (S^{k-2})^k \to \mathbb{R}^k,$$

$$(q, N_1, \ldots, N_k) \to [\tilde{Z}^{k-1}(q_1; q, N_1), \ldots,$$

$$\tilde{Z}^{k-1}(q_{k-1}; q, N_{k-1}), \tilde{Z}^{k-1}(q_1; q, N_k)].$$

The extension of this definition to any E_{ij}^k is immediate.

The following consequence obtains:

Lemma 6.   *Let $(p, M) \in E_{ij}^k$ be regularly degenerate. Then,*

   (i)   *(p, M) is regular (in the sense of regularity for points in E^k);*
   (ii)   *(q, N) and (q, N') (defined as before) are regular in E^{k-1}.*

Proof: The proof of (i) is immediate because from the consistency axioms, the Jacobian matrix $D\Psi_{1,k}^k$ at $(q, N_1, \ldots, N_k)$ is a submatrix of $D\hat{Z}^k$ at (p, M). In particular, if the former is of full rank, so is the latter. For (ii), note that the Jacobian matrix $D\hat{Z}^{k-1}$ in (q, N) is identical to $D\Psi_{1,k}^k$ without its last row. If the latter is onto a neighborhood of zero in $\mathbb{R}^k$, the former is onto a neighborhood of zero in $\mathbb{R}^{k-1}$. The same argument applies to (q, N').   ∎

It can be noted, incidentally, that the properties (i) and (ii) of Lemma 6 are necessary but not sufficient. In other words, the property of regular degeneracy is stronger than regularity of (p, M) (for the mapping defining SSE of cardinal k) and of both (q, N) and (q, N') (for the mapping defining SSE of cardinal $k-1$).[4] However, as we shall argue later, it is not "much" stronger.

As previously, the regular degeneracy property gives information on the local structure of E_{ij}^k. Specifically, we can show the following:

---

[4] As an example, assume that (p, M) is such that

   $D_p \hat{Z}^k(p, M)$ is of rank k,
   $D_q \hat{Z}^{k-1}(q, N)$ and $D_q \hat{Z}^{k-1}(q, N')$ are of rank $(k-1)$,
   $D_M \hat{Z}^k(p, M)$ is of rank zero (i.e., locally, $\hat{Z}^k$ does *not* depend on transition probabilities).

Then (i) and (ii) are fulfilled; however, $D\Psi_{1,k}^k$ has only $(k-1)$ nonzero columns (i.e., $D_q \Psi_{1,k}^k$ is of rank $(k-1)$ and $D_{N^1, \ldots, N^k} \Psi_{1,k}^k$ is of rank zero), so it cannot be locally *onto*. For instance, the reader can check that, for any matrix M, $(\bar{p}, M) \in E^k$ is degenerate but not regularly degenerate though (i) and (ii) may perfectly be fulfilled.

Lemma 7. *Let $(\mathring{p}, \mathring{M}) \in E_{ij}^{k}$ be regularly degenerate, where $\mathring{M}$ is interior to $\mathfrak{M}_{k}$. Then there exists an open neighborhood U' of $(\mathring{p}, \mathring{M})$, such that the set $\bar{E}^{k}$ of* nondegenerate *SSE in $E^{k} \cap U'$ is an open, dense subset of $E^{k} \cap U'$.*

In other words, if $(\mathring{p}, \mathring{M})$ is regularly degenerate, then in any "small" neighborhood of $(\mathring{p}, \mathring{M})$ there exists a nondegenerate SSE; in fact, almost all SSE near $(\mathring{p}, \mathring{M})$ are nondegenerate.

Proof: Because $(\mathring{p}, \mathring{M})$ is regular, $E^{k} \cap U'$ is a smooth manifold of dimension $k^{2} - k$; and the set of nondegenerate SSE is obviously open in this manifold.

Now, consider the mapping φ:

$$\mathbb{R}_{+}^{k-1} \times \mathfrak{M}_{k} \to \mathbb{R}^{k},$$

$$(q, M) \to [\tilde{Z}^{k-1}(q_{1}; q, N_{1}), \ldots, \tilde{Z}^{k-1}(q_{k-1}; q, N_{k-1}), \tilde{Z}^{k-1}(q_{1}; q, N_{k})],$$

where N is constructed from M as explained before. Pose $\mathring{q} = (\mathring{p}_{1}, \ldots, \mathring{p}_{k-1})$ and $(\mathring{p}, \mathring{M})$ is a regular point of φ. Because $\tilde{Z}^{k-1}$ is smooth, there exists a neighborhood V of $(\mathring{q}, \mathring{M})$ in which all points are regular; in particular, 0 is a regular value of the restriction of φ to V. A consequence is that $\varphi^{-1}(0)$ is a smooth manifold of dimension $k^{2} - k - 1$; moreover, $\varphi^{-1}(0)$ is locally diffeomorphic to $E_{1,k}^{k}$ [consider the mapping $(q, M) \to (q, q_{1}, M)$]. Because $E_{1,k}^{k}$ is locally diffeomorphic to $\mathbb{R}^{k^{2}-k}$, thus, for a small enough U', the complement $\bar{E}_{1,k}^{k}$ of $E_{1,k}^{k}$ in $E^{k} \cap U'$ is dense in $E^{k} \cap U'$.

The same argument applies to $\bar{E}_{i,j}^{k}$ for all i, j. Finally,

$$\bar{E}^{k} \cap U' = \bigcap_{i,j \leq k} \bar{E}_{i,j}^{k}$$

is dense, as a finite intersection of dense subsets.   ■

b   *The main result*

We can now prove the main result.

Definition. *An SSE (p, M) in E^{k} is* strongly regular

  (i)   *if it is regular,*
  (ii)   *if it is degenerate (then it is regularly degenerate).*

Proposition 2. *Let (p, M) be a strongly regular SSE with M interior to $\mathfrak{M}_{k}$. There exists an open neighborhood U of (p, M) in $\mathbb{R}_{+}^{k} \times \mathfrak{M}_{k}$ such that*

(i) $E^k \cap U$ is a smooth manifold of dimension $k^2 - k$; and
(ii) the set of nondegenerate SSE in U is a dense, open subset of $E^k \cap U$.

Proof: The proof of (i) is a direct consequence of Lemmas 5 and 6. Moreover, if (p, M) is degenerate, then (ii) is implied by Lemma 7. If (p, M) is nondegenerate, note that the set of nondegenerate SSE is open; thus, for U small enough, every SSE in U is nondegenerate.   ■

In other words, assuming strong regularity, one can characterize the local structure of the set of SSE of cardinal k. Under this hypothesis, E^k is locally diffeomorphic to $\mathbb{R}^{k^2 - k}$; in particular, SSE of cardinal k exist in any neighborhood of (p, M). Moreover, almost all of these SSE are of order k.

Finally, Lemmas 5–7, as well as Proposition 3, consider only matrices that are interior to $\mathfrak{M}_k$. However, the same arguments apply to the boundary of $\mathfrak{M}_k$, the only difference being that the manifolds mentioned would become, in that case, manifolds with boundaries. The transposition is left to the interested reader.

It must be clear, from previous remarks that not all points in E^k are strongly regular; for instance, $(\bar{p}, M)$ is not regularly degenerate, whatever M. This suggests defining the following set:

$$\Sigma^k = \{(p, M) \in E^k \text{ s.t. } \forall i, p_i \neq \bar{p}\}.$$

Now, a natural question is the following: Are the SSE in Σ^k strongly regular? We conjecture that the answer is positive, at least, generically. Naturally, giving a precise meaning (and proof) to this conjecture would require additional work. Particularly, it is likely to require a systematic use of transversality theory, a mathematical investment that may look excessive in our context. An informal support to the conjecture can, however, be obtained as follows. Consider the equations $\hat{Z}^k(\bar{p}, M) = 0$ or $\hat{Z}^{k-1}(q, N) = \hat{Z}^{k-1}(q, N') = 0$, and replace them by $\hat{Z}^k(p, M) = \epsilon$, $\hat{Z}^{k-1}(q, N) = \epsilon'$, $\hat{Z}^{k-1}(q, N') = \epsilon''$, with $\epsilon \in \mathbb{R}^k$ and $\epsilon', \epsilon'' \in \mathbb{R}^{k-1}$. From Sard's theorem, for almost all $(\epsilon, \epsilon', \epsilon'')$, *all* solutions to these equations are regular. This suggests that even if the conjecture is not true for some given $\tilde{Z}$, it should become true after any slight change in $\tilde{Z}$.

Moreover, the conjecture, even if only the weakest form we can think of is true, has several interesting consequences. We shall briefly mention three of them.

1. Consider an economy with SSE of order $k - 1$. From any such SSE (q, N) with $q \neq \bar{p}$ for all i, it is easy to construct an SSE of cardinal k [take $p_i = q_i$ for $i \leq k - 1$, $p_k = p_1$; define M_i $(i \leq k - 1)$ by $m_{i1} = m_{ik} = n_{i1}/2$,

and $m_{ij} = n_{ij}$ otherwise; then pose $M_k = M_1$]. When this SSE is regularly degenerate, Proposition 2 then implies that SSE of order k exist in any neighborhood. By induction, this suggests that, generically over $\tilde{Z}$, if an economy admits an SSE (q, N) of order 2, with $q_1, q_2 \neq \bar{p}$, then it admits SSE of any order. In particular, from Proposition 2, consider an economy such that $|Z_1/Z_2| < 1$; generically, this economy exhibits sunspots of any order.

2. Let M be a Markov matrix in $\overset{\circ}{\mathfrak{M}}_k$ such that (p, M) is in Σ^k for some $p \in \mathbb{R}_+^k$. Consider the canonical projection from E^k to $\mathfrak{M}_k$:

$$(p, M) \rightarrow M.$$

From Sard's theorem, the set of singular values of this (trivially smooth) mapping is null. Hence, for almost all SSE matrices M, the projection is locally *onto*. Since (p, M) is regular, both E^k and $\mathfrak{M}_k$ have, locally, the structure of $k^2 - k$ manifolds; so the projection is, locally, a diffeomorphism. Hence, for almost all M, all matrices in a (small enough) neighborhood of M are sunspot matrices; and almost all of them are associated with SSE of order k.

3. Assume that (p, M) is an SSE, where M is a $(k \times k)$ cycle matrix. As mentioned before, (p, M) is not necessarily a cycle of order k because the price vector p may be degenerate. However, we know from the remarks above that in any small neighborhood of (p, M), there exist SSE of order k. The fact that SSE of order k can be found arbitrarily close to (p, M) can be expressed in probabilistic terms: For all T and $\epsilon > 0$, there exists an SSE of order k such that the probability of observing, during T period, a deviation from a purely cyclical behavior, is less than ϵ. In particular, *if the stationary state is indeterminate, then for any even integer k, our conjecture implies the existence of SSE of order k arbitrarily close (in the sense just defined) of cycles of order k.*

5   "Local" sunspots: the bifurcation viewpoint

Existence theorems of Section 3 rest upon local as well as global restrictions of the excess-demand function under consideration. The nature of the local restrictions suggests that they are valid in a broad class of economic problems covered by our model. The global properties – that is, the boundary assumptions and the uniqueness of the stationary state – are likely to be more restrictive. For example, the reader is invited to check that, in the simple OG model, the introduction of government expenditures à la Sargent (1984) at the same time creates a second stationary state and invalidates our boundary conditions (at least as a condition bearing on the whole domain of prices).

Our global results do rest upon the global assumptions we have just recalled. However, these global results have local counterparts that are bifurcations results. This fact is not surprising if one remembers that the local considerations of bifurcation theory and the global viewpoint of the Poincaré–Hopf theorem refer to a similar core of mathematical arguments.

We do not intend to provide a full development of the bifurcations point of view here. We want only to provide some insights on the local counterparts of our global results, restricting ourselves to formal support only from existing results (i.e., Guesnerie, 1986).

Let us note first that we are considering bifurcations in the space of Markov matrices and *not* in the space of economies – that is, again with the point of view of Azariadis and Guesnerie (1986) rather than the point of view of Grandmont (1986b).

Consider then a one-dimensional family of $(k \times k)$ Markov matrices indexed by a parameter α, and compute

$$\text{Det}\left[M(\alpha) + \frac{Z_1}{Z_2} I\right] = \Psi(\alpha).$$

The bifurcations are bifurcations from the stationary state (with price $\bar{p}, \bar{p}, \ldots$) toward stationary SSE that are local sunspots in the sense of definition 2. Such bifurcations are associated with the fact that the Jacobian of the mapping $p \rightarrow p - \hat{Z}(p, M(\alpha))$ in $\bar{p}$ has an eigenvalue equal to $+1$ (the other ones being outside the unit circle). But the fact that $I - D\hat{Z}$ has an eigenvalue of 1 is itself equivalent to the fact that $D\hat{Z}$ is singular, that is (from Lemma 2), to the fact that $\Psi(\alpha) = 0$. The bifurcations we are looking for will thus occur at a point $\bar{\alpha}$, around which $\Psi(\alpha)$ changes its sign.

The following result provides an example of a bifurcations statement toward SSE of order 2.

Proposition 3. *Consider a stationary state, and let Z_1, Z_2 be the derivatives of the deterministic excess-demand function, as previously defined, at this stationary state.*

Now consider a one-dimensional family of (2×2) Markov matrices $M(\alpha)$ and a number $\bar{\alpha}$ such that

(i) $m_{12}(\bar{\alpha}) + m_{21}(\bar{\alpha}) = 1 + \dfrac{Z_1}{Z_2};$

(ii) $\left. \dfrac{\partial(m_{12} + m_{21})(\alpha)}{\partial \alpha} \right|_{\alpha = \bar{\alpha}} > 0.$

Then, for any neighborhood N of $(\bar{p}, \bar{p})$ in $\mathbb{R}^{2n}$, there exists a $\alpha \neq \bar{\alpha}$ such that N contains a vector $p(\alpha)$ such that $[p(\alpha), M(\alpha)]$ is an SSE.

Proof: This statement is a special case of theorem 4 in Guesnerie (1986). To see that it is enough to check that all the conditions of the theorem are fulfilled, note that the matrix B of the general theorem reduces to the one-dimensional matrix $-Z_2/Z_1$ whose unique eigenvalue is $-Z_2/Z_1$. ∎

The reader should notice that the preceding statement applies to any stationary equilibrium when the system has several of them. For example, in the simple OG model, it signals bifurcations matrices at the Samuelsonian stationary point with backward-bending labor supply when the bifurcation is the one studied in Azariadis and Guesnerie (1986). But in the OG model with government expenditures, the statement signals local sunspots in the neighborhood of the high inflation stationary state, even when labor supply is not backward-bending; a fact well in line with the more global analysis of this situation found in Grandmont (1986a) as well as with the previous example of Farmer and Woodford (1983). The bifurcations toward SSE of order k could be pursued along the lines suggested; it is clear, for instance, that local SSE (of any order) cannot exist around the stationary state unless $|Z_1/Z_2| \leq 1$. Here we shall note only that the bifurcations result of Proposition 3, together with the results of Section 4, imply, at least generically, the existence of local sunspots of any order in the neighborhood of any stationary state such that $|Z_1/Z_2| < +1$. Again this fact is compatible with the (more precise) insights obtained from a different perspective by Grandmont (1986b) in the (more specific) context of the OG model with one representative consumer.

6 Conclusion

We have been concerned with stationary sunspot equilibria in one-dimensional, one-step forward-looking economic systems. The first examples of such SSE have been provided by Azariadis (1981) and Farmer and Woodford (1983). Elements of theory of such a phenomenon, initially brought forth by Azariadis and Guesnerie (1982, 1986) and Spear (1984) have been completed by further works of Grandmont (1986a, b), Peck (1988), and Woodford (1986). This chapter, building on the initial contributions, adds another stone.

The issue of existence of SSE in one-dimensional, one-step forward-looking dynamic systems should not be considered as settled. It is outside the scope of this chapter to write a list of unresolved questions (some arise directly from our earlier comments). We should like, however, to point out that when sunspot beliefs are based on time-independent processes that are somewhat less well-behaved than the one we considered here (such as the processes of money supply in Lucas-type models, which are Markovian but do not admit an invariant distribution), the study of (time-independent) sunspot equilibria raises mathematical issues that are extremely different from those coming into the picture here (see Chiappori and Guesnerie, 1986, 1988). If one considers that such exogenous processes are economically important, then the present study, together with its predecessors, does not exhaust our understanding of sunspot equilibria of economic relevance, even in the simplest (one-dimensional, one-step forward-looking) framework.

REFERENCES

Azariadis, C. (1981), "Self-fulfilling prophecies," *Journal of Economic Theory,* 25, 380–96.
Azariadis, C., and Guesnerie, R. (1982), "Prophéties créatice et persistance des théories," *Revue Economique,* 33, 787–806.
  (1986), "Sunspots and cycles," *Review of Economic Studies,* 53, 725–36.
Cass, D., and Shell, K. (1983), "Do sunspots matter?" *Journal of Political Economy,* 91, 193–227.
Chiappori, P. A., and Guesnerie, R. (1986), "Lucas equation, indeterminacy, and non neutrality," Working Paper, EHESS, Paris.
  (1988), "Self fulfilling prophecies: the sunspot connection," Working Paper, EHESS, Paris.
Farmer, R., and Woodford, M. (1983), "Self-fulfilling prophecies and the business cycle," mimeo., University of Pennsylvania.
Grandmont, J. M. (1986a), "Stabilizing competitive business cycles," *Journal of Economic Theory,* 40(1), 57–76.
  (1986b), "Local bifurcations and stationary sunspots," mimeo., CEPREMAP.
Guesnerie, R. (1986), "Stationary sunspot equilibria in a *N*-commodity world," *Journal of Economic Theory,* 40(1), 103–27.
Milnor, J. (1965), *Topology from the Differentiable Viewpoint,* Charlottesville: University Press of Virginia.
Peck, J. (1988), "On the existence of sunspot equilibria in an overlapping generations model," *Journal of Economic Theory,* 44(1).
Sargent, T. J. (1984), "Consumption, Loans, and Currency: II," unpublished lecture notes.
Shell, K. (1977), "Monnaie et allocation intertemporelle," CNRS Seminaire d'economètrie de M. Edmond Malinvaud, Paris, November. [Title and abstract in French; text in English.]
Spear, S. (1984), "Sufficient conditions for the existence of sunspot equilibria," *Journal of Economic Theory,* 35, 360–70.
Woodford, M. (1986), "Stationary sunspot equilibria in a finance constrained economy," *Journal of Economic Theory,* 40(1), 128–37.
  (1988), "Imperfect financial intermediation and complex dynamics," this volume.

CHAPTER 3

Local bifurcations and stationary sunspots

Jean-Michel Grandmont

Abstract: This paper analyzes the relations between deterministic intertemporal equilibria with perfect foresight and stationary sunspot equilibria near a stationary state. The study takes place within the framework of an overlapping-generations model, in which the deterministic dynamics are described by a one-dimensional difference equation and employs elementary geometrical arguments. One verifies that a stationary sunspot equilibrium exists in *every* neighborhood of the Golden Rule if and, in general, only if, it is stable in the deterministic dynamics. One shows also, by looking at what happens when a local bifurcation occurs, that a stationary sunspot equilibrium can exist in *some* neighborhood of the Golden Rule even when it is unstable in the deterministic dynamics.

The purpose of this chapter is to progress toward a better understanding of the relationships that may exist between the local behavior of deterministic intertemporal equilibria and stationary Markov sunspot equilibria near a stationary state, in economies with characteristics that are constant over time.

We use a simple version of the overlapping-generations model, in which the state variable is one dimensional, that was employed in this context by Azariadis (1981) and Azariadis and Guesnerie (1986). If we stay close enough to the stationary state, things are almost linear. Stationary Markov sunspot equilibria exist then in *every* neighborhood, however small, of the stationary state if and, in general, only if it is deterministically locally indeterminate. The set of such sunspot equilibria is then infinite dimensional. Similar results were obtained in the study of various specific examples by Guesnerie (1986), Woodford (1984, 1986), Laitner (1986), and Grandmont (1985b, 1986).

Matters are further complicated if we look at what happens a little further from the stationary state, but still near it, because the deterministic

This work was supported by National Science Foundation Grant SES-83-20669 at the Institute for Mathematical Studies in the Social Sciences, Stanford University, Stanford, California.

45

dynamics may then involve small but significant nonlinearities. We shall show that in the simple context under consideration, one can get more information on that issue through the theory of bifurcations. Suppose that we look at a one-parameter family of economies having a stationary state that changes stability at some point. Bifurcation theory describes exactly what deterministic intertemporal equilibria look like in the vicinity of the stationary state immediately before and after the bifurcation takes place. One can then characterize the set of stationary Markov sunspot equilibria, and its relationships with the set of deterministic intertemporal equilibria, near the stationary state. In particular, we shall show that stationary Markov sunspot equilibria can exist in *some* neighborhood of the stationary state, even though it is deterministically locally determinate.

As was said earlier, our study is carried out in a one-dimensional framework that permits a simple geometrical analysis. It remains to be seen whether the methods presented here can be extended to a more realistic multidimensional framework.

1   Households' behavior

We consider a discrete time model with overlapping generations (OG) of households. There are no bequests and no population growth. Households live two periods; we assume that they are all alike or, equivalently, that there is a single representative household in each generation. There is a single good. When young, households supply labor and save their wage earnings by holding money balances; they consume when they are old.

· The tastes of a generation are represented by the separable utility function $V_1(\ell^* - \ell) + V_2(c)$, where $0 \leq \ell^* - \ell \leq \ell^*$ is leisure (ℓ is labor supply) and $c \geq 0$ is consumption of the good. We assume the following throughout:

(1.a) $\ell^* > 0$.

(1.b)   *The utility functions V_1 and V_2 are continuous on $[0, \ell^*)$ and $[0, +\infty)$. They are k-times continuously differentiable with $k \geq 4$, on $(0, \ell^*)$ and $(0, +\infty)$, respectively, with $V'_\tau(a) > 0$, $V''_\tau(a) < 0$, $\lim_{a \to 0} V'_1(a) = +\infty$.*

a   *The deterministic case*

We look first at the behavior of a representative household under certain conditions. Consider a young household, at any date, that observe the current money wage $w \geq 0$ and expects the money price $p^e > 0$ of the good

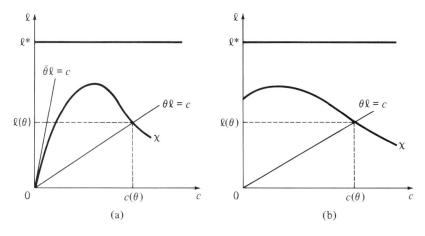

Figure 1

to prevail at the next date. It has to choose its current labor supply $0 \leq \ell \leq \ell^*$, its current money demand $m \geq 0$, and its future consumption $c \geq 0$ so as to maximize its utility function subject to $w\ell = m$ and $p^e c = m$. The solution is unique; and c, ℓ, and m are positive if and only if $\theta = w/p^e$ exceeds $\bar{\theta} = V_1'(\ell^*)/\lim_{c \to 0} V_2'(c)$.

It is easily seen from the first-order conditions of the problem that if $\theta > \bar{\theta}$, the optimum pair (ℓ, c) is the unique solution satisfying $\ell > 0$, $c > 0$, of the system

$$v_1(\ell) = v_2(c) \quad \text{and} \quad \theta\ell = c, \tag{1}$$

in which v_1 and v_2 are defined, for $0 \leq \ell < \ell^*$ and $c > 0$, by

$$v_1(\ell) = \ell V_1'(\ell^* - \ell) \quad \text{and} \quad v_2(c) = cV_2'(c). \tag{2}$$

The function v_1 is increasing and maps $[0, \ell^*)$ onto $[0, +\infty)$. Thus we can define the household's *offer curve* by the equation $\ell = \chi(c)$, where

$$\chi(c) = v_1^{-1}[v_2(c)], \quad \text{for } c > 0 \text{ and } \chi(0) = 0. \tag{3}$$

Then, for any $\theta > \bar{\theta}$, as shown in Figure 1, the optimum values of c and ℓ are obtained as the unique intersection verifying $c > 0$, $\ell > 0$, of the line $\theta\ell = c$ with the offer curve. When $0 \leq \theta \leq \bar{\theta}$, this intersection reduces to the origin.

The case $\lim_{c \to 0} cV_2'(c) = 0$ is described in Figure 1a, whereas Figure 1b represents the case in which this relation does not hold.[1] In all cases, the

---

[1] The specification of the households' sector is taken from Reichlin (1986) and Woodford (1986). See also Benhabib and Laroque (1988). The specification used in Grandmont (1985a) is isomorphic to the case considered here, up to a reinterpretation of the variables, when $V_2(c) = V(\ell_2^* + c)$ with $\ell_2^* > 0$. This corresponds to Figure 1a.

functions v_1, v_2, and χ are $(k-1)$ times continuously differentiable for $0 \le \ell < \ell^*$ or $c > 0$. Moreover, χ has a positive fixed point that is then unique if and only if $\bar{\theta} < 1$; it corresponds to $\theta = 1$.

It is useful to note at this stage that the elasticity of the function χ; that is, $\epsilon_\chi = c\chi'(c)/\chi(c)$, for $c > 0$, is given by

$$\epsilon_\chi = \frac{1 - R_2(c)}{1 + [\ell/(\ell^* - \ell)]R_1(\ell^* - \ell)}, \tag{4}$$

with $\ell = \chi(c)$, where R_τ is the coefficient of relative risk aversion of V_τ; that is, $R_\tau(a) = -aV_\tau''(a)/V_\tau'(a) > 0$, for $a > 0$ and each $\tau = 1, 2$.

b   *Uncertainty*

In preparation for the analysis of sunspot equilibria, we look at the household's behavior under uncertainty. Consider a young agent at any date, who observes the current money wage $w \ge 0$ and expects the prices $p^e = (p_1^e, ..., p_r^e)$ to prevail at the next date, with probability $q_j \ge 0$, $j = 1, ..., r$, where $p_j^e > 0$ for all j. The agent has to choose her current labor supply ℓ, her current money demand $m \ge 0$, and her future *contingent* consumption c_j so as to maximize her *expected utility* $V_1(\ell^* - \ell) + \sum_j q_j V_2(c_j)$ subject to

$$w\ell = m \quad \text{and} \quad p_j^e c_j = m, \quad \text{for } j = 1, ..., r. \tag{5}$$

Again, the solution is unique; and from the first-order conditions, each of the quantities ℓ, m, and c_j is positive if and only if $\bar{\theta} < \sum_j q_j \theta_j$, where $\theta_j = w/p_j^e$. When this relation holds, labor supply and future contingent consumption constitute the unique solution verifying $\ell > 0$, $c_j > 0$, of the system

$$v_1(\ell) = \sum_j q_j v_2(c_j) \quad \text{and} \quad \theta_j \ell = c_j, \quad \text{for all } j. \tag{6}$$

2   Intertemporal equilibria and sunspots

We consider a simple version of the overlapping-generations model in which the money stock is constant and equal to $M > 0$ and the good is perishable and produced from labor in each period with no production lag, one unit of labor yielding one unit of output.

There are competitive markets for labor, output, and money at each date. At a monetary equilibrium, consumption of the old trader at date t (i.e., c_t) is equal to his real money balance $\mu_t = M/p_t > 0$, in which $p_t > 0$ is the equilibrium money price of the good. Clearly c_t is also equal to the current equilibrium output y_t and labor supply ℓ_t. Profit maximization

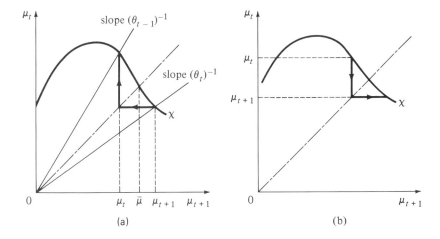

Figure 2

implies then that the equilibrium real wage is unity, so that we can identify equilibrium money wages and prices at all dates, $w_t = p_t$ for all t.

a   *Deterministic intertemporal equilibria*

We first look at the case in which the households are certain about future
prices and have perfect foresight. A deterministic *intertemporal (monetary) equilibrium* is an infinite sequence of money prices $p_t > 0$, $t \geq 1$,
such that markets clear at all dates. As noted earlier, one has $\mu_t = c_t =
\ell_t$ along such an equilibrium. Thus, from the first-order condition (1), one
can define equivalently such an intertemporal equilibrium as a sequence of
positive real balances $\mu_t = M/p_t$ that satisfy, for all t, $v_1(\mu_t) = v_2(\mu_{t+1})$ or

$$\mu_t = \chi(\mu_{t+1}). \tag{7}$$

Figure 2a describes the *backward perfect foresight (bpf)* dynamics on
real balances implied by (7) by means of the offer curve, as well as the
dynamics of the corresponding gross real interest rates $\theta_t = p_t/p_{t+1}$. The
same figure can be used to generate intertemporal equilibria in which
time goes *forward*. The trick is to reverse the direction of the arrows:
Start from the offer curve, go vertically to the 45° line, and horizontally
back to the offer curve (see Fig. 2b). There exists a monetary stationary
state that is unique, if and only if $\bar{\theta} < 1$. It corresponds to $\theta_t = 1$ or to $\mu_t =
\bar{\mu}$ for all t, where $\bar{\mu}$ is the unique positive fixed point of χ.

b   *Stationary sunspot equilibria*

We consider now the same economy and look at the case in which traders believe that prices and quantities are affected by random factors (sunspots), though they do not influence the "fundamental" characteristics of the economy, and in which this belief turns out to be self-fulfilling, in equilibrium.

Assume that the traders observe a Markov process of signals s_t (sunspots) that belong to $S = \{s_1, \ldots, s_r\}$ with known transition probabilities $q_{ij} > 0$. Assume further that households believe these signals to be perfectly correlated with equilibrium prices through the relation

$$p_i = f(s_i), \quad \text{all } i, \text{ with } 0 < p_r < \cdots < p_{i+1} < p_i < \cdots < p_1. \quad (8)$$

Note that here, as in the previous section, the equilibrium real wage is unity at all dates, so we do not need to distinguish between money wages and prices.

The belief (8) generates a *stationary Markov sunspot equilibrium (smse)* with r states corresponding to the given sunspot process if it is self-fulfilling, that is, if $p = p_i$ indeed clears the market when the sunspot s_i is observed, for each $i = 1, \ldots, r$ and at each date.

Note that here also, every date and in any equilibrium corresponding to the observation of an arbitrary value of the sunspot, the real balance M/p is equal to the equilibrium values of output, of consumption, and of the labor supply. Thus, if the households have the belief (8), from the first-order condition (6), the price p that achieves equilibrium at some date when the sunspot s_i is observed is given by

$$v_1\left(\frac{M}{p}\right) = \sum_j q_{ij} v_2\left(\frac{M}{p_j}\right).$$

An smse can therefore be equivalently defined by real balances $\mu_i = M/p_i$ that satisfy

$$0 < \mu_1 < \cdots < \mu_r < \infty \quad \text{and} \quad v_1(\mu_i) = \sum_j q_{ij} v_2(\mu_j), \quad \text{all } i. \quad (9)$$

Equilibrium real balances then follow a Markov chain on $\{\mu_1, \ldots, \mu_r\}$ with transition probabilities $q_{ij} > 0$. Conversely, any such Markov chain of real balances can be interpreted as a stationary sunspot equilibrium, by constructing a Markov process on S with transition probabilities $q_{ij} > 0$, provided that the underlying probability space is rich enough.

Studying the *set* of stationary Markov sunspot equilibria, with r states, amounts therefore to analyzing the set of real balances (μ_i) and of transition probabilities $q_{ij} > 0$ that verify (9).

c   *A constructive global characterization*

The set of smse is easily characterized in this particular case, as shown in Grandmont (1985b, 1986). Consider real balances μ_i and transition probabilities $q_{ij} > 0$ that satisfy (9). Let m, n be integers such that $v_2(\mu_n) \leq v_2(\mu_i) \leq v_2(\mu_m)$ for all i. It follows then from (9) that $v_2(\mu_n) < v_1(\mu_i) < v_2(\mu_m)$ for all j, or equivalently,

$$\chi(\mu_n) < \mu_1 < \cdots < \mu_r < \chi(\mu_m). \tag{10}$$

One cannot have $\mu_n < \mu_m$ in this model because there would then exist more than one monetary stationary state. Thus, if one considers an smse, there are two real balances $\mu_m < \mu_n$ that verify (10).

Consider, conversely, real balances $0 < \mu_1 < \cdots < \mu_r$, with $\mu_m < \mu_n$ that satisfy (10). Then there are transition probabilities verifying (9). They are given by

$$q_{im} = \frac{v_1(\mu_i) - v_2(\mu_n) - \sum_{j \neq m, n} q_{ij}[v_2(\mu_j) - v_2(\mu_n)]}{v_2(\mu_m) - v_2(\mu_n)}, \tag{11}$$

$$q_{in} = \frac{v_2(\mu_m) - v_1(\mu_i) - \sum_{j \neq m, n} q_{ij}[v_2(\mu_m) - v_2(\mu_j)]}{v_2(\mu_m) - v_2(\mu_n)}, \tag{12}$$

in which the $q_{ij} > 0$ are chosen arbitrarily for $j \neq m, n$, subject to the constraints that $q_{im} > 0$ and $q_{in} > 0$, that is,

$$\sum_{j \neq m, n} q_{ij}[v_2(\mu_j) - v_2(\mu_n)] < v_1(\mu_i) - v_2(\mu_n),$$

$$\sum_{j \neq m, n} q_{ij}[v_2(\mu_m) - v_2(\mu_j)] < v_2(\mu_m) - v_1(\mu_i). \tag{13}$$

Clearly, given the real balances (μ_i), the set of such transition probabilities q_{ij}, $i = 1, \ldots, r$, $j \neq m, n$, is nonempty [think of the case in which all q_{ij} in (13) are close to 0], convex, open and thus of dimension $r(r-2)$.

To sum up this discussion, *the real balances (μ_i) define a stationary Markov sunspot equilibrium, with r states – in the sense that there are corresponding transition probabilities $q_{ij} > 0$ that verify (9) – if and only if there exist $\mu_m < \mu_n$ that satisfy (10)*. The corresponding transition probabilities are given (nonuniquely) by (11), (12), and (13). Obviously, the stationary state $\bar{\mu}$ must belong to the interval (μ_m, μ_n).

d   *Local sunspots*

We apply now the foregoing characterization to ϵ-*local sunspot equilibria*, that is, stationary Markov sunspot equilibria such that the corresponding real balances stay within ϵ of the stationary state $\bar{\mu}$, for ϵ small.

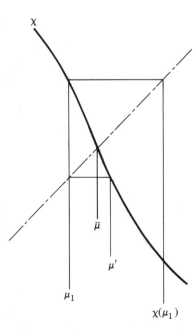

Figure 3

Assume that $\chi'(\bar{\mu}) \neq 0$, and choose ϵ small enough to ensure that $\chi'(\mu)$ keeps the same sign on the interval $(\bar{\mu} - \epsilon, \bar{\mu} + \epsilon)$, as well as on its image by the map χ. If an ϵ-local sunspot equilibrium is to exist, then, in view of (10), the offer curve must be decreasing on these intervals, and one can require $m = 1$, $n = r$ in the previous characterization. It follows that *if ϵ has been chosen in this way, an ϵ-local sunspot equilibrium is characterized by real balances that satisfy $|\mu_i - \bar{\mu}| < \epsilon$ and*

$$\chi^2(\mu_1) < \chi(\mu_r) < \mu_1 < \cdots < \mu_r < \chi(\mu_1) < \chi^2(\mu_r), \qquad (14)$$

in which $\chi^2 = \chi \circ \chi$ is the *second iterate* of the map χ.

Any such ϵ-local sunspot equilibrium can thus be generated through the following procedure. First one looks for μ_1 close to and on the left of $\bar{\mu}$ such that $\chi^2(\mu_1) < \mu_1$. Since χ is decreasing near $\bar{\mu}$, there is a unique μ' in $[\bar{\mu}, \chi(\mu_1)]$ such that $\chi(\mu') = \mu_1$. Then μ_r must be chosen in the interval $[\mu', \chi(\mu_1)]$; see Figure 3 (of course μ_r has to be also within ϵ of $\bar{\mu}$, which will be always verified if μ_1 itself is close enough to the stationary state). Finally, the other values of μ_i, $i \neq 1, r$, can be distributed arbitrarily in the interval (μ_1, μ_r) and the corresponding transition probabilities can be generated (again, nonuniquely) through (11), (12), and (13).

3   Local determinateness and sunspots

An immediate consequence of the preceding analysis is that if we assume away the exceptional cases $\chi'(\bar{\mu}) = 0$ and $\chi'(\bar{\mu}) = -1$, there are ϵ-local sunspot equilibria for every $\epsilon > 0$ if and only if the stationary state is deterministically locally indeterminate.

The notion of local determinateness pertains to the behavior of deterministic intertemporal equilibria near the stationary state $\bar{\mu}$. Formally, we say that a deterministic intertemporal equilibrium is an ϵ-*local equilibrium* if μ_t stays within ϵ of $\bar{\mu}$ for all $t \geq 1$. The stationary state is then *locally determinate* if there exists $\epsilon > 0$ such that there is no ϵ-local equilibrium other than the stationary state itself. It is *locally indeterminate* otherwise.

Local determinateness is governed by the behavior of the trajectories generated by the difference equation that is obtained by inverting locally equation (7) (which is always possible when $\chi'(\bar{\mu}) \neq 0$). Note that in view of (4),

$$\chi'(\bar{\mu}) = \frac{1 - R_2(\bar{\mu})}{1 + [\bar{\mu}/(\ell^* - \bar{\mu})]R_1(\ell^* - \bar{\mu})},\tag{15}$$

so that $\chi'(\bar{\mu})$ is always less than 1. Intuitively, everything else being equal, $\chi'(\bar{\mu})$ decreases as the utility function V_2 becomes more concave, that is, as $R_2(\bar{\mu})$ gets larger. If $\chi'(\bar{\mu}) > -1$, intertemporal equilibria starting close enough to $\bar{\mu}$ have to move away from it: The stationary state is *locally determinate;* see Figure 4a. If $\chi'(\bar{\mu}) < -1$ and if ϵ is small enough, for *every* μ_1 close enough to $\bar{\mu}$, there exists an ϵ-local equilibrium $(\mu_t)_{t \geq 1}$ with initial condition μ_1. Given μ_1, such an intertemporal equilibrium is in fact unique, and it converges eventually to $\bar{\mu}$: The stationary state is *locally indeterminate;* see Figure 4b. Thus, if we assume away the cases $\chi'(\bar{\mu}) = 0$ and $\chi'(\bar{\mu}) = -1$, the stationary state is locally indeterminate if and only if $\chi'(\bar{\mu}) < -1$.

The characterization of sunspot equilibria given in the previous section implies immediately that ϵ-local sunspot equilibria exist for all ϵ if and only if the stationary state is locally indeterminate, whenever $\chi'(\bar{\mu}) \neq 0$ and $\chi'(\bar{\mu}) \neq -1$. If $\chi'(\bar{\mu}) \neq 0$, we can apply the constructive characterization given in (14) and Figure 3. Then there are ϵ-local sunspot equilibria for every ϵ if and only if there exists a sequence μ^k that tends to $\bar{\mu}$ such that $\chi^2(\mu^k) < \mu^k < \bar{\mu}$ for all k. If one remarks next that $(\chi^2)'(\bar{\mu}) = [\chi'(\bar{\mu})]^2$, and if one assumes away the case $\chi'(\bar{\mu}) = -1$, such a sequence exists if and only if $\chi'(\bar{\mu}) < -1$. This implies the following proposition.[2]

---

[2] The result was proved in a similar model in Grandmont (1986). For related results, see Azariadis and Guesnerie (1986), Guesnerie (1986), Woodford (1984, 1986), and Laitner (1986).

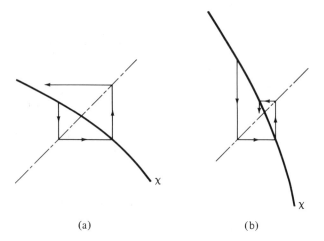

(a)   (b)

Figure 4

Proposition 1.   *Assume $\chi'(\bar{\mu}) \neq 0$ and $\chi'(\bar{\mu}) \neq -1$. Then there exist ϵ-local sunspot equilibria for every $\epsilon > 0$ if and only if $\chi'(\bar{\mu}) < -1$.*

Remark: These results can be refined, in the cases for which $\chi'(\bar{\mu}) = 0$ and $\chi'(\bar{\mu}) = -1$, by looking at higher-order derivatives. The flavor of the results is the same.

4   Local bifurcations and sunspots

Asking for the existence of local sunspot equilibria in *every,* however small, neighborhood of the stationary state is very demanding. There may be cases in which stationary sunspot equilibria do exist in the vicinity of $\bar{\mu}$ but *not arbitrarily near it.* To get information about the circumstances under which this can obtain, we look at what happens when there is a local bifurcation of the deterministic dynamics implied by (7); we can also hope to get a better understanding of the relations that exist between deterministic and sunspot equilibria.

a   *Deterministic bifurcations*

We want first to analyze the local behavior of deterministic intertemporal equilibria when the stationary state changes stability in the dynamics implied by (7). To this effect, we index the characteristics of the economy by a real number λ in some open neighborhood U of 0, say $(\ell_\lambda^*, V_{\tau\lambda})$, and assume that the slope of the associated offer curves at the stationary state goes through -1 at $\lambda = 0$.

(4.a) ℓ_λ^* [respectively, $V_{\tau\lambda}(a)$] is 4-times continuously differentiable on U [respectively, $U \times (0, +\infty)$] and $\bar\theta_{1\lambda} = V'_{1\lambda}(\ell_\lambda^*)/\lim_{c\to 0} V'_{2\lambda}(c) < 1$ for all λ in U.

Assumption (4.a) implies that the corresponding offer curves χ_λ are 3-times continuously differentiable on $U \times (0, +\infty)$ and that for each λ in U, there is a unique monetary stationary state $\bar\mu_\lambda > 0$. The next assumption states that the map χ_λ undergoes a *flip bifurcation* at $\lambda = 0$.

(4.b) $\chi_0(\mu_0) = -1$ *and* $\dfrac{d}{d\lambda}[\chi'_\lambda(\bar\mu_\lambda)]|_{\lambda=0} < 0.$

The theory tells us that we should expect a cycle of period 2 to appear near $\bar\mu_\lambda$ for λ small enough. Such a cycle can be identified with a positive fixed point of $\chi_\lambda^2 = \chi_\lambda \circ \chi_\lambda$ that differs from the stationary state $\bar\mu_\lambda$. For each λ, of course, $\bar\mu_\lambda$ is a fixed point of χ_λ^2. By differentiation, one gets immediately that $(\chi_\lambda^2)'(\bar\mu_\lambda) = [\chi'_\lambda(\bar\mu_\lambda)]^2$, which implies in view of assumption (4.b) that

$$(\chi_0^2)'(\bar\mu_0) = +1 \quad \text{and} \quad \frac{d}{d\lambda}[(\chi_\lambda^2)'(\bar\mu_\lambda)]|_{\lambda=0} > 0. \tag{16}$$

Further differentiation shows that the second derivative of χ_0^2 at $\bar\mu_0$ vanishes. The shape of χ_0^2 near $\bar\mu_0$ is thus governed by the sign of the third derivative of χ_0^2.

We consider the "generic" case in which $(\chi_0^2)'''(\bar\mu_0) \neq 0$. It is easily seen that this expression is equal to $-\{2\chi_0'''(\bar\mu_0) + 3[\chi_0''(\bar\mu_0)]^2\}$ and that it is closely related to the value of the Schwarzian derivative of χ_0 at $\bar\mu_0$. Indeed the Schwarzian derivative of a thrice continuously differentiable map f from the real line into itself is defined as

$$Sf(x) = \frac{f'''(x)}{f'(x)} - \frac{3}{2}\left[\frac{f''(x)}{f'(x)}\right]^2,$$

whenever $f'(x) \neq 0$. Since $\chi_0'(\bar\mu_0) = -1$, we have therefore

$$2S\chi_0(\bar\mu_0) = (\chi_0^2)'''(\bar\mu_0). \tag{17}$$

We consider two cases.

Case 1: $S\chi_0(\bar\mu_0) < 0$

The corresponding graph of χ_0^2 near $\bar\mu_0$ is pictured in Figure 5b. Remark that the assumption implies that $\bar\mu_0$ is asymptotically stable in the bpf

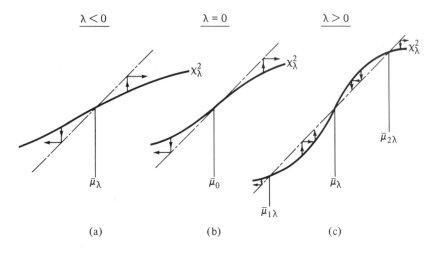

Figure 5.   Case 1: $S\chi_0(\bar{\mu}_0) < 0$. Arrows indicate intertemporal equilibria, every two periods.

dynamics (7), although $\chi_0'(\bar{\mu}_0) = -1$. The graphs of χ_λ^2 near $\bar{\mu}_\lambda$ are represented in Figures 5a and 5c for λ small, negative, and positive. If $\lambda \leq 0$, there is no cycle of period 2 near $\bar{\mu}_\lambda$ and no intertemporal equilibrium, other than $\mu_t = \bar{\mu}_\lambda$, for all $t \geq 1$, that stays near the stationary state (Figs. 5a, b). If $\lambda > 0$, there is a unique cycle of period 2, $\bar{\mu}_{1\lambda}, \bar{\mu}_{2\lambda}$ near the stationary state. Moreover, there exists an intertemporal equilibrium corresponding to the initial condition μ_1 that stays near $\bar{\mu}_\lambda$ for all $t \geq 1$ if and only if μ_1 lies in the interval $[\bar{\mu}_{1\lambda}, \bar{\mu}_{2\lambda}]$. Given such a μ_1, the associated intertemporal equilibrium is unique, is contained in $[\bar{\mu}_{1\mu}, \bar{\mu}_{2\lambda}]$, and converges to $\bar{\mu}_\lambda$ whenever μ_1 does not belong to the period 2 orbit.

Case 2: $S\chi_0(\bar{\mu}_0) > 0$

The corresponding graphs of χ_λ^2 near the stationary state, for small λ, are represented in Figure 6. There the unique cycle $\bar{\mu}_{1\lambda}, \bar{\mu}_{2\lambda}$, appears for λ negative (Fig. 6a). In all cases, for any initial condition μ_1 near $\bar{\mu}_\lambda$, there is a unique intertemporal equilibrium that stays near $\bar{\mu}_\lambda$. If $\lambda \geq 0$, all such intertemporal equilibria converge to the stationary state. When $\lambda < 0$, they converge to the cycle of period 2, provided that μ_1 differs from $\bar{\mu}_\lambda$.

The following formal result summarizes the preceding discussion.

Given λ in U and $\epsilon > 0$, we say that *the intertemporal equilibrium* $(\mu_t)_{t \geq 1}$ *is an ϵ-local equilibrium if* μ_t *stays within* ϵ *of the stationary state* $\bar{\mu}_\lambda$ *for all* $t \geq 1$.

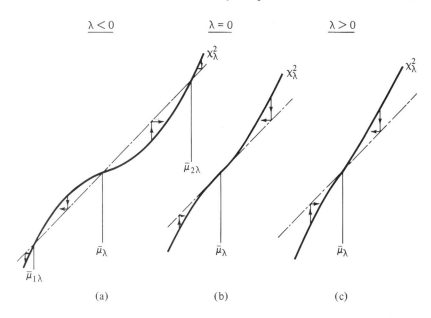

Figure 6.   Case 2: $S\chi_0(\bar{\mu}_0) > 0$. Arrows indicate intertemporal equilibria, every two periods.

Theorem 1.   *Consider a one-parameter family of economies satisfying assumptions* (4.a) *and* (4.b).

1 *Let* $S\chi_0(\bar{\mu}_0) < 0$. *Then there exist* $\lambda_1 < 0$, $\lambda_2 > 0$, *and* $\epsilon > 0$ *such that the following hold:*
   a *If* $\lambda_1 < \lambda \leq 0$, *there is no ϵ-local equilibrium other than the stationary state* $\bar{\mu}_\lambda$.
   b *If* $0 < \lambda < \lambda_2$, *there is a unique cycle of period* 2, *that is,* $\bar{\mu}_{1\lambda}, \bar{\mu}_{2\lambda}$, *within ϵ of the stationary state, and all ϵ-local equilibria lie in* $[\bar{\mu}_{1\lambda}, \bar{\mu}_{2\lambda}]$. *Given* μ_1 *in that interval, there is a unique ϵ-local equilibrium with initial condition* μ_1. *It is contained in* $[\bar{\mu}_{1\lambda}, \bar{\mu}_{2\lambda}]$ *and converges to the stationary state when* $\mu_1 \neq \bar{\mu}_{1\lambda}, \bar{\mu}_{2\lambda}$.
2 *Let* $S\chi_0(\bar{\mu}_0) > 0$. *Then there exist* $\lambda_1 < 0$, $\lambda_2 > 0$, *and* $\epsilon > 0$ *such that for any λ in* (λ_1, λ_2) *and any μ_1 within ϵ of the stationary state* $\bar{\mu}_\lambda$, *there is a unique ϵ-local equilibrium with initial condition* μ_1. *Moreover, the following hold:*
   a *If* $\lambda_1 < \lambda < 0$, *there is a unique cycle of period* 2, *that is,* $\bar{\mu}_{1\lambda}, \bar{\mu}_{2\lambda}$ *within ϵ of the stationary state. Any ϵ-local equilibrium other than the stationary state converges to the period-2 orbit.*

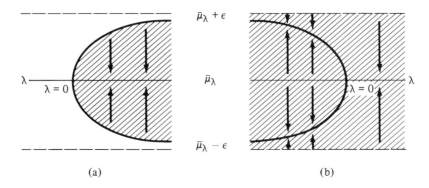

Figure 7. (a) Case 1. (b) Case 2.

    b   *If $0 \le \lambda < \lambda_2$, all ϵ-local equilibria converge to the stationary state $\bar{\mu}_\lambda$.*

Proof: The existence of cycles and their asymptotic stability is a local version of Whitley (1983, proposition 1.2), derived by applying it to the family of offer curves χ_λ and reversing time or, more directly, to the family of local inverses χ_λ^{-1} near the stationary states $\bar{\mu}_\lambda$. The statements concerning ϵ-local equilibria are then straightforward consequences of these stability properties.   ■

    Figure 7 translates the preceding result into a qualitative picture in the plane (λ, μ), within a band of $\pm \epsilon$ on each side of the stationary state $\bar{\mu}_\lambda$. Shaded areas describe the regions filled by deterministic ϵ-local equilibria. Arrows show where they converge, as $t \to +\infty$, for each λ.

    b   *Local sunspots*

We investigate now the relationships between ϵ-local sunspot equilibria and cycles in the above bifurcating family. The principle of the approach is straightforward: We assume that λ_1, λ_2, and ϵ in Theorem 1 have been chosen small enough to enable us to apply the constructive characterization given in (14) and Figure 3.

    It is clear that in Case 1, that is, $S\chi_0(\bar{\mu}_0) < 0$, as described in Figure 5, no local sunspot equilibrium exists for $\lambda \le 0$ because $\chi_\lambda^2(\mu) > \mu$ for all μ close to but less than $\bar{\mu}_\lambda$. By contrast, for $\lambda > 0$ there are infinitely many ϵ-local sunspot equilibria. Each of them can be generated from an arbitrary μ_1 in the interval $(\bar{\mu}_{1\lambda}, \bar{\mu}_\lambda)$. The support $\{\mu_1, \dots, \mu_r\}$ of every ϵ-local sunspot equilibrium is contained in the interval $(\bar{\mu}_{1\lambda}, \bar{\mu}_{2\lambda})$ determined by the orbit of period 2, and the union of these supports is the whole interval.

In this case, ϵ-local sunspot equilibria exist only for $\lambda > 0$, and there are then infinitely many of them in every neighborhood of the stationary state. The qualitative picture is much different in the second case, that is, when $S\chi_0(\bar{\mu}_0) > 0$ (Fig. 6). There, stationary local sunspot equilibria exist in the vicinity of the stationary state for *all* values of the parameter λ, and the union of the supports $\{\mu_1, \ldots, \Gamma_r\}$ of local sunspot equilibria fills the whole neighborhood of the stationary state. For $\lambda \geq 0$ (Fig. 7b), stationary local sunspot equilibria exist in every neighborhood of $\bar{\mu}_\lambda$. But for $\lambda < 0$ (Fig. 7a), there are *no* stationary sunspot equilibria that lie arbitrarily near the stationary state: For every $\lambda < 0$, the closure of the support $\{\mu_1, \ldots, \mu_r\}$ of every ϵ-local sunspot equilibrium contains in its interior the interval determined by the period-2 cycle, $[\bar{\mu}_{1\lambda}, \bar{\mu}_{2\lambda}]$.

One notices a fact that may be of potential generality, namely, that in each of the two cases the union of the supports $\{\mu_1, \ldots, \mu_r\}$ of ϵ-local sunspot equilibria coincides with the union of deterministic ϵ-local intertemporal equilibria. Thus the shaded areas in the bifurcation diagram of Figure 7 represent also the regions filled by the supports $\{\mu_1, \ldots, \mu_r\}$ of stationary local sunspot equilibria in each type of bifurcation.

The following formal result summarizes the preceding discussion.

Theorem 2. *Consider a one-parameter family of economies satisfying assumptions (4.a) and (4.b), and let the parameters $\lambda_1, \lambda_2, \epsilon$ appearing in Theorem 1 be small enough.*

1 *Let $S\chi_0(\bar{\mu}_0) < 0$. Then if $\lambda_1 < \lambda \leq 0$, there is no ϵ-local sunspot equilibrium. If $0 < \lambda < \lambda_2$, there are infinitely many ϵ-local sunspot equilibria in every neighborhood of the stationary state, and the union of the supports $\{\mu_1, \ldots, \mu_r\}$ of these sunspot equilibria is $(\bar{\mu}_{1\lambda}, \bar{\mu}_{2\lambda})$.*

2 *Let $S\chi_0(\bar{\mu}_0) > 0$. Then, for each λ, the union of the supports $\{\mu_1, \ldots, \mu_r\}$ of ϵ-local sunspot equilibria is the whole interval $(\bar{\mu}_\lambda - \epsilon, \bar{\mu}_\lambda + \epsilon)$. If $\lambda_1 < \lambda < 0$, for every ϵ-local sunspot equilibrium one has $\mu_1 < \bar{\mu}_{1\lambda} < \bar{\mu}_{2\lambda} < \mu_r$. If $0 \leq \lambda < \lambda_2$, there are infinitely many stationary local sunspot equilibria in every neighborhood of $\bar{\mu}_\lambda$.*

Remark 1: In Case 1 (respectively, Case 2), the family χ_λ undergoes a so-called supercritical (respectively, subcritical) bifurcation. Had we considered instead the local inverses χ_λ^{-1}, the family χ_λ^{-1} would have undergone a subcritical flip bifurcation in Case 1 and a supercritical one in Case 2. Figure 7 can be interpreted as the "bifurcation diagram" of χ_λ^{-1}.

Remark 2: In view of (15), the sort of bifurcation discussed here will occur if one increases the concavity of the utility function V_2. It follows from footnote 1 and Grantmont (1985a, lemma 4.6) that with the specification

$$V_1(a) = \frac{a^{1-\alpha_1}}{1-\alpha_1} \quad \text{and} \quad V_2(c) = \frac{(\ell_2^* + c)^{1-\alpha_2}}{1-\alpha_2},$$

the map χ has a negative Schwarzian derivative whenever $\alpha_1 \leq 1$, $\alpha_2 \geq 2$, at all $\mu > 0$ such that $\chi'(\mu) \neq 0$ if $\ell_2^* \geq 0$, and also at $\mu = 0$ if $\ell_2^* > 0$.

REFERENCES

Azariadis, C. (1981), "Self-fulfilling prophecies," *Journal of Economic Theory,* 25, 380–96.
Azariadis, C., and Guesnerie, R. (1986), "Sunspots and cycles," *Review of Economic Studies,* 53, 725–38.
Benhabib, J., and Laroque, G. (1988), "On competitive cycles in productive economies," *Journal of Economic Theory,* 45, 145–70.
Grandmont, J. M. (1985a), "On endogenous competitive business cycles," *Econometrica,* 53, 995–1045.
    (1985b), "Cycles concurrentiels endogènes," *Cahiers du Séminaire d'Econométrie.*
    (1986), "Stabilizing competitive business cycles," in *Nonlinear Economic Dynamics,* ed. by J. M. Grandmont, San Diego: Academic Press.
Guesnerie, R. (1986), "Stationary sunspot equilibria in an *N*-commodity world," in *Nonlinear Economic Dynamics,* ed. by J. M. Grandmont, San Diego: Academic Press.
Laitner, J. (1986), "Dynamic determinacy and the existence of sunspot equilibria," mimeo., University of Michigan, Ann Arbor.
Reichlin, P. (1986), "Equilibrium cycles in an overlapping generations economy with production," in *Nonlinear Economic Dynamics,* ed. by J. M. Grandmont, San Diego: Academic Press.
Shell, K. (1977), "Monnaie et allocation intertemporelle," CNRS Séminaire d'econométrie de M. Edmond Malinvaud, 21 November. [Title and abstract in French; text in English.]
Symposium on Nonlinear Economic Dynamics (1986), *Journal of Economic Theory 40.* Reprinted as J. M. Grandmont (ed.), *Nonlinear Economic Dynamics,* San Diego: Academic Press.
Whitley, D. (1983), "Discrete dynamical systems in dimensions one and two," *Bull. London Math. Soc.,* 15, 177–217.
Woodford, M. (1984), "Indeterminacy of equilibrium in the overlapping generations model: a survey," mimeo., Columbia University.
    (1986), "Stationary sunspot equilibria in a finance constrained economy," in *Nonlinear Economic Dynamics,* ed. by J. M. Grandmont, San Diego: Academic Press.

CHAPTER 4

On the nonequivalence of the
Arrow–securities game and the
contingent-commodities game

James Peck and Karl Shell

Abstract: We analyze two imperfectly competitive economies that face intrinsic and/or extrinsic uncertainty. The economies differ only in the structure of the markets for insurance. One economy is the Arrow-securities market game, and the other is the contingent-commodities market game. We show that for each game there is a Nash equilibrium in which all markets are open. The games are not equivalent, even though the corresponding competitive economies are.

In particular, we show that *no* Nash equilibrium allocation from the Arrow-securities game in which some income is transferred across states of nature is a Nash-equilibrium allocation for the contingent-commodities game. There is an immediate corollary for the special case in which uncertainty is purely extrinsic: A sunspot Nash-equilibrium allocation for the Arrow-securities game that is not a mere lottery over Nash-equilibrium allocations for the corresponding certainty game (i.e., the game without insurance markets) is never a Nash-equilibrium allocation for the contingent-commodities game.

These two games differ because the effects of the market power of individual traders depend on the way markets are organized. We conclude that the notion of "complete markets" makes sense only when applied to competitive economies. Imperfectly competitive economies are sensitive to details about market structure, even though these details are inessential for competitive economies.

1   Introduction and summary

Consider two competitive economies that differ only in the structure of their insurance markets. The first economy has a full set of markets for

We acknowledge the support of both the National Science Foundation under Grant SES-8606944 and the Center for Analytic Economics at Cornell University. We thank V. V. Chari, Aditya Goenka, Jim Jordan, Rody Manuelli, Roger Myerson, Andy Postlewaite, Steve Spear, and Raghu Sundaram for their comments. An earlier version of this work was presented at the Conference on Economic Complexity (Austin, Texas, May 27–9, 1987). Andreu

contingent commodities. A contingent commodity is a contract, bought or sold before nature moves, to deliver one unit of commodity i after state s has occurred.[1] The second economy has a full set of markets for trading spot commodities after the state of nature is revealed. Before the state is revealed, individuals trade on a full set of markets for Arrow securities. An Arrow security is a contract to deliver one unit of account[2] if state s occurs, otherwise nothing.[3] Under perfect competition, these two economies are equivalent in the sense that a competitive-equilibrium allocation for one economy is also a competitive-equilibrium allocation for the other.

We show that this equivalence does not extend to imperfectly competitive economies. To do so, we construct two strategic market games, the contingent-commodities game and the Arrow-securities game. The games, which differ only in the structure of their insurance markets, are analogous to the corresponding competitive economies. We build on the market-game price-formation model of Shapley and Shubik.[4] For specificity, we adopt the sell-all variants of these two games: spot-commodity offers and contingent-commodity offers are assumed to be equal to endowments; markets are "thick." Offers of Arrow securities are not prespecified because they are purely financial instruments.[5] In this chapter, all Arrow securities are inside securities; that is, endowments of Arrow securities are assumed to be zero.

Our result is the following: Let x' be an interior[6] (i.e., open-market) Nash-equilibrium allocation for the Arrow-securities game in which some

Footnote *(cont.)*

Mas-Colell was the discussant. His comments were extraordinarily useful and stimulating. Errors and other shortcomings must be blamed on the authors.

[1] See Debreu (1959, chap. 7, pp. 98–102); but the idea of "contingent commodity" or "commodity claim" goes back to Arrow (1953, sect. II).

[2] This implies that in each state the purchasing power of the corresponding Arrow security is positive or that, without loss of generality, its price in terms of "state s unit of account" is unity.

[3] See Arrow (1953, sect. III).

[4] See, for example, Shubik (1973), Shapley (1976), Shapley and Shubik (1977), Postlewaite and Schmeidler (1978), and Peck and Shell (1985, 1988). Another variant of the contingent-commodities game is analyzed in Dubey and Shubik (1977).

[5] Our nonequivalence result still holds when securities offers are prespecified, no matter the level at which they are specified. Nash equilibria in which offers of state s securities are zero (and hence bids for state s securities are zero) entail the closing of the market for state s securities. Then there is no way to transfer income into or out of state s. Do not think about these equilibria until later because they are not consistent with Arrow-securities with payoffs measured in *state s units of account*.

[6] An interior Nash equilibrium is one in which some bids are positive on each market. A market on which some bids are positive is called an open market. Hence, at an interior Nash equilibrium, the aggregate of the bids on each market is positive.

security market is active (i.e., some income is transferred across states of nature), and let x'' be a Nash-equilibrium allocation for the contingent-commodities game. Then *necessarily x' differs from x''*.

Applying this nonequivalence proposition to the case in which uncertainty is purely extrinsic (i.e., the case in which all the economic fundamentals are certain) yields the following corollary: An interior sunspot equilibrium allocation for the Arrow-securities game that is not a mere lottery[7] over Nash-equilibrium allocations for the certainty market game (the corresponding market game without insurance markets) cannot be a Nash-equilibrium allocation to the contingent-commodities game.

This very strong nonequivalence result applies only to finite economies. As the number of consumers becomes large through replication, the Nash equilibria of the contingent-commodities game converge to the competitive equilibria of the contingent-commodities economy, and the Nash equilibria of the Arrow-securities game converge to the competitive equilibria of the Arrow-securities economy. Hence, as one would expect, in the limit the sets of open-market equilibria for the two games are identical.[8] *The games are basically different from one another except in the limit, where competition is perfect.*

Comparative statics analysis for imperfect competition is more complicated than for perfect competition. In each case, the set of equilibrium allocations does depend on market structure, but the competitive model is special because in this case the comparative statics become trivial after "market completeness" is achieved. For example, a full set of contingent-commodities markets represents complete markets for the competitive model in the sense that the opening of additional markets does not affect the set of competitive-equilibrium allocations. This ultimate insensitivity of competitive allocations to the opening of additional markets is an important theorem in comparative statics, one that is used (and abused) regularly in economic analysis. There is no such powerful notion of market completeness that can be adopted for noncompetitive (or imperfectly competitive) environments.

---

[7] We could replace "mere lottery over Nash-equilibrium allocations" with "correlated equilibrium." See Peck and Shell (1985) for an analysis of correlated equilibrium in market games without intrinsic uncertainty. In this chapter, however, only perfectly correlated (symmetric-information) signals are considered. It remains to be seen whether or not our nonequivalence proposition can be extended to the asymmetric-information environment of Peck and Shell (1985).

[8] This would be true if the Arrow securities pay in state-specific units of account. If the Arrow securities are purely financial, then the state s security could have purchasing of zero in terms of state s commodities. Hence, the set of perfectly competitive equilibria in the contingent-claims economy would be a subset of the competitive equilibria in the Arrow-securities economy.

Many other aspects of market structure do not matter in the model of perfect competition but can matter very much in, for example, market games:

> *Wash sales.* Whether or not wash sales of commodities are permitted affects the Nash equilibria of a market game. In the competitive economy, only net trades matter; restrictions on wash sales have no effect.
>
> *Short sales.* Restrictions on short sales affect the equilibria in market games but have no effect on competitive economies if markets are complete so that they include some perfect borrowing and lending markets. If short sales are disallowed or restricted, then the Nash-equilibrium allocations are Pareto optimal only if the endowments are Pareto optimal.
>
>   We have shown (Peck and Shell, 1988) that in the market game that allows arbitrarily large short sales and enforces strong interpersonal bankruptcy rules there is a Nash-equilibrium allocation arbitrarily close to Pareto optimality, even if there are only few players. Restrictions on short sales can matter very much when competition is not perfect.
>
> *Bundling.* In the competitive model with complete markets, the equilibrium allocation is not affected by adding markets for new goods if new goods are merely bundles of old goods. The addition of new bundled goods can affect the Nash-equilibrium allocations of a market game.
>
> *Trading rounds.* Retrading (or recontracting) has no effect on the final allocation in perfectly competitive economies with complete markets. In the market game, however, retrading expands the Nash-equilibrium set. In the one-stage market game without short sales, Nash-equilibrium allocations are (nearly) efficient only if the endowment is (nearly) efficient. We have shown that, in the market game with retrading, there are dynamically consistent Nash-equilibrium paths that yield Pareto-optimal allocations in the limit as the number of rounds becomes large. (See Peck and Shell, 1987.) Retrading can matter very much when competition is not perfect. (There are many other equilibrium paths in the market game with retrading. Not all of these equilibria are efficient in the limit.)
>
> *Other dynamic issues.* Because of births and deaths, participation on markets is naturally restricted. (See Cass and Shell, 1983, sect. III, pp. 198–202.) This restriction on market participation affects both competitive economies and market games.

In dynamic games, strategies can be history dependent. History dependence and problems of dynamic consistency raise issues that arise in games but do not arise in competitive economies with complete markets.

Real versus financial securities. Even in the competitive model there is a difference between a full set of *financial* Arrow securities and a full set of *real* Arrow securities. Financial securities can be worthless (in terms of commodities) in a prespecified spectrum of states, thus endogenously closing an arbitrary spectrum of markets. This does not happen with real securities. Hence, the set of competitive equilibria for an economy with (say) a full range of real Arrow securities (i.e., those that pay in commodities or unit of account) is a subset of the set of competitive equilibria for an economy with a full range of purely financial Arrow securities. The difference between the two sets is the set of equilibria in which some of the markets are (endogenously) closed. This phenomenon carries over to the market-game model, but the matter is further complicated. In the market-game model, because there is no such thing as complete markets, mixing financial securities with real securities will affect the Nash-equilibrium allocations.

In Section 2, we present the economic fundamentals on which the market games and the corresponding competitive economies are based. In Section 3, the contingent-commodities game is introduced. Existence of interior (i.e., open-market) Nash equilibrium and the limiting properties of the replicated economy follow directly from results in the literature. In Section 4, the Arrow-securities game is introduced. The existence of interior Nash equilibrium is demonstrated. The details of the proof are assembled in the appendix. Section 4 also provides the limiting properties for the replicated economy. Section 5 contains the statement and proof of our nonequivalence proposition, as well as some intuition about why it is true. Some concluding remarks are presented in Section 6.

2   The economy

We consider an economy with n traders (or consumers), each of whom is a von Neumann–Morgenstern expected-utility maximizer. There are r states of nature, indexed by the letter s, with α and β referring to specific states. Before the state is revealed, traders know the probability of each state s, which is denoted $\pi(s)$. When the state is revealed, all traders know which state has occurred, that is, information is symmetric, and expectations are rational.

There are ℓ commodities, and ℓ is a (finite) integer. The letters i and j denote specific commodities or index the commodities, depending on the context. Traders receive an endowment of commodities, which can depend on the state of nature, with $\omega_h^i(s)$ denoting the endowment of trader h of commodity i in state s. We assume that we have

$$\omega_h(s) = [\omega_h^1(s), \ldots, \omega_h^i(s), \ldots, \omega_h^\ell(s)] \in \mathbb{R}_{++}^\ell \quad \text{for all } h \text{ and } s.$$

By $x_h^i(s)$, we mean the consumption of trader h of commodity i in state s. We assume that we have

$$x_h(s) = [x_h^1(s), \ldots, x_h^i(s), \ldots, x_h^\ell(s)] \in \mathbb{R}_+^\ell \quad \text{for all } h \text{ and } s.$$

Consumer h's utility v_h can be expressed as

$$v_h(x_h) = \sum_s \pi(s) u_h[x_h(s)].$$

The consumption set of consumer h is the nonnegative orthant

$$\{x_h \mid x_h \in \mathbb{R}_+^{r\ell}\}.$$

Utility is assumed to be strictly monotonic, strictly concave, and differentiable on the strictly positive orthant $\mathbb{R}_{++}^{r\ell}$. Also, we assume that the closure of all indifference surfaces going through the strictly positive orthant is contained in the strictly positive orthant. The boundary of the consumption set, the points with at least one zero component, is the indifference surface of least utility.[9]

In Sections 3 and 4, we define, respectively, the contingent-commodities game and the Arrow-securities game. In the former game, traders buy and sell contingent commodities before the state is revealed, with delivery taking place afterward. This is simply a Shapley–Shubik model with $r\ell$ trading posts.[10] In the latter game, traders buy and sell Arrow-securities before the state is revealed. Afterward, securities are delivered and consumers participate on a spot market with complete knowledge of the state and the endowment. The prices of each of the r securities and the ℓ spot-

[9] The closure assumption on indifference surfaces along with the von Neumann–Morgenstern utility assumption is somewhat restrictive, guaranteeing that no consumer will risk zero consumption in any state. However, this assumption is used only in the existence argument and has no bearing on the nonequivalence result. It has the benefit of permitting a less severe bankruptcy rule for the securities game. Punishment would occur only for observed violations. Planned violations in nonobserved states could then go unpunished because no one would risk zero consumption in any state of nature that occurs with positive probability.

[10] All bids are made in terms of unit of account and all contingent commodities must pass through the market.

market prices (which may depend on the state) are determined by the clearing of bids and offers à la Shapley and Shubik. (See Peck and Shell, 1985, for a more complete description.)

3   The contingent-commodities game

We assume that there is a trading post for each contingent commodity. The strategy set for consumer h is

$$\{[\hat{b}_h^1(1), \ldots, \hat{b}_h^\ell(1); \ldots; \hat{b}_h^1(s), \ldots, \hat{b}_h^\ell(s); \ldots;$$

$$\hat{b}_h^1(r), \ldots, \hat{b}_h^\ell(r)] \mid \hat{b}_h^i(s) \geq 0 \text{ for all } i, s\} \subset \mathbb{R}_+^{\ell r}.$$

Here, the scalar $\hat{b}_h^i(s)$ denotes the bid of consumer h on the commodity i–state s trading post. All state-contingent endowments pass through the trading posts so consumers sell their entire endowments to finance their bids. The final allocation is determined as follows.[11]

$$
\left.
\begin{aligned}
x_h^i(s) &= \frac{\hat{b}_h^i(s) \, \Sigma_k \, \omega_k^i(s)}{\Sigma_k \, \hat{b}_k^i(s)} && \text{if the solvency constraint (2)} \\
&&& \text{is satisfied,} \\
&= 0 && \text{otherwise.}
\end{aligned}
\right\}
\quad (1)
$$

The solvency constraint is that bids for contingent commodities must be financed by sales of contingent commodities. We must have

$$\sum_s \sum_j \left[\hat{b}_h^j(s) - \frac{\omega_h^j(s) \, \Sigma_k \, \hat{b}_k^j(s)}{\Sigma_k \, \omega_k^j(s)} \right] \leq 0. \qquad (2)$$

The unit of account, in which bids are made, can be normalized freely.

Our regularity conditions are sufficient to guarantee the existence of an interior (i.e., open-market) Nash equilibrium. For the proof, see Peck and Shell (1985). We claim that when we replicate, the limiting economy is competitive.

Claim 1.   *Let $\eta^1, \eta^2, \ldots, \eta^\nu, \ldots$ be a sequence of symmetric, uniformly interior Nash equilibria for the contingent-commodities game, where there are ν traders of each of the n "types." Let η be a limit point of the sequence (η^ν). Then η results in a competitive allocation.*

Proof: The claim and its proof are standard in the literature. See, for example, Shapley (1976), Shapley and Shubik (1977), Mas-Colell (1982), or Peck and Shell (1985).   ■

---

[11] To complete the model, we (like others before us) specify that in the unlikely event that all bids on a given trading post are zero, the endowments of this good are confiscated and the consumption of this commodity is zero.

4   The Arrow-securities game

The Arrow-securities game has a securities market that meets before the uncertainty is resolved, followed by a spot market that meets after the state has been observed. On the securities market there is a trading post for each of the r Arrow securities. An Arrow security is a contract to have one dollar[12] delivered if a given state occurs. Purchases of Arrow securities for one state must be financed by sales of securities for other states. A strategy must specify the offers at each Arrow-security post, the bids at each Arrow-security post, and the bids at each spot-market post for each state of nature.

More formally, the strategy set for consumer h is

$$\{[..., \tilde{b}_h^1(s), ..., \tilde{b}_h^\ell(s), ...; ..., \tilde{b}_h^m(s), ...; ..., \tilde{q}_h^m(s), ...]$$
$$\text{satisfying } \tilde{b}_h^i(s) \geq 0 \text{ for all } i \text{ and } s, \text{ and } \tilde{b}_h^m(s) \geq 0 \text{ for all } s,$$
$$\text{and } \tilde{q}_h^m(s) \geq 0 \text{ for all } s\} \subset \mathbb{R}_+^{r(\ell+2)}.$$

The scalar $\tilde{b}_h^i(s)$ is the bid of consumer h on the commodity i–state s spot market, and $\tilde{b}_h^m(s)$ and $\tilde{q}_h^m(s)$ refer to the bids and offers, respectively, on the state s security market. The units of $\tilde{b}_h^m(s)$ can be freely normalized, but it may be convenient to normalize them as dollars. The units of $\tilde{q}_h^m(s)$ are (state s) dollars. The units of $\tilde{b}_h^i(s)$ are state s units of account, but it will be convenient to set the state s unit of account equal to one state s dollar.

The final allocation is determined as follows:

$$
x_h^i(s) = \frac{\tilde{b}_h^i(s) \sum_k \omega_k^i(s)}{\sum_k \tilde{b}_k^i(s)} \quad
\left.
\begin{array}{l}
\text{if the budget constraint (4)} \\
\text{holds and the securities} \\
\text{constraint (5) holds,}[13]
\end{array}
\right\} \quad (3)
$$
$$
= 0 \qquad\qquad\qquad \text{otherwise.}
$$

The solvency constraint is that, in each state, bids must be financed by the sum of sales income and net securities income. For all h and s, we must have

$$\sum_j \tilde{b}_h^j(s) \leq \sum_j \left[\omega_h^j(s) \frac{\sum_k \tilde{b}_k^j(s)}{\sum_k \omega_k^j(s)}\right] + \left[\frac{\tilde{b}_h^m(s) \sum_k \tilde{q}_k^m(s)}{\sum_k \tilde{b}_k^m(s)}\right] - \tilde{q}_h^m(s). \quad (4)$$

---

[12] We change from the introduction. Arrow-securities are now purely financial. The value of state s Arrow money in terms of state s commodities could possibly be zero. Any pre-specified spectrum of markets could be closed with the remainder open. This is a fundamental property of money and other purely financial assets: They can always be worthless; in fact, they must be worthless if people imagine them to be.

[13] If we have $\sum_k \tilde{b}_k^i(s) = 0$ (so, of course, $\tilde{b}_h^i(s) = 0$), then by assumption we interpret the ratio $\tilde{b}_h^i(s)/\sum_k \tilde{b}_k^i(s) = 0/0$ to be equal to zero.

The securities constraint, that purchases of securities are financed by sales of securities, requires that we have, for each h,

$$\sum_s \left[\tilde{b}_h^m(s) - \frac{\tilde{q}_h^m(s) \sum_k \tilde{b}_k^m(s)}{\sum_k \tilde{q}_k^m(s)} \right] \leq 0. \tag{5}$$

Some comments are in order about constraints (4) and (5). The expression

$$\frac{\tilde{b}_h^m(s) \sum_k \tilde{q}_k^m(s)}{\sum_k \tilde{b}_k^m(s)} - \tilde{q}_h^m(s)$$

represents the net number of state s securities purchased by trader h, where one security pays off one dollar in state s. The expression

$$\frac{\sum_k \tilde{b}_k^m(s)}{\sum_k \tilde{q}_k^m(s)}$$

can be interpreted as the price of the state s security, so condition (5) amounts to

$$\sum_s (\text{net purchases of security } s)(\text{price security } s) \leq 0.$$

Also, we handle the possibility of a security post with zero bids or offers by the convention that $0/0 = 0$: When the bids on a post are zero, the offers are confiscated, and *vice versa*.

Consumer h seeks to maximize $v_h = \sum_s \pi(s) u_h[x_h(s)]$, where $u_h[x_h(s)]$ is the utility derived from the certain consumption of $x_h(s)$. A Nash equilibrium is defined in the usual way as a vector of best-response strategies. The Arrow-securities game always exhibits Nash equilibria of the following type: Bids and offers on the securities markets are zero, so no income can be transferred between states. Each of the isolated spot markets plays out a Nash equilibrium for the subgame, which is known to exist (see Peck and Shell, 1985). No trader would want to make a positive bid or offer on the security markets because it would be confiscated; no trader would want to change his spot-market behavior because each spot-market subgame exhibits a Nash equilibrium.

In the Nash equilibria described earlier, the security markets are closed. We shall show that there are always interior Nash equilibria in which there are positive bids on each security market and spot market, but first we prove the following Lemma.

Lemma 1. *All Nash equilibria are individually rational in the sense that consumers receive at least as high a utility as that of their endowments.*

Proof: Consumer h assures his endowment with the following strategy, given the strategies of the other players,

$$\left.\begin{aligned}
\tilde{b}_h^i(s) &= \frac{\omega_h^i(s)\,\Sigma_{k\neq h}\,\tilde{b}_k^i(s)}{\Sigma_{k\neq h}\,\omega_k^i(s)} \\[2mm]
\tilde{b}_h^m(s) &= \frac{\tilde{q}_h^m(s)\,\Sigma_{k\neq h}\,\tilde{b}_k^m(s)}{\Sigma_{k\neq h}\,\tilde{q}_k^m(s)}
\end{aligned}\right\} \quad s=1,2,\dots,r,\ \ i=1,2,\dots,\ell.$$

Thus, $\tilde{q}_h^m(s)$ can be chosen arbitrarily, and the endowment is feasible. For the above strategy not to dominate the Nash-equilibrium strategy for consumer h, his expected utility must be no less than he could achieve by consuming his endowment in each state.   ∎

Remark: Lemma 1 is a well-known result in the market-game literature. We elevate it to lemma status merely for emphasis.

Definition 1.   *For $b \in \Delta^{nr} \times \Delta^{n\ell} \times \cdots \times \Delta^{n\ell}$, define the following augmented bids:*

$$d_h^i(s) = \max[b_h^i(s), \epsilon],$$

$$d(s) = [d_h(s), d_{-h}(s)],$$

$$d_h^m(s) = \max[b_h^m(s), \epsilon].$$

Proposition 1.   *Given our maintained assumptions on utility functions and endowments, the Arrow-securities game has an interior Nash equilibrium.*

Proof: The standard way to prove the existence of a Nash equilibrium is to define an adjustment function based on utility maximizing responses to bids of the other players, and then to find a fixed point of that mapping. The problem here is that when everyone except consumer h is bidding zero on some market, the maximizing response of consumer h is not well-defined. In this proof, we augment the bids to some level ϵ, so that the adjustment function is well-defined and continuous. Then we show that, for small enough ϵ, each component of the fixed point is greater than ϵ. The proof appears in the appendix. It is similar in structure to the proof in Peck and Shell (1985, proposition 2.23, pp. 17–29).   ∎

The Arrow-securities game, just like the contingent-commodities game, becomes competitive in the limit as we replicate the economy.

Claim 2.   *Let $\eta^1, \eta^2, \dots, \eta^\nu, \dots$ be a sequence of symmetric, uniformly interior Nash equilibria for the Arrow-securities game, where there are ν traders of each of the n "types." Let η be a limit point of the sequence (η^ν). Then η results in a competitive allocation.*

Proof: The claim and its proof are standard in the market-games literature. See, for example, Shapley (1976), Shapley and Shubik (1977), Mas-Colell (1982), and Peck and Shell (1985). ■

5 Nonequivalence of the contingent-commodities game and the Arrow-securities game

A complete set of Arrow-securities markets followed by a spot market has the same set of interior competitive equilibria as a complete set of contingent-commodities markets. We have claimed that when we replicate the consumers, Nash equilibria of the limiting contingent-commodities game are competitive and *interior* Nash equilibria of the limiting Arrow-securities game are competitive, so the two games yield the same set of *interior* Nash equilibria in the limit.

With a finite number of consumers, both the contingent-commodities game and the Arrow-securities game have inefficient interior Nash equilibria. We shall show that these two market structures are not equivalent. We go further. We show that an interior Nash-equilibrium allocation of the Arrow-securities game in which some income is transferred across states cannot be a Nash-equilibrium allocation of the corresponding contingent-commodities game.

To build some intuition, consider the noninterior competitive equilibria of the two economies. The contingent-commodities economy has only interior Nash equilibria; in this economy, markets cannot be closed endogenously. The Arrow-securities economy typically has many noninterior competitive equilibria because any pattern of open and closed securities markets is consistent with competitive equilibrium. Closed securities markets correspond to those states in which money is worthless. If (even) the state α security is worthless in state α, then the economy in state α is isolated from the economy in the other states of nature. Within state α, trades can still take place in terms of the state α unit of account, but no income can be transferred into or out of state α. Thus, when we include noninterior competitive equilibria, the contingent-commodities economy and the Arrow-securities economy are clearly nonequivalent.

In the contingent-commodities economy, trading commodity 1α for commodity 2β is very much like trading commodity 1α for commodity 2α. In the competitive Arrow-securities economy, these trades are similar only when it is possible to transfer income between state α and state β via the securities market. If, for example, the state β securities market is closed, then the first (interstate) trade is impossible even though the second (intrastate) trade is possible.

When consumers have market power, their actions affect the equilibrium price. It is far from obvious that trading on contingent-commodities markets induces the same price distortions that arise from trading on securities markets and spot markets. In fact, the distortions are different.

The nonequivalence of the Arrow-securities game and the contingent-commodities game can be motivated by the following observation. Consider a consumer who wants to trade commodity 1 in state α for commodity 2 in state β. Under the market structure of the contingent-commodities game, only the prices of these two contingent commodities will be affected by the trade. This effect on prices is of the same sort as the effect on prices of a trade of commodity 1α for commodity 2α. In the contingent-commodities game, when the consumer transfers income from state α to state β, he does so without directly distorting the terms of other interstate trades. Because there is just one budget constraint, income can be transferred between states with complete flexibility.

Under the market structure of the Arrow-securities game, the consumer must sell state-α securities and buy state-β securities and then use the securities income to buy commodity 2 in state β. This action affects the price of the securities, so the terms of trade between each commodity in state α and each commodity in state β are directly affected. Hence, in the Arrow-securities game, there is an asymmetry between trading commodity 1α for commodity 2β (an interstate trade) and trading commodity 1α for commodity 2α (an intrastate trade). There is no such asymmetry in the contingent-commodities game.

Next we state our formal nonequivalence result.

Proposition 2. *Let $\hat{b} = (\hat{b}_1, \dots, \hat{b}_h, \dots, \hat{b}_n) \in \mathbb{R}_+^{r\ell}$ be an interior Nash equilibrium of the contingent-commodities game, and let $\tilde{b} = (\tilde{b}_1, \dots, \tilde{b}_h, \dots, \tilde{b}_n)$ be an interior Nash equilibrium of the Arrow-securities game, where*

$$\tilde{b}_h = \{\tilde{b}_h^1(s), \dots, \tilde{b}_h^\ell(s), \tilde{b}_h^m(s), \tilde{q}_h^m(s)\}_{s=1}^{s=r} \in \mathbb{R}_+^{r(\ell+2)}.$$

Assume that all of the securities markets are open and that some consumer is a net purchaser of securities in some state. Then $\hat{b}$ and $\tilde{b}$ result in different allocations.

Proof: Because $\hat{b}$ and $\tilde{b}$ are interior solutions to the utility-maximization problem, we have the following first-order conditions:

$$\hat{\lambda}_h = \pi(s) \left\{ \frac{\partial u_h[x_h(s)]}{\partial x_h^i(s)} \right\} \left[\frac{\Sigma_{k \neq h} \hat{b}_k^i(s)}{\Sigma_{k \neq h} \omega_k^i(s)} \right] \left[\frac{\Sigma_k \omega_k^i(s)}{\Sigma_k \hat{b}_k^i(s)} \right]^2, \qquad (6)$$

which must hold for all h, i, and s, along with conditions (1) and (2). The scalar $\hat{\lambda}_h$ is the Lagrangean multiplier on the budget constraint, condition (2).

$$\tilde{\lambda}_h(s) = \pi(s) \left\{ \frac{\partial u_h[x_h(s)]}{\partial x_h^i(s)} \right\} \left[\frac{\Sigma_{k \neq h} \tilde{b}_k^i(s)}{\Sigma_{k \neq h} \omega_k^i(s)} \right] \left[\frac{\Sigma_k \omega_k^i(s)}{\Sigma_k \tilde{b}_k^i(s)} \right]^2, \qquad (7)$$

and

$$\frac{\tilde{\lambda}_h(s)}{\tilde{\lambda}_h} = \frac{\sum_{k \neq h} \tilde{q}_k^m(s)}{\sum_{k \neq h} \tilde{b}_k^m(s)} \left[\frac{\sum_k \tilde{b}_k^m(s)}{\sum_k \tilde{q}_k^m(s)} \right]^2, \tag{8}$$

which must hold along with conditions (3), (4), and (5) for all h, i, and s. The scalar $\tilde{\lambda}_h(s)$ is the Lagrangean multiplier on the state s budget constraint, condition (4), and $\tilde{\lambda}_h$ is the multiplier on the securities constraint, condition (5).

Conditions (1), (2), and (6) are necessary and sufficient for $\hat{b}$ to be an optimal solution, and conditions (3), (4), (5), (7), and (8) are necessary and sufficient for $\tilde{b}$ to be an optimal solution. Even though the utility functions are not jointly concave functions of bids and offers, one can set up corresponding concave programming problems in *allocation space*. Any strategies satisfying (1), (2), and (6) or (3), (4), (5), (7), and (8) satisfy the first-order conditions of these concave programming problems, which guarantees that our conditions are necessary and *sufficient* for an optimum.

Suppose that the conclusion of the proposition is false. Then we have

$$\hat{b}_h^i(s) \frac{\sum_k \omega_k^i(s)}{\sum_k \hat{b}_k^i(s)} = \tilde{b}_h^i(s) \frac{\sum_k \omega_k^i(s)}{\sum_k \tilde{b}_k^i(s)} \quad \text{for all } h, i, \text{ and } s. \tag{9}$$

Using equations (6) and (7) for commodities i and j and simplifying, we have

$$\left[\frac{\sum_k \hat{b}_k^j(s)}{\sum_k \hat{b}_k^i(s)} \right]^2 \left[\frac{\sum_{k \neq h} \hat{b}_k^i(s)}{\sum_{k \neq h} \hat{b}_k^j(s)} \right] = \left[\frac{\sum_k \tilde{b}_k^j(s)}{\sum_k \tilde{b}_k^i(s)} \right]^2 \left[\frac{\sum_{k \neq h} \tilde{b}_k^i(s)}{\sum_{k \neq h} \tilde{b}_k^j(s)} \right]. \tag{10}$$

Equations (9) and (10) imply

$$\frac{\hat{b}_h^i(s)}{\tilde{b}_h^i(s)} = \frac{\hat{b}_h^j(s)}{\tilde{b}_h^j(s)}.$$

Thus, there is a function of s, $c(s)$, for which we have for all h and i,

$$\hat{b}_h^i(s) = c(s)\tilde{b}_h^i(s). \tag{11}$$

[If there is only one commodity, equation (11) follows immediately from equation (9)].

Going back to equations (6) and (7), we have for all h and s, $c(s)\hat{\lambda}_h = \tilde{\lambda}_h(s)$. Therefore, we also have $\tilde{\lambda}_h(\alpha)/\tilde{\lambda}_h(\beta) = c(\alpha)/c(\beta)$ for any choice of α and β. That is, the ratio of Lagrangean multipliers for any two states is the same for all consumers. From equation (8), we have for all consumers

$$\left[\frac{\sum_{k \neq h} \tilde{q}_k^m(\alpha)}{\sum_{k \neq h} \tilde{b}_k^m(\alpha)} \right] \left[\frac{\sum_k \tilde{b}_k^m(\alpha)}{\sum_k \tilde{q}_k^m(\alpha)} \right]^2 \left[\frac{\sum_{k \neq h} \tilde{b}_k^m(\beta)}{\sum_{k \neq h} \tilde{q}_k^m(\beta)} \right] \left[\frac{\sum_k \tilde{q}_k^m(\beta)}{\sum_k \tilde{b}_k^m(\beta)} \right]^2 = \frac{c(\alpha)}{c(\beta)}. \tag{12}$$

Define $p^m(s)$, the price of an Arrow security (or "Arrow money") in state s by

$$p^m(s) = \frac{\Sigma_k \tilde{b}_k^m(s)}{\Sigma_k \tilde{q}_k^m(s)}.$$

Let α be a state for which some consumer is a net purchaser of securities (there is one by hypothesis), let H_{buy} be the set of consumers who are net purchasers of state α securities, and let H_0 be the set of consumers who have zero net trades of state α securities. Let H_{sell} be the set of net sellers of state α securities. The sets H_{buy} and H_{sell} are both nonempty. For $h \in H_{\text{buy}}$, $h' \in H_{\text{sell}}$, and for $\tilde{q}_h^m(\alpha) \neq 0$, we have

$$\frac{\tilde{b}_{h'}^m(\alpha)}{\tilde{q}_{h'}^m(\alpha)} < p^m(\alpha) < \frac{\tilde{b}_h^m(\alpha)}{\tilde{q}_h^m(\alpha)}. \tag{13}$$

From inequality (13), we have

$$\frac{\Sigma_{k \neq h}\, \tilde{b}_k^m(\alpha)}{\Sigma_{k \neq h}\, \tilde{q}_k^m(\alpha)} = \frac{p^m(\alpha) - [\tilde{b}_h^m(\alpha)/\Sigma_k \tilde{q}_k^m(\alpha)]}{1 - [\tilde{q}_h^m(\alpha)/\Sigma_k \tilde{q}_k^m(\alpha)]}$$

$$< \frac{p^m(\alpha) - [\tilde{q}_h^m(\alpha)p^m(\alpha)/\Sigma_k \tilde{q}_k^m(\alpha)]}{1 - [\tilde{q}_h^m(\alpha)/\Sigma_k \tilde{q}_k^m(\alpha)]}.$$

The last expression equals $p^m(\alpha)$, which implies

$$\frac{\Sigma_{k \neq h}\, \tilde{q}_k^m(\alpha)}{\Sigma_{k \neq h}\, \tilde{b}_k^m(\alpha)} > \frac{1}{p^m(\alpha)}. \tag{14}$$

Furthermore, inequality (14) also holds for the case of $\tilde{q}_h^m(\alpha) = 0$. For h', a similar argument to that used to establish (14), but with the inequalities reversed, yields

$$\frac{\Sigma_{k \neq h'}\, \tilde{q}_k^m(\alpha)}{\Sigma_{k \neq h'}\, \tilde{b}_k^m(\alpha)} < \frac{1}{p^m(\alpha)}. \tag{15}$$

Combining condition (14) with equation (12), yields

$$\frac{\Sigma_{k \neq h}\, \tilde{b}_k^m(\beta)}{\Sigma_{k \neq h}\, \tilde{q}_k^m(\beta)} < \frac{[p^m(\beta)]^2 c(\alpha)}{p^m(\alpha)c(\beta)}$$

for all β. Equation (12) is satisfied for consumer h', so for all β we have

$$\frac{\Sigma_{k \neq h'}\, \tilde{b}_k(\beta)}{\Sigma_{k \neq h'}\, \tilde{q}_k^m(\beta)} > \frac{[p^m(\beta)]^2 c(\alpha)}{p^m(\alpha)c(\beta)}. \tag{16}$$

For each consumer $h_0 \in H_0$, we have

$$\frac{\Sigma_{k \neq h_0}\, \tilde{b}_k^m(\beta)}{\Sigma_{k \neq h_0}\, \tilde{q}_k^m(\beta)} = \frac{[p^m(\beta)]^2 c(\alpha)}{p^m(\alpha)c(\beta)}.$$

For $h \in H_{\text{buy}}$ and $h' \in H_{\text{sell}}$, we have that

$$\frac{\Sigma_{k \neq h}\, \tilde{b}_k^m(s)}{\Sigma_{k \neq h}\, \tilde{q}_k^m(s)} < \frac{\Sigma_{k \neq h'}\, \tilde{b}_k^m(s)}{\Sigma_{k \neq h'}\, \tilde{q}_k^m(s)} \qquad (17)$$

holds for all states s.

A typical state β falls into one of two categories.

Case 1: For all $h \in H_{\text{buy}}$, we have $[\Sigma_{k \neq h}\, \tilde{b}_k^m(\beta)]/[\Sigma_{k \neq h}\, \tilde{q}_k^m(\beta)] < p^m(\beta)$. Here all consumers in H_{buy} are net buyers of state-β securities, so we have

$$\sum_{k \in H_{\text{buy}}} [\tilde{b}_k^m(\beta) - \tilde{q}_k^m(\beta)\, p^m(\beta)] > 0. \qquad (18)$$

Case 2: For some $h \in H_{\text{buy}}$, we have

$$\frac{\Sigma_{k \neq h}\, \tilde{b}_k^m(\beta)}{\Sigma_{k \neq h}\, \tilde{q}_k^m(\beta)} \geq p^m(\beta). \qquad (19)$$

From condition (17), we have for all $h' \in H_{\text{sell}}$

$$\frac{\Sigma_{k \neq h'}\, \tilde{b}_k^m(\beta)}{\Sigma_{k \neq h'}\, \tilde{q}_k^m(\beta)} > p^m(\beta),$$

so all consumers in H_{sell} are net sellers of state-β securities. Therefore,

$$\sum_{k \in H_{\text{sell}}} [\tilde{b}_k^m(\beta) - \tilde{q}_k^m(\beta)\, p^m(\beta)] < 0$$

holds. For consumers in H_0, we have

$$\sum_{k \in H_0} [\tilde{b}_k^m(\beta) - \tilde{q}_k^m(\beta)\, p^m(\beta)] \leq 0,$$

which implies

$$\sum_{k \in H_{\text{buy}}} [\tilde{b}_k^m(\beta) - \tilde{q}_k^m(\beta)\, p^m(\beta)] > 0.$$

Since inequality (18) holds for each of the two categories into which state β may fall, we have

$$\sum_{k \in H_{\text{buy}}} \sum_s [\tilde{b}_k^m(s) - \tilde{q}_k^m(s)\, p^m(s)] > 0,$$

which means for some $h \in H_{\text{buy}}$,

$$\sum_s [\tilde{b}_h^m(s) - \tilde{q}_h^m(s)\, p^m(s)] > 0$$

holds, contradicting the securities constraint, inequality (5). Our supposition that $\tilde{b}$ and $\hat{b}$ result in the same allocation is false, and the proposition is proved. ∎

6   Concluding remarks

1. Our nonequivalence result (Proposition 2) is very strong. The set of Nash equilibria for the Arrow-securities game in which income is transferred across states is *disjoint* from the set of Nash equilibria for the contingent-commodities game. The sets are not merely different, they have no element in common. Careful reading of the proof of Proposition 2 shows that this result is not restricted to the sell-all variants but applies to any of these games in which offers are harmonized (i.e., the same in each of the two games). What would follow if offers were unrestricted (except that they not exceed endowments of commodities) in both games? One would then have to compare the set of all interior Nash equilibria for the Arrow-securities game with unrestricted offers to the set of all interior Nash equilibria for the contingent-commodities game with unrestricted offers. We conjecture that the two corresponding (big) sets of equilibrium allocations are different, but this remains to be shown.

2. In this chapter, we assume that information is symmetric. We see no reason why our nonequivalence result should not be extendable to include asymmetric information in rational-expectations games, but this also remains to be seen. For purely extrinsic uncertainty, the question would be: Is there a Nash-equilibrium allocation to the securities game that is not a correlated-equilibrium allocation to the certainty game but that is a Nash equilibrium to the contingent-commodities game?

3. The comparative statics for the competitive model is different from that for the imperfectly competitive model. Under competition, there is sense to the notion of complete markets. When markets are complete, adding further markets leaves the equilibrium allocation unaltered. In the imperfectly competitive environment, markets are *inherently incomplete*. Adding markets typically alters the set of Nash-equilibrium allocations.

Appendix

Proof of Proposition 1:   Let

$$z_h = [z_h^1(1), ..., z_h^i(s), ..., z_h^\ell(r); z_h^m(1), ..., z_h^m(r)]$$

be the value of y_h that maximizes

$$v_h\{y_h^m(1), ..., y_h^m(r), [y_h^i(s)]_{i,s}; [d_{-h}^m(s)]_s, [d_{-h}(s)]_s\},$$

subject to the budget and securities constraints (4) and (5), given that $\tilde{q}_h^m(s) = Q$ holds for all h and s. The bids of others, possibly augmented by ϵ, are taken as fixed for consumer h's maximization problem; see Definition (1). The values of Q and ϵ will be specified later.

The optimal bid for consumer h, z_h, is then a well-defined function of everyone's bids b. Define the adjustment functions $b_h^j(s) \to [b_h^j(s)]'$ and $b_h^m(s) \to [b_h^m(s)]'$ by

$$[b_h^j(s)]' = \frac{z_h^j(s)}{\sum_k \sum_j z_k^j(s)},$$

and

$$[b_h^m(s)]' = \frac{z_h^m(s)}{\sum_k \sum_s z_k^m(s)}.$$

Claim 3. *The set of consumption vectors that give consumer h at least as much utility as $v_h(\omega_h)$ without violating the resource constraints of the economy K_h is* (i) *a compact set in $\mathbb{R}_{++}^{r\ell}$ and* (ii) *bounded away from the axes by the positive scalars $\zeta_h^i(s)$ for $i = 1, 2, \ldots, \ell$ and $s = 1, 2, \ldots, r$.*

Proof of Claim 3: (i) K_h is the intersection of two closed sets and is therefore closed. Since resources are bounded, K_h is bounded, which implies K_h is compact.

(ii) The closure assumption on preferences guarantees that each point in the upper contour set to the indifference surface through ω_h is strictly positive. The set K_h is a subset of this upper contour set. On K_h, the pointwise distance to the axes is bounded above zero, because it is a continuous function on a compact set and therefore attains its minimum. ∎

Claim 4. *For all s, and for $b \in \Delta^{nr} \times \Delta^{n\ell} \times \cdots \times \Delta^{n\ell}$, there are positive scalars $\underline{\theta}$ and $\bar{\theta}$, independent of b and ϵ, such that*

$$\underline{\theta} \le \sum_k \sum_j z_k^j(s) \le \bar{\theta}.$$

Proof of Claim 4: From (4), the utility-maximizing bids $z_h^j(s)$ satisfy

$$\sum_j z_h^j(s) \le \max_{h,j} \left[\frac{\omega_h^j(s)}{\sum_k \omega_h^j(s)} \right] \left[\sum_{k \ne h} \sum_j d_k^j(s) + \sum_j z_h^j(s) \right] + nQ.$$

Let ϵ be chosen less than $1/n\ell$. Since we have $b \in \Delta^{nr} \times \Delta^{\ell n} \times \cdots \times \Delta^{\ell n}$, the expression $\sum_{k \ne h} \sum_j d_k^j(s)$ must be less than 2. Therefore, we have

$$\sum_j z_h^j(s) \le \frac{1}{1 - \max_{h,j}[\omega_h^j(s)/\sum_k \omega_k^j(s)]} \left[2 \max_{h,j} \left\{ \frac{\omega_h^j(s)}{\sum_k \omega_k^j(s)} \right\} + nQ \right].$$

Thus, $\sum_k \sum_j z_k^j(s) \le \bar{\theta}$, where $\bar{\theta}$ is defined to be equal to

$$\bar{\theta} = \frac{n\{2 \max_{h,j}[\omega_h^j(s)/\sum_k \omega_k^j(s)] + nQ\}}{1 - \max_{h,j}[\omega_h^j(s)/\sum_k \omega_k^j(s)]}.$$

From Lemma 1 and Claim 3, it is clear that $z_h^j(s)$ must put consumer h's allocation in the set K_h. Define the positive scalar ς by $\varsigma = \min_{h,j,s}[\varsigma_h^j(s)]$. There must be some h and some i for which we have $\sum_{k \neq h} d_k^i(s) \geq 1/n\ell$, because of the normalization. For x_h to be in K_h, the inequality

$$\varsigma \leq x_h^i(s) = \frac{z_h^i(s) \sum_k \omega_k^i(s)}{z_h^i(s) + \sum_{k \neq h} d_k^i(s)}$$

must hold. Thus, we have

$$z_h^i(s) \leq \frac{\varsigma/n\ell}{\sum_k \omega_k^i(s)}. \tag{20}$$

We define $\underline{\theta}$ to be equal to the right-hand side of inequality (20). It follows that

$$\sum_k \sum_j z_k^j(s) \geq \underline{\theta}. \qquad \blacksquare$$

Claim 5. *For* $b \in \Delta^{nr} \times \Delta^{n\ell} \times \cdots \times \Delta^{n\ell}$, *there are positive scalars* $\underline{\phi}$ *and* $\bar{\phi}$ *(independent of b and ϵ) for which we have*

$$\underline{\phi} \leq \sum_k \sum_s z_k^m(s) \leq \bar{\phi}.$$

Proof of Claim 5: From the securities constraint (5), we have

$$\sum_s z_h^m(s) \leq \frac{1}{n} \sum_s \left[\sum_{k \neq h} d_k^m(s) + z_h^m(s) \right].$$

Because we have $[b_1^m(1), \ldots, b_n^m(r)] \in \Delta^{nr}$, we have $\sum_s z_h^m(s) \leq 1/(n-1)$. Therefore, we also have

$$\sum_k \sum_s z_k^m(s) \leq \frac{n}{n-1} = \bar{\phi}.$$

From (4), it follows that we have

$$0 \leq \sum_j z_h^j(s) \left\{ 1 - \max_{h,j} \left[\frac{\omega_h^j(s)}{\sum_k \omega_k^j(s)} \right] \right\}$$

$$\leq \max_{h,j} \left[\frac{\omega_h^j(s)}{\sum_k \omega_k^j(s)} \right] \left[\sum_{k \neq h} \sum_j d_k^j(s) \right] + Q \left[\frac{n z_h^m(s)}{\sum_{k \neq h} d_k^m(s) + z_h^m(s)} - 1 \right].$$

Using the normalization of $b(s)$ and the fact that $\sum_{k \neq h} \sum_j d_k^j(s) < 2$, we can manipulate the last expression to yield

$$\frac{n z_h^m(s)}{\sum_{k \neq h} d_k^m(s)} \geq 1 - \max_{h,j} \left[\frac{\omega_h^j(s)}{\sum_k \omega_k^j(s)} \right] \frac{2}{Q}. \tag{21}$$

Condition (21) must hold for all h and s. By the normalization of securities bids, there must be some consumer h and some state s for which we have $\Sigma_{k \neq h} d_k^m(s) \geq (1/nr)$. For that h and that s, we have

$$z_h^m(s) \leq \frac{1}{n2r} \left\{ 1 - \max_{h,j} \left[\frac{\omega_h^j(s)}{\Sigma_k \omega_k^j(s)} \right] \right\} \frac{2}{Q}.$$

As long as we choose Q to satisfy

$$Q \geq 4 \max_{h,j,s} \left[\frac{\omega_h^j(s)}{\Sigma_k \omega_k^j(s)} \right], \tag{22}$$

we have $z_h^m(s) \geq 1/2n^2r$. Therefore, we have

$$\sum_k \sum_s z_k^m(s) \geq \frac{1}{2n^2r},$$

so $\underline{\phi}$ is defined to be equal to $1/2n^2r$. ∎

Claim 6. *The mapping $b \to b'$ has a fixed point. That is, there exists $\overset{*}{b} = [\overset{*}{b}{}_h^i(s)]_{h,i,s}$ with the property*

$$\overset{*}{b}{}_h^i(s) = \frac{\overset{*}{z}{}_h^i(s)}{\Sigma_k \Sigma_j \overset{*}{z}{}_k^j(s)} \tag{23}$$

and

$$\overset{*}{b}{}_h^m(s) = \frac{\overset{*}{z}{}_h^m(s)}{\Sigma_k \Sigma_s \overset{*}{z}{}_k^m(s)}, \tag{24}$$

where $\overset{*}{d}{}_h^i(s) = \max(\overset{*}{b}{}_h^i(s), \epsilon)$ and $\overset{*}{z}_h$ is consumer h's utility-maximizing bid given $\overset{*}{d} = \{\overset{*}{d}{}_h^i(s)\}_{h,i,s}$.

Proof of Claim 6: The function that takes b into b' is the composition of continuous functions, since the denominators are bounded above zero, and thus this function is continuous. Also, this function maps a compact, convex subset of $\mathbb{R}^{nr(\ell+2)}$ into itself. The proof of Claim 6 then follows directly from Brouwer's fixed-point theorem. ∎

Claim 7. *For some choice of ϵ, $0 < \epsilon < 1/n\ell$, we have at the fixed point $\overset{*}{b}{}_h^i(s) > \epsilon$ for all h, i, and s.*

To prove Claim 7, we suppose it were not true, and we consider two cases. Intuitively, Case 1 represents too low a price for some commodity i in state s, which is never possible. Case 2 represents a price for commodity i that is not too low, so each consumer h must bid at least some amount to put himself in K_h. By choosing ϵ below that amount, Claim 7 is proved.

Proof of Claim 7:   Suppose Claim 7 is false. For some h, i, and s, $\overset{*}{b}{}^i_h(s) \leq \epsilon$ occurs for all positive ϵ. Because K_h is compact, each consumer's marginal rate of substitution within K_h is bounded. There are $\gamma^{i,j}_h(s,s')$ and $\delta^{i,j}_h(s,s')$ such that

$$\gamma^{i,j}_h(s,s') \leq \mathrm{MRS}_{i,j,s,s'} \leq \delta^{i,j}_h(s,s').$$

Let the positive scalar γ be defined by $\gamma = \min_{i,j,k,s,s'}[\gamma^{i,j}_k(s,s')]$. Also, let M_1 be given by

$$M_1 = \max_{h,i,j,s,s'} \left\{ \frac{\sum_{k \neq h} \omega^i_k(s)[\sum_k \omega^j_k(s')]^2}{[\sum_k \omega^i_k(s)]^2[\sum_{k \neq h} \omega^j_k(s')]} \right\},$$

which is well-defined because endowments are positive and finite. Then, define M by

$$M = \frac{[1+\bar{\theta}]^2 M_1}{\min(\underline{\theta},1)\gamma}.$$

We know that for some consumer h' and commodity j, we have $\overset{*}{b}{}^j_{h'}(s) \geq 1/n\ell$.

Case 1: $\sum_k \overset{*}{d}{}^i_k(s) \leq 1/n\ell M$

There must be some consumer (call her h'') for whom $\overset{*}{b}{}^i_{h''}(s)$ is less than the sum of the other consumers' possibly augmented bids on that market. Since h'' will choose a point in $K_{h''}$, and since the first-order conditions for utility maximization are necessary and sufficient for an optimum, we have

$$\gamma \leq \frac{\dfrac{\partial u_{h''}}{\partial x^i_{h''}(s)}}{\dfrac{\partial u_{h''}}{\partial x^j_{h''}(s)}} = \frac{\left[\dfrac{\overset{*}{z}{}^i_{h''}(s) + \sum_{k \neq h''} \overset{*}{d}{}^i_k(s)}{\sum_k \omega^i_k(s)}\right]^2 \left[\dfrac{\sum_{k \neq h''} \omega^i_k(s)}{\sum_{k \neq h''} \overset{*}{d}{}^i_k(s)}\right]}{\left[\dfrac{\overset{*}{z}{}^j_{h''}(s) + \sum_{k \neq h''} \overset{*}{d}{}^j_k(s)}{\sum_k \omega^j_k(s)}\right]^2 \left[\dfrac{\sum_{k \neq h''} \omega^j_k(s)}{\sum_{k \neq h''} \overset{*}{d}{}^j_k(s)}\right]}.$$

Therefore, we have

$$\gamma \leq \left[\frac{M_1 \sum_{k \neq h''} \overset{*}{d}{}^j_k(s)}{\sum_{k \neq h''} \overset{*}{d}{}^i_k(s)}\right]\left[\frac{\overset{*}{z}{}^i_{h''}(s) + \sum_{k \neq h''} \overset{*}{d}{}^i_k(s)}{\overset{*}{z}{}^j_{h''}(s) + \sum_{k \neq h''} \overset{*}{d}{}^j_k(s)}\right]^2. \tag{25}$$

We have the following facts:

$$\overset{*}{z}{}^i_{h''}(s) + \sum_{k \neq h''} \overset{*}{d}{}^i_k(s) < \bar{\theta}\overset{*}{b}{}^i_{h''}(s) + \frac{1}{n\ell M} < \frac{1}{n\ell M}(\bar{\theta}+1)$$

and

$$\overset{*}{z}{}^j_{h''}(s) + \sum_{k \neq h''} \overset{*}{d}{}^j_k(s) > \underline{\theta}\overset{*}{b}{}^j_{h''}(s) + \sum_{k \neq h''} \overset{*}{d}{}^j_k(s) > \frac{1}{n\ell}[\min(\underline{\theta},1)].$$

The last inequality holds whether or not h' and h'' are equal. Combining the above inequalities with inequality (25) implies that

$$\gamma < \frac{M_1(\bar{\theta}+1)[\dot{z}_{h''}^i(s) + \sum_{k \neq h''} \dot{d}_k^i(s)]}{M[\min(\underline{\theta},1)]\sum_{k \neq h''}\dot{d}_k^i(s)}$$

holds. From (23) and Claim 4, we have

$$\gamma < \left\{\frac{M_1(\bar{\theta}+1)}{M[\min(\underline{\theta},1)]}\right\}\left[1 + \frac{\bar{\theta}\dot{b}_{h''}(s)}{\sum_{k \neq h''}\dot{d}_k^i(s)}\right].$$

Consumer h'' was chosen because her bid is less than $\sum_{k \neq h''}\dot{d}_k^i(s)$, so we have

$$\gamma < \frac{M_1(1+\bar{\theta})^2}{M[\min(\underline{\theta},1)]},$$

which contradicts the definition of M.

Case 2: $\sum_k \dot{d}_k^i(s) > 1/n\ell M$

For consumer h to be in K_h, we must have

$$\zeta < \frac{\dot{z}_h^i(s)\sum_k \omega_k^i(s)}{\dot{z}_h^i(s) + \sum_{k \neq h}\dot{d}_k^i(s)} < \frac{\dot{z}_h^i(s)\sum_k \omega_k^i(s)}{\sum_{k \neq h}\dot{d}_k^i(s)}.$$

Because $\dot{d}_h^i(s) = \epsilon$ holds, we have $\sum_{k \neq h}\dot{d}_k^i(s) + \epsilon > 1/n\ell M$. Thus, there is a positive value of ϵ, say ϵ_1, below which $\sum_{k \neq h}\dot{d}_k^i(s) \geq 1/n\ell M$ holds. As long as we choose ϵ below ϵ_1, we have

$$\zeta < \frac{\bar{\theta}\epsilon \sum_k \omega_k^i(s)}{1/n\ell M}.$$

Choose ϵ to satisfy

$$0 < \epsilon < \min\left[\frac{1}{n\ell}, \epsilon_1, \frac{\zeta}{\bar{\theta}\sum_k \omega_k^i(s)n\ell M}\right], \tag{26}$$

so that we have a contradiction. ∎

Claim 8. *There is a choice of ϵ, satisfying (26), below which we have at the fixed point $\dot{b}_h^m(s) > \epsilon$ for all h and s.*

To prove Claim 8, we suppose it were not true, and we consider two cases. Case 1 represents too low a price for state-α securities, which is impossible. Case 2 represents a price that is not too low, so each consumer must bid at least some amount to achieve positive income in state α. By choosing ϵ below that amount, Claim 8 is proved.

Proof of Claim 8: Suppose Claim 8 is false. For some h and some α, $\overset{*}{b}{}_h^m(\alpha) \leq \epsilon$ holds for all positive ϵ. We know that for some consumer h' and some β, we have $\overset{*}{b}{}_h^m(\beta) \geq 1/nr$. Define M_2 by the equation

$$M_2 = \frac{(1+\bar{\phi})^2(\bar{\theta}+1)(1+M\bar{\theta})M_1}{\min(\underline{\phi},1)\min(\underline{\theta},1)}.$$

Case 1: $\sum_k \overset{*}{d}{}_k^m(\alpha) \leq 1/nrM_2$

There must be some consumer h'' for whom we have

$$\overset{*}{b}{}_{h''}^m(\alpha) \leq \sum_{k \neq h''} \overset{*}{d}{}_k^m(\alpha).$$

Because consumer h'' will choose a point in $K_{h''}$ and because the first-order conditions for utility maximization are necessary and sufficient for an optimum, we have, for i and j,

$$\gamma \leq \left\{ \frac{\pi(\alpha)\dfrac{\partial u_{h''}[x_{h''}(\alpha)]}{\partial x_{h''}^i}}{\pi(\beta)\dfrac{\partial u_{h''}[x_{h''}(\beta)]}{\partial x_{h''}^j}} \right\} = \left[\frac{\overset{*}{z}{}_{h''}^m(\alpha)+\sum_{k \neq h''}\overset{*}{d}{}_k^m(\alpha)}{\overset{*}{z}{}_{h''}^m(\beta)+\sum_{k \neq h''}\overset{*}{d}{}_k^m(\beta)} \right]^2 \left[\frac{\sum_{k \neq h''}\overset{*}{d}{}_k^m(\beta)}{\sum_{k \neq h''}\overset{*}{d}{}_k^m(\alpha)} \right]$$

$$\times \left[\frac{\sum_k \omega_k^i(\alpha)}{\sum_k \omega_k^i(\beta)} \right]^2 \left[\frac{\sum_{k \neq h''}\omega_k^j(\beta)}{\sum_{k \neq h''}\omega_k^j(\alpha)} \right] \left[\frac{\sum_{k \neq h''}\overset{*}{d}{}_k^j(\beta)}{\sum_{k \neq h''}\overset{*}{d}{}_k^i(\alpha)} \right]$$

$$\times \left[\frac{\overset{*}{z}{}_{h''}^i(\alpha)+\sum_{k \neq h''}\overset{*}{d}{}_k^i(\alpha)}{\overset{*}{z}{}_{h''}^j(\beta)+\sum_{k \neq h''}\overset{*}{d}{}_k^j(\beta)} \right]^2. \tag{27}$$

We can choose commodity j to satisfy $\sum_k \overset{*}{d}{}_k^j(\beta) \geq 1/\ell$; and by Case 1 of Claim 7, we can choose i to satisfy $1/n\ell M \leq \sum_k \overset{*}{d}{}_k^i(\alpha) \leq 1/\ell$.

It follows from inequality (27) that we have

$$\gamma < \left[\frac{\overset{*}{z}{}_{h''}^m(\alpha)+\sum_{k \neq h''}\overset{*}{d}{}_k^m(\alpha)}{\overset{*}{z}{}_{h''}^m(\beta)+\sum_{k \neq h''}\overset{*}{d}{}_k^m(\beta)} \right]^2 \left[\frac{\sum_{k \neq h''}\overset{*}{d}{}_k^m(\beta)}{\sum_{k \neq h''}\overset{*}{d}{}_k^m(\alpha)} \right] \left[\frac{M_1(\bar{\theta}+1)(1+M\bar{\theta})}{\min(\underline{\theta},1)} \right].$$

We also know that

$$\overset{*}{z}{}_{h''}^m(\alpha)+\sum_{k \neq h''}\overset{*}{d}{}_k^m(\alpha) < \bar{\phi}\overset{*}{b}{}_{h''}^m(\alpha)+\frac{1}{nrM_2} < \frac{1}{nrM_2}(1+\bar{\phi})$$

and

$$\overset{*}{z}{}_{h''}^m(\beta)+\sum_{k \neq h''}\overset{*}{d}{}_k^m(\beta) > \underline{\phi}\overset{*}{b}{}_{h''}^m(\beta)+\sum_{k \neq h''}\overset{*}{d}{}_k^m(\beta) > \min(\underline{\phi},1)\left(\frac{1}{nr} \right)$$

hold. The last inequality holds whether or not h' and h'' are equal. Thus, we have

$$\gamma < \frac{(1+\bar{\phi})}{\min(\underline{\phi},1)M_2} \left[1+\frac{\overset{*}{z}{}_{h''}^m(\alpha)}{\sum_{k \neq h''}\overset{*}{d}{}_k^m(\alpha)} \right] \frac{M_1(\bar{\theta}+1)(1+M\bar{\theta})}{\min(\underline{\theta},1)}. \tag{28}$$

Consumer h'' bids less on the α security market than the sum of the augmented bids of the other consumers. This fact, conditions (24) and (28), and the bounds on the securities bids imply that

$$\gamma < \frac{(1+\bar{\phi})^2 M_1(\bar{\theta}+1)(1+M\bar{\theta})}{\min(\underline{\phi},1)M_2 \min(\underline{\theta},1)},$$

which contradicts the definition of M_2.

Case 2: $\sum_k \dot{d}_k^m(\alpha) > 1 n r M_2$

From condition (4) and the fact that $\dot{b}_h^m(\alpha) \le \epsilon$, we have that

$$0 < 2 \max_{j,h}\left[\frac{\omega_h^j(\alpha)}{\sum_k \omega_k^j(\alpha)}\right] + \frac{\epsilon n Q}{(1/nrM_2)} - Q$$

must hold. Thus, we have

$$\frac{2 \max_{j,h,s}[\omega_h^j(s)/\sum_k \omega_k^j(s)]}{Qn^2 rM_2} < \frac{Q - 2 \max_{j,h}[\omega_h^j(\alpha)/\sum_k \omega_k^j(\alpha)]}{Qn^2 rM_2} < \epsilon.$$

By choosing ϵ less than

$$\frac{2 \max_{j,h}[\omega_h^j(\alpha)/\sum_k \omega_k^j(\alpha)]}{Qn^2 rM_2},$$

but positive, we have a contradiction. ∎

Claim 9. *Choose ϵ greater than 0 and satisfying*

$$\epsilon < \min\left[\frac{1}{n\ell}, \epsilon_1, \left\{\frac{\varsigma}{\bar{\theta}\sum_k \omega_k^j(s)n\ell M}\right\}_{j,s}, \frac{2 \max_{j,h,s}[\omega_h^j(s)/\sum_k \omega_k^j(s)]}{Qn^2 rM_2}\right]$$

and choose Q so that

$$Q > 4 \max_{j,h,s}\left[\frac{\omega_h^j(s)}{\sum_k \omega_k^j(s)}\right]$$

holds. Then the fixed point $\dot{b}$ (combined with the security market bids of Q for each consumer and state) constitutes an interior Nash equilibrium.

Proof of Claim 9: We have shown that $\dot{b} = \dot{d}$. Conditions (23) and (24) hold at the fixed point, where $\dot{z}_h$ is now consumer h's utility-maximizing bid given $\dot{b}$.

When $\sum_k \sum_i \dot{z}_k^i(s) > 1$ for some s, we have $\dot{b}_h^i(s) < \dot{z}_h^i(s)$ for all h and i. Thus, consumer h wants to increase all his bids, so at $\dot{b}$ there is slack in his state s budget constraint. That is, we have

$$\sum_j \dot{b}_h^j(s) < \sum_j \left[\frac{\omega_h^j(s) \sum_k \dot{b}_k^j(s)}{\sum_k \omega_k^j(s)} \right] + \frac{\dot{b}_h^m(s) nQ}{\sum_k \dot{b}_k^m(s)} - Q.$$

Summing over h, we reach a contradiction.

When $\sum_k \sum_i \dot{z}_k^i(s) < 1$ for some s, we have $\dot{b}_h^i(s) > \dot{z}_h^i(s)$ for all h and i. Consumer h wants to decrease all his bids, so at $\dot{b}$ his bids must not have been feasible in state s. That is, we have

$$\sum_j \dot{b}_h^j(s) > \sum_j \left[\frac{\omega_h^j(s) \sum_k \dot{b}_k^j(s)}{\sum_k \omega_k^j(s)} \right] + \frac{\dot{b}_h^m(s) nQ}{\sum_k \dot{b}_k^m(s)} - Q.$$

Summing over h, we reach a contradiction, which implies $\sum_k \sum_i \dot{z}_k^i(s) = 1$.

When $\sum_k \sum_s \dot{z}_k^m(s) > 1$, we have $\dot{b}_h^m(s) < \dot{z}_h^m(s)$ for all h and s. Consumer h, given the other securities bids, wants to increase all his bids, which means there is slack in his securities constraint. Thus, we have

$$\sum_s \dot{b}_h^m(s) < \frac{1}{n} \sum_s \sum_k \dot{b}_k^m(s).$$

Summing over h, we reach a contradiction.

When $\sum_k \sum_s \dot{z}_k^m(s) < 1$, we have $\dot{b}_h^m(s) > \dot{z}_h^m(s)$. Consumer h wants to reduce all his securities bids, which means his securities constraint is violated at $\dot{b}$. Thus, we have

$$\sum_s \dot{b}_h^m(s) > \frac{1}{n} \sum_s \sum_k \dot{b}_k^m(s).$$

Summing over h, we reach a contradiction, which implies $\sum_k \sum_s \dot{z}_k^m(s) = 1$.

Conditions (23) and (24) reduce to the following:

$$\dot{b}_h^i(s) = \dot{z}_h^i(s)$$

and

$$\dot{b}_h^m(s) = \dot{z}_h^m(s).$$

Given $\dot{b}$ and Q, each consumer optimizes by not deviating from $\dot{b}$. Because $\dot{b}_h^m(s)$ is positive for all h and s, no consumer gains from changing $\tilde{q}_h^m(s)$ away from Q.[14] Thus, we have found an interior Nash equilibrium for the Arrow-securities game, completing the proof of Proposition 1. ∎

[14] See Peck and Shell (1985) for the proof. Because optimizing with respect to $q_h^m(s)$ and $b_h^m(s)$ yields the same interior first-order conditions, fixing $q_h^m(s)$ and solving for $b_h^m(s)$ is a solution to the problem in which $q_h^m(s)$ is not fixed. See Peck and Shell (1985, sect. 2.1, pp. 11–13) for further elucidation of this point.

REFERENCES

Arrow, K. J. (1953), "Le rôle des valeurs boursieres pour la repartition la meilleure des risques," *Econométrie,* Paris: CNRS, pp. 41–8. [Translated as "The role of securities in the optimal allocation of risk-bearing," *Review of Economic Studies,* 31(2), (1964), 91–6.]

Cass, D., and Shell, K. (1983), "Do sunspots matter?" *Journal of Political Economy,* 91(2), 193–227.

Debreu, G. (1959), *Theory of Value,* New York: Wiley.

Dubey, P., and Shubik, M. (1977), "Trade and prices in a closed economy with exogeneous uncertainty, different levels of information, money and compound futures markets," *Econometrica,* 45(7), 1657–80.

Mas-Colell, A. (1982), "The Cournotian foundations of Walrasian equilibrium theory: an exposition of recent theory," in *Advances in Economic Theory,* ed. by W. Hildenbrand, New York: Cambridge University Press, pp. 183–224.

Peck, J., and Shell, K. (1985), "Market uncertainty: sunspot equilibria in imperfectly competitive economies," CARESS Working Paper No. 85-21, University of Pennsylvania. Revised version appears as "Market uncertainty: correlated equilibrium and sunspot equilibrium in imperfectly competitive economies," Center for Analytic Economics Working Paper No. 88-22, Cornell University, May 1988.

 (1987), "Liquid markets and efficiency," mimeo., Northwestern University, April. Abstracted version forthcoming in *Game Theory and Applications: Proceedings of the 1987 International Conference, Ohio State University, Columbus, Ohio,* ed. by T. Ichiish, A. Neyman, and Y. Tauman, Academic Press.

 (1988), "Liquid markets and competition," Center for Analytic Economics Working Paper No. 88-25RRR, Cornell University, October.

Postlewaite, A., and Schmeidler, D. (1978), "Approximate efficiency of non-Walrasian Nash equilibria," *Econometrica,* 46(1), 127–35.

Shapley, L. (1976), "Noncooperative general exchange," in *Theory and Measurement of Economic Externalities,* ed. by S. A. Y. Lin, New York: Academic Press, 155–75.

Shapley, L. and Shubik, M. (1977), "Trade using one commodity as a means of payment," *Journal of Political Economy,* 85(5), 937–68.

Shubik, M. (1973), "Commodity money, oligopoly, credit and bankruptcy in a general equilibrium model," *Western Economic Journal,* 11, 24–38.

PART II

Bubbles, instability, and hyperinflation

CHAPTER 5

Endogenous financial-production cycles in a macroeconomic model

Duncan K. Foley

The concept of a path of exponential growth at a constant rate arises naturally in theories of capitalist economies in which some part of profit (or, indeed, of income in general) is reinvested in production. It appears to be unusual, however, to observe a capitalist economy on such a path for very long (in historical terms). Instead, capitalist economies typically undergo a cyclical path of accumulation, alternating periods of higher than average growth with periods of lower than average growth.

Two general strategies for explaining this fact present themselves. One assumes that the steady-state growth path is stable and that external shocks constantly perturb the economy from that path (see Frisch, 1933). The other, which offers the possibility of a self-contained explanation of cyclical motion, assumes that the steady-state growth path is unstable, and so the economy can never be observed on it. If a linear model of accumulation is locally unstable, it is also globally unstable, and real capitalist economies never make unbounded excursions away from the steady-state growth path. As Samuelson (1939), Kaldor (1940), Goodwin (1950, reprinted in Goodwin, 1982), and Hicks (1950) discovered, and as Blatt (1983) emphasizes, this objection does not hold in nonlinear models. In a nonlinear model a local instability of the steady-state growth path can be contained by nonlinear effects to prevent the economy from exploding. This chapter continues the exploration of this line of thinking by considering the role that financial effects might have in globally stabilizing a growth model whose steady state is made locally unstable by a strong investment accelerator.

To focus sharply on the relation between finance and investment, we shall study a model of an economy that consists essentially only of capitalist

I would like to thank Jesse Benhabib, Charles Wilson, Michael Woodford, Richard Day, Gerard Dumenil, Dominique Levy, and Richard Goodwin for conversations that helped me to clarify my thinking on this problem.

firms. Section 1 explains in general terms the type of microeconomic be-havior of the firm that would be necessary to produce the macroeconomic effects studied later on. Section 2 analyzes the dynamic behavior of a sin-gle firm. In Section 3 the macroeconomic conditions linking the individual firms are set out. Section 4 presents a simplified macroeconomic model in which all the firms are identical in behavior and initial conditions, expec-tations of future sales are formed adaptively, and outside money grows at a constant rate. Under plausible assumptions on the reaction functions, this model exhibits a stable limit cycle in financial and production vari-ables. The magnitude and period of this cycle are calculated. In Section 5 we consider the effect of two simple monetary policy rules on the stability of the model: A monetary policy keyed to the current level of sales or pro-duction is destabilizing in this setting whereas a monetary policy keyed to financial conditions is stabilizing. Section 6 looks briefly at the problems raised for this model by the assumption of perfect foresight. If the lags in production planning have the right relation to other parameters of the model, it can exhibit cycles even with perfect foresight. Thus, vigorous pursuit of information by private decision makers need not in and of it-self eliminate the possibility of cyclical instability. A final section discusses some related papers.

1   The firm and finance

We consider a capitalist firm that hires labor and other inputs to produce a product for sale at a profit. We suppose, for the sake of simplifica-tion, that the firm combines labor and other inputs in fixed proportions and denote the money cost of a unit of output as u. Because the produc-tion process takes time, the firm will always have some value tied up in stocks of inputs and partly finished goods. When the output emerges from the production process, it enters inventories of finished goods awaiting sale. The firm faces a downward-sloping individual demand schedule that shifts over time as the state of aggregate demand in the whole economy changes. To reflect the influence of size of the firm on market share, sup-pose that the position of the firm's demand schedule also depends posi-tively on its inventories of finished goods. In this chapter we shall con-sider the case in which the firm demand schedule has a rectangular shape, and so the firm simply must accept a level of sales equal to a certain pro-portion of its inventory of finished goods at a given price p. This assump-tion is consistent with an unvarying price of output in terms of money. A more sophisticated version of the model would consider the firm's abil-ity to trade off sales for profit margin by changing its price.

Suppose further that this firm operates in a simple financial environment in which a government issues fiat money and distributes it to firms in proportion to their existing money balances.

This stylized firm, though it has no choices about the technique of production, faces important decisions about the management of its financial assets and the timing of production. If it is costly for the firm to carry inventories of finished goods, but larger inventories increase its market share, the firm will make higher long-run profits in the face of a shifting individual demand schedule if it schedules production to come on the market at a time when demand is strong, rather than at a time when demand is weak. Because the firm must use money to buy inputs, if it incurs rising costs as it turns over its money balances more rapidly, it also makes higher long-run profits if it manages its money-holding correctly.

The money value tied up in the firm's operations is expressed in the balance sheet:

Assets	*Liabilities and Net Worth*
Money M	
Productive capital X	Net worth $E = M + X$

In this simplified balance sheet, productive capital includes stocks of inputs, goods in process, and inventories of finished goods awaiting sale. A more sophisticated treatment would separate strictly productive capital from finished-goods inventories.

The critical decision variable for the firm is its level of capital outlays C to hire labor and purchase inputs into production. Here we shall assume that the firm follows a rule-of-thumb policy with regard to C. (A full intertemporal optimizing analysis of a firm of this kind can be found in Foley, 1987b.) The firm forms an expectation of the profitability of capital outlays at the current moment, a rate of return r. It also has a rate of return benchmark ρ, which depends on its current state of liquidity $m = M/X$. The less liquid the firm is, the higher is the benchmark rate of return. We assume that capital outlays as a proportion of existing productive capital rise with the difference between r and ρ:

$$C = c[r - \rho[m]]X, \quad c' > 0, \quad \rho' < 0. \tag{1}$$

2 Laws of motion

For an individual firm, we can write down the laws of motion that determine the evolution of its balance sheet:

$$\dot{M} = S - C + gM, \tag{2}$$

$$\dot{X} = C - (1 - q)S, \tag{3}$$

where S is the sales of the firm, C is capital outlays, and q is profit as a proportion of sales, which is fixed by the assumption of given unit costs and a given price. The classical-Marxist tradition argues that the average profit margin in a whole capitalist system depends on the relation between the standard of living of workers and labor productivity. Here productive capital is valued at cost. gM represents the government's distribution of money to the firms, where g is the factor of proportionality between existing and new money. Clearly g is also the growth rate of the aggregate money stock. We can write these equations in intensive form as

$$\dot{m} = \frac{\dot{M}}{X} - \frac{m\dot{X}}{X} = s - c - mc + m(1-q)s + gm$$

$$= (1+m)(s-c) - mqs + gm, \tag{4}$$

$$\frac{\dot{X}}{X} = c - (1-q)s = c - s + qs, \tag{5}$$

where $s = S/X$.

3   An ensemble of capitalist firms

If we have a large collection of such firms, we can write a closed dynamic model for the evolution of its state. Assume that workers spend all their wages instantly and that all profits are retained by firms in their effort to grow rapidly. Then the source of demand for the products of firms will be the capital outlays of other firms, either directly, or indirectly through workers' spending wages.

The actual pattern of spending can be quite complex in a general model involving differences in pricing policies and hence profit margins. In all models it must be true that in the aggregate

$$S = C. \tag{6}$$

4   A simple dynamic model

The simplest approach to analyzing the dynamics of this system is to assume that all the firms are identical in behavior and initial conditions. Then the motion of a particular firm will be a model of the whole system. If all the firms are identical, (6) implies that $s = c$ for every firm. Then (4) becomes

$$\dot{m} = -mqs + gm = m(g - qc[r - \rho[m]]). \tag{7}$$

Now we can close the dynamic model by specifying the evolution of r, the expectation of profitability. For example, if expectations of profitability adapt to actual instantaneous rates of profit, $qs = qc$, we have

$$\dot{r} = \alpha(qc[r - \rho[m]] - r), \quad \alpha > 0. \tag{8}$$

Equations (7) and (8) constitute a simple closed model of the motion of this ensemble of identical capitals.

The equilibrium of this system has $r^* = qc^* = g$ and $g = qc[g - \rho[m^*]]$. To examine the stability of the system around the steady state, look at the linearization:

	m	r
$\dot{m}$	$qc'\rho'm^*$	$-qc'm^*$
$\dot{r}$	$-\alpha qc'\rho'$	$\alpha(qc'-1)$

The characteristic equation of this system is

$$\lambda^2 - (\alpha(qc'-1) + qc'\rho'm^*)\lambda - \alpha qc'\rho'qc'm^* + qc'\rho'm^*\alpha(qc'-1)$$
$$= \lambda^2 - (\alpha(qc'-1) - qc'\sigma)\lambda + \alpha qc'\sigma$$

For notational convenience σ is written for $|\rho'm^*|$, the semielasticity of the shadow rate of return to money with respect to the liquidity ratio m, evaluated at the equilibrium point.

This system becomes unstable as the bifurcation parameter

$$\mu = \alpha(qc'-1) - qc'\sigma$$

passes through 0, as a result, say, of increasing c' or of increasing α.

The resulting unstable system has a limit cycle with frequency near $\omega = \sqrt{\alpha\sigma qc'}$ if $c'' < 0$.

In this expression for ω, α has the dimensions 1/unit time, qc' is a pure number (an elasticity) close to 1, and $\sigma = |\rho'|m^*$ is a semielasticity (of the shadow rate of return to money with respect to liquidity) that has the dimensions 1/unit time. The real business cycle has a period $T = 5-6$ years or an angular frequency $\omega = 2\pi/T$ of about 1 radian per year. If $\alpha\sigma qc' \approx 1$, the model's cycle frequency would be consistent with the period of the real business cycle. If we think of qc' as being close to 1, then an α of between 1 and 10 (corresponding to a time constant of adaptive expectations of between 1 year and 1 month) would require a semielasticity of the shadow rate of return to money with respect to liquidity of between 1 and 0.1.

This model is a case of the Hopf bifurcation analyzed by Guckenheimer and Holmes (1983, chap. 3, especially pp. 150–6). Let us assume that the function c is quadratic or approximate it by the first three terms of its Taylor expansion:

$$c[r - \rho[m]] = c^* + c'((r - r^*) - \rho'(m - m^*)) + c''((r - r^*) - \rho'(m - m^*))^2, \tag{9}$$

where c^* is the value of c at the equilibrium. Then, making the substitution $m' = m - m^*$, and $r' = r - r^*$, we have

$$\dot{m}' = (m' + m^*)(-qc'(r' - \rho'm') - qc''(r' - \rho'm')^2), \tag{10}$$

$$\dot{r}' = \alpha(qc'(r' - \rho'm') + qc''(r' - \rho'm')^2 - r'). \tag{11}$$

Here it is convenient to make the further substitution

$$z' = (qc'm^*/\omega)(r' - \rho'm')$$

to yield the system, remembering that $\omega^2 = -\alpha qc'\rho'm^*$ and that at the bifurcation, $\mu = \alpha(qc' - 1) + \rho'qc'm^* = 0$:

$$\dot{m}' = \omega z' - \omega \frac{m'}{m^*}z' + \alpha\rho'\frac{c''}{c'}(z')^2 + \alpha\rho'\frac{c''}{c'}\frac{m'}{m^*}(z')^2 \tag{12}$$

$$\dot{z}' = \omega m' + \rho'qc'm'z' + (\alpha + \rho'm^*)\frac{\omega}{m^*}\frac{c''}{c'}(z')^2 + \rho'\omega\frac{c''}{c'}\frac{m'}{m^*}(z')^2. \tag{13}$$

This is exactly the normal form system analyzed by Guckenheimer and Holmes (1983, pp. 152–3). They show that such a system has a surface of periodic solutions in the center manifold, which is a stable limit cycle if the coefficient a defined by them is negative. For the system (12) and (13), we can explicitly calculate:

$$a = \frac{1}{4}\left(\frac{c''}{c'}\right)\left(\frac{\alpha\rho'}{qc'm^*}\right)\left(\alpha\left(\frac{c''}{c'}\right) - qc'\right). \tag{14}$$

Because $\alpha > 0$, $c' > 0$, $\rho' < 0$, a sufficient condition for $a < 0$ is that $c'' < 0$. Thus, if $c'' < 0$, this model will exhibit a stable limit cycle near $\mu = 0$. The amplitude of this cycle is proportional to μ (see Guckenheimer and Holmes, 1983, p. 151), and its frequency will be close to ω.

In this cycle, liquidity as measured by m and profit expectations as measured by r are out of phase with each other. The profit rate–interest rate differential in this model depends on m and is large when m is large. The resulting cycle begins with a low r and an increasing m, which increases the profit rate–interest rate differential. At some point, the growth of the capital as the system goes into a boom begins to reduce m, and the profit rate–interest rate differential becomes smaller. Eventually m becomes so small that it chokes off the expansion of capital outlays, and the system turns down. Liquidity continues to decline until the actual profit rate is below the growth rate of money, when the interest rate begins to fall more slowly than the profit rate. Eventually the system becomes so liquid that a new expansion can start.

5   Monetary policy and stability

Monetary-fiscal policy can affect the stability of this kind of model. One possible policy rule would be to expand money in periods when the profit rate and sales were low, and contract money when the profit rate and sales were high, to "lean against the wind," so to speak. In this case the rate of growth of money $\theta = g - h(qc - g)$, where $h > 0$. The rate of growth of money rises when the profit rate (or sales) falls below the long-run equilibrium level, and conversely. In this situation, equation (7) becomes

$$\dot{m} = (g - h(qc - g) - qc)m = (1 - h)(g - qc)m. \tag{7a}$$

The characteristic equation of the system now becomes

$$\lambda^2 - (\alpha(qc' - 1) - (1 - h)qc'\sigma)\lambda + (1 - h)\alpha qc'\sigma.$$

An increase in h, the policy parameter, increases the coefficient μ, thus making it more likely that the system will be unstable and increasing the amplitude of the limit cycle in the case in which it is unstable. At the same time, the increase in h lowers the frequency of the limit cycle oscillation ω. Thus, a leaning against the wind monetary policy of this kind is destabilizing in this type of model.

We can see why this happens if we consider the nature of the limit cycle in this model. The profit rate (or sales) and the liquidity of the enterprises move out of phase with each other. Thus, when the profit rate is at its peak, relative liquidity is already declining at a rate that is as high as any that is reached over the cycle. When the profit rate is at its trough, the derivative of liquidity is at its peak. The monetary-fiscal policy modeled above adds money when the profit rate is at its trough and withdraws it when the profit rate is at its peak, thus exacerbating the cyclical motion.

This observation suggests that a monetary-fiscal policy aimed at stabilizing m, the measure of liquidity, would stabilize output and sales as well. If we suppose that $\theta = g - h(m/m^*)$, we have

$$\dot{m} = \left(g - h\left(\frac{m}{m^*}\right) - qc \right)m. \tag{7b}$$

Now, the characteristic equation of the system is

$$\lambda^2 - (\alpha(qc' - 1) - qc'\sigma - h)\lambda + (\alpha qc'\sigma - h\alpha(qc' - 1)).$$

This policy reduces μ, thus reducing the chance of instability and lowering the amplitude of the limit cycle in the case in which the model is unstable. This type of policy would stabilize the economy in the sense of reducing the amplitude of the limit cycle.

A policy that stabilizes the liquidity of the firms will, in this model, also stabilize the difference between the profit rate and the firms' benchmark rate of return, which is assumed to depend only on the liquidity ratio m. Because information on the actual level of profit rates is elusive in real economies, in which all the firms are not alike, and there is a considerable dispersion of profit rates, this type of policy may be difficult for a monetary-fiscal authority to achieve.

6   Perfect-foresight cycles

This simple model requires adaptive expectations, so that despite its regular recurrence, firms are always caught by surprise in the course of the cycle. Is it possible to have perfect foresight in this model and still produce regular cycles?

If expected profitability is equal to current actual profitability, perfect foresight cycles are impossible; but a consideration of the reason for this shows under what conditions perfect foresight cycles would be possible. A perfect foresight solution with expected profitability equal to actual current profitability would require (7) to continue to hold, but now (8) would have to be replaced by

$$r = qc[r - \rho[m]]. \tag{15}$$

If r is cyclical, say, $r = g + \tilde{r} \cos \omega t$, equation (7) becomes

$$\frac{\dot{m}}{m} = -\tilde{r} \cos \omega t, \tag{16}$$

which has the solution $\ln m = \ln m^* - (\tilde{r}/\omega) \sin \omega t$. Thus $\ln m$ is out of phase with r. Now, if we approximate

$$qc[r - \rho[m]] = g + qc'((r - g) + \sigma(\ln m - \ln m^*))$$

and

$$\ln m = \ln m^* - (\tilde{r}/\omega) \sin \omega t,$$

we have

$$r = g + \tilde{r} \cos \omega t = g + qc'\tilde{r} \cos \omega t - qc'\sigma\left(\frac{\tilde{r}}{\omega}\right) \sin \omega t. \tag{17}$$

This equation can hold only if $qc' = 1$ and $\sigma = 0$, in which case the liquidity effect has disappeared, and the system has neutrally stable cycles of arbitrary amplitude.

But this analysis suggests a modification of the basic model that will yield perfect foresight cycles. If current capital outlay plans are made, not on the basis of the current profit rate, but on the basis of the profit rate expected at some future time, the relevant expected profit rate would also have a phase shift. If this phase shift were of the right size, the cyclical solution would still exist. This assumption is quite reasonable because capital outlay plans yield saleable output at some point in the future. It is at that future time that the condition of the market determines the profitability of the outlay. (Foley, 1987b, analyzes this type of model more completely.)

Let π be the expected profit rate relevant to capital outlays, so that $c[\pi - \rho[m]]$, and we can approximate

$$qc[\pi - \rho[m]] = g + qc'((\pi - g) + \sigma(\ln m - \ln m^*)). \tag{18}$$

On a cyclical path where $r = qc = g + \tilde{r} \cos \omega t$, (10) will still force $\ln m$ to be out of phase with r, so that $\ln m = \ln m^* - (\tilde{r}/\omega) \sin \omega t$. Substituting in (18), we have

$$\tilde{r} \cos \omega t = qc'(\pi - g) - qc'\sigma\left(\frac{\tilde{r}}{\omega}\right) \sin \omega t, \tag{19}$$

which solves to

$$\pi = g + \tilde{r}\left[\frac{\cos \omega t + (qc'\sigma/\omega) \sin \omega t}{qc'}\right], \quad \text{or} \tag{20}$$

$$\pi = g + \tilde{r}\left(\frac{\sqrt{1 + (qc'\sigma/\omega)^2}}{qc'}\right) \cos[\omega t - \theta], \tag{21}$$

where $\tan \theta = \sigma qc'/\omega$. If $\sqrt{1 + (qc'\sigma/\omega)^2}/qc' \approx 1$, then we have

$$\pi \approx g + \tilde{r} \cos[\omega t - \theta]. \tag{22}$$

Thus it is possible for this model to exhibit perfect foresight cycles, but the parameters of the model must lie in a particular relation to each other and to the typical frequency of the business cycle for this to work.

In this formulation of the model, σ is the semielasticity of the shadow rate of return to money with respect to liquidity, with the dimension 1/unit time, because of the way equation (16) is written. The condition $\sqrt{1 + (qc'\sigma/\omega)^2}/qc' \approx 1$ would require $\sigma^2 \approx 1 - (1/(qc')^2)$ if $\omega = 1$. The phase lag $\theta = \arctan(qc'\sigma/\omega)$. The time lag corresponding to θ is $\tau = \theta/\omega$. The time lags corresponding to σ between 0.1 and 1 are 0.1 to 0.7 years when $\omega \approx 1$.

In the perfect-foresight version of this model, firms correctly predict a cyclical movement in aggregate demand and make their plans looking forward to the profit rate that will be relevant to their current capital outlays. They also consult their current liquidity position. Current profit rates and liquidity move out of phase, but prospective profit rates and liquidity move in phase with each other.

7   Related studies

There has been a considerable flow of work on the problem of the dynamic behavior of economic systems in the past two decades, much of it inspired by Goodwin's early models and by his 1967 (reprinted in Goodwin, 1982) model of a cycle between accumulation and income distribution in the classical-Marxist tradition. Many of these models build on Kaldor's unstable macroeconomic model as well (e.g., V. Torre, 1977). A broad sampling of very recent work in this vein appears in Goodwin, Kruger, and Vercelli (1984) and Semmler (1986). Recent work on the existence of cyclical equilibrium paths in neoclassical overlapping-generations models with perfect foresight (Benhabib and Day, 1982; Grandmont, 1985) uses mathematical techniques connected with dynamic stability, despite the fact that the neoclassical equilibrium model is not in the strict sense a dynamic model.

Benhabib and Miyao (1981), Schinasi (1982), and Semmler (1985) study macroeconomic models with limit cycles in which money and finance play a central role. Woodford (1986) shows that liquidity constraints can lead to cyclical equilibrium paths in a full equilibrium model where agents' horizons are long compared with the period of the cycle.

REFERENCES

Benhabib, J., and Miyao, T. (1981), "Some new results on the dynamics of the generalized Tobin model," *International Economic Review,* 22(3), 589–96.
Benhabib, J., and Day, R. H. (1982), "A characterization of erratic dynamics in the overlapping generations model," *Journal of Economic Dynamics and Control,* 4, 37–55.
Blatt, J. M. (1983), *Dynamic Economic Systems: A Post-Keynesian Approach,* Armonk: M. E. Sharpe.
Foley, D. (1986), "Stabilization policy in a nonlinear business cycle model," in *Competition, Instability, and Nonlinear Cycles,* ed. by W. Semmler, Berlin: Springer-Verlag, 200–11.
    (1987a), "Liquidity-profit rate cycles in a capitalist economy, *Journal of Economic Behavior and Organization,* 8, 363–76.
    (1987b), "A Marxian–Keynesian model of accumulation with money," mimeo., Barnard College.
Frisch, R. (1933), "Propagation problems and impulse problems in dynamic economics," in *Readings in Business Cycles,* American Economic Association, Homewood: Irwin, 1965.
Goodwin, R. M. (1982), *Essays in Economic Dynamics,* London: Macmillan.
Goodwin, R. M., Kruger, M., and Vercelli, A., eds. (1984), *Nonlinear Models of Fluctuating Growth,* Berlin: Springer-Verlag.
Grandmont, J.-M. (1985), "On endogenous competitive business cycles," *Econometrica,* 53(5), 995–1046.

Guckenheimer, J., and Holmes, P. (1983), *Nonlinear Oscillations, Dynamical Systems, and Bifurcations of Vector Fields,* New York: Springer-Verlag.

Hicks, J. R. (1950), *A Contribution to the Theory of the Trade Cycle,* Oxford Clarendon.

Kaldor, N. (1940), "A model of the trade cycle," *Economic Journal,* 50, 78–92.

Kalecki, M. (1969), *Studies in the Theory of Business Cycles: 1933–1939,* Homewood: Irwin.

Keynes, J. M. (1936), *The General Theory of Employment, Interest, and Money,* London: Macmillan.

Samuelson, P. A. (1939), "A synthesis of the principle of acceleration and the multiplier," *Journal of Political Economy,* 47(6), 786–97.

Schinasi, G. (1982), "Fluctuations in a dynamic, intermediate-run ISLM model: applications of the Poincaré–Bendixson Theorem," *Journal of Economic Theory,* 28, 369–75.

Semmler, W. (1985), "Financial crisis as bifurcation in a limit cycle model: a nonlinear approach to Minsky crisis," mimeo., Department of Economics, New School for Social Research, 65 Fifth Avenue, New York.

    ed. (1986), *Competition, Instability, and Nonlinear Cycles,* Berlin: Springer-Verlag Lecture Notes in Economics and Mathematical Systems.

Torre, V. (1977), "Existence of limit cycles and control in a complete Keynesian system by theory of bifurcations," *Econometrica,* 45(6), 1457–66.

Woodford, M. (1986), "Stationary sunspot equilibria in a finance constrained economy," *Journal of Economic Theory,* 40(1), 128–37.

CHAPTER 6

Speculative bubbles and exchange of information on the market of a storable good

L. Broze, C. Gourieroux, and A. Szafarz

1   Introduction

This chapter is a study of the evolution of the equilibrium price of a good (coffee, for instance) that can be both traded for speculative purposes and consumed. However, our focus is on the effects of speculative trading, hence we specify a very simple excess-supply function for the good. The speculative demands are derived from the portfolio choice problem of risk-averse traders who can invest in a risky and a riskless asset. We then derive explicit forms of speculative bubbles and discuss the effects of various factors on the evolution of the equilibrium price. The basic model assumes homogeneous rational expectations. An extension to heterogeneous information is also given.

The model we consider is related to previous works by Grossman (1976), Danthine (1978), and Kawai (1983). The speculators' maximization of constant absolute risk-aversion utility functions leads to a dynamic stochastic mean-variance model that includes rational expectations.

In the context of *linear* rational-expectations (RE) models, the phenomenon of multiple equilibria is now well-known. The introduction of nonlinearities makes the resolution of the model much harder because the known techniques are based only on linearity. Therefore, as a first step in our analysis, we extend to mean-variance rational-expectations models the solution method developed in Broze, Gourieroux, and Szafarz (1985) for the linear case. From the expressions of equilibrium paths that we obtain, it is possible to derive some interesting properties concerning the importance of speculative bubbles.

Section 2 of this chapter presents the basic model, and Section 3 resolves it in a general way. The set of all possible solutions is described by means of an arbitrary stochastic process that is interpreted as the prediction

101

error made by speculators when forecasting the risky asset price. Moreover, the more restricted, but still quite large, class of linear stationary solutions can be fully covered with the use of a single real parameter.

Section 4 is devoted to the analysis of speculative bubbles. It is based on a comparison between the respective rates of increase in price of the riskless and the risky assets. The effects due to variations in the structural coefficients' values are discussed. The additional parameter, resulting from "nonuniqueness" in RE models, also affects the size of the bubbles. Furthermore, it has an appealing interpretation as the level of confidence that speculators have in their own expectations.

Section 5 addresses a model in which the speculators have access to heterogeneous information. It is shown that some information can be conveyed from the most- to the least-informed traders through the price of the speculative commodity. More precisely, a minimal level of information is required to benefit from such a transmission of information.

Section 6 concludes with some additional remarks and perspectives.

2   The model

The basic model includes two assets that can be traded at each point in time. The first asset is riskless; it has a price fixed to unity and pays r "dollars" at the end of each period, and this constant return r ($r > 0$) is assumed to be known by everyone. The second asset, considered to be risky, takes the form of a material good, storable for speculative purposes, that can be bought at the beginning of period t at unit price p_t and sold at the end of the period at a new price p_{t+1} (unknown at time t).

The complete specification of the model will be given by setting the demand function of the speculators and the excess-supply function for the storable good.

a   Demand function of the speculators

To describe the evolution of traders' portfolios, we follow the usual approach based on the optimization of an expected utility function conditional on the currently available information. In the basic model we assume that all traders have the same endowments, preferences, and beliefs. Thus we consider only the case of a single agent.

At the end of period $t-1$, the agent is endowed with stocks of the two types of assets: M_{t-1} for the riskless asset and X_{t-1} for the risky one. At the beginning of period t, he may realize his assets and modify the composition of his portfolio. His wealth is given by

$$W_t = p_t X_{t-1} + RM_{t-1},$$

where $R = 1 + r$. Let (M_t, X_t) denote the new portfolio. The budget constraint is then

$$W_t = p_t X_{t-1} + RM_{t-1} = p_t X_t + M_t. \tag{1}$$

To determine the allocation (M_t, X_t) the agent has a myopic optimization behavior: He maximizes his expected utility one period ahead with reference to a nondecreasing concave utility function $U(W_t)$ depending only on wealth.

Let I_t denote the available information. The agent's behavior is summarized by the following program:

$$\max_{X_t, M_t} E[U(W_{t+1}) \mid I_t] = E[U(p_{t+1}X_t + RM_t) \mid I_t], \tag{2}$$

$$\text{s.t.:} \ \ p_t X_t + M_t = W_t.$$

Generally such a program has no simple explicit solution. Therefore we specify an exponential form for the utility function:

$$U(W_t) = -\exp(-\eta W_t), \quad \eta > 0, \tag{3}$$

where η, the coefficient of absolute risk aversion, is assumed constant. The expected utility is thus given by

$$E[U(W_{t+1}) \mid I_t] = E\{-\exp[-\eta(p_{t+1}X_t + RM_t)] \mid I_t\}.$$

The quantities X_t and M_t chosen by the agent are known at time t. The expected utility depends only on the conditional distribution of the future price p_{t+1} given the information set I_t. With a normal conditional distribution, the expected utility depends only on the conditional mean $E(p_{t+1} \mid I_t)$ and the conditional variance $V(p_{t+1} \mid I_t)$ (equal to the residual variance). More precisely, normality implies that

$$E[U(W_{t+1}) \mid I_t] = -\exp\left[-\eta E(W_{t+1} \mid I_t) + \frac{\eta^2}{2}V(W_{t+1} \mid I_t)\right]$$

$$= -\exp\left\{-\eta[E(p_{t+1} \mid I_t)X_t + RM_t] + \frac{\eta^2}{2}X_t^2 V(p_{t+1} \mid I_t)\right\}. \tag{4}$$

Taking into account the budget constraint (1), we can substitute for one of the quantities, say $M_t = W_t - p_t X_t$, and obtain from (4):

$$E[U(W_{t+1}) \mid I_t]$$

$$= -\exp\left\{-\eta[X_t(E(p_{t+1} \mid I_t) - Rp_t) + RW_t] + \frac{\eta^2}{2}X_t^2 V(p_{t+1} \mid I_t)\right\}. \tag{5}$$

Writing the first-order condition yields a demand function for the risky asset:

$$X_t = \frac{E(p_{t+1}|I_t) - Rp_t}{\eta V(p_{t+1}|I_t)}. \tag{6}$$

From now on this particular form of the demand function will be used. It is restrictive for two obvious reasons. First, it depends only on the transition between the past and the future by means of the conditional mean and variance. Second, the trader's demand does not depend on his wealth W_t. These restrictions afford decisive advantages in terms of the tractability of the model. Indeed, the demand depends only on current expectations $E(p_{t+1}|I_t)$, $V(p_{t+1}|I_t)$ instead of on both current and lagged expectations $E(p_{t+1}|I_{t-j})$, $V(p_{t+1-j}|I_{t-j})$, $j = 0, 1, 2, \ldots$.

However, specification (6) of the demand is sufficiently flexible to take into account risk aversion and leads to a model in which the certainty equivalent principle does not apply.

b   *Excess-supply function of storable good*

The net supply of the storable good is the sum of the previous stock X_{t-1} and the excess of current production Q_t over domestic demand C_t. This excess supply can be deduced from producers' and consumers' behavior. We take here a simple description of this excess-supply function, assuming linearity with respect to the current price:

$$Q_t - C_t = \alpha p_t + u_t, \quad \alpha > 0, \tag{7}$$

where $u = (u_t)$ denotes an exogenous stochastic process summarizing all the stochastic factors that affect production and domestic demand at time t.

c   *Equilibrium condition*

For the risky asset, the equilibrium condition at time t is

$$X_t = X_{t-1} + Q_t - C_t.$$

Because the demand function X_t and the excess supply $Q_t - C_t$ are specified, respectively, by equations (6) and (7), this condition becomes

$$\frac{E(p_{t+1}|I_t) - Rp_t}{\eta V(p_{t+1}|I_t)} = \frac{E(p_t|I_{t-1}) - Rp_{t-1}}{\eta V(p_t|I_{t-1})} + \alpha p_t + u_t. \tag{8}$$

An equilibrium price path is thus defined as a stochastic process $(p_t, t > 0)$ satisfying equation (8) for any nonnegative value of t.

3   Evolution of the equilibrium price

Equation (8) is the starting point of the description of the equilibrium price paths. It is a dynamic rational-expectation model including nonlinearities due to the presence of conditional variances.

It is well-known that linear models containing future rational expectations have multiple solutions. We first examine if this nonuniqueness property arises in the nonlinear model considered. To solve equation (8), we make use of the method given in Broze, Gourieroux, and Szafarz (1985) for linear RE models. We assume that the information set I_t contains at least the current and present values of the exogenous process $u = (u_t)$ and that I_t is nondecreasing in time (no loss of information). The following result gives the set of all equilibrium price paths satisfying equation (8).

Property 1.   *The solutions $p = (p_t)$ of the system of equilibrium conditions* (8) *are obtained by solving the stochastic difference equations,*

$$\frac{p_{t+1} - \epsilon_{t+1} - Rp_t}{\eta E(\epsilon_{t+1}^2 \mid I_t)} = \frac{p_t - \epsilon_t - Rp_{t-1}}{\eta E(\epsilon_t^2 \mid I_{t-1})} + \alpha p_t + u_t, \quad \forall t, \qquad (9)$$

for any possible choice of $\epsilon = (\epsilon_t)$ as a martingale difference sequence, that is, as a process orthogonal to the past $E(\epsilon_t \mid I_{t-1}) = 0$, $\forall t$.

Proof: See Appendix 1.   ■

It can be seen from the proof that ϵ_t can be interpreted as the error made in forecasting the equilibrium price,

$$\epsilon_t = p_t - E(p_t \mid I_{t-1}).$$

Property 1 describes the phenomenon of multiple solutions. An equilibrium path is not uniquely determined by the knowledge of the past. Even if past prices p_t, $t \le t_0$, are given (i.e., if past values ϵ_t, $t \le t_0$, are given), the future values $\epsilon_{t_0+1}, \epsilon_{t_0+2}, \ldots$ of the martingale difference sequence can be chosen arbitrarily. Hence, there will be an infinity of price evolutions compatible with a given past. To illustrate this point, let us assume that the market is not opened to speculators until date t_0. Until t_0 the prices coincide with the usual equilibrium prices in the absence of speculation, that is, $p_t^0 = -u_t/\alpha$, $t \le t_0$. The price p_{t_0+1} is determined according to the future participation of speculators in the market. To simplify the problem, consider the case of an exogenous process u for which the components u_t are independent, with mean m_t and variance σ_t^2. The price p_{t_0+1} satisfies the following:

$$\frac{p_{t_0+1}-\epsilon_{t_0+1}-Rp_{t_0}}{\eta E(\epsilon_{t_0+1}^2\,|\,I_{t_0})}=\frac{p_{t_0}-\epsilon_{t_0}-Rp_{t_0-1}}{\eta E(\epsilon_{t_0}^2\,|\,I_{t_0-1})}+\alpha p_{t_0}+u_{t_0}.$$

Because $p_{t_0}=p_{t_0}^0=-u_{t_0}/\alpha$, $\epsilon_{t_0}=p_{t_0}-E(p_{t_0}\,|\,I_{t_0-1})=p_{t_0}+m_{t_0}/\alpha$, it follows that

$$\frac{p_{t_0+1}-\epsilon_{t_0+1}-(R/\alpha)u_{t_0}}{\eta E(\epsilon_{t_0+1}^2\,|\,I_{t_0})}=\frac{-m_{t_0}/\alpha+(R/\alpha)u_{t_0-1}}{(\eta/\alpha^2)\sigma_{t_0}^2}.$$

The expression for p_{t_0+1} is given by

$$p_{t_0+1}=-\frac{R}{\alpha}u_{t_0}+\frac{\alpha\eta E(\epsilon_{t_0+1}^2\,|\,I_t)}{\sigma_{t_0}^2}[-m_{t_0}+Ru_{t_0-1}]. \qquad (10)$$

Each choice of variable ϵ_{t_0+1} orthogonal to the past leads to a different price p_{t_0+1}.

It is interesting to note that the price $p_{t_0+1}^0=-u_{t_0+1}/\alpha$, associated with no speculators, is not a possible solution. The associated prediction error is $\epsilon_{t_0+1}^0=-u_{t_0+1}/\alpha+m_{t_0+1}$. By substituting this in the right-hand side of equation (10), we obtain a variable

$$p_{t_0+1}=-\frac{R}{\alpha}u_{t_0}+\left(-\frac{u_{t_0+1}}{\alpha}+m_{t_0+1}\right)+\frac{1}{\alpha}\frac{\eta\sigma_{t_0+1}^2}{\sigma_{t_0}^2}[-m_{t_0}+Ru_{t_0-1}],$$

which in general is different from $p_{t_0+1}^0=-u_{t_0+1}/\alpha$.

It is also interesting to note that Property 1 is valid without any assumption on the stochastic structure of the exogenous process u and without any restriction concerning the solutions. Mean-variance RE models are often solved under the assumption that the conditional variance of the price $V(p_{t+1}\,|\,I_t)$ is time-independent (see, e.g., Kawai, 1983); under this additional condition the study of a mean-variance model is similar to the analysis of a linear RE model and the risk-aversion feature disappears. To illustrate the consequences of this stationarity restriction on the second-order moment, consider the simple case in which the exogenous process u is a sequence of independent and identically distributed variables with mean m and variance σ^2.

A subset of all possible prediction errors is given by

$$\epsilon_t=f(t)[u_t-m],$$

where f is any deterministic function. The process ϵ is a martingale difference sequence because

$$E(\epsilon_{t+1}\,|\,I_t)=E\{f(t+1)[u_{t+1}-m]\,|\,I_t\}$$
$$=f(t+1)E[(u_{t+1}-m)\,|\,I_t]=0.$$

For the price paths corresponding to these particular forms of ϵ, the mean-square prediction error on the price is

$$V(p_{t+1} \mid I_t) = E(\epsilon_{t+1}^2 \mid I_t) = \sigma^2 f^2(t+1).$$

Because f is an arbitrary function, the mean-variance model is compatible with any kind of time heteroscedasticity of the price. Furthermore, even if the solutions considered are restricted to those having a constant conditional variance, the value of this constant $V(p_{t+1} \mid I_t)$ is fixed by the model (because p_t is endogenous) and, therefore, cannot be taken as an additional structural parameter.

4 Speculative bubbles

a *Asymptotic behavior of the solutions*

Consider a totally risk-averse agent in the sense that for her the parameter $\eta = \infty$. Her portfolio contains only the riskless asset, and one unit of this asset-hold at time 0 gives her a return R^t at time t.

Symmetrically a (money) unit of the risky asset-hold at time 0 gives a stochastic return of p_t/p_0. Because it is natural for agents holding the risky asset to benefit from a risk premium, one may intuitively expect that the ratio p_t/p_0 will (on average) be larger than R^t. Moreover, since agents' expectations have a direct effect on the price level, one can also hypothesize that the more risk averse the trader, the higher the discrepancy between the ratio p_t/p_0 and the certain return R^t.

We now proceed to a formal analysis of these ideas. To simplify the presentation, we assume that the exogenous process u has an asymptotically stationary moving-average representation:

$$u_t = m + \sum_{i=0}^{\infty} \alpha_i \bar{\bar{\eta}}_{t-i} = m + A(B)\bar{\bar{\eta}}_t, \quad \sum_{i=0}^{\infty} |\alpha_i| < \infty, \quad \alpha_0 = 1, \qquad (11)$$

where m is the mean of u_t ($\forall t \geq 0$) and $(\bar{\bar{\eta}})$ is an independent white noise with variance σ^2. The values of $\bar{\bar{\eta}}_t$ associated with negative indices are fixed to zero.

The available information set is $I_t = \{\bar{\bar{\eta}}_t, p_t, \bar{\bar{\eta}}_{t-1}, p_{t-1}, \dots\}$. We also restrict the analysis to solutions having the following form:

$$\begin{aligned} p_t &= \mu_t + \psi(B)\bar{\bar{\eta}}_t \\ &= \mu_t + \psi_0 \bar{\bar{\eta}}_t + \psi_1 \bar{\bar{\eta}}_{t-1} + \cdots + \psi_1 \bar{\bar{\eta}}_{t-1} + \cdots, \end{aligned} \qquad (12)$$

where μ_t is the (time dependent) mean of the price, and $(\bar{\bar{\eta}})$ is the innovation of the exogenous process.

This class of processes is rather large. It may contain stationary as well as nonstationary solutions. Nonstationarity can appear not only through the mean but also through the moving-average coefficients because the sequence (ψ_j) is not necessarily summable. The previous restrictions have the advantage of providing a large parametric class of solutions.

Property 2. *The equilibrium price paths having the representation,*

$$p_t = \mu_t + \psi(B)\tilde{\bar{\eta}}_t,$$

are such that $\psi(B)$ verifies,

$$\psi(B) = \frac{\psi_0 - \psi_0 B + BA(B)\eta\psi_0^2\sigma^2}{1 - (1+R+\alpha\eta\psi_0^2\sigma^2)B + RB^2},$$

and the sequence (μ_t) verifies,

$$\mu_{t+1} - \mu_t(R+1+\alpha\eta\psi_0^2\sigma^2) + R\mu_{t-1} = \eta\psi_0^2\sigma^2 m, \quad t \geq 0,$$

where the value of ψ_0 can be chosen arbitrarily.

Proof: See Appendix 2.   ■

A price increase greater than R^t can be described in two ways, through the mean and/or through the stochastic part $\psi(B)\tilde{\bar{\eta}}_t$. In fact, the moving-average operator $\psi(B)$ has the form of a rational operator $\psi(B) = \Theta(B)/\Phi(B)$. Although the mean of the stochastic part is always zero, unstable roots of $\Phi(B)$ might have great effects on the variability of prices. More precisely, one has to check whether $\Phi(B)$ has roots lying in the unit circle that are smaller than $1/R$.

Consequently, we should study first the behavior of (μ_t) and then that of $[\psi(B)\tilde{\bar{\eta}}]$. However, both can be analyzed together because the difference equation satisfied by the mean price is

$$\Phi(B)\mu_{t+1} = \eta\psi_0^2\sigma^2 m.$$

Thus, a divergent mean and a divergent variance occur simultaneously according to the values taken by the roots of the equation

$$\Phi(x) = 0,$$

$$Rx^2 - (1+R+\alpha\eta\psi_0^2\sigma^2)x + 1 = 0. \tag{13}$$

Equation (13) is equivalent to

$$\alpha\eta\psi_0^2\sigma^2 x = (1-x)(1-Rx).$$

Because $\eta > 0$, $R \geq 1$, and $\alpha > 0$, the curves given by $y = \alpha\eta\psi_0^2\sigma^2 x$ and $y = (1-x)(1-Rx)$ have the forms shown in Figure 1. Consequently, the roots x_1 and x_2 of Eq. (13) are real and such that

$$0 \leq x_1 \leq \frac{1}{R} \leq 1 \leq x_2.$$

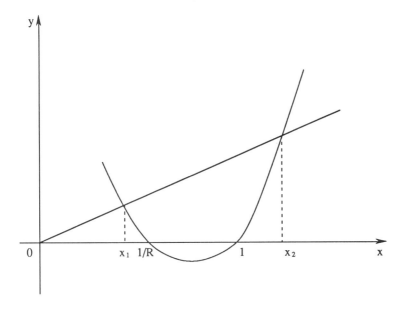

Figure 1

Thus, except in the case in which suitable initial conditions give a constant sequence (μ_t) *and* where ψ_0 is chosen so that the explosive root of $\Phi(B)$ cancels with a corresponding root of $\Theta(B)$,[1] any solution, $p_t = \mu_t + \psi(B)\tilde{\tilde{\eta}}_t$, asymptotically increases with rate $1/x_1^t$, that is, faster than the return on the riskless asset (see Fig. 2).

This phenomenon is clearly related to the phenomenon described in the literature on speculative bubbles (see, e.g., Flood and Garber, 1980; Diba and Grossman, 1983). Here speculative bubbles are defined with reference to the evolution of the return on the riskless asset. Usually, bubbles are seen as deviations from a market fundamental. A possible interpretation of our approach would be to consider the zero value of ψ_0 as corresponding to a fundamental path.

---

[1] We do not analyze further these limit cases because they are not economically plausible. First, they describe a situation in which prices of the risky asset would be stationary whereas the riskless asset would have exponentially increasing prices $(1/R^t)$. Second, the very special constraints required to ensure stationarity of (p_t) are associated with a zero-measure set.

In fact, the only appealing limit case could be $\psi_0 = 0$ together with $\mu_t = 1/R^t$, $t \ge 0$, corresponding to equivalence between the risky and riskless assets (i.e., absence of the risky asset).

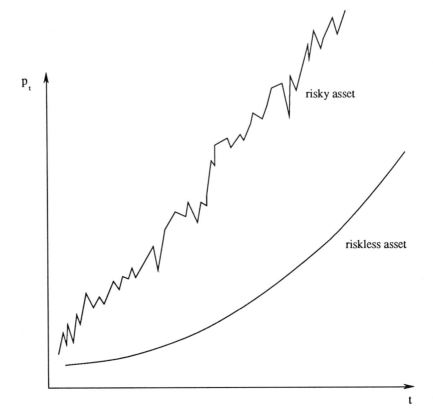

Figure 2

b   *Comparative statics*

The ratio $(1/R)/x_1$ can be viewed as a natural descriptive index of the asymptotic importance of the bubble. This ratio (c) is

$$c(\alpha\eta\psi_0^2\sigma^2 R) = \frac{2}{1+R+\alpha\eta\psi_0^2\sigma^2 - \sqrt{(1+R+\alpha\eta\psi_0^2\sigma^2)^2 - 4R}}.$$

This index takes values from 1 to $+\infty$. It increases with α, η, ψ_0^2, and σ^2, and depends negatively on R. It takes the value

$$\frac{2}{2+\alpha\eta\psi_0^2\sigma^2 - \sqrt{(2+\alpha\eta\psi_0^2\sigma^2)^2 - 4}}$$

when $R = 1$, and the value 0 when R tends to infinity.

The structural parameters that have positive effects on the size of the bubbles are α, which relates excess supply to the current price; η, the risk-aversion parameter; and σ^2, the variability of excess supply. The additional parameter ψ_0 can take any real value, each value corresponding to a specific solution of the model (for given initial values). Thus, for given structural parameters, the various possible paths do not give the same risk premium to the agents. This premium can vary considerably, depending on the equilibrium path followed by the economic system, that is, on the value of ψ_0. An intuitive explanation of this result is the following: The parameter ψ_0 has an interpretation in terms of the mean-square-prediction error on the future price. This is so because

$$V[p_{t+1} - E(p_{t+1} \mid I_t)] = V[\psi_0 \tilde{\eta}_{t+1}] = \psi_0^2 \sigma^2,$$

where σ^2 is the variance of the (innovation of the) exogenous process.

Hence, $|\psi_0|$ can be seen as a measure of the level of confidence the agent has in his own expectations. For instance, if the agent has no precise prediction of the price (even if these predictions are optimal ex post), the consequence is a faster increase in the price to balance a risk viewed as important. Note that ψ_0 is related to the degree of confidence the agent has in his prediction and not to the structural variability of the exogenous environment. The latter is captured by the value of σ^2.

In summary, the three kinds of parameters are α and σ^2, which describe excess supply; η, which corresponds to the speculators' risk aversion; and the coefficient ψ_0, which is specific to the speculative market.

Furthermore, the additional dimension resulting from the presence of ψ_0 might also admit other interpretations, depending on the characteristics of the speculative good. Consider for instance a market in which cartels are sometimes observed among producers. It is known that a cartel organization makes prices more stable whereas periods without cartels generally present more price fluctuations and greater uncertainty. In this framework, the parameter ψ_0 can be seen as an estimation by the speculators of the monopolistic degree of the market. However, this is only one possible interpretation. Generally, the prediction error of the agents will depend on numerous economic phenomena.

c   *Case in which the price is a sufficient statistic for the available information*

Among the various possible solutions, some may depend on an information set I_t that includes only the current price p_t. These solutions are found by considering the stochastic part: $x_t = \psi(B) \tilde{\eta}_t$. To determine the dependence on present and past prices, we first derive the autoregressive form

$$\frac{\psi_0}{\psi(B)} x_t = \psi_0 \tilde{\tilde{\eta}}_t.$$

The past is summarized by the last observed value if the autoregressive lag operator has degree one.

From Property 2, we have

$$\frac{\psi_0}{\psi(B)} = \frac{1+(1+R+\alpha n\psi_0^2\sigma^2)B+RB^2}{1-B+BA(B)\eta\psi_0\sigma^2},$$

and a necessary condition is that the denominator has degree one. This implies $A(B)=1$, using the normalities condition $\alpha_0=1$.

Therefore, there can exist paths corresponding to "perfect markets" only if the exogenous process has serially independent components. Under this condition, we have

$$\frac{\psi_0}{\psi(B)} = \frac{1+(1+R+\alpha n\psi_0^2\sigma^2)B+RB^2}{1-B(1-\eta\psi_0\sigma^2)}.$$

This rational operator reduces to a polynomial of degree one if and only if $1/(1-\eta\psi_0\sigma^2)$ is a root of the numerator. This gives the condition

$$(1-\eta\psi_0\sigma^2)^2-(1-\eta\psi_0\sigma^2)(1+R+\alpha\eta\psi_0^2\sigma^2)+R=0$$

$$\Leftrightarrow \eta\sigma^2\psi_0[\psi_0^2\alpha\eta\sigma^2+\psi_0(\eta\sigma^2-\alpha)-R]=0$$

$$\Leftrightarrow \alpha\eta^2\sigma^4\left[\left(\psi_0-\frac{1}{\alpha}\right)\left(\psi_0-\frac{1}{\eta\sigma^2}\right)+R\right]=0.$$

The solution $\psi_0=0$ is a limit case corresponding to two riskless assets. Other solutions may exist when the discriminant is nonnegative, that is, $(\alpha+\eta\sigma^2)^2/(4\alpha\eta^2\sigma^2)>R$. If the structural coefficients α, η, and σ^2 satisfy this inequality, two nontrivial solutions correspond to the situation in which the present price conveys all useful information.

5   Heterogeneous beliefs

a   A generalization

Thus far we have considered situations in which all traders have the same behavior, have the same risk aversion, and use the same information about the various stochastic factors that determine the price at date t. In this section we generalize this formulation and consider various categories of traders with a distribution of risk aversions and available information throughout these categories.

As previously, we shall derive an equilibrium condition, but now the market-clearing price will naturally depend on all traders' information. The resolution of such RE models including various kinds of expectations is rather complicated; and this is the first aspect we examine. Let each category of traders be denoted by an index i, $i = 1, \ldots, n$, and let β_i denote the number of agents in each category. We assume homogeneity within categories; hence, all agents in category i have the same aversion η_i and the same information I_t^i.

The equilibrium condition then becomes

$$\sum_{i=1}^{n} \beta_i \frac{E(p_{t+1} \mid I_t^i) - Rp_t}{\eta_i V(p_{t+1} \mid I_t^i)} = \sum_{i=1}^{n} \beta_i \frac{E(p_t \mid I_{t-1}^i) - Rp_{t-1}}{\eta_i V(p_t \mid I_{t-1}^i)} + \alpha p_t + u_t. \quad (14)$$

From now on we assume that the conditional variances (which, in general, are random variables) coincide with their means, that is, the residual variances:

$$V(p_t \mid I_{t-1}^i) = E[p_t - E(p_t \mid I_{t-1}^i)]^2.$$

This slight modification simplifies the resolution of the model while keeping its main characteristics. In particular, the equality between conditional and residual variance is satisfied when the information sets are generated by independent white noise and linear moving-average solutions are considered.

To enable tractable results, it is useful to add some restrictions concerning the distribution of the information sets. We assume that these sets can be ordered in the following way:

$$I_t^n \subset I_t^{n-1} \subset \cdots \subset I_t^1, \quad \forall t.$$

The agents of type n are the least informed, and the agents of type 1 dominate the others in this respect. To limit the advantage possessed by the most informed, we assume that, at time $t + 1$, the least informed have more than the maximal information that was available during the previous period:

$$I_t^1 \subset I_{t+1}^n, \quad \forall t.$$

To illustrate these restrictions on the information sets, we consider the case in which, at time t, agents of category i know past and present values of some variables $x^1, \ldots, x^i$ and only past values of some others $x^{i+1}, \ldots, x^n$.

In such a case, $I_t^i = (x_t^1 \cdots x_t^i, x_{t-1}^1 \cdots x_{t-1}^i, x_{t-1}^{i+1} \cdots x_{t-1}^n, \ldots)$, and it is easily checked that the information sets increase with i and are such that $I_t^1 \subset I_{t+1}^n$. With such sets, the information changes when new values of the variables x become available.

Property 3. *If, for any t: $(p_t, u_t) \in I_t^n \subset I_t^{n-1} \subset \cdots \subset I_t^1 \subset I_{t+1}^n$, the solutions of the equilibrium condition* (14) *necessarily satisfy the following equation:*

$$\left[\sum_{i=1}^{n} \frac{\beta_i}{\eta_i}\right] \frac{E(p_{t+1} | I_t^1) - Rp_t}{V(p_{t+1} | I_t^1)} = \left[\sum_{i=1}^{n} \frac{\beta_i}{\eta_i}\right] \frac{E(p_t | I_{t-1}^1) - Rp_{t-1}}{V(p_t | I_{t-1}^1)} + \alpha p_t + u_t.$$

(15)

Proof: See Appendix 3.   ∎

This result is derived by showing that, at equilibrium, all agents held the same expectations:

$$E(p_{t+1} | I_t^1) = E(p_{t+1} | I_t^2) = \cdots = E(p_{t+1} | I_t^n).$$

The heterogeneity of the information sets has no effect on the prediction of the future price. Being more informed does not provide any advantage. Because current and past prices (and exogenous variables u_t) are included in all information sets, the previous result can be interpreted as a property relating to the transmission of relevant information through the equilibrium price path. The less-informed traders learn that prices contain information and use this knowledge to improve their predictions. In some sense the market is efficient.

The previous result on the transmission of information through the equilibrium price seems to be valid only if the exogenous process belongs to all the information sets. To illustrate this point, let us consider two different agents with available information satisfying

$$p_t \in I_t^2 \subset I_t^1 \subset I_{t+1}^2.$$

In addition, we assume that the first agent knows the present value of u_t and that the second agent does not have this information; that is,

$$u_t \in I_t^1, \quad u_t \notin I_t^2.$$

The equilibrium condition is

$$\frac{E(p_{t+1} | I_t^1) - Rp_t}{\eta_1 V(p_{t+1} | I_t^1)} + \frac{E(p_{t+1} | I_t^2) - Rp_t}{\eta_2 V(p_{t+1} | I_t^2)}$$

$$= \frac{E(p_{t+1} | I_{t-1}^1) - Rp_{t-1}}{\eta_1 V(p_t | I_{t-1}^1)} + \frac{E(p_t | I_{t-1}^2) - Rp_{t-1}}{\eta_2 V(p_t | I_{t-1}^2)} + \alpha p_t + u_t. \quad (16)$$

Taking the conditional expectation of both sides of this equation with respect to I_t^2 and substracting from (16), we obtain

$$E(p_{t+1} | I_t^1) - E(p_{t+1} | I_t^2) = [u_t - E(u_t | I_t^2)] \eta_1 V(p_{t+1} | I_t^1).$$

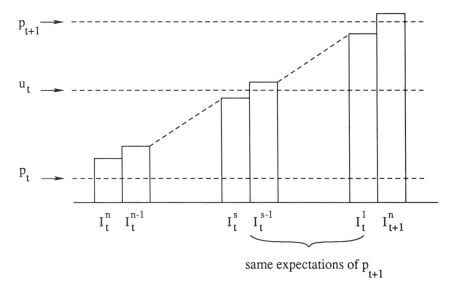

Figure 3

By assumption, u_t does not belong to I_t^2, and therefore $u_t \neq E(u_t \mid I_t^2)$. This implies that at the equilibrium the expectations of the two categories of agents differ. More precisely, we note that the difference between these expectations, $E(p_{t+1} \mid I_t^1) - E(p_{t+1} \mid I_t^2)$, is related to the prediction error made by agent 2 in approximating the value of u_t. The agent who knows u_t has a clear advantage in terms of the precision of his price expectations.

This result does not depend on the number of categories. If at least one agent has information concerning the exogenous process u_t, the difference between the expectations of any two agents is given by

$$E(p_{t+1} \mid I_t^i) - E(p_{t+1} \mid I_t^j) = [E(u_t \mid I_t^i) - E(u_t \mid I_t^j)] \eta_i V(p_{t+1} \mid I_t^i).$$

Therefore, it appears that even if agents are rational and observe the current price, the market is not necessarily efficient. To profit from this transmission of information, it is necessary to hold a minimal level of information concerning p_t and u_t. Knowledge of the current price is in general assumed for all the agents. Knowledge of u_t requires an additional piece of information such as the value of excess supply $Q_t - C_t$. We can distinguish two kinds of agents: Those possessing the minimal level of information (and having the same expectations) and the other agents. The levels of information are shown in Figure 3.

Appendix 1: Proof of Property 1

(i)   *Necessary condition*

We have only to note that the prediction error on the price

$$\epsilon_t = p_t - E(p_t | I_{t-1})$$

is a martingale difference sequence. Then it is possible to replace, in system (8), $E(p_t | I_{t-1})$ by $p_t - \epsilon_t$ and $V(p_t | I_{t-1}) = E\{[p_t - E(p_t | I_{t-1})]^2 | I_{t-1}\}$ by $E(\epsilon_t^2 | I_{t-1})$, which gives system (9).

(ii)   *Sufficient condition*

Conversely, let us consider a solution of system (9) associated with a given martingale difference sequence $\epsilon = (\epsilon_t)$.

Taking conditional expectations of each member of (9), given I_t, we obtain

$$\frac{E(p_{t+1} | I_t) - E(\epsilon_{t+1} | I_t) - Rp_t}{\eta E(\epsilon_{t+1}^2 | I_t)} = \frac{p_t - \epsilon_t - Rp_{t-1}}{\eta E(\epsilon_t^2 | I_{t-1})} + \alpha p_t + u_t.$$

Because ϵ is a martingale difference sequence, this equation reduces to

$$\frac{E(p_{t+1} | I_t) - Rp_t}{\eta E(\epsilon_{t+1}^2 | I_t)} = \frac{p_t + \epsilon_t - Rp_{t-1}}{\eta E(\epsilon_t^2 | I_{t-1})} + \alpha p_t + u_t.$$

Subtracting this relation from (9), we have

$$\frac{p_{t+1} - \epsilon_{t+1} - E(p_{t+1} | I_t)}{\eta E(\epsilon_{t+1}^2 | I_t)} = 0,$$

that is, $\epsilon_{t+1} = p_{t+1} - E(p_{t+1} | I_t)$.

Finally, replacing, in (9), ϵ_t by this expression, we obtain the equilibrium condition (8).   ∎

Appendix 2: Proof of Property 2

The particular form of the solutions implies that the prediction error is such that

$$\epsilon_t = p_t - E(p_t | I_{t-1}) = \psi_0 \tilde{\eta}_t,$$

and consequently that $E(\epsilon_{t+1}^2 | I_t) = \psi_0^2 \sigma^2$.

Replacing ϵ by this expression in the equilibrium condition (9), we have

$$\frac{p_{t+1} - \psi_0 \tilde{\eta}_{t+1} - Rp_t}{\eta \psi_0^2 \sigma^2} = \frac{p_t - \psi_0 \tilde{\eta}_t - Rp_{t-1}}{\eta \psi_0^2 \sigma^2} + \alpha p_t + u_t.$$

Distinguishing the deterministic and stochastic parts in this relation, we obtain

$$\psi(B)\bar{\bar{\eta}}_{t+1} - \psi_0\bar{\bar{\eta}}_{t+1} - R\psi(B)\bar{\bar{\eta}}_t = \psi(B)\bar{\bar{\eta}}_t - \psi_0\bar{\bar{\eta}}_t - R\psi(B)\bar{\bar{\eta}}_{t-1}$$
$$+ \eta\psi_0^2\sigma^2[\alpha\psi(B)\bar{\bar{\eta}}_t + A(B)\bar{\bar{\eta}}_t]$$

and

$$\mu_{t+1} - R\mu_t = \mu_t - R\mu_{t-1} + \eta\alpha\psi_0^2\mu_t + \eta\psi_0^2\sigma^2 m.$$

These two equalities simplify to give

$$\psi(B) = \frac{\psi_0 - \psi_0 B + \eta\psi_0^2\sigma^2 BA(B)}{1 - (1 + R + \alpha\eta\psi_0^2\sigma^2)B + RB^2}$$

and $\mu_{t+1} - \mu_t(1 + R + \alpha\eta\psi_0^2\sigma^2) + R\mu_{t-1} = \eta\psi_0^2\sigma^2 m$. ∎

Appendix 3: Proof of Property 3

Let us take the conditional expectation of the equilibrium condition with respect to I_t^2. We obtain

$$\beta_1 \frac{E(p_{t+1}|I_t^2) - Rp_t}{\eta_1 V(p_{t+1}|I_t^1)} + \sum_{i=2}^{n} \beta_i \frac{E(p_{t+1}|I_t^i) - Rp_t}{\eta_i V(p_{t+1}|I_t^i)}$$
$$= \sum_{i=1}^{n} \beta_i \frac{E(p_t|I_{t-1}^i) - Rp_{t-1}}{\eta_i V(p_t|I_{t-1}^i)} + \alpha p_t + u_t.$$

Subtracting from the equilibrium condition, we deduce the equality of the two first expectations,

$$E(p_{t+1}|I_t^2) = E(p_{t+1}|I_t^1),$$

and also the equality of the associated prediction error,

$$V(p_{t+1}|I_t^2) = V(p_{t+1}|I_t^1).$$

Taking into account these equalities, the equilibrium condition implies that

$$\left(\frac{\beta_1}{\eta_1} + \frac{\beta_2}{\eta_2}\right) \frac{E(p_{t+1}|I_t^1) - Rp_t}{V(p_{t+1}|I_t^1)} + \sum_{i=3}^{n} \beta_i \frac{E(p_{t+1}|I_t^i) - Rp_t}{\eta_i V(p_{t+1}|I_t^i)}$$
$$= \left(\frac{\beta_1}{\eta_1} + \frac{\beta_2}{\eta_2}\right) \frac{E(p_t|I_{t-1}^1) - Rp_{t-1}}{V(p_t|I_{t-1}^1)}$$
$$+ \sum_{i=3}^{n} \beta_i \frac{E(p_t|I_{t-1}^i) - Rp_{t-1}}{\eta_i V(p_t|I_{t-1}^i)} + \alpha p_t + u_t.$$

This is a model similar to the initial equilibrium conditions, in which the two first categories have been aggregated and use the same information I_t^1. The weight of this aggregate is $\beta_1 + \beta_2$, and the risk-aversion coefficient is

$$\frac{1}{\beta_1 + \beta_2} \left(\frac{\beta_1}{\eta_1} + \frac{\beta_2}{\eta_2} \right)^{-1} = \eta_{1,2}.$$

It is, of course, possible to apply the same approach at each step, successively taking the conditional expectations with respect $I_t^3, I_t^4, \ldots$. We then deduce the equality of all the predictions:

$$E(p_{t+1} \mid I_t^1) = E(p_{t+1} \mid I_t^2) = \cdots = E(p_{t+1} \mid I_t^n).$$

Replacing in the equilibrium condition, we obtain the equation of Property 3.   ∎

REFERENCES

Broze, L., Gourieroux, C., and Szafarz, A. (1985), "Solutions of dynamic linear rational expectations models," *Econometric Theory*, 1, 341–68.

Danthine, J. P. (1978), "Information, future prices and stabilizing speculation," *Journal of Economic Theory*, 17, 79–98.

Diamond, D. W., and Verrechia, R. E. (1981), "Information aggregation in a noisy rational expectations economy," *Journal of Financial Economics*, 9, 221–35.

Diba, B. T., and Grossman, H. I. (1983), "Rational asset price bubbles," Working Paper 1059, National Bureau of Economic Research.

Fair, R. C., and Taylor, J. B. (1983), "Solution and maximum likelihood estimation of dynamic non-linear rational expectations models," *Econometrica*, 51, 1169–84.

Flood, R. P., and Garber, P. M. (1980), "Market fundamentals versus price-level bubbles: the first tests," *Journal of Political Economy*, 8, 745–70.

Grossman, S. J. (1976), "On the efficiency of comparative stock markets where traders have diverse information," *Journal of Finance*, 31, 573–85.

Grossman, S. J., and Stiglitz, J. E. (1980), "On the impossibility of informationally efficient markets," *American Economic Review*, 70, 393–408.

Hansen, L. P., and Sargent, T. J. (1980), "Formulating and estimating linear rational expectations models," *Journal of Economic Dynamics and Control*, 2, 7–46.

(1982), "Instrumental variables procedures for estimating linear rational expectations models," *Journal of Monetary Economics*, 9, 263–96.

Hansen, L. P., and Singleton, K. J. (1962), "Generalized instrumental variables estimation of non-linear rational expectations models," *Econometrica*, 50, 1269–86.

Hellwig, M. F. (1982), "Rational expectations equilibrium with conditioning on past prices: a mean-variance example," *Journal of Economic Theory*, 26, 279–312.

Kawai, M. (1983), "Price volability of storable commodities under rational expectations in spot and futures markets," *International Economic Review*, 24, 435–59.

CHAPTER 7

Least-squares learning and the dynamics of hyperinflation

Albert Marcet and Thomas J. Sargent

1   Introduction

In this chapter we use a stability argument based on a least squares learning mechanism to challenge a theory of hyperinflation that was suggested by Sargent and Wallace (1985). Sargent and Wallace used a model consisting of a portfolio balance equation and a government budget constraint. They showed that under rational expectations, the model possesses a continuum of equilibria, all but one of which have average inflation rates that converge to the higher of two possible stationary values. Along paths converging from below to the high stationary value for inflation, real balances will be falling and inflation rising. Sargent and Wallace (1985) suggested that movements along such paths could be used to explain patterns that were observed in a variety of hyperinflationary episodes. Fischer (1984) has described paths of this sort as a process "sliding down the Laffer curve" for the inflation tax.

Instead of assuming rational expectations, we assume that agents form expectations about the future price level by using a least squares regression of price on lagged price. We show that, under least squares learning, the economy can behave in two ways: either it converges to the *low inflation* rate, stationary rational-expectations equilibrium, or no equilibrium exists. The high-equilibrium stationary inflation rate is the attractor under the rational-expectations dynamics, but it is not the attractor under the least squares learning dynamics.

This difference is noteworthy for reasons related to Samuelson's "correspondence principle." In particular, the comparative statics at the low inflation rate equilibrium are "classical," with an everlasting increase in

We thank Jess Benhabib for a useful conversation. Sargent's research was supported by grant number NSF/SES8508935 from the National Science Foundation to the University of Minnesota.

119

the government deficit *raising* the stationary inflation rate.[1] The comparative statics are perverse at the high stationary inflation rate in that a permanent increase in the deficit *lowers* the stationary inflation rate. Furthermore, for some high settings for the deficit for which there exist equilibria under rational expectations, there exists no equilibrium under least squares learning. Thus, under learning a higher permanent deficit either is associated with a higher stationary inflation rate or else it precludes equilibrium.

This chapter is related to our earlier papers on convergence of least squares learning to rational-expectations equilibria (see Marcet and Sargent 1987a, 1987b). Although this approach resembles the one we took earlier, there are important technical differences due to the "explosive" nature of the price and money series under hyperinflation. The present work serves as a limited excursion into the general subject of convergence of least squares learning schemes in nonstationary self-referential systems. Section 2 describes the basic model and its dynamics under rational expectations. Section 3 describes the dynamics of the system under least squares learning and provides some simulations designed to illustrate our results. Section 4 draws some conclusions.

2   Dynamics under rational expectations

To focus on the issues in the simplest context, we analyze a nonstochastic version of the model studied by Sargent and Wallace (1985).[2] The model consists of the equations

$$P_t = \lambda E_t^* P_{t+1} + \gamma h_t, \quad 0 < \lambda < 1, \ 0 < \gamma, \tag{1}$$

and

$$h_t = \theta h_{t-1} + \xi P_t, \quad 1 \le \theta \le \lambda^{-1}, \ \xi > 0,$$
$$h_0 \text{ given}, \quad P_t, h_t \ge 0. \tag{2}$$

---

[1] The "unpleasant monetarist arithmetic" of Sargent and Wallace (1981) rests on their having assumed that for $t > T$, the system will rest at the *lower* stationary inflation rate that finances the government budget deficit.

[2] Sargent and Wallace (1985) describe a stochastic version of the model in which each of equations (1) and (2) is disturbed by a serially correlated shock. For the case in which the disturbance processes are covariance stationary, the results of this chapter would continue to govern the limiting behavior of the model under least squares learning. The reason is that a system of explosive stochastic difference equations driven by homoscedastic errors exhibits behavior that quickly degenerates to that of the corresponding nonstochastic system. If we made the disturbance innovation variances blow up at just the right rate, by setting the parameter μ in Sargent and Wallace (1985), we might modify the model so that, appropriately transformed, the earlier results of Marcet and Sargent (1987a) could apply.

Here P_t is the price level, h_t the per capita level of currency, and $E_t^* P_{t+1}$ the public's expectation of the price level at $t+1$ based on information at t. Equation (1) is a version of Cagan's (1956) portfolio balance schedule, and (2) is a version of the government budget constraint, which states that the government finances a constant per capita real deficit of ξ by creating currency. In terms of the Sargent and Wallace (1985) model, the parameter $\theta = (1+n)^{-1}$, where n is the growth rate of the population. The initial currency stock h_0 is given. When supplemented with a mechanism for forming $E_t^* P_{t+1}$, the model determines equilibrium sequences for $\{P_t, h_t\}_{t=0}^{\infty}$.

Sargent and Wallace (1981, 1985) have studied this model under rational expectations or "perfect foresight." Their findings can be briefly summarized as follows. Impose rational expectations by requiring that

$$E_t^* P_{t+1} = \beta_t P_t, \tag{3a}$$

where

$$\beta_t = \frac{P_{t+1}}{P_t}. \tag{3b}$$

The variable β_t is the gross inflation rate between t and $t+1$. Substituting (3) into (1) using (2) and rearranging leads to the following restriction on equilibrium β_t sequences:

$$\beta_{t+1} = (\lambda^{-1} + \theta - \xi \gamma \lambda^{-1}) - \theta \lambda^{-1} \cdot \frac{1}{\beta_t}. \tag{4}$$

A rational-expectations equilibrium for $\{P_t, h_t\}_{t=0}^{\infty}$ is determined by a $\{\beta_t\}_{t=0}^{\infty}$ sequence that satisfies the difference equation (4). Provided that the deficit satisfies $\xi < \xi_{\max} = \frac{\lambda}{\gamma}[\theta + \lambda^{-1} - 2(\theta \lambda^{-1})^{1/2}]$, there are two stationary points of (4), denoted $\beta_1^* < \beta_2^*$ as depicted in Figure 1.[3] It turns out that (1)–(3) leaves us free to pick any initial value β_0 for β_t so long as $\beta_0 \in [\beta_1^*, \lambda^{-1})$, where β_1^* is the lower fixed point of (4) and λ^{-1} is the value of β at which (1) asserts that zero real balances are demanded. The upper fixed point is stable, being the attractor for all paths starting from $\beta_0 \in (\beta_1^*, \lambda^{-1})$. Only if the initial $\beta_0 = \beta_1^*$ can the system attain the low inflation stationary state. Thus, there is a continuum of equilibria indexed by $\beta_0 \in [\beta_1^*, \lambda^{-1})$, all but one of which have gross inflation rates converging to the higher stationary point β_2^*. Any $\{\beta_t\}_{t=0}^{\infty}$ that satisfies (4) with $\beta_0 \in [\beta_1^*, \lambda^{-1})$ is an equilibrium. Except for the case in which $\beta_0 = \beta_1^*$, all equilibria have the property that $\lim_{t \to \infty} \beta_t = \beta_2^*$.

---

[3] The roots (β_1^*, β_2^*) of the characteristic equation are given by

$$(\beta_1^*, \beta_2^*) = \{(\lambda^{-1} + \theta - \gamma \xi \lambda^{-1}) \pm [(\lambda^{-1} + \theta - \gamma \xi \lambda^{-1})^2 - 4\theta/\lambda]^{1/2}\}/2.$$

The roots satisfy $\theta < \beta_1^*, \beta_2^* < \lambda^{-1}$. By setting $\theta \geq 1$ and $\xi > 0$, we assure that the only potential limit points of the model involve gross inflation rates exceeding unity.

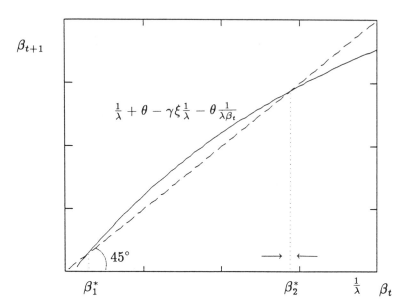

β_{t+1}

$\frac{1}{\lambda} + \theta - \gamma\xi\frac{1}{\lambda} - \theta\frac{1}{\lambda\beta_t}$

$45°$

β_1^* β_2^* $\frac{1}{\lambda}$ β_t

Figure 1.   Any $\{\beta_t\}_{t=0}^{\infty}$ with $\beta_0 \in [\beta_1^*, \lambda^{-1})$ is an equilibrium. Except for the case in which $\beta_0 = \beta_1^*$, all equilibria have the property that $\lim \beta_t = \beta_2^*$.

From Figure 1, we see that the comparative statics at the lower stationary point β_1^* are classical in the sense that increases in the deficit to be financed by currency creation raise the value of β_1^*. (An increase in the deficit ξ lowers the curve $[\lambda^{-1}+\theta-\gamma\xi\lambda^{-1}]-\theta\lambda^{-1}/\beta_t$ in Figure 1.) At the higher stationary point β_2^*, the comparative statics are perverse, an increase in the deficit decreasing the equilibrium stationary inflation rate. Figure 1 indicates that among the continuum of equilibria, almost all of them converge to the higher inflation stationary point with the perverse comparative statics.

This concludes our treatment of the dynamics of the model under rational expectations. Next we study how the dynamics change when least squares learning replaces the hypothesis of rational expectations.

3   Dynamics with least squares learning

We return to the system formed by (1) and (2) and now complete the system with the least squares learning mechanism

$$E_t^* P_{t+1} = \beta_t P_t, \tag{5a}$$

where

$$\beta_t = \left[\sum_{s=1}^{t-1} P_{s-1}^2\right]^{-1}\left[\sum_{s=1}^{t-1} P_s P_{s-1}\right]. \tag{5b}$$

Equation (5b) makes the β_t used to form expectations the coefficient in a linear least squares regression of P_s on P_{s-1}, using data up through $t-1$.

We begin by studying the behavior of the model when the expectations of the agents are given by the time-invariant rule:

$$E_t^* P_{t+1} = \beta P_t \quad \text{for all } t, \tag{6}$$

where β is some arbitrary number. When agents' expectations are given by (6), equations (1) and (2) can be solved to yield

$$P_t = \frac{\gamma}{(1-\lambda\beta)} h_t, \tag{7a}$$

$$h_t = S(\beta)h_{t-1}, \tag{7b}$$

and

$$P_t = S(\beta)P_{t-1}, \quad \text{where } S(\beta) \equiv \frac{1-\lambda\beta}{1-\lambda\beta-\gamma\xi}\theta. \tag{7c}$$

These equations provide a solution for $\{P_t, h_t\}_{t=0}^{\infty}$ so long as $\beta < (1-\gamma\xi)/\lambda$. However, when β does not satisfy this inequality, no equilibrium exists that satisfies the nonnegativity constraints imposed on P_t and h_t: If $\beta \in [(1-\gamma\xi)/\lambda, \lambda^{-1})]$, then $S(\beta) < 0$, and from (7c) it follows that the price level will be negative in some period; if $\beta \geq \lambda^{-1}$, it follows from (7a) that either h_t or P_t will be negative.

The function S, which is graphed in Figure 2, maps a perceived law of motion for P_t into an actual law of motion for P_t. A stationary or time-invariant rational-expectations equilibrium can be regarded as a fixed point of S. We formalize this in the following:

Definition. *A time-invariant rational-expectations equilibrium is given by a perceived law of motion of the form $E_t^* P_{t+1} = \beta^* P_t$, for some $\beta^* = S(\beta^*)$.*

From (7c) it follows that

$$S(\beta) - \beta = \lambda\left\{\frac{\beta^2 - (\theta + \lambda^{-1} - \xi\gamma\lambda^{-1})\beta + \theta\lambda^{-1}}{(1-\lambda\beta-\xi\gamma)}\right\}.$$

The equation $S(\beta) - \beta = 0$ has two solutions that are identical to β_1^* and β_2^*, the two possible rest points of (4).

As in Marcet and Sargent (1987b), the operator S largely governs convergence of a least squares learning scheme. We now turn to the analysis of the dynamics of the model under learning. We use the following:

$S(\beta_t)$

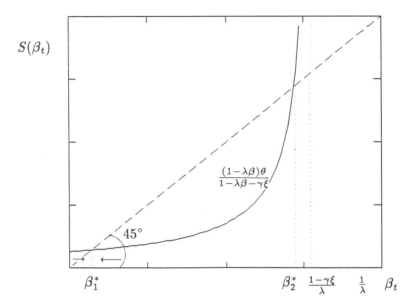

Figure 2.   There are two fixed points of S, β_1^* and β_2^*. $S(\beta)$ goes to ∞ as β approaches $(1+\gamma\xi)/\lambda$. The fixed point β_1^* is stable under iterations on $S(\cdot)$ whereas the fixed point β_2^* is unstable.

Definition.   *An equilibrium under learning is a set of nonnegative sequences for* $\{\beta_t, P_t, h_t\}_{t=0}^{\infty}$ *that satisfy* (1), (2), *and* (5a, b).

Thus, we want to analyze the system formed by equations (1), (2), and (5a, b). For this purpose, it is convenient to represent (5b) in the recursive form employed extensively by Ljung and Söderström (1983):

$$\beta_t = \beta_{t-1} + \frac{1}{t} R_{t-1}^{-1} P_{t-2}[P_{t-1} - \beta_{t-1} P_{t-2}], \tag{8a}$$

$$R_t = R_{t-1} + \frac{1}{t}[P_{t-1}^2 - R_{t-1}]. \tag{8b}$$

Equations (8) are easily derived from (5b), using the fact that

$$R_t = \sum_{s=1}^{t-1}(P_{s-1})^2 + R_0.$$

To start the system formed by (1), (2), and (8) we require "priors" in the form of initial values for β_0 and R_0, and we require the initial value for h_0.

Equations (1), (2), and (5a) can be solved to yield

$$P_t = \frac{\gamma}{(1-\lambda\beta_t)} h_t,$$ (9a)

$$h_t = S(\beta_t) h_{t-1},$$ (9b)

$$P_t = S(\beta_t) \frac{1-\lambda\beta_{t-1}}{1-\lambda\beta_t} P_{t-1},$$ (9c)

where S has been defined in (7c).

Substituting (9c) into (8) and rearranging gives

$$\beta_t = \beta_{t-1} + g_{t-1} \left[\frac{(1-\lambda\beta_{t-2})}{(1-\lambda\beta_{t-1})} S(\beta_{t-1}) - \beta_{t-1} \right],$$ (10)

where

$$g_{t-1} = \frac{P_{t-2}^2}{R_0 + \sum_{j=1}^{t-1} P_{s-1}^2}.$$ (11)

Given initial conditions (β_0, R_0, h_0), equations (9), (10), and (11) determine the sequence $\{P_t, h_t, \beta_t\}_{t=0}^{\infty}$ so long as $\beta_t < (1-\gamma\xi)/\lambda$ for all t. It is possible to show that no equilibrium for h_t and P_t exists when $\beta_t > (1-\gamma\xi)/\lambda$ for some t. In this case, the supply of money is larger than the demand at any price level,[4] in which case the model provides no solution for P_t and h_t. We shall see below that, in certain cases, β_t does threaten to exceed $(1-\gamma\xi)/\lambda$ for some period t. When this happens we say that no equilibrium exists.[5]

We seek to study the limiting behavior of $\{\beta_t\}$ determined by the system (9), (10), (11). Our analysis of this system is contained in Proposition 3.

[4] We can write the supply and demand for money at t in the following way:

$$h_t^d = P_t(1-\gamma\beta_t)/\gamma$$
$$h_t^s = \theta h_{t-1} - \xi P_t.$$

It is easy to see that an equilibrium P_t and h_t does not exist when β_t is larger than $(1-\gamma\xi)/\lambda$ by using a graph of h_t^s and h_t^d against P_t. In this case, we have that the slope of the demand curve is smaller than the slope of the supply curve. Because $h_{t-1} > 0$, the supply and demand curves in period t never cross.

[5] In saying that no equilibrium exists, we mean that there exist no sequences of positive numbers $\{\beta_t, P_t, h_t\}_{t=0}^{\infty}$ that satisfy (1), (2), (5a,b), and the given initial conditions for (h_0, β_0, R_0). For cases in which there exists a perfect foresight equilibrium but *not* an equilibrium under the learning scheme (5a,b), we could restore existence of equilibrium by modifying the learning scheme as follows. Let the learning scheme be (8a,b) when (8a) implies $\beta_t < (1-\gamma\xi)/\lambda - \delta$, for some small positive number δ; and $\beta_t = (1-\gamma\xi)/\lambda - \delta$ when (8a) implies that $\beta_t \geq (1-\lambda\xi)/\lambda - \delta \equiv \bar{\beta}$. In cases where no equilibrium exists under the learning scheme (8a,b), but one does exist under perfect foresight, this altered learning scheme will converge to a rational-expectations equilibrium in which the perceived gross rate of inflation remains $\bar{\beta}$ and the actual gross rate of inflation remains $S(\bar{\beta}) > \bar{\beta}$.

To understand the results, it is helpful to study the behavior of two difference equations that differ from (12) but share some limiting properties. The first difference equation is determined by iterates of S, namely,

$$\beta_n = S(\beta_{n-1}).$$

The second difference equation is

$$\beta_t = (1 - g_{t-1})\beta_{t-1} + g_{t-1}S(\beta_{t-1}).$$

Proposition 1 states properties of the first of these difference equations, and Proposition 2 states properties of the second. These properties will be used to interpret our results about convergence of (10), which is the equation that actually governs $\{\beta_t\}$.

Proposition 1. *For every $\beta_0 \in (0, \beta_2^*)$, iterates of S, $\beta_n = S^n(\beta_0)$, converge to β_1^* as $n \to \infty$. If $\beta_0 > \beta_2^*$, iterates of S will eventually become larger than $(1 - \gamma\xi)/\lambda$, so that no equilibrium exists.*

Proof: From the shape of $S(\beta)$. ∎

Figure 2 depicts $S(\beta)$. It indicates how, under iterations on S, either the *lower* fixed point β_1^* is stable or the iterations send $S^n(\beta_0)$ to the region where no equilibrium exists for the learning model. Which alternative occurs depends on whether β_0 is larger or smaller than β_2^*. The local stability of S at β_1^* can be verified by evaluating S' at β_1^*.

Least squares learning is governed by (10), which differs from being simply iterations on $S(\cdot)$ due to the presence of the term g_{t-1} and the term $(1 - \lambda\beta_{t-2})/(1 - \lambda\beta_{t-1})$. We now represent equation (10) as

$$\beta_t = (1 - g_{t-1})\beta_{t-1} + g_{t-1}\frac{(1 - \lambda\beta_{t-2})}{(1 - \lambda\beta_{t-1})}S(\beta_{t-1}). \tag{12}$$

From (11), it follows that g_{t-1} obeys $0 < g_{t-1} < 1$. Further, it turns out that g_t is bounded away from zero, as the following lemma makes precise. This lemma will be useful in several parts of this chapter.

Lemma 1. *If $\beta_t \to \bar{\beta} > 1$, then $g_t \to [1 - S(\bar{\beta})^{-2}]$.*

Proof: Using repeated substitution in (9c) and simplifying, we can write P_t in terms of the initial price:

$$P_t = \prod_{i=0}^{t} S(\beta_i)\frac{1 - \lambda\beta_0}{1 - \lambda\beta_t}P_0.$$

From this equality and the definition of g_t in (11), we have

$$g_t = \frac{\prod_{i=0}^{t} S(\beta_i)^2}{\sum_{\tau=0}^{t} \prod_{i=0}^{\tau} S(\beta_i)^2 (1-\lambda\beta_t)^2/(1-\lambda\beta_\tau)^2} = \left[\sum_{\tau=0}^{t} \phi_{\tau,t} \frac{(1-\lambda\beta_t)^2}{(1-\lambda\beta_\tau)^2} \right]^{-1},$$

where

$$\phi_{\tau,t} = \prod_{i=\tau+1}^{t} S(\beta_i)^{-2}.$$

Now, given any $\epsilon > 0$ and using $\beta_t \to \bar{\beta}$, we can choose T such that if $\tau, t > T$

$$S(\beta_t)^{-2} < S(\bar{\beta})^{-2} + \epsilon \quad \text{and} \quad \frac{1-\lambda\beta_t}{1-\lambda\beta_\tau} < 1 + \epsilon.$$

Also, since $\bar{\beta}, S > 1$, we can choose ϵ small enough so that $S(\bar{\beta})^{-2} + \epsilon < 1$. Then $\phi_{\tau,t} < [S(\bar{\beta})^{-2} + \epsilon]^{t-\tau-1}$, and the following inequality is satisfied:

$$g_t > \left[\sum_{\tau=0}^{T-1} \phi_{\tau,t} \frac{1-\lambda\beta_0}{1-\lambda\beta_t} + \sum_{\tau=T}^{t} [S(\bar{\beta})^{-2} + \epsilon]^{t-\tau-1}(1+\epsilon) \right]^{-1}. \quad (13)$$

Now, consider the ϕ's under the first summation sign, where $\tau < T$. Since $S(\beta)^{-2} < 1$, we have

$$\phi_{\tau,t} = \prod_{i=\tau+1}^{t} S(\beta_i)^{-2} \to 0 \quad \text{as } t \to \infty,$$

and the first summation sign on the right-hand side of (13) goes to zero as $t \to \infty$. Therefore, the following inequality is satisfied:

$$\liminf_{t\to\infty} g_t \geq \liminf_{t\to\infty} \left[\sum_{i=0}^{t} [S(\bar{\beta})^{-2} + \epsilon]^i (1+\epsilon) \right]^{-1} = \frac{1 - S(\bar{\beta})^{-2} - \epsilon}{1+\epsilon}.$$

Because this is true for any $\epsilon > 0$ small enough, we can conclude that

$$\liminf g_t \geq 1 - S(\bar{\beta})^{-2}.$$

With a similar line of argument, we can conclude that

$$\limsup g_t \leq 1 - S(\bar{\beta})^{-2}.$$

The usual properties of lim sup and lim inf imply that the limit of g_t exists and that it equals $1 - S(\bar{\beta})^2$. ∎

It is useful to compare (12) with the following closely related equation:

$$\beta_t = (1-g_{t-1})\beta_{t-1} + g_{t-1}S(\beta_{t-1}). \quad (14)$$

From the previous lemma, there emerges the following proposition:

Proposition 2. *In the difference equation (14), β_t converges to β_1^* for any $\beta_0 \in (0, \beta_2^*)$. If $\beta_0 > \beta_2^*$, β_t will get to the region where no equilibrium exists.*

Proof: We shall consider three cases: $\beta_0 \in [\beta_1^*, \beta_2^*)$, $\beta_0 \in [0, \beta_1^*)$, and $\beta_0 > \beta_2^*$. Given some integer t, if $\beta_1^* < \beta_t < \beta_2^*$, then $\beta_1^* < S(\beta_t) < \beta_t$; and from (14) it is clear that because g_t is between zero and one, $\beta_1^* < \beta_{t+1} < \beta_t$. Hence, if $\beta_0 \in (\beta_1^*, \beta_2^*)$, $\{\beta_t\}$ converges (because it is decreasing), and β_1^* is a lower bound. From Lemma 1 it follows that $\{\beta_t\}$ cannot converge to any $\beta > \beta_1^*$; if it did, the fact that $S(\beta) < \beta$ and that g_t is bounded away from zero would eventually drive β_t below β. Hence, $\beta_t \to \beta_1^*$.

A similar argument works for the case in which $\beta_0 \le \beta_1^*$.

If $\beta_0 > \beta_2^*$, $S(\beta_t) > \beta_t$; so $\{\beta_t\}$ is increasing. Because S grows with no bound as β_t grows, from Lemma 1 we have the second part of this proposition. ∎

One reason we have studied equation (14) is that in least squares learning models it is usually just this kind of equation that describes the evolution of the beliefs β_t. In other words, at every period, the beliefs β_t are obtained by adjusting β_{t-1} toward $S(\beta_{t-1})$ by a small amount (see Marcet and Sargent, 1987a, b). In effect, relative to iterating on $S(\cdot)$, (14) slows convergence by making β_t a convex linear combination of $S(\beta_{t-1})$ and β_{t-1}.

Now look at equation (12), which actually describes the dynamics of the system with least squares learning in the present model. Equation (12) makes β_t a convex linear combination of β_{t-1} and $S(\beta_{t-1})(1 - \lambda\beta_{t-2})/ (1 - \lambda\beta_{t-1})$. When $\{\beta_t\}$ is changing slowly, the term $(1 - \lambda\beta_{t-2})/(1 - \lambda\beta_{t-1})$ will be close to unity, so that the behavior of (12) can normally be expected to be close to that of (14).

However, consider a case in which $\{\beta_t\}$ is embarked along a path that seems to be converging to β_1^* from below. Along this path,

$$\frac{1 - \lambda\beta_{t-2}}{1 - \lambda\beta_{t-1}} > 1,$$

because $\beta_{t-2} < \beta_{t-1} < \lambda^{-1}$. Thus, (12) makes β_t a convex linear combination of β_{t-1} and a number *exceeding* $S(\beta_{t-1})$. This creates the possibility that, if g_{t-1} is large enough, β_t can *exceed* $S(\beta_{t-1})$. In itself, this possibility creates no necessary impediment to convergence of $\{\beta_t\}$ to β_1^*, provided that $S(\beta_{t-1}) \cdot (1 - \lambda\beta_{t-2})/(1 - \lambda\beta_{t-1}) < \beta_2^*$. However, if $S(\beta_{t-1}) \cdot (1 - \lambda\beta_{t-2})/(1 - \lambda\beta_{t-1}) > \beta_2^*$ and if g_t is sufficiently large, we can have that $\beta_t > \beta_2^*$, which causes β_t to diverge away from β_1^* toward the region where there is no equilibrium.

This possible failure of β_t to converge to β_1^* from below is more likely to happen when β_2^* is close to β_1^*. The stationary gross inflation rates β_1^* and β_2^* approach the common value $(\theta/\lambda)^{1/2}$ as the deficit ξ approaches from below the maximal feasible value of $\xi_{max} = (\lambda/\gamma)[\theta + \gamma^{-1} - 2(\theta/\lambda)^{1/2}]$.

By driving ξ very close to ξ_{max} we have been able to produce examples that realize the nonconvergence possibilities described.

Another circumstance that makes it possible for $\{\beta_t\}$ to jump over both stationary inflation rates is when the initial beliefs are much smaller than β_1^*. In this case, for the first few periods $S(\beta_t)$ is much larger than β_t (see Fig. 2), so β_t can be considerably larger than β_{t-1}. In this case, the ratio $(1-\lambda\beta_{t-2})/(1-\lambda\beta_{t-1})$ will be much larger than 1, making $\{\beta_t\}$ more likely to go above β_2^*.

Next, we present our main proposition (Proposition 3), which describes the dynamics of the model. The main results are the following:

1   β_1^* is locally stable if and only if the constant $K_1 \equiv (1-\beta_1^{*-2})\lambda\beta_1^*/(1-\lambda\beta_1^*)$ is less than one. In general, there are levels of deficit $\xi < \xi_{max}$ for which $K_1 > 1$; in these cases, β_1^* is unstable.
2   β_2^* is always unstable; hence, β_1^* is the only candidate for a limit point.
3   If β_t ever becomes larger than β_2^*, β_t will be eventually pushed over the singularity $(1-\gamma\xi)/\lambda$, into the region with no equilibrium.

Note that these results are quite similar to the ones described in Proposition 2. The only difference is that now the constant K_1 plays a role in preventing convergence and we are restricted to local stability. Global stability is out of the question, as the simulations at the end of this section illustrate.

In the next paragraphs we provide an intuitive justification for the local stability results of Proposition 3. We approximate the law of motion of β_t with a second-order linear difference equation. The true law of motion for β_t can be written as

$$\beta_t = [\beta_{t-1} + g_{t-1}(S(\beta_{t-1}) - \beta_{t-1})] + \left[g_{t-1}\frac{\lambda S(\beta_{t-1})}{1-\lambda\beta_{t-1}}(\beta_{t-1} - \beta_{t-2})\right]. \quad (15)$$

This equation is obtained by adding and subtracting $g_{t-1}S(\beta_{t-1})$ from equation (10) and rearranging. The first term in brackets in the right-hand side of (15) is the usual term of least squares learning mechanisms, which we discussed in Proposition 2; the second term in brackets is an additional term that appears in this model because of the ratio $(1-\lambda\beta_{t-2})/(1-\lambda\beta_{t-1})$ in (10).

Now we perform the following approximations: linearize (15) around β_1^* and substitute g_{t-1} by $g^1 \equiv (1-\beta_1^{*-2})$, which is its limiting value when $\beta_t \rightarrow \beta_1^*$, (see Lemma 1). With these approximations we obtain

$$\beta_t \simeq g^1[1-S'(\beta_1^*)](\beta_1^* - \beta_t) + K_1(\beta_{t-1} - \beta_{t-2}), \quad (16)$$

where K_1 is defined as before and $S'(\beta_1^*) = \partial S(\beta_1^*)/\partial\beta$.

Finally we rewrite (16) as

$$\beta_t - \{K_1 - g^1[1 - S'(\beta_1^*)] + 1\}\beta_{t-1} + K_1\beta_{t-2} \simeq g^1[1 - S'(\beta_1^*)]\beta_1^*,$$

which is a second-order linear difference equation in β_t. It is easy to check that the usual conditions for stability are met if and only if $K_1 \leq 1$. These conditions are checked in the appendix, Lemma 2.

To prove that β_2^* is unstable, we can linearize around β_2^*, and we proceed similarly. From Lemma 3, in the appendix, we have that the corresponding difference equation is unstable.

Proposition 3.   *Let $K_1 = (1 - \beta_1^{*-2})\lambda\beta_1^*/(1 - \lambda\beta_1^*)$.*

(i)   *If $K_1 \leq 1$, β_0 is close enough to β_1^*, and g_0 is close to $g^1 = 1 - \beta_1^{*-2}$, then $\beta_t \to \beta_1^*$. If $K_1 > 1$, then $\beta_t \nrightarrow \beta_1^*$.*
(ii)   *β_t can only converge to β_1^* or β_2^*.*
(iii) *$\beta_t \to \beta_2^*$ if and only if $\beta_0 = \beta_2^*$.*
(iv)   *If $\beta_{t'} \geq \beta_2^*$ for some t', then $\{\beta_t\}$ will become larger than $(1 - \gamma\xi)/\lambda$.*

Proof: The algorithm can be rewritten as

$$\beta_t = \beta_{t-1} + g_{t-1}\left[S(\beta_{t-1})\frac{1 - \lambda\beta_{t-2}}{1 - \lambda\beta_{t-1}} - \beta_{t-1}\right],$$

$$\beta_{t-1} = \beta_{t-1}, \tag{17}$$

$$g_t = \left\{(g_{t-1})^{-1}\left[S(\beta_{t-1})\frac{1 - \lambda\beta_{t-2}}{1 - \lambda\beta_{t-1}}\right]^{-2} + 1\right\}^{-1}.$$

Here, the first equation is just (10); the last equation follows from (11), dividing the numerator and denominator by P_{t-2}^2, using (9c), and rearranging.

Letting $\alpha_t \equiv [\beta_t, \beta_{t-1}, g_t]$, we can rewrite (17) as

$$\alpha_t = H(\alpha_{t-1}), \tag{18}$$

where $H: R^3 \to R^3$ is defined by the right-hand side of (17). Then the evolution of β_t is completely described by iterations on H as in equation (18).

It is useful to write the algorithm in terms of iterations on H for two reasons: (1) We can appeal to the usual theorem that says α_t can only converge to a fixed point $\alpha^* = H(\alpha^*)$, and for local convergence it is necessary and sufficient that all eigenvalues of $\partial H(\alpha)/\partial\alpha|_{\alpha = \alpha^*}$ be less than one in modulus; (2) also, (18) describes the evolution of β_t without reference to P_t, an explosive variable that cannot converge.

Proof of part (i):   Let $\alpha_1^* \equiv [\beta_1^*, \beta_1^*, (1 - \beta_1^{*-2})]$. Clearly, $\alpha_1^* = H(\alpha_1^*)$. Also,

$$\frac{\partial H}{\partial \alpha}\bigg|_{\alpha = \alpha_1^*}$$

$$= \begin{bmatrix} K_1 - (1-\beta_1^{*-2})[1-S'(\beta_1^*)]+1 & -K_1 & 0 \\ 1 & 0 & 0 \\ h_{31}' & h_{32}' & -\beta^{*-2}[(g^1)^{-1}\beta_1^{*-2}+1]^{-2} \end{bmatrix},$$

where h_{31}' and h_{32}' are terms that we do not need to calculate. We shall check that all the eigenvalues of this matrix are less than 1 in absolute value if and only if $K_1 \leq 1$. This is enough to prove local stability of iterations on H, and therefore it is enough to prove local stability of β_t.

First, the $(3,3)$ element is one such eigenvalue and

$$|-\beta_1^{*-2}[(g^1)^{-1}\beta_1^{*-2}+1]^{-2}| \leq [(g^1)^{-1}\beta_1^{*-2}+1]^{-2} = (g^1)^2 < 1,$$

where we have used $\beta_1^* \geq 1$ and the fact that g^1 is the fixed point of the third element in H.

The other two eigenvalues are given by the eigenvalues of the upper-left (2×2) submatrix. These are the inverse of the roots of the polynomial analyzed in the appendix; from Lemma 2, it follows that all eigenvalues are stable if and only if $K_1 \leq 1$.

Proof of part (ii): If $\beta_t \to \beta$, then from Lemma 1, $g_t \to 1-\beta^{-2}$. So, if β_t converges to β, then α_t converges to $\alpha \equiv [\beta, \beta, 1-\beta^{-2}]$. But if $\beta \neq \beta_1^*, \beta_2^*$, α cannot be a fixed point of H, and either $\beta = \beta_1^*$ or $\beta = \beta_2^*$.

Proof of part (iii): If $\beta_0 = \beta_1 = \beta_2^*$, then $\beta_t = \beta_2^*$, $\forall t$. If $\beta_0 \neq \beta_2^*$, then $\beta_t \to \beta_2^*$ only if all eigenvalues of $\partial H/\partial \alpha|_{\alpha = \alpha_2^*}$ are less than one in modulus. Proceeding in a similar manner as in part (i) and using Lemma 3 in the appendix, we see that one eigenvalue is always strictly larger than one.

Proof of part (iv): Let t' be the *first* time that $\{\beta_t\}$ exceeds β_2^*. Then $S(\beta_{t'}) \geq \beta_{t'}$ and $\beta_{t'-1} < \beta_{t'}$, so that $S(\beta_{t'})(1+\lambda\beta_{t'-1})/(1-\lambda\beta_{t'}) > \beta_{t'}$; using an obvious inductive argument, we conclude that $\{\beta_t\}_{t=t'}^\infty$ is increasing, and all that is left to show is that β_t has no bound. But this follows from (12), Lemma 1, and the fact that $S(\beta) \to \infty$ as $\beta \to (1-\gamma\xi)/\lambda$. ∎

We end this section with some simulations that illustrate the behavior postulated by Proposition 3 and that justify our earlier claims in this section about nonconvergence when the initial condition β_0 is far from β_1^* and when ξ is high.

In Figures 3–8 we plot series $\{\beta_t\}$ for six sets of parameter values. In all the simulations, $\theta = \gamma = 1$ and $\lambda = 0.09$; only β_0 and ξ vary across figures. For these parameters the maximum deficit sustainable under rational

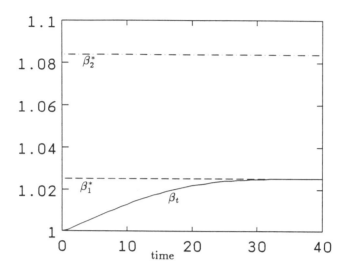

Figure 3.   The perceived rate of inflation when $\xi = 0.0019$, $\beta_0 = 1$.

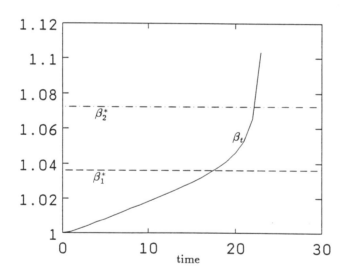

Figure 4.   The perceived rate of inflation when $\xi = 0.00234$, $\beta_0 = 1$.

expectations is $\xi_{max} = 0.00263$. Notice that the number of periods is different in each figure, depending on how long it took for β_t to converge to β_1^* or to exceed $(1 - \gamma\xi)/\lambda$, in which case no equilibrium exists. The two horizontal lines represent β_1^* and β_2^*.

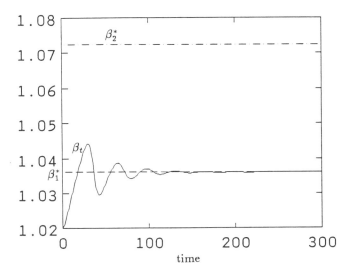

Figure 5.   The perceived rate of inflation when $\xi = 0.00234$, $\beta_0 = 1.02$.

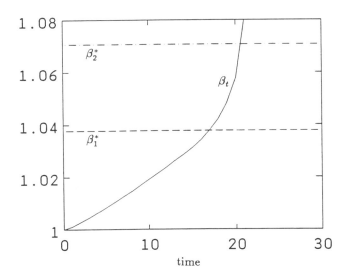

Figure 6.   The perceived rate of inflation when $\xi = 0.0024$, $\beta_0 = 1$.

In Figure 3 the deficit is rather low, and $\{\beta_t\}$ converges very quickly. In Figure 4 the deficit has been increased and, for the same initial condition as before ($\beta_0 = 1$), β_t eventually exceeds $(1 - \gamma\xi)/\lambda$. However, if we move the initial conditions closer to β_1^*, the algorithm converges, as Figure 5 shows.

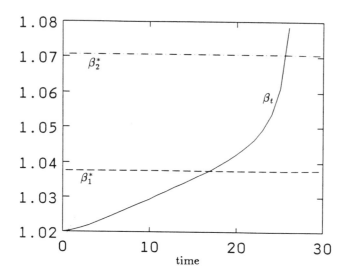

Figure 7.   The perceived rate of inflation when $\xi = 0.0024$, $\beta_0 = 1.02$.

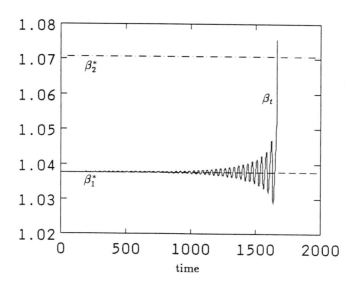

Figure 8.   The perceived rate of inflation when $\xi = 0.0024$, $\beta_0 = 1.0376$.

For the deficits of Figures 3, 4, and 5, the corresponding K_1 is less than 1 ($K_1 = 0.58$ for Fig. 3 and 0.94 for Figs. 4 and 5). Figures 6, 7, and 8 correspond to a deficit that implies $K_1 = 1.008$; β_t fails to converge even in Figure 8, where the initial condition is within 0.0001 of β_1^*. This illustrates part (i) of Proposition 3. It also shows how the system oscillates in a way typical of certain second-order, unstable difference equations.

4   Conclusion

The dynamics under least squares learning provide little comfort for those, like Sargent and Wallace (1985), who would like to interpret hyperinflations as reflecting perfect foresight equilibria that "slide along the slippery side of the Laffer curve." Roughly speaking, if an equilibrium exists under least squares learning, the inflation rate converges to the low inflation stationary rational-expectations equilibrium. At this equilibrium, the comparative statics are classical: An increase in the permanent government deficit leads to an increase of the stationary inflation rate.

For deficits sufficiently close to the maximum sustainable deficit under rational expectations, it can occur that there exists *no* equilibrium under least squares learning, even though there exists a continuum of rational-expectations equilibria.[6]

Appendix

In the text we have argued informally that local stability around β_1^* or β_2^* can be approximated by a second-order linear difference equation; in the proof of Proposition 3 we have used the approach of analyzing iterations on the mapping H. In either approach, stability around β_i^* obtains if and only if all the zeros of the following polynomial in Z,

$$Z^2 - \frac{K_i + 1(1 - \beta_i^{*-2})[1 - S'(\beta_i^*)]}{K_i} Z + \frac{1}{K_i} = 0, \qquad (19)$$

are larger than one in modulus, where $K_i = (1 - \beta_i^{*-2})\lambda\beta_i^* / (1 - \lambda\beta_i^*)$ for $i = 1, 2$.

Lemma 2.   *For $i = 1$, all the zeros of* (19) *are larger than one in modulus if and only if $K_1 \le 1$.*

Proof: Let $\bar{S} = S'(\beta_1^*)$. The zeros are

$$Z^+, Z^- = \frac{K_1 + 1 - g^1(1 - \bar{S}) \pm \sqrt{[K_1 + 1 - g^1(1 - \bar{S})]^2 - 4K}}{2K_1}.$$

---

[6] Marcet and Sargent (1987b) contains an analysis of stationary stochastic learning models that applies to the present model when $\theta < 1$ and $\xi = 0$, in which case

$$\beta_1^* = \theta < 1 \quad \text{and} \quad \beta_2^* = \lambda^{-1} > 1.$$

When the deficit ξ is driven toward zero from above, notice that the singularity of S and the fixed point β_2^* in Figure 2 approach one another. Marcet and Sargent show how $\beta_t \to \theta$.

With complex roots, $|Z^+| = |Z^-| = (K_1)^{-1/2}$, which is greater than 1 if and only if $K_1 < 1$. With real roots, since $\bar{S} < 1$, we have

$$Z^+ < \frac{K_1 + 1 + \sqrt{(K_1+1)^2 - 4K_1}}{2K_1} = \frac{K_1 + 1 + |K_1 - 1|}{2K_1}. \tag{20}$$

If $K_1 \leq 1$, then $|K_1 - 1| = 1 - K_1$, and $Z^+ < 1/K_1$. From this and the fact that $Z^+ \cdot Z^- = (K_1)^{-1}$, we have

$$Z^- = \frac{1}{K_1 Z^+} > 1.$$

Because $Z^+ > Z^-$, both roots are larger than one.

If $K_1 > 1$, then $|K_1 - 1| = K_1 - 1$, and from (20) it follows that

$$Z^+ < \frac{K_1 + 1 + K_1 - 1}{2K_1} = 1;$$

because $0 < Z^- < Z^+$, both roots are unstable.　■

Lemma 3.　*If we take $i = 2$ in (19), at least one root is less than one in absolute value.*

Proof:　Let $\bar{S} = S'(\beta_2^*)$. The key to this proof will be that $\bar{S} > 1$. Now, we have real roots because $[K_2 + 1 - g^2(1 - \bar{S})]^2 - 4K_2 > (K_2 + 1)^2 - 4K_2 = (K_2 - 1)^2 > 0$. Denote these roots by Z^+, Z^-.

From steps similar to those in Lemma 2, the inequality in (20) is reversed by virtue of $\bar{S} > 1$. If $K_2 \leq 1$, then $Z^+ > 1/K_2$; again using $Z^+ \cdot Z^- = 1/K_2$, we get $Z^- < 1$. Because $Z^- > 0$, $|Z^-| < 1$. If $K_2 > 1$, then $Z^+ > 1$ and $Z^- = 1/(K_2 Z^+) < 1/K_2 < 1$.　■

REFERENCES

Cagan, P. (1956), "The monetary dynamics of hyperinflation," in *Studies in the Quantity Theory of Money,* ed. by M. Friedman, University of Chicago Press, Chicago.

Fischer, S. (1984), "The economy of Israel," in *Monetary and Fiscal Policies and Their Application,* Carnegie-Rochester Conference Series 20, ed. by K. Brunner and A. H. Meltzer, Amsterdam: North Holland, 7-52.

Ljung, L., and Söderström, T. (1983), *Theory and Practice of Recursive Identification,* Cambridge: Massachusetts Institute of Technology Press.

Marcet, A., and Sargent, T. J. (1987a), "Convergence of least squares learning mechanisms in self referential linear stochastic models," manuscript, December.

　(1987b), "Convergence of least squares learning in environments with hidden state variables and private information," manuscript, December 1987.

Sargent, T. J., and Wallace, N. (1981), "Some unpleasant monetarist arithmetic," Federal Reserve Bank of Minneapolis Quarterly Review, Fall.

(1985), "Identification and estimation of a model of hyperinflation with a continuum of sunspot equilibria," University of Minnesota discussion paper, September. Subsequently published as "Inflation and the government budget constraint," in *Economics Policy in Theory and Practice,* ed. by A. Razin and E. Sadka, Macmillan, London, 1987.

PART III

Empirical tests for chaos

A comparison between the conventional econometric approach to structural inference and the nonparametric chaotic attractor approach

William A. Barnett and Seungmook S. Choi

1   Introduction

a   *The issue*

During the past ten years, deterministic chaos has become an important part of nonlinear dynamics and has become widely used in deductive theory in many areas of scientific research. More recently, the newer work on chaotic attractor sets has enabled the use of developments in nonlinear dynamics as tools for nonparametric dynamical inference. The relevant techniques involve the application of such currently exotic areas of research as Mandelbrot's fractal geometry, Hausdorf measure on sets of fractional dimension, and asymptotic strange-attractor sets. It is natural to ask whether the investment of time necessary to incorporate these new tools into econometrics would be profitable, or whether the already available tools in econometrics already possess the same capabilities as those potentially presented by nonparametric chaotic inference. In this chapter, we investigate the relationship between conventional statistical methods and chaotic attractor methods. We find that neither is a substitute for the other. In fact, the objectives of either approach are not easily defined in terms of the language of the other.

b   *Overview*

A deep, new scientific methodology is beginning to take form as a result of dramatic recent advances in nonlinear dynamics.[1] During the past

This research was partially supported by NSF grant SES 8305162.

[1] Furthermore, a strong case for the use of nonlinear dynamics as the fundamental general paradigm in science has been made by Prigogine (1980).

decade in mathematics and physics, strange attractors, bufurcation theory, and deterministic chaos have increasingly been applied in many fields.[2] The reason for the interest is evident: The recent advances have generated the capability to produce deterministic solution paths that have the characteristics of stochastic processes and hence have the properties usually seen in real data. These results, in addition to being directly empirically useful, can be derived directly from the relevant structural theory without the need to introduce ad hoc additive or exogenous stochastics, although the inclusion of such uninformative additive noise to represent measurement error is also possible in these methods. Furthermore, the resulting solution paths can exhibit the appearance of unpredictability and of structural change when in fact there has been no shift in the model's structure at all. In other words, empirically useful results, applicable even to very long run data, become available without the need to introduce any free parameters.

In fact, a measure theoretic approach exists for interpreting chaotic solution paths as realizations of stochastic processes, so that mathematical chaos can be viewed as a means of producing *a deterministic origin for stochastic processes.* Hence, the literature on deterministic chaos can produce a theoretically deep explanation for stochastic phenomena. Structural theory and stochastics become linked through the use of new advances in measure theory and fractal geometry. Stochastic processes and time series methods are not eliminated or replaced, but rather they are explained, in the sense that structural theory and stochastics become linked and thereby acquire common theoretical origins. Theory becomes relevant to those aspects of modeling that previously had possessed no deductive origins. Only pure white noise, as from measurement error, remains outside the domain of this new work and therefore must be removed by conventional filtering methods to find the potentially informative (not pure white) stochastic signal that remains.

Once it is found that observed data can be explained from a chaotic attractor model, the possibility then exists of recovering information about the unknown model that produced the observed data path. In this chapter

---

[2] For surveys of much of that literature, see Barnett and Chen (1986, 1988a, b), Brock and Dechert (1988), and Nicholis and Nicholis (1984). Applications to economic theory were pioneered by Benhabib and Day (1980, 1981, 1982) and Stutzer (1980). For additional important contributions to economic theory, see Day (1982, 1983, 1985), Grandmont (1985), and Schinasi (1979, 1981, 1982). For an earlier use in empirical economic inference, see Brock (1986). Related research on empirical applications can be found in Brock and Chamberlain (1986), Brock and Dechert (1988), Brock, Dechert, and Scheinkman (1986), Brock and Sayers (1986), Frank and Stengos (1986, 1987), Hinich and Patterson (1985), Kalaba and Tesfatsion (1986), Ramsey and Yuan (1987), Sayers (1985), and Scheinkman and LeBaron (1986).

we review the results of an ongoing research project that has been successful in identifying economic chaotic attractors from long time series of unusually high quality data, and we compare the resulting inferences with those that could be produced from more conventional econometric inference procedures. We display the results of a Monte Carlo study that investigates the reliability of the inferences produced by those conventional inference procedures. We find that the kinds of inferences that can be produced from chaotic attractor theory are not easily or dependably produceable by better known econometric inference procedures.

This result is particularly striking considering the fact that conventional structural econometric theory is based on statistical methods having origins extending back a century whereas the chaotic attractor approach finds its origins in the three-year-old laboratory research on experimental chaos in turbulent fluid flow. The latter literature is intimately connected with recent innovations in fractal geometry and measure theory. The reason that this very new work on chaotic attractors already has produced useful inference algorithms is that this approach seeks to produce inferences of a sort that have rarely been the subject of conventional statistical approaches. The source of these new capabilities is that all of the information contained in the structure of the unknown dynamical system in state space can be shown to be embedded in the geometry of the chaotic attractor fractal, which asymptotically produces the stochastic behavior of the solution paths in phase space. The ability to pass from the fractal geometry of the asymptotic chaotic attractor in phase space back to the unknown dynamical system in state space is fundamental to the capabilities of the chaotic attractor approach.

The chaotic attractor approach is not a substitute for conventional structural modeling or for time-series methods, but rather provides the link between the two. That link provides the potential to permit time-series data on solution paths to be used nonparametrically to uncover the structure of unknown dynamical models in state space. But to appreciate that potential, one must recognize that chaotic attractor methods are in their infancy and currently have very limited capabilities. For an extensive discussion of some of the possible capabilities, see Prigogine and Stengers (1984) and Prigogine (1980).

2   The new results from nonlinear dynamics

a   *Deterministic chaos*

The relevant mathematical theory deals with very deep modeling in the sense that all sources of the system's dynamics are endogenized, so that the system itself then produces its own dynamics. In particular, let us define s_t to be the vector of state variables at period t. The state vector is of dimension S. The state vector is defined to contain all information that is relevant to the behavior of the economy during period $t+1$. It therefore follows, almost tautologically, that there must exist a function f (called the *deterministic dynamical system* or law of motion) such that $s_{t+1} = f(s_t)$ for all t. We need not assume that all or any of the state variables are actually observed. We also certainly need not assume that we know f. However, we do observe a variable m_t during period t. Clearly, m_t must depend on the state vector; hence, there must exist an *observer function g* such that $m_t = g(s_t)$ for every t. The space that contains all possible paths of the state vector is called the *state space* and has dimension S.

Because the dimension of state space is huge, there is likely to be a tremendous number of choices of state vectors s_t and dynamical systems f that can explain the existing data on m_t deterministically. However, in the spirit of all economic theory and of all science, the literature on chaotic dynamics seeks to produce the simplest useful explanation for the observed data path. Hence, we shall be seeking the lowest-dimensional state space that can be used to produce a self-generating deterministic explanation of the past, present, and future behavior of the data series m_t. We might expect that the resulting minimum dimension could be very low because it has been shown that very simple, small neoclassical economic models can produce richly complex chaotic dynamics.

If the function f is monotonically increasing or monotonically decreasing, the state vector will forever trend in one direction. Such simple trends do not produce interesting (i.e., stochastic-appearing) results in this approach, so we assume that f has at least one turning point. In applications, we might, for example, assume that our data have been detrended so that f is not monotonic. Under the very general and highly abstract assumptions just made, it has been shown in the mathematics and physics literature that m_t can evolve over time in a remarkable number of ways, from simple convergence to a constant, to cycling, to deterministic chaos having the properties of almost any kind of informative stochastic process. Much is now known about all of the possible regimes, including the conditions producing transition between regimes. The source of this theoretical richness is the nonlinearity of f and the feedback produced by the definition of the function f. Feedback-induced dynamics is produced by the resulting nonlinear iterations on the function f. Beginning at some initial condition s_0, the sequences or paths produced for s_t and m_t by iteration on f are called the *orbits* or *trajectories*.

For our purposes, chaotic dynamical systems can be viewed as deterministic systems that produce solution paths that appear to be stochastic.[3] The approach becomes noninformative when the data are *pure* white noise; in that case, any exact deterministic explanation would have to be infinitely complex, so no possible finite amount of information about the state vector could produce any information whatsoever relative to m_{t+1}.

Similarly, the use of chaotic attractors in inference becomes ineffective when there exists a great deal (high noise-to-signal ratio) of pure white noise induced by substantial measurement error. Then the currently available algorithms cannot always extract the signal from the noise. As a result, data quality is of great importance in empirical applications of mathematical chaos to economics.

Differences in opinion between the various macroeconomic schools of thought amount to differences in opinion about the degree of depth of modeling needed to capture the source of the system's dynamics. Keynesians often argue that the system's dynamics can be produced from within the structure of the private sector. The monetarist model requires endogenizing the central bank's reaction function. Rational expectations modeling and the related "new classical economics" have produced their own dynamical models, which typically require endogenizing private sector expectations (especially about relative prices) consistently with the economy's structure and also endogenizing all sources of governmental shocks to the private sector; the resulting econometric specifications reveal the economy's "deep parameters." The linearity assumptions common in models in all three traditions have rarely been viewed as inherent to the economic theory but rather as simplifying local approximations. In fact, formidable literatures on endogenous business cycles exist in each of the three traditions. The empirical inference techniques that we use from chaotic dynamics require no prior assumptions about the depth of modeling needed to endogenize the system's dynamics and hence are *not* dependent upon one's views about the source of the system's dynamics. In fact, the techniques are totally nonparametric and specification-free.

b   *Strange attractor theory*

Attractor sets, and especially strange attractors, play an important role in chaotic dynamics. We now define the concept of a *strange* (or chaotic)

---

[3] Nevertheless, a rigorous and formal definition for chaos exists in the mathematics literature. In particular, a time sequence is *chaotic*, or turbulent, if the sequence has the following three properties: *sensitive dependence* on the initial conditions (called the *seed*), a form of stationarity, and nonperiodicity. Sensitive dependence on initial conditions is defined to mean that if two initial conditions are very close together, then the two induced time paths of m_t will initially diverge exponentially (i.e., as if produced stochastically).

attractor. First, collect the cluster (limit) points of the sequence (s_t) into a set S called the *attractor*. The sequence (s_t) is produced, through its definition, by successive iterations on the function f. In the limit, the orbits are trapped or "locked in" by that attractor set so long as the initial condition s_0 is sufficiently close to the attractor set.[4] Once trapped by the attractor set (i.e., for sufficiently large t), the orbit will wander in or near the attractor set forever, and the behavior of the trapped paths in the attractor set are influenced by the geometry of the attractor set.

If the sequence converges to a fixed point, then the attractor is a singleton set containing that one limit point and therefore has dimension zero. We can imagine the sequence to be drawn by some attraction to the limit point, so that the sequence necessarily must eventually converge to the limit point. If, however, the attractor set contains two points, the sequence will be attracted simultaneously by two separated points and therefore will oscillate between points in two separate sequences, each of which converges to a different limit point. The same system frequently can exhibit either of the above solution-path characteristics for different values of the system's parameters. The original single limit point *bifurcates* (or fissions) into two cluster points if the parameters are changed to cause the stable solution paths to become oscillatory.

The transition to chaos often proceeds as follows. As the parameters of the model are further shifted, the two cluster points, which coincided at their birth from the bifurcation, separate farther and farther apart. Eventually, succeeding bifurcation points are passed at predictable values of the parameters. The number of cluster points doubles each time that bifurcation occurs, and every point in the attractor bifurcates simultaneously. The potential richness of the observed behavior that can be produced increases as the number of points in the attractor set increase.[5]

In the limit, after the infinite sequence of bifurcations has converged, the attractor set can have an infinite number of points. In such cases, which can produce transition to chaos, the attractor set is usually a *fractal*, which is a Cantor set of fractional Hausdorf dimension.[6] We then say that the attractor set is a chaotic or *strange attractor*. Chaos is *not* an exceptional case that can be approached only in an unattainable limit.

---

[4] The *basin*, or domain of attraction, induced by an attractor set is the closure of the set of initial conditions (seeds) such that the orbit originating at the initial condition will eventually be trapped by the attractor set.

[5] If the behavior is periodic, the attractor is a closed loop (a limit cycle). If the behavior is n-periodic, the attractor is an n-torus. In all of those cases, points that are initially close will remain close for all time.

[6] Fractals are the sets made famous by Mandelbrot (1977).

Chaos can be reached from predictable values of the parameters of the relevant nonlinear models. The potential explanatory power of strange attractors is tremendous because they can attract a sequence into deterministic behavior that is sufficiently complex and turbulent to appear to be stochastic.

Because orbits produced from nearby initial conditions can initially diverge rapidly (exponentially), a "statistical" view of the generated phenomena becomes natural. In addition, a beautiful form of mathematical order can be found in the resulting "chaos" – an order of a deeper kind than the more transparent kind encountered prior to the transition to chaos.[7]

c   *Empirical inference capabilities of chaotic dynamics and strange attractors*

A number of techniques are widely used in physics to detect chaos. However, not all of the approaches developed by physicists are applicable in economics because most of those methods require a large amount of data to assure sufficient precision. Here we consider only one technique, the computation of correlation dimension. Not only is that technique useful for detecting chaos with less than 1,000 data points, but in addition the computation of correlation dimension is particularly interesting due to the unusual sort of statistical inference made possible from its use. That inference is an example of the potential capability of chaotic attractors to permit solution paths in phase space to be used to produce nonparametric dynamical inferences about totally unknown dynamical structural systems in state space, when we do not even know the identities or number of state variables in the system. But first we describe the fundamental relationship between phase space and state space.

(i)   *Phase space embedding*
It can be shown that strange attractors are never topological manifolds, which have integer dimensions, but rather are fractals, which are Cantor sets having noninteger dimensions and zero volumes (relative to Lebesgue measure). A measure theoretic method, based upon Hausdorf measure, exists for measuring the dimension of a fractal. The resulting noninteger-valued dimension of a strange attractor is called its *fractal dimension,* which measures the number of independent degrees of freedom relevant

---

[7] See Prigogine and Stengers (1984). In particular, strange attractors (as well as fractals in general) are characterized by an infinite regress of detail, with a never-ending nesting of pattern within pattern as one magnifies the attractor set.

to the system's dynamical behavior.[8] *The attractor is defined to be strange if and only if the attractor's dimension is noninteger valued, that is, if the attractor is a fractal.*

The attractor set is a subset of the state space, though we typically have no measured values of the state vector s_t. We have measured values only of m_t; hence, it is important to have a means of relating fractal dimension to the potential values of m_t. Takens (1980, p. 369) has related them through an embedding theorem, which can be understood as follows. Select a state vector from the basin set; iterate on (g, f) repeatedly $(n-1)\tau$ times, where time delay τ and embedding dimension n are preselected; and then stack the resulting n values of m_t into an n-dimensional vector, with successive elements of the vector being separated by τ periods. If the first observation in the n-history is m_t, then we can designate the resulting n-history at t by $\mathbf{m}(n, \tau)_t$, where we define

$$\mathbf{m}(n, \tau)_t = (m_t, m_{t+\tau}, m_{t+2\tau}, \ldots, m_{t+(n-1)\tau}), \tag{1}$$

at each t. For notational simplicity, the τ will usually be dropped in $\mathbf{m}(n, \tau)_t$. The existence of the argument τ should be understood.

The space of those n-histories, $\mathbf{m}(n, \tau)_t$, for a fixed choice of n is called *phase space,* and the selected value of n is called the *embedding dimension.* As defined in that manner, phase space has delay coordinates. The set of phase space trajectories for all possible initial conditions for the state vector within the basin set is called the *phase portrait* of the system.

(ii)   *Dimensionality measures*

Suppose the construction of $\mathbf{m}(n)_t$ for fixed embedding dimension is repeated for each possible value of s_t within the basin set.[9] Designate the resulting set of n-history vectors by $J(n)$. Then the Hausdorf dimension of $J(n)$ is computed. This computation is repeated for successively larger values of n. Takens (1980, p. 369) proved that the limiting dimension of $J(n)$ as $n \to \infty$ equals the fractal dimension of the strange attractor in state space. We shall call that theorem the *Takens embedding theorem.* Hence, we can define the dimension of the strange attractor in state space in terms solely of n-histories, $\mathbf{m}(n)_t$, of observable values of m_t.[10] Hence,

---

[8] In general, the dimension of a set is the amount of information needed to specify the position of a point on the set to within a given accuracy. If the attractor is a Euclidean object (i.e., topological manifold), any of the methods to be described of measuring attractor dimension produces the Euclidean dimension of the attractor.

[9] In empirical applications, the set of initial conditions is restricted to the set of state vector values that produced the set of observed values of m_t.

[10] In fact, Takens proved an even stronger result. He proved that there exists a deterministic dynamical system (coupled recursion relation) F_n in phase space for any fixed embedding

a strange attractor exists in phase space if and only if a strange attractor exists in state space, and the dimensions of the attractors are the same in both spaces.

The Hausdorf dimension of a strange attractor, whether computed in phase space or directly in state space, is extremely difficult to compute. As a result, more easily computed approximations have been proposed. The most notable examples are the Grassberger–Procaccia correlation dimension and the information dimension. Physical scientists now consider the Grassberger and Procaccia (1983a, b) method to be the best.[11]

We first define the Grassberger–Procaccia method of measuring the dimension of $J(n)$. The dimension measure resulting from that method is called the *correlation dimension* of $J(n)$ because the procedure uses the correlation function $C_n(\epsilon)$, defined by

$$C_n^*(\epsilon) = \frac{\#\{(i,j): \|\mathbf{m}(n)_i - \mathbf{m}(n)_j\| < \epsilon,\ 1 \le i \le N_n,\ 1 \le j \le N_n,\ i \ne j\}}{N_n^2 - N_n}, \quad (2)$$

where $N_n = N - (n-1)\tau$ is the number of n-histories that can be produced from a sample of size N with time lag τ, and $\#A$ denotes the cardinality of (number of distinct points in) the set A. In particular, the Grassberger–Procaccia correlation dimension of $J(n)$ is defined to be

$$D(n) = \lim_{\epsilon \to 0} \frac{\log_2 C_n^*(\epsilon)}{\log_2 \epsilon}. \quad (3)$$

If we then take the limit as the embedding dimension goes to infinity, as suggested by the Takens embedding theorem, we get the correlation dimension of the strange attractor in state space,

$$D = \lim_{n \to \infty} D(n). \quad (4)$$

In practice, with a well-behaved chaotic model, the value of $D(n)$ "saturates" (i.e., attain its limit) at some finite level of n called the saturation embedding dimension n_S. The correlation dimension of the strange attractor then is $D(n_S)$. At the opposite extreme, saturation is never attained if the data are white noise. In that case, all dimensions of phase space are used by the data at every embedding dimension, and $D(n) = n$ at all n. As a result, D equals infinity for white noise.

---

dimension n such that a one-to-one correspondence exists between the dynamical properties (in particular, all conjugate invariants) of $\mathbf{s}_{t+1} = f(\mathbf{s}_t)$ in state space and the dynamical properties of $\mathbf{m}(n)_{t+1} = F_n[\mathbf{m}(n)_t]$ in phase space. Those invariant properties include the dimension concepts to be discussed.

[11] See Barnett and Chen (1986, 1988a, b) for further background and discussion.

The reason for definition (3) is easily seen from the fact that at sufficiently small ϵ, Grassberger and Procaccia showed that the correlation function can be written approximately in the form

$$\log_2 C_n^*(\epsilon) = \log_2 k + D(n) \log_2 \epsilon, \tag{5}$$

where k is a constant. Hence, (3) follows by dividing (5) by $\log_2 \epsilon$, and letting $\epsilon \to 0$. From (5) we see that we alternatively can define $D(n)$ by

$$D(n) = \lim_{\epsilon \to 0} \frac{\partial \log_2 C_n(\epsilon)}{\partial \log_2 \epsilon}, \tag{6}$$

which is, in fact, the form used in practice. The procedure is to select a small value for ϵ, but not to go all the way to zero because data noise tends to dominate at extremely small values of ϵ. As a result, (6) must be used rather than (3) because, for small nonzero values of ϵ, the intercept of the plot of $\log_2 C_n(\epsilon)/\log_2 \epsilon$ against $\log_2 \epsilon$ remains nonzero.

Observe that the algorithm does not assume that no noise exists, but rather that removal of the pure white noise errors can reveal an underlying process that is stochastic – but also informative. The probability distribution of that process is called intrinsic because it is produced by the unknown system and hence contains information about that dynamical system. The removed white noise is called extrinsic stochasticity because its distribution is uninformative and hence extrinsic to the system and thereby to any relevant endogenous theory.

In particular, $\log_2 C_n(\epsilon)$ is plotted against $\log_2 \epsilon$ to permit measurement of the slope, $\partial \log_2 C_n(\epsilon)/\partial \log_2 \epsilon$, versus $\log_2 \epsilon$. At sufficiently low value for $\log_2 \epsilon$, the slope reaches a plateau before noise begins to dominate and produce further variation of the slope at even lower values of $\log_2 \epsilon$. The value of the slope along the plateau is used as $D(n)$.[12] By (4), the limiting value of $D(n)$, approximated by the value of $D(n)$ at the saturation embedding dimension, is the fractal dimension D.

We would expect from the Takens embedding theorem that D measures the dimension of the strange attractor in state space, despite the fact that $D(n)$ at all finite n is produced from vectors in phase space. In fact, Grassberger and Procaccia have shown that D can indeed be written in terms of the state vectors s_t $(1 \le t \le N)$ as

$$D = \lim_{\epsilon \to 0} \frac{\log_2 C^*(\epsilon)}{\log_2 \epsilon}, \tag{7}$$

---

[12] It is important not to exceed the lowest candidate for a saturation embedding dimension because the number of observations in phase space rapidly declines as the embedding dimension increases. With too few points in phase space, the ability to identify the linear region quickly disappears.

where

$$C^*(\epsilon) = \lim_{N \to \infty} \frac{\#\{(i, j): \|\mathbf{s}_i - \mathbf{s}_j\| < \epsilon,\ 1 \le i \le N,\ 1 \le j \le N,\ i \ne j\}}{N^2 - N}. \tag{8}$$

For sufficiently large n and N, the limiting correlation dimension can be found with reasonable accuracy. Grassberger and Procaccia showed that the limiting correlation dimension D is less than, but nevertheless closely approximates, the Hausdorf fractal dimension of the strange attractor. We use the Grassberger–Procaccia procedure for computing fractal dimensions for strange attractors.

The next integer larger than the fractal dimension of the strange attractor clearly provides a lower bound to the dimension of the space that can contain the attractor. Furthermore, because the attractor set is a subset of the state space, it follows that the next integer larger than the fractal dimension also provides a lower bound to the dimension of the state space that could contain state vector paths ($\mathbf{s}_t$) capable of producing the observed orbit of m_t. Because the Grassberger–Procaccia correlation dimension D is less than the Hausdorf fractal dimension, we see that the correlation dimension D of the strange attractor is also a lower bound to the dimension S of the state space.

All of the preceding conclusions, including the existence of the postulated limits, hold if the state vector orbits are generated in accordance with a deterministic dynamical model consistent with the existence of (f, g). This is a powerful result because it provides a *lower bound to the number of variables that can be used to produce an entirely theoretical explanation for endogenous evolution of m_t*. That result follows from the fact that $m_t = f(\mathbf{s}_t)$, and the dimension of $\mathbf{s}_t$ is S. This minimum dimensionality inference is the one that interests us in this chapter because that inference illustrates the capability of chaotic attractors to permit time-series data to be used in producing inferences about the dynamical system in state space – in this case, about the minimum dimensionality of that space.

It is important, however, to recognize that the simplest chaotic deterministic model that can produce the observed path of m_t need not be the model that actually did produce the observed data. In fact, in experimental applications the fractal dimension is typically very much smaller than the number of variables that actually produced the observed data. Only when the attractor is not chaotic (strange) is that lower bound tight.

Also, again observe that the procedure implicitly acknowledges the existence of pure white noise in the data, which is extracted when ϵ is not permitted to decline all the way to zero. Hence, the deterministic explanation that is being identified by this procedure applies to the signal that remains after removal of the noise. However, the signal itself is stochastic in the sense that it is chaotic and hence follows a nonwhite informative process. It is the intrinsic probability distribution of that informative process that produces the minimum dimensionality inference, in which the intrinsic probability distribution is generated from a measure defined on the strange attractor set. The extrinsic probability distribution is that of the removed white noise process.

3   Data requirements

a   *The issue*

As discussed previously, data quality is very important in applying the existing techniques for uncovering the dynamics of nonlinear systems. The white noise produced from measurement error complicates the use of existing methods for extracting information from strange attractors because such data error gives a fuzzy appearance to strange attractor sets. In addition, it seems reasonable to presume that the variable used as the measured variable m_t should be an "important" one, because the empirical techniques currently available for extracting empirical information from chaotic orbits use the observed orbit of only one variable to reconstruct the dynamics of the complete (simplest compatible) system in state space.

There is no inherent reason to believe that economic data are more noisy than data produced in the physical sciences. Many techniques from classical statistics require most variables to be exogenous; but fully nonstochastic exogenous variables usually can be acquired only as control variables in controlled experiments. As a result, it is often believed that inference procedures applied to economic data, which typically are not produced in controlled experiments, are greatly complicated by "noisy" economic data. Although simultaneity bias created by endogeneity of many variables is certainly a problem for classical statistical inference procedures, endogeneity is *not* a problem for the use of strange attractor theory. The distinction between endogenous and exogeneous variables is irrelevant to chaos; in fact, the power of chaotic dynamics lies in its ability to produce stochastic-appearing solution paths. The usefulness of deterministic mathematical chaos requires only that the data be of high quality, so that the amounts of purely white noise produced by measurement error are not so great as to swamp the intrinsic stochasticity of the informative process produced by the unknown dynamical system.

There is no reason to believe that completely disaggregated economic data are necessarily inherently more noisy, in the sense of possessing large measurement error, than data produced from controlled experiments in the physical sciences. However, almost all available economic data are aggregated both over goods and over economic agents, and that aggregation can indeed induce white noise into the aggregated data. Hence, the problem for the empirical use of deterministic chaos and strange attractor theory is not that economic data are not produced from controlled experiments, but rather that the data are aggregated, and aggregation bias can introduce noise into the aggregated data.

Most governmental data are produced from Laspeyres or Paasche indexes, which are only first-order approximations to the true aggregation theoretic aggregate. The resulting second-order remainder terms could possibly produce a troublesome amount of noise for the nonlinear inference procedures currently available from the physics literature. Although the money supply would be an "important" variable, the official Federal Reserve System simple-sum monetary aggregates are not even first-order approximations and, hence, have first-order remainder terms that certainly are too large for our purposes. In addition, the techniques that we seek to use in this research benefit substantially from the largest possible sample sizes.

b   *A successful example*

We believe that a data series potentially well-suited to the objectives of this research is the weekly data on the Divisia monetary aggregates. Barnett's (1980, 1981, 1983, 1984a, 1987) Divisia monetary aggregates are second-order approximations to the exact aggregation theoretic monetary service flows produced by the corresponding monetary asset components. As a result, the remainder terms are only third-order and have been shown to be less than the round-off error in the component data. Furthermore, the monetary service flows in the economy are important variables. Barnett and Chen (1986, 1988a, b) used both the Divisia demand monetary aggregates and the Divisia supply monetary aggregates as data in our tests for chaos. For purposes of comparison, they also used the official simple-sum monetary aggregates and IBM common stock daily returns. Barnett and Chen found that some of those data series, mostly from among the Divisia monetary aggregates series, passed all of the available tests for chaos and produced low-dimensionality estimates, usually equal to two. The inference then is that some very simple (though unknown) model in state space could explain most of the observed variability in those data (up to the small amount of removed white-noise error). The monetary aggregates that did not produce well-defined dimensions perhaps either are low-quality noisy aggregates having substantial aggregation or data error or are good-quality aggregates that cannot be controlled by a small number of control variables, so the state-space dimension must be very large.

Barnett and Chen's (1986, 1988a, b) results are consistent with the relevant aggregation theory. At the lowest level of aggregation M1, little substitution has been internalized by aggregation; hence, many explanatory variables should be expected in the demand function and supply functions. Therefore those aggregates should be expected to be volatile and difficult to control without the use of many policy instruments. In other words, the minimum dimension of the state space must be large, as was found in those cases by Barnett and Chen.

Barnett and Chen found that the Divisia aggregates more frequently passed the tests for low-dimensional chaos than the simple-sum aggregates. That finding is precisely as should be expected from the aggregation theory. The simple-sum index is not even a first-order approximation to the exact aggregation theoretic aggregate, and such zero-order approximations produce tremendous aggregation error. We should expect to find extremely high noise in the simple-sum monetary aggregates.[13]

4   The conventional econometric approach

a   *The issue*

As we have observed, the most ambitious objective of strange-attractor theory is to permit the use of fractal geometry as a tool for uncovering the unknown structure of the system in state space, even if there are no observations on any state variables, no knowledge about the structure of the system, and no knowledge about the identities or even the number of state variables. The procedure embeds the output of the observer function into phase space, and the vectors in phase space are asymptotically embedded into the strange attractor, which is a fractal possessing a great deal of information about the unknown dynamical system in state space. It is this potential for uncovering structural information nonparametrically from stochastic processes in phase space that gives chaotic inference its uniquely interesting capabilities.

As we have seen, one such structural inference has become available: We are able to compute a lower bound to the dimension of the state space. This inference is especially interesting because in all sciences, including

---

[13] The exception was the simple-sum M2 aggregate. We do not know the reason for the favorable results with simple-sum M2; however, it has been observed previously that M2 is the only simple-sum monetary aggregate that has ever been found to perform well in comparisons with the Divisia monetary aggregates in other tests. See Barnett (1982).

economics, there is a natural interest in determining the simplest theory (perhaps à la Milton Friedman's methodology of positive economics) that can explain the data. The Grassberger–Procaccia algorithm does indeed produce a lower bound to the complexity (dimensionality) needed to explain the data; therefore, the objective of that algorithm clearly is important in economics.

The limitations of that algorithm are evident from the preceding discussion. The algorithm is univariate in the sense that it can be used only with observer functions that map into scalar observations. This limitation guarantees that large samples are needed because time-series observations on only one variable cannot adequately identify the dimensionality of high-dimensional systems without very large sample size. There just is not enough information in a small sample of observations on a scalar variable to enable the attractor set to uncover details about a high-dimensional system. Hence, with small systems the algorithm either is not applicable or produces an extremely conservative lower bound for dimensionality. In any case, even with large samples, the algorithm does not produce an unbiased or even consistent dimensionality estimate because the estimate is always a lower bound. Some of these limitations have been at least partially offset by recent research on the sampling distribution of the test statistic, but there is no doubt that until a multivariate extension of the algorithm is acquired, the usefulness of its inference in econometrics is limited.

Despite the limitations of that algorithm and the very early stages of development of the relevant literature, it nevertheless is interesting to ask whether conventional econometric or statistical inference procedures can provide a clearly preferable alternative. As we shall argue in the remaining sections of this chapter, conventional inference procedures do not produce an easy alternative. The nature of the inference is such that conventional statistical procedures are not easily applicable.

b   *The alternatives*

There appear to be three logical possibilities for conventional econometric approaches to estimating minimum dimensionality: the time-series approach, the structural nonnested hypothesis-testing approach, and the structural nested hypotheses-testing approach. The time-series approach seems to be the least promising of the three alternatives. Time-series methods usually are most useful in producing inferences about the properties of time-series data. Those methods typically are not very effective in passing back into another space (state space) to produce structural inferences; that asymptotic passage between spaces is the most powerful potential capability of strange-attractor theory. The second alternative, structural nonnested hypotheses testing, is difficult to assess. Nonnested hypotheses testing is itself controversial. For example, what are the power functions of such a test? Perhaps even more troublesome is the fact that the problem is difficult to formulate in such a fashion. One would have to consider the possibility of the existence of an infinite number of nonnested structural models that would have to be compared by hypothesis tests to find the dimensionality estimate. But even then, it would be unclear how the inference would compare with the Grassberger–Procaccia estimate. In that latter case, the idea is to find the simplest model and hence its dimensionality. Hypotheses-testing methods, whether nested or nonnested, typically seek the sole correct model rather than the simplest model. The simplest model is presumably found by rejecting statistically insignificant high dimensions.

This leads us to the third alternative, testing nested hypotheses. This most conventional and oldest of statistical approaches also appears to be the most promising of conventional nonchaotic approaches. In this case, we maintain that only one true model exists, and we seek to produce its greatest possible simplification. In particular, we seek to decrease the number of variables in the true model, which has a potentially immense number of variables. The relevant approach, therefore, is testing for the conditions for exact aggregation over variables. The resulting inference produces a behaviorally indistinguishable lower-dimensional model. The lower-dimensional model remains a true model in the sense that, under exact aggregation, all economic agents act in exact accordance with the simplified model when the aggregated variables are measured in the manner dictated by exact aggregation theory. Testing for minimum dimensionality then becomes testing for the highest degree of possible exact aggregation.

The fundamental necessary condition for exact aggregation is blockwise weak separability because weak separability is the clustering condition required for exact aggregation; and in the linearly homogeneous case, it also follows that the separable subfunction factored out of the disaggregated model is the exact aggregator function for aggregating over the weakly separable clustered components. Hence, testing for minimum dimensionality is equivalent to testing for the highest level of exact aggregation or, more precisely, for that weakly separable blocking that produces the minimum number of blocks in the partition of the vector of variables. In the rest of this chapter, we shall use Monte Carlo methods to investigate the reliability of the available tests for blockwise weak separability.

We conduct those experiments for the case of a single consumer and seek to determine the available capabilities to test for weak separability of a consumer's utility function. However, even if we were to find that those capabilities are formidable, the conventional approach would still be far from easy to use because we would have to deal with the troublesome problems of aggregating over economic agents jointly with aggregating over goods. At the very least, we would probably need to require that every consumer's utility function and every firm's production function be blockwise weakly separable in the same blocks of goods. Nevertheless, we need not consider those deep issues because we shall see that even testing for blockwise weak separability of one consumer's utility function may very well be beyond the state of the art in conventional econometric inference.[14]

c   *Blockwise weak separability*

Separability assumptions on functional structure have received a great deal of attention from econometricians and economic theorists during the last two decades. The practical importance of separability results from three facts:

(1)   Separability provides the fundamental linkage between aggregation over goods and the maximization principles in economic theory.[15]
(2)   Separability provides the theoretical basis for partitioning the economy's structure into sectors.
(3)   Separability provides a theoretical hypothesis that can produce powerful parameter restrictions, permitting great simplification in estimation of large demand systems.[16]

In this study, we are motivated by the first of these objectives, but our results would be relevant to any of the three motivations for testing for weak separability. Separability is a fundamental testable hypothesis, and the

---

[14] Although factor analysis may appear to be a conventional econometric approach to measuring minimum dimensionality, that approach cannot be used to uncover an unknown structural model from the properties of its solution path. Factor analysis typically is used to produce revealing orthogonal transformations of fully known models, rather than to uncover the structure of unknown models. Hence, factor analysis, although similar in spirit to the Grassberger–Procaccia inference, does not have comparable capabilities to those of strange-attractor theory. We therefore do not pursue the factor analysis analogy.

[15] See, e.g., Green (1964, theorem 4).

[16] See, e.g., Barten (1964, 1968), Byron (1970), and Barnett (1977).

testing of separability hypotheses has, in recent years, been considerably facilitated by the development of new demand models based upon flexible functional forms.[17]

However, flexible functional forms are structured, by definition, solely for the purpose of providing local approximations; as a result, the approximation properties of those models over finite regions are not well understood. A number of approaches have been used to explore the regional and global properties of flexible functional forms and to determine the effects of structural restrictions, such as separability, upon the local properties of such models.[18] For example, Blackorby, Primont, and Russell (1977) proved that the global imposition of separability destroys the local flexibility property of flexible functional forms. It has more recently been argued that the difficulties associated with testing separability can be circumvented by conducting and interpreting the tests locally. We use that local interpretation of "approximate" separability in this study. We also try Varian's new nonparametric test. The reliability of the various available tests for separability has never been determined. In particular, nothing is known about the power of the available tests of separability other than that the theoretical result proved by Blackorby, Primont, and Russell tends to cast doubt on that power.

Barnett and Choi (1987) carefully examined the capability of flexible functional forms to provide correct inferences. Specifically, in that paper we produced Monte Carlo experiments based on data generated by the three-good WS-branch utility function, which is blockwise weakly separable. The flexible functional forms that we used for inference with the simulated data were the translog (TL), the absolute price version of the Rotterdam model (RM), the generalized Leontief (GL), and the third-order translog (3TL).[19] We here collect those aspects of our results that

---

[17] See Barnett (1983) for a formal mathematical definition of flexibility and for proofs of theorems relating flexibility to various desirable properties of models.

[18] See, e.g., Wales (1977), Guilkey and Lovell (1980), Guilkey, Lovell, and Sickles (1983), Byron (1984), Gallant (1981), Caves and Christensen (1980), Barnett (1985), Barnett and Lee (1985), and Barnett, Lee, and Wolfe (1985, 1987).

[19] Other models have been proposed for separability testing. Woodland (1978) proposed a modified translog model for testing separability on the production side, but we omit that model in our study because we consider only consumption models. In addition, Woodland's approach is not completely general because his test is only applicable to certain preselected separability hypotheses. Blackorby, Schworm, and Fisher (1986) have proposed a newer, and very promising, test of blockwise weak separability in the production context. That approach, based upon Diewert and Wales' (1987) symmetric generalized Barnett model, has not yet been adapted to consumer demand modeling and hence has not been used in our study.

are relevant to exact aggregation over goods and analyze the implications of those results for testing for blockwise weak separability.

Varian (1982, 1983, 1985) has introduced a nonparametric procedure for testing hypotheses about consumer (or producer) behavior. He developed a computational algorithm that can check whether a given data set is consistent with the maximization hypothesis. The advantage of this procedure is that it does not require a particular functional form and therefore potentially can avoid problems that may arise as a result of model misspecification. Varian's approach is particularly useful in testing for the consistency of data with theory. However, the available nonparametric approach to separability hypothesis testing is not satisfactory. That approach checks sufficient but not necessary conditions for the data to satisfy a separable structure. Those sufficient conditions are so restrictive that the test is very strongly biased toward rejection. Nevertheless, we tested the procedure with the Pascal program (2nd version) developed by Varian and with the data generated from the three-good Cobb–Douglas function without random disturbances. We could find no case in which Varian's sufficient conditions for separability were satisfied, despite the fact that the three-good Cobb–Douglas function is completely strongly separable and therefore separable in all blockings of goods.

5   Separability, duality, and elasticities of substitution

Assume that a preference structure is represented by a twice-differentiable, strictly quasiconcave utility function U with a finite number $N+M$ of goods, each having strictly positive marginal utility:

$$U = u(\mathbf{x}, \mathbf{y}),$$

where $\mathbf{x} = (x_1, \dots, x_N)$ and $\mathbf{y} = (y_1, \dots, y_M)$. If there exists an aggregator function F such that

$$U = u(\mathbf{x}, \mathbf{y}) = U(\mathbf{x}, F(\mathbf{y})), \tag{9}$$

then $\mathbf{y}$ is said to be weakly separable from $\mathbf{x}$ in u.[20] If the aggregator function is also homothetic, $\mathbf{y}$ is said to be homothetically separable from $\mathbf{x}$ in u. For the corresponding indirect utility function, there then exists a homothetic price aggregator function P such that

$$V = v(\bar{\mathbf{q}}, \bar{\mathbf{p}}) = V(\bar{\mathbf{q}}, P(\bar{\mathbf{p}})), \tag{10}$$

[20] Note that the separability structure is asymmetric, i.e., $\mathbf{x}$ is not separable from $\mathbf{y}$ in u unless there exists a function G such that $U = u(\mathbf{x}, \mathbf{y}) = U[G(\mathbf{x}), F(\mathbf{y})]$. For an executive discussion of separability, see Blackorby, Primont, and Russell (1978) and Goldman and Uzawa (1964).

where $\bar{\mathbf{q}} = (\bar{q}_1, \ldots, \bar{q}_N)$ and $\bar{\mathbf{p}} = (\bar{p}_1, \ldots, \bar{p}_M)$ are the expenditure normalized price vectors for $\mathbf{x}$ and $\mathbf{y}$, respectively.[21] Therefore, if one is interested in testing a homothetic separability hypothesis on a direct utility function, the test can be carried out by testing homothetic separability of the indirect utility function. However, if the data are consistent with separability but not with homothetic separability, a test for separability of the indirect utility function cannot be used to test for separability of the direct utility function. Because the flexible functional forms that we consider in this study are approximations to the indirect utility function, we consider only the homothetic case to assure the existence of a separable dual structure between the approximated indirect and unknown direct utility functions.[22]

a   *Elasticities of substitution under homothetic separability*

In the two-good case, elasticities of substitution are rather easily computed, but the computational problems become much greater with three or more goods. However, if a utility function is homothetically separable, the computational difficulties can be reduced considerably by the use of a relationship between micro and aggregate (macro) elasticities of substitution. The microelasticity of substitution here is the elasticity of substitution between elementary goods, and the aggregate elasticity of substitution is the elasticity of substitution between exact aggregates over a weakly separable group of goods. Diewert (1974) developed such a relationship in the case of Hicksian aggregation, which does not require separability but does require constant relative prices within the aggregated block of goods. Barnett and Choi (1987) derived the analogous result in the case of blockwise weak separability, without the need for constant relative prices.

Suppose the quantity aggregator function, $F(\mathbf{y})$, in (1) is linearly homogeneous. Then from (2) it follows that the linearly homogeneous function $P(\bar{\mathbf{p}})$ exists. Define $\bar{P}$ such that

$$P = P(\bar{\mathbf{p}}). \tag{11}$$

It is well known from aggregation theory that $Y = F(\mathbf{y})$ and $\bar{P}$ are the consistent quantity and (normalized) price aggregates, respectively. The corresponding nonnormalized price aggregate is acquired by multiplying both sides of (11) by total expenditure, $\mathbf{p} \cdot \bar{\mathbf{q}}$, on the aggregated goods to obtain

---

[21] In particular, if $(\mathbf{q}, \mathbf{p})$ are the corresponding nonnormalized prices, and if I is total expenditure on $(\mathbf{x}, \mathbf{y})$, then $(\bar{\mathbf{q}}, \bar{\mathbf{p}}) = (\mathbf{q}, \mathbf{p})/I$.

[22] In a few cases we did run the more complicated separability tests without homotheticity. The conclusions were not altered in any substantive ways.

$$P = P(\mathbf{p}).\tag{11a}$$

The following result was proved by Barnett and Choi (1987).

Theorem 1. *Suppose a utility function is homothetically separable as in (9). Let $Y = F(\mathbf{y})$ be the consistent quantity aggregate for $\mathbf{y}$. Then the elasticity of substitution between x_n and Y is equal to the elasticity of substitution between x_n and any elementary good y_k in $\mathbf{y}$.*

In fact, Theorem 1 immediately implies a result that Berndt and Christensen (1973) derived.[23] We state that result as a corollary to Theorem 1.

Corollary 1 (Berndt and Christensen). *If a utility function is homothetically separable as in Eq. (9), then the elasticity of substitution between x_n and y_k is independent of k for any fixed n.*

When a utility function is homothetically separable, Theorem 1 and Corollary 1 make the computation of elasticities of substitution much easier. For example, suppose the utility function is of the following form:

$$U = U(q_1(y_1, y_2), q_2(y_3, y_4)),$$

where (y_1, y_2) are homothetically separable from (y_3, y_4), and vice versa. The two aggregator functions are q_1 and q_2. At a given point, the elasticity of substitution between y_1 and y_2 or between y_3 and y_4 can be computed by treating q_1 and q_2 as individual utility functions. The elasticity of substitution between any good in block 1 and any good in block 2 is easily computed as the elasticity of substitution between the two aggregates Q_1 and Q_2 at the given data point, where $Q_1 = q_1(y_1, y_2)$ and $Q_2 = q_2(y_3, y_4)$.[24]

b   *Supernumerary quantities, elasticities of substitution, and income elasticities*

Homotheticity in consumer demand analysis is regarded as too restrictive because it implies unitary income elasticity of demand for all goods. However, a utility function that is homothetic in supernumerary quantities (quantities in excess of fixed committed quantities) is not homothetic in the elementary quantities. Hence, a homothetic utility function

---

[23] The converse, however, is not true, since Corollary 1 does not imply our Theorem 1.

[24] This equality is easily proved as follows. Replace $q_2(y_3, y_4)$ by Q_2 and use Theorem 1 to produce the elasticities of substitution between Q_2 and the arguments of q_1. Then replace $q_1(y_1, y_2)$ by Q_1 and use Theorem 1 to produce the elasticities of substitution between Q_1 and the arguments of q_2. Our conclusion now follows immediately.

can be converted into a nonhomothetic function by translating the quantities into supernumerary quantities. Such affine homothetic utility functions are often called quasihomothetic. The utility function that we use to generate our Monte Carlo data is quasihomothetic. Barnett and Choi (1987) derived some formulas that simplify computation of elasticities when preferences are quasihomothetic.

Let $\mathbf{x} = (x_1, \ldots, x_n)$ be a vector of quantities of elementary goods, and let $\mathbf{a} = (a_1, \ldots, a_n)$ be an n-dimensional vector of constant committed quantities. Consider a well-defined utility function $u = U(\mathbf{y})$, where $\mathbf{y} = \mathbf{x} - \mathbf{a}$ is the n-dimensional supernumerary quantity vector. Suppose function U is homothetic in $\mathbf{y}$. Because U is homothetic in $\mathbf{y}$, the income elasticities of demand for the y_i are unitary for all i, though the income elasticities of demand for the x_i are not necessarily unitary. The following theorem, derived by Barnett and Choi (1987), provides formulas relating the income and substitution elasticities for the x_i to the corresponding elasticities for the y_i. The formulas are very useful because the elasticities for the supernumerary quantities are of much simpler form than those for the elementary goods.

Theorem 2.   *Suppose a utility function is of the form* $u = U(\mathbf{y}) = U(\mathbf{x} - \mathbf{a})$, *as defined above. Let* $\mathbf{p}$ *be the vector of prices of the goods* $\mathbf{x}$. *Let* ξ_{ij} *be the elasticity of substitution between* y_i *and* y_j. *Then the elasticity of substitution* σ_{ij} *between* x_i *and* x_j *and the income elasticity of demand* η_j, *for* x_j, *are as follows:*

$$\sigma_{ij} = \xi_{ij} \cdot \frac{1}{1 - \bar{\mathbf{p}} \cdot \mathbf{a}} \cdot \frac{(x_j - a_j)(x_i - a_i)}{x_j x_i} \tag{12}$$

and

$$\eta_j = \frac{1}{1 - \bar{\mathbf{p}} \cdot \mathbf{a}} \cdot \frac{x_j - a_j}{x_j}, \tag{13}$$

where $\bar{\mathbf{p}} = (\bar{p}_1, \ldots, \bar{p}_n)$ *is the expenditure normalized price vector* $\mathbf{p}/m$ *for total expenditure* $m = \mathbf{p} \cdot \mathbf{x}$.

The use of the formulas (12) and (13) is much easier computationally than the direct derivation of the elasticities by the usual methods. For example, the usual direct method for deriving elasticities of substitution requires the computation of second derivatives, which is not required in either of our formulas. We use the results obtained in this section to compute those elasticities from the utility function adopted to produce our Monte Carlo data.

6   The true utility function

We have chosen Barnett's (1977) nonhomothetic WS-branch utility tree as the underlying true utility function in generating our Monte Carlo data.

In this model, the individual aggregator ("category") functions in the tree are in the form of the generalized quadratic mean of order ρ, as is the macro utility function defined over those aggregates. The WS-branch utility tree is the generalization to blockwise weak separability of the S-branch utility tree, which is blockwise strongly separable. The WS-branch model is the only blockwise weakly separable utility function specification of which we are aware. In addition, the specification is a flexible functional form when there are no more than two goods in each block and no more than two blocks. Those conditions are the ones under which we use the model.[25]

The generalized quadratic mean of order ρ is of the following form:

$$U(q_1, \ldots, q_m) = A\left(\sum_i \sum_j B_{ij} q_i^\rho q_j^\rho\right)^{1/2\rho}, \tag{14}$$

where $\rho < 1/2$ and $B_{ij} > 0$ for all i, j, $\sum_i \sum_j B_{ij} = 1$, $B_{ij} = B_{ji}$ for $i \neq j$, and $A > 0$. These inequalities ensure the monotonicity and quasiconcavity of the function.[26] To introduce a weakly separable structure, each q_r is treated as an aggregate rather than as an elementary good, so that (14) becomes the macro function defined over the quantity aggregates. The aggregator functions producing the aggregates are of the form $q_r = q_r(\mathbf{x}_r)$, where $\mathbf{x}_r$ is a subvector of $\mathbf{x}$. We assume that these aggregator functions also take the same form as (14). The resulting nested two-stage structure of means of order ρ produces the WS-branch utility function.

Because the three-good case is considered in our experiments, the true utility function used to generate our data is specified as follows. Let x_1, x_2, and x_3 denote the quantity consumed of each good. The true utility function is

$$U = U(q_1(x_1, x_2), q_2(x_3))$$
$$= A(B_{11} q_1^{2\rho} + 2B_{12} q_1^\rho q_2^\rho + B_{22} q_2^{2\rho})^{1/2\rho} \tag{15}$$

where $q_1 = q_1(x_1, x_2)$ and $q_2 = q_2(x_3) = x_3 - a_3$ are aggregator functions. The function q_1 has the same form as (15) in the supernumerary quantities $\mathbf{y} = \mathbf{x} - \mathbf{a}$ with $\mathbf{x} = (x_1, x_2, x_3)$:

$$q_1 = q_1(x_1, x_2)$$
$$= (A_{11} y_1^{2\delta} + 2A_{12} y_1^\delta y_2^\delta + A_{22} y_2^{2\delta})^{1/2\delta}. \tag{16}$$

The parameters in (15) and (16) are subject to the same restrictions as the corresponding parameters in (14). Without loss of generality, the parameter A can be set to 1.0 because the selection of A produces only monotonic

---

[25] The model previously has been used primarily in recursive estimation of demand systems based on the model's hierarchical utility tree structure (see, e.g., Barnett, 1977).

[26] See Kadiyala (1972).

transformations of the utility function. Goods x_1 and x_2 are weakly separable in U from x_3. If $B_{12} = 0$, then (x_1, x_2) are also blockwise strongly separable from x_3.[27]

Because both the aggregator function (16) and the macro function (15) have identical specifications, the properties to be discussed apply equally to all of those functions. The B_{12} and A_{12} coefficients are called the interaction coefficients. If all of the interaction coefficients are zero, then all of the aggregator and macro functions are constant elasticity of substitution (CES), and the nested utility tree produced by them is the S-branch tree, which is blockwise strongly separable between blocks and completely strongly separable within each block. Unlike the CES function, the generalized quadratic mean of order ρ with nonzero interaction coefficient does not have constant elasticity of substitution and is not strongly separable.

7   Data generation

The experiments are performed over a sample size of 60 preselected quantity and total-expenditure points. We solve for the values of the parameters of the macro and category utility functions, (15) and (16), that yield preselected values for the elasticities of substitution at the median data point. We then substitute those parameter values into the WS-branch inverse demand system and solve for the price values corresponding to the preselected quantity and expenditure values. For each set of quantity and price values, we add white noise to the quantity values in a manner that preserves the total expenditure stream. This step is repeated 50 times by randomly selecting 50 noise vectors from the assumed disturbance distribution. Hence, there are 50 data sets for each selection of the WS-branch model's elasticities of substitution. Accordingly, we shall estimate the parameters of the approximating specifications 50 times for each of the selections of the true elasticities of substitution.[28]

To obtain the initial preselected quantity and expenditure values for the above Monte Carlo data generation procedure, we could generate a

---

[27] Because there is only one good in the x_3 block, the separability structure is symmetric in the sense that x_3 is weakly separable in U from x_1 and x_2. Also observe that the macro function $q_1(x_1, x_2)$, is not homothetic in (x_1, x_2), despite the fact that q_1 is homothetic in the supernumerary quantity variables.

[28] This data generation procedure is very similar to that used by Guilkey and Lovell (1980) and Guilkey, Lovell, and Sickles (1983). However, we use additive errors whereas they used multiplicative errors. Although we here report only our results with additive errors, we also tried multiplicative errors without affecting any of our conclusions. In addition, our true model, the WS-branch, is more general than the true model used to generate the data in the other two studies. To permit testing for weak separability, our use of the WS-branch true model was necessary.

set of random data from a first-order autoregressive scheme. Alternatively, we could use an actual observed data time series. We adopt the latter alternative and use the consumption quantities and total expenditures from Barnett (1981, appendix D), whose annual data series span an unusually long time period, extending back into the late nineteenth century. From Barnett's observations on U.S. consumption of perishables, semidurables, and services, we use the first 60 observations for the purpose of the experiments.[29] For details of the data generation procedure, see the appendix of Barnett and Choi (1987).

8   The approximation functions

a   *The translog approximation*

The first empirical specification we consider is the translog (TL) approximation to the indirect utility function,

$$\ln V(\bar{\mathbf{p}}) = \alpha_0 + \sum_{i \in N} \alpha_i \ln \bar{p}_i + \sum_{j \in N} \sum_{k \in N} \beta_{jk} \ln \bar{p}_j \ln \bar{p}_k, \tag{17}$$

where $\bar{\mathbf{p}}$ is the expenditure normalized price vector and ln is the natural log operator. The following share equations result from the use of Roy's identity:

$$\omega_i = \frac{\alpha_i + \sum_j \beta_{ij} \ln \bar{p}_j}{\sum_k \alpha_k + \sum_k \sum_j \beta_{kj} \ln \bar{p}_k}, \quad i = 1, 2, 3. \tag{18}$$

We impose the usual identifying normalization, $\sum_k \alpha_k = -1$.

Blackorby, Primont, and Russell (1977) have shown that global imposition of weak separability on the translog causes the aggregator function to take a very restrictive form. As a result, the translog cannot be used effectively to test for global separability because such a test would be a joint test for separability and for an unrealistically restrictive specification for the resulting aggregator functions. As a result, Jorgenson and Lau (1975) and Denny and Fuss (1977) suggest the use of an approximate local separability test, by which, under the null hypothesis, separability need be satisfied only at the unit vector $\bar{\mathbf{p}} = 1$.

If x_1 and x_2 are separable from x_3, then that local separability restriction becomes

$$\frac{\alpha_1}{\alpha_2} = \frac{\beta_{13}}{\beta_{23}} \tag{19}$$

---

[29] We did not use Barnett's data on durables or leisure consumption because our study was restricted for computational reasons to the use of three-good models.

More precisely, condition (19) is that p_1 and p_2 are separable from p_3 at $\bar{\mathbf{p}} = 1$ in V because the restriction is obtained from the indirect utility function V. However, we are seeking to test blockwise separability of goods in U, not blockwise separability of prices in V.

Unless the utility function is homothetically separable, blockwise separability of U is not equivalent to blockwise separability of V. As a result, when the data are generated from (15) and (16) with nonzero (a_1, a_2, a_3), the translog test of (19) may be inappropriate to our objectives. To avoid this problem, we concentrate most of our experimental efforts on testing for homothetic separability, when the data are generated from the WS-branch model under homothetic separability restrictions. In these cases, homotheticity also is imposed upon the approximating specifications, such as the translog.

The linear homogeneity restriction on translog is that

$$\sum_j \beta_{ij} = 0 \quad \text{for all } i. \tag{20}$$

The imposition of (20) does not destroy the second-order flexibility property of translog so long as the data are produced from a homothetic utility function.[30]

b   *The third-order translog approximation*

The third-order translog (3TL) is obtained by adding to equation (17) the third-order term of the Taylor series expansion in the logarithms about $\bar{\mathbf{p}} = 1$. The resulting specification for the indirect utility function V is

$$\ln V(\bar{\mathbf{p}}) = \theta_0 + \sum_{i \in N} \theta_i \ln \bar{p}_i + \frac{1}{2} \sum_{j \in N} \sum_{k \in N} \theta_{jk} \ln \bar{p}_j \ln \bar{p}_k$$

$$+ \frac{1}{6} \sum_{j \in N} \sum_{k \in N} \sum_{h \in N} \theta_{jkh} \ln \bar{p}_j \ln \bar{p}_k \ln \bar{p}_h. \tag{21}$$

Applying Roy's identity produces the share equations,

$$\omega_i = \frac{\theta_i + \sum_j \theta_{ij} \ln \bar{p}_j + (1/2) \sum_j \sum_h \theta_{ijh} \ln \bar{p}_j \ln \bar{p}_h}{\sum_k \theta_k + \sum_k \sum_j \theta_{kj} \ln \bar{p}_j + \sum_k \sum_j \sum_h \beta_{kjh} \ln \bar{p}_j \ln \bar{p}_h} \tag{22}$$

for $i = 1, 2, 3$. As with the second-order translog, $\sum_k \theta_k = -1$ is a convenient identifying normalization. The number of parameters has increased dramatically by the inclusion of the third-order terms. In the three-good

---

[30] The reason for the preservation of this flexibility property under homotheticity is that local and global homotheticity are mathematically equivalent for the translog. Hence, the global homotheticity restrictions, (20), are no stronger than local flexibility at the point, $\mathbf{p} = 1$.

case before any further theoretical restrictions are imposed, the total number of parameters is 18 whereas there are only 8 parameters in the unrestricted second-order translog.

Hayes (1986) derived the parameter restrictions for approximate (local) separability and homotheticity. In the three-good case, if $\bar{p}_1$ and $\bar{p}_2$ are separable from $\bar{p}_3$, the restrictions for separability at $\bar{\mathbf{p}} = 1$ are the following:

$$\theta_{i3} = \rho\theta_i \qquad \text{for } i = 1, 2, \tag{22a}$$

$$\theta_{ij3} = \rho\theta_{ij} + \varsigma_1\theta_i\theta_j \quad \text{for } i, j = 1, 2, \tag{22b}$$

$$\theta_{i33} = \varsigma_2\theta_i \qquad \text{for } i = 1, 2, \tag{22c}$$

where ρ, ς_1, and ς_2 are additional parameters to be estimated.

The restrictions for local homotheticity at the point $\mathbf{p} = 1$ are as follows:

$$\sum_j \theta_{ij} = \psi_1\theta_i \qquad \text{for } i = 1, 2, 3, \tag{23a}$$

and

$$\sum_j \theta_{ijh} = \psi_1\theta_{ij} + \psi_2\theta_i\theta_j \quad \text{for } i, j = 1, 2, 3, \tag{23b}$$

where ψ_1 and ψ_2 are additional parameters to be estimated. As a special case, global linear homogeneity restrictions are obtained by setting both ψ_1 and ψ_2 equal to zero. When the global linear homogeneity restrictions are imposed, the total number of parameters to be estimated becomes nine. If the restrictions for approximate separability are imposed in addition to the (global) linear homogeneity restrictions, the number of parameters to be estimated becomes six. Note that the restrictions (22c) are redundant if the linear homogeneity conditions are imposed.

The elasticities of substitution for the 3TL can be derived from Diewert's (1974) formula to obtain

$$\sigma_{ik} = 1 + \frac{E \cdot \theta_{ik}}{A_i A_k} - \sum_h \frac{\theta_{kh}}{A_k} - \sum_h \frac{\theta_{ih}}{A_i} + \sum_{jh} \frac{\theta_{jh}}{E}$$

$$+ E \cdot \sum_c \frac{\theta_{ikc}\ln\bar{p}_c}{A_i A_k} - \sum_h \sum_c \frac{\theta_{hkc}\ln\bar{p}_c}{A_k} - \sum_h \sum_c \frac{\theta_{hic}\ln\bar{p}_c}{A_i}$$

$$+ \sum_g \sum_h \sum_c \frac{\theta_{ghc}\ln\bar{p}_c}{E} \quad \text{for } i \neq k,$$

and

$$\sigma_{ii} = 1 + E \cdot \frac{\theta_{ii}}{A_i^2} + 2\sum_h \frac{\theta_{ih}}{A_i} + \sum_{jh} \frac{\theta_{jh}}{E} + E \cdot \sum_c \frac{\theta_{ikc}\ln\bar{p}_c}{A_i^2}$$

$$- 2\sum_h \sum_c \frac{\theta_{hic}\ln\bar{p}_c}{A_i} + \sum_g \sum_h \sum_c \frac{\theta_{ghc}\ln\bar{p}_c}{E} - \frac{E}{A_i} \quad \text{for all } i,$$

where

$$E = \sum_k \theta_k + \sum_k \sum_j \theta_{kj} \ln \bar{p}_j + \sum_k \sum_j \sum_h \beta_{kjh} \ln \bar{p}_j \ln \bar{p}_h$$

and

$$A_i = \theta_i + \sum_j \theta_{ij} \ln \bar{p}_j + \frac{1}{2} \sum_j \sum_h \theta_{ijh} \ln \bar{p}_j \ln \bar{p}_h.$$

c   *The generalized Leontief model*

The third approximating empirical specification we consider is the generalized Leontief (GL) model:

$$V(\bar{\mathbf{p}}) = \alpha_0 + 2 \sum_{i \in N} \alpha_i \bar{p}_i^{1/2} + \sum_{j \in N} \sum_{k \in N} \beta_{jk} \bar{p}_j^{1/2} \bar{p}_k^{1/2}. \tag{24}$$

Its share equations are

$$\omega_i = \frac{\alpha_i v_i + \sum_j \beta_{ij} v_i v_j}{\sum_k \alpha_k v_k + \sum_k \sum_j \beta_{kj} v_k v_j} \quad \text{for } i = 1, 2, 3, \tag{25}$$

where $v_i = p_i^{1/2}$. For an identifying normalization, we set the denominator of the share equation to equal one at $\bar{\mathbf{p}} = 1$.

Let the generalized Leontief be linearly homogeneous. It then follows from Euler's theorem that

$$V = \sum_{i \in N} \frac{\partial U}{\partial \bar{p}_i} \cdot \bar{p}_i$$
$$= \sum_{i \in N} \alpha_i \bar{p}_i^{1/2} + \sum_{i \in N} \sum_{j \in N} \beta_{ij} \bar{p}_i^{1/2} \bar{p}_j^{1/2}.$$

By (24), the following equality must hold:

$$\sum_{i \in N} \alpha_i \bar{p}_i^{1/2} = \alpha_0 + 2 \sum_{i \in N} \alpha_i \bar{p}_i^{1/2}.$$

To produce approximate (local) linear homogeneity, the above restriction can be imposed at the point of approximation. As a special case, the above equality holds globally for all $\bar{\mathbf{p}}$, if $\alpha_0 = \alpha_1 = \cdots = \alpha_n = 0$. These global restrictions are widely used as the means of testing for or imposing homotheticity with the generalized Leontief model, and we also do so.[31]

To obtain the separability condition, consider again the case in which $\bar{p}_i$ and $\bar{p}_j$ are separable from $\bar{p}_k$, where $i \neq j \neq k$. The definition of separability directly leads to

---

[31] Although the use of global homotheticity is conventional in this context, it nevertheless should be observed that, unlike the translog, the generalized Leontief model does not retain its local flexibility property under the global homotheticity restrictions. The reason is that global homotheticity is stronger than local homotheticity for the generalized Leontief, whereas global and local homotheticity are equivalent for the translog.

$$\alpha_i \beta_{jk} - \alpha_j \beta_{ik} + \sum_{h \in N} (\beta_{jh} \beta_{ik} - \beta_{ih} \beta_{jk}) = 0$$

at the point $\bar{p} = 1$. We use this restriction in testing for approximate separability.

d   *The Rotterdam model*

The final approximating specification we consider is the Rotterdam model (RM) in its absolute price version. The model's specification before addition of stochastic disturbances is

$$\tilde{\omega}_{i,t} Dx_{i,t} = \mu_i D\tilde{m}_t + \sum_{j \in N} \pi_{ij} Dp_{j,t} \tag{26}$$

for $i = 1, 2, 3$ and $N = \{1, 2, 3\}$, where $\tilde{\omega}_{i,t} = (1/2)(\omega_{i,t+1} + \omega_{i,t})$, $D\tilde{m}_t = \sum_i \tilde{\omega}_{i,t} Dx_{i,t}$, and the log change operator D is defined such that $Dx_{i,t} = \log x_{i,t} - \log x_{i,t-1}$. The parameter μ_i locally approximates the marginal budget share of the ith good, and π_{ij} locally approximates the Slutsky compensated function $(p_i p_j / m) \cdot \partial x_i / \partial p_j |_{\text{utility constant}}$. The matrix of π_{ij} coefficients is called the Slutsky matrix. The parameters of the model are subject to the following theoretical constraints:

$\sum_i \mu_i = 1$;
$\sum_j \pi_{ij} = 0$;
$[\pi_{ij}]$ is symmetric and negative semidefinite.

The model in its aggregated form was proved to be a flexible functional form by Barnett (1979a, b), and in its disaggregated form by Mountain (1988).[32]

The first and second constraints are Engel aggregation and homogeneity of demand, respectively. Symmetry and negative semidefiniteness of $[\pi_{ij}]$ are directly related to the condition of local quasiconcavity of the utility function. In case of the other models we consider, quasiconcavity of the utility function can be tested at each data point by checking the negative semidefiniteness of $[\sigma_{ij}]$.[33] However, in the case of the Rotterdam model, the test can only be conducted locally. The model cannot be used to test curvature conditions globally because the Slutsky matrix is estimated only at the point of approximation.[34]

The condition for local blockwise weak separability of the Rotterdam model is

---

[32] Also see Barnett (1984b) on that subject.
[33] See Barnett, Lee, and Wolfe (1985) for the formulas for the elasticities of substitution of the translog and generalized Leontief models.
[34] The value of the Slutsky matrix at other points cannot be determined because the Rotterdam model is not integrable.

$$\pi_{ij} = c\mu_i\mu_j, \tag{27}$$

for goods i and j in different blocks, where c is constant.[35] The elasticities of substitution for the Rotterdam model are obtained as functions of the predicted expenditure shares ω_i^* from the following formula:

$$\sigma_{ij} = \frac{\pi_{ij}}{\omega_i^*\omega_j^*} \quad \text{for all } i,j.$$

As shown by Theil (1971, p. 646), the predicted value shares can be computed from $\omega_{it}^* = \omega_{it} - \epsilon_{it}^*$, for all i and t, where ω_{it}^* is the predicted value share of the ith good during period t, ω_{it} is the observed value shares of the ith good during period t, and ϵ_{it}^* is the residual during period t of the ith estimated equation of the model.

With the Rotterdam model, the test for separability does not require imposition of homotheticity because the separability conditions for that model were derived directly from the Slutsky equation; hence, they are conditions for separability of the direct utility function U in goods, rather than for the indirect utility function V in prices.

9   Estimation

We employed a full information maximum-likelihood (FIML) estimation and used the asymptotic log likelihood ratio test statistic $(-2\log\lambda)$ to test for separability. We first performed all of the experiments with homogeneity restrictions imposed a priori on all models except for the Rotterdam model. The linear homogeneity restrictions were imposed not only on the approximating specifications but also on the WS-branch model used to generate the data. Except for the Rotterdam model, all of the other approximating specifications required the imposition of linear homogeneity of preferences to permit the separability hypothesis to be interpreted in terms of direct utility rather than solely in terms of indirect utility. Despite the resulting failure of self-duality of separability, we also conducted some tests for separability when preferences were not required to be homothetic. Because we found no marked differences in our conclusions, we report only the results under homogeneity restrictions.

In our experiments, goods 1 and 2 were blockwise separable from good 3 in the WS-branch true model used to generate the data. If the WS-branch also is homothetic, then $\sigma_{13} = \sigma_{23}$, and we needed only to specify the two free substitution elasticities, σ_{12} and σ_{13}. Our experiments can be grouped together into six general categories:

[35] See Barnett (1981, theorem 5.1) or Barnett (1979b).

1   The value of the elasticity of substitution between the two goods in the separable block (σ_{12}) was set to be similar in value to that of the elasticity of the remaining free substitution elasticity (σ_{13}).

2   The value of σ_{12} was set to be low.

3   The value of σ_{13} was set to be low.

4   The value of σ_{12} was set to be equal to unity.

5   The value of σ_{13} was set to be equal to unity.

6   The value of either σ_{12} or σ_{13} was set to be twice as large as that of the other.

In each of the above six general groups, several specific experiments were conducted; hence, there were six sets of experiments. The results generated from each of the six sets of experiments are reported, respectively, in Tables 1–6. Each table contains the results that were generated from one group of experiments with all of the specified approximate models: the translog, the Rotterdam model, the generalized Leontief, and the third-order translog.

The first two columns in each table are the true values of σ_{12} and σ_{13} at the median data point in each experiment.[36] The hypothesis-testing results for testing blockwise weak separability are reported in the remaining columns. Those results are the rejection rates of the null hypothesis over 50 replications at the 1%, 5%, and 10% levels of significance.[37]

We conducted the experiments both with blockwise strongly separable structure (with zero interaction coefficients) in the WS-branch generating model, and with blockwise weakly separable structure. The interpretation of results is substantially clarified in the strongly separable cases because the WS-branch aggregator and macro functions become CES under strong separability. Then the elasticities of substitution are not dependent on the observation; hence, evaluation of the estimates of elasticities of substitution and their use in testing for separability are straightforward globally. We found that our conclusions about the relative merits of the models were usually unchanged by the use of strong separability rather than weak separability. Hence, we often report only the more easily interpreted results using blockwise strong separability. In those cases, any given blocking is either both weak and strongly separable or is neither. As a result, there is no loss in validity in using that generated data to compare tests of blockwise weak separability.

[36] Alternatively, the true elasticities reported can be viewed as the average elasticities over the data points because there were only negligible differences between the elasticities obtained at the median data point and the average elasticities over the data points for the entire experiment.

[37] In the tables, the words "true" and "false" refer to the null hypothesis. See Barnett (1976) for the derivation of the test statistic and its limiting distribution.

An exception is the case in which σ_{12} is close to σ_{13}. If those two elasticities are exactly equal, the true function then becomes the three-good CES function. In that case, the null hypothesis of separability cannot be false because any one of the three goods is always separable from the other two goods. As a result, whenever all elasticities of substitution are similar (i.e., in Table 1), blockwise weak separability without blockwise strong separability is used in generating the data. For purposes of comparison, an assortment of other results with blockwise weak separability is supplied in Table 7.

10   Results

Separability requires that the elasticity of substitution between any good in a separable block and any good outside the block be independent of the good inside the block. Hence, imposition of separability is equivalent to equating certain elasticities of substitution. However, in Table 1 all true elasticities of substitution are equal at the median data point, regardless of whether the null is true or false, and as a result, if the point estimates are of high quality, the imposition of the null will have little effect on the point estimates and therefore on the likelihood function. In the cases displayed in Table 1, good-quality point estimates are of little use in testing the null, unless the precisions of the point estimates are very high.

There should, therefore, be substantial differences among the true substitution elasticities σ_{12} and σ_{13} for the separability tests to be statistically reliable. Tables 2–6 show much improvement in the performances of the four approximations in testing separability, though not for all cases. In particular, the rejection rates are often low when the null is false and high when the null is true. The performance of each approximating specification in testing separability is summarized as follows:

> When the elasticity of substitution σ_{12} in the aggregator function is very low (Table 2), the statistical power of the separability tests using the four approximations is usually not high.[38] There are two exceptions: (1) the generalized Leontief when σ_{13} is relatively low[39] and (2) the third-order translog when the value of σ_{13} is not far from unity.
>
> When the elasticity of substitution between aggregates, σ_{13} is very low (Table 3), all approximating specifications usually provide

[38] The term *statistical power* is used here to mean the probability of accepting the null hypothesis when it is true as well as the probability of rejecting the null hypothesis when it is false.

[39] See the case in which $\sigma_{12} = 0.1$ and $\sigma_{13} = 0.3$.

Table 1. *Summary of experiments, for similar true elasticities of substitution*

Approximate function	True elasticities of substitution σ_{12}	σ_{13}	Estimated elasticities of substitution σ_{12}	σ_{13}	σ_{23}	Regularity violation percentage	Separability rejection percentage 10% level True	False	5% level True	False	1% level True	False
Translog	0.10	0.10	−7.108 (26.459)	6.581 (49.603)	−0.030 (5.044)	92.1	88.0	0	88.0	0	88.0	0
			−8.751 (20.415)	−0.799 (7.332)	−1.305 (4.445)	75.2						
			4.016 (5.404)	−0.342 (2.731)	0.445 (1.112)	91.0						
Rotterdam			4.318 (9.377)	2.764 (3.167)	0.439 (0.235)	51.2 (46.0)	48.0	32.0	32.0	22.0	24.0	14.0
			19.562 (33.438)	1.468 (8.865)	0.500 (0.215)	35.7 (32.0)						
			10.874 (14.842)	1.156 (1.508)	0.443 (0.259)	44.1 (38.0)						
Leontief			0.132 (0.068)	0.134 (0.038)	0.131 (0.012)	21.8	0	24.0	0	14.0	0	0
			0.131 (0.070)	0.128 (0.026)	0.133 (0.012)	23.1						
			0.151 (0.025)	0.114 (0.022)	0.129 (0.011)	21.4						
Trans3rd			0.178 (11.305)	26.945 (63.065)	0.641 (0.274)	96.6	100.0	100.0	100.0	100.0	100.0	100.0
			−1.592 (12.984)	−0.833 (16.463)	−0.407 (0.927)	93.5						
			−6.829 (38.586)	38.182 (85.298)	2.764 (5.059)	81.3						
Translog	0.30	0.30	0.069 (0.033)	0.116 (0.033)	0.288 (0.017)	48.6	12.0	10.0	2.0	6.0	0	0
			0.060 (0.029)	0.101 (0.015)	0.294 (0.012)	50.5						
			0.062 (0.032)	0.125 (0.029)	0.291 (0.017)	47.5						
Rotterdam			0.323 (0.073)	0.365 (0.074)	0.346 (0.052)	21.8 (8.0)	12.0	10.0	4.0	6.0	0	0
			0.321 (0.073)	0.354 (0.060)	0.351 (0.048)	20.8 (14.0)						
			0.322 (0.055)	0.366 (0.070)	0.347 (0.049)	21.9 (18.0)						
Leontief			0.328 (0.026)	0.326 (0.028)	0.299 (0.016)	21.5	20.0	18.0	4.0	12.0	2.0	4.0
			0.325 (0.024)	0.321 (0.012)	0.301 (0.011)	22.5						
			0.329 (0.022)	0.324 (0.022)	0.298 (0.016)	22.6						
Trans3rd			0.010 (0.040)	0.121 (0.048)	0.360 (0.019)	54.1	30.0	74.0	18.0	68.0	6.0	60.0
			0.022 (0.040)	0.179 (0.011)	0.358 (0.008)	48.0						
			0.091 (0.038)	0.161 (0.032)	0.390 (0.018)	42.7						

174

Table 1 *(cont.)*

Approximate function	True elasticities of substitution		Estimated elasticities of substitution			Regularity violation percentage	Separability rejection percentage					
							10% level		5% level		1% level	
	σ_{12}	σ_{13}	σ_{12}	σ_{13}	σ_{23}		True	False	True	False	True	False
Translog	0.60	0.60	0.582 (0.044)	0.596 (0.056)	0.594 (0.033)	28.5	34.0	12.0	24.0	6.0	4.0	0
			0.571 (0.036)	0.578 (0.017)	0.603 (0.016)	29.7						
			0.585 (0.046)	0.592 (0.045)	0.593 (0.036)	27.7						
Rotterdam			0.629 (0.123)	0.643 (0.112)	0.601 (0.098)	19.2 (20.0)	22.0	8.0	18.0	2.0	2.0	0
			0.623 (0.118)	0.620 (0.091)	0.613 (0.082)	18.8 (20.0)						
			0.622 (0.102)	0.652 (0.115)	0.607 (0.094)	20.2 (10.0)						
Leontief			0.597 (0.040)	0.609 (0.053)	0.594 (0.032)	27.4	34.0	12.0	18.0	6.0	4.0	0
			0.588 (0.033)	0.593 (0.016)	0.602 (0.016)	24.2						
			0.601 (0.041)	0.603 (0.042)	0.592 (0.035)	25.5						
Trans3rd			0.571 (0.056)	0.573 (0.079)	0.611 (0.041)	27.6	24.0	30.0	20.0	18.0	12.0	8.0
			0.566 (0.040)	0.595 (0.013)	0.619 (0.013)	30.3						
			0.572 (0.052)	0.580 (0.051)	0.625 (0.036)	29.7						
Translog	0.80	0.80	0.805 (0.055)	0.820 (0.074)	0.790 (0.044)	18.3	40.0	14.0	24.0	6.0	4.0	0
			0.791 (0.045)	0.797 (0.021)	0.802 (0.020)	15.8						
			0.809 (0.058)	0.810 (0.058)	0.788 (0.049)	17.9						
Rotterdam			0.848 (0.164)	0.844 (0.145)	0.784 (0.131)	15.4 (16.0)	22.0	4.0	18.0	2.0	4.0	0
			0.839 (0.157)	0.812 (0.117)	0.801 (0.107)	15.1 (12.0)						
			0.837 (0.137)	0.857 (0.151)	0.792 (0.127)	16.4 (20.0)						
Leontief			0.783 (0.052)	0.802 (0.072)	0.793 (0.044)	17.2	38.0	14.0	24.0	6.0	4.0	0
			0.769 (0.042)	0.780 (0.021)	0.805 (0.021)	14.9						
			0.788 (0.055)	0.795 (0.056)	0.791 (0.048)	16.5						
Trans3rd			0.793 (0.066)	0.779 (0.102)	0.802 (0.054)	17.5	26.0	28.0	20.0	18.0	12.0	8.0
			0.794 (0.047)	0.801 (0.018)	0.805 (0.018)	16.5						
			0.788 (0.062)	0.789 (0.062)	0.814 (0.046)	15.6						

Translog	1.00	1.00	1.012 (0.067)	1.029 (0.093)	0.986 (0.057)	15.9	58.0	36.0	36.0	24.0	6.0	10.0
			0.995 (0.038)	1.023 (0.014)	1.023 (0.014)	14.0						
			0.972 (0.057)	0.972 (0.057)	1.004 (0.057)	10.5						
Rotterdam			1.069 (0.207)	1.046 (0.180)	0.969 (0.165)	18.3 (16.0)	22.0	4.0	18.0	2.0	8.0	0
			1.058 (0.196)	1.007 (0.143)	0.991 (0.132)	18.0 (20.0)						
			1.055 (0.173)	1.065 (0.187)	0.980 (0.161)	19.7 (12.0)						
Leontief			0.971 (0.064)	0.996 (0.090)	0.992 (0.056)	12.5	40.0	12.0	24.0	4.0	4.0	0
			0.952 (0.051)	0.966 (0.025)	1.008 (0.025)	7.5						
			0.976 (0.069)	0.987 (0.070)	0.989 (0.062)	11.4						
Trans3rd			0.997 (0.076)	0.977 (0.127)	1.000 (0.066)	14.9	26.0	22.0	20.0	18.0	10.0	12.0
			1.001 (0.054)	1.002 (0.023)	1.002 (0.023)	13.4						
			0.990 (0.072)	0.990 (0.072)	1.012 (0.054)	11.5						
Translog	1.20	1.20	1.211 (0.079)	1.233 (0.111)	1.183 (0.069)	28.7	42.0	12.0	26.0	6.0	4.0	0
			1.190 (0.063)	1.199 (0.029)	1.201 (0.029)	31.2						
			1.224 (0.083)	1.225 (0.083)	1.176 (0.074)	30.1						
Rotterdam			1.291 (0.249)	1.250 (0.215)	1.155 (0.200)	20.7 (26.0)	22.0	2.0	18.0	2.0	10.0	0
			1.278 (0.237)	1.204 (0.169)	1.183 (0.157)	20.1 (14.0)						
			1.274 (0.209)	1.274 (0.224)	1.169 (0.196)	19.5 (26.0)						
Leontief			1.159 (0.076)	1.190 (0.109)	1.192 (0.068)	26.8	42.0	14.0	24.0	6.0	4.0	0
			1.136 (0.060)	1.154 (0.029)	1.212 (0.030)	28.0						
			1.165 (0.083)	1.181 (0.084)	1.189 (0.076)	25.5						
Trans3rd			1.193 (0.086)	1.173 (0.151)	1.202 (0.078)	25.6	26.0	22.0	20.0	18.0	10.0	10.0
			1.196 (0.061)	1.203 (0.027)	1.206 (0.028)	29.7						
			1.185 (0.081)	1.186 (0.081)	1.217 (0.062)	29.3						

Table 1 *(cont.)*

Approximate function	True elasticities of substitution		Estimated elasticities of substitution			Regularity violation percentage	Separability rejection percentage					
							10% level		5% level		1% level	
	σ_{12}	σ_{13}	σ_{12}	σ_{13}	σ_{23}		True	False	True	False	True	False
Translog	1.50	1.50	1.505 (0.098)	1.533 (0.139)	1.479 (0.087)	16.7	44.0	12.0	26.0	6.0	4.0	0
			1.478 (0.077)	1.489 (0.035)	1.503 (0.036)	13.9						
			1.515 (0.108)	1.519 (0.108)	1.474 (0.098)	17.0						
Rotterdam			1.627 (0.314)	1.557 (0.268)	1.435 (0.252)	16.9 (16.0)	22.0	2.0	18.0	2.0	10.0	0
			1.611 (0.298)	1.499 (0.209)	1.471 (0.194)	16.4 (26.0)						
			1.604 (0.263)	1.588 (0.279)	1.453 (0.249)	15.0 (16.0)						
Leontief			1.442 (0.095)	1.482 (0.137)	1.491 (0.087)	17.4	48.0	14.0	30.0	6.0	6.0	0
			1.390 (0.078)	1.427 (0.028)	1.507 (0.028)	16.7						
			1.449 (0.104)	1.471 (0.106)	1.488 (0.097)	16.2						
Trans3rd			1.483 (0.102)	1.468 (0.189)	1.508 (0.095)	16.8	32.0	22.0	20.0	18.0	12.0	10.0
			1.480 (0.072)	1.505 (0.035)	1.520 (0.035)	14.4						
			1.472 (0.097)	1.475 (0.098)	1.530 (0.076)	15.8						
Translog	3.00	3.00	2.947 (0.192)	2.998 (0.277)	2.961 (0.180)	13.7	46.0	14.0	26.0	10.0	6.0	0
			2.889 (0.148)	2.904 (0.068)	3.014 (0.070)	12.8						
			2.954 (0.215)	2.986 (0.217)	2.957 (0.203)	16.7						
Rotterdam			3.321 (0.639)	3.085 (0.533)	2.834 (0.515)	15.4 (22.0)	22.0	6.0	22.0	2.0	10.0	0
			3.287 (0.607)	2.973 (0.407)	2.911 (0.382)	16.5 (12.0)						
			3.267 (0.539)	3.161 (0.553)	2.877 (0.513)	15.7 (16.0)						
Leontief			2.866 (0.189)	2.932 (0.275)	2.981 (0.179)	18.9	48.0	14.0	28.0	10.0	6.0	0
			3.475 (0.012)	1.490 (0.005)	1.597 (0.005)	14.5						
			2.868 (0.212)	2.926 (0.215)	2.980 (0.202)	17.7						
Trans3rd			2.896 (0.189)	2.961 (0.374)	3.059 (0.182)	14.7	32.0	30.0	24.0	14.0	14.0	10.0
			2.834 (0.138)	3.022 (0.072)	3.140 (0.073)	12.4						
			2.869 (0.181)	2.894 (0.183)	3.128 (0.146)	11.2						

Translog	5.00	5.00	4.852 (0.318)	4.939 (0.463)	4.945 (0.304)	22.1	48.0	12.0	26.0	10.0	6.0	0
			4.750 (0.243)	4.778 (0.112)	5.038 (0.117)	20.7						
			4.855 (0.358)	4.931 (0.363)	4.943 (0.343)	20.7						
Rotterdam			5.580 (1.074)	5.129 (0.889)	4.704 (0.867)	18.2 (16.0)	22.0	6.0	22.0	2.0	10.0	0
			5.524 (1.019)	4.943 (0.672)	4.836 (0.633)	19.0 (28.0)						
			5.487 (0.910)	5.263 (0.919)	4.780 (0.865)	18.3 (22.0)						
Leontief			4.763 (0.314)	4.869 (0.461)	4.969 (0.303)	20.5	48.0	14.0	28.0	10.0	6.0	0
			4.659 (0.240)	4.702 (0.113)	5.066 (0.118)	19.7						
			4.761 (0.355)	4.867 (0.361)	4.970 (0.342)	21.1						
Trans3rd			4.758 (0.305)	4.966 (0.623)	5.138 (0.298)	20.4	34.0	32.0	30.0	18.0	16.0	10.0
			4.609 (0.234)	5.025 (0.123)	5.303 (0.127)	20.6						
			4.710 (0.294)	4.770 (0.298)	5.286 (0.242)	17.9						

Table 2. *Summary of experiments, for very low true elasticity of substitution in aggregator function*

Approximate function	True elasticities of substitution σ12	True elasticities of substitution σ13	Estimated elasticities of substitution σ12	Estimated elasticities of substitution σ13	Estimated elasticities of substitution σ23	Regularity violation percentage	Separability rejection percentage 10% level True	10% level False	5% level True	5% level False	1% level True	1% level False
Translog	0.10	0.10	−7.108 (26.459)	6.581 (49.603)	−0.030 (5.044)	92.1	88.0	0	88.0	0	88.0	0
			−8.751 (20.415)	−0.799 (7.332)	−1.305 (4.445)	75.2						
			4.016 (5.404)	−0.342 (2.731)	0.445 (1.112)	91.0						
Rotterdam			4.318 (9.377)	2.764 (3.167)	0.439 (0.235)	51.2 (46.0)	48.0	32.0	32.0	22.0	24.0	14.0
			19.562 (33.438)	1.468 (8.865)	0.500 (0.215)	35.7 (32.0)						
			10.874 (14.842)	1.156 (1.508)	0.443 (0.259)	44.1 (38.0)						
Leontief			0.132 (0.068)	0.134 (0.038)	0.131 (0.012)	21.8	0	24.0	0	14.0	0	0
			0.131 (0.070)	0.128 (0.026)	0.133 (0.012)	23.1						
			0.151 (0.025)	0.114 (0.022)	0.129 (0.011)	21.4						
Trans3rd			0.178 (11.305)	26.945 (63.065)	0.641 (0.274)	96.6	100.0	100.0	100.0	100.0	100.0	100.0
			−1.592 (12.984)	−0.833 (16.463)	−0.407 (0.927)	93.5						
			−6.829 (38.586)	38.182 (85.298)	2.764 (5.059)	81.3						
Translog	0.10	0.30	−0.028 (0.667)	−0.681 (1.658)	0.314 (0.036)	51.2	100.0	0	100.0	0	100.0	0
			2.294 (4.699)	5.767 (12.308)	0.697 (2.143)	72.4						
			0.220 (0.518)	−0.171 (1.447)	0.293 (0.029)	52.9						
Rotterdam			−0.124 (0.188)	0.040 (2.875)	0.353 (0.040)	32.1 (28.0)	16.0	84.0	8.0	78.0	0	48.0
			−0.039 (0.104)	1.036 (0.769)	0.355 (0.042)	33.4 (42.0)						
			0.109 (0.067)	0.265 (0.299)	0.249 (0.040)	33.6 (32.0)						
Leontief			−0.026 (0.026)	0.476 (0.044)	0.335 (0.012)	32.7	32.0	100.0	22.0	100.0	8.0	100.0
			−0.022 (0.026)	0.525 (0.027)	0.325 (0.013)	33.3						
			0.116 (0.016)	0.127 (0.018)	0.274 (0.012)	23.4						
Trans3rd			65.376 (129.430)	−2.293 (0.441)	33.281 (64.409)	86.6	100.0	100.0	100.0	100.0	100.0	100.0
			−0.269 (1.253)	−1.417 (0.309)	0.758 (0.403)	84.4						
			−1.789 (1.445)	−3.354 (0.849)	0.270 (0.492)	77.3						

0.10	0.60	Translog	1.120 (1.678)	1.119 (0.616)	0.465 (0.025)	33.9	100.0	100.0	100.0	100.0	100.0	98.0
			8.086 (15.887)	7.721 (14.419)	0.713 (0.031)	38.1						
			1.188 (3.512)	1.933 (6.777)	0.198 (0.015)	41.8						
		Rotterdam	−0.271 (0.312)	2.783 (3.190)	0.469 (0.054)	36.2 (16.0)	12.0	90.0	10.0	64.0	0	36.0
			−0.326 (0.455)	3.772 (5.023)	0.458 (0.065)	35.1 (32.0)						
			0.124 (0.082)	0.268 (0.220)	0.267 (0.040)	33.5 (34.0)						
		Leontief	−0.224 (0.032)	0.818 (0.059)	0.693 (0.021)	37.3	100.0	100.0	100.0	100.0	100.0	100.0
			−0.244 (0.029)	1.042 (0.042)	0.692 (0.022)	44.5						
			0.049 (0.019)	0.052 (0.020)	0.461 (0.016)	43.1						
		Trans3rd	−1.399 (0.200)	−0.247 (0.184)	0.663 (0.050)	75.5	62.0	100.0	54.0	100.0	32.0	100.0
			−1.450 (0.217)	−0.094 (0.131)	0.711 (0.014)	74.6						
			−0.980 (0.125)	−1.952 (0.261)	0.697 (0.017)	76.0						
0.10	0.80	Translog	0.475 (0.385)	0.918 (0.212)	0.526 (0.035)	34.2	100.0	100.0	100.0	96.0	100.0	36.0
			1.404 (2.940)	1.023 (0.153)	1.020 (0.009)	45.2						
			−2.107 (5.339)	−4.075 (9.456)	0.217 (0.015)	42.4						
		Rotterdam	−0.125 (0.154)	1.246 (0.918)	0.457 (0.060)	36.6 (26.0)	10.0	48.0	8.0	36.0	2.0	8.0
			−0.090 (0.268)	0.897 (1.874)	0.444 (0.078)	34.7 (22.0)						
			0.104 (0.106)	0.190 (0.252)	0.268 (0.041)	33.8 (42.0)						
		Leontief	−0.332 (0.037)	1.015 (0.068)	0.915 (0.030)	36.3	100.0	100.0	100.0	100.0	100.0	100.0
			−0.380 (0.033)	1.366 (0.054)	0.934 (0.032)	43.1						
			0.038 (0.017)	0.039 (0.017)	0.531 (0.015)	45.3						
		Trans3rd	−1.721 (0.273)	0.388 (0.169)	0.883 (0.056)	66.9	60.0	100.0	46.0	100.0	24.0	100.0
			−1.742 (0.313)	0.389 (0.115)	0.842 (0.020)	67.0						
			−1.054 (0.132)	−1.865 (0.239)	0.753 (0.017)	75.0						

Table 2 *(cont.)*

Approximate function	True elasticities of substitution σ12	σ13	Estimated elasticities of substitution σ12	σ13	σ23	Regularity violation percentage	Separability rejection percentage 10% level True	False	5% level True	False	1% level True	False
Translog	0.10	1.00	0.414 (0.280)	0.825 (0.215)	0.483 (0.049)	35.9	100.0	44.0	100.0	12.0	90.0	4.0
			-0.428 (1.504)	1.063 (0.092)	1.024 (0.013)	46.6						
			0.138 (0.703)	-0.106 (1.200)	0.220 (0.016)	42.5						
Rotterdam			-0.036 (0.117)	0.760 (0.790)	0.410 (0.065)	35.9 (24.0)	12.0	18.0	6.0	8.0	4.0	2.0
			0.001 (0.179)	0.868 (0.854)	0.406 (0.086)	37.3 (30.0)						
			0.059 (0.178)	0.084 (0.387)	0.267 (0.041)	32.0 (22.0)						
Leontief			-0.422 (0.041)	1.180 (0.074)	1.115 (0.039)	35.1	100.0	100.0	100.0	100.0	100.0	100.0
			-0.493 (0.037)	1.634 (0.071)	1.134 (0.049)	42.8						
			0.032 (0.017)	0.033 (0.018)	0.580 (0.016)	50.0						
Trans3rd			-2.133 (0.461)	0.926 (0.215)	1.053 (0.064)	61.1	58.0	100.0	40.0	100.0	28.0	100.0
			-1.909 (0.682)	0.945 (0.109)	0.985 (0.026)	61.0						
			-1.108 (0.139)	-1.825 (0.232)	0.792 (0.016)	75.1						
Translog	0.10	1.20	0.508 (0.281)	0.656 (0.234)	0.373 (0.058)	35.8	100.0	4.0	96.0	0	48.0	0
			-3.442 (5.404)	0.360 (0.860)	0.945 (0.022)	40.6						
			0.511 (0.564)	0.510 (0.934)	0.217 (0.016)	40.9						
Rotterdam			1.518 (2.937)	4.621 (7.962)	0.354 (0.069)	34.5 (30.0)	14.0	4.0	8.0	2.0	4.0	0
			0.039 (0.149)	0.808 (0.591)	0.361 (0.091)	37.3 (32.0)						
			-0.247 (0.737)	-0.498 (1.415)	0.265 (0.042)	33.0 (20.0)						
Leontief			-0.493 (0.044)	1.309 (0.079)	1.286 (0.047)	35.5	100.0	100.0	100.0	100.0	100.0	100.0
			-0.579 (0.042)	1.820 (0.092)	1.256 (0.072)	42.3						
			0.030 (0.018)	0.030 (0.019)	0.615 (0.017)	52.7						
Trans3rd			-3.534 (2.404)	1.587 (0.442)	1.201 (0.073)	59.3	46.0	100.0	36.0	100.0	20.0	100.0
			-0.259 (5.233)	1.124 (1.034)	1.139 (0.033)	61.8						
			-1.141 (0.143)	-1.793 (0.227)	0.819 (0.016)	76.3						

Table with parameter blocks. First block: 0.10, 1.50. Second block: 0.10, 3.00.

Model			%	%	%	%	%	%	Coeff 1 (s.e.)	Coeff 2 (s.e.)	Coeff 3 (s.e.)	
Translog	0.10	1.50	100.0	0	96.0	0	80.0	0	0.363 (0.165)	0.178 (0.261)	0.175 (0.064)	46.4
									6.140 (11.215)	3.080 (4.322)	0.859 (0.022)	35.7
									0.381 (0.169)	0.285 (0.272)	0.208 (0.016)	43.7
Rotterdam			24.0	0	14.0	0	4.0	0	0.076 (0.163)	0.365 (0.605)	0.276 (0.074)	40.0 (44.0)
									0.117 (0.153)	0.668 (0.501)	0.298 (0.099)	36.7 (30.0)
									0.281 (0.342)	0.462 (0.635)	0.262 (0.042)	34.2 (36.0)
Leontief			100.0	100.0	100.0	100.0	100.0	100.0	−0.564 (0.048)	1.430 (0.088)	1.481 (0.063)	36.7
									−0.698 (0.045)	2.074 (0.084)	1.402 (0.045)	44.7
									0.030 (0.016)	0.031 (0.016)	0.649 (0.018)	50.8
Trans3rd			30.0	100.0	20.0	100.0	18.0	100.0	−123.970 (243.561)	35.529 (68.237)	1.404 (0.090)	57.2
									−1.443 (5.873)	1.901 (2.396)	1.379 (0.044)	62.3
									−1.172 (0.147)	−1.756 (0.223)	0.847 (0.016)	74.6
Translog	0.10	3.00	6.0	6.0	6.0	6.0	6.0	4.0	−0.576 (5.818)	−0.091 (20.755)	4.518 (1.826)	55.7
									0.721 (0.259)	0.884 (0.246)	0.673 (0.019)	34.4
									0.609 (0.163)	0.618 (0.251)	0.164 (0.018)	47.0
Rotterdam			36.0	18.0	26.0	12.0	10.0	0	0.445 (0.227)	−0.233 (0.351)	0.066 (0.084)	78.3 (74.0)
									1.135 (1.666)	0.809 (1.590)	0.080 (0.163)	57.9 (54.0)
									0.156 (0.210)	0.234 (0.376)	0.251 (0.044)	34.0 (28.0)
Leontief			100.0	94.0	100.0	84.0	100.0	70.0	−0.435 (0.079)	1.057 (0.176)	1.484 (0.142)	38.7
									0.522 (0.132)	−0.592 (0.237)	−0.422 (0.168)	97.7
									0.033 (0.015)	0.033 (0.015)	0.717 (0.021)	46.8
Trans3rd			88.0	100.0	86.0	100.0	66.0	100.0	−3.176 (1.438)	1.157 (0.562)	1.406 (0.426)	62.7
									−2.730 (5.056)	2.514 (4.277)	4.027 (3.366)	68.3
									−1.225 (0.154)	−1.667 (0.212)	0.906 (0.017)	71.6

Table 2 *(cont.)*

Approximate function	True elasticities of substitution σ_{12}	σ_{13}	Estimated elasticities of substitution σ_{12}	σ_{13}	σ_{23}	Regularity violation percentage	Separability rejection percentage 10% level True	False	5% level True	False	1% level True	False
Translog	0.10	5.00	0.285 (4.514)	−4.253 (18.083)	3.843 (1.302)	60.6	14.0	14.0	14.0	14.0	14.0	14.0
			0.549 (0.111)	0.613 (0.130)	0.608 (0.018)	33.1						
			0.587 (0.212)	0.575 (0.324)	0.133 (0.019)	50.4						
Rotterdam			0.578 (0.461)	−0.767 (0.523)	−0.026 (0.089)	93.9 (96.0)	40.0	54.0	26.0	30.0	12.0	10.0
			−0.243 (1.389)	−0.667 (1.042)	−0.028 (0.170)	67.9 (60.0)						
			0.458 (0.517)	0.771 (0.935)	0.245 (0.045)	33.5 (22.0)						
Leontief			0.022 (0.106)	0.062 (0.229)	0.771 (0.182)	55.9	100.0	2.0	100.0	2.0	100.0	2.0
			1.037 (0.057)	−1.707 (0.126)	−1.140 (0.076)	100.0						
			0.033 (0.015)	0.033 (0.014)	0.746 (0.020)	48.5						
Trans3rd			−1.676 (0.324)	−0.733 (0.351)	0.542 (0.131)	70.8	100.0	100.0	100.0	100.0	100.0	100.0
			−1.374 (0.225)	−0.301 (0.299)	0.564 (0.086)	71.5						
			−1.238 (0.156)	−1.622 (0.208)	0.930 (0.017)	67.5						

Table 3. *Summary of experiments, for very low true elasticity of substitution between aggregates*

Approximate function	True elasticities of substitution		Estimated elasticities of substitution			Regularity violation percentage	Separability rejection percentage					
							10% level		5% level		1% level	
	σ_{12}	σ_{13}	σ_{12}	σ_{13}	σ_{23}		True	False	True	False	True	False
	0.10	0.10										
Translog			−7.108 (26.459)	6.581 (49.603)	−0.030 (5.044)	92.1	88.0	0	88.0	0	88.0	0
			−8.751 (20.415)	−0.799 (7.332)	−1.305 (4.445)	75.2						
			4.016 (5.404)	−0.342 (2.731)	0.445 (1.112)	91.0						
Rotterdam			4.318 (9.377)	2.764 (3.167)	0.439 (0.235)	51.2 (46.0)	48.0	32.0	32.0	22.0	24.0	14.0
			19.562 (33.438)	1.468 (8.865)	0.500 (0.215)	35.7 (32.0)						
			10.874 (14.842)	1.156 (1.508)	0.443 (0.259)	44.1 (38.0)						
Leontief			0.132 (0.068)	0.134 (0.038)	0.131 (0.012)	21.8	0	24.0	0	14.0	0	0
			0.131 (0.070)	0.128 (0.026)	0.133 (0.012)	23.1						
			0.151 (0.025)	0.114 (0.022)	0.129 (0.011)	21.4						
Trans3rd			0.178 (11.305)	26.945 (63.065)	0.641 (0.274)	96.6	100.0	100.0	100.0	100.0	100.0	100.0
			−1.592 (12.984)	−0.833 (16.463)	−0.407 (0.927)	93.5						
			−6.829 (38.586)	38.182 (85.298)	2.764 (5.059)	81.3						
	0.30	0.10										
Translog			−88.088 (288.251)	−3.574 (13.266)	0.950 (2.970)	81.3	0	100.0	0	100.0	0	92.0
			−4.296 (92.348)	−0.299 (5.277)	0.805 (3.232)	80.3						
			64.813 (204.714)	−5.289 (10.329)	1.029 (1.794)	72.3						
Rotterdam			39.364 (85.169)	0.226 (0.198)	0.432 (0.498)	31.5 (34.0)	24.0	38.0	22.0	30.0	14.0	12.0
			102.366 (162.403)	0.424 (0.268)	0.412 (0.413)	29.2 (22.0)						
			30.808 (45.874)	0.260 (0.165)	0.513 (0.433)	30.7 (24.0)						
Leontief			0.993 (0.093)	0.138 (0.017)	0.124 (0.014)	26.9	0	100.0	0	100.0	0	100.0
			0.990 (0.090)	0.136 (0.013)	0.126 (0.012)	27.5						
			1.066 (0.320)	1.649 (3.942)	−0.580 (2.930)	98.8						
Trans3rd			−197.462 (461.026)	18.299 (38.746)	6.664 (14.511)	84.9	94.0	100.0	78.0	100.0	50.0	100.0
			51.991 (98.732)	−7.427 (13.738)	−2.678 (5.976)	81.5						
			−32.400 (359.997)	0.623 (1.940)	0.426 (1.208)	71.5						

Table 3 (cont.)

Approximate function	True elasticities of substitution σ_{12}	σ_{13}	Estimated elasticities of substitution σ_{12}	σ_{13}	σ_{23}	Regularity violation percentage	Separability rejection percentage 10% level True	10% level False	5% level True	5% level False	1% level True	1% level False
Translog	0.60	0.10	−20.834 (69.139)	−0.196 (2.657)	−0.103 (1.558)	62.4	0	100.0	0	100.0	0	92.0
			88.689 (226.978)	2.202 (6.859)	−1.002 (3.030)	62.7						
			16.177 (125.591)	−1.634 (7.043)	−1.144 (5.327)	69.1						
Rotterdam			235.599 (584.901)	0.266 (0.268)	0.126 (0.877)	28.8 (30.0)	16.0	74.0	14.0	66.0	2.0	42.0
			285.132 (563.664)	0.318 (0.209)	0.341 (0.244)	29.0 (26.0)						
			237.133 (453.908)	0.268 (0.264)	−0.176 (1.220)	31.1 (24.0)						
Leontief			2.103 (0.170)	0.128 (0.014)	0.126 (0.015)	31.1	0	100.0	0	100.0	0	100.0
			2.095 (0.159)	0.126 (0.012)	0.127 (0.012)	30.8						
			1.282 (0.004)	3.337 (5.625)	−3.077 (7.324)	94.2						
Trans3rd			−90.865 (216.993)	−0.731 (1.675)	−0.048 (1.906)	67.2	12.0	100.0	10.0	100.0	6.0	100.0
			−0.1E+04 (********)[a]	13.803 (28.319)	6.573 (26.797)	64.4						
			239.867 (495.250)	0.276 (0.684)	−2.639 (4.896)	56.9						
Translog	0.80	0.10	−3.964 (12.815)	−0.580 (2.973)	−0.074 (2.460)	54.9	0	100.0	0	100.0	0	84.0
			1.429 (11.497)	−0.672 (3.024)	−0.447 (2.794)	54.9						
			12.945 (54.377)	−0.013 (0.658)	−0.461 (0.967)	67.8						
Rotterdam			1387.640 (********)[a]	0.709 (0.969)	0.613 (0.779)	30.8 (34.0)	18.0	86.0	12.0	80.0	2.0	54.0
			1337.687 (********)[a]	0.621 (0.778)	0.424 (0.296)	30.0 (24.0)						
			1423.917 (********)[a]	0.627 (0.853)	0.655 (0.477)	33.4 (16.0)						
Leontief			2.821 (0.228)	0.125 (0.013)	0.126 (0.016)	33.8	0	100.0	0	100.0	0	100.0
			2.814 (0.210)	0.123 (0.012)	0.128 (0.012)	33.5						
			1.319 (0.005)	1.121 (0.217)	−0.183 (0.320)	92.4						
Trans3rd			62.398 (259.420)	−1.858 (3.571)	0.018 (2.024)	64.7	10.0	100.0	8.0	100.0	4.0	100.0
			5310.019 (********)[a]	−18.884 (38.744)	−18.763 (37.017)	61.5						
			17.346 (126.371)	0.294 (0.740)	0.249 (0.641)	52.1						

Model													
Translog	1.00	0.10	32.402 (36.612)	−0.282 (0.415)	−0.388 (0.597)	56.0	0	100.0	0	100.0	0	98.0
			−319.920 (812.959)	3.269 (4.755)	2.119 (1.257)	57.6						
			17.069 (33.360)	0.418 (0.619)	−0.190 (0.582)	69.2						
Rotterdam			264.951 (624.341)	0.206 (0.137)	0.128 (0.524)	30.9 (22.0)	18.0	92.0	8.0	84.0	2.0	62.0
			84.120 (700.477)	0.251 (0.112)	−0.082 (1.007)	31.0 (32.0)						
			146.060 (276.815)	0.215 (0.178)	0.566 (0.416)	36.5 (30.0)						
Leontief			3.549 (0.284)	0.123 (0.012)	0.127 (0.016)	33.1	0	100.0	0	100.0	0	100.0
			3.541 (0.261)	0.122 (0.011)	0.128 (0.012)	33.0						
			1.935 (0.017)	1.834 (0.866)	−0.973 (1.143)	94.3						
Trans3rd			146.280 (355.309)	−0.470 (1.649)	−1.504 (1.853)	64.6	10.0	100.0	10.0	100.0	8.0	100.0
			0.1E+05 (********)[a]	−1.033 (1.408)	−43.237 (83.424)	60.1						
			−350.062 (688.710)	−4.739 (9.737)	0.180 (1.023)	58.9						
Translog	1.20	0.10	−502.766 (********)[a]	0.102 (0.246)	2.389 (4.530)	59.7	0	100.0	0	100.0	0	100.0
			55.803 (62.466)	0.119 (0.255)	0.133 (0.354)	57.6						
			−7.594 (42.566)	0.664 (0.676)	0.458 (0.821)	65.9						
Rotterdam			646.503 (********)[a]	0.195 (0.137)	0.367 (0.381)	31.7 (18.0)	18.0	98.0	8.0	88.0	0	70.0
			863.252 (********)[a]	0.240 (0.108)	0.239 (0.363)	31.7 (20.0)						
			390.452 (736.463)	0.186 (0.209)	0.489 (0.509)	38.5 (36.0)						
Leontief			4.255 (0.328)	0.123 (0.012)	0.128 (0.015)	33.5	0	100.0	0	100.0	0	100.0
			4.247 (0.304)	0.122 (0.011)	0.129 (0.012)	33.4						
			−0.918 (0.376)	0.291 (0.108)	1.229 (0.078)	91.9						
Trans3rd			269.281 (655.515)	0.091 (1.016)	−0.831 (1.371)	64.3	26.0	100.0	12.0	100.0	8.0	100.0
			440.361 (********)[a]	0.066 (1.308)	0.389 (2.085)	62.5						
			172.609 (475.039)	−1.186 (2.980)	0.665 (1.361)	78.9						

Table 3 (cont.)

Approximate function	True elasticities of substitution σ12	σ13	Estimated elasticities of substitution σ12	σ13	σ23	Regularity violation percentage	Separability rejection percentage 10% level True	10% False	5% level True	5% False	1% level True	1% False
Translog	1.50	0.10	261.459 (326.857)	0.435 (0.387)	-0.129 (1.063)	58.7	0	100.0	0	100.0	0	100.0
			464.354 (643.937)	0.400 (0.333)	-1.825 (3.639)	58.0						
			12.394 (24.798)	1.002 (0.667)	0.477 (0.591)	64.4						
Rotterdam			188.297 (427.724)	0.200 (0.130)	0.265 (0.199)	31.2 (18.0)	14.0	98.0	6.0	94.0	0	76.0
			237.328 (480.977)	0.234 (0.105)	0.242 (0.215)	34.1 (16.0)						
			14.285 (36.841)	0.142 (0.154)	0.404 (0.292)	39.0 (30.0)						
Leontief			5.316 (0.406)	0.123 (0.013)	0.128 (0.016)	36.4	0	100.0	0	100.0	0	100.0
			5.304 (0.377)	0.122 (0.012)	0.130 (0.012)	37.2						
			-0.905 (0.675)	-0.172 (1.707)	1.683 (3.862)	87.1						
Trans3rd			212.413 (********)[a]	0.479 (2.245)	-0.336 (1.580)	65.2	60.0	100.0	40.0	100.0	12.0	100.0
			*-0.3E+04 (********)[a]	-0.579 (1.194)	-0.647 (3.546)	58.0						
			-7.146 (61.995)	-0.302 (0.606)	-0.132 (0.187)	84.0						
Translog	3.00	0.10	103.252 (415.458)	0.853 (1.197)	1.428 (1.613)	58.5	0	100.0	0	100.0	0	100.0
			762.447 (********)[a]	1.428 (1.703)	0.738 (2.170)	58.9						
			1.923 (6.222)	0.551 (0.227)	-0.062 (0.690)	81.5						
Rotterdam			630.338 (********)[a]	0.204 (0.127)	0.305 (0.188)	34.3 (20.0)	10.0	100.0	6.0	96.0	0	80.0
			708.291 (********)[a]	0.233 (0.103)	0.296 (0.194)	35.3 (28.0)						
			36.398 (84.199)	0.376 (0.467)	0.194 (0.618)	43.0 (42.0)						
Leontief			10.678 (0.795)	0.122 (0.013)	0.129 (0.016)	36.7	0	100.0	0	100.0	0	100.0
			10.656 (0.736)	0.121 (0.012)	0.131 (0.012)	37.8						
			2.628 (0.037)	-0.321 (0.364)	2.184 (0.527)	79.2						
Trans3rd			-145.277 (858.455)	0.989 (3.638)	1.462 (4.453)	66.2	100.0	100.0	100.0	100.0	96.0	100.0
			-440.948 (********)[a]	0.112 (0.947)	-0.223 (0.690)	54.9						
			-21.291 (56.402)	-0.793 (0.779)	-0.166 (0.099)	88.8						

Translog	5.00	0.10	−0.1E+05 (*******)[a]	−4.674 (9.974)	4.069 (10.131)	62.4	0	100.0	0	100.0	0	100.0
			1086.578 (*******)[a]	−0.180 (2.968)	−1.676 (6.521)	63.4						
			−4.580 (15.300)	1.251 (0.039)	1.583 (0.413)	86.1						
Rotterdam			1283.105 (*******)[a]	0.206 (0.127)	0.290 (0.184)	35.7 (30.0)	6.0	100.0	6.0	98.0	0	84.0
			1427.773 (*******)[a]	0.234 (0.104)	0.318 (0.202)	36.3 (36.0)						
			−5.579 (56.625)	0.123 (0.155)	0.770 (0.671)	51.9 (52.0)						
Leontief			17.823 (1.314)	0.121 (0.013)	0.130 (0.016)	38.2	0	100.0	0	100.0	0	100.0
			17.787 (1.216)	0.120 (0.011)	0.131 (0.012)	39.6						
			2.950 (0.051)	−0.208 (0.487)	2.022 (0.717)	80.4						
Trans3rd			−850.537 (*******)[a]	0.033 (1.493)	1.472 (3.292)	70.0	100.0	100.0	100.0	100.0	100.0	100.0
			0.1E+06 (*******)[a]	0.513 (1.610)	−50.255 (99.034)	51.7						
			−30.139 (41.830)	−0.602 (0.295)	0.204 (0.815)	90.6						

[a] (*******) indicates a number greater than 1000.

187

Table 4. *Summary of experiments, for unitary true elasticity of substitution in aggregator function*

Approximate function	True elasticities of substitution		Estimated elasticities of substitution			Regularity violation percentage	Separability rejection percentage					
							10% level		5% level		1% level	
	σ_{12}	σ_{13}	σ_{12}	σ_{13}	σ_{23}		True	False	True	False	True	False
Translog	1.00	0.10	32.402 (36.612)	−0.282 (0.415)	−0.388 (0.597)	56.0	0	100.0	0	100.0	0	98.0
			−319.920 (812.959)	3.269 (4.755)	2.119 (1.257)	57.6						
			17.069 (33.360)	0.418 (0.619)	−0.190 (0.582)	69.2						
Rotterdam			264.951 (624.341)	0.206 (0.137)	0.128 (0.524)	30.9 (22.0)	18.0	92.0	8.0	84.0	2.0	62.0
			84.120 (700.477)	0.251 (0.112)	−0.082 (1.007)	31.0 (32.0)						
			146.060 (276.815)	0.215 (0.178)	0.566 (0.416)	36.5 (30.0)						
Leontief			3.549 (0.284)	0.123 (0.012)	0.127 (0.016)	33.1	0	100.0	0	100.0	0	100.0
			3.541 (0.261)	0.122 (0.011)	0.128 (0.012)	33.1						
			1.935 (0.017)	1.834 (0.866)	−0.973 (1.143)	94.3						
Trans3rd			146.280 (355.309)	−0.470 (1.649)	−1.504 (1.853)	64.6	10.0	100.0	10.0	100.0	8.0	100.0
			0.1E+05 (********)[a]	−1.033 (1.408)	−43.237 (83.424)	60.1						
			−350.062 (688.710)	−4.739 (9.737)	0.180 (1.023)	58.9						
Translog	1.00	0.30	1.456 (0.098)	0.269 (0.026)	0.266 (0.022)	25.0	24.0	100.0	10.0	100.0	2.0	100.0
			1.450 (0.070)	0.267 (0.012)	0.267 (0.012)	22.0						
			0.253 (0.303)	0.350 (0.264)	0.430 (0.038)	34.5						
Rotterdam			1.525 (0.216)	0.329 (0.059)	0.351 (0.062)	22.8 (20.0)	18.0	98.0	6.0	94.0	2.0	94.0
			1.522 (0.204)	0.326 (0.048)	0.352 (0.054)	22.7 (20.0)						
			0.979 (0.319)	0.441 (0.061)	0.454 (0.056)	19.5 (8.0)						
Leontief			1.391 (0.073)	0.303 (0.024)	0.308 (0.021)	25.9	16.0	100.0	14.0	100.0	2.0	100.0
			1.379 (0.055)	0.298 (0.011)	0.312 (0.011)	23.1						
			0.261 (0.025)	0.256 (0.024)	0.475 (0.016)	17.9						
Trans3rd			1.410 (0.086)	0.288 (0.045)	0.313 (0.029)	20.3	24.0	100.0	20.0	100.0	10.0	100.0
			1.446 (0.062)	0.305 (0.009)	0.304 (0.010)	22.7						
			0.120 (0.085)	0.285 (0.067)	0.478 (0.045)	32.2						

Translog	1.00	0.60	1.223 (0.078)	0.611 (0.054)	0.589 (0.039)	27.1	38.0	100.0	26.0	100.0	6.0	100.0
			1.206 (0.056)	0.597 (0.016)	0.598 (0.017)	25.4						
			0.777 (0.130)	0.781 (0.128)	0.719 (0.053)	21.1						
Rotterdam			1.257 (0.207)	0.632 (0.111)	0.606 (0.110)	19.5 (22.0)	22.0	68.0	18.0	52.0	4.0	36.0
			1.246 (0.193)	0.613 (0.086)	0.618 (0.088)	18.2 (18.0)						
			1.077 (0.197)	0.762 (0.107)	0.688 (0.102)	16.4 (16.0)						
Leontief			1.170 (0.070)	0.598 (0.052)	0.600 (0.039)	23.8	36.0	100.0	20.0	100.0	6.0	100.0
			1.153 (0.051)	0.584 (0.016)	0.610 (0.017)	22.2						
			0.690 (0.055)	0.701 (0.056)	0.741 (0.037)	19.3						
Trans3rd			1.198 (0.079)	0.584 (0.085)	0.610 (0.049)	21.0	34.0	100.0	24.0	100.0	14.0	100.0
			1.212 (0.053)	0.604 (0.014)	0.604 (0.014)	24.9						
			0.614 (0.077)	0.630 (0.075)	0.717 (0.047)	29.2						
Translog	1.00	0.80	1.114 (0.072)	0.822 (0.073)	0.788 (0.049)	16.0	44.0	100.0	26.0	100.0	4.0	90.0
			1.096 (0.054)	0.800 (0.020)	0.800 (0.021)	11.5						
			0.969 (0.091)	0.970 (0.090)	0.845 (0.056)	20.3						
Rotterdam			1.160 (0.207)	0.839 (0.146)	0.785 (0.139)	16.5 (22.0)	22.0	32.0	20.0	20.0	8.0	2.0
			1.149 (0.194)	0.809 (0.114)	0.803 (0.110)	14.5 (8.0)						
			1.071 (0.182)	0.930 (0.147)	0.838 (0.133)	15.7 (18.0)						
Leontief			1.068 (0.067)	0.797 (0.071)	0.796 (0.049)	13.9	38.0	98.0	24.0	98.0	4.0	86.0
			1.049 (0.051)	0.775 (0.020)	0.809 (0.021)	8.2						
			0.888 (0.066)	0.902 (0.067)	0.866 (0.051)	14.7						
Trans3rd			1.094 (0.077)	0.779 (0.107)	0.804 (0.057)	13.0	26.0	98.0	22.0	94.0	12.0	76.0
			1.103 (0.053)	0.802 (0.018)	0.802 (0.018)	12.6						
			0.928 (0.073)	0.929 (0.072)	0.817 (0.053)	18.3						

189

Table 4 (cont.)

Approximate function	True elasticities of substitution σ_{12}	σ_{13}	Estimated elasticities of substitution σ_{12}	σ_{13}	σ_{23}	Regularity violation percentage	Separability rejection percentage 10% level True	10% False	5% level True	5% False	1% level True	1% False
Translog	1.00	1.20	0.911 (0.062)	1.236 (0.111)	1.185 (0.062)	20.8	38.0	90.0	24.0	86.0	4.0	76.0
			0.895 (0.054)	1.201 (0.029)	1.201 (0.029)	25.4						
			0.950 (0.034)	0.950 (0.034)	1.163 (0.056)	17.9						
Rotterdam			0.977 (0.207)	1.254 (0.211)	1.155 (0.188)	20.8 (16.0)	22.0	12.0	18.0	8.0	8.0	0
			0.968 (0.198)	1.207 (0.172)	1.181 (0.153)	20.1 (10.0)						
			1.033 (0.167)	1.170 (0.224)	1.113 (0.187)	19.9 (26.0)						
Leontief			0.875 (0.061)	1.196 (0.109)	1.189 (0.061)	17.9	38.0	84.0	24.0	82.0	4.0	72.0
			0.858 (0.052)	1.158 (0.029)	1.207 (0.030)	17.8						
			0.970 (0.068)	0.976 (0.068)	1.136 (0.070)	16.3						
Trans3rd			0.900 (0.079)	1.176 (0.144)	1.199 (0.077)	21.6	24.0	72.0	20.0	60.0	8.0	38.0
			0.900 (0.054)	1.204 (0.028)	1.204 (0.028)	27.0						
			0.907 (0.069)	0.906 (0.069)	1.261 (0.054)	18.0						
Translog	1.00	1.50	0.763 (0.058)	1.543 (0.137)	1.483 (0.066)	19.2	36.0	100.0	22.0	100.0	4.0	100.0
			0.750 (0.054)	1.500 (0.036)	1.500 (0.035)	20.4						
			0.897 (0.058)	0.897 (0.058)	1.392 (0.072)	18.0						
Rotterdam			0.840 (0.208)	1.564 (0.253)	1.438 (0.217)	17.8 (18.0)	20.0	40.0	18.0	20.0	8.0	8.0
			0.833 (0.203)	1.505 (0.215)	1.466 (0.182)	18.7 (18.0)						
			0.997 (0.161)	1.280 (0.272)	1.299 (0.220)	18.6 (36.0)						
Leontief			0.735 (0.057)	1.494 (0.134)	1.483 (0.065)	19.0	42.0	100.0	22.0	100.0	4.0	100.0
			0.717 (0.053)	1.434 (0.027)	1.494 (0.027)	20.5						
			0.881 (0.066)	0.882 (0.066)	1.383 (0.078)	19.1						
Trans3rd			0.756 (0.102)	1.478 (0.165)	1.501 (0.101)	18.3	22.0	98.0	20.0	98.0	6.0	96.0
			0.753 (0.055)	1.506 (0.035)	1.506 (0.035)	20.8						
			0.740 (0.061)	0.737 (0.062)	1.603 (0.056)	19.6						

1.00	3.00	Translog	0.036 (0.062)	3.051 (0.219)	2.990 (0.069)	28.4	12.0	100.0	4.0	100.0	0	100.0
			0.038 (0.061)	2.996 (0.070)	2.996 (0.069)	30.0						
			0.543 (0.057)	0.551 (0.056)	2.428 (0.092)	31.5						
		Rotterdam	0.141 (0.235)	3.081 (0.408)	2.898 (0.325)	30.0 (30.0)	16.0	100.0	12.0	98.0	4.0	78.0
			0.150 (0.237)	2.996 (0.406)	2.906 (0.307)	30.4 (36.0)						
			0.854 (0.147)	1.358 (0.348)	1.979 (0.306)	16.8 (18.0)						
		Leontief	0.039 (0.062)	2.990 (0.218)	2.948 (0.068)	31.3	22.0	100.0	12.0	100.0	2.0	100.0
			0.042 (0.061)	2.845 (0.069)	2.963 (0.069)	28.7						
			0.529 (0.058)	0.514 (0.056)	2.401 (0.090)	32.7						
		Trans3rd	0.006 (0.152)	3.020 (0.255)	3.049 (0.174)	27.8	12.0	100.0	6.0	100.0	0	100.0
			0.032 (0.060)	3.018 (0.077)	3.021 (0.073)	28.9						
			0.387 (0.055)	0.373 (0.057)	2.592 (0.068)	32.6						
1.00	5.00	Translog	−0.911 (0.091)	5.029 (0.277)	4.998 (0.119)	40.4	2.0	100.0	0	100.0	0	100.0
			−0.904 (0.078)	4.994 (0.117)	4.993 (0.115)	40.1						
			0.400 (0.050)	0.422 (0.048)	3.142 (0.078)	27.3						
		Rotterdam	−0.791 (0.305)	5.058 (0.581)	4.881 (0.463)	38.3 (42.0)	20.0	100.0	12.0	100.0	4.0	100.0
			−0.768 (0.306)	4.966 (0.620)	4.853 (0.453)	39.9 (30.0)						
			0.767 (0.137)	1.263 (0.317)	2.396 (0.330)	17.6 (18.0)						
		Leontief	−0.885 (0.091)	4.986 (0.284)	4.891 (0.119)	40.1	28.0	100.0	12.0	100.0	0	100.0
			−0.825 (0.078)	4.650 (0.113)	4.843 (0.114)	34.2						
			0.391 (0.056)	0.371 (0.053)	3.086 (0.084)	29.4						
		Trans3rd	−0.934 (0.226)	5.047 (0.352)	5.048 (0.279)	41.8	12.0	100.0	6.0	100.0	0	100.0
			−0.919 (0.070)	5.029 (0.135)	5.037 (0.125)	44.2						
			0.308 (0.052)	0.292 (0.054)	3.189 (0.075)	28.2						

[a] (*******) indicates a number greater than 1,000.

Table 5. *Summary of experiments, for unitary true elasticity of substitution between aggregates*

Approximate function	True elasticities of substitution		Estimated elasticities of substitution			Regularity violation percentage	Separability rejection percentage					
							10% level		5% level		1% level	
	σ_{12}	σ_{13}	σ_{12}	σ_{13}	σ_{23}		True	False	True	False	True	False
Translog	0.10	1.00	0.414 (0.280)	0.825 (0.215)	0.483 (0.049)	35.9	100.0	44.0	100.0	12.0	90.0	4.0
			−0.428 (1.504)	1.063 (0.092)	1.024 (0.013)	46.6						
			0.138 (0.703)	−0.106 (1.200)	0.220 (0.016)	42.5						
Rotterdam			−0.036 (0.117)	0.760 (0.790)	0.410 (0.065)	35.9 (24.0)	12.0	18.0	6.0	8.0	4.0	2.0
			0.001 (0.179)	0.868 (0.854)	−0.406 (0.086)	37.3 (30.0)						
			0.059 (0.178)	0.084 (0.387)	0.267 (0.041)	32.0 (22.0)						
Leontief			−0.422 (0.041)	1.180 (0.074)	1.115 (0.039)	35.1	100.0	100.0	100.0	100.0	100.0	100.0
			−0.493 (0.037)	1.634 (0.071)	1.134 (0.049)	42.8						
			0.032 (0.017)	0.033 (0.018)	0.580 (0.016)	50.0						
Trans3rd			−2.133 (0.461)	0.926 (0.215)	1.053 (0.064)	61.1	58.0	100.0	40.0	100.0	28.0	100.0
			−1.909 (0.682)	0.945 (0.109)	0.985 (0.026)	61.0						
			−1.108 (0.139)	−1.825 (0.232)	0.792 (0.016)	75.1						
Translog	0.30	1.00	−0.047 (0.027)	1.035 (0.073)	1.000 (0.026)	37.2	22.0	100.0	8.0	100.0	2.0	100.0
			−0.032 (0.021)	0.966 (0.008)	0.973 (0.007)	26.1						
			0.175 (0.021)	0.148 (0.022)	0.766 (0.026)	32.0						
Rotterdam			−0.030 (0.084)	1.136 (0.158)	0.969 (0.102)	35.0 (20.0)	18.0	100.0	10.0	96.0	4.0	82.0
			−0.022 (0.084)	1.076 (0.165)	0.973 (0.100)	32.7 (20.0)						
			0.253 (0.047)	0.412 (0.111)	0.636 (0.091)	21.1 (26.0)						
Leontief			−0.050 (0.026)	1.033 (0.072)	1.020 (0.025)	34.3	20.0	100.0	14.0	100.0	2.0	100.0
			−0.052 (0.025)	1.076 (0.027)	1.017 (0.025)	40.0						
			0.168 (0.022)	0.167 (0.022)	0.800 (0.028)	32.4						
Trans3rd			−0.097 (0.054)	0.984 (0.092)	1.023 (0.060)	36.8	12.0	100.0	10.0	100.0	4.0	100.0
			−0.078 (0.031)	1.002 (0.025)	1.002 (0.021)	40.9						
			0.030 (0.039)	−0.018 (0.040)	0.926 (0.032)	61.2						

Method													
Translog	0.60	1.00	0.404 (0.036)	1.032 (0.091)	0.991 (0.039)	26.0	44.0	100.0	28.0	100.0	4.0	100.0
			0.392 (0.028)	1.025 (0.012)	1.023 (0.011)	30.0						
			0.508 (0.041)	0.507 (0.041)	0.918 (0.048)	17.9						
Rotterdam			0.442 (0.126)	1.063 (0.172)	0.967 (0.136)	24.5 (16.0)	18.0	52.0	14.0	40.0	6.0	16.0
			0.439 (0.124)	1.019 (0.150)	0.985 (0.120)	22.4 (28.0)						
			0.580 (0.095)	0.797 (0.180)	0.845 (0.138)	17.6 (20.0)						
Leontief			0.399 (0.035)	1.011 (0.088)	0.989 (0.039)	27.4	32.0	100.0	14.0	100.0	4.0	100.0
			0.392 (0.034)	0.984 (0.025)	0.998 (0.025)	26.9						
			0.510 (0.041)	0.509 (0.041)	0.913 (0.048)	16.6						
Trans3rd			0.402 (0.079)	0.980 (0.106)	0.995 (0.068)	26.7	22.0	100.0	18.0	100.0	2.0	100.0
			0.397 (0.040)	1.002 (0.023)	1.002 (0.022)	30.1						
			0.387 (0.051)	0.378 (0.051)	1.077 (0.041)	20.0						
Translog	0.80	1.00	0.708 (0.050)	1.031 (0.093)	0.988 (0.049)	19.4	62.0	96.0	38.0	88.0	10.0	80.0
			0.683 (0.025)	1.023 (0.010)	1.022 (0.010)	22.0						
			0.793 (0.056)	0.793 (0.056)	0.939 (0.056)	9.2						
Rotterdam			0.755 (0.164)	1.052 (0.176)	0.967 (0.154)	18.2 (28.0)	22.0	16.0	18.0	10.0	6.0	2.0
			0.748 (0.159)	1.011 (0.146)	0.989 (0.127)	16.2 (24.0)						
			0.816 (0.131)	0.957 (0.187)	0.922 (0.152)	16.4 (16.0)						
Leontief			0.686 (0.049)	1.022 (0.090)	0.989 (0.049)	18.5	36.0	96.0	24.0	88.0	4.0	80.0
			0.673 (0.043)	0.972 (0.025)	1.003 (0.025)	15.3						
			0.773 (0.054)	0.777 (0.055)	0.940 (0.056)	8.5						
Trans3rd			0.700 (0.071)	0.978 (0.118)	0.997 (0.065)	16.9	24.0	82.0	20.0	74.0	8.0	62.0
			0.699 (0.047)	1.002 (0.023)	1.002 (0.023)	17.6						
			0.705 (0.060)	0.704 (0.061)	1.058 (0.047)	6.0						

Table 5 *(cont.)*

Approximate function	True elasticities of substitution σ_{12}	σ_{13}	Estimated elasticities of substitution σ_{12}	σ_{13}	σ_{23}	Regularity violation percentage	Separability rejection percentage 10% level True	False	5% level True	False	1% level True	False
Translog	1.20	1.00	1.316 (0.084)	1.028 (0.092)	0.985 (0.062)	23.4	68.0	90.0	56.0	88.0	22.0	64.0
			1.240 (0.056)	0.980 (0.012)	0.980 (0.013)	18.0						
			1.151 (0.074)	1.152 (0.075)	1.052 (0.063)	23.1						
Rotterdam			1.383 (0.250)	1.043 (0.182)	0.970 (0.173)	19.2 (10.0)	22.0	26.0	20.0	14.0	10.0	2.0
			1.370 (0.235)	1.005 (0.141)	0.994 (0.135)	17.3 (18.0)						
			1.294 (0.218)	1.141 (0.184)	1.026 (0.168)	20.7 (26.0)						
Leontief			1.255 (0.080)	0.992 (0.090)	0.996 (0.061)	19.4	44.0	88.0	24.0	86.0	4.0	62.0
			1.232 (0.060)	0.964 (0.025)	1.012 (0.025)	17.7						
			1.085 (0.080)	1.105 (0.082)	1.065 (0.066)	19.5						
Trans3rd			1.293 (0.089)	0.975 (0.131)	1.003 (0.069)	22.0	30.0	86.0	22.0	80.0	10.0	60.0
			1.303 (0.060)	1.002 (0.022)	1.002 (0.023)	22.4						
			1.153 (0.084)	1.152 (0.083)	1.006 (0.064)	20.6						
Translog	1.50	1.00	1.770 (0.110)	1.027 (0.091)	0.984 (0.067)	16.0	60.0	100.0	40.0	100.0	18.0	100.0
			1.729 (0.039)	1.022 (0.011)	1.023 (0.012)	16.4						
			1.201 (0.091)	1.202 (0.091)	1.175 (0.066)	31.3						
Rotterdam			1.853 (0.315)	1.040 (0.183)	0.972 (0.181)	18.2 (26.0)	22.0	52.0	22.0	38.0	10.0	22.0
			1.835 (0.293)	1.004 (0.139)	0.996 (0.138)	18.2 (14.0)						
			1.654 (0.290)	1.218 (0.180)	1.079 (0.175)	19.3 (14.0)						
Leontief			1.678 (0.103)	0.989 (0.089)	1.000 (0.066)	19.3	44.0	100.0	26.0	100.0	4.0	100.0
			1.650 (0.073)	0.962 (0.025)	1.018 (0.026)	21.5						
			1.131 (0.091)	1.161 (0.093)	1.186 (0.067)	28.0						
Trans3rd			1.737 (0.112)	0.972 (0.134)	1.007 (0.076)	16.8	30.0	100.0	24.0	100.0	10.0	100.0
			1.754 (0.071)	1.002 (0.022)	1.002 (0.023)	17.5						
			1.108 (0.101)	1.107 (0.100)	1.105 (0.074)	25.5						

Translog	3.00	1.00	4.038 (0.233)	1.024 (0.087)	0.983 (0.077)	17.3	68.0	100.0	56.0	100.0	30.0	100.0
			4.023 (0.043)	1.038 (0.008)	1.040 (0.009)	16.8						
			0.920 (0.108)	0.919 (0.110)	1.532 (0.056)	22.2						
Rotterdam			4.210 (0.643)	1.035 (0.183)	0.977 (0.197)	21.9 (24.0)	26.0	96.0	18.0	94.0	6.0	90.0
			4.174 (0.589)	1.001 (0.134)	1.002 (0.144)	20.5 (18.0)						
			3.564 (0.711)	1.367 (0.166)	1.207 (0.188)	20.6 (20.0)						
Leontief			3.799 (0.217)	0.983 (0.086)	1.012 (0.076)	24.5	42.0	100.0	30.0	100.0	8.0	100.0
			3.744 (0.140)	0.960 (0.025)	1.030 (0.026)	24.9						
			0.949 (0.343)	0.961 (0.304)	0.743 (1.502)	27.3						
Trans3rd			3.971 (0.231)	0.969 (0.125)	1.016 (0.091)	17.3	36.0	100.0	24.0	100.0	12.0	100.0
			4.011 (0.133)	1.000 (0.023)	1.000 (0.024)	15.9						
			1.161 (0.094)	0.171 (0.092)	1.754 (0.078)	52.1						
Translog	5.00	1.00	7.058 (0.392)	1.023 (0.085)	0.982 (0.081)	34.1	98.0	100.0	98.0	100.0	94.0	100.0
			5.967 (0.019)	0.954 (0.005)	0.951 (0.006)	25.0						
			0.744 (0.210)	0.739 (0.214)	1.650 (0.069)	23.8						
Rotterdam			7.354 (1.078)	1.033 (0.182)	0.981 (0.202)	26.1 (28.0)	28.0	100.0	18.0	100.0	6.0	98.0
			7.296 (0.984)	1.001 (0.132)	1.005 (0.146)	28.5 (30.0)						
			6.409 (1.259)	1.405 (0.167)	1.257 (0.197)	23.1 (18.0)						
Leontief			6.628 (0.366)	0.981 (0.084)	1.018 (0.080)	31.1	44.0	100.0	32.0	100.0	8.0	100.0
			6.538 (0.230)	0.960 (0.025)	1.036 (0.026)	29.5						
			4.923 (0.211)	−1.289 (5.678)	7.216 (28.771)	100.0						
Trans3rd			6.976 (0.385)	0.975 (0.112)	1.015 (0.095)	29.6	36.0	100.0	24.0	100.0	8.0	100.0
			7.019 (0.220)	0.998 (0.026)	0.998 (0.028)	32.5						
			−0.107 (0.082)	−0.090 (0.078)	2.016 (0.075)	92.3						

Table 6. *Summary of experiments, for one true elasticity of substitution approximately twice as big as the others*

Approximate function	True elasticities of substitution σ_{12}	σ_{13}	Estimated elasticities of substitution σ_{12}	σ_{13}	σ_{23}	Regularity violation percentage	Separability rejection percentage 10% level True	10% False	5% level True	5% False	1% level True	1% False
Translog	0.10	0.30	−0.028 (0.667)	−0.681 (1.658)	0.314 (0.036)	51.2	100.0	0	100.0	0	100.0	0
			2.294 (4.699)	5.767 (12.308)	0.697 (2.143)	72.4						
			0.220 (0.518)	−0.171 (1.447)	0.293 (0.029)	52.9						
Rotterdam			−0.124 (0.188)	0.040 (2.875)	0.353 (0.040)	32.1 (28.0)	16.0	84.0	8.0	78.0	0	48.0
			−0.039 (0.104)	1.036 (0.769)	0.355 (0.042)	33.4 (42.0)						
			0.109 (0.067)	0.265 (0.299)	0.249 (0.040)	33.6 (32.0)						
Leontief			−0.026 (0.026)	0.476 (0.044)	0.335 (0.012)	32.7	32.0	100.0	22.0	100.0	8.0	100.0
			−0.022 (0.026)	0.525 (0.027)	0.325 (0.013)	33.3						
			0.116 (0.016)	0.127 (0.018)	0.274 (0.012)	23.4						
Trans3rd			65.376 (129.430)	−2.293 (0.441)	33.281 (64.409)	86.6	100.0	100.0	100.0	100.0	100.0	100.0
			−0.269 (1.253)	−1.417 (0.309)	0.758 (0.403)	84.4						
			−1.789 (1.445)	−3.354 (0.849)	0.270 (0.492)	77.3						
Translog	0.30	0.10	−88.088 (288.251)	−3.574 (13.266)	0.950 (2.970)	81.3	0	100.0	0	100.0	0	92.0
			−4.296 (92.348)	−0.299 (5.277)	0.805 (3.232)	80.3						
			64.813 (204.714)	−5.289 (10.329)	1.029 (1.794)	72.3						
Rotterdam			39.364 (85.169)	0.226 (0.198)	0.432 (0.498)	31.5 (34.0)	24.0	38.0	22.0	30.0	14.0	12.0
			102.366 (162.403)	0.424 (0.268)	0.412 (0.413)	29.2 (22.0)						
			30.808 (45.874)	0.260 (0.165)	0.513 (0.433)	30.7 (24.0)						
Leontief			0.993 (0.093)	0.138 (0.017)	0.124 (0.014)	26.9	0	100.0	0	100.0	0	100.0
			0.990 (0.090)	0.136 (0.013)	0.126 (0.012)	27.5						
			1.066 (0.320)	1.649 (3.942)	−0.580 (2.930)	98.8						
Trans3rd			−197.462 (461.026)	18.299 (38.746)	6.664 (14.511)	84.9	94.0	100.0	78.0	100.0	50.0	100.0
			51.991 (98.732)	−7.427 (13.738)	−2.678 (5.976)	81.5						
			−32.400 (359.997)	0.623 (1.940)	0.426 (1.208)	71.5						

Translog	0.30	0.60	0.130 (0.023)	0.555 (0.058)	0.581 (0.020)	34.5	42.0	100.0	30.0	100.0	8.0	100.0
			0.123 (0.023)	0.493 (0.020)	0.596 (0.016)	34.1						
			0.200 (0.022)	0.181 (0.023)	0.529 (0.023)	26.9						
Rotterdam			0.159 (0.070)	0.702 (0.118)	0.600 (0.075)	29.7 (30.0)	16.0	70.0	14.0	66.0	4.0	38.0
			0.159 (0.070)	0.663 (0.108)	0.611 (0.071)	25.8 (20.0)						
			0.281 (0.049)	0.432 (0.112)	0.494 (0.076)	20.0 (14.0)						
Leontief			0.153 (0.022)	0.636 (0.052)	0.602 (0.021)	28.7	20.0	100.0	8.0	100.0	0	100.0
			0.153 (0.023)	0.638 (0.018)	0.602 (0.016)	30.7						
			0.249 (0.024)	0.250 (0.024)	0.540 (0.025)	14.0						
Trans3rd			0.084 (0.050)	0.520 (0.069)	0.619 (0.039)	38.5	24.0	100.0	18.0	100.0	4.0	100.0
			0.055 (0.033)	0.560 (0.014)	0.649 (0.011)	39.2						
			0.216 (0.056)	0.186 (0.053)	0.637 (0.026)	27.8						
Translog	0.60	0.30	0.640 (0.062)	0.238 (0.028)	0.282 (0.021)	28.3	40.0	100.0	28.0	100.0	8.0	100.0
			1.815 (0.003)	1.002 (0.000)	1.002 (0.000)	13.2						
			0.433 (0.369)	0.497 (0.327)	0.338 (0.068)	31.6						
Rotterdam			0.834 (0.130)	0.335 (0.063)	0.348 (0.059)	21.0 (14.0)	16.0	78.0	2.0	74.0	0	48.0
			0.830 (0.125)	0.330 (0.051)	0.351 (0.052)	20.8 (20.0)						
			0.619 (0.136)	0.420 (0.057)	0.412 (0.052)	16.2 (14.0)						
Leontief			0.785 (0.046)	0.309 (0.025)	0.303 (0.019)	23.2	18.0	100.0	12.0	100.0	2.0	100.0
			0.777 (0.036)	0.302 (0.011)	0.307 (0.011)	23.5						
			0.367 (0.029)	0.360 (0.028)	0.399 (0.016)	17.2						
Trans3rd			0.618 (0.049)	0.251 (0.046)	0.328 (0.025)	20.6	26.0	100.0	20.0	100.0	10.0	100.0
			0.658 (0.043)	0.274 (0.009)	0.321 (0.009)	21.8						
			0.265 (0.053)	0.380 (0.042)	0.380 (0.036)	24.8						

Table 6 (cont.)

Approximate function	True elasticities of substitution σ12	σ13	Estimated elasticities of substitution σ12	σ13	σ23	Regularity violation percentage	Separability rejection percentage 10% level True	False	5% level True	False	1% level True	False
Translog	0.60	1.20	0.307 (0.035)	1.243 (0.105)	1.193 (0.040)	34.1	30.0	100.0	10.0	100.0	2.0	100.0
			0.303 (0.036)	1.213 (0.030)	1.201 (0.029)	37.5						
			0.450 (0.039)	0.449 (0.039)	1.078 (0.051)	16.8						
Rotterdam			0.349 (0.130)	1.271 (0.196)	1.156 (0.152)	27.9 (44.0)	18.0	74.0	14.0	68.0	4.0	36.0
			0.349 (0.128)	1.220 (0.179)	1.173 (0.138)	26.2 (24.0)						
			0.559 (0.093)	0.821 (0.199)	0.948 (0.154)	16.7 (22.0)						
Leontief			0.302 (0.035)	1.211 (0.101)	1.188 (0.040)	33.6	30.0	100.0	10.0	100.0	2.0	100.0
			0.298 (0.035)	1.180 (0.029)	1.196 (0.029)	35.6						
			0.448 (0.040)	0.445 (0.039)	1.072 (0.052)	15.6						
Trans3rd			0.308 (0.084)	1.186 (0.118)	1.197 (0.077)	30.6	18.0	100.0	12.0	100.0	4.0	100.0
			0.311 (0.041)	1.207 (0.029)	1.196 (0.027)	38.6						
			0.293 (0.049)	0.278 (0.049)	1.258 (0.043)	29.2						
Translog	1.20	0.60	1.546 (0.095)	0.614 (0.053)	0.586 (0.041)	24.0	36.0	100.0	16.0	100.0	2.0	100.0
			1.708 (0.002)	1.004 (0.000)	1.004 (0.000)	13.1						
			0.765 (0.152)	0.770 (0.149)	0.777 (0.049)	22.0						
Rotterdam			1.572 (0.250)	0.630 (0.111)	0.607 (0.112)	20.5 (26.0)	22.0	82.0	18.0	76.0	4.0	54.0
			1.560 (0.232)	0.612 (0.085)	0.619 (0.089)	20.3 (20.0)						
			1.309 (0.253)	0.791 (0.105)	0.714 (0.105)	16.6 (18.0)						
Leontief			1.457 (0.084)	0.596 (0.051)	0.603 (0.041)	20.8	38.0	100.0	22.0	100.0	6.0	100.0
			1.436 (0.060)	0.582 (0.016)	0.612 (0.017)	17.9						
			0.645 (0.054)	0.658 (0.055)	0.805 (0.036)	14.7						
Trans3rd			1.513 (0.094)	0.585 (0.084)	0.611 (0.052)	21.5	34.0	100.0	22.0	100.0	10.0	100.0
			1.530 (0.061)	0.606 (0.014)	0.599 (0.015)	22.2						
			0.450 (0.085)	0.474 (0.081)	0.820 (0.050)	22.7						

Translog	0.80	1.50	0.463 (0.045)	1.548 (0.132)	1.488 (0.053)	18.3	34.0	100.0	14.0	100.0	2.0	100.0
			0.457 (0.045)	1.510 (0.036)	1.499 (0.035)	21.0						
			0.628 (0.052)	0.629 (0.052)	1.357 (0.069)	19.6						
Rotterdam			0.525 (0.170)	1.568 (0.243)	1.440 (0.197)	19.1 (20.0)	18.0	68.0	14.0	56.0	4.0	24.0
			0.523 (0.168)	1.510 (0.217)	1.462 (0.174)	19.0 (20.0)						
			0.759 (0.124)	1.082 (0.254)	1.208 (0.201)	18.6 (8.0)						
Leontief			0.449 (0.045)	1.501 (0.128)	1.481 (0.053)	18.2	30.0	100.0	14.0	100.0	4.0	100.0
			0.439 (0.045)	1.446 (0.031)	1.491 (0.031)	19.1						
			0.614 (0.052)	0.610 (0.052)	1.350 (0.068)	16.7						
Trans3rd			0.461 (0.106)	1.485 (0.150)	1.501 (0.101)	18.1	22.0	100.0	14.0	100.0	4.0	100.0
			0.465 (0.049)	1.508 (0.037)	1.498 (0.035)	22.9						
			0.446 (0.053)	0.436 (0.054)	1.570 (0.051)	25.7						
Translog	1.50	0.80	1.888 (0.114)	0.823 (0.071)	0.785 (0.055)	11.2	46.0	100.0	26.0	100.0	4.0	100.0
			1.861 (0.079)	0.804 (0.020)	0.798 (0.021)	12.5						
			0.974 (0.091)	0.974 (0.091)	1.031 (0.052)	19.0						
Rotterdam			1.945 (0.315)	0.834 (0.147)	0.789 (0.149)	14.3 (14.0)	22.0	78.0	18.0	70.0	6.0	46.0
			1.928 (0.291)	0.806 (0.111)	0.807 (0.114)	13.9 (16.0)						
			1.665 (0.310)	1.030 (0.140)	0.915 (0.142)	16.6 (24.0)						
Leontief			1.777 (0.105)	0.791 (0.069)	0.803 (0.055)	14.5	40.0	100.0	26.0	100.0	4.0	100.0
			1.750 (0.073)	0.771 (0.021)	0.817 (0.021)	15.0						
			0.868 (0.073)	0.893 (0.075)	1.050 (0.050)	9.6						
Trans3rd			1.850 (0.115)	0.777 (0.109)	0.809 (0.066)	14.6	34.0	100.0	24.0	100.0	8.0	100.0
			1.872 (0.072)	0.803 (0.018)	0.796 (0.019)	11.1						
			0.640 (0.090)	0.648 (0.088)	1.049 (0.063)	7.3						

Table 6 *(cont.)*

Approximate function	True elasticities of substitution σ12	σ13	Estimated elasticities of substitution σ12	σ13	σ23	Regularity violation percentage	Separability rejection percentage 10% level True	False	5% level True	False	1% level True	False
Translog	1.50	3.00	0.773 (0.082)	3.043 (0.256)	2.968 (0.101)	17.3	30.0	100.0	16.0	100.0	2.0	100.0
			0.759 (0.080)	2.943 (0.069)	2.998 (0.069)	16.5						
			1.017 (0.096)	1.017 (0.095)	2.755 (0.129)	19.3						
Rotterdam			0.933 (0.323)	3.093 (0.464)	2.878 (0.390)	19.6 (32.0)	18.0	76.0	16.0	68.0	4.0	36.0
			0.930 (0.316)	2.995 (0.416)	2.915 (0.341)	21.5 (18.0)						
			1.420 (0.234)	2.052 (0.486)	2.356 (0.400)	19.4 (18.0)						
Leontief			0.752 (0.081)	2.974 (0.253)	2.955 (0.101)	19.7	32.0	100.0	16.0	100.0	4.0	100.0
			0.731 (0.080)	2.836 (0.068)	2.997 (0.070)	18.9						
			1.072 (0.093)	1.058 (0.092)	2.669 (0.134)	15.2						
Trans3rd			0.716 (0.189)	2.988 (0.296)	3.064 (0.202)	18.3	14.0	100.0	12.0	100.0	2.0	100.0
			0.714 (0.077)	3.008 (0.074)	3.066 (0.073)	18.7						
			0.880 (0.074)	0.878 (0.076)	2.996 (0.086)	19.6						
Translog	3.00	1.50	3.718 (0.225)	1.524 (0.135)	1.483 (0.111)	9.3	48.0	100.0	28.0	100.0	6.0	100.0
			3.658 (0.147)	1.484 (0.035)	1.512 (0.037)	9.7						
			1.637 (0.142)	1.655 (0.146)	2.035 (0.100)	13.2						
Rotterdam			3.991 (0.647)	1.552 (0.277)	1.439 (0.288)	16.4 (20.0)	24.0	86.0	18.0	74.0	10.0	54.0
			3.952 (0.595)	1.497 (0.202)	1.482 (0.207)	14.7 (12.0)						
			3.472 (0.643)	1.933 (0.261)	1.680 (0.279)	17.3 (26.0)						
Leontief			3.557 (0.216)	1.475 (0.134)	1.511 (0.110)	13.8	72.0	100.0	64.0	100.0	10.0	100.0
			3.319 (0.046)	1.417 (0.014)	1.514 (0.014)	15.2						
			1.539 (0.135)	1.609 (0.142)	2.050 (0.099)	11.9						
Trans3rd			3.666 (0.224)	1.461 (0.196)	1.524 (0.127)	9.8	40.0	100.0	32.0	100.0	16.0	100.0
			3.674 (0.135)	1.510 (0.034)	1.541 (0.035)	9.0						
			1.011 (0.156)	1.011 (0.157)	2.077 (0.125)	12.4						

	3.00	5.00										
Translog			1.995 (0.166)	5.007 (0.444)	4.945 (0.207)	20.7	34.0	100.0	18.0	100.0	4.0	100.0
			1.945 (0.153)	4.806 (0.112)	5.022 (0.116)	20.3						
			2.471 (0.193)	2.464 (0.192)	4.560 (0.259)	12.7						
Rotterdam			2.380 (0.637)	5.152 (0.807)	4.785 (0.720)	22.3 (14.0)	20.0	50.0	18.0	40.0	8.0	18.0
			2.365 (0.620)	4.988 (0.684)	4.867 (0.590)	21.6 (22.0)						
			2.990 (0.488)	3.973 (0.879)	4.182 (0.737)	20.4 (18.0)						
Leontief			1.955 (0.165)	4.932 (0.441)	4.944 (0.207)	23.9	34.0	100.0	22.0	100.0	4.0	100.0
			1.897 (0.152)	4.700 (0.112)	5.034 (0.117)	24.4						
			2.425 (0.191)	2.411 (0.190)	4.561 (0.258)	15.3						
Trans3rd			1.861 (0.290)	4.980 (0.533)	5.151 (0.335)	20.0	22.0	100.0	14.0	98.0	6.0	98.0
			1.790 (0.141)	5.001 (0.124)	5.230 (0.123)	20.1						
			2.085 (0.144)	2.103 (0.146)	5.198 (0.158)	15.8						
	5.00	3.00										
Translog			5.823 (0.365)	3.005 (0.277)	2.989 (0.219)	20.8	48.0	100.0	30.0	100.0	8.0	100.0
			5.715 (0.239)	2.917 (0.068)	3.050 (0.072)	18.2						
			3.406 (0.289)	3.500 (0.300)	3.773 (0.215)	14.8						
Rotterdam			6.483 (1.091)	3.105 (0.557)	2.844 (0.574)	17.1 (22.0)	24.0	64.0	20.0	56.0	10.0	32.0
			6.415 (1.010)	2.989 (0.403)	2.937 (0.403)	16.1 (8.0)						
			5.794 (1.037)	3.722 (0.536)	3.215 (0.563)	17.5 (10.0)						
Leontief			5.675 (0.358)	2.947 (0.275)	3.020 (0.219)	19.9	48.0	100.0	30.0	100.0	6.0	100.0
			5.572 (0.235)	2.860 (0.069)	3.082 (0.072)	16.7						
			3.290 (0.282)	3.444 (0.295)	3.799 (0.214)	17.3						
Trans3rd			5.769 (0.355)	2.956 (0.398)	3.074 (0.242)	17.6	58.0	100.0	50.0	100.0	30.0	100.0
			5.651 (0.228)	3.058 (0.072)	3.201 (0.074)	16.3						
			2.914 (0.331)	2.946 (0.336)	3.633 (0.257)	12.2						

Table 7. *Summary of experiments, for true functions having a weakly separable structure*

Approximate function	True elasticities of substitution σ_{12}	σ_{13}	Estimated elasticities of substitution σ_{12}	σ_{13}	σ_{23}	Regularity violation percentage	Separability rejection percentage 10% level True	10% False	5% level True	5% False	1% level True	1% False
Translog	0.10	0.30	2.011 (2.942)	5.344 (9.071)	0.310 (0.030)	54.8	100.0	0	100.0	0	100.0	0
			−1.355 (3.902)	−4.281 (8.519)	−0.208 (2.236)	74.6						
			0.303 (0.930)	0.114 (2.780)	0.312 (0.026)	55.3						
Rotterdam			−0.063 (0.088)	0.793 (1.064)	0.358 (0.041)	33.1 (34.0)	20.0	88.0	6.0	80.0	0	42.0
			−0.037 (0.084)	1.252 (0.670)	0.361 (0.042)	35.2 (26.0)						
			0.114 (0.063)	0.284 (0.250)	0.260 (0.040)	34.0 (28.0)						
Leontief			−0.018 (0.024)	0.456 (0.044)	0.331 (0.012)	31.4	28.0	100.0	22.0	100.0	4.0	100.0
			−0.014 (0.024)	0.501 (0.024)	0.323 (0.013)	34.0						
			0.117 (0.017)	0.127 (0.018)	0.273 (0.011)	24.0						
Trans3rd			−0.761 (1.143)	−1.916 (0.336)	0.337 (0.563)	86.3	100.0	100.0	100.0	100.0	98.0	100.0
			−1.271 (1.945)	−1.195 (0.257)	0.374 (0.630)	83.1						
			−0.999 (0.397)	−2.666 (0.547)	0.482 (0.097)	78.6						
Translog	0.10	0.60	2.253 (3.851)	1.789 (1.800)	0.503 (0.024)	41.3	100.0	100.0	100.0	100.0	100.0	100.0
			−0.217 (0.625)	0.638 (0.738)	0.963 (0.075)	44.6						
			0.131 (0.381)	−0.055 (0.721)	0.234 (0.014)	41.5						
Rotterdam			−0.114 (0.147)	1.093 (0.874)	0.492 (0.061)	36.2 (30.0)	14.0	90.0	4.0	76.0	2.0	38.0
			−0.118 (0.108)	1.143 (0.514)	0.484 (0.064)	38.0 (32.0)						
			0.132 (0.054)	0.269 (0.131)	0.279 (0.044)	30.8 (22.0)						
Leontief			−0.213 (0.028)	0.799 (0.057)	0.688 (0.022)	37.6	100.0	100.0	100.0	100.0	96.0	100.0
			−0.234 (0.026)	1.010 (0.039)	0.688 (0.023)	44.0						
			0.052 (0.019)	0.055 (0.020)	0.460 (0.015)	40.1						
Trans3rd			−1.182 (0.152)	−0.118 (0.147)	0.665 (0.048)	74.3	58.0	100.0	46.0	100.0	24.0	100.0
			−1.214 (0.150)	0.021 (0.100)	0.711 (0.011)	73.9						
			−0.826 (0.084)	−1.644 (0.189)	0.688 (0.017)	78.6						

Translog	1.00	0.30	1.459 (0.098)	0.268 (0.026)	0.265 (0.022)	25.0	24.0	100.0	10.0	100.0	2.0	100.0
			1.453 (0.070)	0.266 (0.012)	0.266 (0.012)	23.1						
			0.192 (0.229)	0.300 (0.198)	0.433 (0.028)	33.5						
Rotterdam			1.530 (0.217)	0.328 (0.059)	0.350 (0.062)	22.9 (12.0)	18.0	98.0	6.0	94.0	2.0	94.0
			1.526 (0.204)	0.325 (0.048)	0.351 (0.054)	21.0 (20.0)						
			0.980 (0.320)	0.439 (0.061)	0.453 (0.056)	18.2 (6.0)						
Leontief			1.393 (0.073)	0.302 (0.024)	0.307 (0.021)	24.8	16.0	100.0	14.0	100.0	2.0	100.0
			1.381 (0.055)	0.297 (0.011)	0.311 (0.011)	25.5						
			0.260 (0.025)	0.255 (0.024)	0.473 (0.016)	17.4						
Trans3rd			1.412 (0.086)	0.288 (0.045)	0.313 (0.029)	19.8	24.0	100.0	20.0	100.0	10.0	100.0
			1.449 (0.063)	0.304 (0.009)	0.304 (0.010)	22.5						
			0.113 (0.086)	0.282 (0.066)	0.481 (0.045)	32.8						
Translog	1.00	0.60	1.223 (0.078)	0.610 (0.054)	0.589 (0.039)	23.6	38.0	100.0	26.0	100.0	6.0	100.0
			1.207 (0.056)	0.597 (0.016)	0.597 (0.017)	24.9						
			0.795 (0.149)	0.799 (0.146)	0.712 (0.053)	23.0						
Rotterdam			1.257 (0.207)	0.632 (0.111)	0.605 (0.109)	18.7 (22.0)	22.0	68.0	18.0	52.0	4.0	36.0
			1.246 (0.193)	0.612 (0.086)	0.617 (0.088)	19.6 (26.0)						
			1.077 (0.197)	0.762 (0.107)	0.688 (0.102)	16.5 (14.0)						
Leontief			1.170 (0.070)	0.598 (0.052)	0.600 (0.039)	24.1	36.0	100.0	20.0	100.0	6.0	100.0
			1.153 (0.051)	0.583 (0.016)	0.609 (0.017)	22.1						
			0.689 (0.055)	0.700 (0.056)	0.741 (0.037)	19.7						
Trans3rd			1.198 (0.079)	0.584 (0.085)	0.610 (0.049)	21.8	32.0	100.0	24.0	100.0	14.0	100.0
			1.212 (0.053)	0.604 (0.014)	0.604 (0.014)	23.6						
			0.613 (0.077)	0.629 (0.075)	0.718 (0.047)	27.6						

Table 7 (cont.)

Approximate function	True elasticities of substitution		Estimated elasticities of substitution			Regularity violation percentage	Separability rejection percentage					
							10% level		5% level		1% level	
	σ_{12}	σ_{13}	σ_{12}	σ_{13}	σ_{23}		True	False	True	False	True	False
Translog	0.30	1.00	−0.045 (0.027)	1.035 (0.074)	0.999 (0.026)	41.1	16.0	100.0	10.0	100.0	0	100.0
			−0.054 (0.021)	1.033 (0.013)	1.027 (0.011)	44.0						
			0.176 (0.021)	0.149 (0.022)	0.768 (0.026)	32.4						
Rotterdam			−0.029 (0.084)	1.135 (0.158)	0.969 (0.102)	33.9 (36.0)	18.0	100.0	10.0	96.0	4.0	82.0
			−0.021 (0.084)	1.075 (0.165)	0.973 (0.100)	32.9 (38.0)						
			0.253 (0.048)	0.413 (0.111)	0.637 (0.091)	21.0 (16.0)						
Leontief			−0.048 (0.026)	1.033 (0.072)	1.020 (0.025)	33.8	20.0	100.0	14.0	100.0	2.0	100.0
			−0.051 (0.025)	1.075 (0.027)	1.016 (0.025)	40.0						
			0.169 (0.022)	0.167 (0.022)	0.801 (0.028)	30.2						
Trans3rd			−0.096 (0.054)	0.983 (0.092)	1.024 (0.060)	37.4	12.0	100.0	10.0	100.0	4.0	100.0
			−0.077 (0.031)	1.002 (0.025)	1.002 (0.021)	41.1						
			0.030 (0.039)	−0.017 (0.040)	0.927 (0.032)	62.3						
Translog	0.60	1.00	0.404 (0.036)	1.032 (0.091)	0.991 (0.039)	27.2	46.0	100.0	30.0	100.0	10.0	100.0
			0.389 (0.018)	1.015 (0.016)	1.014 (0.015)	30.0						
			0.508 (0.041)	0.508 (0.041)	0.918 (0.048)	16.1						
Rotterdam			0.443 (0.126)	1.063 (0.172)	0.967 (0.136)	22.6 (22.0)	18.0	52.0	14.0	40.0	6.0	16.0
			0.440 (0.125)	1.019 (0.150)	0.985 (0.120)	21.3 (24.0)						
			0.580 (0.095)	0.797 (0.180)	0.845 (0.138)	17.1 (18.0)						
Leontief			0.399 (0.035)	1.011 (0.088)	0.989 (0.039)	28.1	32.0	100.0	14.0	100.0	4.0	100.0
			0.393 (0.034)	0.984 (0.025)	0.998 (0.025)	27.2						
			0.510 (0.041)	0.509 (0.041)	0.913 (0.048)	17.2						
Trans3rd			0.403 (0.079)	0.980 (0.106)	0.995 (0.068)	23.9	22.0	100.0	18.0	100.0	2.0	100.0
			0.398 (0.040)	1.002 (0.023)	1.002 (0.022)	30.6						
			0.388 (0.051)	0.379 (0.051)	1.077 (0.041)	20.0						

204

Model	0.80	1.50								
Translog	0.464 (0.045)	1.546 (0.132)	1.487 (0.053)	18.3	34.0	100.0	14.0	100.0	2.0	100.0
	0.458 (0.045)	1.509 (0.036)	1.498 (0.035)	20.8						
	0.629 (0.052)	0.630 (0.052)	1.356 (0.069)	16.8						
Rotterdam	0.526 (0.170)	1.567 (0.243)	1.439 (0.197)	18.6 (26.0)	18.0	68.0	14.0	56.0	4.0	24.0
	0.524 (0.168)	1.508 (0.217)	1.461 (0.174)	20.6 (26.0)						
	0.760 (0.125)	1.082 (0.254)	1.208 (0.201)	19.0 (10.0)						
Leontief	0.450 (0.045)	1.500 (0.128)	1.480 (0.053)	18.6	32.0	100.0	14.0	100.0	4.0	100.0
	0.441 (0.044)	1.443 (0.029)	1.489 (0.029)	20.5						
	0.615 (0.052)	0.611 (0.052)	1.349 (0.068)	18.3						
Trans3rd	0.461 (0.106)	1.485 (0.150)	1.502 (0.101)	19.8	22.0	100.0	16.0	100.0	4.0	100.0
	0.466 (0.049)	1.507 (0.037)	1.497 (0.035)	24.1						
	0.447 (0.053)	0.437 (0.054)	1.570 (0.051)	25.9						

Model	1.20	0.60								
Translog	1.545 (0.094)	0.613 (0.053)	0.586 (0.041)	23.0	38.0	100.0	26.0	100.0	6.0	100.0
	1.526 (0.066)	0.601 (0.016)	0.595 (0.017)	23.2						
	0.779 (0.172)	0.783 (0.169)	0.773 (0.054)	19.1						
Rotterdam	1.571 (0.250)	0.630 (0.111)	0.607 (0.112)	19.1 (18.0)	22.0	82.0	18.0	76.0	4.0	54.0
	1.559 (0.232)	0.611 (0.085)	0.619 (0.089)	21.2 (22.0)						
	1.308 (0.253)	0.790 (0.105)	0.714 (0.105)	17.2 (20.0)						
Leontief	1.456 (0.084)	0.595 (0.051)	0.602 (0.041)	20.8	38.0	100.0	22.0	100.0	6.0	100.0
	1.435 (0.060)	0.582 (0.016)	0.612 (0.017)	17.8						
	0.644 (0.054)	0.658 (0.055)	0.805 (0.036)	16.9						
Trans3rd	1.512 (0.093)	0.585 (0.084)	0.611 (0.052)	20.2	34.0	100.0	22.0	100.0	10.0	100.0
	1.529 (0.061)	0.606 (0.014)	0.600 (0.015)	20.5						
	0.450 (0.085)	0.474 (0.081)	0.820 (0.050)	21.8						

Table 7 (cont.)

Approximate function	True elasticities of substitution		Estimated elasticities of substitution			Regularity violation percentage	Separability rejection percentage					
	σ_{12}	σ_{13}	σ_{12}	σ_{13}	σ_{23}		10% level		5% level		1% level	
							True	False	True	False	True	False
Translog	1.50	3.00	0.779 (0.082)	3.021 (0.255)	2.955 (0.101)	16.1	30.0	100.0	16.0	100.0	2.0	100.0
			0.765 (0.080)	2.929 (0.068)	2.983 (0.069)	16.0						
			1.027 (0.103)	1.027 (0.102)	2.733 (0.144)	19.2						
Rotterdam			0.941 (0.322)	3.070 (0.461)	2.862 (0.389)	21.1 (30.0)	18.0	74.0	18.0	66.0	4.0	36.0
			0.938 (0.316)	2.974 (0.412)	2.897 (0.340)	21.1 (20.0)						
			1.422 (0.234)	2.046 (0.484)	2.348 (0.399)	18.0 (12.0)						
Leontief			0.758 (0.082)	2.952 (0.252)	2.942 (0.101)	18.4	32.0	100.0	16.0	100.0	4.0	100.0
			0.738 (0.080)	2.822 (0.068)	2.982 (0.070)	18.8						
			1.077 (0.093)	1.064 (0.092)	2.659 (0.134)	15.8						
Trans3rd			0.704 (0.189)	2.986 (0.296)	3.073 (0.203)	17.9	14.0	100.0	12.0	100.0	2.0	100.0
			0.718 (0.077)	2.999 (0.074)	3.058 (0.073)	16.5						
			0.882 (0.074)	0.880 (0.076)	2.989 (0.086)	21.0						

high statistical power. There are two exceptions: (1) the Rotterdam model when σ_{12} is low[40] and (2) the third-order translog when σ_{12} is either low or very high.[41]

When the value of either σ_{12} or σ_{13} is close to one (Tables 4 and 5), the Rotterdam model and the third-order translog require a wider gap between σ_{12} and σ_{13} than any other models in order to provide reasonably high statistical power of the tests.

When σ_{12} is larger than σ_{13}, the statistical power is usually higher than in the converse case (see Tables 2–6).

The approximate (local) separability tests conducted with the generalized Leontief model were seldom worse than those with the translog. In addition, we found no clear superiority of the third-order translog over the regular translog. In fact, in many cases the regular translog provides higher statistical power than the third-order translog.

11   Conclusions

a   The Monte Carlo results

In many cases Barnett and Choi (1987) found that all of the models did reasonably well in terms of producing accurate elasticity point estimates and also in terms of producing a reasonably low percentage of violations of the theoretical regularity conditions. However, relative to the separability testing criterion, we have found that all models usually did poorly. The early theoretical speculations on this subject by Blackorby, Primont, and Russell (1977) appear to be confirmed and are not altered by the use of recent attempts to circumvent those problems.

In particular, the problem is not solved by conducting the test at a point rather than globally or by the use of Varian's nonparametric test. The third-order translog produced no systematic gains over the regular translog. In addition, the well-known small-sample bias of the asymptotic likelihood ratio test toward rejection cannot be used to explain the poor performance of the separability tests because acceptance of false hypotheses was equally as common as rejection of true hypotheses.

It appears that blockwise separability, whether weak or strong, is a subtle structural hypothesis that is difficult to test.[42] We believe that newer,

---

[40] See the case in which $\sigma_{12} = 0.3$ and $\sigma_{13} = 0.1$.

[41] See the cases in which $\sigma_{13} = 0.1$ and $\sigma_{12} = 0.3$ or $\sigma_{12} = 3.0$ or $\sigma_{12} = 5.0$.

[42] Most of the reported results are conducted under the simplest of circumstances: global homotheticity. It seems inconceivable that complicating the separability tests further by introducing nonhomotheticity would produce systematic improvements in the separability testing results. In fact, we found no such improvements when we reran some of these tests in the nonhomothetic cases.

more sophisticated separability tests are needed, perhaps such as the test recently proposed by Blackorby, Schworm, and Fisher (1986) in a production context,[43] or the seminonparametric approach advocated by Gallant (1981) and Barnett and Jonas (1983) in infinite-dimensional parameter space.[44] Blockwise separability is fundamental to all empirical economic research because, without separability, the structure of the economy is necessarily prohibitively difficult to model empirically. New approaches to testing for separability, and thereby for the existence of dimension-reducing exact aggregation, merit much research.

b   *The comparison with chaotic inference*

As we have seen, the conventional structural econometric approach to estimation of minimum dimensionality is, after years of development, still of questionable reliability, even when applied to the decisions of only one economic agent. In fact, that approach does not appear ever to have been applied to the estimation of the minimum degree of complexity (dimensionality) of the structure of an entire economy. Nevertheless, most econometric models of economies are intended to represent a model of minimal complexity because unnecessary dimensionality is usually to be avoided when sample size is finite.

Despite the many limitations of the popular Grassberger–Procaccia algorithm, and despite the fact that the relevant literature is only about three years old, the new chaotic inference can produce a minimum dimensionality estimate. The hope of mathematicians that strange-attractor theory eventually can be used to uncover large amounts of information about unknown systems from the dynamical properties of their solution paths may be realized in the not too distant future. We agree with Prigogine and Stengers (1984) that the recent birth of the field of chaotic inference, when combined with fractal geometry and measure theory, presents exciting prospects for innovations in inference procedures in the sciences. In addition, it recently has been shown that the new procedures can be adapted to use in conventional sampling theoretic statistical inference.[45]

The usefulness of the related literature on bifurcation theory in mathematics already has been shown to be of importance to economic theorists.

---

[43] That approach uses Diewert and Wales' (1987) new symmetric generalized Barnett model, which appears to be the only currently available model that has been proven to remain flexible under the null hypothesis of weak separability and hence to circumvent the separability–inflexibility issue raised by Blackorby, Primont, and Russell (1977).

[44] Gallant (1981) uses the infinite-order Fourier series for asymptotic inferences, whereas Barnett and Jonas (1983) have proposed the use of the infinite-order Müntz–Szatz series in the same manner.

[45] See, e.g., Ramsey and Yuan (1987) and Brock, Dechert, and Scheinkman (1986).

REFERENCES

Barnett, W. A. (1976), "Maximum likelihood and iterated Aitken estimation of nonlinear systems of equations," *Journal of the American Statistical Association,* 71, 354–60.

(1977), "Recursive subaggregation and a generalized hypocycloidal demand model," *Econometrica,* 45, 1117–36.

(1979a), "Theoretical foundations for the Rotterdam model," *Review of Economic Studies,* 46, 109–30.

(1979b), "The joint allocation of leisure and goods expenditure," *Econometrica,* 45, 1117–36.

(1980), "Economic monetary aggregates: an application of index number and aggregation theory," *Journal of Econometrics,* 14 (September), 11–48.

(1981), *Consumer Demand and Labor Supply: Goods, Monetary Assets, and Time,* Amsterdam: North-Holland.

(1982), "The optimal level of monetary aggregation," *Journal of Money, Credit, and Banking,* 14(4), pt. 2, 687–710.

(1983), "New indices of money supply and the flexible Laurent demand system," *Journal of Business and Economic Statistics,* 1(1), 7–23.

(1984a), "Recent monetary policy and the Divisia monetary aggregates," *American Statistician,* 38 (August), 165–72.

(1984b), "On the flexibility of the Rotterdam model: a first empirical look," *European Economic Review,* 24, 285–9.

(1985), "The minflex-Laurent translog flexible functional form," *Journal of Econometrics,* 30, 33–44.

(1987), "The economic theory of monetary aggregation," in *New Approaches to Monetary Economics,* Proceedings of the Second International Symposium in Economic Theory and Econometrics, ed. by W. Barnett and K. Singleton, Cambridge: Cambridge University Press.

Barnett, W. A., and Chen, P. (1986), "Economic theory as a generator of measurable attractors," *Mondes en Developpement,* 14(453); reprinted in *Laws of Nature and Human Conduct: Specificities and Unifying Themes,* ed. by I. Prigogine and M. Sanglier, G.O.R.D.E.S., Brussels, pp. 209–24.

(1988a), "The aggregation-theoretic monetary aggregates are chaotic and have strange attractors: an econometric application of mathematical chaos," in *Dynamic Econometric Modeling,* Proceedings of the Third International Symposium in Economic Theory and Econometrics, ed. by W. Barnett, E. Berndt, and H. White, Cambridge: Cambridge University Press, 199–246.

(1988b), "Deterministic chaos and fractal attractors as tools for nonparametric dynamical econometric inference," *Mathematical Computer Modeling,* 10, 275–96.

Barnett, W. A., and Choi, S. (1987), "A Monte Carlo study of tests of blockwise weak separability," *Journal of Business and Economic Statistics,* forthcoming.

Barnett, W. A., and Jonas, A. (1983), "The Müntz-Szatz demand system: an application of a globally well behaved series expansion," *Economics Letters,* 11, 337–42.

Barnett, W. A., and Lee, Y. W. (1985), "The global properties of the minflex Laurent, generalized Leontief, and translog flexible functional forms," *Econometrica,* 53, 1421–37.

Barnett, W. A., Lee, Y. W., and Wolfe, M. D. (1985), "The three-dimensional global properties of the minflex Laurent, generalized Leontief, and translog flexible functional forms," *Journal of Econometrics,* 30, 3–31.

(1987), "A comparison of the global properties of the two minflex Laurent flexible functional forms," *Journal of Econometrics,* 36, 281–98.

Barten, A. P. (1964), "Consumer demand functions under condition of almost additive preferences," *Econometrica,* 32, 1–38.

(1968), "Estimating demand functions," *Econometrica,* 36, 213–51.

Benhabib, J., and Day, R. H. (1980), "Erratic accumulation," *Economics Letters,* 6(2), 113–17.

(1981), "Rational choice and erratic behavior," *Review of Economic Studies,* 48, 459–71.

(1982), "A characterization of erratic dynamics in the overlapping generation model," *Journal of Economic Dynamics and Control,* 4, 27–55.

Berndt, E. R., and Christensen, L. R. (1973), "The internal structure of functional relationships: separability, substitution, and aggregation," *Review of Economic Studies,* 40, 403–10.

Blackorby, C., Primont, D., and Russell, R. R. (1977), "On testing separability restrictions with flexible functional forms," *Journal of Econometrics,* 5, 195–209.

(1978), *Duality, Separability, and Functional Structure,* New York: Elsevier North-Holland.

Blackorby, C., Schworm, W., and Fisher, T. (1986), "Testing for the existence of input aggregates in an economy production function," working paper, University of British Columbia, Department of Economics.

Brock, W. (1986), "Distinguishing random and deterministic systems: abridged version," *Journal of Economic Theory,* 40(1), 168–94.

Brock, W., and Chamberlain, G. (1986), "Spectral analysis cannot tell a macroeconometrician whether his time series came from a stochastic economy or a deterministic economy," SSRI Working Paper 8419, Department of Economics, University of Wisconsin, Madison.

Brock, W., and Dechert, W. D. (1988), "Theorems on distinguishing deterministic and random systems," in *Dynamic Econometric Modeling,* Proceedings of the Third International Symposium in Economic Theory and Econometrics, ed. by W. Barnett, E. Berndt, and H. White, Cambridge: Cambridge University Press, 247–68.

Brock, W., Dechert, W. D., and Scheinkman, J. A. (1986), "A test for independence based on the correlation dimension," working paper, Economics Department, University of Wisconsin, Madison.

Brock, W., and Sayers, C. L. (1986), "Is the business cycle characterized by deterministic chaos?" Working Paper 8617, Social Systems Research Institute, University of Wisconsin, Madison.

Byron, R. P. (1970), "A simple method for estimating demand systems under separable utility assumptions," *A Review of Economic Studies,* 37, 261–74.

(1984), "On the flexibility of the Rotterdam model," *European Economic Review,* 24, 285–9.

Caves, D., and Christensen, L. (1980), "Global properties of flexible functional forms," *American Economic Review,* 70, 422–32.

Day, R. (1982), "Irregular growth cycles," *American Economic Review,* 72, 406–14.

(1983), "The emergence of chaos from classical economic growth," *Quarterly Journal of Economics,* May, pp. 201-13.

(1985), "Dynamical systems theory and complicated economic behavior," *Environment and Planning B: Planning and Design,* 12, 55-64.

Denny, M., and Fuss, M. (1977), "The use of approximation analysis to test for separability and the existence of consistent aggregates," *American Economic Review,* 67, 404-18.

Diewert, W. E. (1974), "A note on aggregation and elasticities of substitution," *Canadian Journal of Economics,* VII, no. 1, 12-20.

Diewert, W. E., and Wales, T. J. (1987), "Flexible functional forms and global curvature conditions," *Econometrica,* 55, 43-68.

Frank, M. Z., and Stengos, T. (1986), "Measuring the strangeness of gold and silver rates of return," working paper, Department of Economics, University of Guelph, Guelph, Ontario, July.

(1987), "Some evidence concerning macroeconomic chaos," working paper, Department of Economics, University of Guelph, Guelph, Ontario, February.

Gallant, A. R. (1981), "On the bias in flexible functional forms and an essentially unbiased form: the Fourier flexible form," *Journal of Econometrics,* 15, 211-45.

Goldman, S. M., and Uzawa, H. (1964), "A note on separability in demand analysis," *Econometrica,* 32, 387-98.

Grandmont, J. M. (1985), "On endogenous competitive business cycles," *Econometrica,* 53, 995-1045.

Grassberger, P., and Procaccia, I. (1983a), "Measuring the strangeness of strange attractors," *Physica 90,* 189-208.

(1983b), "Characterization of strange attractors," *Physical Review Letters,* 50(5), 346-49.

Green, H. A. J. (1964), *Aggregation in Economic Analysis,* Princeton: Princeton University Press.

Guilkey, D., and Lovell, C. (1980), "On the flexibility of the translog approximation," *International Economic Review,* 21, 137-47.

Guilkey, D., Lovell, C., and Sickles, C. (1983), "A comparison of the performance of three flexible functional forms," *International Economic Review,* 24, 591-616.

Hayes, K. (1986), "Third-order translog utility functions," *Journal of Business and Economic Statistics,* 4, 339-46.

Hinich, M. J., and Patterson, D. M. (1985), "Identification of the coefficients in a non-linear time series of the quadratic type," *Journal of Econometrics,* 30, 112-21.

Jorgenson, D., and Lau, L. (1975), "The structure of consumer preferences," *Annals of Economic and Social Measurement,* 4, 49-102.

Kadiyala, K. R. (1972), "Production functions and elasticity of substitution," *The Southern Economic Journal,* XXXVIII, 281-4.

Kalaba, R., and Tesfatsion, L. (1986), "Flexible least squares," MRG Working Paper M8616, University of Southern California, Los Angeles.

Mandelbrot, B. (1977), *Fractals, Form, Chance, and Dimension,* San Francisco: W. H. Freeman.

Mountain, D. C. (1988), "The Rotterdam model: an approximation in variables space," *Econometrica,* 56, 477-84.

Nicholis, C., and Nicholis, G. (1984), "Is there a climatic attractor?" *Nature,* 311, 529–32.

Prigogine, I. (1980), *From Being to Becoming,* New York: W. H. Freeman.

Prigogine, I., and Stengers, I. (1984), *Order Out of Chaos: Man's New Dialogue with Nature,* New York: Bantam.

Ramsey, J. B., and Yuan, H.-J. (1987), "The statistical properties of dimension calculations using small data sets," working paper, New York University, Department of Economics.

Sayers, C. (1985), "Work stoppages: exploring the nonlinear dynamics," University of Wisconsin, Madison, Department of Economics, July.

Scheinkman, J. A., and LeBaron, B. (1986), "Nonlinear dynamics and stock returns," working paper, University of Chicago.

Schinasi, G. J. (1979), "A nonlinear dynamic disequilibrium model of macroeconomic fluctuations under monetary and fiscal policy: a theoretical and empirical study," unpublished doctoral dissertation, Columbia University.

(1981), "A nonlinear dynamic model of short run fluctuations," *Review of Economic Studies,* 48, 649–56.

(1982), "Fluctuations in a dynamic intermediate-run IS-LM model: applications of the Poincaré-Bendixon theorem," *Journal of Economic Theory,* 28, 369–75.

Stutzer, M. (1980), "Chaotic dynamics and bifurcations in a macro model," *Journal of Economic Dynamics and Control,* 2, 353–76.

Takens, F. (1980), "Detecting strange attractors in turbulence," in *Dynamical Systems and Turbulence,* Lecture Notes in Mathematics No. 898, ed. by D. Rand and L. Young, Berlin: Springer-Verlag, 366–82.

Theil, H. (1971), *Principles of Econometrics,* New York: Wiley.

Varian, H. R. (1982), "The nonparametric approach to demand analysis," *Econometrica,* 50(4), 945–73.

(1983), "Non-parametric tests of consumer behavior," *Review of Economic Studies,* 50, 99–110.

(1985), "Non-parametric analysis of optimizing behavior with measurement error," *Journal of Econometrics,* 30, 445–58.

Wales, T. J. (1977), "On the flexibility of flexible functional forms: an empirical approach," *Journal of Econometrics,* 5, 183–93.

Woodland, A. D. (1978), "On testing weak separability," *Journal of Econometrics,* 8, 383–98.

CHAPTER 9

Nonlinear dynamics and GNP data

José A. Scheinkman and Blake LeBaron

1   Introduction

There has been a revival of interest among theorists in nonlinear models of growth and fluctuations. In contrast with the earlier work by Goodwin (1951), Hicks (1950), and others, the new models explicitly incorporate maximizing agents, competitive behavior, and rational expectations. An example of the latest type of model is implicit in Boldrin and Montrucchio (1986). There they show that, for any twice continuously differentiable function $f(\ )$ that maps a compact set into itself, there exists a neoclassical growth model that possesses for its solution a capital stock sequence k_t that solves an equation $k_{t+1} = f(k_t)$. Because such a neoclassical growth model gives exactly the same solution as a dynamic competitive-equilibrium model with perfect foresight, the Boldrin–Montrucchio theorem can be used to establish the theoretical possibility that even a rather simple deterministic setup can give rise to a time path that is as if generated by an arbitrary deterministic dynamics.

These and other examples (e.g., Grandmont, 1985) seem to put the nonlinear deterministic models of fluctuations on a theoretical footing that equals that of the stable systems buffeted by exogenous shocks that constitute the underpinning of linear – really log-linear – macroeconometric models. From an empirical point of view, matters are quite different. It seems unlikely that a low-order deterministic system accounts for observed economic data even if one allows for measurement error. On the other hand, both types of models are particular cases of one, such as

$$z_{t+1} = f(z_t, \epsilon_t),$$

where, for each t, z_t is a vector of "state variables" and ϵ_t a random variable. Hence it seems natural to ask whether f depends nonlinearly on z_t.

We thank John Cochrane for conversations. This version was prepared while J. Scheinkman was at CEREMADE. The NSF, through grant SES 8420930, provided research support.

The rather good fit of low-order autoregressive models to aggregate data seems to challenge the view that nonlinearities are important in actual economic time series. This in turn is answered with the aid of examples such as the following (Granger, 1980):

$$z_t = au_{t-1}z_{t-1} + u_t,$$

where u_t is independent and identically distributed (i.i.d.) with mean zero, which generates serially uncorrelated output. Further, there are now a series of deterministic examples that show that simple nonlinear maps can generate output that looks, from the viewpoint of linear time series analysis, as if they were generated by i.i.d. sampling. Motivated by these examples, Takens (1983) and Grassberger and Procaccia (1983) developed algorithms to try to distinguish between these possibilities. These have proved quite successful in distinguishing between deterministic and "random" data generated by theoretical models and have been able to accommodate even a combination of a nonlinear deterministic system and small amounts of noise (Ben-Mizrachi et al., 1984). Barnett and Chen (1988), Brock (1986), Brock and Sayers (1986), Frank and Stengos (1986, 1987), Scheinkman (1985), and Scheinkman and LeBaron (1986) applied these techniques to economic data. Although the presence of nonlinearities was detected in some series (Barnett's Divisia monetary aggregates, U.S. employment, investment, gold and silver returns, and stock returns), Brock and Sayers (1986) show that one could not reject the hypothesis that detrended U.S. quarterly (1947–1985) real GNP was generated by an AR(2) process using the Grassberger–Procaccia–Takens (GPT) measure of correlation dimension.

Though the GPT estimate can distinguish whether the residuals of the AR(2) regression are truly white if an infinite data set is available and has worked fairly well in practice, no asymptotic distribution theory was available until recently. This gap was filled by Brock, Dechert, and Scheinkman (1986; henceforth BDS) who produced distribution theory for statistics based on the GPT dimension estimate. First, we apply here the BDS statistics on a series of per capita yearly GNP (1872–1986) to test for the presence of nonlinearities. Our aim is not so much to demonstrate the presence of such nonlinearities in this time series but to be able to explore the various issues that arise in trying to apply the tests developed in BDS. We show that the BDS tests can be used to reject the leading linear models for this series. This result, though encouraging, is not definite. With the aid of an example that is developed in Section 2 we explain why this rejection could in principle be due to a nonconstant variance. We try to account for this problem by using weighted least squares, and the residuals of the weighted least squares regression are again shown to fail the BDS test. We also discuss the possible introduction of dummy variables that seem to account for much of the nonlinearity. Second, we apply the test to a seasonally adjusted monthly series of U.S. industrial production growth rates and find stronger evidence of nonlinearities. This same series had already been found to exhibit nonlinearities, with the aid of the bispectral test (cf. Hinich, 1982), by Ashley and Patterson (1986).

There are good practical reasons to try to detect nonlinearities in macro data. Economists have long understood the importance of estimating parameters of taste and technology to evaluate policy intervention. The results of Boldrin and Montrucchio show that one can generate a policy function in a nonlinear deterministic model that is, from the linear point of view, exactly as if it were generated from a log-linear stochastic growth model. The following example, which is a variation on the logistic, illustrates this.

Let

$$f(x) = x^{\{a(1-\ln x) + b[(\ln x)^2 - 1]\}},$$

with a and b chosen such that the max of $f(x)$ for $x \in [1, e]$ is obtained when $\ln x = \lambda$ and equals e, the base of natural logarithm. For $\lambda = 0.5$ we obtain $a = 4$, $b = 0$, and we have "logistic chaos" in the natural logarithms. For $\lambda = 0.56$, the data generated by using $k_{t+1} = f(k_t)$ exhibit no significant correlation (in the logarithms) except in the first lag, in samples of size up to 1000. Since f maps $(1, e)$ back into itself and is C^2, the conditions of the Boldrin–Montrucchio theorem are satisfied. Further, a regression of k_t on k_{t+1} yields

$$k_{t+1} = 0.467 + (0.088) k_t + u_t, \tag{$*$}$$

which is, of course, compatible with a model with a single agent with logarithmic utility function and dynamics given by

$$x_{t+1} = u_t (x_t - c_t)^{0.088},$$

where u_t is i.i.d. Although ($*$) is not even near to fitting any real data we know of, this illustrates the use of the Boldrin–Montrucchio results in generating log-linear-like data from deterministic models.

Note that for this information to be useful it is necessary to be able to estimate the nonlinearity present. We think the ideas behind the correlation dimension and the BDS tests can be used for estimating the nonlinearity, and we are now working on this.

2 The BDS statistics

Let $X_1, X_2, \ldots, X_N$ be independent with a common distribution F. For each $\epsilon > 0$, let $I_\epsilon : \mathbf{R}^2 \to \mathbf{R}$ be the indicator function of the set

216   **José A. Scheinkman and Blake LeBaron**

$$B_\epsilon = \{(z, y) \in \mathbf{R}^2 \mid |z - y| \le \epsilon\},$$

that is, $I_\epsilon(z, y) = 1$ if $(z, y) \in B_\epsilon$, $I_\epsilon(z, y) = 0$ otherwise. For each $n \ge 2$ and $m \ge 1$, let

$$C(m, n, \epsilon)(X_1, \ldots, X_N) = \frac{2}{n(n-1)} \sum_{1 \le i < j \le n} \prod_{k=0}^{m-1} I_\epsilon(X_{i+k}, X_{j+k}),$$

which is well defined whenever $N > n + m$.

Remark: Note that if we consider the m-histories $y_t = (X_t, \ldots, X_{t+m-1})$, then the correlation dimension of $\{y_t\}_{t=0}^\infty$ is given by

$$d = \lim_{\epsilon \to 0} \left\{ \frac{\ln[\lim_{n \to \infty} C(m, n, \epsilon)(X_1, \ldots, X_{n+m})]}{\ln \epsilon} \right\}$$

if the right-hand side is well defined.
   Also let

$$C(\epsilon) = EI_\epsilon(X_i, X_j) \quad \text{and} \quad K(\epsilon) = E[I_\epsilon(X_i, X_j)I_\epsilon(X_j, X_k)].$$

Brock, Dechert, and Scheinkman (1986) prove the following:

Theorem 1.   *For any $m > 1$, as $n \to \infty$,*

$$\frac{\sqrt{n}}{\sigma} \{C(m, n, \epsilon) - [C(1, n, \epsilon)]^m\} \xrightarrow{d} N(0, 1),$$

where

$$\sigma = (-mC^{m-1}, 1)^T \Sigma(-mC^{m-1}, 1)$$

and

$$\Sigma_{11} = 4(K - C^2),$$

$$\Sigma_{22} = 4(K^m - C^{2m}) + 8 \sum_{j=1}^{m-1} (K^{m-j}C^{2j} - C^{2m}),$$

$$\Sigma_{12} = 2(K + K^m + 2KC^{m-1} - (C + C^m)^2)$$
$$+ 4 \sum_{j=1}^{m-1} (KC^{m-1} + K^{m-j}C^{2j} - C^{1+m} + C^{2m}) - \tfrac{1}{2}(\Sigma_{11} + \Sigma_{22}),$$

$$\Sigma_{21} = \Sigma_{12}.$$

Further, in computing σ, we can use $C(1, n, \epsilon)$ in place of C, and $K(1, n, \epsilon)$ in place of K.

   Note that the BDS statistic is based on the idea that for i.i.d. systems the probability that the vector $(X_i, X_{i+1}, \ldots, X_{i+m-1})$ is within ϵ of

$(X_j, X_{j+1}, \ldots, X_{j+m-1})$ in the maximum norm (L^∞) is exactly the mth power of the probability that X_i is within ϵ of X_j.

Besides the BDS statistics we also show graphs (Figs. 1 and 3 to 5) in which we plot, for a fixed m and ϵ, the pairs (t, τ) such that

$$d[(X_t, X_{t+1}, \ldots, X_{t+m-1}), (X_\tau, X_{\tau+1}, \ldots, X_{\tau+m-1})] < \epsilon.$$

This graph, called a *recurrence plot,* was introduced by Eckmann, Kamphorst, and Ruelle (1987). It serves to examine whether the near neighbors are mostly in a particular subset of the series or are homogeneously spread. The lack of homogeneity could in principle indicate that each part of the series is actually generated by a different system, and the rejection of the null could be a result of this. The following example illustrates our point.

Example 1: Suppose the first N points of a data set with $2N$ points are independent and uniformly distributed in $(-\frac{1}{2}, \frac{1}{2})$ and the second N points are independent and uniformly distributed in $(-\alpha, \alpha)$. Let $\frac{1}{2} > \epsilon > 2\alpha$, and write

$$p_1 = \text{Prob}\{|X_i - X_j| < \epsilon \mid j < i \le N\},$$
$$p_2 = \text{Prob}\{|X_i - X_j| < \epsilon \mid i < N < j\},$$
$$p_3 = \text{Prob}\{|X_i - X_j| < \epsilon \mid N < i < j\};$$

then $p_3 = 1$, $p_1 = 2\epsilon - \epsilon^2$, and $p_2 \approx 2\epsilon$. Further,

$$C(1, 2N, \epsilon) \approx \frac{1}{4}(p_1 + 2p_2 + 1) \approx \frac{1}{4}(6\epsilon - \epsilon^2 + 1),$$

$$C(2, 2N, \epsilon) \approx \frac{1}{4}(p_1^2 + 2p_2^2 + 1) \approx 3\epsilon^2 + \epsilon^4 - \frac{\epsilon^3}{4} + \frac{1}{4},$$

$$C(2, 2N, \epsilon) - [C(1, 2N, \epsilon)]^2 \approx \frac{1}{16}(3 - 12\epsilon + 14\epsilon^2 - 4\epsilon^3 + 3\epsilon^4),$$

which is greater than 0 for all ϵ in $(0, 1)$. Hence the BDS statistic rejects, as it should, the null of an i.i.d. system, but it would be wrong to attribute the departure from the null to interesting nonlinearities.

Notice that in this example the recurrence plot would show many pairs (t, τ) with $\min(t, \tau) > N$ and relatively few with $\min(t, \tau) < N$. This graph is useful here in detecting the presence of two separate systems.

As a numerical example, consider the case in which $N = 100$ and $\alpha = 2^{-5}$. Then the BDS statistics we get are

$$\frac{\sqrt{200}}{\sigma}\{C(2, 200, \epsilon) - [C(1, 200, \epsilon)]^2\} = 14.04$$

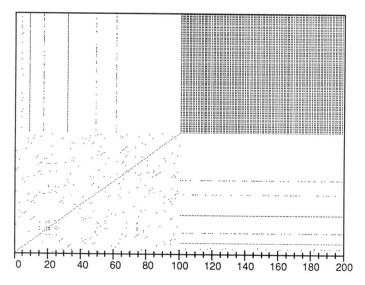

Figure 1.   Uniform random $[-1/2, 1/2]$ and $[-1/32, 1/32]$; $d = 2$, $\epsilon = 1/2$ standard.

and

$$\frac{\sqrt{200}}{\sigma}\{C(3, 200, \epsilon) - [C(1, 200, \epsilon)]^3\} = 22.67,$$

where ϵ equals one-half the standard deviation of the whole series. Figure 1 presents the recurrence plot for this example. Note that most of the pairs are in the upper right-hand corner.

In principle one could deal with this problem by estimating separately the variance of the residuals for the first and second halves of the data set and renormalizing the parts so that they have equal variance. This is not entirely satisfactory because it implies that the original linear model was incorrectly specified. A better method is to admit that the variance of the residuals change across the two periods and use generalized least squares. For U.S. GNP data, for the linear models we tried, the post-1947 residuals exhibit a much lower variance.

3   Data and tests

a   GNP 1870–1986

In testing the whiteness of GNP residuals two points are crucial. First, the residuals are computed from a regression model and thus are not i.i.d.

Second, the series is rather short compared with the ones studied in the BDS paper. Although a result analogous to Theorem 1 seems to hold for residuals of linear models, we take a more direct tack to the problem. We start by fitting a linear model to the original data. We discuss later the alternative linear models considered. For each linear model we generate comparison sets in the following manner (this process is closely related to Efron, 1982, chap. 5.):

1 Extract residuals from the original fitted model. Call these $\{e_t\}_{t=k}^{N}$. (k depends on the lag length of the fitted model.)
2 Resample from this data set with replacement generating a new "scrambled" sample of residuals e_t^*.
3 Using the original model and estimated parameters, regenerate a linear model using the new scrambled residual series.
4 Estimate the linear model again on this generated series, giving a new residual series $\hat{e}_t$.
5 Get BDS statistics from this residual series $\hat{e}_t$.

We then compare the test statistics in our data with the distribution of test statistics in 250 comparison data sets and report the percentage of the comparison data sets that gave at least as large a value for the test statistics.

The next problem we face is selecting a linear model. The data contain known linearities and trends. We want to fit the data to the "best" linear model and proceed by examining the residuals. With GNP data there is some controversy as to what is the best model. The main question is whether the data are difference stationary,

$$(1-L)y_t = \mu + A(L)e_t, \quad e_t \text{ i.i.d.,}$$

or trend stationary,

$$y_t = bt + A(L)e_t.$$

Cochrane (1986) uses the technique of looking at variance differences, $k^{-1}\mathrm{var}(y_t - y_{t-k})$, to estimate the size of the random-walk component in real per capita GNP. This test is based on the fact that in a random walk the variance just shown must increase in proportion to t. He finds the ratio of the variance of the random-walk component to first differences is about $\frac{2}{5}$. This indicates that there is a large mean reverting component in annual GNP growth. Cochrane continues by simulating some linear models to find which best fits his results for per capita GNP. He finds that an AR(2) with trend

$$(1-L-L^2)y_t = bt + e_t$$

best replicates the variance differences of the data. Through most of this chapter we shall use variations of this model. However, recognizing that this controversy continues, we also looked at results for the differenced series as well.

The data used are the natural logs of real GNP/Capita for the United States from 1870 through 1986. For the years through 1947, the data are from Friedman and Schwartz (1982). Postwar data are from the *Economic Report of the President*, 1986.

First we test the AR(2) with trend residuals.

Regression ($R^2 = 0.99$)

		standard deviation
Constant	-1.31	(0.31)
Lag 1	1.09	(0.09)
Lag 2	-0.30	(0.09)
Trend	0.0036	(0.00089)

BDS ($\epsilon = \frac{1}{2}$ Std.)

Dimension 2	5.77	(0.00)
Dimension 3	7.11	(0.00)

For the regression, the numbers in parentheses are the standard errors from ordinary least squares (OLS). For the BDS statistics, the numbers in parentheses are the proportion of 250 simulation runs for the appropriate model with BDS statistics lying outside $[-C_s, C_s]$, where C_s is the statistic for the original data. The BDS statistics clearly reject that an AR(2), such as that used here with i.i.d. residuals, could have generated the original data. Figure 2 plots the residual series, and Figure 3 is the recurrence plot discussed earlier. In Figure 2 the reduction in variance can be seen directly. Figure 3 shows many of the neighbor pairs clustering in the upper right-hand corner, which corresponds to the postwar period. Although this does not imply that the variance change is causing the significant C, it does suggest that it could be a major factor.

To examine whether these results depend on what type of stationarity is present, we took first differences of the log GNP/Capita. An AR(10) was identified using the partial autocorrelation function (PACF), and after estimation its residuals appear white. (Their autocorrelations are within the 95 percent confidence region of zero.) The residuals are then tested as before, using the BDS statistics.

Regression ($R^2 = 0.22$)

		standard deviation
Constant	0.02	(0.008)
Lag 1	0.20	(0.092)
Lag 2	-0.01	(0.091)

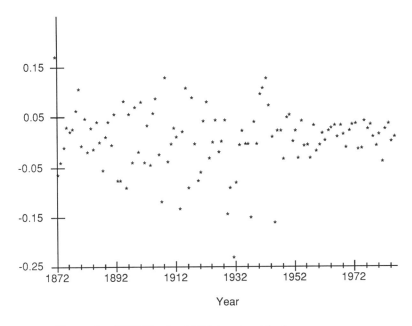

Figure 2.   GNP/Capita AR(2)-trend residuals.

Lag 3	−0.08	(0.091)
Lag 4	−0.20	(0.091)
Lag 5	−0.24	(0.091)
Lag 6	0.17	(0.091)
Lag 7	−0.04	(0.091)
Lag 8	−0.05	(0.091)
Lag 9	−0.22	(0.087)
Lag 10	−0.01	(0.087)

BDS ($\epsilon = \frac{1}{2}$ Std.)

Dimension 2	2.68	(0.08)
Dimension 3	3.13	(0.07)

Figure 4 is the recurrence plot for this series. The results and the plots have not changed. This series contains the same postwar bunching as in the first set of residuals.

As was mentioned before, changes in variance in a purely random system can cause the BDS statistic to reject the null hypothesis. Our data do have lower variances in the postwar period, and the recurrence plots appear to show a large number of close pairs there. We shall attempt to account for this by fitting a single linear relationship [AR(2) with trend] but allowing the residuals to have different variances before and after

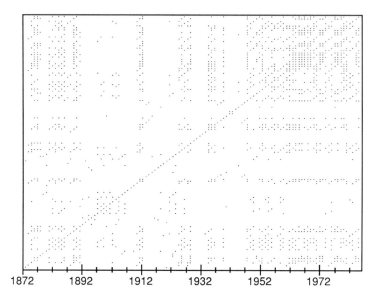

Figure 3.   GNP/Capita AR(2)-trend residuals; $d = 2$, $\epsilon = 1/2$ standard.

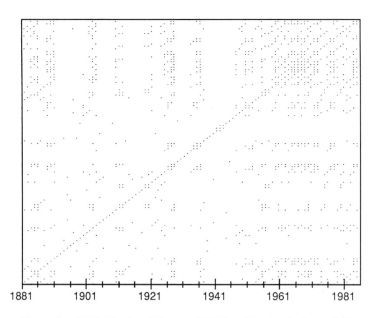

Figure 4.   GNP/Capita difference AR(10) residuals; $d = 2$, $\epsilon = 1/2$ standard.

1947. To estimate this we use generalized least squares (GLS). This simple case, in which the residuals are still uncorrelated, is also known as weighted least squares. We estimate the variances of the residuals by running our AR(2) with trend on the original data and then split the residuals and estimate the variances separately. These are used in running the final GLS estimates of the data and generating adjusted residuals for the BDS statistics. This two-step procedure is described in Theil (1971).

GLS results

Subperiod standard deviations
    1872–1946, $\sigma = 0.073$
    1947–1986, $\sigma = 0.024$

Regression (GLS) ($R^2 = 0.99$)

		standard deviation
Constant	−1.38	(0.32)
Lag 1	1.04	(0.08)
Lag 2	−0.27	(0.07)
Trend	0.0039	(0.00092)

BDS ($\epsilon = \frac{1}{2}$ Std.)
Dimension 2	3.14	(0.044)
Dimension 3	3.28	(0.068)

Notice in Figure 5 that neighbors no longer appear "clumped" in the postwar period. So variance adjustment has eliminated some of the problem. It has reduced the BDS statistics, but they are still in the tails of the simulations. (Note: The simulations exactly replicate the procedure used for model estimation. The series is generated using the scrambled normalized residuals multiplied by an appropriate scale factor for the subperiod.)

In the following test we proceed as in the last test except that, for all the regressions run, dummy variables are added for the periods 1930–1939 and 1940–1945. The addition of dummies reduces the significance of the BDS statistics. These results suggest that accounting for these unusual periods will eliminate the detectable nonlinearities in the data.

Subperiod standard deviations
    1872–1946, $\sigma = 0.063$
    1947–1986, $\sigma = 0.024$

Regression ($R^2 = 0.99$)

		standard deviation
Constant	−2.54	(0.36)
Lag 1	0.87	(0.08)

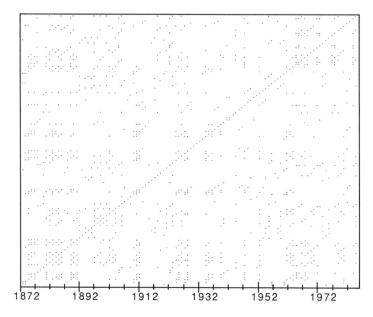

Figure 5.   GNP/Capita WLS AR(2), trend, residuals; $d = 2$, $\epsilon = 1/2$ standard.

Lag 2	−0.28	(0.06)
Trend	0.0072	(0.0010)
1930–1939	−0.13	(0.03)
1940–1945	0.04	(0.02)

BDS ($\epsilon = \frac{1}{2}$ Std.)

Dimension 2	1.83	(0.23)
Dimension 3	2.52	(0.16)

b   *Monthly growth rates in U.S. industrial production*

We examine here a series of seasonally adjusted monthly growth rates in industrial production (Feb. 1947 to Feb. 1987). This series contains over 450 points. This large number of observations turns out to be important for the behavior of the BDS statistics. On the other hand, there is the possibility that the seasonal adjustment is, in fact, responsible for some of the nonlinearities observed. An AR(24) was identified (again using PACF) and estimated on the monthly growth rates, and the residuals were found to be "white."

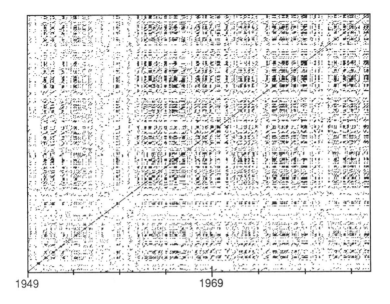

1949   1969

Figure 6.   Industrial production AR(10) residuals; $d = 2$, $\epsilon = 1/2$ standard.

BDS ($\epsilon = \frac{1}{2}$ Std.)
    Dimension 2   4.68   (0.00)
    Dimension 3   6.02   (0.00)
    Dimension 4   7.50   (0.00)
    Dimension 5   8.21   (0.00)

The recurrence plot (Figure 6) seems to show none of the clumping that appeared in the GNP series.

4   Conclusions

We have used the methods developed by BDS to test for the presence of nonlinearities in a time series of U.S. real per capita GNP. The results are mixed: The tests rejected the AR(2) with trend model, but part of that rejection may stem from a change in variance through the period. Although the tests still rejected the model once we allowed for different variances in the periods 1872–1946 and 1947–1986, it failed to reject the model after dummies for the great depression (1930–1939) and World War II (1940–1945) were introduced. This last point should perhaps be further explored: The introduction of dummy variables destroys certain similarities of patterns across distinct periods, for example, making a period that includes years in 1940–1945 that was previously similar to a period at the end of the eighteenth century now distinct. The results are definitely more encouraging for the longer data series of industrial production, pointing perhaps to the limitations of the tests when dealing with short series. Although our intentions were somewhat methodological, the results certainly buttress other evidence of nonlinearities in macroeconomic data. Brock and Sayers (1986) contains a useful discussion of the literature as well as a presentation of original evidence.

One of the difficulties in applying the BDS tests is that one needs first to commit to a particular linear structure. Although the residuals of the structure considered here look white, those of other more complicated (or perhaps simpler!) linear relationships will also look white, and no detectable nonlinearities may be then left. The test for the presence of nonlinearities based on the estimated bispectrum (cf. Hinich, 1982) has the advantage of detecting nonlinearities in any stationary time series. The test seems to have less power than the BDS test (cf. Brock, Dechert, and Scheinkman, 1986). It also has problems detecting some forms of nonlinearities, as in the example in Ashley and Patterson (1986):

$$x_{t+1} = x_t + ax_t(x_t - 1)(x_t + 1),$$

which presents no difficulty for the BDS statistics. Nonetheless, the fact that the estimation of the linear system may introduce dependence on the residuals is a definite advantage of the bispectral test.

REFERENCES

Ashley, R., and Patterson, D. (1986), "Linear versus nonlinear macroeconomies: a statistical test," Department of Economics, Virginia Polytechnic Institute and State University, Blacksburg.

Barnett, W., and Chen, P. (1988), "The aggregation-theoretic monetary aggregates are chaotic and have strange attractors," in *Dynamic Econometric Modeling,* Proceedings of the Third International Symposium in Economic Theory and Econometrics, ed. by W. Barnett, E. Berndt, and H. White, Cambridge: Cambridge University Press, 199–245.

Ben-Mizrachi, A., et al. (1984), "Characterization of experimental (noisy) strange attractors, *Physical Review (A),* 29, 975.

Boldrin, M., and Montrucchio, L. (1986), "On the indeterminacy of capital accumulation paths," *Journal of Economic Theory,* 40, 26–39.

Brock, W. (1986), "Distinguishing random and deterministic systems: abridged version," *Journal of Economic Theory,* 40, 168–95.

Brock, W., Dechert, W. D., and Scheinkman, J. (1986), "A test for independence based on the correlation dimension," University of Wisconsin-Madison and University of Chicago.

Brock, W., and Sayers, C. (1986), "Is the business cycle characterized by deterministic chaos?" SSRI W.P. #8617, Department of Economics, University of Wisconsin-Madison.

Cochrane, J. (1986), "How big is the random walk component of GNP?" Department of Economics, University of Chicago.

Eckman, J. P., Kamphorst, S. O., Ruelle, D. (1987), "Recurrence plots of dynamical systems," Départment de Physique Théorique, Université de Genève, and IHES, F-91440 Bures-sur-Yvette.

Efron, B. (1982), The Jackknife, the Bootstrap, and Other Resampling Plans, Philadelphia: SIAM.

Frank, M. Z., and Stengos, T. (1986), "Measuring the strangeness of gold and silver rates of return," Discussion Paper #1986-13, Economics, University of Guelph, Ontario.

(1987), "Some evidence concerning macroeconomic chaos," Department of Economics, University of Guelph, Ontario.

Friedman, M., and Schwartz, A. J. (1982), Monetary Trends in the United States and the United Kingdom, Their Relation to Income, Prices and Interest Rates, 1867-1975, Chicago: University of Chicago Press.

Goodwin, R. M. (1951), "The nonlinear accelerator and the persistence of business cycles," Econometrica, 19, 1-17.

Grandmont, J. M. (1985), "On endogenous competitive business cycles," Econometrica, 53, 995-1045.

Granger, C. (1980). "Forecasting white noise," Working Paper 80-31, University of California at San Diego.

Grassberger, P., and Procaccia, I. (1983), "Measuring the strangeness of strange attractors," Physica (D), 9, 189.

Hicks, J. R. (1950), A contribution to the theory of the trade cycle, Clarendon: Oxford University Press.

Hinich, M. (1982), "Testing for Gaussianity and linearity of stationary time series," Journal of Time Series Analysis, 3, 169-76.

Sayers, C. (1986), "Workstoppages: exploring the nonlinear dynamics," University of Wisconsin-Madison.

Scheinkman, J. A. (1985), "Distinguishing deterministic from random systems: An examination of stock returns," manuscript prepared for the Conference on Nonlinear Dynamics, Centre de Recherché de Mathematíques de la Decision (CEREMADE) at the University of Paris IX.

Scheinkman, J., and LeBaron, B. (1986), "Nonlinear dynamics and stock returns," Department of Economics, University of Chicago.

Takens, F., (1983), "Distinguishing determininstic and random systems," in Nonlinear Dynamics and Turbulence, ed. by G. Borenblatt, G. Loos, and D. Joseph, Boston: Pitman Advanced Publishing Program, pp. 315-33.

Theil, H. (1971), Principles of Econometrics, New York: John Wiley and Sons.

PART IV

Chaos and informational complexity in economic theory

CHAPTER 10

Paths of optimal accumulation in two-sector models

Michele Boldrin

1   Introduction

The 1980s have witnessed an increasing attention by the profession to endogenous, deterministic explanations of the erratic dynamic behavior of many macro variables. Examples of this new line of research are Benhabib and Day (1982), Benhabib and Nishimura (1979, 1985), Grandmont (1985), and most of the works collected in Grandmont (1986).

Attention is centered on the notion of chaos as an appropriate qualitative description of the observed oscillations. Empirical efforts (especially Barnett and Chen, 1986; Brock and Sayers, 1988; and LeBaron and Scheinkman, 1986) suggest that, indeed, some strange attractors may be behind certain data.

A sound economic theory for the emergence of chaos in pure exchange OG economies is provided in both Benhabib and Day (1982) and Grandmont (1985). On the other hand, no reasonable economic arguments have been provided to justify chaotic competitive dynamics in optimal-growth models with a representative consumer. Benhabib and Nishimura (1979, 1985) provide an argument for periodic cycles but do not address the existence of more complicated phenomena. That the latter are possible and perfectly consistent with the generally maintained assumptions is, however, an implication of the general theory developed in Boldrin and Montrucchio (1984, 1986); see also Deneckere and Pelikan (1986) for related results.

A preliminary version of this chapter was circulated in August 1986, under the same title, as Technical Report #502 of the Institute of Mathematical Studies in the Social Sciences, Stanford University, Stanford, Ca. I am very grateful to the Institute, and to Mordecai Kurz in particular, for the kind hospitality and financial support provided during summer 1986. Financial support from the A. P. Sloan Foundation through a Dissertation Fellowship is also gratefully acknowledged. I am indebted to Jess Benhabib, Raymond Deneckere, Lionel McKenzie, Luigi Montrucchio, Paul Romer, and José Scheinkman for several helpful discussions, criticisms, and suggestions that greatly improved the article.

This chapter attempts to provide a rationale for the existence of chaotic competitive-equilibrium paths within the context of a simple, aggregated optimal-growth model with two sectors and an infinitely living consumer. We show that the emergence of chaotic orbits is linked to dynamic changes in the profitability conditions between the two sectors – changes that, in turn, have their origins in the technological structure of the economy. In particular, it is proved that under certain simplifying assumptions, such conditions can be expressed in terms of factor-intensity reversal and high discounting. In the more general case, a high degree of impatience is still needed, whereas the reversal assumption can be replaced by the hypothesis of a uniformly larger capital/labor ratio in the consumption sector, together with a relatively high sensitivity of the price of the investment good to changes in the output of the same sector for low values of the aggregated capital stock. An analytic example that uses a constant elasticity of substitution (CES) and a Leontief production function is used to illustrate the working of the general theorems.

A few words of caution should be added about the notion of chaos that we are using. The two main theorems give sufficient conditions for "topological chaos" (see Definition 3). It is well known that such behavior can be unobservable. This is a point that is stressed, for example, in Grandmont (1987). The existence of "observable chaos" (see Definition 4) cannot be generally proved for this class of models due to unavoidable computability constraints, which are briefly discussed in the main text. We provide a corollary showing that, under regularity assumptions, observable chaos can be derived.

The chapter proceeds as follows: Section 2 describes the model and characterizes the dynamic competitive equilibrium. Section 3 derives a standard dynamic programming problem from which the competitive equilibrium can be computed. Section 4 contains the main theorems as well as the applications to our example.

2   Intertemporal competitive equilibrium in a two-sector economy

a   *The model*

We deal with a competitive economy in which a pure consumption good and a pure capital good are produced and traded over time. Only one representative agent exists. He lives forever and takes as given the sequence of triples $\{w_t, r_t, q_t\}$, $t = 0, 1, 2, \ldots$, denoting the labor wage rate w, the gross capital rental r, and the price of capital q in every period t. These variables are expressed in units of the consumption good, which has its price fixed at 1 in all periods. Our price system is then a current-value system at every time t. We assume perfect foresight.

The preferences of the consumer are described by a standard utility function $u(c_t)$ depending on the current level of consumption:

U1) u is an increasing, concave function from $[0, \infty)$ into $[0, \infty)$, C^2 on $(0, \infty)$.

In each period the consumer is endowed with one unit of labor time, which he supplies inelastically at the current wage rate, and with an amount k_t of capital stock, which is left over from previous consumption-saving decisions and which he supplies inelastically to the productive sectors. At any time his budget constraint is

$$c_t + q_t[k_{t+1} - (1-\mu)k_t] = r_t k_t + w_t, \tag{1}$$

where μ is the capital depreciation rate. Given the initial capital stock k_0, the problem of the consumer amounts to pick-up sequences of consumption c_t and gross saving $[k_{t+1} - (1-\mu)k_t]$ to maximize the present value of his lifetime utility under the period-by-period budget constraint (1). Formally, we write:

(PC) Max $\sum\limits_{t=0}^{\infty} u(c_t)\delta^t$, s.t. (1), all $t = 0, 1, 2, \dots$, and a given k_0.

Here δ denotes the discount factor.

On the production side we assume the existence of two industries that are distinguished because of the different technologies available and different outputs. They can be imagined as being composed of a large number of identical competitive firms. Constant returns to scale are assumed to hold in both sectors. We summarize this with two production functions:

$$y^1 = F^1(k^1, \ell^1), \qquad y^2 = F^2(k^2, \ell^2), \tag{2}$$

where superscript 1 denotes the consumption sector and 2 denotes the capital good sector; k^i, ℓ^i, $i = 1, 2$, are the quantities of capital and labor used as inputs in either of the two industries. With regard to (2) we state the following:

T1) F^i, $i = 1, 2$, is linear homogeneous in its arguments. Also, $F^2(0, x) = 0$ for all x in R_+.

T2) F^i, $i = 1, 2$, is an increasing and concave function from $[0, \infty) \times [0, \infty)$ into $[0, \infty)$, of class C^2 in the interior of its domain. F^i is strictly concave in each separate factor.

The following hypothesis is also useful:

T3)   There exists a $\bar{k} \in (0, \infty)$ such that $F^2(k, 1) < \mu k$ for all $k > \bar{k}$ and that $F^2(k, 1) > \mu k$ for all $k < \bar{k}$.

Firms take the price sequence $\{w_t, r_t, q_t\}$ as given. Their optimal decision problems reduce to the choice of factors-demand sequences $\{k_t^i, \ell_t^i\}$ that maximize the present discounted value of the stream of future profits. Therefore, the consumption-good sector solves

(PF^1)   Max $y_t^1 - r_t k_t^1 - w_t \ell_t^1$, s.t. $y_t^1 \le F^1(k_t^1, \ell_t^1)$, all t,

and the capital good solves

(PF^2)   Max $q_t y_t^2 - r_t k_t^2 - w_t \ell_t^2$, s.t. $y_t^2 \le F^2(k_t^2, \ell_t^2)$, all t.

Given this description of agents' behavior, it is natural to define a competitive equilibrium (with perfect foresight) in the following way:

Definition 1.   *An intertemporal competitive equilibrium (ICE) is given by price sequences $\{w_t, r_t, q_t\}$ and quantity sequences*

$$\{y_t^1, y_t^2, k_t^1, k_t^2, \ell_t^1, \ell_t^2, c_t, k_t\}$$

such that:

   a. *$\{c_t\}$ and $\{k_t\}$ solve (PC), given $\{w_t, r_t, q_t\}$;*
   b. *y_t^1, k_t^1 and ℓ_t^1 solve (PF^1), given $\{w_t, r_t\}$, all $t = 0, 1, 2, \ldots$;*
   c. *y_t^2, k_t^2 and ℓ_t^2 solve (PF^2), given $\{w_t, r_t, q_t\}$, all $t = 0, 1, 2, \ldots$;*
   d. *$c_t = y_t^1$, $y_t^2 = k_{t+1} - (1-\mu)k_t$, $k_t = k_t^1 + k_t^2$, $1 = \ell_t^1 + \ell_t^2$, all $t = 0, 1, 2, \ldots$.*

The existence of such ICE can be proved by standard arguments. Moreover, we can write an infinite-horizon maximization problem whose solutions are ICE for our two-sector economy.

Proposition 1.   *Consider the economy described by (PC), (PF^1), and (PF^2) under assumptions U1) and T1) and T2). Consider a set of quantity sequences satisfying Definition 1. Then they also solve the following problem:*

(P1) $\max \sum\limits_{t=0}^{\infty} u(c_t)\delta^t$, s.t. $c_t \le T(k_t, y_t^2)$, $k_{t+1} = (1-\mu)k_t + y_t^2$,

where

(T) $T(k_t, y_t^2) = \max y_t^1 = F^1(k_t^1, \ell_t^1)$, s.t. $y_t^2 \le F^2(k_t^2, \ell_t^2)$,
$k_t \ge k_t^1 + k_t^2$, $1 \ge \ell_t^1 + \ell_t^2$, $\ell_t^i \ge 0$, $k_t^i \ge 0$, $i = 1, 2$.

The reciprocal is also true.

We omit the proof of this statement. It can be easily derived by adopting the arguments of Becker (1981).

b   *Optimal sequences*

Before moving ahead in the analysis of the intertemporal problem (P1), let us discuss the nature of problem (T). The existence of a solution is guaranteed by standard arguments. The nature of such a solution has been extensively studied in the literature, and we shall make heavy use of the existing results in the sequel. The reader is referred to Kuga (1972), Hirota and Kuga (1971), and Benhabib and Nishimura (1979) for the proofs.

Let us denote the chosen input levels with $k^1(k, y)$, $\ell^1(k, y)$, $k^2(k, y)$, and $\ell^2(k, y)$. These are continuously differentiable functions under the maintained assumptions. The *production possibility frontier* (PPF), $T(k, y)$, is then equal to $F^1[k^1(k, y), \ell^1(k, y)]$. It turns out to be concave and, under some weak technical conditions, twice continuously differentiable. In particular, for interior values of k^i, ℓ^i we have

$$T_1(k, y) = F_1^1(k^1, \ell^1) = qF_1^2(k^2, \ell^2) \geq 0, \tag{3}$$

$$T_2(k, y) = -\frac{F_j^1(k^1, \ell^1)}{F_j^2(k^2, \ell^2)} \leq 0, \quad j = 1, 2. \tag{4}$$

Additional information on the nature of T can be obtained by exploiting some duality relations. Because this is also standard we summarize here only the essential results.

From problem (T) one has

$$r(k, y) = T_1(k, y) \quad \text{and} \quad q(k, y) = -T_2(k, y), \tag{5}$$

where, we recall, the price of the consumption good is taken to be the numeraire. The Hessian matrix of T can then be written as

$$\begin{bmatrix} T_{11} & T_{12} \\ T_{21} & T_{22} \end{bmatrix} = \begin{bmatrix} \dfrac{\partial r}{\partial k} & \dfrac{\partial r}{\partial y} \\ -\dfrac{\partial q}{\partial k} & -\dfrac{\partial q}{\partial y} \end{bmatrix}. \tag{6}$$

Define the cost function that solves the dual of T as $p = p(\omega)$, where $p = [1, q]$ and $\omega = w/r$. In extensive form we can write

$$1 = a_{11}(\omega)r + a_{21}(\omega)w,$$
$$q = a_{12}(\omega)r + a_{22}(\omega)w, \tag{7}$$

where the a_{ij} indicate the cost-minimizing input coefficients of the two sectors. By totally differentiating (7), using the necessary conditions for cost minimization, and using the fact that $d\omega/\omega = dw/w - dr/r$ to simplify, we obtain

$$\frac{dq}{d\omega} = [a_{22}a_{11} - a_{12}a_{21}]r^2. \tag{8}$$

From the assumption $T \in C^2$ we have $T_{12} = T_{21}$, and therefore,

$$\frac{\partial r}{\partial y} = -\frac{\partial q}{\partial k} = -\frac{\partial q}{\partial \omega}\frac{\partial \omega}{\partial k}. \tag{9}$$

Therefore (6) can be written

$$\begin{bmatrix} T_{11} & T_{12} \\ T_{21} & T_{22} \end{bmatrix} = \begin{bmatrix} \dfrac{\partial r}{\partial k} & -\dfrac{\partial q}{\partial \omega}\dfrac{\partial \omega}{\partial k} \\ -\dfrac{\partial q}{\partial \omega}\dfrac{\partial \omega}{\partial k} & -\dfrac{\partial q}{\partial y} \end{bmatrix}, \tag{10}$$

which can now be completely signed:

$$T_{11} = \frac{\partial r}{\partial k} \le 0, \qquad T_{22} = -\frac{\partial q}{\partial y} \le 0, \qquad T_{11}T_{22} - (T_{12})^2 \ge 0; \tag{11}$$

and, given that $\partial \omega/\partial k > 0$ (see Intriligator, 1971, p. 420),

$$T_{12} = -\frac{\partial q}{\partial \omega}\frac{\partial \omega}{\partial k} \lessgtr 0, \tag{12}$$

according to (8). The interpretation of the a_{ij} implies that T_{12} is positive when the capital good sector is more capital intensive than the consumption good sector and negative in the opposite case. T_{12} vanishes when both sectors have the same capital intensity for a given factor–price ratio. Assumptions T1)–T3) do not restrict our economy to either of the two patterns. Which of the two situations will turn out true at a given time depends on the relative degrees of convexity of the unit isoquants of F^1 and F^2, together with the prevailing factor–price ratio at that time. Because the latter depends, in turn, on k and y in the general dynamic problem, the sign of T_{12} can change along the chosen optimal accumulation path.

The case in which T_{12} can be either positive or negative is considered in our example.

Example: In this simple example we shall use

$$F^1(k^1, \ell^1) = [ak_1^\rho + (1-a)\ell_1^\rho]^{1/\rho}, \quad a \in (0,1), \ \rho \in (-\infty, 1),$$

$$F^2(k^2, \ell^2) = \min\left\{\ell^2, \frac{k_2}{\gamma}\right\}, \quad \gamma \in (0, 1).$$

Notice that F^2 is not of class C^2; this choice has been dictated by computability reasons. Had we chosen F^2 to be, for example, a second CES, we would have not been able to work out an explicit form for T. Simplicity also recommends that we use $u(c_t) = c_t$. Problem (T) now is

$$\max[ak_1^\rho + (1-a)\ell_1^\rho]^{1/\rho}, \quad \text{s.t. } y \leq \min\left\{1 - \ell_1, \frac{k - k_1}{\gamma}\right\}.$$

The straightforward solution gives a PPF of the type:

$$T(k, y) = [a(k - \gamma y)^\rho + (1-a)(1-y)^\rho]^{1/\rho}. \tag{13}$$

Such a T is of class C^2 on the interior of its domain, which is the following set:

$$D = \left\{(k, y) \in [0,1] \times [0,1]; \text{ s.t. } 0 \leq y \leq \frac{k}{\gamma}\right\}.$$

It is also strictly concave in its second argument everywhere on D except the vertical line $x = \gamma$.

Let us now turn our attention to the intertemporal problem (P1). Given any initial condition, a unique optimal solution to (P1) exists that is also supported by a sequence of competitive prices. McKenzie (1986) gives a proof of this under conditions much weaker than ours. For heuristic purposes we consider here the associated Lagrangean:[1]

$$L = \sum_{t=0}^\infty \{u(c_t) + p_t^1[T(k_t, y_t) - c_t] + p_t^2[(1-\mu)k_t + y_t - k_{t+1}]\}\delta^t. \tag{14}$$

The first-order conditions for interior solutions are as follows:

$$u'(c_t) = p_t^1, \tag{15a}$$

$$p_t^1 T_2(k_t, y_t) = -p_t^2, \tag{15b}$$

$$p_{t+1}^2 = \frac{p_t^2}{\delta(1-\mu)} - \frac{p_{t+1}^1 T_1(k_{t+1}, y_{t+1})}{1-\mu}, \tag{15c}$$

$$c_t = T(k_t, y_t), \tag{15d}$$

$$k_{t+1} = (1-\mu)k_t + y_t. \tag{15e}$$

It is easy to see that (15a–d) together with the "dated" version of (5) completely "price" our competitive economy. By construction, these prices

---

[1] See Dechert (1978) for an exact justification of the use of this formalism in our class of models.

are current-value prices. Set $p_t^1 = 1$ and $p_t^2 = q_t$, all t, then the sequence of Lagrange multipliers $\{w_t, r_t, q_t\}$ solving (P1) and (T) are the competitive prices associated to the ICE quantities $\{c_t, k_t, y_t, k_t^1, k_t^2, \ell_t^1, \ell_t^2\}$. Finally, by massaging (15a–e), the Euler equation for the interior optimal paths $\{k_t\}$ can be derived:

$$u'[T(k_t, k_{t+1} - (1-\mu)k_t)]\,T_2(k_t, k_{t+1} - (1-\mu)k_t)$$
$$+ \delta u'[T(k_{t+1}, k_{t+2} - (1-\mu)k_{t+1})]$$
$$\cdot \{T_1(k_{t+1}, k_{t+2} - (1-\mu)k_{t+1}) - (1-\mu)T_2(k_{t+1}, k_{t+2} - (1-\mu)k_{t+1})\} = 0.$$
$$(16)$$

We conclude this part by stating (without proof) the following well-known proposition.

Proposition 2.   *Let u, F^1, and F^2 satisfy conditions U1), T1), and T2). If there exist sequences $\{c_t, y_t, k_t\}$ satisfying (15a–e) plus the transversality condition $\lim \delta^t q_t k_t = 0$, for $t \to \infty$, then $\{c_t, y_t, k_t\}$ solves (P1).*

3   **Dynamic programming**

a   *The value function and the optimal policy function*

The previous discussion should have clarified the economic content of the problem:

(P) $W_\delta(k_0) = \max \sum\limits_{t=0}^{\infty} V(k_t, k_{t+1})\delta^t$, s.t. $(k_t, k_{t+1}) \in D$, k_0 given in K,

where the following are assumed:

A1) D is a compact and convex subset of R_+^2. We assume $(0,0) \in D$ and $(0, y) \notin D$, all $y > 0$.

A2) $V: D \to R_+$ is a concave function, strictly concave in its second argument, continuous on D, and C^2 on D. We assume $V_1(x, y) \geq 0$ and $V_2(x, y) \leq 0$, all $(x, y) \in D$.

A3)   The discount factor δ lies in $[0, 1)$.

Let us relate A1) and A2) to U1) and T1)–T3). T3) implies that for all $k > \bar{k}$, $T(k, \mu k) < 0$, and for all $k < \bar{k}$, $T(k, \mu k) > 0$; hence production of capital is limited to the interval $K = [0, \bar{k}]$. The feasible values (k_t, k_{t+1}) of initial stock–final stock pairs belong to $D \subset K \times K$. Denote as $y = f(k)$ the solution to $T(k, y) = 0$; the set D is defined as

$$D = \{(k, k') \in K \times K, \text{ s.t. } (1-\mu)k \leq k' \leq (1-\mu)k + f(k)\},$$

which is obviously compact and convex. The second part of A1) follows directly from T1). Finally, A2) comes from setting

$$V(k, k') = u[T(k, k' - (1 - \mu)k)]$$

and U1) and T2). Because we want to concentrate our analysis on the features of the model that are implications of different technological assumptions, we make the simplifying hypothesis:

Ū1)   The utility function has the linear form $u(c_t) = c_t$.

It is worth stressing that Ū1) is of no harm to the generality of the analysis. All the results can be replicated with minor changes by adopting a generic utility function. The dynamic programming approach to the study of (P) considers the equivalent problem

$$W_\delta(k_0) = \max\{V(k_0, k_1) + \delta W_\delta(k_1), \text{ s.t. } (k_0, k_1) \in D\}. \qquad (17)$$

A solution to (17) is a map $\tau_\delta: K \to K$, with graph contained in D. We call this map the (optimal) policy function of (P). The whole sequence of optimal capital stocks solving (P) is then described as the dynamical system: $k_{t+1} = \tau_\delta(k_t)$. We shall study the asymptotic properties of the accumulation paths by means of the map τ_δ.

To enhance the economic significance of what follows we point out that the knowledge of the optimal sequence $\{k_t\}$ is enough to deduce the paths over time of all the price sequences and the quantity sequences listed in the definition of an ICE in Section 2. In particular, one would like to know how the capital stock price evolves over time. In fact, stock prices are much more easily observable than quantities, which makes it possible to test the implications of the model. The problem has a simple solution.[2]

Definition 2.   *Let $f: X \to X$ and $g: Y \to Y$ be two maps, with X and Y any pair of topological spaces. We say that f and g are topologically conjugate if there exists a homeomorphism $h: X \to Y$ such that $h \cdot f = g \cdot h$. The homeomorphism h is called a topological conjugacy.*

Theorem 1.   *Assume $\tau: K \to K$ is an interior solution to (P) under A1)–A3). Let $\theta: [0, \infty) \to [0, \infty)$ be such that $q_{t+1} = \theta(q_t)$, with q_t defined as in (7). Then τ and θ are topologically conjugate.*

Proof: By the definition of q_t and the result of Benveniste and Scheinkman (1979) it is obvious that

---

[2] The problem was posed to me by José Scheinkman.

$$q_t = \delta W'(k_{t+1}),$$

where W' is the first derivative of the value function. Also, $q_{t-1} = \delta W'(k_t)$, and because k_{t+1} is optimal given k_t, we can write

$$q_{t-1} = \delta W'(k_t), \qquad q_t = \delta W'[\tau(k_t)].$$

Because W is strictly concave, W' is a homeomorphism from K into $[0, \infty)$. Hence,

$$q_t = \theta(q_{t-1}), \quad \text{with } \theta = \delta W' \cdot \tau \cdot (W'\delta)^{-1}. \qquad \blacksquare$$

Corollary 1.   *Under* A1)–A3), *if k^* is an optimal steady state (OSS) for τ_δ, then $q^* = \delta W'(k^*)$ is an OSS for θ_δ, and if $\{k_t(k_0)\}$ is an orbit of τ_δ with initial condition k_0, then $\{q_t\} = \delta\{W'[k_t(k_0)]\}$ is an orbit for θ_δ. In short, the dynamics of k_t over K is identical, up to a monotonically decreasing homeomorphism, to that of q_t over R_+.*

Proof: It follows from Theorem 1˙and Proposition (A.1) in Appendix A. $\qquad \blacksquare$

Remark 1:   The assumptions $V \in C^1$ and τ_δ interior are critical to obtain the result. In fact, if differentiability of the value function W_δ is not guaranteed, we have to use the supergradient set of $W_\delta(k_t)$ to obtain the price q_t. But the supergradient correspondence, even if monotonic, does not need to be lower-hemicontinuous. Therefore, we cannot claim the existence of a continuous, monotonic selection that realizes the topological conjugacy between prices and quantities in the nondifferentiable case.

Example: Problem (P) for our model economy is

$$\max \sum_{t=0}^{\infty} \{a[k_t(1+\gamma-\gamma\mu) - \gamma k_{t+1}]^\rho + (1-a)[1-k_{t+1}-(1-\mu)k_t]^\rho\}^{1/\rho}\delta^t,$$

s.t. $(k_t, k_{t+1}) \in D,$

where

$$D = \left\{(x, y) \in [0, 1/\mu] \times [0, 1/\mu], \text{ s.t. } (1-\mu)x \le y \le (1-\mu)x + \frac{x}{\gamma}\right\}.$$

It is apparent that we shall not be able to put it in the form (17), essentially because the nonlinear structure of our V makes it impossible (to the author) to find an explicit form for the value function $W_\delta(k_0)$. Consequently, we shall not compute the policy function for our example. This is generally the case for this class of problems when nonlinearities are

introduced. It explains why, in the theoretical part, we search for information on the τ_δ that can be directly computed from the V, in particular
from the associated Euler equation.

4   Exotic dynamics

a   *Optimal cycles and optimal chaos*

It is well known that the dynamical system τ_δ that solves (P) exhibits
regular behaviors for certain parameter values. The Turnpike theorems
(see McKenzie, 1986) assure that for any V satisfying (A.2) there exists a
value of the discount factor close enough to 1 to guarantee that all optimal paths, from any initial condition, eventually converge to a unique
steady state. The point of our research is to show that, in general, this is
not the case for smaller δ and to provide conditions under which very
irregular dynamics are optimal. The work of Benhabib and Nishimura
(1985) gives sufficient conditions for the existence of optimal period-two
cycles. In the two-sector setup these amount to a consumption-good sector that is more capital/labor intensive than the investment sector in an
appropriate neighborhood of the steady state, together with an appropriate value of δ. This is theorem 1 from Benhabib and Nishimura (1985).
It exploits the fact that the τ_δ is downward sloping, with a slope at the
steady state that crosses the value -1 when the discount factor passes
through a threshold. This creates the period-two cycles by means of a
flip bifurcation. In any case, a monotonic policy function cannot produce orbits more complicated than that, as can be easily checked.

Therefore, we need to know what determines the slope of the policy
function. The answer is again provided by Benhabib and Nishimura (1985,
theorem 2).

Theorem 2.   *Let $\{k_t\}$ be an optimal path. Let $\{k_t, k_{t+1}) \in \text{int}(D)$, and
let* A1)–A3) *hold. Then:*

(i)   *If $V_{12}(x, y) > 0$ for all $(x, y) \in \text{int}(D)$, $k_t < k_{t+1}$ implies $k_{t+1} \leq k_{t+2}$. If $(k_{t+1}, k_{t+2}) \in \text{int}(D)$, $k_t < k_{t+1}$ implies $k_{t+1} < k_{t+2}$ (i.e., τ_δ is strictly increasing on interior segments of K).*

(ii)   *If $V_{12}(x, y) < 0$ for all $(x, y) \in \text{int}(D)$, $k_t < k_{t+1}$ implies $k_{t+1} \geq k_{t+2}$. If $(k_{t+1}, k_{t+2}) \in \text{int}(D)$, $k_t < k_{t+1}$ implies $k_{t+1} > k_{t+2}$ (i.e., τ_δ is strictly decreasing on interior segments of K).*

Proof: See Benhabib and Nishimura (1985, theorem 2).   ∎

In our model we have

$$V_{12}(k_t, k_{t+1}) = T_{12}[k_t, k_{t+1} - (1-\mu)k_t] - (1-\mu)T_{22}[k_t, k_{t+1} - (1-\mu)k_t].$$
(18)

Equation (12) implies that we have to assume either a factor-intensity reversal and a large negative magnitude of T_{12} relative to $(1-\mu)T_{22}$, or a more capital-intensive consumption sector with relative magnitudes of T_{12} and $(1-\mu)T_{22}$ such that (18) has opposite signs over different subsets of the interior of D. For the sake of simplicity we shall take the first road in its most extreme version:

A4)   The PPF T is derived from F^1 and F^2 satisfying T1) and T2) and such that there exists one and only one factor-intensity reversal. Moreover, the depreciation factor μ equals 1.

Under (Ũ1) and A4), we have $T(k_t, k_{t+1}) = V(k_t, k_{t+1})$. Then we can prove the following:

Lemma 1.   *Under* (Ũ1) *and* A4), *if*

$$(k^*, k^{*\prime}) \in D$$

are such that $V_{12}(k^*, k^{*\prime}) = 0$, *then* $V_{12}(k^*, k') = 0$ *for all* k' *feasible from* k^*.

Proof: See Appendix A.   ∎

All-in-all we have the following proposition:

Proposition 3.   *Under* A1), A2), A4), *and* (Ũ1) *the following is true:* τ_δ *is increasing on* $[0, k^*]$ *and decreasing on* $[k^*, \bar{k}]$ *for all* $\delta \in [0, 1)$.

Proof: By Lemma 1, $V_{12} = 0$ only along the vertical line $k_t = k^*$ in the (k_t, k_{t+1}) plane. From Theorem 2 and the fact that $\tau_\delta(0) = 0$ from A1), if τ_δ is not identically zero on K, it must increase in $[0, k^*]$ and decrease in $[k^*, \bar{k}]$.   ∎

Example: Our pair of production functions clearly satisfy the first part of A4); in fact, any pair of distinct CES production functions exhibit factor-intensity reversal as long as they are not both Leontief, Cobb–Douglas, or linear. If we set also $\mu = 1$, then our $V(k_t, k_{t+1})$ becomes

$$[a(k_t - \gamma k_{t+1})^\rho + (1-a)(1 - k_{t+1})^\rho]^{1/\rho}.$$

The second derivative V_{12} is zero for $k_{t+1} = 1$ or for $k_t = \gamma$, positive on the interior of D for all $k_t \in [0, \gamma)$, and negative for all $k_t \in (\gamma, 1]$. Lemma 1 is therefore also satisfied with $k^* = \gamma$ (the boundary value $k_{t+1} = 1$ does not matter here). Simple manipulations of the Euler equation,

$$-[a(k_{t-1} - \gamma k_t)^\rho + (1-a)(1-k_t)^\rho]^{1/\rho - 1}$$

$$\cdot [(1-a)(1-k_t)^{\rho-1} + a\gamma(k_{t-1} - \gamma k_t)^{\rho-1}]$$

$$+ \delta a[a(k_t - \gamma k_{t+1})^\rho + (1-a)(1-k_{t+1})^\rho]^{1/\rho-1} \cdot (k_t - \gamma k_{t-1})^{\rho-1} = 0,$$

$$(19)$$

show that the unique, interior steady-state $k(\delta)$ can be expressed as

$$k(\delta) = \left\{ 1 + (1-\gamma)\left[\frac{1-a}{a(\delta-\gamma)} \right]^{1/(1-\rho)} \right\}^{-1}. \tag{20}$$

Therefore, for $\delta \in [0, \gamma]$ we have no interior state, and for $\delta \in (\gamma, 1)$ we have a unique interior steady state that is on the upward-sloping branch of τ_δ for $\delta < \gamma[1 + (1-a)/a\gamma^\rho]$ and on the downward-sloping branch for $\delta > \gamma[1 + (1-a)/a\gamma^\rho]$ (see Appendix B for the computations). Some additional algebra shows that there exists a pair of values of δ greater than $\gamma[1 + (1-a)/a\gamma^\rho]$ but smaller than 1 at which Theorem 1 of Benhabib and Nishimura (1985) is verified, so our model economy exhibits dynamic competitive equilibria that are cycles of period two. Once again, the algebra is in Appendix B. We start our search for chaos by defining it.

Definition 3. *We say that $\tau_\delta \colon K \to K$ has topological chaos if there exists a period-three cycle for τ_δ on K.*

If τ_δ has period three, then by the Sarkovskij theorem it also has cycles of any other period, and by Li and Yorke (1975) there exist a nondenumerable set $S \subset K$ and an $\epsilon > 0$ such that, for every pair x and y in S with $x \neq y$,

$$\lim \sup |\tau_\delta^n(x) - \tau_\delta^n(y)| \geq \epsilon$$

and

$$\lim \inf |\tau_\delta^n(x) - \tau_\delta^n(y)| = 0,$$

and for all $x \in \text{Per}(\tau_\delta)$ and $y \in S$,

$$\lim \sup |\tau_\delta^n(x) - \tau_\delta^n(y)| > 0.$$

The latter is a weak form of sensitive dependence on initial conditions. It is weak because (a) given S we do not need to be able to pick x and y arbitrarily close to each other, and (b) even if it is uncountable, the set S can have Lebesgue measure zero in K. A stronger form of chaos,[3] that we call *observable chaos,* satisfies the following definition.

---

[3] See Grandmont (1987) for a discussion of the relevance of these two different forms of chaos in economic modeling.

Definition 4. $\tau_\delta\colon K \to K$ *has observable chaos if there exists a measure* μ *on K that is invariant with respect to* τ_δ, *absolutely continuous, and ergodic.*

Unfortunately, it is almost impossible to check if τ_δ satisfies Definition 4 without knowledge of its functional form. Because this is the case in most of the applications of our theory, we shall concentrate our attention on topological chaos (however, see Corollary 2). The following lemma is crucial to our analysis. It is a well-known result from the theory of one-dimensional discrete dynamical systems.

Lemma 2. *Let* $\tau_\delta\colon K \to K$ *be continuous. Then* τ_δ *has cycles of period three if and only if there exist distinct intervals* $K^1 \subset K$ *and* $K^2 \subset K$, *such that*

$$\tau_\delta(K^1) \supset K^2 \quad \text{and} \quad \tau_\delta(K^2) \supset (K^1 \cup K^2).$$

Our strategy is that of looking for computable conditions on V such that Lemma 2 is satisfied by the associated policy function. In the first case we need to replace A1) with the following:

Ã1) D is a compact and convex subset of $K \times K$, such that

(i) $(0,0) \in D$,
(ii) $(k,0) \in D$ for all $k \in K$, and
(iii) there exists a $k^1 \le k^*$ such that $(k, \bar k) \in D$ for all $k \ge k^1$.

The implications of Ã1) on F^1 and F^2 should be clear. The only stringent condition is (iii).

We need three lemmas.

Lemma 3. *A path* $\{k_t^*\}$ *such that* rel int $\Gamma(k_{t-1}^*) \cap$ rel int $\Gamma^{-1}(k_{t+1}^*) \ne \emptyset$ *for all t, with* Γ *defined as* $\Gamma(x) = \{y \in K, \text{ s.t. } (x, y) \in D\}$ *is an optimal solution to problem* (P) *if and only if*

$$V(k_{t-1}^*, y) + \delta V(y, k_{t+1}^*)$$

is maximized at $y = k_t^*$ *for all* $t = 0, 1, \ldots$,

Proof: See Appendix A. ∎

Lemma 4. *Assume* $\tau_\delta(\bar k) = 0$ *for given* δ. *Then, under* Ã1), A2), A3), *and* A4), $\tau_\delta(k^*) = \bar k$ *if and only if* $V(k^*, k) + \delta V(k, 0)$ *is increasing in k.*

Proof: Apply Lemma 3. ∎

Lemma 5. *Assume $\tau_\delta(0) = 0$ for given δ. Then, under $\tilde{A}1$), A2), and A4), $\tau_\delta(\bar{k}) = 0$ if and only if $V(\bar{k}, k) + \delta V(k, 0)$ is decreasing in k.*

Proof: Apply Lemma 3.   ∎

Lemma 6. *Assume there exists an $\epsilon > 0$ with $[0, \epsilon] \subset \Gamma(0)$. Then, under $\tilde{A}1$), A2), A3), and A4), $\tau_\delta(0) = 0$ if and only if $V(0, k) + \delta V(k, 0)$ is decreasing in k.*

Proof: Apply Lemma 3.   ∎

Remark 2: The three preceding lemmas provide conditions for the path $\{k^*, \bar{k}, 0, 0, \ldots\}$ to be optimal that can be easily verified and require only that V be subdifferentiable on D. If the assumption $V \in C^2$ is used, then we can check that Lemmas 4, 5, and 6 are satisfied if $\delta \in C(V)$, where

$$C(V) = \left\{ \delta \in (0, 1), \text{s.t.} \ \frac{|V_2(k^*, \bar{k})|}{V_1(\bar{k}, 0)} \leq \delta \leq \frac{\min\{|V_2(\bar{k}, 0)|, |V_2(0, 0)|\}}{V_1(0, 0)} \right\}.$$

In this case our result reduces to Proposition 7 of Deneckere and Pelikan (1986). It is obvious (see also the later proof of Theorem 3) that topological chaos is obtained under the previous assumptions.

It is easy to check that strict concavity of V in either of its two arguments bounds $C(V)$ away from $\underline{\delta} = |V_2(k^*, 0)|/V_1(0, 0)$, which is the largest value of δ that makes τ_δ identically zero. At the same time, there is nothing in our model that assures that $C(V)$ is not empty. Hence we must assume it explicitly:

A5) V satisfies A2) and A4) and is such that $C(V)$ is not empty.

The hypothesis that there exists an $\epsilon > 0$ such that $[0, \epsilon] \subset \Gamma(0)$, which we used in Lemma 6, is not satisfied by a large class of production functions that are typically used by economists (e.g., our own example). One may then want to consider the case in which $\Gamma(0) = \{0\}$. By using the three Lemmas 4, 5, and 6, we can prove the following theorem.[4]

Theorem 3. *Assume that, for a given sequence $\{\epsilon_n\}_{n=0}^{\infty}$, $\epsilon_n > 0$, $\epsilon_n \to 0$ as $n \to \infty$, the condition of Lemma 6 is satisfied with $\epsilon = \epsilon_n$ for all n. Then,*

---

[4] I would like to thank Raymond Deneckere for pointing out a mistake in a previous formulation and proof of this theorem. He has subsequently generalized the result by providing a necessary, as well as sufficient, condition for $\tau_\delta(\bar{k}) = 0$ when $\Gamma(0) = \{0\}$ (see Deneckere, 1988). I also am grateful to him for several suggestions that helped to prove Theorem 4.

under the maintained hypotheses $\tilde{A}1$), A2), A3), A4), *and* A5), τ_δ *has topological chaos when* $\delta \in C(V)$ *even if* $\Gamma(0) = \{0\}$.

Proof: To the sequence $\{\epsilon_n\}_{n=0}^\infty$ we can associate a sequence of policy functions θ_n and the sequence of subsets $C_n(V) \subset (0,1)$, where, for each n, $C_n(V)$ contains all the δ's that guarantee the satisfaction of Lemmas 4, 5, and 6. Then, $\theta_n(k^*) = \bar{k}$, $\theta_n(\bar{k}) = 0$, and $\theta_n(0) = 0$, all n. As the sequence θ_n converges uniformly to τ_δ for $n \to \infty$, and given δ, we have that $\tau_\delta(k^*) = \bar{k}$, $\tau_\delta(\bar{k}) = 0$, $\tau_\delta(0) = 0$ for $\delta \in C(V)$, where $C(V)$ is the limit of $C_n(V)$, nonempty by hypothesis. The conclusion then follows from Lemma 2. ∎

Corollary 2. *Under the assumptions of Theorem 3 and the regularity hypothesis that τ_δ has a negative Schwartzian derivative everywhere on K for $\delta \in C(V)$, the dynamical system τ_δ exhibits observable chaos.*

Proof: Notice that $\tau_\delta[\tau_\delta(k^*)] = 0$ for $\delta \in C(V)$; that is, the unique critical point is mapped onto the unstable fixed point at the origin. For a theorem of Collet and Eckmann[5] this implies that τ_δ has no stable periodic orbits and, in fact, displays a unique invariant, ergodic and absolutely continuous measure on K. ∎

Example: Theorem 3 cannot be applied directly to our V. The reason is that though Lemmas 4 and 5 are satisfied for a large class of parameters, the version of Lemma 6 that is used in Theorem 3 is satisfied by our example only when the discount factor is less than γ. We already know that in this case the policy function has no interior steady state, and its graph lies all below the 45° line. Examples of economies that do satisfy Theorem 3 can, in any case, be provided. We shall not investigate this here but refer the reader to the examples given in Boldrin and Montrucchio (1984, 1986) and Deneckere and Pelikan (1986).

The conditions of Theorem 3, even for well-behaved problems, are often not realized. It may be surprising to discover that linear homogeneity of the production functions simplifies the search for chaotic accumulation paths. We have the following.

Lemma 7. *Under assumptions A1)–A4), if*

$$V_2(k, k^*) + \delta V_1(k^*, k') = 0$$

has a solution $k = G(k^*, k')$, then G is independent from k'.

---

[5] I do not report here either the test of the theorem or the intuition behind it in order to avoid a long technical digression. As a matter of fact, the results we are using come from

Proof: By the implicit function theorem,

$$\frac{\partial k}{\partial k'} = -\frac{\delta V_{12}(k^*, k')}{V_{22}(k, k^*)}.$$

By Lemma 2, $V_{12}(k^*, \cdot) = 0$, independently of the second argument. ∎

Remark 3: A way of restating the lemma is to say that the preimage of the critical point k^* under the policy function τ_δ is independent from the image of k^* under τ_δ.

We can now state our last theorem.

Theorem 4. *Consider problem* (P) *under* A1)–A4). *Assume there exists an interval* $C(V) \subset (0,1)$ *such that for all* $\delta \in C(V)$ *the following conditions are satisfied at such* δ:

(i) $V_2(x, k^*) + \delta V_1(k^*, \cdot) = 0$ *has a solution* $k_1 \in (0, k^*)$,
(ii) $V_2(x, k_1) + \delta V_1(k_1, k^*) = 0$ *has a solution* $k_2 \in (k^*, \bar{k}]$, *and*
(iii) $V_2(x, k_2) + \delta V_1(k_2, k_1) = 0$ *has a solution* $k_3 \in \mathbb{R}_+$.

Then τ_δ *has topological chaos.*

Proof: Notice that if k^* has any preimage other than itself, $k_1 < k^*$ must hold. Therefore (i) implies that $M = \tau_\delta(k^*) > k^*$. We do not know if $k_2 \leq M$. This can be detected from (iii). In fact, $k_2 > M$ would imply that k_2 has no preimage. Hence, $k_1 = \tau_\delta(k_2) > \tau_\delta(M)$. Now, set $I_1 = [k_1, k^*]$ and $I_2 = [k^*, M]$. Then, $\tau_\delta(I_1) = [k^*, M] = I_2$ and $\tau_\delta(I_2) = [\tau_\delta(M), M] \supset [k_1, M] = (I_1 \cup I_2)$. The theorem then follows from Lemma 2. ∎

Remark 4: This theorem, so to speak, is just a computational device but it is very useful when the direct criterion of Theorem 3 fails. Our example fits this theorem, but we cannot go through other computations here. Notice that if we set $\rho = 0$, then we have the Cobb–Douglas case. Scheinkman (1984) first conjectured that chaos may exist in such a case. The analysis contained in Boldrin and Deneckere (1987) shows that he was right because the conditions of Theorem 4 are satisfied. We also show, in the same paper, that the general CES case presented here does meet the conditions of Theorem 4 and that the values of the discount factor for which this is true increase when the degree of substitutability between factors, as measured by ρ, decreases. In particular, it seems that for ρ negative, chaos obtains for δ in the interval $[0.2, 0.4]$, which are values enormously larger than those obtained in previous examples.

the work of various authors, among whom are the named Collet and Eckmann. A statement, without proof, can be found in Grandmont (1987) as theorem D.1.9.

5   Conclusions

In this paper we study the dynamic competitive equilibrium of an aggregate, neoclassical, two-sector model under the hypothesis that all markets clear at each time and that all agents are identical maximizers with infinite, perfect foresight. We concentrate on the technological side of the model and show that a source for endogenous sustained oscillations can be found in the changes of relative profitability between the two sectors. This, in turn, is brought about by shifts in the relative capital–labor intensities. We adopt the idea of chaotic dynamics as a qualitative representation of sustained, apparently stochastic oscillations. Two sets of conditions are obtained under which the optimal accumulation paths (and the related competitive prices and quantities sequences) are chaotic. The theoretical results are applied to a simple example. In particular, we claim that the idea that oscillations are optimal only when the discount factor is extremely small is not true in general. In fact, as the degree of factors substitutability in the economy decreases, chaos and cycles may appear for discount factors that are "fairly large."

It is clear, nevertheless, that such an abstract and overly simplified setup cannot be proposed as a complete macro model. It simply shows that there is room for an endogenous explanation of competitive business cycles.

Appendix A

Proposition A.1. *If two maps $f: I \to I$ and $g: J \to J$ are topologically conjugate through the homeomorphism h, then for every invariant set $C \subset I$, $h(C) \subset J$ is invariant, and for every invariant set $C' \subset J$, $h^{-1}(C') \subset I$ is invariant.*

Proof: Trivial.   ∎

Corollary 1 follows from the fact that the OSS and the orbits of τ_δ are invariant sets for τ_δ.

Proof of Lemma 1:   Consider an Edgeworth box for problem T when the capital stock is k^* and there exists a level of future capital stock k^{*1} such that $V_{12}(k^*, k^{*1}) = 0$. Let $c^* = T(k^*, k^{*1})$ and $y^* = k^{*1} - (1 - \mu)k^*$. The two isoquants of F^1 and F^2 associated with c^* and y^* are tangent at a point (k^1, ℓ^1), $(k^* - k^1, 1 - \ell^1)$, at which the two sectors have the same capital intensity. Such a point must be on the diagonal of the box. Linear homogeneity implies that all the points on the diagonal are points of tangency for some isoquants (c, y) with $0 \leq c \leq T(k^*, 0)$ and $0 \leq y \leq f(k^*)$. The PPF then coincides with the diagonal in this case; and, therefore, $V_{12}[k^*, y + (1 - \mu)k^*] = 0$ for all y. ∎

Proof of Lemma 3: Necessity is obvious. We shall prove sufficiency by showing that our condition implies that there exists a price sequence $\{q_t\}$ such that

$$V(k_t^*, k_{t+1}^*) + \delta q_{t+1} k_{t+1}^* - q_t k_t^* \geq V(x, y) + \delta q_{t+1} y - q_t x \quad (A1)$$

for all $(x, y) \in D$. The latter, together with the transversality condition that is trivially satisfied in our model, has been shown in McKenzie (1974) to be sufficient for optimality of $\{k_t^*\}$, extending a result of Weitzman (1973) to the discounted case.

From our hypothesis, we have

$$V(k_{t-1}^*, k_t^*) + \delta V(k_t^*, k_{t+1}^*) \geq V(k_{t-1}^*, y) + \delta V(y, k_{t+1}^*)$$

for all $y \in$ rel int $\Gamma(k_{t-1}^*) \cap$ rel int $\Gamma^{-1}(k_{t+1}^*) \neq \emptyset$.

Set

$$G(x) = V(k_{t-1}^*, x) + \delta V(x, k_{t+1}^*).$$

The last inequality means that zero is a supergradient of G at k_t^*, that is, $0 \in \partial G(k_t^*)$. From Rockafellar (1970, theorem 23.8) we have also that $0 \in [\partial_2 V(k_{t-1}^*, k_t^*) + \delta \partial_1 V(k_t^*, k_{t+1}^*)]$; therefore, there exists a sequence of vectors $\{q_t\}$ such that $-q_{t+1} \in \partial_2 V(k_{t-1}^*, k_t^*)$, $q_t \in \delta \partial_1 V(k_t^*, k_{t+1}^*)$. This in turn implies that $(q_t/\delta, -q_{t+1}) \in \partial V(k_t^*, k_{t+1}^*)$ and by definition that

$$V(k_t^*, k_{t+1}^*) \geq V(x, y) + q_t(k_t^* - x) - \delta q_{t+1}(k_{t+1}^* - y),$$

which is equivalent to (A1). ∎

Appendix B

The first- and second-order partial derivatives of our PPF are easy to compute. We leave it to the reader. The Euler equation at an interior steady-state k reduces to

$$[a(k - \gamma k)^\rho + (1 - a)(1 - k)^\rho]^{1/\rho - 1}$$
$$\cdot [(\delta - \gamma)a(k - \gamma k)^{\rho - 1} - (1 - a)(1 - k)^{\rho - 1}] = 0,$$

from which (20) can be obtained after a few manipulations. We are interested in parameter values at which the steady-state $k(\delta)$ lies on the downward-sloping arm of τ_δ (i.e., it is larger than γ). This is necessary to obtain cycles and chaos. From (20) one has

$$k(\delta) \in \begin{cases} (0, \gamma) & \text{for } \gamma < \delta < \gamma[1 + (1-a)/a\gamma^\rho], \\ (\gamma, 1) & \text{for } \gamma[1 + (1-a)/a\gamma^\rho] < \delta < 1. \end{cases}$$

To guarantee that $\gamma[1 + (1-a)/a\gamma^\rho]$ is less than one, we need to impose $a > [1 + \gamma^{\rho-1}(1-\gamma)]^{-1}$, which is understood from now on.

To consider the local stability of $k(\delta)$ and the possibility of period-two cycles bifurcating around it, we have to compute the pair of eigenvalues associated with the linearized Euler equation in a neighborhood of $k(\delta)$. These are the roots λ, of $\delta V_{12}\lambda^2 + (V_{22} + \delta V_{11})\lambda + V_{12} = 0$, where $V_{ij} = V_{ij}[k(\delta), k(\delta)]$, $i, j = 1, 2$. In our case this reads

$$\delta \frac{\gamma - k(\delta)}{1 - k(\delta)} \lambda^2 - \left[\left(\frac{\gamma - k(\delta)}{1 - k(\delta)} \right)^2 + \delta \right] \lambda + \frac{\gamma - k(\delta)}{1 - k(\delta)} = 0.$$

The two eigenvalues are

$$\lambda_1 = \frac{1 - k(\delta)}{\gamma - k(\delta)} \quad \text{and} \quad \lambda_2 = \frac{\gamma - k(\delta)}{[1 - k(\delta)]\delta}.$$

Substituting (20) into the preceding equations gives

$$\lambda_1 = \frac{(1-a)^{1/(1-\rho)}}{\gamma(1-a)^{1/(1-\rho)} - [a(\delta - \gamma)]^{1/(1-\rho)}}$$

and

$$\lambda_2 = \delta^{-1} \left\{ \gamma - \left[\frac{a(\delta - \gamma)}{1-a} \right]^{1/(1-\rho)} \right\}.$$

For values of δ larger than γ, λ_1 behaves as

$$\lambda_1 = \begin{cases} [1/\gamma + \infty) & \text{for } \gamma \leq \delta < \gamma[1 + (1-a)/a\gamma^\rho], \\ [-1, 0) & \text{for } \gamma + (1+\gamma)^{1-\rho}(1-a)/a \leq \delta, \\ (-\infty, -1] & \text{for } \gamma[1 + (1-a)/a\gamma^\rho] < \delta \leq \gamma + (1+\gamma)^{1-\rho}(1-a)/a. \end{cases}$$

The behavior of λ_2 is analogous, even if not all the critical values can be explicitly computed. Anyhow, λ_2 is a decreasing function of δ in the interval $[\gamma, 1)$, with $\lambda_2(\gamma) = 1$ and $\lambda_2(1) < -1$ for

$$a > (1+\gamma)^{1-\rho}[1 - \gamma + (1+\gamma)^{1-\rho}]^{-1}.$$

Assuming that (a, γ, ρ) satisfy the latter inequality and denoting with δ^{00} the unique solution to $\lambda_2(\delta) = -1$, we have

$$\lambda_2 = \begin{cases} [0, 1] & \text{for } \gamma \leq \delta \leq \gamma[1 + (1-a)/a\gamma^\rho], \\ [-1, 0] & \text{for } \gamma[1 + (1-a)/a\gamma^\rho] \leq \delta \leq \delta^{00}, \\ (-\infty, -1) & \text{for } \delta^{00} < \delta. \end{cases}$$

To prove that there exists a period-two cycle for some value of $\delta > \gamma[1 + (1-a)/a\gamma^\rho]$, we adopt the sufficient conditions given in Theorem 1 of Benhabib and Nishimura (1985). They amount to showing that there exists a δ^0 and an interval $[\delta^-, \delta^+]$ in $[\gamma(1 + (1-a)/a\gamma^\rho), 1)$ such that $B(\delta) = V_{22}(\delta) + \delta V_{11}(\delta) - (1 + \delta)V_{12}(\delta)$ satisfies

$$B(\delta) \begin{cases} > 0 & \text{for } \delta \in [\delta^-, \delta^0), \\ = 0 & \text{for } \delta = \delta^0, \\ < 0 & \text{for } \delta \in (\delta^0, \delta^+], \end{cases}$$

where $V_{ij}(\delta) = V_{ij}[k(\delta), k(\delta)]$, $i, j = 1, 2$.

For our model, $B(\delta)$ reads

$$B(\delta) = f[k(\delta), k(\delta)]\{[k(\delta) - \gamma]^2 + \delta[1 - k(\delta)]^2 + (1 + \delta)[\gamma - k(\delta)][1 - k(\delta)]\},$$

where the function f is always negative. Therefore we have

$$B(\delta) \begin{cases} > 0 & \text{for } \gamma[1 + (1-a)/a\gamma^\rho] \le \delta < \delta^{00}, \\ = 0 & \text{for } \delta = \delta^{00}, \\ < 0 & \text{for } \delta^{00} < \delta < \delta^0, \\ = 0 & \text{for } \delta = \delta^0 = \gamma + (1 + \gamma)^{1-\rho}(1-a)/a, \\ > 0 & \text{for } \delta > \delta^0, \end{cases}$$

where δ^{00} solves $\delta + \gamma = [a(\delta - \gamma)/(1-a)]^{1/(1-\rho)}$; that is, it is such that $\lambda_2(\delta^{00}) = -1$.

Therefore, cycles of period-two exist around both δ^0 and δ^{00}.

REFERENCES

Barnett, W., and Chen, P. (1986), "The aggregation-theoretic monetary aggregates are chaotic and have strange attractors," in *Nonlinear Econometric Modeling,* Proceedings of the Third International Symposium in Economic Theory and Econometrics, ed. by W. Barnett, E. Berndt, and H. White, Cambridge: Cambridge University Press.

Becker, R. (1981), "The duality of a dynamic model of equilibrium and an optimal growth model: the heterogeneous capital goods case," *Quarterly Journal of Economics,* 96, 271–300.

Benhabib, J., and Day, R. (1982), "A characterization of erratic dynamics in the overlapping generations model," *Journal of Economic Dynamics and Control,* 4, 37–55.

Benhabib, J., and Nishimura, K. (1979), "The Höpf bifurcation and the existence and stability of closed orbits in multisector models of optimal economic growth," *Journal of Economic Theory,* 21, 421–44.

    (1985), "Competitive equilibrium cycles," *Journal of Economic Theory,* 35, 284–306.

Benveniste, L., and Scheinkman, J. A. (1979), "On the differentiability of the value function in dynamic models of economics," *Econometrica,* 47, 727–32.

Boldrin, M., and Deneckere, R. (1987), "Simple growth models with very complicated dynamics," mimeo., University of Chicago and Northwestern University, May.

252   **Michele Boldrin**

Boldrin, M., and Montrucchio, L. (1984), "The emergence of complex dynamics in models of optimization over time: the role of impatience," *Rochester Center for Economic Research,* University of Rochester, WP No. 7, October.
(1986), "On the indeterminacy of capital accumulation paths," *Journal of Economic Theory,* 40, 26–39.
Brock, W. (1986), "Distinguishing random and deterministic systems: abridged version," *Journal of Economic Theory,* 40, 168–95.
Brock, W., and Sayers, C. (1988), "Is the business cycle characterized by deterministic chaos?" *Journal of Monetary Economics,* 22, 71–90.
Dechert, D. (1978), "ℓ_∞-multipliers with an application to discrete time optimal control problems," *MRG* WP#7826, University of Southern California, August.
Deneckere, R. (1988), "An improved sufficiency condition for complex dynamics in optimal growth models," mimeo., Northwestern University, June.
Deneckere, R., and Pelikan, S. (1986), "Competitive chaos," *Journal of Economic Theory,* 40, 13–25.
Devaney, R. L. (1986), *An Introduction to Chaotic Dynamical Systems,* Menlo Park, Calif.: Benjamin/Cummings.
Grandmont, J. M. (1985), "On endogenous competitive business cycles," *Econometrica,* 53, 995–1096.
ed. (1986), *Nonlinear Economic Dynamics,* New York: Academic Press.
(1987), "Non-linear difference equations and sunspots: an introduction," Lecture Notes, IMSSS, Stanford University, July.
Hirota, M., and Kuga, K. (1971), "On an intrinsic joint production," *International Economic Review,* 12, 87–98.
Intriligator, M. D. (1971), *Mathematical Optimization and Economic Theory,* Englewood Cliffs, N.J.: Prentice-Hall.
Kuga, K. (1972), "The factor-price equalization theorem," *Econometrica,* 40, 723–36.
LeBaron, B., and Scheinkman, J. A. (1986), "Nonlinear dynamics and stock returns," *Journal of Business,* forthcoming.
Li, T., and Yorke, J. (1975), "Period three implies chaos," *American Mathematical Monthly,* 82, 985–92.
McKenzie, L. (1974), "Turnpike theorems with technology and welfare function variable," in *Mathematical Models in Economics,* ed. by J. Los and M. W. Los, New York: American Elsevier.
(1986), "Optimal economic growth and turnpike theorems," in *Handbook of Mathematical Economics,* vol. III, ed. by K. Arrow and M. Intriligator, New York: North-Holland.
Rockafeller, T. (1970), *Convex Analysis,* Princeton, N.J.: Princeton University Press.
Sarkovskij, A. N. (1964), "Coexistence of cycles of a continuous map of a line into itself," *Ukrainian Mat. Z.,* 16, 61–71.
Scheinkman, J. (1984), "General equilibrium models of economic fluctuations: a survey of theory," mimeo., University of Chicago, July.
Weitzman, M. (1973), "Duality theory for infinite horizon convex models," *Management Science,* 19, 783–89.

CHAPTER 11

Economic growth in the very long run: on the multiple-phase interaction of population, technology, and social infrastructure

Richard H. Day and Jean-Luc Walter

> Our ultimate goal is to form laws of cultural dynamics.
> — *Paul Martin*

> The archaeological data suggest that we must...break
> away from the assumption that human cultures are
> inherently stable.... — *Mark Nathan Cohen*

Abstract: Economic growth in the very long run is described by a mutiple-phase, dynamic process with potentially complex dynamics during transitions between regimes. Technology is assumed to rest on a managerial–administrative infrastructure that influences natality, productivity, and mortality. A population adopts a temporarily efficient techno-infrastructure and determines the population of its heirs. Growth can occur within a regime by the reorganization of population into new groups, but this process cannot continue forever because of externalities. A way out exists in the adoption of a new regime. Economic and social evolution is possible, but the probability of escape from an old regime need not be unity. Fluctuations can occur with or without reswitching, and under certain conditions a population can be trapped in a complex pattern of growth, fluctuation, reswitching, and collapse. It is shown that realistic scenarios can be generated by the model. The chapter concludes with a formal analysis of the possible events and the construction of probabilities that describe the chance that phases will switch and that various kinds of qualitative histories can unfold.

The theory of economic growth that flourished after midcentury was motivated, at least in part, by the exponential trend in aggregate output exhibited by the industrialized countries during the preceding century or

The present study was initially stimulated by discussions at Harvard in 1976 with J. Sablov concerning the Classic Mayan Collapse. Sablov later organized an advanced seminar of the

253

two. Indeed, Tinbergen referred to his contribution as "a theory of the trend," and Solow's seminal work reflected the same stylized fact. That stylized fact, however, is only a relatively short-run movement from the perspective of archaeologists for whom a generation or even a century is a short period, and who think in terms of millennia when contemplating changes in human culture. Although the details become increasingly obscure in the more remote reaches of time, scientists in this field have established a reasonably clear picture of human socioeconomic development in its broadest terms. That development has taken us from the epoch of hunting and food collecting to horticultural settlements and complex, nonliterate societies, then to the historical epoch of urban civilization, household agriculture, and trading empires, and very recently to the industrialized economy. Some pundits believe we are already in the midst of a transition to a new epoch of postindustrialization.

At some places and times the transition between epochs seems to have been smooth; at others, crises seem to have occurred with "jumping" and "reswitching" prior to successful adoption of a new regime. Moreover, examples exist in which a rapid collapse and reversion to a preceding regime seems to have occurred. Population fluctuations within a particular way of life appear in the archaeological and historical records, and in some well-known cases of relatively isolated cultures, the socioeconomic process seems to have been stuck in a more or less stationary or fluctuating state for very long periods of time.

The present contribution provides a model of this complex picture of socioeconomic evolution. Economic growth is described by a multiple-phase, dynamic process. The effective use of a technology (or set of technologies) is assumed to rest on an associated social system that incorporates managerial–administrative practice and measures for public health,

Footnote *(cont.)*

Center for American Studies in Santa Fe in the fall of 1978 involving archaeologists M. Aldenderfer, L. Cordell, G. Low, C. Renfrew, and E. Zubrow, a mathematician K. Cooke, a philosopher J. Bell, and the first author, an economist. A book resulted with essays by the participants: Sablov (1980). Further inspiration was provided by successive interdisciplinary conferences sponsored by Ilya Prigogine's Institute in Theoretical and Applied Thermodynamics in March 1982 and March 1984, and by a continuing interdisciplinary seminar led by A. Iberall (physics) and including A. Moore and D. White (anthropology), L. Goldberg (biology), R. Baum and D. Wilkerson (political science), P. Wohlmuth (law), and the first author (economics). All of the computations and diagrams for this study were prepared by Weihong Huang. Section 4 of this chapter has benefited from discussions with Guilio Pianigiani. Although the first author's original notes on the subject were set down more than a decade ago, and these served as the basis for a lecture on the subject at the University of Paris in the spring of 1985, it was during a month of research at Gunnar Eliasson's Industrial Institute for Economic and Social Research in October 1986 that he finally began to put these ideas into a form suitable for publication.

welfare, and defense. Natality, productivity, and mortality are all assumed to depend on this social system. A *regime* consists of more or less independent *groups,* each organized within a technology–social system pair that we call a techno-infrastructure. A population adopts a temporarily efficient techno-infrastructure and determines the population of its heirs. Although expansion within a group is limited by internal diseconomies of group size, growth can occur in a regime by the reorganization of population into new groups. This process cannot continue forever because of external diseconomies associated with the total population. A way out exists in the adoption of a new technology and its associated infrastructure. The probability of escape from an old regime need not be unity, however. Fluctuations can occur with or without reswitching. Under certain conditions a population can be trapped in a complex pattern of growth, fluctuation, collapse, reversion to an old regime, and renewed growth.

Although the picture that emerges is very different in some ways from the models of growth that have dominated economic thinking until now, it is built up from classical ingredients: the interaction of population, productivity, and reproductive behavior. But there are crucial new elements that, when added to the classical assumptions, lead away from stationary states or steady, balanced growth.

The present introduction to this theory is divided into four parts:

1   a background survey of the major epochs and the hypotheses of social infrastructure, productivity, and demoeconomic behavior on which the analysis rests;
2   the statement of a formal model that expresses these hypotheses;
3   an illustration of the kinds of histories that can be generated by the model and an explanation of how a variety of scenarios that seem like "real world" developments can occur; and
4   an introduction to the mathematical analysis of processes of this kind.

1   Background

a   *The epochs*

Some 50 millennia ago, when modern people replaced their Neanderthal predecessors, the change was associated with an improvement in social organization and technology. According to Butzer (1977), the new bands were probably twice the size of the earlier groups. Their hunting–gathering technology involved an expanded ensemble of specialized stone implements of consummately skilled manufacture for various tasks of killing game, processing food, and fabricating clothing and habitations. This great advance was apparently made possible by an improved brain, as well as by vocal organs that yielded a distinct advantage in communication and hence in social interaction. The new linguistic capacity may also have been intimately related to a superior creative capacity that made possible the striking improvement in technology and the adaptation to virtually every nook and cranny of the globe, a process that came to an end some 10,000 years ago when the world (both old and new) was essentially filled with representatives of the hunting and gathering culture.

Binford (1968) and, in an especially comprehensive treatise, Cohen (1977) demonstrate that during the closing of the global frontier, three roughly coincident developments occurred: the disappearance of the megafaunal species, the appearance of villages, and the domestication of plants and animals. The subsequent agricultural and herding societies, based on horticulture and animal husbandry, marked the beginning of a transition to a new epoch that spread throughout a very large part of the world. The new culture displayed considerably more variety of technology and social style, and it supported a denser population. As this new culture spread, and it seems to have done so quite steadily, human numbers exhibited a worldwide surge. "Earlier" peoples were displaced, settled themselves, or fused into larger, more productive groups than before. Hunting cultures gradually retreated into remote areas relatively unsuited for agricultural activity.

About 3,000–5,000 years ago urban–agricultural societies began to organize into centrally controlled, bureaucratically administered city states that used writing and accounting to monitor and control economic transactions. Sagan (1985) suggests that these early civilizations were preceded by intermediate, complex societies that possessed roads, schools, police, standing armies, and bureaucracies but not written languages, prominent examples of which persisted in Africa and Polynesia until the European commercial expansion. In any event, the emergence about 1,500 B.C. of empires based on widespread trading networks made possible a great increase in specialization and a pronounced expansion again in productivity. Another surge in population followed. Social, cultural, and scientific progress of various kinds occurred throughout this age, leading, after the Renaissance, to a breakthrough to a new commercial age when nation states and trading empires spread their civilizations throughout much of the world. Then came the industrial revolution, based on power technology and large-scale capital. It led to still another surge in productivity and population and, compared to previous rates of increase, a truly explosive one, due in large measure to the decrease in mortality rates that accompanied this regime.

This in barest outline is the grand dynamics of *Homo sapiens sapiens*. The actual number of epochs used in describing it is somewhat arbitrary.[1] More importantly, in the major epochs that mark these vast rearrangements of human activity and numbers, various goods, techniques, rules of behavior, and institutional forms were invented, innovated, diffused, and abandoned in overlapping waves of activity and organization, a process that has accelerated with growing amplitude and shortening period. Economic evolution is, thus, much richer and more varied than this brief sketch portrays. What is crucial to the present analysis, however, is the practical existence of distinct socioeconomic epochs.[2]

b   *The techno-infrastructure*

The key to understanding the significance of epochs for the theory of economic growth is the explicit recognition that each one is based on a distinct managerial–administrative infrastructure. Butzer already emphasized the point that it was more efficient organization that enabled humans to specialize in the harvest of dominant species (mammoth, horse, etc.) and to adopt quasipermanent settlements, religion, and specialization in the production of weapons and other implements.

When agriculture emerged, higher levels of organization and more complex societies evolved with it. People assembled into villages; classes and political organizations emerged. The increasingly intensive systems of cultivation required them. A literate elite, large-scale public architecture, a standing military, and a permanent bureaucracy characterized civilized urban centers based on irrigated agriculture, all stemming from the need to organize local production and long-distance trade. When the modern industrial economy began to emerge, its growing armies of white- and blue-collar workers depended on their abilities to function appropriately within vast systems of transportation, education, police, justice, and public health. These systems require huge forces of workers and administrators.[3]

---

[1] A splendid, boldly synthetic survey of this vast process that vividly portrays its dynamic character will be found in Barraclough (1984). See also Sherratt (1980) for another helpful overview for the nonspecialist.

[2] Deevey, for example, bases his survey on seven major epochs whereas, at the other extreme, Easterlin (1983) uses three gross epochs, those of hunting and food collecting, settled agriculture, and modern growth. The present theory can actually accommodate as many or as few distinct regimes as is meaningful or that are convenient for the purpose at hand. See Day and Cigno (1978) and Day (1987) for very general expositions.

[3] Barraclough (1984, p. 52). See also Sagan (1985, pp. xvi–xxiii) on complex societies in this context.

Evidently, a salient feature of socioeconomic life in all the great epochs is the division of effort between *managerial and organizational infrastructure* and *work*. The former produces the social cohesion, coordination, and knowledge on which the productivity of labor is based. Given that effort, the work force can effectively process materials and fabricate goods. A technology defines the possibilities for specialization and cooperation. Its effective implementation depends on the existence of the infrastructure and its managerial "know-how," a prerequisite that Boserup (1981) calls the administrative technology.

In the simplest social groups, this infrastructure may be created by many or even all individuals part of the time. Even in paleolithic hunting bands, individuals played distinct, specialized roles of social and religious leadership. Although the term *infrastructure* may exaggerate these functions in such simple societies, the presence of such a division of labor is obviously crucial to cohesiveness in the very large, nonliterate, complex societies and in the huge agglomerations of early civilization and of our own industrial age. It is clear on the basis of these observations that for society to switch from one epoch to another, it is essential for it to possess a large enough population to support the new technology by providing an appropriate infrastructure. The infrastructure requirements constitute a threshold of population that must be surpassed before a transition is possible.

In addition to this lower threshold, there is an upper bound on population beyond which the effective operation of technology with a given infrastructure cannot be maintained. This is because an excessive population cannot be coordinated: The planning, organization, and control of public goods and services cannot be effectively managed. Technology and infrastructure are, therefore, characterized by both lower and upper thresholds that define its *domain of viability*. This combination of production and administrative technology, with its division of effort between work and management (where these terms are broadly conceived) and with its population range of viability, we shall call a *techno-infrastructure*.

In addition to the internal diseconomy caused by expanding group size, due to problems of information, communication, and coordination in a group possessing a fixed infrastructure, there exists also an *external diseconomy,* also determined by the technology, that derives from aggregate population size. It is induced by the absorbing capacity of the environment. The earth's absorbing capacity for peoples possessing a given techno-infrastructure can be stated in terms of the space available, which depends on the technology and which can be expressed in terms of the average population density. The supply of nonhuman resources is diminished when human densities become too large: The productivity of agriculture is reduced due to the scarcity of land, water, and other resources, and the waste-absorbing capacity of the environment is gradually exhausted.

The externality factor is a characteristic of the techno-infrastructure in that the absorbing capacity of the earth depends on the implied way of life. For example, hunting–gathering societies are limited by the available game and natural produce; horticultural societies by the supply of arable land and water; and industrial society by the supplies of water, oxygen, and the waste-absorbing capacity of the environment. A change in regime may overcome a constraint. Once the process of fission and diffusion of groups in a culture has run its course, a change in regime is the only avenue for further development. It is the only avenue, that is, given the absence of technological innovation and diffusion that is "neutral" to the techno-infrastructure in the sense of being compatible with the social system. This latter type of technological change, of course, plays an important role and occurs more or less continually. Its effect, however, is to accelerate growth in a regime, which, as shall become evident, hastens the process of switching among alternative regimes. Consequently, little is lost if in this study we abstract from neutral technological change *to focus on the process of epochal development in the sense defined here.*

c   *Population*

Population size evidently plays an essential role in determining which techno-infrastructures are viable. A sufficient population size is necessary for any productive activity; and after a technology has been adapted, productivity is influenced by growth in numbers. Eventually, this productivity must decline because of internal and external diseconomies. Any idea of well-being must depend on productivity, and this initial formalization of the theory will follow Cohen in using average product as the key variable. If average product is adequate, population can expand. If it is not, the attendant adversity will motivate a reorganization of society in a search for a means to insure survival and to improve welfare. This process of switching is the heart of the matter, but the relation of population to welfare is its crucial antecedent.

Within the limits of survivability, the "demand for children" can be expressed like a demand for any other costly good, but the correlation of net population growth rates with welfare need not be thought of in literally rational terms. When welfare is low enough, no children will survive. When some threshold of material well-being is surpassed, some children will survive; and this surviving number will increase with rising well-being until the choices of individuals, social customs, or biological constraints introduce sufficient pressure to place an upper bound on further expansion.

The connection between productivity and population growth rates was the essence of the classical theory of development, and it has been incorporated in toto by modern anthropological–economic growth theorists such as Cohen and Boserup. Obviously, the connection is subtle and variable, but for purposes of analyzing economic development in the very long run, it would be inadmissible to omit it. For purposes of developing a formal model, the connection must be made precise; this will be done using the standard form, long incorporated by Nelson (1956), Solow (1956), Haavelmo (1956), or more recently by Day (1983) or Day, Kim, and Macunovich (in press).

What we have then is the interaction of population, productivity, welfare, and population growth rates that forms the basis of the classical theory of economic growth. What has been added to the classical theory is the concept of the techno-infrastructure and the explicit incorporation of internal and external diseconomies associated with excessive population within a given technology and administrative framework.

d   *Fission, fusion, and the switch in regime*

The key hypothesis originated by Binford, developed in Boserup and buttressed in a comprehensive survey of the evidence by Cohen, is that population growth brings about a need to switch to progressively more intensive techniques to avoid an excessive decline in well-being and that, in order to switch, an appropriate infrastructure is required. According to this theory, population growth is necessary to bring about major reorganizations of society and is sufficient to create the economic pressures that motivate social transformations.

This process of socioeconomic evolution can be most easily identified at the transition between the hunting and food-collecting epoch and the succeeding epoch of settled agriculture. Under favorable conditions, a hunting and food-collecting band grows. As it does, it draws on a greater and greater area whose scope eventually taxes the energies of the group. Productivity and, hence, welfare begin to fall. At some point the band may split to form two groups or in a more gradual way may "shed" some of its members, who will fuse with others who have separated from other bands to form a new productive entity. The new groups move apart, each occupying about the same space as the original bands and each following essentially the same life as before. In this way (in a process originally described by Birdsell, 1958), an originally small, insignificant population spreads itself throughout all those areas where hunting and food collecting are possible.

The process is slow or fast depending on the yield of the environment, the quality and specialization of implements, and the effectiveness of co-operation in the hunt. Also crucial are the mores of reproduction, conditions of hygiene, and external environmental factors that determine mortality in the group. The process can take place at a very high rate, as shown in recent simulation studies by Martin (1987).

New groups that emerge could choose a new technology, but this may not be possible until there is a large enough population for groups to be fused; or it may be that the old technology makes possible a superior well-being just by splitting the groups, each adopting the same infrastructure-technology pair as before. But once the world becomes "full" – that is, once the external diseconomies of total population using a given techno-infrastructure become prominent enough – well-being cannot be maintained by further group formation. It can be accomplished (given the previously mentioned caveat about neutral technological change) only by a jump to a new techno-infrastructure.

The process of fission that characterized the expansion throughout the epoch of the hunting–gathering band did not disappear at the end of the age. It is still an important phenomenon. Fusion became increasingly important at the beginning of the next regime as formerly disparate groups were conquered and assimilated, or combined among themselves to form new civilizations to oppose the others. Nonetheless, during the spread of civilization, great empires that had once been formed often broke up into smaller geographical units within which growth eventually resumed. The Roman Empire, for example, divided into a considerable number of smaller states. Although population declined in some places, particularly in Rome, population growth in Europe quickly resumed. Similar break-ups and reunifications occurred in China. Although fusion and fission in advanced societies is usually, if not universally, accompanied by war, it seems likely that the underlying economic forces causing these changes include those of population growth, productivity, and the efficacy of administrative technology in a manner described in general and somewhat abstract terms set forth here.

e   *Alternative scenarios of economic development*

The transition to a new techno-infrastructure rests both on its sufficient productivity and on its "reachability." In the absence of a reachable regime, the expansion of population could converge to an equilibrium or, more likely, to a fluctuation in numbers as originally argued by Malthus and in the archaeological literature by Zubrow (1971), who provides evidence of such dynamics in the data on prehistoric agriculture in what is now the southwestern United States. In either case, economic evolution would come to a halt, awaiting the discovery of new techniques and the requisite social forms.

A more extreme result of long-run growth in the absence of a reachable regime is the overshoot of an equilibrium and the collapse of the culture, with an attendant reversion to a preceding, "less advanced" techno-infrastructure. Such a collapse, for which there are several notable examples in the archaeological record (e.g., ancient Egypt and Teotihuacan), could be followed by a new expansion and evolution, but it could also be followed by still another collapse. See Renfrew (1980) and Sablov (1980).

Finally, it may be that a regime is reachable, but because of the previous development history an expansion within a regime is followed by fluctuations with switching and reswitching that delay an eventual permanent transition to a new epoch. Such a scenario seems to mimic events that have been played out at one place or another in former times. Sagan (1985, p. 235), for example, observes that prior to contact with Western culture some societies appear to have spent hundreds of years alternating between band organizations and primitive, kinship societies.

Broadly speaking, however, the general trend of growth has involved a progression from one regime to another, each marked by the increasing size and complexity of its managerial infrastructure and each requiring a striking advance in administrative as well as production technology.

2   A formal model

The grand dynamics of our story can be portrayed by a formal model that illuminates the underlying interaction of population, productivity, welfare, and social organization. The first step is to reconsider the aggregate production function; the second is to summarize the salient features of natality and mortality; and the third step is to combine these classical but now modified ingredients to obtain a more general theory of growth that applies, not just to a single epoch, but to change within epochs and the switching from one techno-infrastructure to another.

a   Production in a group

For simplicity, consider a communal group made of heterosexual pairs and their children. Each pair supplies one adult equivalent of effort to society, either as part of the work force or as part of the infrastructure; the other adult equivalent of effort is used in household production, child rearing, or leisure. The group possesses a technology that rests on a managerial and administrative infrastructure whose presence is necessary for effective production. Given this infrastructure, effective work can be undertaken with the available technology. With this setup, two distinct inputs must be distinguished: administrative or managerial effort M and labor L. If the group size is x (measured in numbers of adult pairs), then $x = M + L$.

According to the theory under consideration, the planning, coordination, and control of economic activity becomes increasingly difficult as group population grows. For simplicity, it can be assumed that for any regime there is some maximum number compatible with any effective socioeconomic order. Let this number be N and call it the *upper viability threshold*. The term $S = N - x$ represents the *social space* or *social slack* within which the group functions. If S is relatively large, a group can increase its population for some time with little depressing effect on productivity. When S is relatively small, there is little room for expansion, and increases in group size begin to lower productivity. If $S \leq 0$, the group cannot function.

Suppose now that the *intragroup production function* can be represented by the product of three factors involving separately the managerial input M, the labor input L, and the social space S; that is, let $f(M, L, S) = g(M)h(L)k(S)$, where $g(\cdot)$, $h(\cdot)$, and $k(\cdot)$ are strictly increasing concave functions on $\Re^+$ with $g(M) = h(L) = k(S) = 0$ for $M, L, S \leq 0$. Suppose also that M is fixed so that it is a parameter for a given group. Then, the production function for the group can be reexpressed as

$$Y = f(x; M, N) := \begin{cases} g(M)h(x-M)k(N-x), & M \leq x \leq N, \\ 0, & x \leq M \text{ or } x \geq N. \end{cases} \tag{1}$$

The separate factors in the production function all have positive marginal productivity. When the constraints implied by the lower and upper thresholds M and N are taken into account, however, group effort as a whole has increasing and then diminishing average productivity and, after a maximum output is reached, declining absolute productivity. The interval (M, N) is the group's *viability domain* given its fixed techno-infrastructure.[4] Group size must exceed M but not N.

---

[4] If effort allocated to management were freely substitutable for work, then we could derive aggregate production as a function of group size alone by using an efficient combination of the two inputs. Thus, we could define $f(x; M, N) := \max_{M, L}\{g(M)h(L)k(S) \mid M + L \leq x, S = N - x\}$. Indeed, any number of separate types of effort could be subsumed in this way. Suppose, however, that there is a residuum of effort that is not substitutable within a given regime. Such a socially nonfungible type of effort is what we associate with the variable M.

b   *Fission, fusion, and the social production function*

Given a fixed techno-infrastructure, a population could expand beyond the feasibility domain for a single group by fission, the splitting of a group, or by shedding and fusion, the formation of a new group from individuals splitting off from existing groups.

Let x be the total population organized into n groups of average size x/n. For n groups, production is

$$nf\left(\frac{x}{n}\right)=Kh\left(\max\left\{0,\ \frac{x}{n}-M\right\}\right)\cdot k\left(\max\left\{0,\ N-\frac{x}{n}\right\}\right),\quad K=g(M).$$

Clearly, $nf(x/n)>0$ on the open interval $V_n:=(nM,nN)$. According to the theory, the processes of fission and shedding and fusion occur so as to maintain temporarily efficient production. Consequently, social production is $\max_{n\in\mathfrak{N}}\{nf(x/n)\}$, where $\mathfrak{N}$ is the set of positive integers. Thus, the production function as a whole is the efficiency frontier of a scalloped sequence of overlapping component functions, each member of which is an integer multiple of its predecessor: n times the range of viability and n times the maximum attainable output. It presumes that, as population expands, groups split or shed and fuse so as to maintain overall population productivity at as high a level as possible.

Eventually, the absorbing capacity of the environment must be exceeded, and this absorbing capacity cannot be expanded by forming new groups. Denote this externality factor by the term $p(x;\bar{x})$, a decreasing function on $[0,\bar{x}]$ with $p(0,\bar{x})=1$ and $p(x,\bar{x})=0$, all $x\geq\bar{x}$. Incorporating this externality, the *social production function* is

$$Y=F(x):=\max_{n\in\mathfrak{N}}\left\{nf\left(\frac{x}{n}\right)\right\}p(x;\bar{x}).\qquad(2)$$

Evidently, population is bounded above by $\bar{x}$. Define $\bar{n}:=\max_n\{nM\leq\bar{x}\}$. Then $\bar{n}$ is the maximum number of groups compatible with $\bar{x}$ and the requirements of the techno-infrastructure.[5]

Figure 1 shows an example in which $\bar{n}=3$. The dotted lines show the successive production functions for 1, 2, and 3 groups when the externality factor does not play a role. The solid lines show how these are modified

---

[5] Evidently, $nf(x/n)\geq0$ for all $x\in V_n$, $n\leq\bar{n}$, and on $V_{\bar{n}}\cap(0,\bar{x})$. Note that the effect of the externality is to compress the production function "downward and backward." Thus, $V_n=(\bar{n}M,\min\{\bar{n}N,\bar{x}\})$ and $F(x)\leq\max_n\{nf(x)\}$. Note that $V_n\cap V_{n+1}$ may be empty. Thus, suppose $N\leq2M$; then $V_1\cap V_2=\emptyset$. In general, if $nN\geq(n+1)M$ then $V_m\cap V_{m+1}=\emptyset$, $m=1,\dots,n$. From this it does *not* follow that $V_n\cap V_{n+1}=\emptyset$ for all n. But suppose $nN\geq(n+1)M$; then $V_n\cap V_{n+1}\neq\emptyset$. If $N\geq2M$ then it follows by induction that $V_n\cap V_{n+1}\neq\emptyset$ for all n.

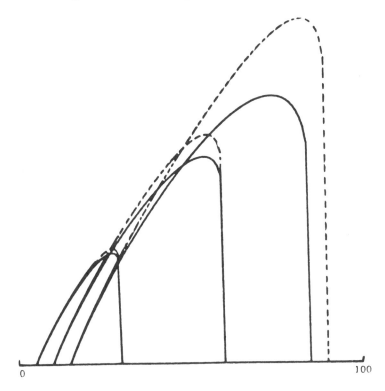

Figure 1. The social production function. Equation (1′) was used for 1, 2, and 3 groups. The parameters are $\beta = 0.9$, $\lambda = 0.1$, $\delta = 0.1$, $M = 5$, $N = 30$, $\bar{x} = 0.85$.

by the externality factor. The social production function is the envelope of the solid lines.

Average productivity, which plays a key role in the theory, is

$$y = \frac{Y}{x} = F(x). \tag{3}$$

Given a social production function like that shown in Figure 1, the graph of average productivity in a regime would be like that shown in Figure 2.

c   *The aggregate social production function and average family welfare*

Suppose now that we have a collection of alternative regimes waiting to be discovered or created in some kind of morphogenesis that occurs when

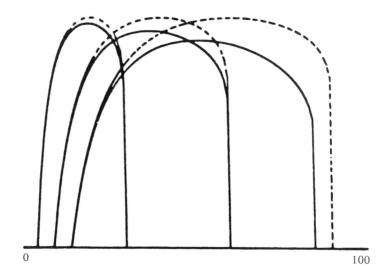

Figure 2.   Average productivity. Using the social production function of Figure 1.

productivity falls, each represented by a technology and by its characteristic threshold parameters. A population can now choose between expansion within a regime by fission and diffusion *or* by a switch in regime.

Let us denote the sequence of alternative technologies by

$$\mathfrak{J} = \{1, 2, 3, \dots\} \subset \mathfrak{N}.$$

Assuming that society uses an efficient technology, the *aggregate production function* is

$$G(x) = \max_{i \in \mathfrak{J}} \{F^i(x)\}, \tag{4}$$

where each F^i is defined by (2) and each component group production function f^i is defined by (1). The aggregate production function is the efficiency frontier of a scalloped sequence of overlapping, scalloped social production functions, each member of which is made up from the basic production function for a single group for a given regime. The aggregate technology $\{[x, G(x)]; x \in \mathfrak{R}^+\}$ is, of course, nonconvex.[6]

The efficiency criterion underlying the aggregate production function implies that the average aggregate product is maximized temporarily and

[6] The set $V^i := \bigcup_{n \in \mathfrak{N}} V_n^i \cap (0, \bar{x})$, where $V_n^i := (nM^i, nN^i)$, is the feasibility domain for each technology $i \in \tau$; the set $V^* := \bigcup_{i \in \tau} V^i$ is the *aggregate feasibility domain* for G defined on $\mathfrak{J}$. The set $\mathfrak{R}^+ \setminus V^* := V^0$ is the *null domain* given the menu $\mathfrak{J}$.

locally over alternative techno-infrastructures so that

$$y = \frac{G(x)}{x} = \frac{\max_{i \in \mathfrak{I}} \{F^i(x)\}}{x} = \max_{i \in \mathfrak{I}} \left\{ \frac{F^i(x)}{x} \right\}. \tag{5}$$

d   *Demoeconomic behavior*

Assume that the time period is a generation. The number of adult pairs being x_t, the total population of adults and children is $P_t = (2 + b_t)x_t$, where b_t is the number of children per female. The maximum number of surviving children per female (Ricardo's "natural rate of growth") depends in general on the average well-being. The actual surviving number may be, and under some conditions actually is, smaller than this natural rate. The actual rate may depend on preferences and social mores. Likewise, the number of children surviving to maturity depends on economic circumstances. Below some starvation level of income, say c_i, naturally, survival is impossible. Above this level the survival rate increases sharply. It approaches unity and possibly dips somewhat at very high income levels.[7]

For the sake of the theory, the net result of these considerations is the specification of a *demoeconomic function* that defines the average number of adult females that emerge in a given period per female existing in the preceding period. Formally, we suppose that $\pi(\cdot)$ is a function of average well-being that is fixed for a given infrastructure but may change when a transition occurs. Thus we index $\pi_i(y)$, $i \in \mathfrak{I}$. We shall assume that $\pi_i(y)$ is quasiconcave for $y \geq c_i \geq 0$ with $\pi_i(y) = 0$, $0 \leq y \leq c_i$, $i \in \mathfrak{I}$. The parameter c_i will be called the *net birth income threshold* for the ith regime. Let $\lambda_i := \sup_{y \geq 0} \pi_i(y)$. Then λ_i is the maximum net rate of population growth in regime i.

e   *Phase structures and regimes*

Given the assumptions made so far, the number of households that emerge in time period $t+1$ from the population of period t, when the latter is organized into groups with the ith techno-infrastructure, is $x_{t+1} = \pi_i(y_t)x_t$. Recalling that the average well-being is assumed to be the average product $y = G(x)/x$, then

$$x_{t+1} = \theta_i(x_t) := \pi_i\left[\frac{F^i(x_t)}{x_t} \right] x_t \tag{6}$$

when the population is organized in the ith techno-infrastructure. The map $\theta_i(\cdot)$ is called the ith *phase structure*.

---

[7] All of this can be encompassed within a standard economic decision-making framework as is outlined in Day, Kim, and Macunovich (in press), which reviews the empirical background.

It could be that for some n, i there exist feasible $x \in (nM^i, nN^i)$ such that $\theta_i(x) = 0$ because $F^i(x)/x < c_i$. If in the course of development from an initial population x_0 such a population is generated, then it is the last because $x = 0$ is a fixpoint for any phase structure (6). This motivates the following:

Definition 1: Regimes and the viability domain.   *The set* $\mathcal{Q}^* := \{x \mid \theta_i(x) > 0 \text{ for some } i\}$ *is called the* viability domain. *Define*

$$I(x) := \min\{\arg\max_{i \in 3}\{F^i(x)\}\} \quad \text{for all } x \in \mathcal{Q}^* \tag{6a}$$

and

$$I(x) := 0 \quad \text{for all } x \in \mathcal{Q}_0 := \mathcal{R} \setminus \mathcal{Q}^*. \tag{6b}$$

Now let

$$\mathcal{Q}_i := \{x \mid I(x) = i\}, \tag{7}$$

the set of populations for which the ith phase structure governs development. *We shall call it the ith* regime. *Thus, when* $x \in \mathcal{Q}_i$, *the ith phase structure determines the succeeding population. The set* $\mathcal{Q}_0$ *is called the* null *regime. For any* $x \in \mathcal{Q}_0$, *the succeeding population is zero, so we define* $\theta_0(x) := 0$ *for all* $x \in \mathcal{Q}_0$.

Obviously, $\mathcal{Q}^* := \bigcup_{i \in 3}\{x \mid F^i(x)/x > c_i\}$.

f   *The multiple-phase dynamic process*

The grand dynamics of demoeconomic development – involving the interaction of population, productivity, technology, and social infrastructure – can now be represented as the *multiple-phase dynamic process,*

$$x_{t+1} = \theta(x_t) := \theta_{I(x_t)}(x_t) = \theta_i(x_t), \quad x_t \in \mathcal{Q}_i. \tag{8}$$

Nothing guarantees that every phase zone is nonempty. An empty phase zone for a given regime means that it is dominated by other uniformly more productive regimes. Moreover, not all techno-infrastructures may be reachable from an initial population. But some history of phases unfolds for any initial population. The *phase progression* $I(x_t)$, $t = 0, 1, \ldots$, represents this history. *It describes economic development as an epochal evolution.*

For change to occur within a given regime, there must be a number n of groups, into which the population is divided, that are compatible with the population viability thresholds M_i and N_i. If regime $\mathcal{Q}_i$ governs growth during period t, then there exists a number of groups, say $n(t)$, such that $n(t)M^i \leq x_t \leq n(t)N^i$.

Begin with an initial population of adult pairs x_0 in some base period. Suppose $I(x_t) = 1$ for $t = 0, \ldots, s_1$ but that the regimes switch and $I(x_t) = i_2$ when $t = s_1 + 1$. The first epoch lasted for s_1 generations. Suppose that $I(x_t) = i_2$ for $t = s_1 + 1, \ldots, s_2$ but not for $t = s_2 + 1$. Then again the regime switches, let us say to i_3. The second epoch lasted $(s_2 - s_1)$ generations. The third regime is i_3 with duration $s_3 - s_1 - s_2$, and so on. In each epoch the number of groups $n_i(t)$ changes when fission or shedding and fusion occurs, so the number of groups in the ith regime forms a sequence n_{ij}, $j = 1, \ldots, g_i$, where n_{i1} is the initial number of groups formed at the switch to regime i. This process can continue so long as there are productive techno-infrastructures to be adopted when a population becomes sufficiently large.

3   "Real world" histories

The model specified above is probably the minimal variation on the classical–neoclassical growth theory that incorporates the new theory of socioeconomic growth in the very long run. Some examples will illustrate how the theory can "explain" some of the more complex patterns of development found in the archaeological–anthropological–economic historical literature.

a   *Specific functional forms*

First, we must adopt specific functional forms for the components of the theory. Consider the group production function for techno-infrastructure i:

$$y = f^i(x) = K_i(x - M_i)^{\beta_i}(N_i - x)^{\gamma_i}, \quad M_i < x < N_i. \tag{1'}$$

Let the externality factor $p(x; \bar{x}_i) := (1 - x/\bar{x}_i)^{\delta_i}$ for $x \in [0, \bar{x}_i]$.[8] The social production function for a given techno-infrastructure can be shown to be

$$y = F^i(x) = K_i \max_{n \in \mathfrak{N}} \left\{ n^{1 - \beta_i - \gamma_i}(x - nM_i)^{\beta_i}(nN_i - x)^{\gamma_i}\left(1 - \frac{x}{\bar{x}_i}\right)^{\delta_i} \right\}. \tag{2'}$$

Next, suppose the demoeconomic function is

$$\pi_i(y) := \max\{0, \min\{\alpha_i(y - c_i), \lambda_i\}\},$$

which gives a positive linear function with positive slope α_i on the interval $[c_i, \lambda_i/\alpha_i - c_i]$.

---

[8] The externality factor could be written in terms of population density. Let d be the maximum possible average density and S the total space available for a given regime. Then $\bar{x} = Sd$.

From these, the ith phase equations must be

$$x_{t+1} = \theta_i(x_t) = \max\{0, \min\{\alpha_i[F^i(x_t) - c_i x_t], \lambda_i x_t\}\}.^9 \qquad (5')$$

The production function (1') is concave on its feasibility domain

$$v^i = (M^i, N^i)$$

when $0 < \beta_i, \gamma_i < 1$. When fission occurs, this function is "stretched," but because of the externality, it may become quasiconcave near $\bar{x}_i$. The function $F^i(\cdot)$ is certainly piecewise quasiconcave and piecewise monotonic. Because $\alpha_i c_i x$ is linear, the term $\alpha_i F^i(x_t) - \alpha_i c_i x_t$ retains essentially the same profile as $F^i(\cdot)$.

Given all this, the ith regime is

$$\mathcal{Q}_i = \left\{x; \frac{F^i(x)}{x} > c_i\right\}, \quad i \in \mathfrak{I}, \qquad \mathcal{Q}_0 := \left\{x; \frac{F^i(x)}{x} \le c_i\right\}.$$

The multiple-phase dynamic process is given by

$$x_{t+1} = \begin{cases} \theta_i(x_t) = \min\{\alpha_i[F^i(x_t) - c_i x_t], \lambda_i x_t\}, & x_t \in \mathcal{Q}_i, \\ 0, & x_t \in \mathcal{Q}_0. \end{cases} \qquad (8')$$

b   *Complex dynamics at the transition*

One of the most striking possibilities in this multiple-phase process is one in which fluctuations occur between the regimes, with switching and re-switching occurring at irregular intervals, and then a permanent switch followed by growth within a succeeding regime. *Development in the long*

---

[9] Note that each phase structure has three potential "subregimes" with corresponding "subphase structures." These are

$$\theta^i(x_t) = \theta^{i0}(x_t) := 0 \quad \text{when } F^i(x_t)/x_t \le c^i, \qquad (7a)$$
$$\theta^i(x_t) = \theta^{i1}(x_t) := \alpha^i F^i(x_t) - \alpha^i c_i x_t \quad \text{when } G^i(x_t)/x_t \le c_i + \lambda^i/d^i, \qquad (7b)$$
$$\theta^i(x_t) = \theta^{i2}(x_t) := \lambda^i x_t \quad \text{when } F^i(x_t)/x_t \ge c^i + \lambda^i/\alpha^i. \qquad (7c)$$

Of course, when $x_t \notin (M^i n, N^i n)$ for some n, then subregime i_0 holds. Suppose there exists an A such that $F^i(x)/x \ge \lambda^i/\alpha^i + c$; then there is a set made up of a finite union of intervals on which $F^i(x)/x \ge \lambda^i/\alpha^i + y^i$, where each interval corresponds to a particular value of n, the efficient number of groups. In this case there must be values of A where subphase i_1 holds.

The switching among subphases within a regime is governed by the average product. When it is below the threshold c, people cannot or will not raise children. Above c_i but below $\lambda_i/\alpha_i + c_i$, the preference for children is manifest but may be less than or greater than the number required for a growing population. When the average product is above $c_i + \lambda_i/\alpha_i$, population growth is exponential, the rate of growth being determined by the adult mortality rate and the minimum of the maximum possible number of children and the maximum desired number of children, λ_i.

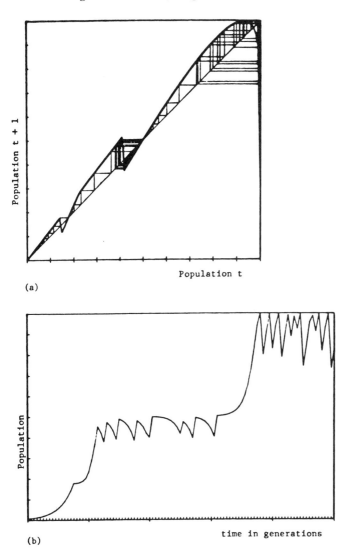

(a)

(b)

Figure 3.   Complex dynamics with reswitching. (a) Phase diagram and (b) implied history.

run is portrayed as a sequence of growth trends interspersed with fluctuations. Smooth transitions can also occur, with monotonic growth continuing at some transitions but fluctuations and crises at others.

In Figure 3a, a phase diagram for equation (8′) using specific parameter values is displayed. In Figure 3b a trajectory beginning from a very

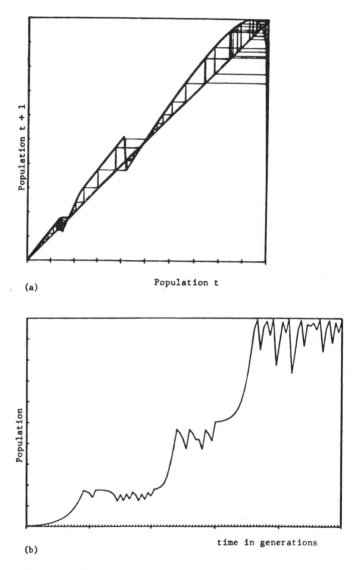

Figure 4.   Complex dynamics with reswitching. (a) Phase diagram and (b) implied history.

small population is shown. After a period of growth, a smooth transition to a second regime occurs. This is followed by growth, then fluctuations with reswitching – a prolonged period of crises, if you will – followed by a successful jump, further growth, and then fluctuations again. Figure 4 presents another phase diagram and trajectory starting from a slightly

Table 1. *The epochs*

Regime	Duration	Number of generations before 1975	Epoch	Beginning population (number of households)
1	40,000–8,000 B.C.	1,680	Hunting and collecting	$0.325K^2$
2	8,000–3,000 B.C·	400	Village agriculture	$1.5K^2$
3	3,000–1,750 B.C.	200	Civilization and trading empires	$25K^2$
4	1,750 A.D.–1,975 A.D.	9	Industrial revolution	$250K^2$

different initial population *but with the same parameters*. In this example, fluctuations with reswitching occur even in the first regime, but eventually a permanent transition comes about. To bring out the potential instabilities inherent in such a process, the parameters have been adjusted so that the probability of switching regimes without fluctuations is very small. Nonetheless, the probability of jumping is 1, as is shown in Theorem 1.

c   *The very long run growth trend*

Consider now the stylized epochs based on Deevey (1960), as shown in Table 1.

Our problem, given this aggregated set of epochs, is to estimate the parameters of equation (8'), so that the regime switchings occur more or less in the order – and with growth in a regime occurring for roughly the duration – presented in the table. A crude set of "guestimated" parameter values that will accomplish this is shown in Table 2.[10]

To record the huge range in the data over so many millennia, log transformations have been used to plot population and output. This has the effect of giving the early epochs, which lasted a long time, a weight comparable to the more recent epochs, which grew at accelerating rates for much shorter durations.

Figure 5a shows the aggregate production function. Figure 5b illustrates the implied average product. Because of the logarithmic scale we

[10] An attempt to estimate parameters using econometric methods would be interesting, perhaps even worthwhile, but not justified for our illustrative purposes and given the data at hand. Crude estimates will be sufficient for illustrative purposes and will give us a good idea if further research along this line is warranted.

Table 2. *Parameter values*

Regime	M	N	≥	K	β	γ	δ	λ
1	5	30	$104K$	7	0.9	0.1	0.1	1.001196
2	40	100	$2.2K^2$	20	0.6	0.1	0.1	1.012167
3	$50K$	$2K^2$	$180K^2$	5	0.6	0.1	0.1	0.014128
4	$5K^2$	$500K^2$	$1.3K^3$	800	0.6	0.1	0.1	1.222845

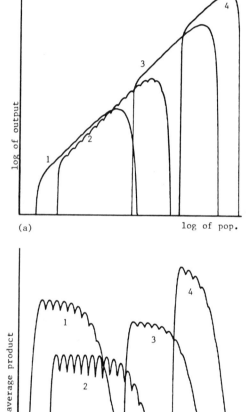

Figure 5.   The aggregate production function and average product with four regimes. (a) Aggregate production and (b) average product. See Table 1.

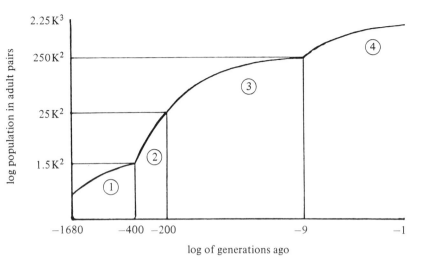

Figure 6. The progress of aggregate population through the four major epochs.

cannot see much of the detail in the former diagram. In contrast, the scalloped profile due to the fission–shedding–fusion process shows up boldly in the latter chart. Figure 6 gives the history of population. Evidently, the model presents a story of socioeconomic evolution that is more or less like that described by Deevey's population data.

4   Mathematical analysis

We have shown that it is possible to construct models using specific functional forms that generate patterns of development reminiscent of those in the record. It is the purpose of this concluding section to derive precise "general" conditions under which these results occur and to give a formal characterization of scenarios that are possible within this framework. For this purpose, history is described by sequences of qualitative events whose conditional probabilities of occurrence can be derived in principle from the underlying parameters of the techno-infrastructure and demoeconomic behavior. The necessary concepts are developed and the central results presented. Proofs of the latter will be found in the appendix.

a   *Trajectories and orbits*

A *trajectory* of (8), with initial condition $x_0 = x$, is a sequence $\tau(x) :=$ $(x_n)_{n=0}^{\infty}$ such that x_{n+1}, x_n satisfy (8) for all n. If $\theta^n(x)$ is the nth iterated map generated from θ, then $\tau(x) = [\theta^n(x)]_{n=0}^{\infty}$. A trajectory is a model-generated history or scenario, and in what follows will be referred to synonymously as such.

b   *Viability*

To keep the number of evolutionary possibilities within reasonable bounds and to simplify the analysis, some regularity conditions will be adopted.

First, assume that the number of distinct infrastructures is finite [i.e., that $\mathfrak{J} = \{1, \ldots, r < \infty\}$]. Next, to insure that $\mathfrak{A}^*$ is a connected set, assume that the infrastructure M_i is less than one-half the upper feasibility bound on group size; that is, assume that $M_i < \frac{1}{2}N_i$ for all $i \in \mathfrak{J}$. Also assume that $M_i < M_{i+1} < \bar{x}_i < \bar{x}_{i+1}$, so that neighboring feasibility domains overlap and are well ordered. If it is also assumed that $\max_x \theta(x) \leq \bar{x}_r$, then it is easily seen that $\theta(\cdot)$ is continuous and maps into $[0, \bar{x}_r]$, but it need not be that $\theta(\mathfrak{A}^*) \subset \mathfrak{A}^*$. Indeed, if M_1 or c_1 is positive, then $\theta(x) = 0$ for any $i \in \mathfrak{J}$ and any x such that $G^i(x)/x < c_i$. Such x will exist sufficiently close to M_1 and $\bar{x}_r$ and perhaps at other populations as well. Hence,

$$\mathfrak{A}_0 \cap (0, \bar{x}_r) \neq \emptyset,$$

and evolution comes to an end for any trajectory that enters $\mathfrak{A}_0$. Such a possibility is worth thinking about because extinction is such a common occurrence in the biological world of which we are a part. Nonetheless, the insights of the present theory are of considerable interest in the absence of such catastrophes, so we shall assume M_1 and c_1 are zero. Then, $\theta(0) = 0 = \theta(\bar{x}_r)$; and, given the previous assumptions, $\theta(x) > 0$ for all $x \in (0, \bar{x}_r)$. Thus, $\mathfrak{A}^* = (0, \bar{x}_r)$ and $\theta(\mathfrak{A}^*) \subset \mathfrak{A}^*$; once the system "starts up," it can continue.[11]

c   *Peaks and tails*

It is evident from the preceding sections that local minima can occur for the map $\theta(\cdot)$ at population levels for which the number of groups in the

---

[11]   Using a function-stretching argument analogous to that exploited in Day (1982), one can now easily derive conditions on the underlying group production functions in $\mathfrak{J}$ for the existence of a "chaos" point $x \in \mathcal{V}^*$ such that $\theta^3(x) < x < \theta(x)$. The implication is that under these conditions, which essentially mean that some technologies are productive enough, there exists an uncountable scrambled set C such that $\omega(C) = C$, where $\omega(C)$ is the limit set for all trajectories originating in C and such that $\tau(x)$ is chaotic in the sense of Li and Yorke (1975) for all $x \in C$.

Moreover, if a point $z \in \mathcal{V}^*$, and if there exists an odd integer n such that $\theta^n(z) < z < \theta(z)$ or such that $\theta^n(z) > z > \theta(z)$, then similarly – according to Li, Misiurewicz, Piani-giani, and Yorke (1982), known as LMPY – a scrambled set exists. Points that satisfy this LMPY condition are easy to find in the sample trajectories shown in Figure 6.

population changes within a given regime, or at populations for which a regime switch occurs (and the preexisting groups are fused to form a smaller, or decomposed to form a larger, number of groups). These local minima, or *tails,* are turning points at which the slope of $\theta(\cdot)$ changes from negative to positive. Between these tails are local maxima, or *peaks,* that are associated with the maximum population possible for a given number of groups within a given regime. For our present purposes the two kinds of switch points, one due to a change in the number of groups and one due to a switch in regime, need not be distinguished.

Let $\beta_0 = 0$, $\beta_1 < \beta_2 < \cdots < \beta_s = \bar{x}_r$ be the $s+1$ local minimizers and let α_i, $i = 1, \ldots, s$, be the local maximizers of θ. Of course, $\beta_{i-1} < \alpha_i < \beta_i$, $i = 1, \ldots, s$. By definition, the peak $\theta(\alpha_i)$ is the maximum emerging population that can occur from established populations in the neighborhood of α_i. Likewise, the tail $\theta(\beta_i)$ is the minimum population that can emerge in the neighborhood of β_i. Note that because of the splitting of socioeconomic groups, s will not be smaller than r.

Now let Z be an interval and let $\theta_Z(\cdot)$ be the restriction of $\theta(\cdot)$ to this interval. It will be assumed that for all $x \in [\beta_{i-1}, \alpha_i]$, θ is strictly increasing and $\theta(x) > x$. It will further be assumed that θ is concave and strictly decreasing on $[\alpha_i, \beta_i]$, $i = 1, \ldots, s$. Thus, θ is not constant in the neighborhood of a peak. These assumptions mean only that θ_i is concave on the relevant parts of its domain. They rule out feasible regimes in which only a contraction can occur. Although models that violate these assumptions would be of considerable interest for describing some kinds of history, to exclude them reduces the number of cases to be explored, which (as shall soon be seen) is still quite large. The instability or local expansiveness of the map θ plays a crucial role in the present theory. Specifically, we shall make use of

Condition E: $\theta'(x) < -1$ for all $x \in (\alpha_i, \beta_i)$.

This condition rules out convergence to a stationary state almost surely. When it prevails, we can get very strong results.

d   *Events*

Now consider the set of trajectories $S := \{\tau(x) \mid x \in (0, \alpha_1)\}$. Our objective is to give a characterization for all trajectories in S. To proceed, we decompose $[0, \bar{x}_r]$ into intervals according to the following definition.

Definition 2: Event thresholds and event zones.   *Set* $\gamma_1 = \beta_0 = 0$, $\gamma_{s+1} = \beta_s = \bar{x}_r$. *For* $i = 2, \ldots, s$, *define* $\gamma_i \in [\beta_{i-1}, \alpha_i]$ *by*

$$\gamma_i = \theta(\gamma_i) \quad \text{if } \theta(\beta_i) \leq \beta_i,$$
$$\gamma_i = \beta_i \quad \text{if } \theta(\beta_i) > \beta_i.$$

The interval $Z_i := [\gamma_i, \gamma_{i+1}]$, $i = 1, \ldots, s$, *will be called the* i*th event zone and the parameter* γ_i *the* i*th event threshold.*

The types of trajectories that occur can now be characterized in terms of these event zones. For this purpose, the following definitions will be used.

Definition 3: Events.   *An event* S_i *is a subset of* $S := \{\tau(x) | x \in [0, \alpha_1]\}$ *defined with reference to the* i*th zone. The* null event N_i *contains trajectories that never reach the* i*th zone; the* reaching event Γ_i *contains all trajectories that surpass the* i*th event threshold. The* touching event Γ_i^* *contains all reaching trajectories whose first element past the* i*th threshold belongs to the* i*th event zone. The* skipping event J_i^k *contains trajectories that skip the* i*th event zone the first time they enter a higher zone (i.e.,* $J_i^k = \Gamma_i \backslash \Gamma_i^*$*); the* growth event J_i^g *contains trajectories that grow monotonically in* Z_i *after initially surpassing the* i*th event threshold and then jump to a higher zone; they may return to* Z_i *or to some lower event zone after this first escape; the* fluctuation and jumping, or local chaos event J_i^{lc}, *contains trajectories that oscillate a finite number of periods and jump to a higher zone after first entering* Z_i*; the* sticking event T_i^s *contains trajectories that do not escape* Z_i*; the* reversion event T_i^r *contains trajectories that touch* Z_i*, revert to an earlier event zone, and never exceed* γ_{i+1}*. The* jumping event $J_i := J_i^g \cup J_i^{lc} \cup J_i^k$ *contains all trajectories that skip* Z_i *or that enter* Z_i *and then jump to a higher zone* Z_j, $j > i$*. The* trapping event $T_i := T_i^s \cup T_i^r$ *contains all trajectories that enter* Z_i *but never reach a higher zone.*

Figure 7 shows a map $\theta(\cdot)$ that satisfies the assumptions made so far. Generally speaking, any trajectories that enter the sets G_i grow, those that enter the sets F_i fluctuate, and those that enter the sets E_i escape to a higher zone.

Consider an initial condition $x_0 \in Z_1$. Note that $Z_1 = (0, \beta_1) = \alpha_1$. Growth in G_1 and a smooth transition to the second regime occurs unless $\theta^s(x_0) = \beta_1$ for some s. Because there are only a countable number of points mapping into β_1, almost all trajectories beginning in $(0, \alpha_1)$ must enter the escape interval E_1. Thus, we can see that the monotonic growth and jump event J_1^g occurs almost surely for x chosen at random in $(0, \alpha_1)$.

In regime 2, growth continues. If the trajectory enters the escape interval E_2, a jump to regime 3 occurs. If, instead, the trajectory enters the interval F_2, then fluctuations emerge. Note that a switch in regime occurs if x_t enters the subinterval (β_2, γ_3), but population declines and regime 2 is re-adopted. As one can see, there is a small interval in F_2 that leads to E_2

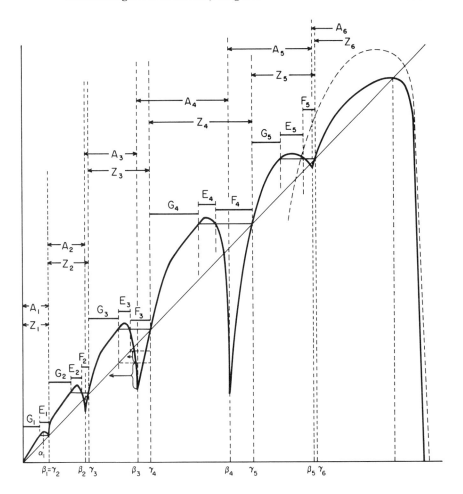

Figure 7. Multiple-phase dynamics. There are six or seven regimes, each exhibiting a different canonical type of transition possibility.

and a successful jump to regime 3. What is the probability of escape when the trajectory enters F_2? Evidently, it is positive. Is it one? That question is answered in the affirmative below when Condition E prevails.

Suppose, then, that the trajectory passes γ_3 and into event zone Z_3. Evidently, if the interval E_3 is entered, we have J_3^g. A jump to regime 4 with further growth would occur. If the interval F_3 were entered, fluctuations with reswitching could occur. Note that there are intervals in F_3 from which trajectories will enter E_3 or G_3. In the former case, escape to the next regime occurs. In the latter case, growth within regime 3 resumes, followed by all the possibilities already noted. Must a jump to regime 4 occur, or could "history" be trapped in regime 3? It is shown below that if Condition E prevails, a jump must occur. If that condition does not hold, then a trapping event could occur with positive probability.

Suppose an escape to regime 4 does occur. As in the previous case, if x_t enters E_4, a transition occurs. But if it enters F_4, fluctuations emerge again with the possibility of switching and reswitching. The trajectory may enter E_4 and escape, emerging into regime 5 and a continuation of growth in G_5. Or it may revert to G_4. If so, growth resumes, and the story is repeated with the possibility of a successful jump or a crisis with fluctuations and reswitching. But there are also small intervals in F_4 that will lead to a reversion to regime 3. If this happens, then all the qualitative histories already described can unfold. Given this possibility of switching, reswitching, and reversion, does the probability of escape equal 1? Or can society be trapped with positive probability into an endless pattern of growth and complex fluctuations among regimes 3, 4, and 5? If Condition E does not hold, then the latter is possible. If it does, growth will resume almost surely.

If a successful jump is made to regime 5 then growth does resume, and (as shown in the diagram) a smooth transition to regime 6 is possible. In contrast, however, if the interval F_5 is entered, the economy is trapped. Inside these interval cycles, chaotic fluctuations or convergence can occur but not escape. Thus, there is a positive probability that a trajectory beginning in the interval $(0, \alpha_1)$ will be trapped in F_5. If Condition E prevails then fluctuations would continue. Otherwise, trajectories would converge to a classical stationary state with positive probability.

If the transition to regime 6 does occur, then population converges to a stationary state. Suppose that the socioeconomic menu is augmented by phase structure 7. Then growth would resume, fluctuations would reemerge, and a reversion to some earlier techno-infrastructure would take place.

e   *Peaks, tails, and types of transitions*

Whether or not jumps, traps, reversions, and so on occur depends essentially on the local peaks and tails of the θ_{Z_i} (the restriction of θ to the ith event zone). To give this observation precise meaning, we specify the following definition.

Definition 4.

(i)   *Let $\theta(\alpha_i) \in Z_{j_i}$. Then $h_i : j_i - i$ will be called the* size *of the ith peak.*

(ii) *The size of the ith tail is*

$t_i = 0 \quad \text{if} \quad \theta(\beta_i) \geq \gamma_{i+1},$

$t_i = 2 + k \quad \text{if} \quad \gamma_{i-k} \leq \theta(\beta_i) < \gamma_{i-k+1}, \quad k = 1, \ldots.$

If $\theta(\beta_i) < \beta_i$ and $h_i \geq 1$, then γ_{i+1} has two preimages in Z_{i1}, say $\phi_i < \psi_i$. Then,

$t_i = 1 \quad \text{if} \quad \psi_i \leq \theta(\beta_i) < \beta_i,$

$t_i = 2 \quad \text{if} \quad \gamma_i \leq \theta(\beta_i) < \psi_i.$

(iii) *The interval $E_i := (\phi_i, \psi_i)$ will be called the ith* escape zone.

(iv) *The interval $F_i := (\psi_i, \gamma_{i+1})$ will be called the ith* fluctuation zone.

The size of the ith peak determines the highest regime reachable from trajectories entering Z_i. The size of the ith tail determines the lowest regime reachable from trajectories entering Z_i. Figure 8 illustrates the types of transitions from one event zone to another and shows how these are determined by the peaks and tails. Three distinct types are shown. In Figure 8a, the probability of escape from Z_i is zero: in part i convergence to a stationary state occurs; in part ii, fluctuations within a fixed regime take place; and in part iii, endless (possibly chaotic) fluctuations occur with reswitching (in the number of groups and/or techno-infrastructures). When such sticking events occur, further development in the sense of transitions to regimes with larger managerial infrastructures and higher productivity cannot occur.

In Figure 8b, there is a positive probability for the monotonic growth and jumping event J_i^g but also a positive probability of the sticking event T_i^s, in which endless chaotic fluctuations are possible.

In Figure 8c, transition types occur in which the probability of jumping from event zone Z_i is unity, but locally chaotic fluctuation with reswitching may occur between an initial period of growth and the jump to a higher regime, or the reversion to a lower regime can occur.

f   *Qualitative history*

We can now think of history as a sequence of qualitative events. To determine the probability of given event sequences, we need to derive a conditional probability measure on the event zone Z_i. To do this, let p be a probability measure on $[0, \alpha_1]$ that is absolutely continuous with respect to Lebesgue measure μ, so that the density of any point $x \in [0, \alpha_1]$ can be represented by a continuous function, say $\delta(\cdot)$, and the probability of "choosing" any $x \in [a, b] \subset [0, \alpha_1]$ is $\int_a^b \delta(x)\, dx$. The density $\delta(\cdot)$ can be used to represent a prior degree of reasonable belief (Jeffries probability) that population in the initial regime occurred within a certain interval.

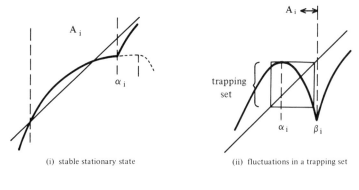

(i) stable stationary state   (ii) fluctuations in a trapping set

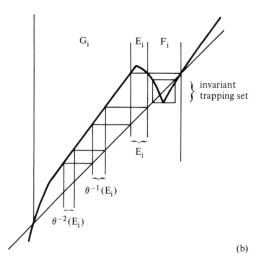

(iii) fluctuations perpetuated
with reswitching   (a)

Figure 8.   Transitions. (a) Type 1: probability of escape $= 0$ (sticking events). (b) Type 2: probability of escape and probability of sticking are positive. (c) Type 3: probability of escape is 1.

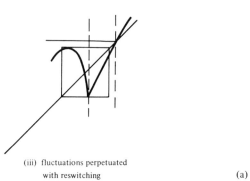

(b)

Figure 8.   Transitions *(continued)*.

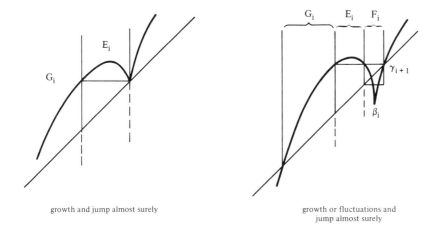

growth and jump almost surely

growth or fluctuations and
jump almost surely

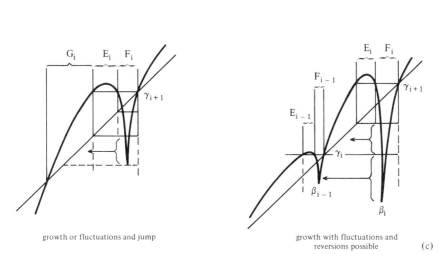

growth or fluctuations and jump

growth with fluctuations and
reversions possible   (c)

Figure 8.   Transitions *(continued)*.

Because the trajectory $\tau(x)$ defines a one-to-one map

$$\tau \colon [0, \alpha_1] \to S := \{[\theta_n(x)]_{n=0}^{\infty}\},$$

the measure p can be considered to be a probability measure on S.

Let S_i be an event in Γ_i, and suppose that $p(\Gamma_i) > 0$. Then $p_i(S_i) := p(S_i)/p(\Gamma_i)$ is the conditional probability of the ith event given that the ith reaching event has occurred.

Using this concept, qualitative history can be given a rigorous treatment within the framework of our theory. Indeed, we have the following theorem whose proof, given in the appendix, characterizes the chance that given trajectories exhibit specific characteristics. We recall that *events* can be associated either with the fission of groups or with the switch in techno-infrastructures.

Theorem 1.

(i) *If* $\Gamma_i^* \neq \emptyset$, $h_i = 0$, *and* $t_i = 1$, *then the* ith *sticking event* T_i^s *has conditional probability one; that is,* $p_i(T_i^s) = 1$.

(ii) *If* $\Gamma_i^* \neq \emptyset$, $h_i \geq 1$, *and* $t_i = 0$, *then the* ith *growth event* J_i^g *has conditional probability one; that is,* $p_i(J_i^g) = 1$.

(iii) *If* $\Gamma_i \neq \emptyset$ *and there exists* $j < i$ *such that* $j + h_j > i$, *then the* ith *skipping event* J_i^k *has conditional positive probability; that is,* $p_i(J_i^k) > 0$.

(iv) *If* $\Gamma_i^* \neq \emptyset$, $h_i \geq 1$, *and* $t_i = 1$, *then the* ith *growth event* J_i^g *and the* ith *sticking event* T_i^s *have positive probability; that is,* $p_i(J_i^g) > 0$, $p_i(T_i^s) > 0$, *and* $p_i(J_i^g) + p_i(T_i^s) = 1$.

(v) *If* $\Gamma_i^* \neq \emptyset$, $h_i \geq 1$, *and* $t_i = 2$ *or* 3, *then the* ith *growth event* J_i^g *and the* ith *local chaos event* J_i^{lc} *have positive probability. Moreover, if Condition E is satisfied, then the probability of jumping is unity; that is,* $p(J_i) = p(J_i^g) + p(J_i^{lc}) = 1$. *If this condition is not satisfied, then the probability of sticking in* Z_i *is nonnegative; that is,* $p(T_i^s) \geq 0$ *and* $p(J_i^g) + p(J_i^{lc}) + p(T^s) = 1$.

(vi) *If* $i \geq 2$, $\Gamma_i^* \neq \emptyset$, $h_i = 0$, *and* $t_i < 3$, *then the* ith *trapping and reversion event* T_i^r *has positive probability. If in addition Condition E is satisfied, then* $p_i(T_i^r) = 1$.

(vii) *If* $i \geq 2$, $\Gamma_i^* \neq \emptyset$, $h_i \geq 1$, *and* $t_i < 2$, *then the* ith *growth event* J_i^g *and the* ith *reversion event have positive probability. If in addition Condition E is satisfied, then* $p(J_i^g) + p(T_i^r) = 1$.

Consider now sequences of events $S_1, \ldots, S_q$ that constitute a qualitative history in terms of the event zones $Z_1, \ldots, Z_q$. Suppose, for example, that $p(T_1) > 0$. Then $p(N_i) > 0$, $i = 2, \ldots, q$. History could be trapped in the first event zone with positive probability, experiencing endless fluctuations, perhaps with reswitching between phase structures θ_1 and θ_2 in the interval (ψ_1, γ_2).

Suppose, by way of contrast, that $h_j \geq 1$, with $j = 1, \ldots, \tau - 1$. Then we have $p[\theta(x) \in \bigcap_{j=1}^{r-1} J_j] > 0$. If, in addition, $t_j \neq 1$ with $j = 1, \ldots, r-1$, then $p[\tau(x) \in \bigcap_{j=1}^{r-1} J_j] = 1$. If, however, $t_j = 1$ for some $1 \leq j < r$, then evolution would have a positive probability of being trapped in a set bounded by the $j + 1$ event threshold γ_{j+1}.

In this way we can give an exact meaning to the probability of occurrence of any qualitative history. If we are dealing with an unstable system, trajectories that do not get trapped evolve. Those that are trapped fluctuate, and those that are trapped and have large tails revert almost surely. These facts are stated formally in the last two theorems, which are simple corollaries of Theorem 1.

Theorem 2: Evolving trajectories.

(i) *Suppose that $\Gamma_i \neq \emptyset$, $h_i \geq 1$, and that Condition E prevails for all Z_j, $j = 1, \dots, i$.*

(ii) *Let $G_i := \{\tau(x) \in \Gamma_i \mid \text{there exists no } t \text{ such that } \theta^t(x) \in [\psi_j, \gamma_{j+1}] \text{ with } t_j = 1, \ 0 \leq j \leq i\}$.*

(iii) *Suppose that for all Z_j, $j = 1, \dots, i$, Condition E prevails.*

Then, for all $\tau(x) \in G_i$, there exists n such that $\theta^n(x) > \gamma_{i+1}$.

Recall that the interval $[\psi_j, \gamma_{j+1}]$ traps all trajectories that enter if $t_j = 1$. The theorem states that almost all trajectories that are not trapped will evolve if the humps are big enough ($h_i \geq 1$) and the map is expansive in the zone of fluctuation.

On the other hand, if the hump is small ($h_i = 0$) and the tail large, almost all trajectories will revert to a zone of lesser index:

Theorem 3: Reverting trajectories. *Suppose that $p(\Gamma_i^*) > 0$, $h_i = 0$, $t_i > 2$, and Condition E_i prevails. Then for any $\tau(x) \in \Gamma_i^*$, $p_i(T_i^r) = 1$.*

5   Summary

1 Evolution in this theory is driven by an unstable, deterministic (intrinsic) process, not by a random shock (extrinsic) process.

2 Nonetheless, the probabilities of various possible historical scenarios can be derived in terms of sequences of qualitative events.

3 If the socioeconomic menu is finite, then evolution in terms of continued progression to higher regimes eventually comes to an end.

4 If the map $\theta(\cdot)$ is unstable and closed, then history must involve endless fluctuations, eventually sticking with a given regime or cycling in a nonperiodic fashion through an endless reversion sequence of regimes.

5 If, by way of contrast, there were one last reachable regime with a stable stationary state, world history could converge after possibly many periods of local chaos to a classical equilibrium.

It is easy to see that the probability of trapping events is increased if *ceteris paribus* successive infrastructures are "large." They must occur if at least one peak is "small" ($h_i = 0$). But a given hump h_i can be increased by *decreasing* the successive infrastructure M_{i+1} while maintaining productivity [increase $g(M_{i+1})$]. *Thus, the key to continued evolution is the identification of new socioeconomic infrastructures that overcome the internal and external diseconomies of population.*

An improvement in production within a given techno-infrastructural regime is also a possible way, one that we have not incorporated in the present analysis so as to highlight a new point of view. But it should be clear that improvements in technological productivity alone that leave unchanged the techno-infrastructural thresholds M_i and N_i can only accelerate progress through the several epochs. The moral of the theory would seem to be that it is the creative human faculty focused on the design for group living that is the ultimate resource in a finite world.

Appendix

Proof of Theorem 1:   (i) In this case $\theta(Z_i) \subset Z_i$, so all trajectories that enter Z_i remain there. Because the stationary state in Z_i is unstable, fluctuations persist. These may converge to cycles or they may be chaotic.

(ii) Here $\theta(\beta_i) \geq \beta_i = \gamma_{i+1}$. In this case γ_i and possibly β_i (if $\theta(\beta_i) = \beta_i$) are fix points, but by assumption they are repellant. By concavity $\theta(x) > x$ for all $x \in (\gamma_i, \beta_i)$; so except for the countable sequence $\theta^{-t}(\beta_i) t = 1, \ldots$ (if β_i is a fix point), for all x there must exist an n such that $\theta^n(x) > \beta_i = \gamma_{i+1}$.

(iii) $\Gamma_i \neq \phi$ implies there exists j ($1 \leq j < i$), with $j + h_j > i$ such that $p(J_h) > 1$ for all $1 \leq h \leq j$. Consequently, $\Gamma_j^* \neq \emptyset$ and $p(J_j) = \prod_{h=1}^{j} p(J_h) > 1$. Let E_j be the escape interval in j. It is nondegenerate because $h_j > i - j$. By continuity and concavity of $\theta(\cdot)$ there exists a nondegenerate interval $E_j^{h_j} \subset E_j$ such that $\theta(x) \in Z_{j+h_j}$ for all $x \in E_j^{h_j}$. Let

$$E_j^* := \{\tau(x) \in \Gamma^* - j \mid x_{n_j}(x) \in E_j^{h_j}\}.$$

Then $p_j(E_j^{h_j}) = p(E_j^*)/p(\Gamma_j^*) > 0$ but $p(J_i^k) \geq p_j(E_j^{h_j})$.

(iv) Here $\theta(\beta_i) < \beta_i$, and γ_{i+1} (the event threshold for event $i+1$) has two preimages $\phi < \psi$. Let $\gamma = \gamma_{i+1}$. We shall call the open interval $E := (\phi, \psi)$ the *jump interval* and the set $F := (\psi, \gamma)$ the *fluctuation interval*. Any trajectories that enter E jump to a higher zone [i.e., for any $x_n \in E$, $x_{n+1} = \theta(s_n) > \gamma$]. The set $\gamma^{-n}(E)$, therefore, gives the set of points that jump into a higher zone after $n+1$ periods, and the open set

$$J := \bigcup_{n \in \mathfrak{N}} \theta^{-n}(E)$$

gives the set of all initial conditions that eventually jump.

The map θ_{Z_i} is an increasing C_1 diffeomorphism, so its inverse image $g := \theta_{Z_i}^{-1}$ is likewise an increasing diffeomorphism from $[\gamma_i, \gamma]$ to $[\gamma_i, \phi]$.

For all $x \in (\gamma_i, \phi)$, $\theta(x) > x$, so $g(x) < x$. Let $(\phi^n)_{n \in \mathfrak{N}}$ be two sequences defined by $\phi^{n+1} = g(\phi^n)$ and $\psi^{n+1} = g(\psi^n)$, respectively. Because $g(x) < x$ for all $x \in (0, \phi)$,

$$\phi^{n+1} < \psi^{n+1} < \phi^n < \psi^n$$

for all $n \in \mathfrak{N}$. Because 0 is the only fixpoint on $[\gamma_i, \phi]$, we have

$$\lim_n \phi^n = \lim_n \psi^n = 0.$$

Because ϕ has only a single inverse image on $(0, \psi)$,

$$
\begin{aligned}
\theta^{-1}(E) &= (g(\phi), g(\psi)) &&= (\phi^1, \psi^1) \\
\theta^{-2}(E) &= (g(\phi^1), g(\psi^1)) &&= (\phi^2, \psi^2) \\
&\quad\vdots \\
\theta^{-i}(E) &= (g(\theta^{i-1}), g(\psi^{i-1})) = (\phi^i, \psi^i),
\end{aligned}
$$

so

$$J_i^g = \left\{ \tau(x) \in S \,\middle|\, x \in \bigcup_{i=1}^{\infty} (\theta^i, \psi^i) = J \subset\subset Z_i \right\} \quad \text{and} \quad p(J_i^g) = \sum_{i=1}^{\infty} p(\phi^i, \psi^i) < 1.$$

Obviously, $\theta(F) \subset F$. Moreover, by an argument similar to the preceding, let $T_1^\delta = \{\tau(x) \in S \,|\, x \in \bigcup_{i=1}^{\infty} \theta^{-1}(F)\}$, where $\theta^{-1}(F) = (\theta^{-1}(\psi), \theta^{-1}(\gamma))$. Because $\theta_{[\gamma_i, d_i]}$ is monotonically increasing, any trajectory in S must enter either E or F. Consequently, $p(J_i^g) + p(T_i^\delta) = 1$.

(v) By the same argument as that used in case (iii), the probability of the growth event is positive. Hence, $p(J_i) > 0$. Now consider the fluctuating set $F = [\phi, \psi]$, where ϕ, ψ are the preimages of γ_{i+1}. Because $t_i = 2$, $\phi_i < \theta(\beta_i) < \psi_i$. Hence, there exists a set $E_j^1 \subset F$ such that $\theta(x) \in E_j$ for all $x \in D_j^1$. Hence, all trajectories that enter $\bigcup_t \theta^{-t}(E_j^1)$ escape. But by an argument similar to that used in case (iii), this is a measurable set and so $p(J^{lc}) > 0$.

If $\theta'(x) < -1$ for all $x \in [\psi, \gamma_{i+1}]$ then it is expansive, and from Pianigiani (1981) we conclude that all trajectories escape F [i.e., $p(J_i) = 1$]. An obvious extension of the argument can be used where $t = 3$.

(vi) Obviously, $p(\Gamma_{i+1}) = 0$. Since $t_i < 3$ there exist sets $E_1, \ldots, D_{t_i - 3}$ such that $\theta(x) \in Z_{i-j}$ for all $x \in E_j$, $j = 1, \ldots, t_{i-3}$. But by our familiar techniques we can show that, for almost all $x \in \Gamma_i^*$, $n > n_i(x)$ such that $\theta^n(x) \in E_j$ for some $j = 1, \ldots, t_{i-3}$, so almost all histories revert.

(vii) The result is obtained by combining the arguments for cases (v) and (vi). ∎

REFERENCES

Adams, R. (1956), "Some hypotheses on the development of early civilization," *American Antiquity*, 21, 227–32.

(1978), "Strategies of maximization, stability and resilience in Mesopotamian society, settlement and agriculture," in *Proceedings of the American Philosophical Society,* 122, 329-35.

Barraclough, G., ed. (1984), *The Times Atlas of World History,* rev. ed., Maplewood, N.J.: Hammond, Inc.

Binford, L. (1968), "Post Pleistocene adaptations," in *New Perspectives in Archeology,* ed. by M. Leane, Chicago: Aldine Publishers, Ch. 21.

Birdsell, J. (1957), "Some population problems involving Pleistocene man," in *Cold Spring Harbor Symposia on Quantitative Biology,* 22, 47-69.

(1958), "On population structure in generalized hunting and collecting populations," *Evolution,* 12, 189-205.

Boserup, E. (1975), *The Condition of Agricultural Growth,* Chicago: Aldine Publishers.

(1981), *Population and Technological Change,* Chicago: The University of Chicago Press.

Butzer, K. (1977), "Environment, culture, and human evolution," *American Scientist,* 65, 572-84.

Cohen, M. (1977), *The Food Crisis in Prehistory,* New Haven: Yale University Press.

Day, R. (1981), "Dynamic systems and epochal change," in *Simulations in Archeology,* ed. by J. Sablov, Albuquerque: University of New Mexico Press.

(1982), "Instability in the transition from manorialism," *Explorations in Entrepreneurial History,* 19, 321-38.

(1983), "The emergence of chaos from classical economic growth," *Quarterly Journal of Economics,* 210-13, May.

(1987), "The general theory of disequilibrium economics and economic evolution," in *Economic Evolution and Structural Adjustment,* ed. by D. Batten, J. Casti, B. Johansson, Berlin: Springer-Verlag.

Day, R., and Cigno, A. (1978), *Modelling Economic Change: The Recursive Programming Approach,* Amsterdam: North-Holland.

Day, R., Kim, K.-H., and Macunovich, D. (in press), "Demoeconomic dynamics: A classical analysis," *Journal of Population Economics,* forthcoming.

Deevey, E. (1960), "The human population," *Scientific American,* 203, 194-204 (September).

Easterlin, R. (1983), "The epoch of modern economic growth," lecture presented at the Caltech/Weingart Social Science History Association Conference, March 26, 1983.

Eberts, R. W. (1986), "Estimating the contribution of urban public infrastructure to regional growth," Federal Reserve Bank of Cleveland, W.P. 8610.

Eliasson, G., et al. (1986), *Kunskap Information och Tjä nstar.* Stockholm: IUI, Ch. 4, p. 98.

Flannery, K. (1965), "The ecology of early food production in Mesopotamia," *Science,* 147, 1247-55.

Goodwin, R. (1978), "Wicksell and the Malthusian catastrophe," *The Scandinavian Journal of Economics,* 80, 190-8.

Haavelmo, T. (1956), *A Study in the Theory of Economic Evolution,* Amsterdam: North-Holland.

Hansen, N. (1965), "Unbalanced growth and regional development," *Western Economic Journal,* 4, 3-14.

Helms, J. (1985), "The effects of state and local taxes on economic growth," *Review of Economics and Statistics,* 7, 574-82.

Hole, F., and Heizer, R. (1973), *An Introduction to Prehistoric Archeology,* New York: Holt, Rinehart and Winston, p. 448.

Iberall, I. (1972), *Toward a General Science of Viable Systems,* New York: Mc-Graw-Hill.

Iberall, I., and Soodak, H. (1978), "Physical basis for complex systems – Some propositions relating levels of organization," *Collective Phenomena,* 3, 9–24.

Iberall, I., and Wilkenson, D. (1984), "Human sociogeophysics – Phase I: Explaining the macroscopic patterns of man on earth," *Geo Journal,* 8.2, 171–9; "Human sociogeophysics – Phase II: The diffusion of human ethnicity by remixing," ibid., 9.4, 387–91; "Human sociogeophysics – Phase II (continued): Criticality in the diffusion of ethnicity produces civil society," ibid., 11.2, 152–8.

Jacobs, J. (1970), *The Economy of Cities,* New York: Vintage Books.

Lee, R. (1972), "Population growth," in *Population Growth: Anthropological Implications,* ed. by B. Spooner, Cambridge: The MIT Press.

Li, T., and Yorke, J. (1975), "Period three implies chaos," *American Mathematical Monthly,* 82, 985.

Li, T., Misiurewicz, M., Pianigiani, G., and Yorke, J. (1982), "Odd chaos," *Physics Letters,* 87A, 271–3.

Looney, R., and Federikkson, P. (1981), "The regional impact of infrastructure investment in Mexico," *Regional Studies,* 15, 285–96.

Martin, P. S. (1971), "The revolution in archeology," *Science,* 36, 1–8.

(1987), "Clovisia the beautiful," *Natural History,* 96, 10–13.

Mera, K. (1975), *Income Distribution and Regional Development,* Tokyo: University of Tokyo Press.

MIT (1970), *Man's Impact on the Global Environment,* Cambridge: The MIT Press.

Nelson, R. (1956), "A theory of the low-level equilibrium trap in underdeveloped countries," *American Economic Review,* 46, 894–908.

Pianigiani, G. (1981), "Conditionally invariant measures and exponential decay," *Journal of Mathematical Analysis and Application,* 82, 75–88.

Renfrew, C. (1980), "The simulator as demiurge," in *Simulations in Archeology,* ed. by J. Sablov, Albuquerque: University of New Mexico Press.

Sablov, J., ed. (1980), *Simulations in Archeology,* Albuquerque: University of New Mexico Press.

Sagan, E. (1985), *At the Dawn of Tyranny,* New York: Alfred A. Knopf.

Sherratt, A., ed. (1980), *The Cambridge Encyclopedia of Archeology,* New York: Cambridge University Press.

Smith, V. (1975), "The primitive hunter culture, Pleistocene extinction and the rise of agriculture," *Journal of Political Economy,* 83, 727–55.

Solow, R. (1956), "A contribution to the theory of economic growth," *Quarterly Journal of Economics,* 57, 65–94.

Zubrow, E. (1971), "Carrying capacity and dynamic equilibrium in the prehistoric Southwest," *American Antiquity,* 36, 127–38.

CHAPTER 12

When are small frictions negligible?

Stephen E. Spear

Abstract: This chapter examines the concept of perfect foresight equilibrium in economies with informationally complex dynamics. The first part focuses on a typical example of such an economy, the two-sector neoclassical growth model. Recent results have shown that, for sufficiently small discount rates, this model exhibits optimal capital accumulation trajectories that are chaotic. Using a notion of informational complexity due to Kolmogorov, we quantify the informational burden imposed on agents by the requirement that they actually calculate the optimal trajectory. It is shown that when trajectories depend sensitively on initial conditions, informational complexity grows without bound as the trajectories become longer.

This analysis is then used to show that chaotic dynamics is not necessary for informationally complex dynamics to occur. Sensitive dependence on initial conditions alone is sufficient to generate informationally complex dynamics. We then observe that growing economies depend sensitively on initial conditions and, hence, require precise (and informationally complex) specification of initial conditions for the calculation of perfect-foresight growth paths. These observations suggest the need for reevaluation of the role of frictions, such as measurement error, when the dynamics of an economy is informationally complex.

1 Introduction

In one form or another, the concept of perfect foresight is a central feature of virtually every model of general equilibrium dynamics. Indeed, the idea that agents' expectations should be correct in equilibrium is as obvious a part of the definition of equilibrium as that markets should clear. Although it is possible to argue what the word *correct* ought to mean in a competitive environment without frictions, simple arbitrage

This chapter was prepared for the Conference on Complexity in Economics held at the IC^2, May 1987. I am grateful to the referees of the conference volume and to José Scheinkman for many helpful comments and to Bill Barnett and Karl Shell for their editorial advice.

arguments quickly drive one to the conclusion that perfect foresight or rational expectations is the correct equilibrium concept.

But what of markets operating under small frictions (say, small errors in measurement or in implementing optimal plans)? The usual doctrine holds that the frictionless models represent approximations of how markets subject to small frictions actually operate. Thus, although arbitrage is in fact costly, large deviations from equilibrium can be profitably exploited and do, in fact, drive the economy to something approximating the frictionless equilibrium. If the costs of arbitrage activity are sufficiently small, then the frictions in the economy will be negligible, and the predictions of the frictionless model will be valid.

In this chapter we shall argue that the question of whether or not small frictions are negligible depends very sensitively on the dynamics of the underlying economy and that, in a large class of economies, it may be necessary for agents to devote substantial resources to the process of forecasting. In such a model, the process of forecasting becomes an issue of choice for the agents, and this necessitates a redefinition of what constitutes a "rational" forecast and, hence, an appropriate concept of equilibrium.

The arguments presented here are based on several recent developments in the theory of dynamic economic systems and in applied game theory for models in which the equilibria are chaotic. We shall be concerned primarily with the practical issues of the *complexity* and *computability* of equilibria in dynamic settings.

In the literature on dynamic systems, there are now many examples of nonstochastic economies with perfect-foresight equilibria whose trajectories are chaotic; see, for example, Benhabib and Day (1981, 1982), Grandmont (1985), Deneckere and Pelikan (1986), Boldrin and Montrucchio (1986), and Dana and Montrucchio (1986). These examples occur in models of overlapping generations, multisector growth models, and models of repeated duopoly; so the possibility of chaotic dynamics does not seem to be peculiar to the modeling assumptions. In the case of neoclassical growth models, such trajectories arise as optimal solutions to discounted dynamic programming problems and are known to be unique.

Chaotic dynamics poses forecasting difficulties because of the tremendous informational requirements imposed on agents in calculating equilibrium trajectories. These informational requirements are generated by the sensitive dependence of trajectories on initial conditions and by the consequent need for great precision in specifying initial conditions. Sensitive dependence on initial conditions arises when the mapping that describes the dynamics of the economy is expanding, at least on average.

Such mappings have the effect of magnifying small uncertainties in the specification of initial conditions. In the context of a dynamic economy, the magnification of small risks means that agents must continually devote resources to measurement to insure that optimal plans are implemented with reasonable accuracy. One purpose of this chapter is to examine and quantify the informational requirements imposed by such dynamics and to consider the question of whether the perfect-foresight equilibria of a model can actually be calculated. A related question concerns the resource costs of calculating (or forecasting) approximations to the perfect-foresight equilibrium.

These observations raise several interesting questions about what constitutes an appropriate equilibrium concept for such a model. In the context of a decentralized market economy whose perfect-foresight trajectories are chaotic, we shall show that agents who recognize the effect of the dynamics in magnifying initial uncertainties, and who do not devote any resources to measurement, will be led to forecast stochastic prices, not deterministic perfect-foresight equilibrium prices. This suggests that a rational-expectations equilibrium (REE) concept would be more appropriate to the model. Attempts to prove the existence of simple stationary REE in these models, however, are complicated tremendously by the nonstationarity of the conditional price processes generated by the model. Indeed, stationary REE may not even exist. On the other hand, if agents do undertake repeated measurements, it is clear that the decision of when to measure should be endogenous. This raises issues of how frequently to make measurements, whether to measure periodically or at random intervals, or whether (in models with heterogeneous agents) to simply purchase another agent's forecast from him. In this case, there are also important technical questions about how to define the REE because relevant elements of an agent's information set are being endogenously generated. Attempts to prove the existence of equilibrium are also likely to be complicated by the discrete nature of the decision to measure or not and by the possibility that the results of some agent's measurement activity may be communicated costlessly through the market to other agents, generating free-rider problems. Although we make no attempt to deal with these issues, we hope to show their relevance to the study of economic dynamics.

Given these observations about chaotic models, an obvious question presents itself: How seriously should we take these implications of the chaos literature if we do not believe that real economies exhibit chaotic dynamics? A main observation of this work is that we must take them seriously. The results on the relationship between complexity, information, and dynamics developed in the context of chaotic trajectories can be applied in a nonchaotic context to show that chaotic dynamics are not necessary for informational complexity to arise in a dynamic economic system. Growth alone is sufficient.

2   Information and complexity

By way of motivating the information-theoretic analysis to follow, we briefly examine a model of optimal growth that can exhibit chaotic trajectories. Because our main interest in the model is its policy function (which describes the dynamics of the model), our treatment will be brief. The model is a simple two-sector neoclassical growth model. One sector produces consumption goods, the other produces capital. Capital and labor enter as inputs to production in both sectors. Technology has the standard neoclassical properties. There is a continuum of identical, infinitely-living consumers whose preferences over consumption streams are given by a discounted sum of utilities.

For this model, the usual dynamic programming approach can be applied. Letting x_t denote capital in period t, the optimal-growth problem can be represented as

$$\max_t \sum_t \beta^t V(x_t, x_{t+1}), \quad \text{s.t.} \ (x_t, x_{t+1}) \in K \ \text{for} \ t = 0, 1, 2, \dots . \tag{1}$$

The objective function V is C^2, increasing in x_t (capital today), decreasing in x_{t+1} (capital tomorrow), and strictly concave. The set K is compact and convex in R^2 and such that $\pi_2(K) \subset \pi_1(K)$, where π_i is projection on the ith factor. It is also well known that solutions to this problem exist and are unique; see, for example, McKenzie (1985) for details. Finally, trajectories obtained as solutions to (1) can be generated by a policy function $h(\cdot)$ such that

$$x_{t+1} = h(x_t)$$

and x_0 is given historically. If we let $W(\cdot)$ be the value function determined by the dynamic programming algorithm, then the policy function satisfies the usual Bellman equation $W(x) = V[x, h(x)] + \beta W[h(x)]$.

Within this framework, work by Deneckere and Pelikan (1986) or Boldrin and Montrucchio (1986) shows that for sufficiently small values of the discount factor β, there exist economies whose policy functions generate chaotic trajectories. In particular, Deneckere and Pelikan present an example whose value function is given by

$$W(x) = \frac{100}{3} x - 5x^2$$

and whose policy function is the quadratic logistic map

$$h(x) = 4x(1-x).$$

This map is known to exhibit chaotic trajectories. It shows sensitive dependence on initial conditions and has an invariant measure with density

$$g(x) = [\pi^2 x(1-x)]^{-1/2}.$$

With this example in mind, we now focus on the question of characterizing the complexity of the trajectories generated by the map h. The notion of complexity used here has its basis in information theory and was first given by Kolmogorov (1965). Let $\mathcal{C}$ be a finite set (called an *alphabet*) and σ^N a sequence of elements of $\mathcal{C}$ of length N (called a *word*). The Kolmogorov complexity of the word σ^N is defined as the size (in bits) of the smallest computer program capable of generating σ^N as its output.

The Kolmogorov complexity, though well defined, cannot be effectively calculated, in the sense that there is no algorithm for actually calculating the minimal program (formally, the Kolmogorov complexity of a sequence is given by a partially recursive function of the sequence and may not be computable for some sequences). The Kolmogorov complexity (as just defined) is also *machine specific* because the minimal program for a sequence calculated on one machine usually differs from that calculated on another machine. Nonetheless, the complexity measure is not ambiguous. Kolmogorov (1965) showed that there exists a machine for which the complexity of any word is no greater than that obtained for any other machine. Indeed, if we denote the Kolmogorov complexity of σ for machine A by $K_A(\sigma)$, then the result of Kolmogorov states that there exists a machine B such that, for any machine A,

$$K_B(\sigma) \le K_A(\sigma) + C_A,$$

where C_A is a constant independent of σ and depending only on machine A. By working with machine B (at least abstractly), the Kolmogorov complexity can be well defined. Finally, we note that although there is no effective method for computing $K(x)$, it is frequently possible to analyze how $K(x)$ *changes* when x changes if we can determine what causes x to vary and how this affects the size of any program that calculates x.

To apply this measure of complexity to the dynamic system

$$x_{t+1} = h(x_t) = 4x_t(1-x_t), \quad x_t \in [0,1],$$

we must first represent trajectories of the system as sequences of letters in an alphabet. This is done by representing the trajectories in terms of their symbolic dynamics.

Let $\mathcal{E} = \{E_1, \ldots, E_m\}$ be an open cover of $[0,1]$, and let

$$\Sigma = \overset{\infty}{\underset{0}{\times}} \{1, \ldots, m\}.$$

Define a correspondence

$$\psi: [0,1] \rightrightarrows \Sigma$$

by

$$\sigma = (\sigma_1, \ldots, \sigma_n, \ldots) \in \psi(x) \quad \text{if and only if } h^n(x) \in E_{\sigma_n}.$$

The correspondence ψ characterizes the trajectory starting at x by listing the elements of the cover $\mathcal{E}$ visited in turn by the trajectory. Now, let

$$[\psi(x)]^N = \left\{ \sigma^N = [\sigma_0, \ldots, \sigma_{N-1}] \,\middle|\, x \in \bigcap_{n=0}^{N-1} h^{-n}(E_{\sigma_n}) \right\}.$$

The correspondence $[\psi(x)]^N$ consists of the first N components of symbol sequences of trajectories starting at x. Next, let $K(\sigma^N)$ be the Kolmogorov complexity of σ^N, and define

$$\mathcal{K}(x \,|\, \mathcal{E}) = \limsup_{N \to \infty} \frac{1}{N} \left[\min_{\sigma^N \in [\psi(x)]^N} K(\sigma^N) \right].$$

Finally, let

$$\mathcal{K}(x) = \sup_{\mathcal{E}} \mathcal{K}(x \,|\, \mathcal{E}).$$

We call $\mathcal{K}(x)$ the complexity of the trajectory at x. Intuitively, $\mathcal{K}(x \,|\, \mathcal{E})$ is the asymptotic average of the least-complex symbol sequence (relative to $\mathcal{E}$) associated with the trajectory at x. The complexity $\mathcal{K}(x)$ is then found by varying the cover of $[0,1]$ and taking the supremum. When $\mathcal{K}(x) > 0$, it means that $K(\sigma^N) \to \infty$ at a rate of order $\geq N$; so the length of any minimal program grows at least as fast as the trajectory sequence itself. Intuitively, the number of bits required to specify the sequence directly is roughly the same as is required to specify any program to calculate the sequence. When $\mathcal{K}(x) > 0$, we call the trajectory at x complex, or *algorithmically random*. Such trajectories are also said to be unpredictable.

To understand why maps with chaotic dynamics give rise to complex trajectories, it is helpful to examine the informational basis of the given definition of complexity.

The program size $K(\sigma^N)$ defining the Kolmogorov complexity of σ^N depends on the amount of information required to specify the program. Information, in turn, is a primitive concept measured by the so-called metric entropy of the sequence σ^N. Letting **p** denote a probability distribution on the words σ^N with

$$p_j = \text{prob}(\sigma^N = \sigma_j),$$

the entropy (relative to **p**) of σ^N is

$$H(\sigma^N|_\mathbf{p}) = -\sum_j p_j \log_2 p_j.$$

The information of σ^N is defined by maximizing H over the probability distribution **p**. It is easily verified that H attains a maximum when $p_i = p_j = 1/M$, where $M = |\sigma^N|$ (i.e., each word σ^N is equiprobable). For this case, we define

$$I(\sigma^N) = \log_2 M.$$

Intuitively, when our prior distribution on σ^N is uniform, we are completely ignorant of the actual value of the word σ^N. When σ^N is specified, all uncertainty is resolved and $I(\cdot)$ measures the information revealed by the specification of σ^N. This can also be seen by noting that after σ^N is revealed, our new prior on σ^N would put probability 1 on σ^N, in which case $H = 0$. $I(\sigma^N)$ then measures the change in the entropy due to specifying σ^N.

When considering the informational size of any program that calculates trajectory sequences, we need to consider the following:

1   the fixed amount of information required to specify the operation of the computer and a fixed amount of information specifying the parameters of the map $h(\cdot)$;

2   a variable information input specifying the number of iterations of h to be calculated; and

3   the information required to specify the partition $\mathcal{E}$ of $[0,1]$.

We consider the two variable inputs given by items 2 and 3. Given the partition $\mathcal{E}$, the incremental information required to specify an additional iteration of h depends only on the information required to specify N. This is calculated as follows. Let $s(N)$ be the binary sequence specifying N (i.e., the sequence obtained from the binary expansion of the integer N). Then, because N is finite, there exists an integer k such that $N \leq 2^k$. Hence, we require at most a sequence of length k to specify N. If $N < 2^k$, then specifying $N+1$ requires a sequence $s(N+1)$ of length no more than k. If $N = 2^k$ then $s(N+1)$ will be of length $k+1$. It now follows that the information content of $s(N+1)$ is such that

$$I[s(N+1)] \leq \log_2 \binom{k+1}{k} 2^k.$$

This expression is obtained by noting that given $s(N)$, there are $\binom{k+1}{k}$ different ways to form a sequence of length $k+1$. There are 2^k different ways to form a sequence of length k. It follows that the incremental information required to specify an additional interation of h is

$$I[s(N+1)] - I[s(N)] = \log_2(k+1) + k - k = \log_2(k+1).$$

Hence, the minimal program grows as $\log_2(k+1)$. On the basis of specifying the iteration length, then, the complexity

$$\mathcal{K}(x \mid \mathcal{E}) = \lim_{N \to \infty} \frac{1}{N} \log_2(N+1) = 0.$$

Thus the specification of how many times the map h is to be iterated is *not* the source of the complexity of the trajectories of h. Indeed, because the preceding calculation is purely combinatorial, it makes no reference to the trajectories of h except in specifying iterations and hence cannot be a cause of complexity.

When we examine the informational content of the partition $\mathcal{E}$ used to define the symbolic dynamics of h, however, the dynamics of the system defined by h become important. To see why, suppose the trajectories of map h are converging to a fixed point or stable cycle of finite order. For such a map, the symbol sequences in the symbolic representation of the dynamics are eventually constant or repetitive. In this case, if we refine the partition $\mathcal{E}$ in a neighborhood of the initial point x (which requires specifying the end points of E_j more precisely, requiring more information) then the symbol sequence remains unchanged sufficiently far into its tail. It then follows that $\mathcal{K}(x \mid \mathcal{E})$ is not increased by varying $\mathcal{E}$; in fact, one can show that $\mathcal{K}(x) = 0$ for such maps. Intuitively, calculation of longer trajectories does not require detailed information about where the system starts. In systems exhibiting chaotic dynamics, on the other hand, refining the partition $\mathcal{E}$ typically changes the tails of a symbol sequence and hence affects the calculation of $\mathcal{K}(x)$. To see how this sensitive dependence on initial conditions affects the information required to calculate a trajectory, suppose we summarize our knowledge of the initial point x by specifying a probability distribution on x with density $g(x)$. The information content of this knowledge is given by the Boltzman integral (which is the continuum analog of the entropy measure we defined):

$$H = -\int_0^1 g(x) \log g(x)\, dx.$$

After iterating h once, we obtain a new density $f(y)$ on $y = h(x)$. When supp g is sufficiently small that h is bijective on supp g, we have from the standard change of variable formula,

$$g(x)\, dx = g[h^{-1}(y)] \cdot \frac{1}{|h'[h^{-1}(y)]|}\, dy = f(y)\, dy.$$

Under the new distribution f, the information integral is

$$\hat{H} = -\int_0^1 f(y) \log f(y)\, dy$$

$$= -\int_0^1 g(x) \log\left[\frac{g(x)}{|h'(x)|}\right] dx$$

$$= H + \int_0^1 g(x) \log|h'(x)|\, dx.$$

Hence, the change in information is

$$\Delta H = \int_0^1 g(x) \log|h'(x)|\, dx.$$

In the particular case when g is a δ-function at x, we have

$$\Delta H = \log|h'(x)|.$$

When $|h'(x)| > 1$, so that the map h is expanding at x, we see that $\Delta H > 0$ and information has been *created*. To interpret this, suppose that after one iteration of h we observe that $x \in I_\epsilon$, where I_ϵ is an interval of width $\epsilon > 0$. When $h'(x) > 1$, we can, by iterating the map backward, infer the value of x_0 to a precision better than ϵ. Hence, future observations of values of x_t provide new information about the value of x_0. An equivalent observation is that when h is expanding, small fluctuations or uncertainties about initial conditions are magnified under forward iterations of the map and are suppressed under backward iterations. Note also that the creation or destruction of information by the map h is purely local, being determined by the derivative of h at x.

To measure the information creation or destruction of the map h in global terms, define

$$\bar{\lambda} = \lim_{n \to \infty} \frac{1}{n} \sum_{i=1}^{n} \log|h'(x_i)|,$$

with $x_i = h^i(x_0)$. When $\bar{\lambda} > 0$, the action of h over successive iterations creates information on average; so the calculation of longer trajectories requires increasing amounts of information about initial conditions to determine a given trajectory uniquely. In terms of $\mathcal{K}(x)$, $\bar{\lambda} > 0$ implies that to calculate an additional iteration of h, $\bar{\lambda}$ additional bits of information are required to specify initial conditions to a sufficient precision. It then follows that the information required to calculate a trajectory of length N grows at rate N; hence, $K(\sigma^N)$ diverges at rate N, so that $\mathcal{K}(x) > 0$.

The informational measure of complexity given above is closely related to several well-known measures of complexity in the theory of dynamic systems. We shall focus here on the relationship of $\mathcal{K}(x)$ to the metric entropy and Lyapunov exponents of the dynamic system defined by h. Details of this discussion can be found in Alekseev and Yakobson (1981).

The metric entropy of the dynamic system given by the mapping h is defined as follows. Let μ be an invariant measure for h, and let $\mathcal{E}$ be a measurable partition of $[0, 1]$. Words of length N are elements of $\mathcal{E}^N$; denote the "cell" containing the word σ^N by $E(\sigma^N)$. Then,

$$H(\mathcal{E}^N) = -\sum_{\mathcal{E}^N} \mu[E(\sigma^N)] \log \mu[E(\sigma^N)].$$

Define

$$\mathcal{K}_\mu(h \mid \mathcal{E}) = \lim_{N \to \infty} \frac{1}{N} H(\mathcal{E}^N),$$

$$\mathcal{K}_\mu(h) = \sup_{\mathcal{E}} H_\mu(h \mid \mathcal{E}), \quad \text{and}$$

$$\mathcal{K}(h) = \sup_\mu \mathcal{K}_\mu(h).$$

$\mathcal{K}(h)$ is the metric entropy of the dynamic system defined by h.

For the one-dimensional map h, the Lyapunov exponent of h is just $\bar{\lambda}$ (see, e.g., Guckenheimer and Holmes, 1983, for definitions in the general case). In general, the Lyapunov exponents of a map measure the average expansion or contraction rates of the map in the characteristic directions associated with the map. We then have the following propositions.

Proposition 1.   *For the quadratic logistic map h, $\mathcal{K}(h) = \bar{\lambda}$.*

Proof: See Ruelle (1978).   ∎

Proposition 2.   *If h has an ergodic invariant measure then $\mathcal{K}(x) = \mathcal{K}(h)$.*

Proof: See Alekseev and Yakovson (1981).   ∎

Comment: It is interesting to note that the informational complexity and metric entropy are generally different, with $\mathcal{K}(x, f) \leq \mathcal{K}(f)$ for a given map f. Alekseev and Yakobson present the following example of a symbolic trajectory:

$$\sigma = [0\ 1\ 00\ 01\ 10\ 11\ 000\ 001\ 010\ 011\ 100\ 101\ 110\ 111 \dots].$$

Of course, σ is just the natural numbers in binary form listed in order. As was indicated in our discussion of the information required to calculate longer iterates of a given map, this sequence has informational complexity zero. Nevertheless, the metric entropy of this sequence is $\log 2$. Intuitively, the metric entropy detects only those characteristics of a symbol sequence related to letter frequencies of the sequence.

For the quadratic logistic map example we have been working with, it is easy to calculate $\mathcal{K}(x)$ because a standard ergodic theorem (cf. Cornfeld, Fomin, and Sinai, 1982) implies that

$$\lim_{N \to \infty} \frac{1}{N} \sum_{i=1}^{N} \log|h'(x_i)| = \frac{1}{\pi} \int_0^1 \frac{\log|4(1-2x)|}{[x(1-x)]^{1/2}} \, dx = 1.$$

What conclusions can we draw from the results presented here? The simple two-sector growth model considered at the beginning of the section shows that there are abundant examples of economies in which the unique optimal policy function h has the property that, for almost all initial values of the capital stock, the optimal trajectory is chaotic. In these cases, the sensitive dependence of trajectories on initial conditions means that initial conditions must be specified with extreme precision in order that the trajectory generated by the policy function even approximate the optimal trajectory over long periods of time.

How important are deviations from the optimal trajectory? If we measure in terms of agents' utility, such deviations are not very important. Indeed, because

$$W(x) = V(x, h(x)) + \beta W[h(x)],$$

the first-order conditions for optimality tell us that

$$\frac{dW}{dh} = V_2 + \beta W' = 0;$$

so small deviations in the specification of x_1 from $h(x_0)$ have no effect on W. Errors in measurement of x_0, on the other hand, can have nonnegligible effects because

$$W'(x) = V_1[x, h(x)] > 0.$$

However, if no further errors are made in determining x_t, this utility deviation should not exceed $|W'(x) \, dx|$. For small dx, this deviation is negligible.

The real problem for perfect foresight created by chaotic trajectories comes when we attempt to decentralize the optimal trajectory by introducing prices. Assuming for simplicity that our agents' period utilities are given by $U(x) = x$, the standard pricing relations for optimal growth are given by the following:

$V_2[x_t, x_{t+1}] = -q_t =$ price of capital as an output at t;
$V_1[x_t, x_{t+1}] = \rho_t =$ rental rate of capital as an input;
$\beta = 1/(1+r)$, where r is the interest rate; and
$q_t(1+r) = \rho_{t+1}$ (no asset market arbitrage).

From the dynamic programming description of optimality, we also know that

$$\rho_t = W'(x_t) = W'[h^t(x_0)].$$

Under perfect foresight (and assuming perfect knowledge of x_0), agents forecast ρ_t as given by the preceding equation. However, if measurement or calculation is costly, x_0 will be uncertain. Suppose the agents' knowledge of x_0 is summarized by a probability distribution having mean $\bar{x}_0$ and variance σ^2. In this case, $x_t = h^t(x_0)$ will be a random variable. If the map h is globally contracting then x_t is constant for large t, and we are justified in viewing the equilibrium price sequence of the model as an approximation of the true equilibrium sequence. On the other hand, if $h(x) = 4x(1-x)$ then x_t will not be constant. If agents do not undertake any measurements after the initial one in period 0 then, for t sufficiently large, x_t is a stationary random variable having the distribution with density

$$g(x) = [\pi^2 x(1-x)]^{-1/2}$$

(see Shaw, 1981, for details). In the example that generates this policy function, we also know that $W(x) = (100/3)x - 5x^2$; so $W'(x) = (100/3) - 10x$. Because this is monotonic one can easily check that, for t sufficiently large, ρ_t has density

$$\hat{g}(\rho) = \frac{1}{300\pi} [(100 - 3\rho)(3\rho - 70)]^{-1/2}$$

for $\rho \in [70/3, 100/3]$. Thus, for large t, ρ is nonnegligibly random *ex ante*. Note that the expanding nature of the map h in this example (i.e., the sensitive dependence on initial conditions) magnifies small initial uncertainties into large uncertainties. In the context of an economic growth model, we refer to this process as *risk magnification*.

How should agents who know the map h, the function W, and the distribution of x_0 respond? Obviously, this depends on whether or not they undertake repeated measurements. If they do not, then it is clear they should solve a stochastic optimization problem using the distribution calculated. This distribution would then have to be compared with the resulting distribution of prices and a fixed point obtained to determine a rational-expectations equilibrium. Whether such a stationary, stochastic rational-expectations equilibrium exists for this model is not known at this time. Several important problems arise in trying to show the existence of such an equilibrium. First, it is possible that the model will generate temporary equilibrium trajectories (for a given forecast distribution) that converge to a fixed point and hence generate only deterministic temporary equilibrium price measures. Although it is possible to generate examples in which the temporary equilibrium trajectories are chaotic if the perfect foresight trajectory is, these models possess invariant measures on the price process only asymptotically, if at all. Furthermore, if one examines the conditional probability measures on the temporary equilibrium process associated with a given forecast, it is highly nonstationary.

Second, it is possible that agents want to make frequent measurements or calculations at some cost in resources. The repeated measurement will prevent the risk-magnification effect generated by the model, but analysis of the model will be complicated because decisions of when and how accurately to measure must be treated as endogenous choice variables of the agents in the model. However, even in this case the uncertainty associated with measurement error is not negligible, because it must be constantly monitored to keep the risk-magnification effect under control. Indeed, if an agent values resources sufficiently highly, he may find it optimal to face substantially magnified risk before committing resources to measurement. In either event, the model is nontrivially stochastic.

As the example makes clear, informationally complex environments can substantially alter the nature of competitive equilibrium. In such environments, measurement or calculational frictions play important roles in determining optimal behavior, and it may be unrealistic to model such environments under the assumptions of deterministic perfect foresight over an infinite time horizon.

Whether these observations justify devoting research resources to the more complicated kinds of analysis suggested depends, of course, on how prevalent such informationally complex dynamic systems are in economics. To paraphrase Brock (1986), no economist really believes that observed economic time-series are generated by low-dimensional strange attractors. If informational complexity arises only in such settings, the problems posed for perfect foresight can, and should, be viewed as a mere theoretical curiosity not likely to arise in real economies. However, in the following section we shall argue that, whether or not chaos is likely in real economies, problems with informational complexities of the type discussed arise naturally in common economic settings.

3   Growth

In characterizing informational complexity for chaotic economies, we saw that the Kolmogorov complexity of a trajectory depends fundamentally on whether the dynamic system depends sensitively on initial conditions. This dependence, in turn, is measured by the change in information associated with iterations of the mapping h, given by the formula

$$\Delta H = \log |h'(x)|.$$

When $|h'| > 1$, $\Delta H > 0$ and information is being created locally in a neighborhood of x whenever the map h is iterated. In the previous section, we saw that chaotic dynamic systems having positive Lyapunov exponents depend sensitively on initial conditions, and hence create information (on average) when the map is iterated. Calculation of such trajectories is, therefore, informationally complex.

The analysis of the previous section also shows that chaotic dynamics are sufficient for informational complexity, but not necessary. Any map h that is expanding in a neighborhood of a point x creates information under iteration, at least until the trajectory leaves the neighborhood. A map that is expanding everywhere creates information under all iterations, and hence exhibits informationally complex trajectories. It is also obvious that globally expanding maps depend sensitively on initial conditions; so all of our observations about the information required to calculate long trajectories for chaotic dynamic systems also apply to expanding systems.

Unlike chaotic systems, expanding dynamic systems have been studied extensively in economics and are widely accepted as models of economic growth. Indeed, in the simplest models of growth, capital accumulation takes place in a balanced fashion (steady-state growth) and is driven entirely by population growth, yielding a simple difference equation,

$$k_{t+1} = \eta k_t,$$

where $\eta > 1$ and $\eta - 1$ is the rate of growth of population. Growth can, of course, be driven by factors other than population growth, such as technological improvements or investment in human capital.

In many respects, the questions of how informational complexity affects optimizing behavior, which were raised in the last section in the context of chaotic growth, are more sharply posed in the context of simple, balanced-growth equilibria. We noted that small errors in the determination of initial allocations had negligible effects on utility (at least to first-order effects). Because it is also well known that large discount rates are necessary for chaotic dynamics to arise, it can be argued that – despite the large deviations from optimal trajectories induced by small errors in the specification of initial conditions – the effects of these deviations on agents' objectives are likely to be quite small. For systems in which there is no long-term growth in per capita consumption, it is also easy to calculate bounds on the utility loss associated with deviations from optimality. With large discount rates, these losses are small.

For systems in which per capita consumption is growing and discount rates are not large, however, no such argument is possible. In these systems, the magnification of small initial errors by the growth process can lead to substantial utility losses. The possibility of such magnification of losses imposes a nonnegligible risk on agents that is not taken into account in the formulation of the optimization problem.

Given the obvious fact of growth in real economies and the importance of perfect foresight in models of optimal growth, our observations on the relationship of informationally complex dynamics to expanding maps suggest that some reevaluation of the concept of perfect foresight may be in order. In particular, an attempt to analyze the prediction problem of long-lived agents in a growing economy when the neglected frictions of measurement and calculation are explicitly taken into account would seem a useful exercise.

Toward this end, the remainder of this chapter will focus on two examples of how the interaction of informational complexity and measurement error in a simple optimal-growth model can sharply alter the characterization of when a trajectory is optimal.

The model considered is the one-good, neoclassical capital model with exogenous growth in labor productivity at a fixed positive rate $\eta - 1$. Under this assumption, the effective labor input to production is

$$L_t = \eta^t L_0.$$

We focus on steady-state capital accumulation at a constant ratio of capital to effective labor input, so that

$$K_t = \eta^t K_0.$$

In terms of the ratio of capital to effective labor input,

$$k_t = \frac{K_t}{L_t},$$

steady-state consumption is

$$x_t = f(\hat{k}) - \hat{k},$$

where $\hat{k}$ is such that $f'(\hat{k}) = 1$. Hence, actual consumption is

$$X_t = \eta^t [f(\hat{k}) - \hat{k}] L_0 = \eta^t \hat{\theta}.$$

Note that any deviation from $\hat{k}$ reduces X_t. With

$$X = [X_0, X_1, \ldots],$$

an agent's utility from consumption is given by

$$V(\hat{X}) = \sum_{t=0}^{\infty} \beta^t U[\eta^t \hat{\theta}],$$

where $0 < \beta < 1$, and the period utility function U satisfies the usual properties.

To capture measurement aspects, we assume that by paying a fixed cost C (in terms of consumption), agents can determine X_t at time t by making a measurement that yields a probability distribution on X_t with mean $\eta^t \theta_0$ and variance σ^2, where θ_0 is the actual initial consumption value. At time zero, an initial measurement determines a probability distribution on X_0 with mean $\hat{\theta}$ and variance σ^2.

Except for measurement errors, the economy is assumed to evolve in a deterministic manner. By a simple calculation, one easily determines that in the absence of measurements, the distribution of X_t has mean $\eta^t \hat{\theta}$ and variance $\eta^{2t} \sigma^2$. Our agent's problem is to decide when and if to make any measurements after the initial one in period 0. To illustrate this, we consider a simple example.

Suppose that the production function f and the period utility function U are such that

$$U\{\eta^t[f(\hat{k}) - \hat{k}]L_0\} = -\eta^t(k - \hat{k})^2.$$

Suppose that an initial measurement is made at time 0 and that the actual initial value of k is k_0. At time t, in the absence of measurement, the agent's expected utility is

$$EU_t = -\eta^t \sigma^2 - \eta^t(k_0 - \hat{k})^2.$$

If the agent makes a measurement at t, his expected utility is

$$\begin{aligned} E\bar{U}_t &= -E[\eta^t(k - \hat{k})^2 + C] = -\eta^t E(k - \hat{k})^2 - C \\ &= -\eta^t[\eta^{-t}\sigma^2 + (k_0 - \hat{k})^2] - C \\ &= -\sigma^2 + \eta^t(k_0 - \hat{k})^2 - C. \end{aligned}$$

Note that the variance of the measured initial value of k at time t is $\eta^{-t}\sigma^2$ because the measurement is made at t (with a variance of σ^2) and then is mapped *backward*.

The expected utility difference $E\bar{U}_t - EU_t$ is thus

$$\Delta EU = (\eta^t - 1)\sigma^2 - C.$$

It now follows that $\Delta EU \geq 0$ if $(\eta^t - 1)\sigma^2 \geq C$. Hence, if

$$t \geq \frac{1}{\ln \eta} \ln\left[\frac{\sigma^2 + C}{\sigma^2}\right],$$

the expected utility difference will be positive; and, *ex ante*, the agent will find it optimal to verify his position at some finite time t and then recalculate an optimal trajectory based on the new initial condition.

For this particular example, we also obtain some intuitively appealing comparative statics on the optimal measurement time. For example, if

$C \to 0$, the optimal measurement time is $t = 0$, which can be interpreted as specifying measurement in every period. For $C > 0$, if $\sigma^2 \to \infty$ then $t \to 0$, and again measurement becomes more frequent. On the other hand, if $\sigma^2 \to 0$ then $t \to \infty$, and we are back in the usual, standard, perfect-foresight model.

Note that in this example our agent will recalculate an optimal trajectory after every measurement, so that (formally) the example resembles an overlapping-generations model because the optimization horizon is always finite. It would be interesting to know whether this property persists if we attempt to decentralize the model, examining the stochastic equilibria generated when agents make measurements and then attempt to forecast future prices conditional on their measurements (and other information). Although it is beyond the scope of this chapter to undertake any detailed analysis of this issue, the following example briefly examines the pricing equations that arise in this model.

This example parallels the discussion of pricing in our analysis of the chaotic model. As was the case there, risk magnification in our simple growth example also affects the way agents forecast prices when we attempt to decentralize the economy. For example, with simple growth the steady-state return to capital is $f'(k) = 1$. When we drive the model with exogenous technological improvement, the period-t return to capital is

$$\rho_t = \eta^t f'(k) = \eta^t$$

(along the balanced-growth path). If the initial capital input is subject to small errors in specification or measurement, then the period-t return to capital will be stochastic, having a distribution with mean η^t and variance $\eta^{2t}\hat{\sigma}^2$, where $\hat{\sigma}^2$ is the variance obtained from the function $f'(\cdot)$ when k_0 has variance σ^2. Although we do not have the same nice results on the invariance of the resulting price distribution that we were able to obtain for the chaotic model, it is clear that because of risk magnification, agents in this model who know the pricing function and the distribution of k_0 will forecast stochastic rather than deterministic prices. As in the chaotic model, then, it does not seem reasonable to model the decentralized economy in terms of deterministic perfect foresight.

Although both of these examples are highly stylized and simplified, they do seem to capture the salient feature: Risk-averse agents will find it optimal (eventually) to respond to the magnification of small uncertainties that occurs in dynamic systems that depend sensitively on initial conditions. The examples also suggest that, in situations where risk magnification and related calculational complexities are nontrivial features, seemingly negligible frictions can play a major role in generating fluctuations in observed economic activity.

REFERENCES

Alekseev, V. M., and Yakobson, M. V. (1981), "Symbolic dynamics and hyperbolic dynamic systems," *Physics Reports,* 75, 5.

Benhabib, J., and Day, R. H. (1981), "Rational choice and erratic behavior," *Review of Economic Studies,* 48, 459–72.

(1982), "A characterization of erratic dynamics in the overlapping generations model," *Journal of Economic Dynamics and Control,* 4, 37–55.

Boldrin, M., and Montrucchio, L. (1986), "On the indeterminacy of capital accumulation paths," *Journal of Economic Theory,* 40(1).

Brock, W. A. (1986), "Distinguishing random and deterministic systems: Abridged version," *Journal of Economic Theory,* 40(1).

Cornfeld, I. P., Fomin, S. V., and Sinai, Ya. G. (1982), *Ergodic Theory,* New York: Springer-Verlag.

Dana, R., and Montrucchio, L. (1986), "Dynamic complexity in duopoly games," *Journal of Economic Theory,* 40(1).

Deneckere, R., and Pelikan, S. (1986), "Competitive chaos," *Journal of Economic Theory,* 40, 1.

Grandmont, J. M. (1985), "On endogenous competitive business cycles," *Econometrica,* 53, 5.

Guckenheimer, J., and Holmes, P. (1983), *Non-linear Oscillations, Dynamic Systems, and Bifurcations of Vector Fields,* New York: Springer-Verlag.

Kolmogorov, A. N. (1965), "Three approaches to the quantitative definition of information," *Problems of Information Transmission,* 1, 1.

McKenzie, L. (1985), "Optimal economic growth and turnpike theorems," in *Handbook of Mathematical Economics,* ed. by K. Arrow and M. Intriligator, New York: North-Holland.

Ruelle, D. (1978), "An inequality for the entropy of differentiable maps," *Bulletin of the Brazilian Mathematical Society,* 9, 331.

Shaw, R. (1981), "Strange attractors, chaotic behavior and information flow," *Zeitschrift für Naturforschung,* 36a, 80.

CHAPTER 13

Imperfect financial intermediation and complex dynamics

Michael Woodford

It is now well established that self-sustaining deterministic fluctuations, either periodic or "chaotic," can occur as a perfect-foresight equilibrium phenomenon in well-formulated models of competitive economies. However, existing examples have thus far relied on parameter specifications of a particularly extreme sort that leave open the question of whether such phenomena could occur in a world at all similar to our own. In particular, existing examples have depended either on agents with lifetimes that are short compared with the time scale over which cycles occur (e.g., Benhabib and Day, 1982; Grandmont, 1985) or on agents with very high rates of time preference (e.g., Benhabib and Nishimura, 1979, 1985; Boldrin and Montrucchio, 1986; Deneckere and Pelikan, 1986). In the case of the optimal-growth models considered by these last authors, the high rate of time preference appears to be necessary for endogenous fluctuations to occur because it is known for a quite general technology that the equilibrium steady state is globally stable if the rate of time preference is sufficiently low (Scheinkman, 1976).

We suggest that complex dynamics can occur under less special circumstances in the case of economies that lack the complete set of competitive markets assumed in the preceding references. In particular, we consider here the consequences for equilibrium dynamics, in a simple model, of the absence of a loan market serving to insure equality between the marginal rates of substitution between present and future goods on the part of agents in different circumstances. We show that it is possible in this case to obtain both equilibrium cycles and chaotic equilibrium dynamics, even with a finite number of infinite-lived agents with arbitrarily low rates of time preference. Furthermore, we obtain this result even for the case

I would like to thank Jess Benhabib, Michele Boldrin, and José Scheinkman for helpful discussions, and the National Science Foundation for support.

of a simple one-sector technology whereas, in the optimal-growth framework, a one-sector technology implies global stability of the steady state, regardless of the rate of time preference (Dechert, 1984).

A first example illustrating the possible role of missing financial markets in allowing for equilibrium cycles was provided by Bewley (1986). In Bewley's model, there are two types of infinite-lived agents with exactly complementary patterns of fluctuating endowments. Each agent is able to save (by accumulating capital) but not to borrow from the other; in Bewley's equilibria, the no-borrowing constraint binds on the agent who has the low endowment in each period. Bewley shows that it is possible for a two-period equilibrium cycle to exist even in the case of a one-sector production technology. However, time discounting is still important in allowing Bewley's cycle to occur, insofar as a sufficiently great rate of discount is necessary for the no-borrowing constraint to actually bind in an economy of that sort.

We investigate another structure in which there are two types of infinite-lived agents, but whose positions are not symmetrical; our intent is to capture, in a somewhat stylized way, the distinct roles in the economy of the household and firm sectors, respectively. The failure of financial intermediation in which we are interested is an inability of firms to finance capital expenditures other than out of internally generated funds. Because only one type of agent is assumed to have an opportunity to shift resources over time by accumulating capital goods (i.e., organizing production), discounting of future consumption is not necessary for the marginal rates of substitution of the two types of agents to diverge in the absence of a loan market.

We also go beyond Bewley's result, not only showing that equilibrium cycles are possible but also exhibiting conditions under which equilibrium dynamics are chaotic. Finally, we extend our analysis to the case in which the inability to borrow is not absolute; we assume that a competitive market exists in riskless debt securities but that more complicated contracts are not possible. We show that complex equilibrium dynamics continue to be possible in that case, and for similar reasons.

1   An economy with no external finance

We want to consider an economy with a one-sector production technology in which labor and the produced good of the previous period are used to produce the sole produced good, which can be either consumed or accumulated for use in the following period's production. We assume constant returns to scale and hence can completely specify the production possibilities by specifying a profit function $r(w)$, indicating the maximum possible return for the owner of capital (per unit of capital) if labor is purchasable at a real wage w. (This is just what is often called the *factor price frontier*, though in our model there is no market for the services of capital.)

We assume a profit function with the following properties:

(A.1)   The function $r(w)$ is well defined for all $w > 0$, nonnegative, a continuous function of w, nonincreasing in w, and convex.

These properties necessarily obtain if the profit function is derived from maximization subject to a convex production set; and conversely, by standard duality theory, a well-behaved production set corresponds to any such function $r(w)$.

Given $r(w)$, we let $d(w)$ denote the labor demand correspondence given by the negative of the subgradient of $r(w)$; that is, for any $w > 0$, $d(w)$ is the set of $d \geq 0$ such that $r(w') - r(w) \geq d(w - w')$ for all $w' > 0$. In addition, if

$$\liminf_{w \to 0} d(w) = \bar{d} < \infty, \tag{1}$$

then let $d(0)$ denote the set of $d \geq \bar{d}$; whereas if the limit is infinite, $d(0)$ is empty. Then $d(w)$ is just the set of possible choices of a quantity of labor to employ per unit of capital that are optimal if the real wage is w. It follows from (A.1) that $d(w)$ is an upper hemicontinuous correspondence (i.e., its graph is closed), convex-valued, nonempty for all $w > 0$, and nonincreasing in the sense that if $w_1 > w_2$ then $d_1 \leq d_2$ for any $d_1 \in d(w_1)$ and $d_2 \in d(w_2)$. It will also be useful to define the inverse correspondence $w(d)$ as $w' \in w(d')$ if and only if $d' \in d(w')$. It follows from (A.1) that $w(d)$ is also a convex-valued, upper hemicontinuous correspondence, nonempty for all $d > 0$, and nonincreasing.

We shall also assume that the production technology satisfies the following:

(A.2)   For any $s > 0$, $\lim_{k \to 0} kr(\inf w(s/k)) = 0$.

Here s represents a quantity of labor inputs and k the quantity of capital inputs; the condition says that as the quantity of capital used with the given quantity of labor inputs is reduced to zero, the total returns to the capital employed goes to zero as well if, for each capital/labor ratio, the real wage must be such as to justify that choice of input combination. This condition must obtain if we assume that capital is necessary for production, so that as the quantity of capital used with a given quantity of labor inputs goes to zero, the total product must go to zero. Because for any $w \in w(s/k)$, $kr(w)$ is no greater than the total product obtained using quantities k and s, it follows that $kr(w)$ goes to zero.

These assumptions are standard. We depart from a standard optimal-growth framework, however, first by assuming two distinct types of agents and second by assuming that they are unable to exchange financial claims.[1] The first type of agents we call *entrepreneurs*. These agents alone have the opportunity to accumulate capital and operate the production technology described. We will assume that the *capital goods* are so specific to the particular production opportunities available to a particular entrepreneur that it is not possible for other agents to accumulate capital goods with the intention of renting them to entrepreneurs. We assume for simplicity that entrepreneurs have no labor endowment; they are able to consume only because they are assumed already to own capital (i.e., projects that yield them saleable output if only labor inputs are hired) at the beginning of the first period. The second type of agents we call *workers*. These agents are assumed to supply labor and to finance their consumption out of their wage income; as stated before, they have no opportunity to accumulate capital and organize production, and so will never share in the returns to capital.

To simplify our analysis, we assume that entrepreneurs seek to maximize $\sum_{t=0}^{\infty} \beta^t \log q_t$, where q_t is each entrepreneur's consumption in period t, and β is a discount factor between 0 and 1. (As noted in the introduction, we are most interested in the case in which β is close to 1.) With these preferences, the optimal consumption/savings decision of an entrepreneur is always to consume exactly a fraction $(1 - \beta)$ of his current wealth and to save the remainder. We make this special assumption regarding the intertemporal preferences of entrepreneurs in order to simplify our equilibrium conditions; in this case, they reduce to a first-order, nonlinear, difference equation, a form that greatly facilitates our exhibition of conditions under which chaotic dynamics are obtained. Our results for this case are probably not too special. Because when β is close to 1, it is true for a wide range of utility functions that entrepreneurs want to save almost all of their current wealth when the rate of return to saving is not too large; and so, as here, it turns out that the main determinant of the rate of capital accumulation by entrepreneurs is the rate of profit obtained on their previously invested capital (which determines their wealth), rather than their expectations about future rates of profit. We assume the following relationship between entrepreneur's rate of time preference and the production technology:

---

[1] The heterogeneity is obviosly necessary for our assumption of imperfect financial intermediation to have any consequences. Note that with complete markets, heterogeneous infinite-lived agents with stationary preferences have little effect on the conditions under which a "turnpike" result fails to hold, as shown by Benhabib, Jafarey, and Nishimura (1986).

(A.3) $\lim_{w \to 0} r(w) > \beta^{-1}$; $\lim_{w \to \infty} r(w) < \beta^{-1}$; and r is twice con-
        tinuously differentiable in a neighborhood of w^*, the point
        at which $r(w^*) = \beta^{-1}$.

Inequalities of this sort are familiar from optimal-growth models, where
(as here) they are necessary to insure the existence of an equilibrium in
which the capital stock neither grows without bound nor is run down to
zero. The continuous derivative at w^* enables us to obtain a determinate
steady-state capital stock rather than having to treat the case of an interval of possible steady-state values. The continuous second derivative enables us to state a local stability condition for the steady state in terms of
familiar elasticities, though a more complicated version of Proposition 2
below could be stated without it.

Workers are assumed to maximize $\sum_{t=0}^{\infty} \gamma^t u(c_t, n_t)$, where c_t is each
worker's consumption in period t, n_t his labor supply, and γ a discount
factor. The utility function u is assumed to be monotonically increasing
in c, monotonically decreasing in n, and strictly concave. It is useful to
define $s(w)$ as the labor supply $n \geq 0$ that maximizes $u(wn, n)$, given a
real wage w. We assume the following properties:

(A.4)   The function $s(w)$ is well defined and C^1 for all $w \geq 0$, positive
        for all $w > 0$, and nondecreasing.

Here the only assumption that is at all nonstandard is the assumption that
$s(w)$ is nondecreasing; it is well known that even if both consumption
and leisure are normal goods, a "backward-bending" labor-supply curve
is possible. Here we rule out this case, both to avoid certain complexities
that arise in the description of the equilibrium dynamics in that case (e.g.,
possible nonuniqueness of equilibrium) and to emphasize that the complex behavior exhibited later does not depend on violation of the "gross
substitutability" property in the preferences of either type of agent.[2]

Finally, we assume the following:

(A.5)   If $w_1 > w_2$, then either sup $d(w_1) < $ inf $d(w_2)$, $s(w_1) > s(w_2)$,
        or both.

We do not want to assume either that $d(w)$ must be strictly decreasing or
that $s(w)$ must be strictly increasing, because we want to be able to treat
both the case of a fixed-coefficients production technology and the case of

---

[2] For examples in which a sufficiently sharply backward-bending supply curve produces
complex dynamics, see Benhabib and Day (1982) and Grandmont (1985). Kehoe et al.
(1986) show that gross substitutability guarantees a turnpike property of the perfect-
foresight equilibrium dynamics for general stationary overlapping-generations exchange
economies.

inelastic labor supply. (Examples of each of these kinds are discussed in Section 3.) However, we disallow simultaneous occurrence of these limiting cases in order to obtain a continuous map for the equilibrium dynamics of the capital stock.

Finally, the pivotal assumption of our model is to suppose that, for some reason, no borrowing or lending is possible between agents of the two types. This might be because loan contracts are unenforceable (as in models where agents change locations, such as those considered by Townsend, 1980) or because the entrepreneurs with viable projects, whose investment decisions are modeled here, cannot be distinguished by lenders from sham entrepreneurs who would issue large quantities of debt (could it be sold for any positive price) to finance current consumption, knowing that there would be nothing for their creditors to seize when they default in the following period (as in a model considered by Bryant, 1980).[3] As a consequence, agents of each type have to finance current spending (whether on consumption or investment) entirely out of their own current income. Although such an assumption is plainly extreme, it captures (albeit crudely) an important fact about actual economies – namely, that even in an economy with such well-developed financial institutions as the United States today, a large part of the capital expenditures of the nonfinancial business sector are financed out of internal funds (retained earnings plus depreciation) rather than from external sources.[4] This, together with the fact that it is not hard to think of plausible reasons involving asymmetric information for external funds to be relatively costly, suggests that cyclical variations in the availability of internal funds to business firms may have an important effect on investment spending and hence on the pace of capital accumulation.[5] Our model provides a simple formal representation of an effect of this sort.

---

[3] It is not necessary for our results that the constraint be on the ability of entrepreneurs to borrow. One might equally well suppose that enforcement problems or adverse selection problems prevent entrepreneurs from lending to workers wanting to consume more in the present; who would like to borrow depends on the relative size of β and γ. In either event, both types of agents end up forced to spend exactly their current income. For further discussion, see Woodford (1988, sect. 2.B).

[4] A classic discussion can be found in Duesenberry (1958, chap. 5). For further discussion and references, see Judd and Petersen (1986).

[5] Such effects have often been emphasized in business cycle models that identify fluctuations in investment spending as the main source of fluctuations in business activity. For example, variations in the availability of internal funds are an important regulator of investment spending in Keynes' theory (see Minsky, 1975, pp. 106–16). These views are quite close to the sort of model discussed briefly in Section 4, in which external finance is possible but the amount that entrepreneurs are willing to borrow depends on the level of internal funds. For a modern treatment, grounded on the economics of information and sressing consequences for the propagation of business fluctuations, see Greenwald and Stiglitz (1988).

Because workers are assumed to be unable to accumulate capital and unwilling to accumulate debt issued by entrepreneurs, they are unable to save and so face a budget constraint $c_t = w_t n_t$ each period, where w_t is the real wage in period t. Their optimizing labor supply decision in each period is then just $n_t = s(w_t)$. Labor market clearing accordingly requires

$$\frac{s(w_t)}{k_t} \in d(w_t), \tag{2}$$

where k_t is the capital stock per worker in period t.

Given (A.5) and the monotonicity of $d(w)$, equation (2) has at most one solution for w_t, for any given k_t. Furthermore

$$\limsup_{w \to \infty} d(w) = 0,$$

because any positive limit would be inconsistent with $r(w) \geq 0$ for large w. It follows for any k that for large enough w, $s(w)/k > \sup d(w)$. Furthermore, given our specification of $d(0)$ in the case that (1) holds, either $s(w)/k < \inf d(w)$ for small enough $w > 0$, so that (2) has a solution with $w_t > 0$, or $s(0)/k \in d(0)$, so that $w_t = 0$ is a solution. Let the unique solution to (2) for each $k_t > 0$ be denoted $v(k_t)$. It follows from the continuity assumptions on s and d, and (A.5), that $v(k)$ is a continuous function; it follows from the monotonicity assumptions that $v(k)$ is nondecreasing.

Note also that $v(k) > 0$ for all $k > 0$, except possibly when (1) holds. In the latter case, there must also exist a limit

$$r(0) = \lim_{w \to 0} r(w) < \infty.$$

Extending $r(w)$ to the value $w = 0$ in this way, we insure that $r(v(k))$ is well defined and is a continuous, nonincreasing function of k for all $k > 0$. This indicates the possible rate of return to capital, given clearing of the labor market, when k is the capital stock per worker.

Another consequence of the impossibility of external finance is that the capital accumulated by entrepreneurs each period must equal exactly their desired saving out of the returns that they receive on the capital used for production in that period. (We assume here for simplicity that capital goods are used up entirely in one period's production. Because of the one-sector technology, this involves no loss of generality.) Because the total wealth of entrepreneurs (after receiving period t profits and before spending on period t consumption) is equal to $k_t r(v(k_t))$, their investment decision is

$$k_{t+1} = \beta k_t r(v(k_t)). \tag{3}$$

Equation (3) provides a nonlinear difference equation for the evolution of the capital stock. Given an initial capital stock k_0, the entire sequence

$\{k_t\}$ is uniquely determined. Corresponding to this sequence is a unique sequence of real wages, rates of return on capital, labor supplies, and so on. Thus, for any initial condition k_0, there is a unique equilibrium path for the economy.

It is worth noting that the difference equation (3) is just a special case of the kind of dynamics for the capital stock considered by Day (1982). Day considers a one-sector "neoclassical" growth model in which the fraction of national income saved is allowed to be a function of the aggregate capital stock. Our dynamics are of this kind, where the savings ratio is equal to β times the share of returns to capital in national income (which is a function of the aggregate capital stock). It is, accordingly, perhaps not surprising that we shall find later that endogenous cycles and chaotic equilibrium dynamics are possible in our model. The contribution of the present chapter is to derive such a specification from an optimizing model and to highlight the role of a certain kind of financial constraint in allowing that derivation.

2   Stability of the steady-state equilibrium

Consideration of whether or not self-perpetuating equilibrium fluctuations are possible in such an economy requires investigation of the asymptotic behavior of the trajectories generated by a continuous map f of the positive reals into the nonnegative reals, where $f(k_t)$ is defined as the right-hand side of (3). Propositions 1 and 2 follow immediately from the form of (3) and the assumptions of the previous section.

Proposition 1.   *The map f has a unique fixed point $k^* > 0$; that is, there exists a unique positive steady-state capital stock.*

Proposition 2.   *Let the elasticities of supply and demand for labor, evaluated at the steady state, be defined (respectively) as $e_s = w^*s'(w^*)/s(w^*)$, $e_d = -w^*r''(w^*)/r'(w^*)$. Suppose that $e_s + e_d > 0$. (Because (A.5) guarantees that $s(w)/-r'(w)$ is increasing at w^*, this holds generically.) Let s_n and s_k denote (respectively) the shares of labor and capital in the total product, also evaluated at the steady state. Finally, suppose that $e_s + e_d \neq s_n/2s_k$. (This condition is also generic.) Then, the steady state is locally stable if and only if $e_s + e_d > s_n/2s_k$.*

Proposition 2 indicates that the steady state need not be stable; if there is sufficiently little labor-supply response and labor-demand response to a change in real wages, then it is unstable. The intuition is simple: If both labor demand and labor supply are relatively inelastic, a small increase in the level of the capital stock results in a large increase in the market-clearing real wage and hence a large fall in the rate of return on capital. If the rate of return falls sharply enough, total returns to capital (i.e., $r(v(k))k$), can decrease when k increases, so a higher capital stock in period t results in a lower capital stock in period $t+1$. If the amount by which the capital stock in period $t+1$ is decreased by an increase in period-t capital stock is sufficiently large, the economy will diverge from steady state by oscillations of progressively larger amplitude in the capital stock per worker.

Note the role in this mechanism of the restriction of entrepreneurs to financing investment only out of internal funds. Note also that instability is possible here, despite the assumption of a one-sector production technology, and that the conditions under which the steady state is unstable do not require any assumption that agents discount the future to a great degree. The value of γ does not affect the equilibrium dynamics at all (at least as long as a particular range of values of γ are not necessary to justify our assumption that external finance is impossible), and it is evident that one can construct examples of instability in which β is as close to 1 as one likes.

Note also that our assumption that $s(w)$ is nondecreasing biases our analysis in favor of stability. Because if one had $e_s < 0$, it would be possible to have a larger value for e_d while still having an unstable steady state. For a sufficiently backward-bending labor-supply curve, one might even have $e_s + e_d < 0$, in which case $f'(k^*) > 1$ – an instability of another sort. (Furthermore, with a backward-bending supply curve, $v(k)$ and hence $f(k)$ may not be single-valued for all k, in which case the set of equilibria becomes much more complicated.)

Next we consider global aspects of the equilibrium dynamics. For this purpose it is useful to observe that the dynamics are eventually restricted to a compact interval. Hence we can restrict our attention to the properties of the dynamical system defined on that interval.

Proposition 3.   *Let f be extended to the point $k = 0$ by defining $f(0) = 0$. Then there exists a $\bar{k} < \infty$ such that f maps the compact interval $K = [0, \bar{k}]$ into itself, and is continuous on that interval. Furthermore, for any k_0, the distance of k_t from the set K approaches zero as t goes to infinity.*

Proof: Consider some $\underline{k} > 0$, and let $\underline{w} = v(\underline{k})$ and $\underline{s} = s(\underline{w})$. Then, by (A.4), $s(w) \leq \underline{s}$ for all $w \leq \underline{w}$. It follows that $kr(v(k)) \leq kr(\inf w(\underline{s}/k))$ for all $k < \underline{k}$. Then, from (A.2),

$$\lim_{k \to 0} f(k) = 0.$$

Thus, f is continuous for all $k \geq 0$. It follows immediately that f has a maximum on the interval $[0, k^*]$; let it be denoted $\hat{k}$. Then, if we set $\bar{k} = \max(k^*, \hat{k})$, we obtain an invariant interval. Because $f(k) < k$ for any $k > \bar{k}$, starting from any point outside K, the trajectory monotonically decreases until eventually a point in K is reached (and k_t remains within K thereafter) or until k_t approaches $\bar{k}$ asymptotically. ∎

The extended map f has two fixed points in the interval K, namely, 0 and k^*. But 0 is necessarily an unstable fixed point, because we have established that $f(k) > k$ for all $0 < k < k^*$. Hence Proposition 3 implies that when $e_s + e_d < s_n/2s_k$, so that the steady state k^* is unstable (by Proposition 2), the equilibrium capital stock neither grows without bound nor (for almost all initial conditions) ever converges to a steady-state value. Hence it must cycle forever, either eventually settling into periodic fluctuations or following an aperiodic (chaotic) trajectory.

Although this result gives a sufficient condition for self-sustaining fluctuations, it is not necessary. The following characterization is therefore useful.

Proposition 4.   *Either there exists a two-period equilibrium cycle – that is, a pair k_1, k_2 with $k_1 \neq k_2$ such that $f(k_1) = k_2$ and $f(k_2) = k_1$ – or else every equilibrium converges to one of the fixed points (0 or k^*). If no two-period cycle exists and $f(\bar{k}) > 0$ then, for any $0 < k_0 \leq \bar{k}$, $k_t \to k^*$ as $t \to \infty$.*

Proof: Because f is a continuous map of a compact interval into itself, the first sentence follows from the celebrated theorem of Sarkovskii (1964).[6] If $f(\bar{k}) > 0$ then no point in the interval $(0, \bar{k}]$ is mapped to 0, and because 0 is unstable it follows that no initial conditions in that interval result in a trajectory converging to 0. Hence all must converge to k^*. ∎

Note that Proposition 4 does not rule out the existence of other kinds of cycles (or of chaos); it simply says that when they exist, there will necessarily exist a two-period cycle (possibly unstable). The usefulness of this result is that it is relatively easy to determine whether a given map possesses a two-period cycle; for example, if one knows the shape of the graph of f, one can plot both equations $f(k_1) = k_2$ and $f(k_2) = k_1$ in the k_1-k_2 plane and see where they intersect. The following sufficient conditions for global stability of the steady state are a simple consequence of Proposition 4.

---

[6] For discussion, see Grandmont (1985).

Proposition 5.   *Suppose that $r(w)$ is twice differentiable, so that the elasticities $e_s(w)$ and $e_d(w)$ can be defined for all $w > 0$. If $r(w) > 0$ for all w and if*

$$e_s(w) + e_d(w) > \frac{-wr'(w)}{r(w) + \beta^{-1}} \tag{4}$$

for all $w > 0$, then the steady state k^* is globally stable. In particular, if the elasticity of substitution between capital and labor is no less than 1 for all possible relative factor prices, the steady state k^* is globally stable. That is, $k_t \to k^*$ as $t \to \infty$, for any $k_0 > 0$.

Proof: If $r(w)$ is C^2 then one finds that, for any k such that $v(k) > 0$,

$$f'(k) = \beta \left[r(v(k)) + \frac{v(k)r'(v(k))}{e_s(v(k)) + e_d(v(k))} \right]. \tag{5}$$

If (4) holds for all $w > 0$, one has $f'(k) > -1$ for all k such that $v(k) > 0$. If there exist any $k > 0$ for which $v(k) = 0$ then $f(k) = \beta r(0)k$ for these values of k, so that $f'(k) > 0$. Hence, one has $f'(k) > -1$ globally (except possibly at a single point where f' is not defined); it follows that if $k_2 > k_1$ then $f(k_2) - f(k_1) > k_1 - k_2$. This rules out the existence of a two-period equilibrium cycle. If $r(w) > 0$ for all w then $f(k) > 0$ for all $k > 0$, and so one cannot have $k_t \to 0$ except for $k_0 = 0$. Proposition 4 then implies the global stability of k^*.

When $r(w)$ is C^2, the elasticity of substitution between capital and labor is well defined and equal to $s_k e_d$. Hence, if the elasticity is never less than 1 then one must have

$$e_d(w) \geq s_k(w)^{-1} = 1 - \frac{wr'(w)}{r(w)} > \frac{-wr'(w)}{r(w) + \beta^{-1}}$$

for all $w > 0$. Hence (4) holds because $e_s(w) \geq 0$ by (A.4).   ∎

By a similar argument, one can extend Proposition 2 to show that an elasticity of substitution greater than $\frac{1}{2}$ suffices to guarantee local stability of the steady state. Again, note that these strong conclusions regarding the consequences of a given elasticity of substitution between capital and labor depend on our assumption that the labor-supply curve cannot be backward-bending. If it were, the steady state might be unstable despite the existence of an elasticity of substitution greater than one.

3   Chaotic equilibrium dynamics

We now consider in greater detail the kinds of self-sustaining fluctuations that can occur when the steady state is unstable. The following example illustrates the range of kinds of behavior that are possible. Suppose that labor supply is completely inelastic (and without loss of generality, let it equal 1), and consider a profit function

$$r(w) = \begin{cases} a - (2bw)^{1/2} & \text{for } w \leq a^2/2b, \\ 0 & \text{for } w \geq a^2/2b. \end{cases}$$

(This would result from a production technology according to which k units of capital and n units of labor yield $ak - bk^2/2n$ units of output when $k/n \leq a/b$, and yield $a^2n/2b$ when $k/n \geq a/b$.) One obtains in this case a map

$$f(k) = \begin{cases} \beta(ak - bk^2) & \text{for } k \leq a/b, \\ 0 & \text{for } k \geq a/b. \end{cases}$$

With a transformation of variables, $x_t = (b/a)k_t$, this becomes $x_{t+1} = \beta a x_t (1 - x_t)$ on the interval $[0, 1]$.

This family of quadratic maps has been extensively studied (see, e.g., May, 1976). Our previous assumptions, in particular (A.3), are satisfied if $\beta a > 1$. For $1 < \beta a < 3$, the steady state k^* is globally stable. For $3 < \beta a < 1 + \sqrt{6}$, the steady state is unstable, and almost all initial conditions result in paths that converge to a two-period cycle. As βa is made larger, more and more complicated kinds of equilibrium cycles become possible. It can be shown that for any integer $m > 1$ there exists at least one interval of values for βa, within the interval $(3, 4)$, for which there exists a stable equilibrium cycle of period m.

Furthermore, for all values of βa between a critical value (approximately 3.57) and 4, there exist an uncountably infinite number of initial conditions for which the equilibrium dynamics never settle into any periodic pattern, despite the capital stock's continuing to fluctuate within the compact interval K. In this case we can speak of *chaotic* equilibrium dynamics.[7] But it is of limited interest merely to show that the existence of chaotic trajectories for *some* initial conditions is possible; this does not establish that one should expect to observe such trajectories. In many of the cases just described, the set of initial conditions K that result in chaotic trajectories is of measure zero.[8] It is accordingly of greater interest when a map f is *strongly chaotic* in the sense of the following definition:

(i)   It has at most a countable number of periodic points and all of its periodic points are unstable.

---

[7] For discussion, see Benhabib and Day (1982).

[8] This is a problem with many of the early demonstrations of the possibility of chaotic dynamics in economic models. See Melese and Transue (1986). Our definition of "strongly chaotic" dynamics is more restrictive than Melese and Transue's "thick chaos" but implies it.

(ii)   For almost all initial conditions k_0 in K, there exists a probability measure μ on K that is absolutely continuous with respect to Lebesgue measure [i.e., the measure μ can be described in terms of a density function g so that $\mu(A) = \int_A g(k)\,dk$, for A any measurable subset of K] and that describes the asymptotic frequency distribution for k_t [i.e., for A any measurable subset of K with $\mu(A) > 0$, the asymptotic frequency with which $k_1 \in A$ is equal to $\mu(A)$].

In such a case, the set of initial conditions in K that result in bounded but asymptotically aperiodic (i.e., chaotic) trajectories is of full measure so that the chaotic equilibrium dynamics should be "observable." Furthermore, for almost all initial conditions, the equilibrium dynamics appear stochastic in the sense that the long-run frequency distribution for k_t is given by an absolutely continuous measure.[9] If, in addition, the measure μ is the same for almost all k_0 in K, the equilibrium dynamics are *ergodic;* we do not, however, require this for strong chaos. Our definition of strongly chaotic dynamics corresponds to asymptotic periodicity of the Frobenius–Perron operator (Lasota and Mackey, 1985, sects. 5.3 and 6.4).

Some of the maps associated with the example just described are strongly chaotic; for example, the case $\beta a = 4$. In fact, it is known that the map f is strongly chaotic for a set of values of βa between 3.57 and 4 that is of positive measure (Jakobson, 1981). On the other hand, it is believed that this set contains no intervals, that is, that the contrary case is generic in the sense of obtaining for an open, dense set of parameter values (Collet and Eckmann, 1980; Coppel, 1983). Hence the example might not suffice to establish that strong chaos is a robust possibility among economies of the kind considered here. The following result enables us to determine open sets of parameter values for which strongly chaotic dynamics obtain.

Lemma 1.   *Suppose that $f : K \to K$ is C^2 at all but a finite number of points in K, and* everywhere expanding *in the sense that* $\inf_k |f'(k)| > 1$, *where the infimum is over those points in K where f' is defined. Then f generates* strongly chaotic dynamics. *If f' is discontinuous at only one point then the dynamics are also ergodic.*

Proof: Part (i) of the definition of strongly chaotic dynamics is trivial: Any period-m cycle $(k_1, k_2, \ldots, k_m)$, with f' continuous at k_i for $i = 1, 2, \ldots, m$, is unstable if

$$|Df^m(k_i)| = |f'(k_1)f'(k_2)\cdots f'(k_m)| > 1,$$

[9] For discussion, see Benhabib and Day (1982, p. 53).

and this is guaranteed if f is everywhere expanding. The result is easily obtained as well in the case that f' is discontinuous at k_i for some i, using one-sided derivatives, because both one-sided derivatives of f at such a point are greater than 1 in absolute value. Because $|Df^m| > 1$ at all points where it is defined, and the set of points where it is not defined is finite in number (at most $2^m - 1$), it follows that f^m can have only a finite number of fixed points (at most 2^m). Hence the number of periodic points is countable.

Part (ii) follows from the results of Li and Yorke (1978). Their theorem 1 states that under the hypotheses of the lemma, there exist a finite collection of sets $K_1, \ldots, K_n$ and associated integrable functions $g_1, \ldots, g_n$ such that:

(a) each K_i is a finite union of closed intervals, containing in its interior at least one point at which f' is discontinuous;
(b) $K_i \cap K_j$ contains at most a finite number of points if $i \neq j$;
(c) each g_i is an invariant probability distribution under f, with support K_i; and
(d) any invariant probability distribution g under f can be written as $g = \sum_i a_i g_i$ for some coefficients $\{a_i\}$.

Now if we consider the map f restricted to K_i (call it f_i), it is evident that K_i is an invariant set under f_i; that is, $f_i^{-1}(K_i) = K_i$. Furthermore, there can be no subset A of K_i such that both A and $K_i \setminus A$ have positive measure that is invariant under f_i. For if such a set A existed then f_i restricted to A would also be an invariant distribution under f, but not of the form specified in (d). Hence f is an ergodic transformation of the compact set K_i and thus is a measure-preserving ergodic transformation of the finite measure space $(K_i, \mathbf{B}_i, \mu_i)$, where $\mathbf{B}_i$ is the set of Borel subsets of K_i and μ_i is the absolutely continuous invariant measure generated by the distribution function g_i. Then the Birkhoff ergodic theorem (Lasota and Mackey, 1985, corollary 4.2.2) implies that μ_i describes the long-run frequency distribution of k_t, for almost all initial conditions $k_0 \in K_i$.

Furthermore, in the proof of theorem 2 of Li and Yorke (1978), it is shown that the trajectory $\{k_t\}$ eventually enters one of the sets K_i, for almost all initial conditions $k_0 \in K$. Hence, for almost all initial conditions in K, the long-run frequency distribution of k_t is described by one of the absolutely continuous measures μ_i. This is part (ii) of the definition of strong chaos.

Finally, if there is only one point of discontinuity for f' then, by (a) and (b), $n = 1$ (i.e., there can be only one set K_i). It then follows from (d) that there exists a unique absolutely continuous invariant measure μ, so the dynamics are also ergodic. ∎

The following useful sufficient conditions for strongly chaotic dynamics can now be derived.

Proposition 6. *Suppose that $r(w)$ satisfies condition (1). Suppose that $s(w)$ is twice continuously differentiable, and that $s(0) > 0$. In addition, suppose that there exists a $\bar{w} > 0$ such that $r(w)$ is three times continuously differentiable on the interval $0 < w < \bar{w}$. Suppose furthermore that*

$$e_s(w) + e_d(w) < \frac{-wr'(w)}{r(w) + \beta^{-1}} \tag{6}$$

for all $0 < w \leq \bar{w}$, and that

$$\lim_{w \to 0} \frac{e_s(w) + e_d(w)}{w} < \frac{-r'(0)}{r(0) + \beta^{-1}}, \tag{7}$$

as well. Finally, suppose that

$$\frac{s(\bar{w})}{s(0)} \geq \frac{\beta r(0) r'(\bar{w})}{w(0)}. \tag{8}$$

Then the equilibrium dynamics described by (3) are strongly chaotic. Furthermore, the set of initial conditions for which the equilibrium trajectory appears chaotic is of full measure.

Proof: It is necessary only to establish that the hypotheses suffice to guarantee that f is piecewise C^2 and everywhere expanding, so that Lemma 1 applies. If $r(w)$ satisfies condition (1), so that $r(0) < \infty$ and $r'(0) > -\infty$, and if $s(0) > 0$, it follows that $v(k) = 0$ for all $0 \leq k \leq \bar{k} = s(0)/-r'(0)$. On this subinterval, then, $r(v(k)) = r(0)$, and $f(k) = \beta r(0)k$. It follows that f is C^2 on the interior of this subinterval; and because $r(0) > \beta^{-1}$ by (A.3), it is everywhere expanding. If we set $\tilde{k} = f(\bar{k})$, then (8) simply says that $s(\bar{w}) \geq [-r'(\bar{w})]\tilde{k}$, so that $v(\tilde{k}) \leq \bar{w}$. Then $r(w)$ is C^3 on the subinterval $(v(\bar{k}), v(\tilde{k}))$, and this, together with the fact that $s(w)$ is C^2, guarantees that f is C^2 on the subinterval $\bar{k} < k < \tilde{k}$. For $\bar{k} < k \leq \tilde{k}$, $f'(k)$ is then given by (5). Hence (6) guarantees that $f'(k) < -1$ on this subinterval, and (7) guarantees that the right derivative at $\bar{k}$ is also strictly less than -1.   ∎

It can easily be verified that the conditions assumed in Proposition 6 are not inconsistent with the general assumptions of our model. Consider the case of a fixed-coefficients production technology, in which $b > 0$ units of labor must be used with each unit of capital to produce $ab > \beta^{-1}$ units of the produced good. This yields a profit function $r(w) = b(a - w)$, for $0 \leq w \leq a$. Suppose also that the labor-supply curve is $s(w) = c + ew$, where

$c, e > 0$. Then one can show that all the conditions assumed in Proposition 6 are satisfied if ab is chosen so that $1 < \beta ab < (1 + \sqrt{5})/2$ and ae/c is then chosen so that $\beta ab - 1 \le ae/c < \beta ab/(1 + \beta ab)$. These conditions are all obviously satisfied by an open set of the parameters a, b, c, e, and they can be satisfied regardless of how close β might be to 1.

Furthermore, it is obvious that neither of the functional forms assumed for $r(w)$ and $s(w)$ are essential to the result. [For (1) to hold, it *is* necessary that capital be essential for production, in the sense that there exists a minimum quantity of capital that must be used per worker if anything is to be produced; this quantity is $-r'(0)^{-1}$. And, of course, conditions (6) and (7) require that the substitutability between capital and labor not be too great.] In fact, if one slightly perturbs both $r(w)$ and $s(w)$ in any way – so that the values of $r(w)$ and $s(w)$ are little changed for all $0 \le w \le \bar{w}$ and so that the values of $r'(w)$, $r''(w)$, and $s'(w)$ are also little changed – then the conditions of Proposition 6 will still be satisfied. Hence strongly chaotic dynamics are a robust phenomenon.

4   Consequences of limited external finance: an example

Thus far we have investigated the character of equilibrium dynamics when all capital accumulation must be financed out of internal funds. This is, of course, too extreme an assumption to be realistic. In this section we show that self-sustaining fluctuations are still possible when some amount of external finance is available. In particular, we consider the case where there exists a competitive market in which entrepreneurs can sell riskless debt securities, but other types of financial contracting are impossible.

Consideration of this case allows a significant increase in realism because much more external finance is in fact obtained on straight debt contracts (whether bond issues, commercial paper, or bank loans) than through any kind of contingent contracts, and because the problems caused by asymmetric information are well known to be more serious in the case of equity issues and other contracts whose terms are contingent on the future performance of the firm than in the case of straight debt contracts.[10]

Let us now consider an economy in which debts are enforceable; in particular, let us suppose that in the event of default borrowers can be made subject to some penalty that is sufficiently severe as to induce borrowers always to repay and to lead them to refrain from borrowing when there is any positive probability of their not being able to repay. But let us suppose that entrepreneurs' projects are subject to firm-specific shocks and that the return to a given entrepreneur's investment is observed only

---

[10] See, e.g., Greenwald and Stiglitz (1988).

by that entrepreneur, so that no debt contract that makes repayment contingent on this shock is incentive-compatible.[11]

Then, if an entrepreneur has equity equal to e_t in period t (after repayment of debts incurred in the previous period, and after period-t consumption outlays but before period-t investment expenditures have been made), his choice of a level of capital k_{t+1} to accumulate for use in period-$t+1$ production implies net borrowing in the amount $k_{t+1} - e_t$. Plainly, the entrepreneur will choose $k_{t+1} = 0$ (i.e., he will lend out all of his equity capital) unless the expected return per unit of capital r_{t+1} is at least as great as the interest rate i_{t+1} on riskless loans. On the other hand, when r_{t+1} exceeds i_{t+1}, the entrepreneur's desired capital accumulation (and hence loan demand) need not be unbounded. His willingness to leverage himself may be limited by his desire to avoid default in the event of an adverse productivity shock, which Keynes referred to as "borrowers' risk." One simple way of representing this constraint is to suppose that there is a maximum ratio of debt repayment obligations to expected capital returns that entrepreneurs regard as safe. If we let this ratio be $\theta < 1$, then we may suppose that entrepreneurs subject themselves to the constraint

$$i_{t+1}(k_{t-1} - e_t) \leq \theta r_{t+1} k_{t+1}. \tag{9}$$

An interpretation of (9) is that though the expected return per unit of capital is r_{t+1}, it is possible for the return to be as low as θr_{t-1}; (9) is then simply a no-default constraint. We can suppose that, subject to (9), entrepreneurs seek to maximize their expected returns after repayment of debt obligations.[12] Entrepreneurs then choose $k_{t+1} = 0$ if $r_{t+1} < i_{t+1}$, choose

$$k_{t+1} = \left(\frac{i_{t+1}}{i_{t+1} - \theta r_{t+1}} \right) e_t \tag{10}$$

if $i_{t+1} < r_{t+1} < \theta^{-1} i_{t+1}$, choose any level of capital stock between zero and the amount given in (10) if $r_{t+1} = i_{t+1}$ exactly, and choose an unbounded capital stock if $r_{t+1} \geq \theta^{-1} i_{t+1}$.

In this case, capital accumulation is still very much dependent on the level of entrepreneurial equity (i.e., on the availability of internal funds), despite the existence of a competitive loan market. Accordingly, endogenous fluctuations are still possible for reasons much like those that apply in the case of no external finance at all. Here we content ourselves with the presentation of a simple example. Using techniques like those employed in Section 3, one can show that the properties of this example also hold for other nearby specifications of the technology and of preferences.

---

[11] This sort of argument for the existence of straight debt contracts has been made previously by Diamond (1984), Gale and Hellwig (1984), and Townsend (1979).

[12] A similar sort of financial constraint has been investigated by Gale (1983a, 1983b).

Suppose that there exists a fixed-coefficients production technology in which $\bar{k}$ units of capital must be used with each unit of labor to produce $\bar{r}\bar{k}$ units of output. This corresponds to a profit function $r(w) = \bar{r} - (w/\bar{k})$ for $w \leq \bar{r}\bar{k}$, $r(w) = 0$ for $w \geq \bar{r}\bar{k}$. We can reconcile this deterministic relationship with the firm-specific variability of the returns to capital by supposing that there is a firm-specific shock, observed between the time when capital is accumulated and when labor is hired to work with it, that multiplies the quantity of capital accumulated by a given firm by a random variable with mean 1, whose lowest possible value is θ. Assuming a continuum of firms with independent drawings of the multiplicative factor, the (effective) aggregate capital stock per worker after the shock is still exactly k_{t+1}, the quantity of capital stock per worker accumulated in the previous period. The returns to each unit of effective capital are $r_{t+1} = r(w_{t+1})$, though the returns to physical capital accumulated in the previous period are as low as θr_{t+1} for some entrepreneurs. The aggregate returns to capital in the economy equal the deterministic quantity $r_{t+1}k_{t+1}$.

As a final simplification, suppose that workers supply labor inelastically (one unit each) and that they want to maximize

$$\sum_{t=0}^{\infty} \gamma^t c_t,$$

so that their demand for riskless bonds in any period t is completely elastic as long as $i_{t+1} = \gamma^{-1}$. We ignore here the possibility of a binding constraint $c_t \geq 0$. Because in all the equilibria to be described, the entrepreneurs' demand for capital is bounded above in all periods, we need only give workers some finite endowment of goods each period in addition to their labor endowment to make these equilibria consistent with $c_t \geq 0$. Similarly, we need not worry about the workers' accumulation of bonds failing to satisfy a transversality constraint because workers' wealth can never exceed the aggregate capital stock, which is always bounded. Finally, in all of the equilibria, it will be found that the consumption program of workers satisfies the infinite-horizon budget constraint

$$\liminf_{t \to \infty} \gamma^t d_t \leq 0,$$

where d_t is workers' indebtedness in period t. Because entrepreneurial equity must equal the capital stock plus workers' indebtedness, and the capital stock must be nonnegative, a sufficient condition for the preceding to hold is

$$\liminf_{t \to \infty} \gamma^t e_t = 0,$$

which will be observed to be satisfied by all the equilibria to be exhibited.

Now suppose that aggregate entrepreneurial equity per worker in period t is given by $e_t > 0$. [Because of the form of (10), the assumption of constant returns to scale, and the homothetic preferences of entrepreneurs, it does not matter how this equity capital is distributed across entrepreneurs.] The market-clearing real wage in period $t+1$ will equal zero if $k_t < \bar{k}$, will equal $\bar{r}\bar{k}$ if $k_t > \bar{k}$, and can be anywhere in between if $k_t = \bar{k}$ exactly. Accordingly, the average return per unit of capital r_{t+1} must be expected to be $\bar{r}$ if $k_t < \bar{k}$ and zero if $k_t > \bar{k}$, but might be anything in between if $k_t = \bar{k}$ exactly. This implies that there is a unique expectation r_{t+1} that leads to a capital stock k_{t+1} consistent with that rate of return and a unique such capital stock k_{t+1} for a given value of e_t. Let us suppose that

$$\bar{r} > \gamma^{-1}, \tag{11}$$

so that it is possible for expected returns to be high enough to induce capital accumulation. Then the unique perfect-foresight equilibrium is given by the following regimes:

1 If $\gamma\theta\bar{r} < 1$, then $r_{t+1} = \bar{r}$ and $k_{t+1} = (1-\gamma\theta\bar{r})^{-1}e_t$ for all
   $0 < e_t \leq \bar{e} = (1-\gamma\theta\bar{r})\bar{k}$.
2 $k_{t+1} = \bar{k}$ and $r_{t+1} = (\gamma\theta\bar{k})^{-1}(\bar{k} - e_t)$ for all $\bar{e} \leq e_t \leq (1-\theta)\bar{k}$,
   or simply for $0 < e_t \leq (1-\theta)\bar{k}$ if $\gamma\theta\bar{r} \geq 1$.
3 $k_{t+1} = \bar{k}$ and $r_{t+1} = \gamma^{-1}$ for all $e_t \geq (1-\theta)\bar{k}$.

In regime 1, the level of entrepreneurial equity is insufficient to allow full employment. Accordingly, the real wage is zero, $r_{t+1} = \bar{r}$, and k_{t+1} increases proportionally with an increase in e_t. In regime 2, there is full employment, so $k_{t+1} = \bar{k}$, and r_{t+1} falls to a level sufficient to induce entrepreneurs to accumulate no more capital than $\bar{k}$. The higher the level of entrepreneurial equity, the lower r_{t+1} must fall for this to occur, as long as r_{t+1} remains above γ^{-1}. In regime 3, r_{t+1} has fallen to γ^{-1} and so need fall no further to maintain $k_{t+1} = \bar{k}$ as e_t increases; entrepreneurs no longer necessarily want to leverage themselves to the maximum extent consistent with (9).

Because entrepreneurs consume a fraction $(1-\beta)$ of their net worth each period, the following period's aggregate entrepreneurial equity per worker is given by $e_{t+1} = \beta[r_{t+1}k_{t+1} - \gamma^{-1}(k_{t+1} - e_t)]$. This yields an equation for e_{t+1} as a function of e_t that is piecewise linear:

$$e_{t+1} = \begin{cases} [\beta(1-\theta)\bar{r}/(1-\gamma\theta\bar{r})]e_t, & \text{for } e_t \text{ in regime 1,} \\ [\beta(1-\theta)/\gamma\theta](\bar{k} - e_t), & \text{for } e_t \text{ in regime 2,} \\ [\beta/\gamma]e_t, & \text{for } e_t \text{ in regime 3.} \end{cases}$$

Let us call this function $e_{t+1} = f(e_t)$.

The dynamics of such a piecewise linear map are easily characterized. It is evident that if $\bar{r} < [\beta(-\theta) + \gamma\theta]^{-1}$ then $e_{t+1} < e_t$ for all $e_t > 0$, so e_t must approach zero asymptotically and k_t must as well. In this case, capital is not productive enough to be accumulated in the long run. It is likewise evident that if $\gamma < \beta$ then $e_{t+1} > e_t$ for all $e_t > 0$, and so e_t must grow without bound. In this case, entrepreneurs eventually have no need of external finance, and the basic structure we are investigating here would cease to apply. The case of most interest is that in which

$$\bar{r} > [\beta(1-\theta) + \gamma\theta]^{-1}, \tag{12}$$

$$\beta < \gamma, \tag{13}$$

so that $e_{t+1} > e_t$ for small enough $e_t > 0$ whereas $e_{t+1} < e_t$ for large e_t. In this case there exists a unique positive steady-state level of entrepreneurial equity e^*, which lies in regime 2.

The stability of the steady state obviously depends on the slope of the graph of f in regime 2. If $\beta/\gamma < \theta/(1-\theta)$, it can be shown that the steady state is globally stable; that is, for any initial condition $e_0 > 0$, e_t converges to e^*. On the other hand, if

$$\frac{\beta}{\gamma} > \frac{\theta}{1-\theta}, \tag{14}$$

the steady state is unstable. It is easily shown that when (11)–(13) hold, the compact interval $E = [0, \hat{e}]$ is mapped into itself, where $\hat{e} = \beta(1-\theta)\bar{r}\bar{k}$, if one defines $f(0)$ as the limit of $f(e)$ as e approaches zero from above. Furthermore, for any initial condition, e_t eventually enters E and remains in it forever after. And if 0 is also a fixed point of f, (12) implies that it will be unstable. Hence, when (11)–(14) hold, the level of entrepreneurial equity fluctuates forever within the bounded interval E, never settling down to any steady state, for almost all initial conditions e_0.

In general, for specifications of technology and preferences close to but not identical to this one, these fluctuations in entrepreneurial equity also mean fluctuations in the capital stock and the level of production. In the special case treated here this need not be so, because $k_{t+1} = \bar{k}$ and output equals $\bar{r}\bar{k}$ whenever entrepreneurial equity lies within either regime 2 or regime 3. However, even in the limiting case (of inelastic labor supply and fixed coefficients) considered here, it is possible to insure that fluctuations in the capital stock and in output occur forever in equilibrium, for almost all initial conditions, by insuring that there is no invariant set containing an open interval and wholly contained within regimes 2 and 3. An example would be if, in addition to (11)–(14), we have $\bar{r} \le \beta^{-1}$. Then $\hat{e} \le (1-\theta)\bar{k}$, so that the invariant interval E is contained wholly within regimes 1 and 2.

It follows that f is everywhere expanding, so Lemma 1 applies, and one has strongly chaotic dynamics. The following result shows that it is possible to have strongly chaotic dynamics even when the invariant interval E includes part of regime (3). These additional sufficient conditions for strongly chaotic dynamics are useful because (unlike the condition just discussed) they can be satisfied even for β and γ arbitrarily close to 1.

Proposition 7. *Consider an economy with limited external finance, and suppose that in addition to* (11)–(14) *one has*

$$\frac{\beta(1-\theta)}{\gamma} \geq \max[\gamma\theta\bar{r}, 1-\gamma\theta\bar{r}]. \tag{15}$$

Then equilibrium dynamics are strongly chaotic.

Proof: Suppose first that one has

$$\frac{\beta(1-\theta)}{\gamma} \geq \gamma\theta\bar{r} \geq \frac{1}{2}. \tag{16}$$

The first inequality in (16) suffices to insure that there exists a positive integer k such that

$$\beta\bar{r} \leq \left(\frac{\gamma}{\beta}\right)^k < \frac{\beta(1-\theta)}{\gamma\theta}. \tag{17}$$

The first inequality in (17) implies that $(\beta/\gamma)^k\hat{e} \leq (1-\theta)\bar{k}$, so that there exists no point e in E such that $f^t(e)$ lies in regime 3 for $t = 0, 1, \ldots, k$. Then, for any e in E (except for a finite number of points at which the derivative is not defined),

$$|[f^{k+1}]'(e)| \geq x^k y,$$

where $x = \beta/\gamma$ is the slope of the graph in regime 3, and y is the minimum of the absolute values of the slopes in regimes 1 and 2. The second inequality in (16) insures that the slope of the graph of f in regime 1 is at least as large as the absolute value of the slope in regime 2, so that $y = \beta(1-\theta)/\gamma\theta$. Then the second inequality in (17) states that $x^k y > 1$.

It follows that f^{k+1} is everywhere expanding on E. Because f is piecewise C^2, f^{k+1} is also, and so Lemma 1 applies to f^{k+1}. Then f^{k+1} has no stable periodic points, from which it follows that f has none either. Furthermore, for almost all initial conditions e_0, the sequence $\{e_{n(k+1)}\}$ has a long-run frequency distribution given by some integrable function g. For any such e_0, it follows that the sequence $\{e_t\}$ has a long-run frequency distribution given by the integrable function

$$\hat{g} = (k+1)^{-1}[1+P+P^2+\cdots+P^k]g,$$

where P is the Frobenius–Perron operator. Hence the equilibrium dynamics are strongly chaotic.

If (16) does not hold, then instead one must have

$$1 - \frac{\beta(1-\theta)}{\gamma} \leq \gamma\theta\bar{r} \leq \frac{1}{2}. \tag{18}$$

The argument proceeds along similar lines in this case because the first inequality in (18) implies the existence of a positive integer k such that

$$\beta\bar{r} \leq \left(\frac{\gamma}{\beta}\right)^k < \frac{\beta(1-\theta)\bar{r}}{1-\gamma\theta\bar{r}}.$$

The argument proceeds as before, except that the second inequality in (18) implies that the graph is at least as steep in regime 2 as in regime 1, so that $y = \beta(1-\theta)\bar{r}/(1-\gamma\theta\bar{r})$. One finds that (18) is also a sufficient condition for strong chaos. ∎

Thus the same sort of complex dynamics revealed to be possible in Section 3 continue to be possible even with limited external finance. Furthermore, as in Section 3, self-sustaining equilibrium fluctuations are possible even with a one-sector production technology and arbitrarily low rates of time preference, because conditions (11)–(15) are satisfied (as β and γ are made to approach 1) so long as

$$1 \leq \bar{r} \leq \theta^{-1} - 1$$

and β remains less than γ as both are increased. Because $\bar{r} > 1$ is necessary for there to exist any equilibrium with capital accumulation, the essential precondition for chaotic dynamics with low rates of time preference is that $\theta \leq (1 + \bar{r})^{-1}$. This condition, which states that the acceptable degree of leverage is not too high, is obviously a limitation on the degree to which external finance is feasible.

It is important to note that none of these equilibrium fluctuations would occur in the absence of the imperfect information problem (nonobservability of firm-specific shocks) that prevents financial markets from being complete. If it were possible for contracts to be written contingent upon the firm-specific shocks then, because of the continuum of entrepreneurs subject to independent shocks, complete risk-pooling would occur in equilibrium. Then entrepreneurs would borrow each period to the point where $r_{t+1} = i_{t+1} = \gamma^{-1}$, regardless of their level of internal equity, which [because of (11)] means that there would always be full employment. The dynamics of entrepreneurial equity would be as in regime 3, for all values of e_t, so that entrepreneurial equity would necessarily approach zero asymptotically, but this would have no effect upon the level of production.

5 Concluding remarks

A brief remark is appropriate on the implications of our model of endogenous fluctuations for the possibility and desirability of stabilization policy. The fluctuating equilibria shown to occur for some parameter values are plainly not desirable, because any Pareto optimal allocation of resources must coincide with the equilibrium of some optimal-growth model with the same one-sector technology and so must converge asymptotically to a constant capital stock and a constant level of output.

On the other hand, this does not mean that an intervention that succeeds in preventing self-sustaining fluctuations is for that reason alone an improvement, because the steady-state equilibrium of our model is *not* the stationary allocation to which the Pareto optimal allocations converge. (Typically, the model involves a lower capital stock than occurs in the Pareto optimal stationary allocation and too large a level of consumption by entrepreneurs.) An intervention that was to achieve an efficient use of resources would therefore have to go beyond the mere suppression of cycles and would involve continuing intervention even in the steady state.

It is sometimes argued that although asymmetric information can result in aggregate fluctuations of a kind that would not exist in the case of symmetric information, this does not create a role for stabilization policy because the government could not improve on the allocation of resources unless it possessed information greater than what is assumed to be publicly available. It is also argued that if the government does have access to superior information then it should be able to achieve the desired effects simply by making public its information and otherwise refraining from interference with market processes. Such an argument is certainly incorrect in the case of information imperfections of the kind assumed here. For in order to stabilize, fiscal policy need only be made responsive to aggregate economic conditions (in particular, to the aggregate quantity of entrepreneurial equity per worker), and these are assumed to be perfectly understood by the private sector as well. It is not necessary to assume that the government can somehow get around the moral hazard problem faced by other lenders by observing the firm-specific productivity shocks. The government can make transfers to entrepreneurs as a group, when this is necessary to prevent a collapse of investment, because of the government's power to tax workers as a group; it is this power to tax (without being able to make taxes or transfers contingent upon individual circumstances) that allows the government to stabilize when private contracting cannot. There is thus a role for something like the traditional conception of aggregate fiscal policy, quite distinct from any role the government might have in improving the level of publicly available information.

Imperfect financial intermediation can also make possible endogenous equilibrium fluctuations in another sense than that explored here. Financial constraints of certain sorts result in the existence of "sunspot" equilibria: rational expectations equilibria in which the allocation of resources fluctuates in response to random events that have no intrinsic significance in terms of a change in agents' preferences or in the technological possibilities. This phenomenon is impossible in well-behaved economies with a finite number of infinite-lived agents of the kind considered here, with perfect financial markets.[13] However, in models related to the one described here – models in which, in addition, the role of money is modeled by introducing a cash-in-advance constraint – sunspot equilibria do exist, including some in which endogenous variables such as the capital stock and output follow a stationary stochastic process.[14] In this case, too, the endogenous fluctuations are necessarily inefficient, because a Pareto optimal allocation of resources will never involve unnecessary randomization of this kind when agents are risk averse and technology is convex; though, again, the nonsunspot equilibria of the models referred to are themselves inefficient. Likewise, in this case it is possible to stabilize (in the sense of preventing equilibria of the sunspot type) by making fiscal transfers contingent upon publicly observed aggregate variables, without the government's being able to observe the private information that causes the financial market imperfections.

REFERENCES

Benhabib, J., and Day, R. H. (1982), "A characterization of erratic dynamics in the overlapping generations model," *Journal of Economic Dynamics and Control,* 4, 37–55.
Benhabib, J., and Nishimura, K. (1979), "The Hopf bifurcation and the existence and stability of closed orbits in multi-sector models of optimal economic growth," *Journal of Economic Theory,* 21, 421–44.
   (1985), "Competitive equilibrium cycles," *Journal of Economic Theory,* 35, 284–306.
Benhabib, J., Jafarey, S., and Nishimura, K. (1986), "The dynamics of efficient intertemporal allocations with many agents, recursive preferences, and production," C. V. Starr Center Working Paper No. 86-18, New York University.
Bewley, T. F. (1986), "Dynamic implications of the form of the budget constraint," in *Models of Economic Dynamics,* ed. by H. F. Sonnenschein, New York: Springer-Verlag.
Boldrin, M., and Montrucchio, L. (1986), "On the indeterminacy of capital accumulation paths," *Journal of Economic Theory,* 40, 26–39.

[13] See, e.g., Woodford (1987, 1988).
[14] See, e.g., Woodford (1986, 1988).

Bryant, J. (1980), "Transaction demand for money and moral hazard," in *Models of Monetary Economics,* ed. by J. H. Kareken and N. Wallace, Minneapolis: Federal Reserve Bank.

Collet, P., and Eckmann, J.-P. (1980), *Iterated Maps on the Interval as Dynamical Systems,* Boston: Birkhauser.

Coppel, W. A. (1983), "Maps on an interval," Preprint Series No. 26, Inst. for Math. and Apps., Univ. of Minnesota.

Day, R. H. (1982), "Irregular growth cycles," *American Economic Review,* 72, 406–14.

Dechert, D. W. (1984), "Does optimal growth preclude chaos? A theorem on monotonicity," *Zeitschrift für Nationalokonomie,* 44, 57–61.

Deneckere, R., and Pelikan, S. (1986), "Competitive chaos," *Journal of Economic Theory,* 40, 13–25.

Diamond, D. W. (1984), "Financial intermediation and delegated monitoring," *Review of Economic Studies,* 51, 393–414.

Duesenberry, J. S. (1958), *Business Cycles and Economic Growth,* New York: McGraw-Hill.

Gale, D. (1983a), "Competitive models with Keynesian features," *Economic Journal,* 93, AUTE Conf. Papers Supp., 17–33.

(1983b), *Money: In Disequilibrium,* Cambridge: Cambridge University Press.

Gale, D., and Hellwig, M. (1984), "Incentive compatible debt contracts: The one period problem," I.C.E.R.D. Disc. Paper No. 84/97, London School of Economics.

Grandmont, J. M. (1985), "On endogenous competitive business cycles," *Econometrica,* 53, 995–1045.

Greenwald, B., and Stiglitz, J. E. (1988), "Information, finance constraints, and business fluctuations," in *Finance Constraints, Expectations, and Macroeconomics,* ed. by M. Kohn and S.-C. Tsiang, New York: Oxford University Press.

Jakobson, M. V. (1981), "Absolutely continuous invariant measures for one-parameter families of one-dimensional maps," *Communications in Mathematical Physics,* 81, 39–88.

Judd, K. L., and Petersen, B. C. (1986), "Dynamic limit pricing and internal finance," *Journal of Economic Theory,* 39, 368–99.

Kehoe, T. J., Levine, D. K., Mas-Colell, A., and Woodford, M. (1986), "Gross substitutability in large square economies," mimeo., Cambridge University.

Lasota, A., and Mackey, M. C. (1985), *Probabilistic Properties of Deterministic Systems,* Cambridge: Cambridge University Press.

Li, T., and Yorke, J. A. (1978), "Ergodic transformations from an interval into itself," *Transactions of the American Mathematical Society,* 235, 183–92.

May, R. B. (1976), "Simple mathematical models with very complicated dynamics," *Nature,* 261, 459–67.

Melese, F., and Transue, W. (1986), "Unscrambling chaos through thick and thin," *Quarterly Journal of Economics,* 51, 419–23.

Minsky, H. P. (1975), *John Maynard Keynes,* New York: Columbia University Press.

Sarkovskii, A. N. (1964), "Coexistence of cycles of a continuous map of a line into itself," *Ukrain. Mat. Z.,* 16, 61–71.

Scheinkman, J. A. (1976), "On optimal steady states of *n*-sector growth models when utility is discounted," *Journal of Economic Theory,* 12, 11–30.

Townsend, R. M. (1979), "Optimal contracts and competitive markets with costly state verification," *Journal of Economic Theory,* 21, 1–29.

(1980). "Models of money with spatially separated agents," in *Models of Monetary Economics,* ed. by J. H. Kareken and N. Wallace, Minneapolis: Federal Reserve Bank.

Woodford, M. (1986), "Stationary sunspot equilibria in a finance constrained economy," *Journal of Economic Theory,* 40, 128–37.

(1987), "Three questions about sunspot equilibria as an explanation of economic fluctuations," *American Economic Association Papers and Proceedings,* 77, 93–8.

(1988), "Expectations, finance and aggregate instability," in *Finance Constraints, Expectations, and Macroeconomics,* ed. by M. Kohn and S.-C. Tsiang, New York: Oxford University Press.

PART V

Nonlinear econometric modeling

CHAPTER 14

Modeling with normal polynomial expansions

John Geweke

Abstract: Polynomial expansions of the normal probability density function are proposed as a class of models for unobserved components. Operational procedures for Bayesian inference in these models are developed, as are methods for combining a sequence of such models and evaluation of the hypotheses of normality and symmetry. The contributions of this chapter are illustrated with an application to daily rates of change in stock price.

1   Introduction

The assumption that unobserved stochastic components are normally distributed is common in econometric models. This assumption has the virtue of analytical simplicity and often leads to workable closed-form solutions when alternative or more general assumptions do not. It can be justified by appealing to central-limit theorems, if linearity of the underlying process is axiomatic. Perhaps most important, classical asymptotic distribution theory shows that the incorrect assumption of normality is in many circumstances inconsequential for inference about parameters of interest when sample size is large.

In this chapter we propose operational methods for dispensing with the assumption of normality. The project is motivated by three observations. First, there is no compelling argument that unobserved components in econometric models should be generated by linear processes. Second, the assumption of normality is not without consequence in small samples; neither frequentist nor Bayesian methods regularly permit nonnormality,

An expanded version of this chapter that provides more mathematical and technical detail is available from the author on request. Financial support for this work was provided by NSF Grant SES-8605867 and by a grant from the Pew Foundation to Duke University. Helpful conversations with Ron Gallant are gratefully acknowledged, but the author bears responsibility for any remaining difficulties.

337

and in particular the possibility of exact Bayesian inference is much less appealing if it is bound by the normality assumption. Third, given the current course of developments in computing there is a rapidly expanding class of problems in which it is not essential to obtain analytical solutions.

The generalization of the normal employed in this work is motivated by the well-known expansions introduced by Edgeworth (1896, 1907) and Charlier (1905). The Edgeworth expansion, in particular, is used heavily in analytical improvement of the asymptotic sampling distribution of classical estimators, but its use in modeling random variables directly is much less common; an important exception is contemporaneous work by Gallant and Tauchen (in press) who use a restricted expansion. These expansions cannot be applied directly in a classical approach because their parameters are subject to inequality restrictions that are nonlinear and cannot even be expressed in closed form. In a Bayesian framework with numerical methods this difficulty becomes inessential.

Section 2 introduces the polynomial expansion of the normal and describes the implementation and limitations of classical methods in the context of these models. A numerical Bayesian approach, Monte Carlo integration with importance sampling, is described in Section 3; the reader who is familiar with these methods can skip this section, but it is essential to what follows. In Section 4 these methods are applied to inference about the distribution of daily stock price changes, using the fourth- and eighth-degree expansions of the normal. The assumption of a particular expansion is rather arbitrary, and Section 5 proposes exact operational procedures for the integration of expansions of different orders. The procedures are applied to the daily stock price change data for polynomial expansions of the normal up to tenth degree. The concluding section summarizes the contributions of this work and suggests some directions for research.

2   Polynomial expansions of the normal distribution

Let $\phi(x; \mu, \sigma) = (2\pi)^{-1/2}\sigma^{-1}\exp[-(x-\mu)^2/2\sigma^2]$ be the normal *probability density function* (p.d.f.); let $Q(z; m) \equiv \sum_{j=0}^{m} q_j z^j$ be a polynomial of mth degree, and define $q(x; m, \mu, \sigma) = Q((x-\mu)/\sigma; m)$. The function $f(x)$ is the p.d.f. of a polynomial expansion of the normal if it takes the form $f(x) = q(x; m, \mu, \sigma)\phi(x; \mu, \sigma)$, and if $f(x)$ satisfies the restrictions

$$\int_{-\infty}^{\infty} f(x)\, dx = 1, \tag{1}$$

$$f(x) \geq 0 \ \ \forall x, \tag{2}$$

$$\int_{-\infty}^{\infty} x f(x)\, dx = \mu, \tag{3}$$

$$\int_{-\infty}^{\infty} (x-\mu)^2 f(x)\,dx = \sigma^2. \tag{4}$$

The requirement that $f(x)$ be a p.d.f. introduces a single linear restriction on the q_j through (1) and introduces the nonlinear restrictions $Q(z; m) \geq 0 \ \forall z$ in (2). Restrictions (3) and (4) assure that the polynomial expansion modifies only third- and higher-order moments of the normal; as a practical matter, the parameters q_0, q_1, and q_2 are nearly unidentified in all but enormous samples without these restrictions.

It is easy to see that $\sum_{j=0}^{m} q_j z^j$ is identically nonnegative if and only if the largest j^* for which $q_{j^*} \neq 0$ is even, $q_{j^*} > 0$, and any real roots of $Q(z; m)$ are repeated in even degree. Thus, given $\{q_j\}_{j=0}^{m}$, these conditions are trivial to verify, as discussed in Geweke (1988b, app. B). The polynomial expansions are therefore indexed by $m = 4, 6, 8, \ldots$. Restrictions (1), (3), and (4) can be solved to express q_{m-2}, q_{m-1}, and q_m as respective linear functions of $q_0, \ldots, q_{m-3}$ (Geweke, 1988b, app. B). Hence the mth degree polynomial expansion of the normal has m parameters $\mu, \sigma, q_0, \ldots, q_{m-3}$, which are free up to restriction (2).

The moments of the polynomial expansion can be derived routinely (Geweke, 1988b, app. A). The polynomial expansions can be orthogonalized, with $Q(z; m)$ rewritten in terms of Hermite polynomials, as is typically done in the Gram–Charlier and Edgeworth expansions, but for our purposes there is no need to orthogonalize the polynomials. As m increases, there are wider possibilities for combinations of higher-order moments. Figure 1 illustrates the range of skewness and kurtosis afforded in the case $m = 4$.

Using polynomial expansions to model an unknown p.d.f., given a sample, was first considered by Edgeworth (1916, 1917). Indeed, were it not for restriction (2) this could be accomplished routinely by maximum-likelihood methods (Geweke, 1988b, app. B). Maximization of the likelihood function subject to (2) [in addition to the easily imposed (1), (3), and (4)] is technically difficult, and the present disuse of polynomial expansions is ascribed to this fact by Johnson and Kotz (1970, p. 22). Even if the constrained maximization problem were solved, there would be serious difficulties in conducting inference based on the restricted maximum-likelihood estimator, as discussed in Geweke (1986). These inequality restrictions also preclude an analytical Bayesian approach. Numerical Bayes methods are, in contrast, much simpler and quite direct.

3   Bayesian inference by means of Monte Carlo integration with important sampling

We now turn to an approach to Bayesian inference developed in detail in Geweke (in press), with application to polynomial expansions of the

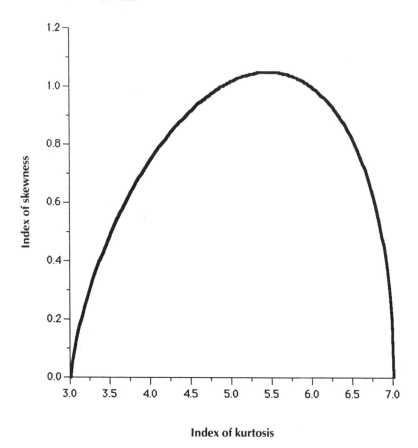

Figure 1.   Skewness and kurtosis, expansion $m = 4$. The combinations of positive skewness and kurtosis *under* the solid line and *above* the horizontal axis can be implied by suitable choice of a fourth-order polynomial expansion. The combinations of negative skewness and kurtosis achievable are the same; i.e., extension to the full vertical axis would show a mirror image about the horizontal axis.

normal distribution. Let $\theta'_{1 \times m} = (\mu, \sigma, q_0, q_1, \ldots, q_{m-3})$ be the vector of parameters, and let $\pi(\theta)$ be a diffuse prior. In subsequent applications we shall use two such priors, each a generalization of the standard uninformative conjugate prior for the normal:

$$\pi_1(\theta) \propto \sigma^{-1}, \tag{5a}$$

$$\pi_2(\theta) \propto \sigma^{-1} \chi_m(q_0, \ldots, q_m); \tag{5b}$$

$$\chi_m(q_0, \dots, q_m) = \begin{cases} 1 & \text{if } q_m(x; \mu, \sigma)\phi(x; \mu, \sigma) \text{ is unimodal,} \\ 0 & \text{if } q_m(x; \mu, \sigma)\phi(x; \mu, \sigma) \text{ is multimodal.} \end{cases}$$

These priors are coherent across degrees of polynomial expansion: that is, the prior for an mth degree expansion, conditional on knowledge that $q_{\ell+1} = \dots = q_m = 0$, $\ell < m$ even, is the same as the prior on the ℓth degree expansion. For $\pi_1(\theta)$, the parameter space Θ consists of all real μ, all positive σ, and all real $q_0, q_1, \dots, q_{m-3}$ such that for q_{m-2}, q_{m-1}, and q_m defined by (1), (3), and (4), restriction (2) is true. For $\pi_2(\theta)$ the parameter space is further restricted to include only those $(q_0, \dots, q_m)$ for which the probability density function is unimodal. The modality of a specified p.d.f. can be evaluated using the results on the derivatives of $f(x)$ provided in Geweke (1988b).

The likelihood function is proportional to

$$L(\theta) = \sigma^{-T} \exp\left[\frac{-\sum_{i=1}^{T}(x_i - \mu)^2}{2\sigma^2}\right] \prod_{i=1}^{T}\left[\sum_{j=0}^{m} q_j\left(\frac{x_i - \mu}{\sigma}\right)^j\right], \qquad (6)$$

and the posterior distribution is proportional to $p(\theta) \equiv \pi(\theta)L(\theta)$. Most Bayesian inference problems can be expressed as the evaluation of the expectation of a function of interest $g(\theta)$ under the posterior,

$$E[g(\theta)] = \frac{\int_\Theta g(\theta)p(\theta)\, d\theta}{\int_\Theta p(\theta)\, d\theta}. \qquad (7)$$

The integrations in (7) cannot be carried out analytically in the present case. Monte Carlo integration provides a systematic numerical approach that can be applied in any situation in which $E[g(\theta)]$ exists, and whose numerical accuracy is readily evaluated. The method was discussed by Hammersly and Handscomb (1964, sect. 5.4) and brought to the attention of econometricians by Kloek and van Dijk (1978).

The main idea is simple. Let $\{\theta_i\}$ be a sequence of k-dimensional random vectors, independent and identically distributed (i.i.d.) in theory and in practice generated by a random number generator on a computer. If the p.d.f. of the θ_i is proportional to $p(\theta)$, then $n^{-1}\sum_{i=1}^{n} g(\theta_i)$ converges almost surely (in n) to $E[g(\theta)]$; if the p.d.f. of the θ_i is proportional to $L(\theta)$, then $n^{-1}\sum_{i=1}^{n} g(\theta_i)\pi(\theta_i)$ converges almost surely (in n) to $E[g(\theta)]$. (All expectation operators are under the posterior.) It is not feasible to generate synthetic variates from $p(\theta)$ or $L(\theta)$ here; indeed, this is possible only in a rather limited set of cases. More generally, suppose the p.d.f. on the θ_i is $I(\theta)$, termed the *importance-sampling density,* and consider approximating $\bar{g} \equiv E[g(\theta)]$ by

$$\bar{g}_n \equiv \frac{\sum_{i=1}^{n}[g(\theta_i)p(\theta_i)/I(\theta_i)]}{\sum_{i=1}^{n}[p(\theta_i)/I(\theta_i)]}.$$

So long as $p(\theta)$ is proportional to a proper posterior distribution, $E[g(\theta)]$ exists, and the support of $p(\theta)$ is included in the support of $I(\theta)$; $\bar{g}_n$ converges almost surely (in n) to $E[g(\theta)]$ (Geweke, in press, theorem 1).

For practical rates of convergence in Monte Carlo integration with importance sampling, it is important that $I(\theta)$ be not too different from $p(\theta)$ and especially important that the weighting function $w(\theta) \equiv p(\theta)/I(\theta)$ not become very large over the support of $p(\theta)$. If $w(\theta)$ is bounded above, and the posterior variance of $g(\theta)$, $\text{var}[g(\theta)]$, exists, then (from Geweke, in press, theorem 2),

$$n^{1/2}(\bar{g}_n - \bar{g}) \Rightarrow N(0, \sigma^2), \quad \sigma^2 \equiv \frac{E\{[g(\theta) - \bar{g}]^2 w(\theta)^2\}}{\int_\Theta p(\theta) \, d\theta}, \tag{8}$$

where the arrow denotes convergence in distribution. If we define $\hat{\sigma}_n^2 \equiv \sum_{i=1}^n [g(\theta_i) - \bar{g}_n]^2 w(\theta_i)^2 / [\sum_{i=1}^n w(\theta_i)]^2$, then $n\hat{\sigma}_n^2 \to \sigma^2$. (Subsequently, we refer to $\hat{\sigma}_n$ as the numerical standard error.) The necessary conditions can be verified analytically, and it is then reasonable to assess numerical accuracy under the assumption $\bar{g}_n \sim N(\bar{g}, \hat{\sigma}_n^2)$ when n is large.

The result (8) indicates that numerical accuracy is adversely affected by large relative values of the weight function; such large values indicate poor approximation of the posterior density by the importance-sampling density. A simple benchmark for comparing the adequacy of importance-sampling distributions is the numerical standard error that would result if the importance-sampling density were the posterior density itself [i.e., $I(\theta) \propto p(\theta)$]. In this case, $\sigma^2 = \text{var}[g(\theta)]$, and the number of replications chosen, n, controls the numerical standard error relative to the posterior standard deviation of the function of interest (e.g., $n = 10,000$ implies that the former will be 1% of the latter). Only in special cases (e.g., Geweke, 1986) is it practical to construct synthetic variates whose distribution is given by the posterior. But because $\text{var}[g(\theta)]$ can also be approximated well by Monte Carlo integration, it is possible to see what the numerical variance would have been had it been possible to generate synthetic random vectors directly from the posterior distribution. We define the *relative numerical efficiency* (RNE) of the importance-sampling distribution for the function of interest $g(\theta)$,

$$\text{RNE} = \frac{\text{var}[g(\theta)]}{\sigma^2}.$$

The RNE is the ratio of the number of replications required to achieve any specified numerical standard error using the posterior density as the importance-sampling density to the number required using the importance-sampling density $I(\theta)$. Numerical values of RNE are routinely computed for each $g(\theta)$ in software developed by the author.

Up to an additive constant, the log-likelihood function can be written

$$-(T+2)\log(\sigma) - \sum_{i=1}^{T} \frac{(x_i - \mu)^2}{2\sigma^2} + \sum_{i=1}^{T} \log\left[\sum_{j=0}^{m} q_j(x_i - \mu)^j\right].$$

As $\sigma \to \infty$, the term $-(T+2)\log(\sigma)$ dominates, suggesting a multivariate Student distribution with $2T - m$ degrees of freedom. As $\mu \to \pm\infty$, the term $-\mu^2/\sigma^2$ dominates, suggesting a multivariate normal distribution. As any $q_j \to \pm\infty$, the constraints (1) and (2) are violated, so the q_j are confined to a compact set. Hence, for the purposes of assuring (8), we could take the importance-sampling density to be multivariate Student with $2T - m$ degrees of freedom. However, as documented in Geweke (in press), such a sampling distribution constructed using the asymptotic variance matrix of the parameter estimates may not suffice because the likelihood function may decline too fast relative to the importance-sampling density in certain directions, leading to enormous values of $w(\theta)$. This problem can be overcome by adjusting the variance matrix of the multivariate sampling density separately along each axis and in each direction to reduce the value of $w(\theta)$.

To describe this procedure exactly, let sgn$^+(\ )$ be the indicator function for nonnegative real numbers, and let sgn$^-(\ ) = 1 - $ sgn$^+(\ )$. Define the k-variate split-Student density $t^*(\hat{\theta}, T, \mathbf{q}, \mathbf{r}, \nu)$ by constructing a member $\mathbf{x}$ of its population: $\omega \sim N(\mathbf{0}, I_k)$; $\zeta \sim \chi^2(\nu)$ independent of ω; $\eta_i = [q_i \operatorname{sgn}^+(\omega_i) + r_i \operatorname{sgn}^-(\omega_i)]\omega_i(\zeta/\nu)^{-1/2}$; $\mathbf{x} = \hat{\theta} + T\eta$. In our application, $\hat{\theta}$ is the maximum likelihood estimator (m.l.e.) of θ *not* subject to the restrictions (2), T is a factorization such that TT' is the inverse of the Hessian evaluated at $\hat{\theta}$, and $\mathbf{x}$ is θ_i. (Computation of $\hat{\theta}$ and the construction of the Hessian are described in Geweke, 1988b.) To choose q_i and r_i, explore along the ith axis $\hat{\theta} + \delta T \mathbf{e}^{(i)}$, where $\mathbf{e}^{(i)}$ is the $k \times 1$ indicator vector and $e_i^{(i)} = \mathbf{e}^{(i)'}\mathbf{e}^{(i)} = 1$. Compute

$$f_i(\delta) = \nu^{-1/2}|\delta|\left\{\left[\frac{p(\hat{\theta})}{p(\hat{\theta} + \delta T \mathbf{e}^{(i)})}\right]^{2/(\nu+k)} - 1\right\}^{-1/2}, \tag{9}$$

and take $q_i = \sup_{\delta > 0} f_i(\delta)$, $r_i = \sup_{\delta < 0} f_i(\delta)$. In practice, the evaluation is carried out for $\delta = 0.5, 1, \ldots, 9.5, 10$. Values of θ_i that do not satisfy (2) are discarded.

Nonrandom sampling from the importance-sampling density can lead to faster rates of convergence. In the *antithetic acceleration* of Monte Carlo integration, synthetic random values θ_i are drawn in pairs (θ_i^A, θ_i^B), with θ_i^A and θ_i^B negatively correlated. The function of interest $g(\theta_i)$ is replaced by $w(\theta_i^A)g(\theta_i^A) + w(\theta_i^B)g(\theta_i^B)$ and the weight $w(\theta_i)$ by $w(\theta_i^A) + w(\theta_i^B)$. For the k-variate split-Student density this method is implemented by setting $\omega_i^A = -\omega_i^B$, $\zeta_i^A = \zeta_i^B$. One can readily verify that the expressions for posterior variance and numerical variance $\hat{\sigma}_n^2$ are appropriate after these substitutions.

If the likelihood function were proportional to the importance-sampling density and if the function of interest $g(\theta)$ were linear, then numerical variance would be zero for all n ($\sigma^2 = 0$). This limiting case is itself uninteresting because it rarely arises; and when it does, the integrals in question can often be evaluated analytically. However, it provides the motivation for antithetic acceleration: Under standard regularity conditions, as sample size increases, the likelihood function becomes locally symmetric and proportional to the importance-sampling density, and functions of interest become locally linear. In Geweke (1988a) it is shown for the case of direct Monte Carlo integration (i.e., *without* importance sampling) numerical variance is of order $0(1/nT)$ without antithetic acceleration, and $0(1/nT^2)$ with antithetic acceleration, where T is sample size. We conjecture that the result holds for Monte Carlo integration with importance sampling, and hence antithetic acceleration would be useful in the present application. (It should be emphasized that only the general efficacy of antithetic acceleration, not the validity of the computations, depends on the conjecture; and in specific applications one can always check computed relative numerical efficiency to assess gains from antithetic acceleration.)

4   An empirical example

To apply the normal polynomial expansions, we have chosen a readily accessible and commonly studied data set: 255 observations on successive daily closing prices of IBM common stock provided by Box and Jenkins (1976, p. 527). This series was transformed to first differences of the logarithms, leaving 254 data points. For the purpose of this illustration we regard these observations as independent and identically distributed. Models that permit departures from these assumptions have turned up only weak evidence against independence (Box and Jenkins, 1976, p. 94) and identical distributions for the observations (Geweke, 1989, sect. 6). If normality is assumed, the maximum-likelihood estimates are $\hat{\mu} = 0.0628$, $\hat{\sigma} = 1.1232$; respective standard errors are 0.0705 and 0.0793. This data set was chosen because of its ready availability, the fact that it has been studied previously, and the widespread belief that financial data of this kind are not normally distributed.

Maximum-likelihood estimation of the parameters of the normal polynomial expansions with this data set was straightforward for polynomials up through order ten. Examples of point estimates and their asymptotic standard errors are provided for $m = 4$ in Table 1 and for $m = 8$ in Table 2.

The modified Newton method described in Geweke (1988b, app. B) was employed, with a convergence criterion $\mathbf{g}'H^{-1}\mathbf{g} < 10^{-9}$, where $\mathbf{g}$ is the gradient and H the Hessian. Convergence required seven iterations (3.94 seconds) for the fourth-order expansion, and nine iterations (11.99 seconds) for the eighth-order expansion, the initial values being the normal maximum-likelihood estimates in each case. The maximum-likelihood estimate satisfies (2) for expansions up to tenth order. The twelfth-order expansion produces what appears to be a highly irregular likelihood surface, and some numerical problems arise in this case as well. As we shall see in the next section, however, there is ample reason to think that nothing is lost by limiting our attention to expansions of order ten and lower.

From the maximum-likelihood estimates of the parameters and the Hessian evaluated at the maximum of the likelihood function, a split-Student importance-sampling density was constructed as described in the previous section. Some experimentation showed that antithetic acceleration produced gains in computational efficiency over random sampling from the importance-sampling density, and that method of sampling was used for all results reported here. Relative numerical efficiency is generally greater for lower-order expansions than for higher order; as discussed in Geweke (1988a), this is to be expected under the reasonable assumption that the log likelihood is more nearly quadratic in the expansions with few parameters. Initial runs with a few hundred replications provided a rough indication of the RNE for the index of kurtosis, used to select the final number of replications. Dividing this RNE into 10,000 provided the number of replications that assure that the numerical standard error $\hat{\sigma}_n$ is about 1% of the posterior standard deviation for the index of kurtosis. This became the number of replications used to compute the results reported here. As suggested in Tables 1 and 2, the required number of replications increases sharply with the order of the polynomial expansion. This is because (1) the split-Student density is a poorer approximation of the posterior density over parameter space Θ as m increases; (2) the log posterior density is less symmetric for higher m, thereby reducing the gains from antithetic acceleration; and (3) a substantial number of drawings are outside Θ – and in the case of $\pi_2(\theta)$ imply multimodal distributions – for higher m. For a given model, required computation time is roughly proportional to the number of replications in Θ in the case of $\pi_1(\theta)$ and to those replications for which the p.d.f. is also unimodal in the case of $\pi_2(\theta)$.

Tables 1 and 2 present detailed results for two selected models. The first column indicates the computed mean of the posterior distribution of the parameter, moment, or function of moments, given; the second is the corresponding standard deviation of the posterior distribution; the third column provides the numerical standard error for the computed mean of the

Table 1. *Fourth-order polynomial expansion of normal rate of daily change of IBM common stock closing prices, 6/29/59–6/30/60*

	Maximum-likelihood estimates	
Parameter	Estimate	Asymptotic standard error[a]
μ	0.0681	0.0729
σ	1.1425	0.0659
q_0	1.2310	0.0552
q_1	−0.1461	0.1172

Posterior moments with prior $\pi_1(\theta)$[b]

Function $g(\theta)$	$E[g(\theta)]$	Std. deviation $[g(\theta)]$	$\hat{\sigma}_n$	RNE(%)
μ	0.0643	0.0748	0.0013	128.6
σ	1.1620	0.0699	0.0013	112.6
q_0	1.2356	0.0519	0.0006	299.4
q_1	−0.0987	0.1142	0.0022	108.5
q_2	−0.4711	0.1039	0.0012	299.4
q_3	0.0329	0.0381	0.0007	108.5
q_4	0.0785	0.0173	0.0002	299.4
$E(X-\mu)^3$	0.3084	0.3898	0.0096	68.8
$E(X-\mu)^4$	9.1811	2.7396	0.0506	122.4
Skewness	0.2459	0.2949	0.0065	85.9
Kurtosis	4.8844	0.4155	0.0049	299.4

Posterior moments with prior $\pi_2(\theta)$[c]

Function $g(\theta)$	$E[g(\theta)]$	Std. deviation $[g(\theta)]$	$\hat{\sigma}_n$	RNE(%)
μ	0.0615	0.0723	0.0007	153.3
σ	1.1492	0.0628	0.0005	221.0
q_0	1.2186	0.0409	0.0005	92.9
q_1	−0.0943	0.1042	0.0011	139.2
q_2	−0.4372	0.0819	0.0010	92.9
q_3	0.0314	0.0347	0.0004	139.2
q_4	0.0729	0.0136	0.0002	92.9
$E(X-\mu)^3$	0.2847	0.3285	0.0036	116.6
$E(X-\mu)^4$	8.4740	2.1510	0.0195	174.2
Skewness	0.2309	0.2592	0.0027	127.0
Kurtosis	4.7489	0.3275	0.0041	92.9

posterior distribution as explained in Section 3; and RNE in the fourth
column is an estimate of the ratio to $\hat{\sigma}_n^2$ of the numerical variance that
would have been reported had it been possible to sample, independently,
from the posterior distribution itself. As an example from Table 1, the
mean and standard deviation of q_2 are -0.4711 and 0.1039, respectively.
The numerical standard error indicates that a 95% frequentist confidence
interval corresponding to the value -0.4711 is $[-0.4735, -0.4687]$; in rep-
etitions of the numerical calculations with randomly chosen initial seeds,
one would expect an interval computed in this way to include the actual
posterior mean about 95% of the time. The RNE of 299.4% indicates
that – had we sampled independently from the posterior density itself –
about three times as many replications would have been required to attain the same degree of numerical accuracy. Computation time for the
2,400 replications on a MicroVAX II was less than ten minutes.

For the fourth-order expansion (Table 1), maximum-likelihood estimates and the means of corresponding posterior densities are fairly close,
and the asymptotic standard errors are quite close to the posterior standard deviations. These observations, and the fact that over 99% of the
Monte Carlo replications from the importance-sampling distribution were
in Θ, indicate that the maximum-likelihood estimates are well within Θ
and that classical asymptotic distribution theory provides a reliable interpretation of the likelihood surface. This is further substantiated by examination of the actual posterior p.d.f. of the functions of interest (not
reported here), which are very nearly normal. The eighth-order expansion (Table 2) shows substantial departure from the asymptotic paradigm,
evidenced in several ways: Maximum likelihood estimates and posterior
means typically differ by half a standard deviation; the maximum-likelihood estimates are in Θ but close to the boundary, as indicated by the fact
that only 54% of the replications drawn from the importance-sampling
density were in Θ; and the split-Student importance-sampling density is
only a moderately good approximation to posterior densities with diffuse
priors over Θ. This is characteristic of situations in which computation
of maximum-likelihood estimates is not complicated operationally by an
inequality restriction such as (2), but the restriction complicates the inter-

Notes to Table 1
[a] Computed as the square root of the approximate diagonal element of the inverse of the
Hessian evaluated at the maximum-likelihood estimate.
[b] 2,400 Monte Carlo replications, in antithetic pairs, of which 2,393 (99.71%) were in Θ;
execution time 0:09:40.
[c] 7,000 Monte Carlo replications, in antithetic pairs, of which 6,963 (99.47%) were in Θ;
execution time 0:28:01.

Table 2. *Eighth-order polynomial expansion of normal rate of daily change of IBM common stock closing prices, 6/29/59–6/30/60*

Maximum-likelihood estimates		
Parameter	Estimate	Asymptotic standard error[a]
μ	0.0566	0.0678
σ	1.1015	0.0676
q_0	1.2513	0.0792
q_1	−0.3638	0.1759
q_2	−0.5784	0.2525
q_3	0.3233	0.1518
q_4	0.1842	0.1272
q_5	−0.0702	0.0348

Posterior moments with prior $\pi_1(\theta)$[b]

Function $g(\theta)$	$E[g(\theta)]$	Std. deviation $[g(\theta)]$	$\hat{\sigma}_n$	RNE(%)
μ	0.0496	0.0693	0.0007	11.2
σ	1.1442	0.0760	0.0007	13.8
q_0	1.2930	0.0733	0.0006	20.0
q_1	−0.2869	0.1742	0.0018	12.1
q_2	−0.6976	0.2225	0.0018	19.2
q_3	0.2482	0.1460	0.0014	13.4
q_4	0.2306	0.1039	0.0008	19.4
q_5	−0.0524	0.0324	0.0003	13.2
q_6	−0.0309	0.0160	0.0001	19.2
q_7	0.0031	0.0021	*	12.3
q_8	0.0017	0.0008	*	17.7
$E(X-\mu)^3$	0.3895	0.3634	0.0038	11.7
$E(X-\mu)^4$	10.4347	3.6148	0.0351	13.2
Skewness	0.3895	0.3634	0.0038	11.7
Kurtosis	5.8546	0.6736	0.0058	16.8

Posterior moments with prior $\pi_2(\theta)$[c]

Function $g(\theta)$	$E[g(\theta)]$	Std. deviation $[g(\theta)]$	$\hat{\sigma}_n$	RNE(%)
μ	0.0533	0.0695	0.0014	5.0
σ	1.1361	0.0743	0.0015	5.1
q_0	1.2706	0.0647	0.0011	6.6
q_1	−0.2511	0.1613	0.0030	5.8
q_2	−0.6299	0.1910	0.0034	6.4
q_3	0.1939	0.1227	0.0022	6.2

Table 2 *(cont.)*

	Posterior moments with prior $\pi_2(\theta)^c$			
Function $g(\theta)$	$E[g(\theta)]$	Std. deviation $[g(\theta)]$	$\hat{\sigma}_n$	RNE(%)
q_4	0.1884	0.0830	0.0015	6.5
q_5	−0.0365	0.0241	0.0004	6.2
q_6	−0.0215	0.0117	0.0002	6.4
q_7	0.0021	0.0015	*	5.9
q_8	0.0012	0.0005	*	6.1
$E(X-\mu)^3$	0.4094	0.3999	0.0085	4.4
$E(X-\mu)^4$	9.3099	3.0731	0.0671	4.2
Skewness	0.3332	0.3076	0.0061	5.0
Kurtosis	5.3936	0.5089	0.0091	6.3

[a] Computed as the square root of the approximate diagonal element of the inverse of the Hessian evaluated at the maximum-likelihood estimate.
[b] 80,000 Monte Carlo replications, in antithetic pairs, of which 46,252 (57.82%) were in Θ; execution time 8:49:35.
[c] 50,000 Monte Carlo replications, in antithetic pairs, of which 29,124 (58.25%) were in Θ; execution time 5:30:51.
* $< 5 \times 10^{-5}$.

pretation of those estimates. The effect of the unimodality constraint incorporated in $\pi_2(\theta)$ is to reduce all central movements of order two and higher and the indices of skewness and kurtosis.

The polynomial expansion of the normal in these two cases indicates substantial departure of our data set from the normal distribution. The even-degree coefficients of the polynomials are nearly all more than two standard deviations from their values $q_0 = 1$, $q_j = 0$ if $j > 0$, in the normal p.d.f. Given the expansion polynomial, moments can be computed as described in Geweke (1988b), and from these the usual measures of skewness and kurtosis can be formed. These moments and measures are additional functions of interest reported in Tables 1 and 2; note that $E(X-\mu)^j$ is here a random quantity because θ is regarded as random. Kurtosis is clearly greater than three, its value in the normal distribution. Odd-degree coefficients are less than one standard deviation from zero in the fourth-order expansion, and between one and two standard deviations from zero in the eighth-order expansion. The expansions indicate a positively skewed distribution with posterior probability about 0.81 in the fourth-order expansion and about 0.87 in the eighth-order expansion; these numbers are not noticeably affected by the imposition of unimodality. The posterior probability of unimodality under the prior $\pi_1(\theta)$ falls substantially in moving from $m = 4$ to $m = 8$, due to the increased scope for multimodality in higher-order expansions. (In the next section we shall take a formal approach to questions whose answer depends on the order of the expansion.)

A given polynomial expansion of the normal implies a probability density function, and hence it implies a probability that the underlying random variable lies between (say) a and b. In the notation of Section 2, the probability is

$$\int_b^a q_m(x; \mu, \sigma)\phi(x; \mu, \sigma)\, dx.$$

Given μ, σ, and $\{q_j\}_{j=0}^m$, this value could be computed numerically in a variety of ways. For present purposes, we are interested in $P[c < X \le c + 0.5]$, where $c = -5, -4.5, \ldots, 4.0, 4.5$. A uniform random variable in the range $[-5.0, -4.975]$ was generated, the p.d.f. $q_m(x; \mu, \sigma)\phi(x; \mu, \sigma)$ was evaluated at the points $x = w + 0.025i$, $i = 0, \ldots, 399$, and the probability in each interval was estimated as the sum over the 20 relevant evaluations of the p.d.f. This method provides an unbiased estimate of the actual probability in the interval, and its accuracy is easy to assess for *any* p.d.f., no matter how complicated. The grid interval was chosen after experimentation showed that the standard deviation in computed interval probabilities due to randomization over w was then consistently less than the numerical standard error $\hat{\sigma}_n$. (There are only 20 points in each interval; but note that the sampling within each interval, conditional on w, is nonrandom. It is not hard to show that the standard error due to randomization over w is inversely proportional to the number of points in the interval, not to the square root of the number in the interval.) This procedure was implemented for each Monte Carlo replication; that is, 400 evaluations of the p.d.f. were undertaken beginning from a randomly selected w in each replication in Θ. Numerical approximation in the computation of interval probabilities is thereby built into the reported values of $\hat{\sigma}_n$. The resulting histograms are provided in Figures 2 and 3, which portray posterior means for the probabilities in each interval. The value of $\hat{\sigma}_n$ is generally less than one percent of the probability and never more than 2×10^{-4} (i.e., less than the eye could detect in these figures).

5   Hypothesis evaluation and integration of models

The polynomial expansions of the normal are chosen not because of a prior belief that they are in any sense "correct" for some (or any) specific value of m; rather, they are selected for their analytical convenience

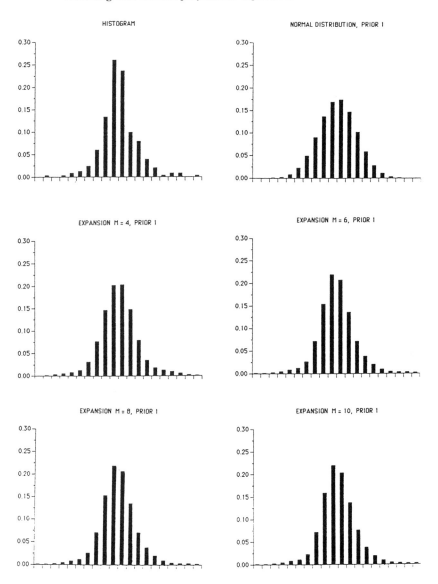

Figure 2. The posterior mean of the probability that the change in daily closing price will be in the interval is shown. The width of each interval is 0.5%. The histogram is the sample distribution of the data points.

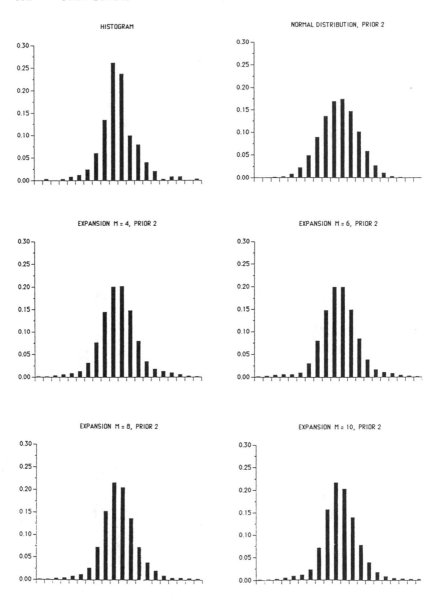

Figure 3.   The posterior mean of the probability that the change in daily closing price will be in the indicated interval is shown. The width of each interval is 0.5%. The histogram is the sample distribution of the data points.

(which is usually the most compelling reason any p.d.f. is selected) and because they permit us to expand systematically the combinations of moments permitted as m increases. In applying this paradigm, one immediately confronts the choice of the range of m that ought to be examined. Because computational requirements increase rapidly with m, this is a question of great practical importance. The issue is not one of choosing the order of the expansion but rather of reaching conclusions about the functions of interest in the context of the family of expansions. Given the numerical methods developed for inference in a single model and described in Section 3, it is fairly straightforward to render operational the formal Bayesian methods for integration of models as well as the evaluation of hypotheses such as normality and symmetry.

To develop the essentials at a fairly high level of generality, let $\Theta^{(j)}$, $L^{(j)}(\theta \mid \mathbf{y})$, π_j, and $\pi^{(j)}(\theta)$ be the parameter spaces, likelihood functions, prior probabilities, and prior densities, respectively, for two models $j = 1, 2$. If

(a) $\int L^{(1)}(\theta \mid \mathbf{y}) \, dy = \int L^{(2)}(\theta \mid \mathbf{y}) \, dy = \text{constant}$, and
(b) the prior distributions $\pi^{(1)}(\theta)$ and $\pi^{(2)}(\theta)$ are jointly normalized so that the distributions are comparable,

then the posterior odds ratio (POR) for model 1 in favor of model 2 is

$$\text{POR}(1, 2) = \frac{\pi_1 \int_{\Theta(1)} \pi^{(1)}(\theta) L^{(1)}(\theta \mid \mathbf{y}) \, d\theta}{\pi_2 \int_{\Theta(2)} \pi^{(2)}(\theta) L^{(2)}(\theta \mid \mathbf{y}) \, d\theta}.$$

It is important to verify conditions (a) and (b). For our likelihood functions, the constant in (a) is $(2\pi)^{T/2}$. Condition (b) obtains if $\int_{\Theta(1)} \pi^{(1)}(\theta) \, d\theta = \int_{\Theta(2)} \pi^{(2)}(\theta) \, d\theta < \infty$. If the priors are improper, then care must be taken to assure that scaling functions are appropriate, as is the case with (5).

In implementing the likelihood function, $L^{(j)}(\theta \mid \mathbf{y})$ is replaced with $L^{*(j)}(\theta \mid \mathbf{y}) \equiv L^{(j)}(\theta \mid \mathbf{y})/L^{(j)}(\hat{\theta}^{(j)})$, which has maximum value 1.0 at $\theta = \hat{\theta}^{(j)}$; the importance-sampling density $I^{(j)}(\theta)$ is replaced by $I^{*(j)}(\theta)$, also normalized to have values near unity in a neighborhood of $\hat{\theta}^{(j)}$; and the computed weights are $w^{*(j)}(\theta_i) = \pi^{(j)}(\theta_i) L^{*(j)}(\theta_i)/I^{*(j)}(\theta_i)$. (The purpose of these normalizations is to avoid overflow or underflow, and their effect is to make the weights about one for a good importance-sampling density.) Adapting some notation from Geweke (in press), let

$$c^{(j)} \equiv \int_{\Theta(j)} \pi^{(j)}(\theta) L^{*(j)}(\theta) \, d\theta \quad \text{and} \quad d^{(j)} = \left[\int_{\Theta(j)} I^{*(j)}(\theta) \, d\theta \right]^{-1}.$$

From the proof of Theorem 1 in Geweke (in press),

$$\bar{w}_n^{*(j)} \equiv n^{-1} \sum_{i=1}^{n} w^{*(j)}(\theta_i) \to c^{(j)} d^{(j)} \equiv \bar{w}^{*(j)}.$$

Hence the logarithm of the numerator or denominator of the posterior odds ratio is approximately

$$\tilde{L} \equiv \log[\bar{w}_n^{*(j)}] - \log[d^{(j)}] + \log[L^{*(j)}(\hat{\theta}|\mathbf{y})], \qquad (10)$$

with the approximation due solely to the fact that $\bar{w}_n^{*(j)}$ is not the same as its almost sure limit $\bar{w}^{*(j)}$. The numerical variance in $\bar{w}_n^{*(j)}$ can be calculated routinely. The value of $\log[d^{(j)}]$ can be determined analytically from the importance-sampling density; in the case of the k-variate split-Student density,

$$\log[d^{(j)}] = -\log\left[\int_{\Theta^{(j)}} I^{*(j)}(\theta)\, d\theta\right] = \frac{1}{4} \sum_{i=1}^{k} \log(q_i r_i) + \log(|T|).$$

From (10), the log posterior odds ratio can be written conveniently as a modification of the log likelihood ratio,

$$\log[\text{POR}(1,2)] = \log\left[\frac{L^{(1)}(\hat{\theta}^{(1)}|\mathbf{y})}{L^{(2)}(\hat{\theta}^{(2)}|\mathbf{y})}\right] + \log\left[\frac{\bar{w}^{*(1)}}{\bar{w}^{*(2)}}\right] - \log\left[\frac{d^{(1)}}{d^{(2)}}\right]. \qquad (11)$$

The term $\log[\bar{w}^{*(1)}/\bar{w}^{*(2)}]$, which is determined numerically, captures the relative variations in the surfaces of the posteriors and accounts for the well-known differences between likelihood ratios and posterior odds ratios; the two would be the same if the posterior densities were proportional. In the case of the normal distribution ($m=2$), we can use, instead of the numerical approximation $\tilde{L}$ in (10), the exact expression

$$\frac{1}{2}\log\frac{2\pi}{T} - \log 2 + \log\left[\Gamma\left(\frac{\nu}{2}\right)\right] - \frac{\nu}{2}\log\frac{\nu s^2}{2},$$

where $\nu = T-1$ (Geweke, 1989, sect. 7).

It is thus straightforward to compute Bayes factors and posterior odds ratios for alternative expansions. In addition, this can be done for all of the expansions with symmetry imposed, which is equivalent to the restrictions $q_j = 0$ for all odd j. Table 3 provides evaluations of the log likelihood function at the maximum $\hat{L}$, the key quantity $\tilde{L}$ of (10) for the computation of Bayes factors, and Bayes factors scaled to be interpreted as posterior probabilities under a uniform prior on m. Observe that in each model, $\hat{L} > \tilde{L}$, as must be the case. In moving to a strictly less parsimonious model, the value of $\hat{L}$ must weakly increase, but $\tilde{L}$ may either rise or fall. Note from Table 3 that when $\hat{L}$ barely rises, $\tilde{L}$ falls substantially, reflecting the well-known penalty ascribed to extraneous parameters by Bayes factors (Zellner and Siow, 1980).

From Table 3, four conclusions about the probability distribution function in the context of polynomial expansions of the normal are warranted:

Table 3. *Comparison of alternative expansions*

	Prior $\pi_1(\theta)$, multimodality permitted; symmetry not imposed		
m	$\hat{L}$	$\tilde{L}$	Posterior probability[a]
2	-156.5	-160.4	2.28×10^{-5}
4	-142.6	-149.8	9.84×10^{-1}
6	-142.2	-153.9	1.51×10^{-2}
8	-139.8	-157.4	4.94×10^{-4}
10	-139.4	-162.2	7.13×10^{-8}

	Prior $\pi_2(\theta)$, unimodality imposed; symmetry not imposed		
m	$\hat{L}$	$\tilde{L}$	Posterior probability[a]
2	-156.5	-160.4	2.84×10^{-5}
4	-142.6	-150.0	9.94×10^{-1}
6	-142.2	-155.1	6.16×10^{-3}
8	-139.8	-158.8	1.51×10^{-4}
10	-139.4	-168.8	6.44×10^{-9}

	Prior $\pi_1(\theta)$, multimodality permitted; symmetry imposed		
m	$\hat{L}$	$\tilde{L}$	Posterior probability[a]
2	-156.5	-160.4	8.16×10^{-6}
4	-143.0	-148.9	7.97×10^{-1}
6	-142.8	-150.6	1.58×10^{-1}
8	-141.8	-151.8	4.40×10^{-2}
10	-141.8	-155.2	1.47×10^{-3}

	Prior $\pi_2(\theta)$, unimodality imposed; symmetry imposed		
m	$\hat{L}$	$\tilde{L}$	Posterior probability[a]
2	-156.5	-160.4	9.72×10^{-6}
4	-143.0	-149.1	8.24×10^{-1}
6	-142.8	-150.9	1.41×10^{-1}
8	-141.8	-152.3	3.39×10^{-2}
10	-141.8	-155.5	1.32×10^{-3}

[a] The prior probability of each expansion is 0.2.

Table 4. *Some posterior probabilities^a*

| | Multimodality prior | | | | | |
| | $\pi_1(\theta)$ | | | $\pi_2(\theta)$ | | |
Prior probability of symmetry:	0.0	1.0	0.2	0.0	1.0	0.2
$P[\text{skewness} > 0]$	0.811	(0)	0.478	0.810	(0)	0.468
$P[\text{skewness} = 0]$	(0)	(1)	0.411	(0)	(1)	0.422
$P[\text{skewness} < 0]$	0.189	(0)	0.111	0.190	(0)	0.109
$P[\text{kurtosis} > 3]$	**	**	**	**	**	**
$P[1\ \text{mode}]$	0.796	0.839	0.813	(1)	(1)	(1)
$P[2\ \text{modes}]$	0.001	*	0.001	(0)	(0)	(0)
$P[3\ \text{modes}]$	0.104	0.013	0.066	(0)	(0)	(0)
$P[4\ \text{modes}]$	*	*	*	(0)	(0)	(0)
$P[5\ \text{modes}]$	0.099	0.149	0.120	(0)	(0)	(0)

^{a} Probabilities that hold identically are indicated parenthetically. * denotes a probability between 0 and 5×10^{-4}; ** denotes a probability between $1 - 5 \times 10^4$ and 1. Reported probabilities are numerically reliable to two significant figures.

1   The hypothesis of normality can be dismissed.
2   If the hypothesis of symmetry has small prior probability, then attention can be confined to the expansion $m = 4$, whose posterior probability exceeds 98% if all expansions receive the same prior probability.
3   Given symmetry, the expansion $m = 4$ has modal probability (assuming once again that all expansions have roughly the same prior probability); but this probability is about 80%, and other expansions – in particular $m = 6$ and $m = 8$ – should not be ignored.
4   We note that the Bayes factor in favor of symmetry is approximately 2.45 : 1 in the fourth-order expansions and increases rapidly with the order of expansion.

Hypotheses about the distribution are investigated formally in Table 4, using a prior probability of 0.2 for symmetry and 0.8 for asymmetry. In all cases the reported probabilities are averages across expansions $m = 2, 4, 6, 8,$ and 10, weighted by the probabilities given in the last column of Table 3. Given asymmetry, a positive index of skewness is about 4.3 times more probable than a negative index. The posterior probability of symmetry (index of skewness zero) is about 0.42, reflecting the Bayes factor in favor of symmetry and the prior probability of 0.2. The hypothesis

Table 5. *Combined posterior means of parameters of interest*[a]

| | Prior $\pi_1(\theta)$: multimodality permitted | | |
$g(\theta)$	$E[g(\theta)]$	Std. deviation $[g(\theta)]$	$\hat{\sigma}_n$
μ	0.0506	0.0697	0.0012
σ	1.1606	0.0697	0.0011
$E(X-\mu)^3$	0.1801	0.2991	0.0083
$E(X-\mu)^4$	9.2093	2.7578	0.0045
Skewness	0.1436	0.2264	0.0056
Kurtosis	4.9223	0.4341	0.0046
	Prior $\pi_2(\theta)$: unimodality imposed		
$g(\theta)$	$E[g(\theta)]$	Std. deviation $[g(\theta)]$	$\hat{\sigma}_n$
μ	0.0488	0.0676	0.0006
σ	1.1498	0.0637	0.0005
$E(X-\mu)^3$	0.1642	0.2495	0.0031
$E(X-\mu)^4$	8.5654	2.2201	0.0192
Skewness	0.1332	0.1970	0.0023
Kurtosis	4.7867	0.3448	0.0042

[a] Prior probability of symmetry is 0.2.

of leptokurtosis is nearly certain; this is perhaps the most obvious way in which the distribution departs from normality. Because of the large posterior probability of $m=4$ relative to other orders of expansion, the posterior probability of unimodality is similar to that reported in Table 1. Odd numbers of modes are more likely than even numbers, which is consistent with the evidence regarding the hypothesis of symmetry. Table 5 presents posterior means for moments unconditional on any particular order of expansion, again employing a prior odds ratio of 4:1 in favor of asymmetry over symmetry and prior odds ratios of 1:1 between any two orders of expansion.

6   Conclusion

Polynomial expansions of the normal distribution were proposed nearly a century ago, and Edgeworth suggested their application to data in 1916.

In this chapter, we have demonstrated a practical method for coping with certain analytical difficulties that have heretofore made Edgeworth's suggestion unworkable. The expansions provide a systematic way to dispense with the often-made assumption of normality in Bayesian approaches to modeling; and numerical Bayesian methods easily cope with the analytical intractabilities of the expansions whereas classical approaches generally do not. Within the framework provided by the polynomial expansions of the normal, it is straightforward to evaluate hypotheses about normality, symmetry, skewness, and kurtosis.

This work has concentrated entirely on the modeling of the probability distribution function of an observed random variable with polynomial expansions of the normal. Although useful here, this approach is even more appealing when applied to unobserved components. One compelling extension of this work is to the linear model – that is, generalizing the mean μ to a linear function of oberved variables $\beta'\mathbf{x}_i$. This extension would systematically remove the normality assumption from the linear model and provide a formal method that is robust against nonnormality of disturbances in the regression model.

REFERENCES

Box, G., and Jenkins, G. (1976), *Time Series Analysis, Forecasting, and Control.* San Francisco: Holden-Day (2nd Ed.).
Charlier, C. F. L. (1905), "Über die Darstellung willkurlicher Funktionen," *Arkiv für Matematik, Astronomi och Fysik,* 2(20), 1–35.
Edgeworth, F. Y. (1896), "The asymmetrical probability curve," *Philosophical Magazine, 5th Ser.,* 41, 90–9.
    (1907), "On the representation of statistical frequency by a series," *Journal of the Royal Statistical Society, Ser. A,* 70, 102–6.
    (1916), "On the mathematical representation of statistical data," *Journal of the Royal Statistical Society, Ser. A,* 79, 455–500.
    (1917), "On the mathematical representation of statistical data," *Journal of the Royal Statistical Society, Ser. A,* 80, 65–83; 266–88; 411–37.
Gallant, A. R., and Tauchen, G. (in press), "Seminonparametric estimation of conditionally constrained heterogeneous processes: Asset pricing applications," *Econometrica.*
Geweke, J. (1986), "Exact inference in the inequality constrained normal linear regression model," *Journal of Applied Econometrics,* 1, 127–41.
    (1988a), "Antithetic acceleration of Monte Carlo integration in Bayesian inference," *Journal of Econometrics,* 38, 73–90.
    (1988b), "Modelling with normal polynomial expansions," ISDS Discussion Paper 88-02, Duke University, Durham, N.C.
    (1989), "Exact predictive densities in linear models with ARCH disturbances," *Journal of Econometrics,* 40, 63–86.
    (in press), "Bayesian inference in econometric models using Monte Carlo integration," *Econometrica.*

Hammersley, J. M., and Handscomb, D. C. (1964), *Monte Carlo Methods.* London: Methuen (1st Ed.).

Johnson, N. L., and Kotz, S. (1970), *Distributions in Statistics: Continuous Univariate Distributions - 1.* New York: Wiley.

Kloek, T., and van Dijk, H. K. (1978), "Bayesian estimates of equation system parameters: An application of integration by Monte Carlo," *Econometrica,* 46, 1–20.

Zellner, A., and Siow, A. (1980), "Posterior odds ratios for selected regression hypotheses," *Trabajos de Estadistica y de Investigacion Operativa,* 31, 585–603.

CHAPTER 15

Hysteresis and the evolution of postwar U.S. and U.K. unemployment

James H. Stock

Abstract: Hysteresis in unemployment can be characterized as a dependence of
the persistence in unemployment on the level of, or on changes in, unemployment.
This chapter presents an empirical investigation of this possible nonlinear behavior, in which the persistence and conditional heteroscedasticity of unemployment
are allowed to depend on its recent history. Both U.S. and U.K. postwar unemployment are found to exhibit substantial nonlinearities of this form, with high
and increasing unemployment corresponding to decreased persistence in both
countries.

1   Introduction

The experience of the United States and Europe during the 1980s has renewed interest in the evident persistence of high levels of unemployment.
Time-series characterizations of this phenomenon take two forms. First, a
statistical interpretation of this persistence, given by Blanchard and Summers (1986a), is that the best forecast of unemployment in a given quarter
is very nearly the unemployment rate in the previous quarter; that is, unemployment appears to have an autoregressive root nearly equal to one.
Second, the notion that some economies can become "stuck" at high levels of unemployment suggests that the serial correlation of the unemployment rate might itself depend on the level of unemployment, with greater
correlation occurring at high rather than at low levels. This second characterization is one interpretation of the proposition that unemployment
might exhibit "hysteresis" as discussed by Tobin (1980) and Blanchard and
Summers (1986a, b, c), in the sense that continuing high unemployment
can be associated with approximately constant inflation rates.

The author thanks R. Cooper, J. Geweke, N. Gottfries, S. R. G. Jones, and T. Sargent for
helpful discussions and suggestions. This chapter was written while the author was visiting
the Institute for International Economic Studies at the University of Stockholm. This research was supported in part by NSF grant #SES-84-08797.

361

Taken together, these two observations suggest that unemployment might exhibit substantial dependence at high levels – close to the dependence of a random walk, with a relatively small innovation variance – but might exhibit less dependence (and a greater innovation variance) at low or at rapidly changing levels. This state-dependent serial correlation can be thought of as a potential "nonlinear" feature of the unemployment series in the sense that it would not be present were unemployment truly generated by a stationary linear time-series model. The idea that unemployment might display important nonlinearities has been investigated before. For example, Neftci (1984) and DeLong and Summers (1986) provide empirical evidence that the evolution of U.S. unemployment is asymmetric over cyclical expansions and contractions; Brock and Sayers (1986) also find evidence of nonlinear structure in the unemployment rate. However, these authors investigate these nonlinearities using statistical techniques that shed little light on the hysteresis hypothesis that the conditional heteroscedasticity or correlation in unemployment depends on its level or its rate of change.

The purpose of this chapter is to examine empirically the persistence and hysteresis of aggregate unemployment. *Persistence* is interpreted as meaning that the largest autoregressive root of the unemployment process is near one, and *hysteresis* is interpreted as state- or time-dependent conditional correlations and heteroscedasticity. One way to look for this latter feature is to apply an existing test for nonlinearities in time-series data. Unfortunately, this approach can yield information about whether nonlinearities are present but rarely elucidates their form. Instead, the strategy adopted here is to study nonlinear patterns in unemployment using a parametric nonlinear time-series model that is unconditionally stationary and mean-reverting but has serial correlation and heteroscedasticity that can depend on the recent history of the series.

The nonlinear time-series model considered here is motivated both by the desire to link conditional dependence with conditional heteroscedasticity and by a simple argument based on flows into and out of unemployment. Specifically, in a precise sense, unemployment evolves more rapidly at higher than at lower flow rates. Thus the unemployment rate can be thought of as having an "operational" time scale that is a nonlinear transformation of the calendar time scale on which it is observed, where the transformation depends on unemployment flow rates. When observed at regular intervals in calendar time, at high flow rates the innovations to unemployment appear large, and the usefulness of lagged unemployment in predicting future unemployment is diminished, relative to periods of low flow rates.

This argument, formalized in Section 2, suggests using a time-deformation model (Stock, 1987, 1988) to analyze the nonlinearities in the unemployment rate. In this model, unemployment is assumed to evolve according to a linear, time-invariant, stochastic differential equation on a (continuous) "economic" or operational time scale. This time scale is nonlinearly related to the calendar time scale on which unemployment is observed, with the time transformation depending on exogenous variables or lagged values of unemployment itself. Qualitatively, the state-dependent autoregressive coefficients inherent in the time-deformation model are capable of capturing the concept of hysteresis informally used to describe the recent European experience.

The empirical analysis begins in Section 3 with an examination of measures of persistence in U.S. and U.K. unemployment in linear, discrete-time, autoregressive models. As has been widely noted, both series have a root near one, with U.K. unemployment exhibiting slightly greater average persistence than the U.S. series.

Estimated time-deformation models are presented in Section 4. The empirical strategy is to estimate several models with different variables determining the transformation between operational and calendar time. The statistical significance of these variables and the estimated transformations themselves summarize the nonlinear patterns being captured by the time-deformation model. Although the theoretical discussion in Section 2 is used to guide the choice of variables to enter the time-scale transformation, the objective of the empirical work is not to test the formal theory but rather to use the theory as a starting point for quantifying nonlinear patterns in unemployment. This investigation reveals statistically significant time-scale nonlinearities that differ in important ways between the United States and the United Kingdom. In both countries, the serial correlation in unemployment appears to be *less* at high levels than at low levels of unemployment. Conclusions from this analysis are summarized in Section 5.

2   Unemployment flows and time deformation

This section provides a theoretical motivation for modeling unemployment as obeying a linear, continuous-time stochastic differential equation in operational time, where operational and calendar time are related by some nonlinear transformation. The development starts with the identity

$$\frac{du}{dt} = \alpha(1-u) - \beta u, \tag{1}$$

where u is the unemployment rate, du/dt is its time derivative, and α and β are, respectively, the instantaneous flow rates into and out of unemployment.

In the context of search theory, if there is no labor-force participation decision, then β in (1) can be interpreted as the probability that an unemployed worker finds a job at a time t multiplied by the fraction of jobs that the worker finds acceptable, given a reservation wage and an assessment of the current distribution of wage offers; see, for example, Diamond (1982) or Pissarides (1985). The flow rate into unemployment α can similarly be interpreted as the probability of a layoff or quit. Theoretical and empirical work in search theory examines the behavior of unemployment under various assumptions about α and β. For example, Pissarides (1985) models β as depending on the reservation wage of workers and on the availability of offers as captured by the ratio of vacancies to unemployment; Bjorklund and Holmlund (1981) consider as well the possibility that price misperceptions result in incorrect judgments concerning the real offer distribution.

Informally, the flow rates α and β determine the speed of evolution of the unemployment process: Unemployment evolves more rapidly at high than at low flow rates. To make this precise, I adopt a particular stochastic specification of α and β. Let $\rho(t)$ be a positive deterministic function of time (this will be relaxed later), and let $\epsilon(t)$ be a mean-zero unforecastable continuous-time innovation with unit variance. For tractability, suppose that the predetermined components of α and β are proportional, so that increased flows into unemployment are associated with increased flows into jobs. In addition, suppose that α and β have a common stochastic component such that an unpredictable increase in α is exactly offset by the same unpredictable decrease in β and that this unpredictable component is proportional to $\rho(t)$. Thus,

$$\alpha = \alpha_0 \rho(t) + \sigma\epsilon(t)\rho(t), \tag{2a}$$

$$\beta = \beta_0 \rho(t) - \sigma\epsilon(t)\rho(t), \tag{2b}$$

where σ, α_0, and β_0 are positive parameters.

Assumption (2) captures some important features of the flow of workers into and out of unemployment. If movements into unemployment arise because workers hope to find better jobs, it is plausible that the predictable parts of the flow rates into and out of unemployment are closely related; this is captured by including the term $\rho(t)$ in the two expressions. In addition, an innovation that induces workers to reduce their quit rate seems likely also to induce the unemployed to accept more jobs, suggesting the opposite signs on the innovation terms in α and β. Finally, the assumption of multiplicative rather than additive errors is consistent with empirical emphases on log-linear specifications. To the extent that workers become unemployed because of layoffs, however, assumption (2) is more problematic. On the one hand, it seems likely that many of the variables entering the decision of unemployed workers to accept an offer also affect the layoff decisions of firms. For example, forecasts of future prices enter into assessments of both the future product demand (and thus of the need for layoffs) and the real value of a nominal wage offer. On the other hand, there is no economic reason that these factors should enter α and β through the single function $\rho(t)$ as presumed in (2). Moreover, (2) assumes that a positive innovation in the layoff rate is associated with an equal decrease in the hiring rate; because layoffs are typically costly, the firm might prefer – in response to an innovation – first to reduce hiring or to lay off by attrition, and only second to lay off current employees directly.[1] The point is not, however, to develop a fully specified model of unemployment flows. Rather, it it merely to motivate a simple nonlinear model of the unemployment rate in which the transition probabilities, and in particular $\rho(t)$, have the interpretation as the rates of change of the operational time scale of unemployment relative to its calendar time scale.

Using the specifications (2) for the flow rates, one can write the unemployment rate in terms of $\rho(t)$ and $\epsilon(t)$ by substituting (2) into (1):

$$\rho(t)^{-1}\frac{du}{dt} = \alpha_0 - \theta u(t) + \sigma\epsilon(t), \tag{3}$$

where $\theta = \alpha_0 + \beta_0$. Because α_0 and β_0 in (2) are positive, it follows that θ is positive, so (3) is stable (a condition assumed henceforth). Note that the differential equation (3) satisfies the integral equation

$$u(t) = \int_{-\infty}^{g(t)} [\alpha_0 + \sigma\bar{\epsilon}(r)]e^{-\theta[g(t)-r]} \, dr, \tag{4}$$

where $g(t) = \int_{-\infty}^{t} \rho(\tau) \, d\tau$ and $\bar{\epsilon}(s) = \epsilon(g^{-1}(s))$, where $g^{-1}(s)$ exists because $\rho(t)$ is positive, so $\epsilon(t) = \bar{\epsilon}(g(t))$.[2]

When unemployment satisfies (4), $g(t)$ can be interpreted as an operational time scale for the unemployment rate. To see this, let $\xi(s)$ denote the continuous-time latent process corresponding to the unemployment

---

[1] See Pissarides (1986, pp. 511–12) for a discussion of "redundancies by wastage" in the United Kingdom.

[2] To verify that (4) is the integral equation corresponding to (3), differentiate (4) and substitute (4) into the resultant expression to obtain $du/dt = \dot{g}\{\alpha_0 + \bar{\epsilon}[g(t)]\} - \theta\dot{g}(t)u(t)$, where $\dot{g}(t) = dg(t)/dt$. The result (3) then obtains by rearranging this expression, using $\dot{g}(t) = \rho(t)$ and $\bar{\epsilon}[g(t)] = \epsilon(t)$.

rate, defined on the operational time scale s, let $s = g(t)$, and let $u(t) = \xi[g(t)]$. Suppose that $\xi(s)$ has the first-order operational time autoregressive representation

$$\frac{d\xi(s)}{ds} = \alpha_0 - \theta\xi(s) + \sigma\bar{\epsilon}(s), \quad s = g(t). \tag{5}$$

Then $\xi(s)$ satisfies the integral equation

$$\xi(s) = e^{-\theta(s-s')}\xi(s') + \int_{s'}^{s} [\alpha_0 + \sigma\bar{\epsilon}(r)]e^{-\theta(s-r)}\,dr. \tag{6}$$

Letting $s' = -\infty$ and $s = g(t)$, and using the assumptions that $u(t) = \xi[g(t)]$ and $\theta > 0$, one obtains from (6) that $u(t)$ obeys (4). Because the integral equations corresponding to (3) and (5) are the same, the non-linear differential equation (3) can be thought of as being the observational time (t) representation of an unemployment process that satisfies a linear first-order differential equation in continuous operational time (s), where the two time scales are linked by $s = g(t)$.[3]

In the first-order case considered here, the integral equation (6) can be rewritten to yield a discrete-time first-order autoregressive representation for the unemployment rate. The nonlinear time-scale transformation introduces nonlinearities in the discrete-time process because the autoregressive coefficient and the variance of the innovation depend on $g(t)$. Let u_t denote the discrete observational time unemployment rate defined on $t = 0, 1, 2, \ldots, T$. Substituting $s = g(t)$ and $s' = g(t-1)$ into (6), one obtains

$$u_t = \delta_t + \gamma_t u_{t-1} + v_t, \tag{7}$$

where

$$\delta_t = \frac{\alpha_0}{\theta}[1 - e^{-\theta\Delta g(t)}]$$

$$\gamma_t = e^{-\theta\Delta g(t)}$$

$$v_t = \sigma \int_{g(t-1)}^{g(t)} e^{-\theta[g(t)-r]}\bar{\epsilon}(r)\,dr,$$

where $\Delta g(t) \equiv g(t) - g(t-1) = \int_{t-1}^{t} \rho(\tau)\,d\tau$. By assumption, $\bar{\epsilon}(t)$ has mean zero and unit variance, so the moments of v_t are

$$Ev_t = 0, \qquad Ev_t^2 = \frac{\sigma^2}{2\theta}[1 - e^{-2\theta\Delta g(t)}].$$

---

[3] In the terminology of subordinated stochastic processes, $g(t)$ is termed a directing process. See Clark (1973) for a discussion when (unlike here) the subordinated process has independent increments.

The continuous-time model (5) and its discrete-time counterpart (7) are first-order univariate time-deformation models. Their properties and several examples are discussed in Stock (1987, 1988). Two features of the model are worth noting here in relation to the previous discussion concerning hysteresis and time-varying transition probabilities.

First, according to (7), the discrete-time unemployment process has a time-varying conditional mean and is heteroscedastic. The extent to which unemployment is persistent on average depends on the root θ in the continuous-time autoregression: A value of θ close to zero implies high average persistence. Relating this to the flows motivation (1) and (2), at low flow rates (i.e., small values of α and β) labor-force turnover in a typical quarter is limited, and the serial dependence in the unemployment rate is high.

Second, the increments of the time transformation are integrals of the deterministic component of the flow rates in (2), that is,

$$\Delta g(t) = \int_{t-1}^{t} \rho(\tau)\, d\tau.$$

When $\Delta g(t)$ is relatively large, many units of operational time occur during a single unit of observational time. In this case, the dependence of u_t on u_{t-1} is diminished, and the variance of ν_t is increased. This formalizes the notion that, in the search-theoretic interpretation of (2), the transition probabilities can be thought of as time-scale parameters: At more intensive levels of search (or during times that search is more productive) and under assumption (2), the unemployment rate literally evolves more rapidly.

The assumptions embodied in (7) will be relaxed in two important ways in the subsequent empirical investigation. First, it has been assumed so far that $\rho(t)$ is a deterministic function of time. If, however, the time-scale transformation is allowed to depend on the past level of unemployment, then the serial correlation in unemployment depends on its own lagged level, as suggested in the discussion of hysteresis in Section 1. Alternatively, the search-theoretic motivation for (1) and (2) suggests that $\rho(t)$ depends on economic variables related to decisions to enter and to leave employment, such as the distribution of reservation wages among job seekers, their misperceptions of real wages, and some measures of job availability such as the vacancy–unemployment ratio. This suggests considering time-scale transformations that depend on a vector of predetermined variables z_{t-1} such that $\epsilon(s)$ is independent of z_{t-1} for $s > t-1$. Specifically, in the empirical analysis we adopt the parametric form used in Stock (1987, 1988),

$$\rho(t) = \frac{\exp(c'z_{t-1})}{T^{-1}\sum_t \exp(c'z_{t-1})}. \tag{8}$$

Note that (8) normalizes $\Delta g(t)$ to be one on average, and ensures that $\Delta g(t) > 0$ for finite c and z_{t-1}.

Second, the model implies that u_t obeys a nonlinear first-order autoregressive process. However, the empirical evidence to be presented suggests that unemployment is better described as a second-order process. Thus the estimated time-deformation models will be based on both first- and second-order continuous-time autoregressions subject to time deformation with time-scale transformations given by (8).[4]

3   Linear time-series properties of unemployment

We first characterize the properties of the U.S. and U.K. unemployment rates in the context of linear models. Both series are quarterly, with observations made on the third month of every quarter.[5]

The unit root and time-trend properties of the unemployment data are examined in Table 1. The first set of statistics tests the hypothesis that unemployment contains a unit root, perhaps with drift, against the alternative that it is stationary, either with a constant mean (the $\hat{\tau}_\mu$ tests) or around a deterministic time trend (the $\hat{\tau}_\tau$ tests). The second set of statistics tests for the presence of a deterministic time trend or a drift.

In the U.S. data, the hypothesis of a unit root is generally rejected at the 10% level in favor of an autoregressive specification in which unemployment is stationary around a time trend. However, in the U.K. data there is little evidence against the unit-root hypothesis using any of the tests. Because of the apparent presence of the unit root in British unemployment, the t-statistic on time in a regression of unemployment on a constant, time, and lag of unemployment has a nonstandard distribution (Fuller, 1976; Sims, Stock, and Watson, in press). However, the test for a drift in first differences of U.K. unemployment is not significant.

---

[4] By assuming that job quitters must wait one period before becoming eligible for a new job offer, Wright (1986) obtains a second-order difference equation for unemployment that he interprets in terms of search theory. His model is of interest here because, as in (1), its parameters depend on transition probabilities that vary over time. The time dependence he analyzes arises because of agents' misperceptions of changes in the nominal wage. He provides no empirical evidence addressing these implied nonlinearities, however, and the evidence in Bjorklund and Holmlund (1981) raises serious questions about Wright's emphasis on nominal wage misperceptions as a primary source of persistence in unemployment.

[5] The U.S. data were obtained from the Citibase data base, and the U.K. data were obtained from OECD *Main Economic Indicators*.

Table 1. *Specification tests in discrete-time autoregressive models of unemployment*

Statistic[a]	United States 1951:1–1985:3[b]		United Kingdom 1961:2–1986:4[b]	
r_1	0.958		0.979	
$\hat{\tau}_\mu$, unit-root test	−2.58[c]	−2.46	−1.10	−0.90
$\hat{\tau}_\tau$, unit-root test	−3.63[d]	−3.64[d]	−2.69	−2.51
t-Statistic on time trend in u_t	2.50[d]	2.63[d]	2.44[d]	2.34[d]
t-Statistic on drift in Δu_t	0.30	0.29	1.01	1.13

[a] The r_1 statistic denotes the first sample autocorrelation. The $\hat{\tau}_\mu$ and $\hat{\tau}_\tau$ statistics testing for a unit root are described in Dickey and Fuller (1979) and tabulated in Fuller (1976). The usual asymptotic critical values were used to evaluate the significance of the t tests for time trends.
[b] 1951:1 denotes the first quarter of 1951, etc.
[c] Significant at the 10% level.
[d] Significant at the 5% level.

The results in Table 1 confirm the evidence of Blanchard and Summers (1986a) from annual data that both series are highly persistent in the sense of having large autoregressive coefficients. Indeed, it is tempting to describe this persistence by suggesting that unemployment is generated by a linear model with a root of exactly one. But such a model provides an unsatisfactory characterization of the process in the long run, because it predicts that unemployment eventually will wander outside the range of 0–100%. One argument used to justify the application of unit-root models to bounded processes is that, in certain applications, they might provide useful locally linear approximations to a globally nonlinear process. However, the informal descriptions of hysteresis as state-dependent second moments suggest that the features of unemployment of particular economic interest are precisely its departures from this linear approximation. This observation, plus the flows analysis of Section 2, suggests taking a closer look at the nonlinear properties of the unemployment rate.

4   Time-deformation models of unemployment

Various time-deformation models of U.S. and British unemployment were estimated using the parametric time-scale transformation (8), where z_{t-1} was a vector of predetermined variables. The parameters were estimated by maximum likelihood under the assumption that the innovation is gaussian. Evaluation of the likelihood involves two technical difficulties. First,

Table 2. *Time-deformation models of U.S. unemployment, 1951:1–1985:3* [a]

Model	Roots	Estimated coefficients c [b], where z_{t-1} is								Log likelihood, $\mathcal{L}$	Likelihood ratio statistic, LR [c]
		u_{t-1}	Δu_{t-1}	$\Delta^2 u_{t-1}$	Δu^+_{t-1}	Δu^+_{t-2}	$(v/u)_{t-1}$	$\Delta(v/u)_{t-1}$	$\Delta^2(v/u)_{t-1}$		
AR(1) operational time process											
1	−0.0036	—	—	—	—	—	—	—	—	−89.599	—
2	−0.0289	0.13 (0.07)	0.88 (0.31)	−0.02 (0.32)	—	—	—	—	—	−80.554	18.09[d]
3	−0.0681	0.10 (0.07)	−0.68 (0.73)	−0.62 (0.54)	4.23 (1.48)	−0.70 (0.86)	—	—	—	−72.394	34.41[d]
4	−0.0500	—	—	—	—	—	−0.50 (0.02)	−0.38 (0.08)	0.16 (0.08)	−65.681	47.84[d]
5	−0.149	0.08 (0.08)	−3.05 (0.67)	1.68 (0.52)	—	—	−0.03 (0.02)	−0.98 (0.14)	0.53 (0.12)	−54.988	69.22[d]
AR(2) operational time process											
6	−0.075, −1.40	—	—	—	—	—	—	—	—	−74.648	—
7	−0.067, −1.46	0.02 (0.03)	0.39 (0.16)	0.07 (0.14)	—	—	—	—	—	−68.792	11.71[d]
8	−0.063, −2.53	0.02 (0.04)	−0.33 (0.36)	0.12 (0.30)	1.85 (0.92)	0.28 (0.46)	—	—	—	−65.555	18.19[d]
9	−0.054, −2.29	—	—	—	—	—	−0.02 (0.01)	−0.19 (0.05)	0.06 (0.04)	−59.269	30.76[d]
10	−0.066, −2.55	−0.01 (0.04)	−1.42 (0.38)	0.89 (0.27)	—	—	−0.02 (0.01)	−0.44 (0.08)	0.23 (0.06)	−52.148	45.00[d]

although the model being estimated is defined in continuous time, the data are collected in discrete time. Second, the nonlinear relation between operational and calendar time implies that data sampled at constant intervals in calendar time are effectively sampled at irregular intervals in operational time. Thus the econometric problem is equivalent to estimating the parameters of a continuous-time process sampled at irregular intervals, where the sampling interval is determined by the time-scale transformation which in turn contains unknown parameters. These difficulties are handled by using the Kalman filter algorithm developed in Stock (1988).

The time-scale variables z_{t-1} were chosen to examine parsimoniously the hysteresis hypothesis discussed in Section 1 and the flows motivation provided in Section 2. The hysteresis hypothesis suggests that the persistence of unemployment is itself state-dependent in the sense that the economy might have a tendency to get stuck at high levels of unemployment. Thus u_{t-1} was included as an explanatory variable in the time scale. Related hypotheses are that the persistence in the process might depend on whether the unemployment rate is increasing or decreasing or on whether the unemployment rate is accelerating or decelerating. Thus Δu_{t-1} and $\Delta^2 u_{t-1} \equiv \Delta u_{t-1} - \Delta u_{t-2}$ were included as elements of z_{t-1} as well. Finally, the persistence of the process might depend on the change in unemployment, but this dependence might differ if unemployment has been increasing rather than decreasing. Consequently, Δu_{t-1}^+ and Δu_{t-2}^+ have also been included, where $\Delta u_{t-1}^+ = \Delta u_{t-1}$ if $\Delta u_{t-1} \geq 0$ and $= 0$ otherwise.

The estimation results for the U.S. data are summarized in Table 2. The theoretical development in Section 2 suggests examining specifications with a first-order autoregressive process in operational time; the results are presented in the first half of the table. Model 1 has no time-deformation effects and so is simply a first-order continuous-time autoregression estimated with evenly spaced discrete observations. Models 2 and 3 examine the hysteresis hypothesis by fitting univariate time-deformation models using lagged unemployment. Both models exhibit statistically significant time-deformation effects based on the likelihood ratio statistic. In the models based on u_{t-1}, Δu_{t-1}, and $\Delta^2 u_{t-1}$, the coefficient on u_{t-1} is positive, indicating a relative increase in the operational time scale at high rates of unemployment, corresponding to a relative *decline* in the persistence of the process at high rates (although this effect is quantitatively slight and, in the case of model 3, statistically insignificant). In particular,

Notes to Table 2

[a] Time transformation is $\Delta g(t) = \exp(c'z_{t-1})/[T^{-1} \sum \exp(c'z_{t-1})]$.

[b] Standard errors (in parentheses) were computed using numerical derivatives.

[c] Tests hypothesis that all time-deformation coefficients are zero.

[d] Significant at the 1% level.

models 2 and 3 provide no evidence that persistence *increases* at high rates of unemployment. In contrast, $\Delta g(t)$ rises substantially when unemployment is increasing. Comparing models 2 and 3, the likelihood ratio statistic indicates that the absolute value of Δu_{t-1} (and its lag) enter the time-scale transformations significantly at the 1% level.

The development in Section 2 also suggests considering variables commonly treated as proximate determinants of flows into and out of unemployment. Thus models 4 and 5 have time-scale transformations based on the vacancy–unemployment ratio (see, e.g., Pissarides, 1985) and its first and second difference. (The Conference Board index of help-wanted advertising is used as the vacancies series.) These models exhibit dramatic time-deformation effects. Both models suggest that an increasing vacancy–unemployment ratio corresponds to a decline in $\Delta g(t)$ and an associated increase in the persistence of unemployment.[6]

Although the discussion of Section 2 was for a first-order model, the restriction that the true model be first order need not be satisfied in the data. The models were therefore reestimated assuming a second-order autoregressive latent process; the results are reported in the second half of the table. In every case the hypothesis that the model is first order can be rejected at the 5% level using the usual likelihood ratio statistics, though the test statistics are substantially smaller for the time-deformation models than for the models with no time deformation. Despite these rejections of the AR(1) specification, the estimated time-scale coefficients are broadly similar for comparable models across the two panels. Additional evidence of the similarity of the estimated transformations is provided by the contemporaneous correlations among them reported in Table 3, with 15 of the 28 correlations exceeding 0.75.[7] The high correlations in comparable AR(1) and AR(2) models provide support for a loose interpretation

---

[6] Using monthly data, Bjorklund and Holmlund (1981) found that vacancies entered significantly into transition probability regressions. The results in Table 2 are consistent with their findings because the v/u ratio is presumed to enter through the transition probabilities α and β.

[7] AR(3) and AR(4) continuous-time latent processes were also estimated. These models typically did not converge, with the most negative root tending toward $-\infty$. This indicates overparameterization of the continuous-time AR models because a continuous-time root of $-\infty$ corresponds to a discrete-time root of 0. As an additional check of the robustness of the estimated time transformations, we reestimated the models in Table 2 including a linear time trend in continuous operational time, though such a specification is largely inconsistent with the spirit of this exercise, which is to model the apparent persistence of high and increasing unemployment using a stable stochastic model. The time transformations estimated with a time trend in the latent process are qualitatively very similar to those reported in Table 2, though in most cases the hypothesis that the time trend is zero can be rejected at the 5% level. These and other unreported results are available from the author upon request.

Table 3. *Correlations of estimated time-scale transformations, United States, 1951:1–1985:3*[a]

Model	2	3	4	5	7	8	9	10
2	1	0.70	0.63	0.31	0.93	0.90	0.92	0.70
3		1	0.79	0.56	0.49	0.92	0.69	0.66
4			1	0.87	0.52	0.81	0.82	0.91
5				1	0.25	0.50	0.56	0.84
7					1	0.77	0.90	0.69
8						1	0.89	0.76
9							1	0.90
10								1

[a] Correlations among $\Delta g(t)$ computed using the estimated models in Table 2.

of these time-scale transformations as changing transition probabilities, as suggested by the development in Section 2, although the test statistics indicate that this interpretation is not strictly warranted.

In summary, two conclusions emerge from Table 2. First, in time transformations based solely on the lagged unemployment rate or its differences, persistence is seen to depend more on the change in unemployment than on the level itself. That is, when U.S. unemployment is stable, it appears to be highly persistent; but a past increase in unemployment is associated with a substantial reduction in its dependence. This suggests that unemployment becomes stuck at a certain level, with high persistence and low innovation variance. However, a large positive innovation is associated with a subsequent reduced dependence and greater innovation variance, that is, with the process becoming unstuck until it moves to a new level with a new and relatively slow operational time scale.

This finding might initially seem unsurprising. In a linear model with positive serial correlation in first differences, a large change in unemployment in one quarter would lead one to forecast a large change in the next. However, the time-deformation results imply something quite different: the greater the increase in one quarter, the *less predictable* is the change in the next. Under a linear specification, this predictability (i.e., serial correlation and heteroscedasticity) is time invariant whereas the test statistics in the final column of Table 2 reject this hypothesis in favor of time deformation.

These results are based on the asymptotic approximation to the likelihood ratio test statistic. To evaluate the adequacy of this approximation in samples of moderate size, a Monte Carlo experiment was performed

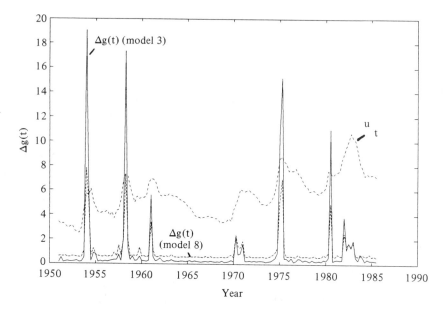

Figure 1.   U.S. unemployment rate and the estimated change in its operational time scale. The estimates of $\Delta g(t)$ are from models 3 and 8 in Table 2.

under the null hypothesis of no time deformation. The results, presented in the appendix, support this application of the asymptotic theory. This reinforces the conclusion that the U.S. unemployment rate exhibits substantial nonlinearities associated with past changes in unemployment.

To gain further insight into the estimated nonlinearity in the unemployment rate, the changes in the time scales estimated using models 3 and 8 have been plotted, along with the unemployment rate, in Figure 1. The spikes in Figure 1 indicate periods of markedly large $\Delta g(t)$, corresponding to sharp drops in the dependence of the process and increases in the conditional discrete time innovation variance. As suggested by the point estimates, these spikes correspond to periods of previously increasing unemployment; this pattern is apparent in both the time transformations plotted, though the magnitudes of the spikes differ. Although they are not plotted here, the other estimated time transformations in Table 2 have the same qualitative features evident in Figure 1, with large spikes during periods of increasing and accelerating unemployment.

Do the same nonlinearities appear in the U.K. data? The estimation results using the U.K. unemployment rate are presented in Table 4. In the

Table 4. *Time-deformation models of U.K. unemployment, 1961:2–1986:4*[a]

Model	Roots	Estimated coefficients c,[b] where z_{t-1} is					Log likelihood, $\mathcal{L}$	Likelihood ratio statistic, LR[c]
		u_{t-1}	Δu_{t-1}	$\Delta^2 u_{t-1}$	Δu^+_{t-1}	Δu^+_{t-2}		
AR(1) operational time process								
1	−0.002	—	—	—	—	—	−27.900	—
2	−0.002	0.11 (0.05)	2.12 (0.49)	−0.15 (0.80)	—	—	−6.145	43.51[d]
3	−0.003	0.09 (0.05)	−2.35 (1.84)	−0.30 (1.49)	6.88 (1.94)	−0.78 (1.87)	−0.220	55.36[d]
AR(2) operational time process								
4	−0.016, −0.432	—	—	—	—	—	16.337	—
5	−0.013, −0.423	0.04 (0.02)	0.036 (0.25)	−0.40 (0.27)	—	—	26.871	21.07[d]
6	−0.015, −0.390	0.05 (0.02)	1.10 (0.70)	−0.85 (0.46)	−0.44 (0.85)	−0.57 (0.54)	27.527	22.38[d]

[a] Time transformation is $\Delta g(t) = \exp(c'z_{t-1})/[T^{-1}\sum \exp(c'z_{t-1})]$.
[b] Standard errors (in parentheses) were computed using numerical derivatives.
[c] Tests hypothesis that all time-deformation coefficients are zero.
[d] Significant at the 1% level.

Table 5. *Correlations of estimated time-scale transformations, United Kingdom, 1961:2–1986:4[a]*

Model	2	3	5	6
2	1	0.90	0.74	0.71
3		1	0.48	0.45
4			1	0.99
5				1

[a] Correlations among $\Delta g(t)$ computed using the estimated models in Table 4.

absence of a measure of vacancies analogous to that used for the U.S. data, only time-deformation models based on lags and lagged differences of unemployment were estimated. All models indicate statistically significant time-deformation effects. However, the evidence against the first-order specification in Table 4 is overwhelming, with χ_1^2 likelihood ratio statistics all exceeding 50. These test results, the small second continuous-time roots reported in the second half of the table, and the differences in the time-scale coefficients in corresponding AR(1) and AR(2) models therefore suggest that the first-order model discussed in Section 2 is sharply inconsistent with the empirical evidence. In addition, the correlations in Table 5 indicate only a modest relation between the two sets of estimated time transformations. The remaining discussion therefore focuses on the estimated second-order models.

An interesting feature of the results is the similarity of the coefficients on u_{t-1} and Δu_{t-1} in model 5 of Table 4 for the United Kingdom to the corresponding coefficients for the U.S. time-deformation models reported in model 7 of Table 2. The primary differences between these two estimated models is the relatively small second root in the British continuous-time model and the opposite signs of the coefficients on $\Delta^2 u_{t-1}$; although an acceleration of unemployment in the United States corresponds to a slight decrease in persistence, a similar acceleration in the United Kingdom corresponds to an increase in persistence.

This difference is reflected in the plots of the respective time transformations. The estimated time transformation from model 6 is plotted in Figure 2; this transformation involves the same time-scale variables as the U.S. transformations plotted in Figure 1. As suggested by the estimated coefficients, $\Delta g(t)$ is greatest (and persistence smallest) at high levels of unemployment and with decelerating unemployment. Accordingly, the

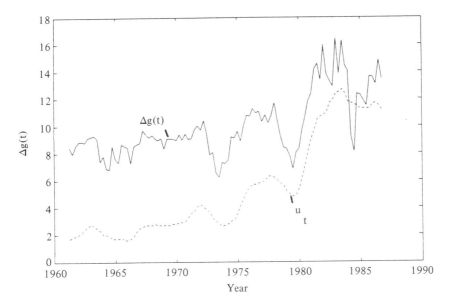

Figure 2. U.K. unemployment rate and the estimated change in its operational time scale. The estimate of $\Delta g(t)$ is from model 6 in Table 4. The plotted values of the time-scale transformation have been scaled up by a factor of ten; the sample average of $\Delta g(t)$ is 1 by construction.

lowest dependence is seen to occur in the 1980s. This contrasts with the view that U.K. unemployment in the early 1980s has exhibited unusually high persistence. Indeed, the opposite appears to be true, at least according to Figure 2.

5   Conclusions

The empirical results of Section 4 indicate substantial and statistically significant nonlinearities in the unemployment process. These findings can be interpreted as indicating a nonlinear relation between the operational and observational time scales of unemployment, a view motivated partly because the time-deformation model captures the qualitative features of state dependence that characterize hysteresis and partly by considering the model of unemployment flows presented in Section 2. This interpretation warrants two caveats. First, although the time-deformation model captures the intuitive notion that unemployment might evolve on a time scale other than calendar time, it imposes a restrictive parameterization on the nonlinearities; other models might detect different nonlinear features in the data. Second, using U.S. data, although the vacancy–unemployment ratio significantly enters the time-scale transformation (as predicted by the search arguments in Section 2), this does not support any particular formulation of search theory or the associated welfare implications. In particular, workers and the unemployed might engage in optimal search, but the set of available jobs could be influenced by macroeconomic policy; this is consistent with the discussions in Blanchard and Summers (1986a, b, c), Pissarides (1986), Gottfries and Horn (1986), and Jones (1987).

The empirical results characterize nonlinear patterns in the unemployment series using a variety of proxies for the time-scale transformation variables. Narrowly interpreted, the results indicate that both U.S. and U.K. unemployment exhibit reduced persistence and greater conditional heteroscedasticity at high than at low rates of unemployment and, more importantly, during times of increasing unemployment.

Interpreting these results somewhat more broadly, these models provide little support for the proposition that unemployment exhibits greater dependence at high than at low levels. Rather, the picture that emerges is: If unemployment has been stable then its dependence is increased. In contrast, if unemployment has been *rising* in the recent past then its dependence is reduced, and the error associated with forecasts of future unemployment increases. This empirical result resembles descriptions of hysteresis in unemployment as shifts between multiple persistent equilibria.

Appendix: A Monte Carlo evaluation of the time deformation MLE

This appendix describes a small Monte Carlo experiment designed to investigate the quality of the asymptotic χ^2 approximation to the distribution of the likelihood ratio statistic testing for the presence of time deformation, under the null hypothesis that there is no time deformation. The data were generated under the maintained assumption that the univariate process obeys a first-order linear stochastic differential equation in continuous operational time.

Two experiments were performed. In both, the data were assumed to obey the stochastic differential equation

$$dX(s) = [\mu - \theta X(s)]\, ds + \sigma d\zeta(s), \quad \mu = 0, \quad \theta = 0.693, \quad \sigma = 1.848,$$

where $\zeta(s)$ is standard Brownian motion and there is no time deformation, so that $s = t$. Thus, by using (7) with $\Delta g(t) = 1$, the pseudodata were generated by the discrete-time AR(1) process $X_t = 0.5X_{t-1} + \nu_t$, where

v_t is independently distributed $N(0,1)$. In the first experiment, the time-scale transformation was of the form (8) and depended on a single lag of x_t; that is,

$$k=1: \quad \Delta g_1(t) = \frac{\exp(cx_{t-1})}{T^{-1}\sum_t \exp(cx_{t-1})}.$$

In the second experiment, the time transformation also depended on the change in x_{t-1}; that is,

$$k=2: \quad \Delta g_2(t) = \frac{\exp(c_1 x_{t-1} + c_2 \Delta x_{t-1})}{T^{-1}\sum_t \exp(c_1 x_{t-1} + c_2 \Delta x_{t-1})}.$$

The unknown parameters are (μ, θ, σ, c) for $k=1$ and $(\mu, \theta, \sigma, c_1, c_2)$ for $k=2$. In both experiments, the likelihood ratio statistic was evaluated by estimating the model subject to the constraint that $c=0$ (or $c_1 = c_2 = 0$) and then not subject to this constraint. Estimation was by maximum likelihood using the modified Kalman filter in Stock (1988). Initial values for the maximization (performed in FORTRAN using the Davidon–Fletcher–Powell maximization algorithm) were $(\mu, \theta, \sigma, c)_0 = (0, 0.5, 0.5, 0)$ for $k=1$ and $(\mu, \theta, \sigma, c_1, c_2)_0 = (0, 0.5, 0.5, 0, 0)$ for $k=2$. Both experiments involved 100 replications with a sample size of 100, requiring a total of 32 hours on an IBM AT. All 400 likelihood maximizations (100 each for the constrained and unconstrained cases with $k=1$ and $k=2$) converged.

As Table 6 indicates, in the Monte Carlo simulations the nominal sizes of the tests based on the likelihood ratio statistic are close to the asymptotic significance level. Although there is some tendency for the size to exceed the level, the standard error associated with these estimates of the size is large (approximately 0.03 for the 10% level entries). However, the results provide no evidence of a dramatic failure of the asymptotic approximation (or the optimization routine), nor is there noticeable deterioration of the asymptotic approximation when two time-deformation parameters are estimated rather than one.

Quantiles of the Monte Carlo distribution of various estimators are presented in Table 7. The estimated autoregressive coefficient is skewed away from zero, being median- but not mean-unbiased in both the restricted and the unrestricted case. There is no noticeable deterioration of the distribution of $\hat{\theta}$ moving from the restricted to the unrestricted case. In addition, the time-deformation parameters appear to be symmetrically distributed around zero in both experiments. Although the range of the estimated time-deformation parameters is large, this does not imply that these parameters would be estimated imprecisely were time deformation in fact present, an issue not addressed in these experiments.

Table 6. *Nominal sizes of likelihood ratio tests for time deformation using asymptotic critical values*[a,b]

	Size[c]	
Level (α)	$k=1$	$k=2$
0.05	0.06	0.08
0.10	0.15	0.17
0.20	0.25	0.21
0.30	0.37	0.28
0.50	0.68	0.50
0.70	0.76	0.71
0.90	0.92	0.89

[a] The critical values for each significance level were taken from tables of the asymptotic $\chi^2_{k;\alpha}$ distribution.

[b] Sample size = 100.

[c] Entries are based on 100 Monte Carlo replications as described in the text. For example, the $k=1$, $\alpha = .05$ entry reports that six of the 100 LR statistics drawn in the $k=1$ experiment indicate rejection of the null of $c=0$ (i.e., of no time deformation) based on the χ^2_1 5% critical value of 3.84.

Table 7. *Percentiles and summary statistics of selected estimators*[a]

Monte Carlo percentile and mean	Quantiles of estimated coefficients when k time-deformation coefficients are estimated[b]					
	$k=0$	$k=1$		$k=2$		
	$-\hat{\theta}$	$-\hat{\theta}$	$\hat{c}$	$-\hat{\theta}$	$\hat{c}_1$	$\hat{c}_2$
10%	-1.06	-1.26	-0.24	-1.15	-0.39	-0.31
30%	-0.86	-0.87	-0.10	-0.86	-0.12	-0.12
50%	-0.72	-0.69	0.00	-0.75	-0.01	-0.02
70%	-0.61	-0.62	0.07	-0.64	0.08	0.13
90%	-0.55	-0.52	0.19	-0.52	0.26	0.37
Mean	-0.85	-0.95	-0.01	-0.83	-0.03	0.01
True value	-0.693	-0.693	0.00	-0.693	0.00	0.00

[a] Sample size = 100.

[b] The restricted estimates in the $k=0$ column were computed imposing the true restriction that there is no time deformation whereas $k=1$ and $k=2$ refer to the number of time-deformation parameters estimated in the unrestricted experiments. Entries in the $k=0$ column are based on 200 Monte Carlo replications (combining the estimates from the $k=1$ and $k=2$ experiments); all other entries are based on 100 Monte Carlo replications.

These experiments were performed under conditions likely to yield good performance of the optimization routine and of the asymptotic theory, that is, a first-order gaussian process with few parameters to estimate and starting values that are not too far from the true values. Nevertheless, the results provide no evidence of an important failure of the algorithm or the asymptotic approximations.

REFERENCES

Bjorklund, A., and Holmlund, B. (1981), "The duration of unemployment and unexpected inflation: An empirical analysis," *American Economic Review,* 71(1), 121–31.

Blanchard, O. J., and Summers, L. H. (1986a), "Hysteresis and the European unemployment problem," *NBER Macroeconomics Annual,* 15–78.

(1986b), "Fiscal increasing returns, hysteresis, real wages and unemployment," National Bureau of Economic Research Working Paper No. 2034.

(1986c), "Hysteresis in unemployment," National Bureau of Economic Research Working Paper No. 2035.

Brock, W. A., and Sayers, C. L. (1986), "Is the business cycle characterized by deterministic chaos?" Working Paper 8617, Social Systems Research Institute, University of Wisconsin, Madison.

Clark, P. K. (1973), "A subordinated stochastic process model with finite variance for speculative prices," *Econometrica,* 41, 135–56.

DeLong, J. B., and Summers, L. H. (1986), "Are business cycles symmetrical?" in *The American Business Cycle,* ed. by R. J. Gordon, Chicago: University of Chicago Press, 166–79.

Diamond, P. A. (1982), "Aggregate demand management in search equilibrium," *Journal of Political Economy,* 90(5), 881–94.

Dickey, D. A., and Fuller, W. A. (1979), "Distribution of the estimators for autoregressive time series with a unit root," *Journal of the American Statistical Association,* 74(366), 427–31.

Fuller, W. A. (1976), *Introduction to Statistical Time Series,* New York: Wiley.

Gottfries, N., and Horn, N. (1986), "Wage formation and the persistence of unemployment," Institute for International Economic Studies Working Paper No. 347, University of Stockholm.

Jones, S. R. G. (1987), "The relationship between unemployment spells and reservation wages as a test of search theory," manuscript, Institute for Advanced Study, Princeton.

Neftci, S. N. (1984), "Are economic time series asymmetric over the business cycle?" *Journal of Political Economy,* 92, 307–28.

Pissarides, C. A. (1985), "Short-run equilibrium dynamics of unemployment, vacancies, and real wages," *American Economic Review,* 75(4), 676–90.

(1986), "Unemployment," *Economic Policy,* 3, 501–41.

Sims, C. A., Stock, J. H., and Watson, M. W. (in press), "Inference in linear time series models with some unit roots," *Econometrica.*

Stock, J. H. (1987), "Measuring business cycle time," *Journal of Political Economy,* 95(6), 1240–61.

(1988), "Estimating continuous time processes subject to time deformation: An application to postwar GNP," *Journal of the American Statistical Association,* 83, 77–85.

Tobin, J. (1980), "Stabilization policy ten years after," *Brookings Papers on Economic Activity,* 1, 19–71.

Wright, R. (1986), "Job search and cyclical unemployment," *Journal of Political Economy,* 94(1), 38–55.

CHAPTER 16

Evidence of nonlinearity in the trade-by-trade stock market return generating process

Melvin J. Hinich and Douglas M. Patterson

Abstract: This chapter presents the results of an investigation into the linear and nonlinear behavior of the continuous-time stock return generating process. The vehicle for studying the continuous-time process is the trade-by-trade price record for 15 of the 30 stocks that make up the Dow Jones Industrial Average. These prices cover a 3 year period. To analyze the data efficiently, sampled returns are constructed for 15-minute and daily intervals. The sampling scheme is designed to avoid the introduction of aliased frequency components into the sampled returns. We find that linearity is rejected more often for daily returns constructed from our sampling scheme than is the case when returns are constructed from daily market closing prices.

1   Introduction

The bispectrum has proven to be an extremely useful tool for detecting certain types of nonlinear behavior in empirical time series. The bispectrum, a complex-valued function of two frequencies, is defined as the double Fourier transform of the third-order cumulant function. If the mechanism generating a time series is such that the third-order cumulant function has some nonzero terms, then the bispectrum will be nonzero and vary with frequency. This fact is the basis for the linearity tests developed by Subba Rao and Gabr (1980) and Hinich (1982). Frequency-domain methods are preferred because the sampling properties of the estimated bispectrum are better understood than those of the estimated third-order cumulants.

Both authors are indebted to John Geweke and three anonymous referees for carefully reading two earlier drafts of the manuscript and for pointing out a number of errors and inconsistencies in the presentation. Any remaining errors are the responsibility of the authors.

Suppose a time series is generated by the continuous-time *linear* model,

$$x(t) = \int_{-\infty}^{\infty} h(\alpha)\epsilon(t-\alpha)\,d\alpha, \tag{1}$$

where $\{\epsilon(t)\}$ is a pure noise process with continuous sample paths (a stationary time series is called "purely noise" if $\epsilon(t_1), \ldots, \epsilon(t_N)$ are independent random variables for all $t_1, \ldots, t_N$). The model of (1) is a fairly general representation of stochastic processes having continuous spectra and a defined probabilistic structure. In physically realizable linear systems, the weighting function $h(t)$, called the *impulse response,* is real, and it equals zero for negative t (causality). If $\{\epsilon(t)\}$ is gaussian, then $\{x(t)\}$ will be gaussian, and the bispectrum will be zero. Alternatively, if $\{\epsilon(t)\}$ is purely noise and nongaussian, then $\{x(t)\}$ will be nongaussian, and the skewness function will be a nonzero constant for all frequency pairs in its domain. Note that (1) is not intended to be an exhaustive definition of the linear model since, for example, a wide variety of point processes are also linear.

The model in (1) will be nonlinear if the input process $\epsilon(t)$ alters the impulse response function $h(t)$. For example, let ϵ_L be a sequence of past values of $\epsilon(t)$ up to and including lag L. Then we might write the impulse response function as

$$h(\epsilon_L, \alpha) = h(\alpha) + \int_0^L a(\beta, \alpha)\epsilon(t-\beta-\alpha)\,d\beta, \tag{2}$$

where $a(\beta, \alpha)$ is another weighting function that is convolved with the input process. If we replace $h(\alpha)$ in (1) with (2), $\{x(t)\}$ will be nonlinear, even if $\{\epsilon(t)\}$ is gaussian. The bispectrum of $\{x(t)\}$ will be nonzero and vary in magnitude over its domain.

The discovery that rates of return to shares of common stock exhibit significant nonlinear behavior was first reported in Hinich and Patterson (1985a). Subsequently, Ashley and Patterson (1986), Scheinkman and Le-Baron (1986), and Brockett, Hinich, and Patterson (1988) have also reported finding nonlinear behavior in stock market rates of return. Note that rates of return rather than share prices are analyzed because price series are highly nonstationary in the mean. Hinich and Patterson and Brockett, Hinich, and Patterson applied the Hinich (1982) bispectrum-based linearity test to daily rates of return of individual common stocks, whereas Ashley and Patterson used a bootstrap linearity test applied to daily rates of return of individual stocks and two market indices. Scheinkman and LeBaron applied their own bootstrap linearity test to a weekly stock market index. In related work, Brock, Dechert, and Scheinkman

(1986) developed a linearity test based on the Grassberger–Procaccia–Takens dimension estimate.

The finding that stock returns are generated by a nonlinear process is particularly surprising because these same returns correspond rather nicely to a white-noise model. This white-noise evidence has led most financial economists (e.g., see Fama, 1965, 1970) to conclude that the stock market cannot be forecast to any economically significant extent. However, nonlinearity implies serial dependence in stock returns and raises the possibility of finding an economically profitable forecasting rule. Although we shall have little to say about nonlinear forecasts in this chapter, it should be noted that Hinich and Patterson (1985b, 1987) have developed a method for identifying the nonzero terms in the quadratic kernel of a Volterra series approximation to a general nonlinear model.

The rates of return used in the studies cited suffer from a problem of aliasing; that is to say, the returns were not properly sampled. The term *aliasing* refers to a phenomenon whereby the high-frequency structure of the source time series is reflected back into the lower frequencies of the sampled series, with the result that the statistics of the sampled series are no longer representative of the underlying source series. Aliasing is a potential problem whenever the analyst works with sampled data. This is true regardless of whether the data are explicitly sampled by the user or have somehow been sampled by the provider or collector of the data used in time-series analysis. The obvious virtue of sampling data is that the sampled record is much shorter than the underlying continuous record, though with many economic time series the continuous record is little more than a theoretical construct because of lags in collecting and collating the information necessary to calculate a single observation of the series. The reader who is unfamiliar with the mathematics of spectral aliasing is directed to Appendix A. The appendix serves as an introduction to the discussion of bispectral aliasing to be presented in Section 2.

In this chapter we study the linear and nonlinear behavior of the continuous-time return generating mechanism by calculating returns from a trade-by-trade record of stock prices. In our analysis of trade-by-trade stock returns we want to work with 15-minute and daily sampled returns to keep the data records to a reasonable length and to make our results comparable to Hinich and Patterson (1985a), where the returns were generated from end-of-day closing prices. Therefore, it will be necessary to pass the trade-by-trade return data through a low-pass filter to avoid aliasing. For example, if the sampling frequency is $f_s = (1/15 \text{ minute})$, then the highest frequency that can be detected without aliasing is $(1/30 \text{ minute})$ or $f_s/2$. The frequency $f_s/2$ is called the Nyquist frequency f_N, and the low-pass filter must be chosen such that it removes the variance in frequencies above f_N. Of course, filtering may remove some of the information contained in the trade-by-trade data, but this is the price we must pay if we want to work with shorter records. On the other hand, the sampled data will more accurately reflect the statistics of the underlying process than would be the case if we simply sampled the price every 15 minutes or at the end of every day.

Hinich and Patterson (and others) used stock returns calculated from end-of-day prices to test the hypothesis that returns are generated by a linear process. The linear hypothesis was rejected for every stock return series that they tested. This rejection should not be interpreted to mean that aliasing is responsible for the nonlinearity found in these daily returns. Aliasing is an identification problem that makes it impossible to separate the true peaks in the estimated bispectrum of a nonlinear process from phantom peaks (in some senses, aliasing is analogous to multicollinearity). Therefore, the nature of the nonlinearity found in daily returns may not be indicative of the form of nonlinearity in the continuous-time (or trade-by-trade) return generating process. If a market participant trades only at the daily close of the stock market, then the returns used by Hinich and Patterson (and other financial researchers) can be defined as the correct process for empirical study. But most market participants execute trades in a trading session, and hence the results to be reported in Section 4 are more indicative of the nonlinear serial dependence faced by typical traders than inferences drawn from end-of-day prices.

The effect of aliasing on the estimated bispectrum of a nonlinear process causes a smearing distortion of the bispectral peaks, with the result that some significant peaks are biased downward whereas other seemingly significant peaks may be phantoms. As a consequence, the bispectral-based linearity test (a global statistic) is biased when the process is nonlinear. In addition, we can no longer interpret the significant peaks as indicating those frequency pairs where nonlinear interaction is taking place.

Section 2 reviews the mathematics of the bispectrum and bispectral aliasing. Of course, a pure noise process cannot be aliased. However, a linear nonwhite process can be aliased, but this does not affect the Hinich linearity test, as will be explained in Section 2. A detailed description of the data base and the sampling scheme employed is presented in Section 3. In Section 4 the bispectral linearity test is applied to 15 stock issues that are also members of the Dow Jones Industrial Average (DJIA). The data cover a three-year period. For each stock, three time series are analyzed: returns sampled every 15 minutes, returns sampled daily, and aliased daily returns (i.e., returns calculated from daily closing prices). We shall illustrate the impact of aliasing on the bispectrum by comparing contour plots of the estimated bispectrum from aliased and unaliased daily returns. Linearity is rejected for all 15 unaliased daily return series at the 5% level, whereas it is rejected for 12 of the aliased daily return series.

2   The mathematics of the bispectrum and bispectral aliasing

Subba Rao and Gabr (1980) and Hinich (1982) have both developed statistical tests, based on the estimated bispectrum, for the detection of nonlinearity in a time series. We shall describe and use the Hinich test because it explicitly exploits the asymptotic distribution of the bispectral estimator. Also, Patterson (1983) has developed a computer algorithm implementing the Hinich test, and Ashley, Patterson, and Hinich (1986) have shown that the test has considerable power to detect stochastic nonlinear dynamics in sample sizes as low as 256.

Because a complete description of the Hinich nonlinearity test based on the estimated bispectrum can be found in Hinich (1982), Hinich and Patterson (1985a), and Ashley, Patterson, and Hinich (1986), a detailed exposition of the implementation of the test will not be presented here; a condensed exposition can be found in Appendix B. For present purposes it suffices to note that the standardized bispectrum gain $(2\Psi^2(f, g)$, defined in equation B5) is a constant for all frequency pairs (f and g) if the generating mechanism of $\{x(t)\}$ is linear.

It is well known that the bispectrum of a discrete time signal is a spatially periodic complex function in two frequency indices, whose principal domain is the closed triangular set $\Omega = \{f, g : 0 \leq f \leq \frac{1}{2}, 0 \leq g \leq f, 2f + g \leq 1\}$. A thorough review of the bispectrum is given by Brillinger and Rosenblatt (1967a, b). For refinements and advances in the statistical methods involving bispectral analysis, see Lii and Rosenblatt (1982), Subba Rao (1983), and Hinich and Wolinsky (1988).

Our plan for the remainder of this section is as follows. First, we define and describe the bispectral density of a continuous-time stochastic process. Later, we prove that the bispectrum of a sampled continuous-time process must be zero in a proper subset of the triangular set Ω if the sampled process is not aliased. This result leads to a test for aliasing.

To review the mathematics of bispectra, let $\{x(t)\}$ denote a real, zero mean, stationary continuous-time stochastic process. Assume that all expected values, sums, and integrals used hold. The *bicovariance function* of the process is $c(u, v) = E\{x(t)x(t+u)x(t+v)\}$, which does not depend on t because the process is stationary. The Fourier transform of $c(u, v)$ is the complex function

$$B(f, g) = \int_{-\infty}^{\infty} \int_{-\infty}^{\infty} c(u, v) \exp[-i2\pi(fu + gv)] \, du \, dv, \qquad (3)$$

called the *bispectrum*. Although this two-frequency index notation is standard, it hides the three-frequency interaction that is so important in applications of bispectral estimation.

To clarify the exposition, we shall use the three-frequency notation $B(f, g, -f-g)$ and the Cramer representation of $x(t)$ used by Brillinger and Rosenblatt (1967a). This representation is

$$x(t) = \int_{-\infty}^{\infty} \exp[i2\pi ft] \, dA_x(f), \qquad (4)$$

where $\{dA_x(f)\}$ is a (complex) stochastic orthogonal increments process, and the integral in (4) is defined in the Stieltjes sense. Because $x(t)$ is real, $dA_x(-f)$ is the complex conjugate of $dA_x(f)$. The spectral density at f of $\{x(t)\}$ is $S(f) \, df = E\{dA_x(f) \, dA_x(-f)\}$, and the bispectral density for $h = -f - g$ is given by

$$B(f, g, h) \, df \, dg = E\{dA_x(f) \, dA_x(g) \, dA_x(h)\}. \qquad (5)$$

From stationarity, $B(f, g, h) \, df \, dg$ is invariant to time translations. For $B(f, g, h) \, df \, dg$ to equal $B(f, g) \, df \, dg$ for all f and g, the sum $f + g + h$ must equal zero.

If $x(t)$ is linear, then we can be more specific about the form of (5). For example, consider the continuous-time linear model defined by expression (1). From Brillinger (1975, exercise 2.13.25 at end of chap. 2), the bispectral density of the linear model is given by

$$B(f, g, h) \, df \, dg = \mu_3 H(f) H(g) H(h), \qquad (6)$$

where the complex-valued function $H(f) = \int h(t) \exp(-2\pi i ft) \, dt$ is called the transfer function of the impulse response $h(t)$, $\mu_3 = E\{\epsilon^3(t)\}$, and $\{\epsilon(t)\}$ is the innovation process. The spectrum of the linear process is $S(f) = \sigma^2 H(f) H(-f)$, where σ^2 is the variance of the innovation process.

Note that the right-hand side of (5) is invariant to permutations of the frequency indices f, g, and $h = -f - g$. Thus the bispectrum's symmetry lines are $g = f$, $h = f$ ($2f = -g$), and $h = g$ ($2g = -f$), as shown in Figure 1. Because $dA_x(-f) = dA_x^*(f)$, $B(-f, -g, -h) \, df \, dg = B^*(f, g, h) \, df \, dg$. This skew symmetry yields another three symmetry lines: $g = -f$, $h = -f$ ($g = 0$), and $h = -g$ ($f = 0$). Thus the pointed cone $C = \{f, g : 0 \le f, 0 \le g \le f\}$ (see Fig. 1) is a principal domain of this continuous-time bispectrum in the (f, g) plane.

Suppose that the process is band limited at frequency f_c. This means that the contribution of frequencies above f_c to the variance of the pro-

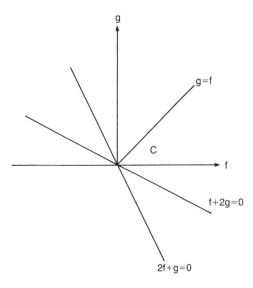

Figure 1. Symmetries of bispectrum $B(f, g)$.

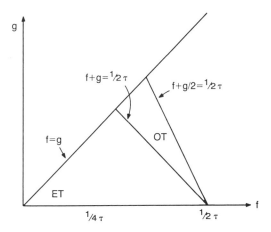

Figure 2. Discrete-time principal domain.

cess is zero, and thus the bispectrum cuts off at $f = \pm f_c$, $g = \pm f_c$, and $f + g = \pm f_c$. Then the continuous-time set of positive support for B's absolute value is the right isosceles triangle $ET = \{f, g : 0 \le f \le f_c, 0 \le g \le f, f + g = f_c\}$ shown in Figure 2.

Next, we describe the principal domain of the discrete-time bispectrum. Consider the sequence $\{x(t_n)\}$ where $t_n = n\tau$ and $1/\tau = 2f_c$ is the sampling rate. Then

$$x(t_n) = \int_{-f_c}^{f_c} \exp[i2\pi f t_n] \, d_\tau A_x(f), \tag{7}$$

where $d_\tau A_x(f) = \sum_n dA_x(f + n/\tau)$ is the sampled data orthogonal increment process (for $n = 0, \pm1, \pm2, \ldots$). The discrete-time spectral density of $\{x(t_n)\}$ is

$$_\tau S(f) \, df = E\{d_\tau A(f) \, d_\tau A(-f)\}. \tag{8}$$

Thus, if the process is linear, $_\tau S(f) \, df = \sigma^2 {}_\tau H(f) {}_\tau H(-f)$, where

$$_\tau H(f) = \sum_k H\left(f + \frac{k}{\tau}\right). \tag{9}$$

This implies that the sampled process can be expressed as the discrete convolution $\sum_n a(m)\epsilon[(n-m)\tau]$, which is the discrete-time definition of a linear time series.

It follows from (5) and (7) that the discrete-time bispectral density $_\tau B \, df \, dg$ is

$$_\tau B(f, g, h) \, df \, dg = E\{d_\tau A_x(f) \, d_\tau A_x(g) \, d_\tau A_x(h)\}$$

$$= \sum_k \sum_m \sum_n B\left(f + \frac{k}{\tau}, g + \frac{m}{\tau}, h + \frac{n}{\tau}\right) df \, dg \tag{10}$$

for $f + g + h + (k + m + n)/\tau = 0$, where the signed integers k, m, n are restricted to keep the indices in B's principal domain (see Brillinger and Rosenblatt, 1967a, p. 190). But B is band limited at f_c, and so the sum is restricted to the k, m, and n such that $0 \le f + k/\tau \le f_c$, $0 \le g + m/\tau \le f_c$, and $0 \le h + n/\tau = (k + m)/\tau - f - g \le f_c$.

Sampling introduces an infinite set of parallel symmetry lines described by $2f + g = n/\tau$ and $f + 2g = n/\tau$. The cone C is cut by both of these symmetry relations. However, for a particular n, say n^*, the line $f + 2g = n^*/\tau$ is at least to the right of the line $2f + g = n^*/\tau$ when both lines are within the cone C drawn in Figure 1. Hence the principal domain of $_\tau B$ is the triangle $\{f, g: 0 \le f \le 1/2\tau, 0 \le g \le f, 2f + g = 1/\tau\}$, which is a proper subset of the cone C. This triangle is the union of the sets ET and OT in Figure 2. From the earlier discussion, we know that the set of positive support for the band-limited continuous-time bispectrum is the triangle ET. But the principal domain of the sampled bispectrum is the union of ET and OT. Hence the question: Can we say anything about the behavior of the sampled bispectrum in the triangle OT? Intuition suggests that the sampled bispectrum is zero in *OT.* We prove that this is the case with the following theorem.

Theorem. *Let the sequence* $\{x(t_n)\}$ *be the sampled, real, zero-mean stationary process defined in* (7). *The underlying continuous-time process is band limited at frequency* f_c *and is sampled at frequency* $2f_c = 1/\tau$. *Then the bispectrum* $_\tau B$ *of* $\{x(t_n)\}$ *is zero in the triangle:*

$$OT = \left\{ f, g : 0 \leq g \leq f, \frac{1}{2\tau} \leq f + g \leq \frac{1}{\tau} - f \right\}. \tag{11}$$

Proof: The theorem will be proved through a contradiction. Suppose $f < f_c$, $g < f_c$, and the point (f, g) is in *OT*; then we have $f + g > 1/2\tau = f_c$. We know from the presentation that follows (10) that in general $0 \leq h + n/\tau = (k + m)/\tau - f - g \leq f_c$. However, band limiting implies that $k = m = 0$ and that $0 \leq h + n/\tau = -f - g \leq f_c = 1/2\tau$. The latter condition holds only when $n = -1$. Thus the only term in the sum (10) to consider is $B(f, g, h - 1/\tau)$, where $h = -f - g + 1/\tau$; but this is $B(f, g, -f - g)$, which is zero because $f + g > f_c$. That is, band limiting means that the bispectrum cuts off at $f + g = \pm f_c$. All the other terms in the sum are zero for similar reasons. It is easy to show that the theorem holds for sampling frequencies greater than $2f_c$. ∎

We next briefly review the Hinich and Wolinsky (1988) test for aliasing. Their test checks whether or not the bispectrum is zero in the triangle *OT* through a simple modification of the Hinich (1982) gaussianity test. The statistic in the Hinich test for gaussianity is the sum of approximately chi-squared statistics over the points in the principal domain grid (see Appendix B). The obvious modification for the problem at hand is to sum the chi-squared statistics only over the triangle *OT.* Under the null hypothesis that there is no aliasing for a sampling rate $1/\tau$, the distribution of the sum is approximately central chi-squared with $2K$ degrees of freedom, where K is the number of grid points in *OT.*

Finally, we consider the impact of aliasing on the Hinich linearity test. The test makes use of the ratio of the absolute value of the bispectrum squared to the triple product of the spectrum at frequencies f, g, and $h = -f - g$. If $x(t_n)$ is linear but not gaussian, then from (6) we have

$$\frac{|_\tau B(f, g, h)|^2}{_\tau S(f) \, _\tau S(g) \, _\tau S(h)} = \frac{\mu_3^2}{\sigma^6}, \tag{12}$$

which is a constant for all frequency pairs in the principal domain. If $x(t_n)$ is aliased, then the ratio will take on the constant value over the triangle

OT. Aliasing does not cause us to reject linearity, just as aliasing does not make a white-noise process look like colored noise. However, if the process is nonlinear, then the ratio in (12) will vary with frequency: A contour plot of (12) will contain a number of sharp peaks. In addition, if $x(t_n)$ is aliased, we shall not be able to distinguish those peaks that are caused by nonlinearity in the continuous-time process from those caused by images (or reflections) of peaks located outside the principal domain as defined by the sampling rate. We conclude that aliasing is an identification, or confounding, problem that does not cause rejection of a linear null hypothesis if the continuous-time process is linear.

3   Data

The master data base used in this study contains a transcription of every trade made on the New York Stock Exchange (NYSE) for the period September 1, 1978 through August 30, 1985. The number of trades totals almost 60,000,000. For the analysis presented here, we selected 15 of the 30 stocks that comprise the Dow Jones Industrial Average (DJIA), which is the most widely followed indicator of stock market performance. The names of the 15 stocks are shown in Table 1. The period chosen for analysis is September 1, 1978 through August 31, 1981. During this period, the 15 stocks traded a total of about 750,000 times. The prices and times of these trades (time is recorded to the nearest minute) form the fundamental data set used in the calculation of returns. After retrieving the trade records from the master data base, the prices were screened for unusually large price changes. The width of the screen was a function of whether the stock was trading either at or below $20.00 a share or above $20.00 a share. Only intraday price changes were screened because legitimate overnight price changes are occasionally rather large. Also, trades that were out of time sequence were eliminated. Finally, the trade prices were adjusted for cash dividends, stock dividends, and stock splits using the adjustment factors from the Daily Master File of the Center for Research in Security Prices (CRSP) at the University of Chicago. It is necessary to adjust for dividends and splits because the price changes associated with these events to not affect the wealth of the stockholders.

The next step in the analysis involved the construction of a minute-by-minute price series for each stock. Trade times are resolved to one-minute intervals in the data base. The process that generates stock market trades is inherently a point process: Trade orders arrive at the market at discrete times, and trades cannot be executed instantaneously. This means that if we sample the trade data, say, at one-minute intervals, there is no guarantee that we will find a trade at every sample point. The scheme used

Table 1. *Summary of gaussianity and linearity tests for 15-minute sampled returns*

Firm	Gaussianity test statistic, H^a	Linearity test statistic, Z^b	Aliasing test statistic, A^c
Allied Corp.	68.9	23.0	20.8
AT&T	47.4	18.2	23.2
DuPont	88.8	17.2	50.2
Exxon	71.6	19.8	42.7
General Electric	43.0	15.6	18.6
General Motors	38.2	18.5	18.6
Philip Morris	35.9	15.8	23.3
Procter & Gamble	29.4	13.8	14.8
Sears Roebuck	22.2	15.8	7.73
Texaco	96.2	23.9	25.6
Union Carbide	27.0	11.7	11.7
U.S. Steel	26.3	14.1	15.9
United Technologies	101.0	30.0	36.0
Westinghouse	40.6	14.9	12.0
F. W. Woolworth	106.0	37.2	21.4

[a] $H = (2\hat{S})^{1/2} - (2n-1)^{1/2}$, where $\hat{S}$ is distributed as a chi-squared with n degrees of freedom. Note that H is approximately distributed as $N(0,1)$ under the null hypothesis of gaussianity. $\hat{S}$ is the sum of the $2|\hat{X}_{f,g}|^2$ over the principal domain. See Appendix B.
[b] Distributed as $N(0,1)$ under the null hypothesis of a linear generating mechanism.
[c] Approximately distributed as $N(0,1)$ under the null hypothesis that the data are unaliased.

here generates a sample for each minute of a 6-hour trading day. If a trade did not occur at a particular sample time, the last traded price prior to the sample time was used. Over the 3-year period, this method produced 270,000 sample prices for each stock. Each price series was converted to a return series by taking the log price relatives [i.e., $\ln(p_t/p_{t-1})$].

To construct the 15-minute sampled return series, the one-minute returns were passed through a low-pass Tukey anti-aliasing digital filter. The choice of the Tukey filter was somewhat arbitrary; a Parzen or Bartlett filter would have been equally effective in removing the high-frequency energy. In the time domain the Tukey filter takes the form of a lag window with base width M. Denote the computed one-minute returns as r_t and the filtered one-minute returns as y_t. Then

$$y_t = \sum_{\ell=-m}^{m} h_\ell r_{t-\ell}, \tag{13}$$

where the weights h_ℓ are given by

$$h_0 = \frac{1}{m+1},$$

$$h_\ell = h_{-\ell} = \frac{1}{m+1}\left(\frac{1}{2} + \frac{1}{2}\cos\frac{j\pi}{m+1}\right), \quad j = 1, 2, \ldots, m, \tag{14}$$

and $m = \text{INT}(M/2) + 1$, with M the base width of the filter. Note that this filter is not causal.

Because realizable filters cannot have an infinite slope at the cutoff frequency, a compromise between aliasing and the loss of information must be made. If we make the base width M wide enough to virtually eliminate any aliasing, then we lose much of the high- and mid-frequency information in the time series. On the other hand, if the base width is on the narrow side, the aliases are reduced but not eliminated. A rule of thumb for this class of filter is to make M twice the Nyquist frequency. With a 15-minute Nyquist period, the rule suggests a 30-minute base width. After some experimentation, a base width of 19 was chosen for the 15-minute filter and 465 minutes (1.29 business days) for the daily filter. Although these selections are somewhat narrow, they do nonetheless substantially attenuate aliases in the data with the benefit that most of the high-frequency information in the data is retained.

The 15-minute returns are calculated by summing the filtered one-minute returns over a 15-minute interval. Suppose we denote a 15-minute return as R, where

$$R = \ln\frac{p_{15}}{p_0}, \tag{15}$$

and p_0 and p_{15} are the prices at $t = 0$ and $t = 15$ minutes (i.e., the beginning and ending prices). Now,

$$\frac{p_{15}}{p_0} = \frac{p_1}{p_0} \times \frac{p_2}{p_1} \times \cdots \times \frac{p_{15}}{p_{14}} \tag{16}$$

and

$$R = \ln\frac{p_{15}}{p_0} = \ln\frac{p_1}{p_0} + \ln\frac{p_2}{p_1} + \cdots + \ln\frac{p_{15}}{p_{14}} = r_1 + r_2 + \cdots + r_{15}, \tag{17}$$

where r_j is the jth one-minute return. To avoid aliasing in $\{R\}$, the r_j in (17) are replaced by the filtered returns y_j.

The unaliased daily returns were constructed in a similar manner using a base width of 465 minutes.

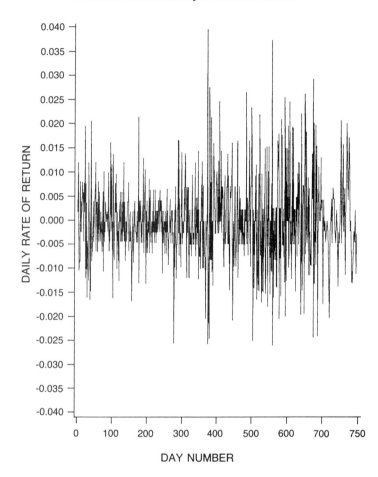

Figure 3.   AT&T aliased daily returns.

Because the anti-aliasing filter averages observations, it introduces serial correlation into the data. This problem is easily overcome by applying a whitening transformation to the output of the 15-minute and daily
filters. To find the appropriate transformation, we passed gaussian white
noise from a random number generator through each filter. Last, an appropriate AR model was fitted to the output of each filter, and the models
were diagnostically checked to ensure that the fitting errors were white.

Figure 3 is a plot of the aliased daily returns for AT&T over the period
September 1, 1978 through August 31, 1981. Figure 4 is a plot of the unaliased daily returns to AT&T over the same period. The differences between the plots are easily noted. First, the variance of the unaliased returns

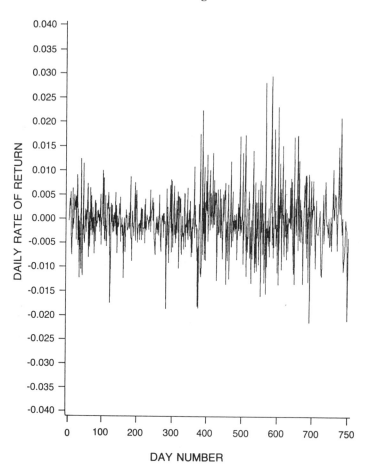

Figure 4.   AT&T unaliased daily returns.

is lower because of the low-pass filtering. Second, the unaliased returns appear to be "smoother" than the aliased returns. As we shall see in the next section, the unaliased returns for all 15-stock series have a greater degree of serial correlation than the aliased returns calculated from end-of-day closing prices.

4   Empirical results

In this section we present the results from applying the bispectrum-based linearity test to the three classes of return data described in Section 3:

namely, the 15-minute unaliased returns, the daily unaliased returns, and the daily aliased returns from the CRSP tapes. Each series for each stock in all three classes covered the same basic time period: September 1, 1978 through August 31, 1981. However, because the base width of the lag window used to construct the unaliased daily returns is 465 minutes wide (1.29 days), complete returns are not available for the first and last days of the sample period, which therefore were not used in the analysis.

Our first result is from the 15-minute returns as reported in Table 1. The first column gives the names of the 15 stocks studied. Again, these stocks were chosen from the 30 stocks that are used to calculate the Dow Jones Industrial Average. The last column of the table lists the Hinich–Wolinsky aliasing test statistic (see Hinich and Wolinsky, 1988; Section 2). The reported test statistic A is approximately distributed as an $N(0, 1)$ variate under the null hypothesis that the series is not aliased. As can be seen in the table, the test statistic is highly significant for all stocks. This is primarily the result of a narrow base width, though the test can also reflect the presence of transients (i.e., embedded coherent signals) in the return generating process for these stocks over the sample period.

The third column of Table 1 shows the linearity test statistic Z for the 15 stocks; Z is defined in equation (B14) in Appendix B. Since $Z \sim N(0, 1)$ under the null hypothesis of a linear generating mechanism, we can easily reject the null hypothesis at the 5.0% level for all 15 of the stock return series.

Finally, the second column in Table 1 reports the gaussianity test statistic for these stocks (of course, a nonlinear process cannot be gaussian). Although there is considerable controversy in the finance area about the probability model responsible for the generation of returns, these results reject gaussianity for all of the series.

The results for the two classes of daily returns are shown in Table 2. For the aliased daily returns we cannot reject linearity at the 5% level for DuPont, General Motors, Philip Morris, Union Carbide, or U.S. Steel. Using the unaliased returns, we fail to reject linearity at the 5% level for DuPont, Exxon, and United Technologies. DuPont is the only return series that we fail to reject for both the aliased and unaliased returns. One might conclude from this evidence that aliasing is affecting the distribution of the test statistics for some of the series.

Figures 5, 6, and 7 show contour plots of the probability that the magnitude of the bispectrum is *not* zero for frequency pairs for three return series: Allied Corporation, AT&T, and DuPont. The probabilities are calculated from the $2|\hat{X}_{f, g}|^2$ estimators defined in equation (B9) of Appendix B. Under the null hypothesis of gaussianity and linearity, the bispectrum is not significantly different from zero. When this null is rejected

Table 2. *Comparison of test statistics for daily returns constructed from trade-by-trade returns and sampled daily returns*

Firm	Unaliased returns		Aliased returns	
	Gaussianity test statistic, H^a	Linearity test statistic, Z^b	Gaussianity test statistic, H^a	Linearity test statistic, Z^b
Allied Corp.	5.18	2.07	6.38	5.50
AT&T	8.81	4.55	7.02	2.24
DuPont	3.09	1.20	−0.73	−1.24
Exxon	3.35	1.25	3.39	2.00
General Electric	3.54	1.85	4.02	2.12
General Motors	3.39	3.05	4.03	1.14
Philip Morris	3.70	3.54	1.93	1.28
Procter & Gamble	7.11	5.53	7.69	2.84
Sears Roebuck	11.2	5.48	7.30	4.84
Texaco	8.25	4.69	11.2	5.34
Union Carbide	2.27	2.24	3.18	1.56
U.S. Steel	10.7	6.53	11.9	0.20
United Technologies	3.24	0.94	4.76	3.62
Westinghouse	2.63	3.82	2.64	2.61
F. W. Woolworth	9.62	7.07	16.2	4.38

[a] $H = (2\hat{S})^{1/2} - (2n-1)^{1/2}$, where $\hat{S}$ is distributed as a chi-squared with n d.f. Note that H is approximately distributed as $N(0,1)$ under the null hypothesis of gaussianity.
[b] Distributed as $N(0,1)$ under the null hypothesis of a linear generating mechanism.

by the data, we would expect to see a number of significant peaks in the bispectrum, as indeed we do in Figures 5, 6, and 7. Obviously, heights greater than 0.95 are significantly different from zero at the 5% level. For example, in Figure 5a contours are plotted for probabilities of 50, 80, 90, and 95%. Part a of each figure plots the probability for the aliased returns, and part b is the contour for the unaliased returns. In comparing parts a and b, note the differences in the locations of the major bispectral peaks, and that the peaks tend to be higher and greater in number for the unaliased returns. All three figures plot the probabilities only within the (triangular) principal domain defined in Appendix B. The region outside the principal domain is suppressed because it only contains mirror images of the bispectrum inside the principal domain.

The horizontal and vertical axes of the contour plots show the frequencies of points in the principal domain measured in cycles per day. In Figure 5a, Allied Corporation has a peak of 0.95 at approximately

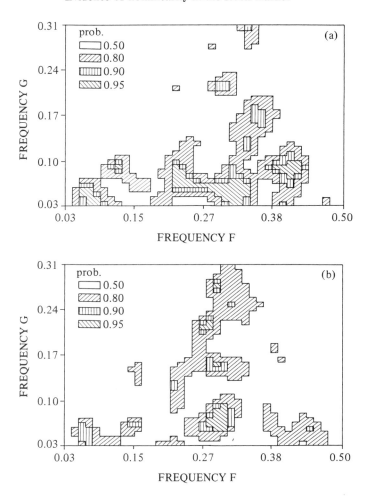

Figure 5.   (a) Probability that estimated bispectrum is not zero, Allied Corp. aliased returns; (b) probability that estimated bispectrum is not zero, Allied Corp. unaliased returns.

(0.4, 0.07). This means that there is interaction between the 0.4 and 0.07 cycles in the aliased daily returns. However, we *do not* see this peak in Figure 5b. If the process were gaussian, we would not find interaction between various frequencies in the sample returns; because the process is both nongaussian and nonlinear, we find *different* skewness at different frequency pairs. The contour plots of Figures 5, 6, and 7 show combinations of frequencies for which interfrequency interaction occurs when the

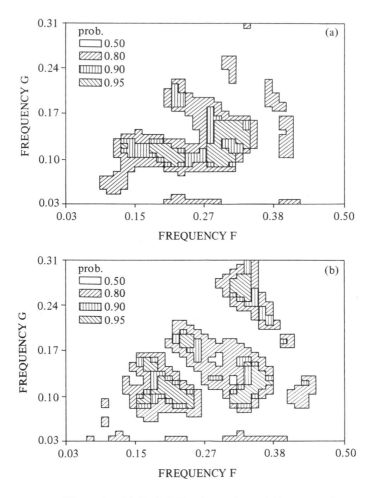

Figure 6.   (a) Probability that estimated bispectrum is not zero, AT&T aliased returns; (b) probability that estimated bispectrum is not zero, AT&T unaliased returns.

input to a nonlinear filter is gaussian white noise. However, because the daily CRSP returns are aliased, the estimated bispectrum for these returns gives a misleading picture of the nature of the nonlinearity in the continuous-time return generating process.

Table 3 presents some interesting evidence concerning the degree of *linear* structure in the aliased and unaliased returns. The second column under the heading "Aliased returns" shows the estimated serial correlation

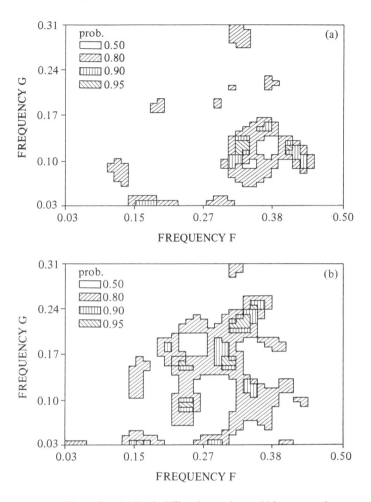

Figure 7.   (a) Probability that estimated bispectrum is not zero, Dupont Corp. aliased returns; (b) probability that estimated bispectrum is not zero, Dupont Corp. unaliased returns.

coefficient for lags of 1, 2, 3, 4, 5, and 6 days. Only three of the lag 1 and lag 2 coefficients exceed two standard errors. This is consistent with other studies in the literature. These low correlations have led most financial economists to conclude that stock returns are white noise and therefore unforecastable. This type of evidence has also been used by theorists to justify the independent and identically distributed (i.i.d.) assumption typically found in mathematical stock market models.

Table 3. *Comparison of estimated serial correlation for daily returns constructed from trade-by-trade returns and sampled daily returns*

	Unaliased returns						Aliased returns					
	Lag (days)						Lag (days)					
Firm	1	2	3	4	5	6	1	2	3	4	5	6
Allied Corp.	0.07	-0.14*	-0.04	-0.04	-0.02	-0.06	0.07	-0.06	0.00	-0.05	-0.07	-0.05
AT&T	0.12*	-0.14*	-0.04	-0.08*	-0.01	0.01	0.03	-0.01	-0.06	-0.06	-0.01	-0.04
DuPont	0.04	-0.07	0.01	-0.09*	0.02	-0.01	-0.05	0.05	0.00	-0.10*	0.05	-0.02
Exxon	0.10*	-0.15*	-0.11*	-0.03	0.06	0.01	0.05	-0.04	-0.10*	-0.04	0.02	0.05
General Electric	0.08*	-0.07	-0.03	-0.04	-0.01	-0.05	0.03	0.03	-0.02	-0.05	-0.02	-0.04
General Motors	0.08*	-0.11*	-0.03	-0.06	-0.01	-0.08*	0.06	-0.02	-0.07	-0.04	-0.02	-0.05
Philip Morris	0.06	-0.08*	-0.04	-0.01	-0.02	-0.03	0.05	-0.01	-0.02	-0.02	-0.02	-0.04
Procter & Gamble	0.13*	-0.04	-0.01	-0.11*	0.01	0.04	0.12*	0.04	-0.04	-0.02	-0.03	0.06
Sears Roebuck	0.02	-0.12*	0.01	-0.05	0.05	-0.02	-0.01	-0.01	-0.05	-0.09*	0.08*	0.00
Texaco	0.04	-0.08*	-0.04	-0.06	0.07	-0.05	-0.04	0.02	-0.06	-0.04	0.07	-0.06
Union Carbide	0.08*	-0.12*	-0.05	-0.08*	0.05	-0.03	0.08*	-0.05	-0.04	-0.08*	0.00	-0.04
U.S. Steel	0.10*	-0.02	-0.07	-0.02	-0.01	-0.05	0.01	0.08*	-0.05	0.00	-0.05	-0.01
United Technologies	0.14*	-0.03	-0.02	-0.05	0.00	-0.01	0.09*	0.04	-0.02	-0.04	-0.01	0.01
Westinghouse	0.05	-0.08*	-0.04	-0.06	0.02	0.00	0.02	-0.01	-0.07	-0.03	0.03	0.00
F. W. Woolworth	0.11*	-0.09*	-0.11*	0.01	0.00	-0.08*	0.00	0.00	-0.07	-0.02	0.00	-0.06

* Coefficient exceeds 2 standard errors.

The lag 1 and lag 2 correlation coefficients estimated from the unaliased returns paint a different picture. As shown in Table 3, these correlations tend to be larger but of the same sign for the unaliased returns. This evidence suggests that we must seriously question the white-noise hypothesis for daily stock returns.

5   Conclusions

Two important conclusions can be drawn from these results. First, the returns from many DJIA stocks are generated by nonlinear stochastic processes, yielding return series that are neither gaussian nor linear (nonlinearity implies serial dependence). Linearity was rejected more frequently for the unaliased returns than for the aliased returns.

Second, the unaliased returns showed a somewhat higher degree of linear serial dependence than did the aliased returns. Whether this linear dependence can be used to form an economically profitable forecasting rule is a question we leave to further research.

Appendix A: Review of spectral aliasing

This appendix reviews the theory of aliasing of sampled data in the context of the spectrum and autocorrelation function.

Consider the continuous time stochastic process $\{x(t)\}$. The covariance function of $\{x(t)\}$ is $c_x(\tau) = Ex(t)x(t+\tau)$ for each lag or lead τ. Assume that the covariance function is absolutely integrable. Then the spectrum of $x(t)$ is defined as the Fourier transform of $c_x(\tau)$; that is,

$$S_x(f) = \int_{-\infty}^{\infty} c_x(\tau) \exp(-i2\pi f\tau)\, d\tau. \tag{A1}$$

The inverse Fourier transform yields the dual relationship

$$c_x(\tau) = \int_{-\infty}^{\infty} S_x(f) \exp(-i2\pi f\tau)\, d\tau. \tag{A2}$$

A process $\{x(t)\}$ is said to be *low pass* if its spectrum $S_x(f)$ is zero for $|f| > f_c$:

$$S_x(f) = 0, \quad |f| > f_c, \tag{A3}$$

as shown in Figure 8a.

We now state the stochastic version of the sampling theorem (see Papoulis, 1965, p. 370, for a proof). If $\{x(t)\}$ is low pass – that is, if its spectrum satisfies (A3) – and if $\{x(t)\}$ is sampled every T units of time with $T = 1/2f_c$, then

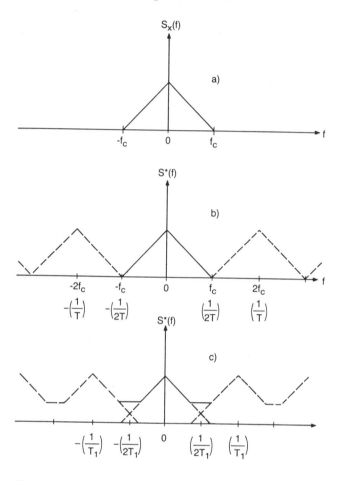

Figure 8.   Spectra of a low-pass process and the sampled process.

$$x(t) = \sum_{-\infty}^{\infty} x(nT) \frac{\sin(2\pi f_c t - n\pi)}{2\pi f_c t - n\pi}, \tag{A4}$$

in the mean-square sense. The theorem says that if the sampling frequency is at least twice f_c, then we can recover $\{x(t)\}$ from the sample sequence $x(nT)$ with zero mean-square error.

Suppose we expand the spectrum $S_x(f)$, as done by Papoulis (1962, p. 51), into a Fourier series in the $(-f_c, f_c)$ interval. Then

$$S_x(f) = \sum_{-\infty}^{\infty} a_n \exp \frac{-in2\pi f}{2f_c} \quad -f_c < f < f_c, \tag{A5}$$

where

$$a_n = \frac{1}{2f_c} \int_{-f_c}^{f_c} S_x(f) \exp \frac{in2\pi f}{2f_c} \, df = Tc_x(nT).$$ (A6)

Equation (A6) states that each coefficient a_n in the expansion of $S_x(f)$ equals the covariance function evaluated at n times the sample period T. The sum,

$$S_x^*(f) = T \sum_{-\infty}^{\infty} c_x(nT) \exp \frac{-in2\pi f}{2f_c},$$ (A7)

is the spectrum of the sampled process (Fig. 8b). It is periodic with period $1/T$ but is equal to $S_x(f)$ in the interval $(-f_c, f_c)$.

Next we want to determine the inverse transform, denoted $c^*(\tau)$, of the periodic sample spectrum $S_x^*(f)$. From (A7) and the fact that the transform of $\exp(-i2\pi f t_0)$ is the delta function $\delta(t - t_0)$, we have

$$c^*(\tau) = \sum_{-\infty}^{\infty} Tc_x(nT)\delta(\tau - nT).$$ (A8)

In other words, $c^*(\tau)$ is a sequence of equally spaced impulses whose envelope is $Tc_x(\tau)$. This means that the covariance function of the sample sequence $x(nT)$ is proportional to the values obtained when the covariance function of $\{x(t)\}$ is sampled every T units of time. Hence, given the function $c^*(\tau)$ and realizing that $c^*(\tau)$ is proportional to the sampled version of $c_x(\tau)$, we can recover the continuous covariance function by invoking the sampling theorem:

$$c_x(\tau) = \frac{1}{T} \sum_{-\infty}^{\infty} c_x^*(nT) \frac{\sin(2\pi f_c - n\pi)}{2\pi f_c - n\pi}.$$ (A9)

If the sampling frequency is less than $2f_c$, then we say that the sequence of sampled values of $\{x(t)\}$ is aliased. Suppose the sampling period is T_1 and $T_1 < 1/2f_c$. The sample spectrum $S_x^*(f)$ will now have a periodicity of $1/T_1$, as we note from (A7). The effect on the sample spectrum $S_x^*(f)$ is illustrated in Figure 8c, where we see that the periodic extension of the spectrum has shifted down into the $(-f_c, f_c)$ interval and distorted the true spectrum. As a consequence, the covariance function of the sampled data is no longer proportional to the sampled version of $c_x(\tau)$.

Appendix B: The Hinich bispectral nonlinearity test

Suppose that $\{x(t)\}$ is a linear process, that is, it can be expressed as

$$x(t) = \sum_{n=0}^{\infty} a(n)u(t-n),$$ (B1)

where $\{u(t)\}$ is purely random (i.e., stationary and serially independent) and the weights $\{a(n)\}$ are fixed. Assuming that $\sum_{n=0}^{\infty}|a(n)|$ is finite, the bispectrum of $\{x(t)\}$ is

$$B_x(f_1, f_2) = \mu_3 A(f_1)A(f_2)A^*(f_1+f_2), \tag{B2}$$

where $\mu_3 = E[U^3(t)]$,

$$A(f) = \sum_{n=0}^{\infty} a(n)\exp(-i2\pi fn), \tag{B3}$$

and $A^*(f)$ is its complex conjugate. Because the spectrum of $\{x(t)\}$ is

$$S_x(f) = \sigma_u^2 |A(f)|^2, \tag{B4}$$

it follows from (B2) that

$$\Psi^2(f_1, f_2) \equiv \frac{|B_x(f_1, f_2)|^2}{S_x(f_1)S_x(f_2)S_x(f_1+f_2)} = \frac{\mu_3^2}{\sigma_u^6}, \tag{B5}$$

for all f_1 and f_2 in Ω.

The left-hand side of (B5) defines the square of the skewness function of $\{x(t)\}$, $\Psi(f_1, f_2)$. Thus the squared-skewness function is a constant if $\{x(t)\}$ is linear. This property is the basis for the Hinich linearity test.

The bispectrum of the stationary process $\{x(t)\}$ can be consistently estimated using a sample $\{x(0), x(1), \ldots, x(N-1)\}$ as follows. Let

$$F_x(j, k) = X\left(\frac{j}{N}\right)X\left(\frac{k}{N}\right)X^*\left(\frac{j+k}{N}\right), \tag{B6}$$

where j and k are integers and

$$X\left(\frac{j}{N}\right) = \sum_{t=0}^{N-1} x(t)\exp\frac{-i2\pi jt}{N}. \tag{B7}$$

$X(0)$ is set to zero; this is equivalent to subtracting the sample mean of $\{x(t)\}$.

$F_x(j, k)$ is an estimator of the bispectrum of $\{x(t)\}$ at frequency pair (j, k). However, it must be smoothed – averaged over adjacent frequency pairs – to obtain the consistent estimator $\hat{B}_x(m, n)$:[1]

$$\hat{B}_x(m, n) = M^{-2} \sum_{j=(m-1)M}^{mM-1} \sum_{k=(n-1)M}^{nM-1} F_x(j, k). \tag{B8}$$

---

[1] Hinich (1982) showed that consistent estimation of $B_x(f_1, f_2)$ requires $N^{0.5} < M < N$. However, the Ashley, Patterson, and Hinich simulation results showed that the finite-sample size of the nonlinearity test converges to the asymptotic size more quickly for values of $M \approx 0.7N^{0.5}$.

$\hat{B}_x(m, n)$ is the average value of $F(j, k)$ over a square of M^2 points, where the centers of the squares are defined by the lattice

$$L = \left\{(2m-1)\frac{M}{2}, (2n-1)\frac{M}{2}; m = 1, \ldots, n \text{ and } m \le \frac{N}{2M} - \frac{n}{2} + \frac{3}{4}\right\}$$

in the principal domain.

This averaging procedure is precisely analogous to smoothing the periodogram to obtain a consistent estimator of the spectrum. As in that case, smoothing reduces the finite sample variance at the cost of introducing bias. Let

$$\hat{X}_{m,n} = \frac{\hat{B}_x(m, n)}{[N/M^2]^{1/2}[\hat{S}_x(g_m)\hat{S}_x(g_n)\hat{S}_x(g_{m+n})]^{1/2}}, \tag{B9}$$

where

$$g_j = \frac{(2j-1)M}{2N} \tag{B10}$$

and S_x is the usual (smoothed) estimator of the power spectrum of $\{x(t)\}$. Hinich (1982) shows that the estimators $2|\hat{X}_{m,n}|^2$ are asymptotically distributed as independent, noncentral chi-squared variates [i.e., $\chi^2(2, \lambda_{m,n})$] with noncentrality parameter

$$\lambda_{m,n} = \frac{2(N/M^2)^{-1}|B_x(m, n)|^2}{S_x(m)S_x(n)S_x(m+n)}, \tag{B11}$$

for all m and n such that the lattice square lies entirely within the principal domain. Later, P denotes the number of such frequency pairs; also, we shall refer to $2|\hat{X}_{m,n}|^2$ as the estimated standardized bispectrum.

Under the null hypothesis that $\{x(t)\}$ is linear, (B11) implies that $\lambda_{m,n}$ is a constant, independent of m and n. This constant is consistently estimated by

$$\hat{\lambda}_0 = \left\{2 \sum_m \sum_n \frac{|\hat{X}_{m,n}|^2}{P}\right\} - 2. \tag{B12}$$

If the null hypothesis is true, then the estimators $2|\hat{X}_{m,n}|^2$ (asymptotically) constitute P independent picks from the $\chi^2(2, \hat{\lambda}_0)$ distribution. They should therefore have a sample dispersion consistent with that distribution. In contrast, if the null hypothesis is false, so that $\{x(t)\}$ is *not* the result of a linear filter applied to i.i.d. noise, then not all $\lambda_{m,n}$ are the same. Consequently, the observations on the estimated standardized bispectrum (i.e., on the values of $2|\hat{X}_{m,n}|^2$) are P independent picks from noncentral chi-squared distributions with differing noncentrality parameters. Therefore, they should have a sample dispersion exceeding that expected under the null hypothesis of linearity. The sum of the $2|\hat{X}_{m,n}|^2$ over the principal domain is used to test the null hypothesis that the bispectrum is zero (a test for gaussianity).

This dispersion can be measured in many ways. Based on the simulation results reported in Ashley, Patterson, and Hinich, we use the 80% quantile of the empirical distribution in the results reported here. This statistic is robust with respect to outliers, and its asymptotic sampling distribution is easily calculated. In particular, David (1970, theorem 9.2) shows that the sample 80% quantile, $\hat{\xi}_{.8}$, is asymptotically distributed as $N(\xi_{.8}, \sigma_0^2)$, where σ_0^2 is consistently estimated by

$$\hat{\sigma}_0^2 = .8(1 - 0.8)f^{-1}(\hat{\xi}_{.8})P^{-1}, \tag{B13}$$

$\xi_{.8}$ is the population 80% quantile of $\chi^2(2, \lambda_0)$, and $f(\cdot)$ is the density function of $\chi^2(2, \hat{\lambda}_0)$. Thus,

$$Z \equiv \frac{\hat{\xi}_{.8}}{\hat{\sigma}_0} \sim N(0, 1) \tag{B14}$$

under the null hypothesis that the time series $\{x(t)\}$ is a realization of a linear process as in (B2).

REFERENCES

Ashley, R., and Patterson, D. (1986), "A nonparametric, distribution-free test for serial independence in stock returns," *Journal of Financial and Quantitative Analysis,* 21(2), 221–7.

Ashley, R. A., Patterson, D. M., and Hinich, M. J. (1986), "A diagnostic test for nonlinear serial dependence in time series fitting errors," *Journal of Time Series Analysis,* 7(3), 165–78.

Brillinger, D. (1975), *Time Series, Data Analysis and Theory,* New York: Holt, Rinehart and Winston.

Brillinger, D., and Rosenblatt, J. (1967a), "Asymptotic theory of kth order spectra," in *Spectral Analysis of Time Series,* ed. by B. Harris, New York: John Wiley, 153–88.

(1976b), "Computation and interpretation of kth order spectra," in *Spectral Analysis of Time Series,* ed. by B. Harris, New York: John Wiley, 189–232.

Brock, W., Dechert, W., and Scheinkman, J. (1986), "A test for independence based on the correlation dimension," unpublished manuscript, Univ. of Wisconsin–Madison.

Brockett, P. L., Hinich, M. J., and Patterson, D. M. (1988), "Bispectral based tests for the detection of Gaussianity and linearity in time series," *Journal of the American Statistical Association,* 83(403), "Applications."

David, H. A. (1970), *Order Statistics,* New York: John Wiley.

Fama, E. (1965), "The Behavior of Stock Market Prices," *Journal of Business,* 38, 34–105.

(1970), "Efficient capital markets: A review of theory and empirical work," *Journal of Finance,* 25, 383–417.

Hinich, M. J. (1982), "Testing for gaussianity and linearity of a stationary time series," *Journal of Time Series Analysis*, 3, 169–76.

Hinich, M., and Patterson, D. (1985a), "Evidence of nonlinearity in daily stock returns," *Journal of Business and Economic Statistics*, 3(1), 69–77.

(1985b), "Identification of the coefficients in a non-linear time series of the quadratic type," *Journal of Econometrics*, 30, 269–88.

(1987), "Fitting a quadratic moving average model to data," Technical Report, Applied Research Laboratories, University of Texas at Austin.

Hinich, M. J., and Wolinsky, M. A. (1988), "A test for aliasing using bispectral analysis," *Journal of the American Statistical Association*, 83(402), "Theory and Methods."

Lii, K. S., and Rosenblatt, M. (1982), "Deconvolution and estimation of transfer function phase and coefficients for non-Gaussian linear processes," *Annals of Statistics*, 10(4), 1195–208.

Papoulis, A. P. (1962), *The Fourier Integral and Its Applications*, New York: McGraw-Hill.

(1965), *Probability, Random Variables, and Stochastic Processes*, New York: McGraw-Hill.

Patterson, D. (1983), "BISPEC: A program to estimate the bispectrum of a stationary time series," *American Statistician*, 37, 323–4.

Scheinkman, J., and LeBaron, B. (1986), "Nonlinear dynamics and stock returns," Economics Working Paper No. 181, University of Chicago.

Subba Rao, T. (1983), "The bispectral analysis of nonlinear stationary time series with reference to bilinear time series models," in *Handbook of Statistics*, Vol. 3, ed. by D. Brillinger and P. Krishnaiah, Amsterdam: North-Holland, chap. 14.

Subba Rao, T., and Gabr, M. (1980), "A test for linearity of stationary time series," *Journal of Time Series Analysis*, 1, 145–58.